Simon & Schuster
HANDBOOK for WRITERS
FIRST CANADIAN EDITION

LYNN QUITMAN TROYKA

JOANNE BUCKLEY

DAVID GATES

Prentice Hall Canada Inc.
Scarborough, Ontario

Canadian Cataloguing in Publication Data

Troyka, Lynn Quitman, 1938–
    Simon & Schuster handbook for writers

1st Canadian ed.
Includes index.
ISBN 0-13-183807-5

1. English language – Rhetoric – Handbooks,
manuals, etc. 2. English language – Grammar –
Handbooks, manuals, etc. I. Buckley, Joanne,
1953– . II. Gates, David, 1952– .
III. Title. IV. Title: Simon and Schuster handbook
for writers. V. Title: Handbook for writers.

PE1408.T76 1995   808'.042   C95–931693–0

© 1996 Prentice-Hall Canada Inc., Scarborough, Ontario
A Viacom Company

ALL RIGHTS RESERVED

No part of this book may be reproduced in any form without permission in writing from
the publisher.

Prentice-Hall, Inc., Englewood Cliffs, New Jersey
Prentice-Hall International (UK) Limited, London
Prentice-Hall of Australia, Pty. Limited, Sydney
Prentice-Hall Hispanoamericana, S.A., Mexico City
Prentice-Hall of India Private Limited, New Delhi
Prentice-Hall of Japan, Inc., Tokyo
Simon & Schuster Asia Private Limited, Singapore
Editora Prentice-Hall do Brasil, Ltda., Rio de Janeiro

ISBN 0-13-183807-5

Acquisitions Editor: Marjorie Munroe
Developmental Editor: Karen Sacks
Copy Editor: Cy Strom
Production Editor: Avivah Wargon
Production Coordinator: Anita Boyle-Evans
Cover Design: Olena Serbyn
Page Layout: Debbie Fleming

Original edition published by Prentice-Hall Inc.
A Division of Simon & Schuster
Englewood Cliffs, New Jersey 07632
Copyright © 1990 by Prentice-Hall Inc.

1 2 3 4 5   00 99 98 97 96

Printed and bound in Canada

Every reasonable effort has been made to obtain permissions for all articles and data
used in this edition. If errors or omissions have occurred, they will be corrected in future
editions provided written notification has been received by the publisher.

We welcome readers' comments, which can be sent by e-mail to
    collegeinfo_pubcanada@prenhall.com

Contents

PART II: Understanding Grammar   *173*

---

7 Parts of Speech and Structures of the Sentence   *72*

---

8 Verbs   *194*

Preface

TO INSTRUCTORS

Scholarship and practice in the teaching of writing and rhetoric have become quite sophisticated today, especially compared to fifty years ago when handbooks for writers began to be widely used. In the *Simon & Schuster Handbook for Writers*, First Canadian Edition, as in its U.S. counterpart, now in its fourth edition, I have sought to wed the best of traditional and contemporary theory to accessible practice.

My stance toward students is that as evolving writers they merit clarity, unwavering support, and respect. I believe that students are empowered, not intimidated, by knowledge. Information about writing processes and products provides students access to critical habits of mind that dramatically increase their chances to fulfil their academic, business, and personal potentials. I have therefore conceptualized the *Simon & Schuster Handbook for Writers*, First Canadian Edition to serve multiple roles in the intellectual lives of students: classroom text, source for students' self-instruction, and comprehensive reference volume for college or university and afterward. Specifically, it contains these features:

- It starts with six chapters about the whole essay, thus establishing contexts for writing.
- It sets the scene with a short first chapter about purposes, audiences, and tone. Using sources for writing is introduced early and connected explicitly to detailed discussions of source-based writing in later chapters.
- It explains that the writing process is rarely linear and always varies with the writer, the topic, and the writing situation.
- It illustrates the variety of writing processes and purposes with four complete student essays. The essay with an information purpose, on women pumping iron, is shown in three drafts, complete with the student's and the instructor's comments on interim drafts.

- It presents (in Chapter 5) an extensive discussion of critical thinking. It offers a sequence for critical thinking; differentiation of the separate processes of summary and synthesis; concrete advice on reading systematically and closely; and specific guidance on writing critically in response to a source illustrated by a student's critical response essay based on her reaction to, and synthesis of, an outside source.
- It devotes an entire chapter to writing argument, with two student essays, each taking a different position on the same topic. The classical model as well as the Toulmin model for argument is discussed and linked to the student essays.
- It covers all topics of grammar, style, language, punctuation, and mechanics, with explanations and examples to facilitate visual as well as verbal learning. Focus on Revising sections apply concepts of revision to matters of grammar, punctuation, and style.
- It explains research writing as three processes: conducting research, understanding the results of that research, and writing a paper based on that understanding. Critical thinking and reading are thereby explicitly integrated into the research process, with greater attention to the roles of synthesis and critical assessment in using sources.
- It includes accessing electronic sources and a "layering strategy" to help even first-time researchers pursue productive research and locate worthwhile sources. Two complete student research papers— one in MLA style and one in APA style—are accompanied by narratives of the students' processes. With the MLA-style research paper, Commentary featuring Process Notes illuminates the student writer's decision-making and composing processes.
- It presents comprehensive coverage of four major documentation styles: MLA, APA, Chicago Manual, and CBE. The pages in these sections are edged in dark blue for instant access. Also, for each style a detailed chart lays out format requirements and other conventions.
- It includes five chapters on writing across the curriculum. Writing about literature is illustrated with three complete student essays, one each on fiction, drama, and poetry. The last two are literary research papers.
- It addresses students for whom English is a second language, offering ESL Notes throughout the text to augment six separate chapters on matters deserving longer discussion.

In writing the *Simon & Schuster Handbook for Writers*, First Canadian Edition, I have sought to be inclusive of all people. Role stereotyping and sexist language are avoided; *man* is almost never used generically for the human race (the few exceptions are contained in quotations from important writers); male and female writers are represented equally in examples; and many ethnic groups are represented in the mix of student and professional writing examples.

To unify this *Handbook* and to avoid its being a grab bag of isolated components, the function of context in writing situations is emphasized. Most exercises contain connected discourse rather than random sentences; when students work the exercises, they experience what writers face when they revise and edit. The content of the exercises, drawn from subjects "across the curriculum," was chosen for its intrinsic interest. Similarly, most clusters of examples have related contents that students can focus on the instruction instead of being distracted by a new topic with each new example.

Also, because students today are strongly oriented toward the visual, I have created many tinted charts and other visual displays for guidelines, checklists, sentence patterns, summaries, flow charts, illustrations, and more. Each item is designed to help students learn new material as well as to refresh their memories afterwards when they want to look up information.

- An ❖ ALERT ❖ system makes students aware of small matters in larger contexts. For example, a brief Punctuation Alert in an explanation of coordination puts into context a particular function of a comma. Full chapters on topics distilled in Alerts complete this dual-entry system, which helps students handle the interplay of variables during writing.
- A degree mark (°) follows all terms that are defined in the Terms Glossary. This identification feature allows students to concentrate on the material at hand, with the assurance that they can easily locate a definition they might need; students no longer need to feel frustrated by what might seem a pileup of unfamiliar words that explain some aspect of writing or language.
- Inside the back cover, a guide on how to use the *Handbook* leads students through four steps for locating information; it also visually displays *Handbook* page elements.
- Response symbols, at the back of the *Handbook*, include notations to acknowledge and praise good student writing, these are intended to be used alongside traditional correction symbols.

As an undergraduate, I never encountered a handbook for writers. Questions about writing nagged at me, so I took to handbooks instantly when I discovered them in graduate school, I'd browse through them, sometimes to locate specific information and sometimes simply to root around and make discoveries. I could not have imagined then that I might some day set my hand to composing such a book. Now that I have completed the fourth U.S. edition of the *Simon & Schuster Handbook for Writers*, on which this Canadian edition was based, I am amazed that I ever had the audacity to start the first edition. This history proves, it seems to me, that anyone can write as long as she or he begins; that a handbook can be an evolving text as long as colleagues and students graciously join in the conversations its pages seek to invite; and that students, empowered by knowledge, can write effectively, even joyfully.

TO STUDENTS

You, along with each student I have ever taught in my writing classes, were in my mind's eye as I wrote this latest edition of the *Simon & Schuster Handbook for Writers*. My goal is to serve you with uncomplicated, yet complete, explanations; contexts for you to enjoy (sometimes even smile at) in the examples and exercises; and a format that gives you quick, easy access to all the information you might want to help you write effectively. If I have succeeded, you will want to keep my handbook as a reference source throughout your college years and afterward.

Given the variety of information that the *Handbook* includes, where might you begin? Few people read it straight through from beginning to end. They browse. I suggest that you become familiar with the contents by scanning the Overview of Contents on the inside front cover, or the more complete Contents list before this Preface, or the detailed Index. When you spot the topic you want, you can turn to it immediately.

You might also want to read the section of this Preface addressed to your instructor. Note especially the explanation of my use of the degree mark: **After a term is introduced and defined, it is marked with a degree symbol (°) to signal that you can find its definition in the Terms Glossary**. Thus, you can move through material in this book with the confidence that you have easy access to the meaning of unfamiliar terms.

The course for which you have bought this book can greatly influence your future. Writing is a skill you need for whatever career path you pursue. The ability to write and communicate clearly is crucial in the modern workplace and in life. I hope my handbook proves to be a trusted companion and friendly resource for many years. Hold onto it throughout your college and university career and beyond so that you can always look up whatever information you might need as a writer. Keep it close at hand in your permanent library, along with a dictionary and other reference books. As you use it, please feel welcome to write me with reactions, suggestions, and questions. Here's the address: Lynn Quitman Troyka, c/o English Editor, Prentice Hall Canada, 1870 Birchmount Road, Scarborough, Ontario M1P 2J7. I promise to answer.

ACKNOWLEDGMENTS

Being able to turn for advice and reactions to a community of colleagues, friends, and family sustained me, affirming once again my conviction that writing is a social act for both writer and reader. Though responsibility for any flaws rests with me, I wish to thank many people for their help.

In composing the *Simon & Schuster Handbook for Writers*, First Canadian Edition, I was privileged to be affiliated with an outstanding group. I want to call particular attention to the spirited collaboration of Joanne Buckley, of the University of Western Ontario, and David Gates. The contributions have added much texture to this *Handbook*. W.H. (Bill) Fricker, Northern Alberta Institute of Technology, has been a good friend to me and my books for many years. At Prentice Hall Canada, freelance editor Cy Strom made magic happen with his sharp eye, keen mind, and graceful pen. Marjorie Munroe, Senior Editor, watched over the project and the people with a gentle hand. Avivah Wargon, Senior Production Editor, steered us expertly and calmly through the daunting maze of book production. Also, John Isley, President, and David Joliffe, Manager, Development & Production Editorial, facilitated everyone's work as only fine leaders can.

In the United States, Jo Ellen Coppersmith, Utah Valley State College, added centrally to the rigour of concept and practice concerning research writing and critical thinking. Victoria Nelson contributed drafts of new exercise content and streamlining of some chapters, Barbara Gaffney lent her expertise to an analysis of my treatment of English as a Second Language (ESL). Other colleagues whose valued contributions I appreciate include Duncan Carter, Portland State University; Jay Don Coppersmith, National Training Specialist in Technology and Research, Jostens Learning Corporation, advisor on documentation updates; Ann B. Dobie, University of Southwestern Louisiana; Michael J. Freeman, Director of the Utah Valley State College Library, advisor on library use in this age of electronic information, Emily R. Gordon, Queensborough Community College; Warren Herendeen, Mercy College, advisor on ESL; Scott Leonard, Youngstown State University, advisor on drafting and revision; Dorothy V. Lindman, Brookhaven College; Alice Maclin, DeKalb College; Darlene Malaska, Youngstown Christian University, advisor on the critical response essay; Patricia Morgan, Louisiana State University; Mary Ruetten, University of New Orleans, advisor on ELS; and Matilda Delgado Saenz, Northlake College, advisor on the Toulmin model for argument.

Among my greatest pleasures in acknowledging others is to thank the many students who generously have given me permission to show their writing as exemplary models in this *Handbook*. I appreciate also the opportunities I have had to meet with hundreds of students to hear their ideas for my handbooks, and I warmly thank all students who have written me letters in which they gracefully shared with me their reactions and suggestions.

Many other faculty helped shape my decisions as I wrote. I am particularly grateful to members of the "Regional Advisory Board for Prentice Hall and Lynn Troyka" who set aside precious days in their busy lives to discuss key issues with me. In the Southeast, they are Peggy Jolly, University of Alabama at Birmingham; Stephen Prewitt, David Lipscomb University; Mary Anne Reiss, Elizabethtown Community College; Michael Thro, Tidewater Community College at Virginia Beach; and Sally Young, University of Tennessee at Chattanooga. In the Southwest, they are Jon Bentley, Albuquerque Technical-Vocational Institute; Kathryn Fitzgerald, University of Utah; Maggy Smith, University of Texas at El Paso; Martha Smith, Brookhaven College; Donnie Yeilding, Central Texas College. I thank also those colleagues who have made specific suggestions in formal reviews as well as letters, e-mail, and relayed messages. They include Susan Ahrens, Valencia Communtiy College; Virginia Anderson, University of Texas at Austin; Christopher Baker, Armstrong State College; Judy L. Burke, Macomb Community College; Jolayne Call, Utah Valley State College; James A. Coleman, Three Rivers Community & Technical College; Paula Gillespie, Marquette University; Jane Hikel, Central Connecticut State University; Sheila McGrory-Klyza, University of Vermont; Patricia McKeague, Moraine Valley Community College; Stuart Morton, Macomb Community College; Marcia Peabody, Mira Costa College; Blue Perry, Valencia Community College; and Don Tighe, Valencia Community College. Special thanks go to Michael Hassett for careful, thorough work, while he was a graduate student, on the writing of student research papers.

Over the course of my writing the prior edition of the *Handbook*, the reviews of many colleagues helped me draft and revise. I renew my thanks to all of them, including Nancy Westrich Baker, Southeast Missouri State University; Norman Bosley, Ocean Community College; Phyllis Brown, Santa Clara University; Robert S. Caim, West Virginia University at Parkersburg; Joe R. Christopher, Tarleton State University; Thomas Copeland, Youngstown State University; Joanne Ferreira, State University of New York at New Paltz and Fordham University; Michael Goodman, Fairleigh Dickinson University; Mary Multer Greene, Tidewater Community College at Virginia Beach; John L. Hare, Montgomery College; Lory Hawkes, DeVry Institute of Technology, Irving; Janet H. Hobbs, Wake Technical Community College; Frank Hubbard, Marquette University; Rebecca Innocent, Southern Methodist University; Ursula Irwin, Mt. Hood Community College; Denise Jackson, Southeast Missouri State University; Margo K. Jang, Northern Kentucky University; Myra Jones, Manatee Community College; Judith C. Kohl, Dutchess Community College; James C. McDonald, University of Southwestern Louisiana; Susan J. Miller, Santa Fe Community College; Jon F. Patton, University of Toledo; Pamela T. Pittman, University of Central Oklahoma; Kirk Rasmussen, Utah Valley State College; Edward J. Reilly, St. Joseph's College; Peter Burton Ross, University of the District of Columbia; Eileen Schwartz, Purdue University of Calumet; Lisa Sebti, Central Texas College; John S. Shea, Loyola University at Chicago; Tony Silva, Purdue University; Bill M. Stiffler, Harford Community College; Jack Summers, Central Piedmont Community College; Vivian A. Thomlinson, Cameron University; Carolyn West, Daytona Beach Community College; and Roseanna B. Whitlow, Southeast Missouri State University.

The staff at U.S. Prentice Hall, Inc./Simon & Schuster has facilitated my writing with extraordinary energy and talent. Central credit goes to Joyce F. Perkins, Senior Development Editor for English, whose voice joins and enhances mine on many pages. She is the dean of English development editors in college publishing today, and as all who have worked with her attest, to collaborate with her is a huge honour. Alison Reeves, Executive Editor for English, a woman of uncommon dedication and ethics, participated vigorously and wisely. Kara Hado, Assistant Development Editor for English, contributed much with unfailing skill. Andrew Roney, Senior Project Manager, shepherded this complex, multifaceted undertaking with gentle humour, a firm hand, and solid professionalism. Hilda Tauber shared her keen eye and mind. Gina Sluss, Executive Marketing Manager for Humanities, informally but crucially part of our editorial team, clarified patiently and inspired frequently. Other people in indispensable roles included J. Phillip Miller, President, Humanities and Social Sciences; D. Anthony English, Editor in Chief for English; Carol Carter, Director of Student Programs; Leslie Osher, Creative Director; Susan Walrath, Designer; Lori Kane, Supervisor of Production Services; Mary Ann Gloriande, Manufacturing Buyer; Bud Therien, Publisher for Art and Music; Kane Tung, Editorial Assistant; and Jennifer Weinberg, Marketing Assistant.

Closer to home are many people who give delightful texture to my life. Ida Morea, my assistant, helps in ways both large and small with her warmth and excellence. Dear friends and family whose understanding and love grace my life include Susan Bartlestone; Kristen Black, with Dan, Lindsey, and Ryan Black; Rita and Hy Cohen; Ruth Davis; Elaine Gilden Dushoff, my cousin; Elliott Goldhush; Warren Herendeen; Kate Morgan Jackson; Edith Klausner, my sister; Myra Kogen; Jo Ann Lavery; Lisa Lavery; Marie Jean Lederman; Marilyn Maiz; Jerrold Nudelman; Belle and Sidney Quitman, my parents; Betty Renshaw; Magdalena Rogalskaja; Shirley and Don Sterns; Marilyn and Ernest Sternglass; Elsie Tischler; Muriel Wolfe; and Gideon and Tzila Zwas. Most of all, I thank my husband, David Troyka, my anchor, sweetheart, and best friend.

Lynn Quitman Troyka

xxiv

Preface to the First Canadian Edition

The first Canadian edition of the *Simon & Schuster Handbook for Writers* places marked emphasis on subject matter, contexts, usages, and methods of proceeding that are quintesessentially Canadian; at the same time, it retains the structure and the coverage of the original *Handbook*. Much consideration has been given to choosing noteworthy and up-to-date examples of Canadian writing to provide a relevant national context. This process of adaptation does not involve simply changing "eagles to beavers," so to speak, but instead demands a Canadian focus in the essays and exercises themselves. This *Handbook* is consequently attuned to issues faced by Canadian writers, including the use of Canadian reference books, Canadian spellings, the metric and Celsius systems, and postal abbreviations. In addition, this *Handbook* treats such themes as Canadian fiction and theatre, aboriginal peoples, ecology, and Canadian contributions to scientific discovery. In producing a Canadian edition of this *Handbook*, we have tried to reflect a broad multicultural perspective that reflects the language issues faced in Canada today.

ACKNOWLEDGMENTS

Joanne Buckley and David Gates would particularly like to acknowledge the contributions of their students and of their editors, Avivah Wargon at Prentice Hall Canada and Cy Strom. A number of reviewers have also made important contributions to this Canadian edition of the *Handbook*. They are Ronald W. Cooley, University of Saskatchewan; Cherry Dalley, Cabot College; Jeffery Donaldson, McMaster University; W.H. (Bill) Fricker, Northern Alberta Institute of Technology; Enid Gossin, Seneca College; Gladys Hindmarch, Capilano College; Ingrid Hutchinson, Fanshawe College; Carol McCandless, Capilano College; and M. Dale Wilkie, University of Alberta.

Joanne Buckley

David Gates

About
the Authors

Lynn Quitman Troyka earned her Ph.D. at New York University and has taught for many years at the City University of New York (CUNY), including Queensborough Community College, the Center for Advanced Studies in Education at the Graduate School, and the graduate program in Language and Literacy at City College.

Dr. Troyka is an author in composition/ rhetoric for the *Encyclopedia of Rhetoric,* 1994. Former editor of the *Journal of Basic Writing,* she has published in journals such as *College Composition and Communication, College English,* and *Writing Program Administration* and in books from Southern Illinois Press, Random House, and Heineman/Boynton/Cook.

Dr. Troyka is the author of the *Simon & Schuster Handbook for Writers,* Fourth Edition, Prentice Hall, 1996; the *Simon & Schuster Quick Access Reference for Writers,* Prentice Hall, 1995; the *Simon & Schuster Concise Handbook,* Prentice Hall, 1992; and *Structured Reading,* Fourth Edition, Prentice Hall, 1995. She is co-author (with John Gerber, Richard Lloyd-Jones, et al.) of *A Checklist and Guide for Reviewing Departments of English,* ADE of the Modern Language Association, 1985; and of *Steps in Composition,* Sixth Edition (with Jerrold Nudelman), Prentice Hall, 1994.

Dr. Troyka has conducted seminars at numerous colleges and universities and at national and international meetings. She is a past chair of the Conference on College Composition and Communication (CCCC), of the College Section of the National Council of Teachers of English (NCTE), and of the Writing Division of the Modern Language Association. Named Rhetorician of the Year in 1993, she has given the 1995 Picket Service Award by CCCC and the NCTE Two-Year College Association. She currently serves as Chair of the Task Force on the Future of CCCC.

"All this information," says Dr. Troyka, "tells what I've done, not who I am. I am a teacher. Teaching is my life's work, and I love it."

Joanne Buckley is English Usage Specialist at the University of Western Ontario in London. She holds an M.Ed. and a Ph.D. in English Language and Literature from that university. She is the author of *Fit to Print: A Canadian Guide to Student Essay Writing*, now in its third edition, and is the co-author, with David Gates, of *Put It in Writing*.

David Gates studied nineteenth-century English literature at McMaster University in Hamilton and the University of Western Ontario in London. He holds a Ph.D. from the University of Western Ontario, where for several years he taught Communications courses. With Joanne Buckley, he is the author of *Put It in Writing*, now in its second edition, published by Prentice Hall Canada in 1995. Mr. Gates currently works in the arts.

SUPPLEMENTARY MATERIALS

As in other editions, the supplementary materials for the first Canadian edition of the *Simon & Schuster Handbook for Writers* assist teachers and students alike to use the text easily and to enhance the learning experience. The following list suggests the range of supplements available with this edition.

Print Supplements for Instructors

- Instructor's Manual
- Troyka with Judith Standford Ann Dobie and Emily R. Gordon
- *Strategies & Resources for Teaching Writing* by Linda Julian with Patricia Kelvin and Scott A. Leonard, Laurel Black, Cynthia L. Myers, and Edgar V. Roberts
- *Teaching Writing Across the Curriculum* by Ann O. Beghard
- *Computers and Writing* by Dawn Rodrigues
- *Teaching Writing* by Phyllis Hastings
- *Answer Key to the Simon & Schuster Workbook for Writers*
- Diagnostic Tests
- Response Symbols Chart

Print Supplements for Students

- *Simon & Schuster Workbook for Writers*, First Canadian Edition, by Lynn Quitman Troyka and Marsha Songer
- *Simon & Schuster Guide to Research and Documentation*
- Prentice Hall/New York Times Contemporary View Program: *Writing*
- *Rough Drafts* by Kathleen Shine Cain
- *Model Research Papers*, Second Edition, by Janette S. Lewis
- *The Research Organizer* by Sue D. Hopke
- *Supplementary Essays for Writers*
- *Preparing for the TASP* by Matilda Degado Saenz
- *Preparing for the CLAST* by Sybil Patterson
- *Webster's Dictionary* offers

Software Supplements

- On-Line Handbook
- Blue Pencil interactive editing program by Bob Bator, Canadian Edition
- Bibliotec bibliography generator

Audio-Visual Supplements

- *Prentice Hall/Simon & Schuster Transparencies for Writers* by Duncan Carter
- *Profiles of a Writer* Video Series
- Prentice Hall Critical Thinking Skills audiocassette

For more information, contact your Prentice Hall representative or write to: Marketing Manager, Prentice-Hall, 1870 Birchmount Road, Scarborough, Ontario M1P 2J7.

Prentice Hall and *The New York Times* proudly cosponsor A Contemporary View, a program designed to enhance student access in the classroom to relevant current information. Through this program, a collection of timely articles from *The New York Times*, one of the world's most distinguished newspapers, supplements the core subject matter of a course. These articles demonstrate the vital, ongoing connection between what is learned in the classroom and what is happening in the world around us. In newspaper format, with a range of articles and opinion pieces on topics of interest to today's students. A *Contemporary View: Writing* not only demonstrates purposeful writing but can serve to initiate it as well.

CREDIT LIST

Writing
An Essay

When you write an essay, you engage in a process. The parts of that process vary with the writer and the demands of the subject. Part One explains all aspects of the act of writing, and of thinking and reading in relation to writing, so that you can evolve your personal style of composing and thereby become an effective writer.

1

1 Thinking About Purposes and Audiences

Why write? In this age of telephones and tape recorders, television and film, computers and communication satellites, why should you bother with writing? The answer has overlapping parts, starting with the inner life of a writer and moving outward.

Writing is a way of thinking and learning. Writing gives you unique opportunities to explore ideas and understand information. By writing, you come to know subjects well and make them your own. Even thirty years later, many people can recall details about the topics and content of essays they wrote in college or university, but far fewer people can recall specifics of a classroom lecture or a textbook chapter. Writing helps you learn and gain authority over knowledge. As you share what you learn, you also teach. When you write for a reader, you play the role of a teacher, someone who knows the material sufficiently well to organize and present it clearly.

Writing is a way of discovering. The act of writing allows you to make unexpected connections among ideas and language. As you write, thoughts emerge and interconnect in ways unavailable until the physical act of writing begins. An authority on writing, James Britton, describes discovery in writing as "shaping at the point of utterance." Similarly, well-known writer E. M. Forster talked about discovery during writing by asking, "How can I know what I mean until I've seen what I said?" You can expect many surprises of insight that come only when you write and rewrite, each time trying to get closer to what you want to say.

Writing creates reading. Writing is a powerful means of communication. It creates a permanent, visible record of your ideas for others to read and ponder. Reading informs and shapes human thought. In an open society, everyone is free to write and thereby to create reading for other people. For that freedom to be exercised, however, the ability to write cannot be concentrated in a few people. All of us need access to the power of the written word.

Writing ability is needed by educated people. In college and university, you must write many different types of assignments. In the workplace, most jobs, even in today's technological society, require writing skill for preparing documents ranging from letters to formal reports. Throughout your life, your writing reveals your ability to think clearly and to use language effectively.

1a Understanding the elements of writing

Writing can be explained by its elements: *Writing is a way of communicating a message to a reader for a purpose.* Each word in this definition carries important meaning. **Communicating** in writing means sending a message that has a destination. The **message** of writing is its content, which originates in your motivation as a writer to engage in one or more of these activities: *observing, remembering, reporting, explaining, exploring, interpreting, speculating, evaluating,* and *reflecting.* The **reader,** usually called the audience, is explained in section 1c. **Purposes** for writing are discussed in section 1b.

1b Understanding purposes for writing

Writing is often defined by its **purpose.** Writing purposes have to do with goals, sometimes referred to as *aims of writing* or *writing intentions.* Thinking about purposes for writing means thinking about the motivating forces that move people to write. As a student, you might assume that your only purpose for writing is to fulfil a class assignment. More is involved, however. Your academic writing will almost certainly address at least one of the major purposes discussed in this section.

The overarching categories for the major purposes for writing are shown in Chart 1. The purposes of writing *to express yourself* and *to create a literary work* contribute importantly to human thought and culture (see 1b-1). This handbook concentrates on the two purposes most prominent and practical in your academic life: *to inform a reader* (1b-2) and *to persuade a reader* (1b-3).

As a writer in college or university, you are challenged to shape the content of your material and the style of your writing to suit your writing purpose.

You have many choices of writing strategies for presenting your message with clarity and impact. These strategies include narrating, describing, illustrating, defining, analyzing and classifying, comparing

---

PURPOSES FOR WRITING*

- to express yourself
- to inform a reader
- to persuade a reader
- to create a literary work

---

and contrasting, drawing an analogy, considering cause and effect, and others; see Chapter 4, especially section 4f.

1 Writing to express yourself

Expressive writing is usually the private recording of your thoughts and feelings. (When expressive writing is intended for public exposure, it becomes more like *literary writing*.) Consider this personal journal entry written by one of the students whose essay appears in Chapter 6; even though it is his private writing, it is published here with his permission.

> When we lived in Manitoba, the fall and winter holidays were my touchstones—the calendar moved along in comforting sequence. I wrapped the snow and foods and celebrations around me like a soft blanket. I burrowed in. Now that we live in Victoria, I don't need that blanket. But I surely do miss it.
>
> —DANIEL CASEY, student

2 Writing to inform a reader

Informative writing seeks to give information and, frequently, to explain it. This writing is known also as **expository writing** because it expounds on, or sets forth, ideas and facts. *Informative writing focuses mainly on the subject being discussed.*

Informative writing includes reports of observations, ideas, scientific data, facts, statistics. It can be found in textbooks, encyclopedias, technical and business reports, nonfiction, newspapers, and magazines.

When you write to inform, you are expected to offer information with a minimum of bias. You aim to educate, not persuade. Like

---

*Adapted from ideas that James L. Kinneavy, a modern rhetorician, discusses in *A Theory of Discourse.* 1971; New York: Norton, 1980.

all effective teachers, you need to present the information completely, clearly, and accurately. The material should be verifiable by additional reading, talking with others, or personal experience. For example, consider this passage that aims to inform the reader.

> In 1914 in what is now Addo Park in South Africa, a hunter by the name of Pretorius was asked to exterminate a herd of 140 elephants. He killed all but 20, and those survivors became so cunning at evading him that he was forced to abandon the hunt. The area became a preserve in 1930, and the elephants have been protected ever since. Nevertheless, elephants now four generations removed from those Pretorius hunted remain shy and strangely nocturnal. Young elephants evidently learn from the adults' trumpeting alarm calls to avoid humans.
>
> —Carol Grant Gould, "Out of the Mouths of Beasts"

This passage is successful because it *communicates* (transmits) a *message* (about young elephants learning to avoid humans) to a *reader* (a person who might become or already is interested in the subject) for a *purpose* (to inform). In this passage, the writer's last sentence states the main idea. The other sentences offer support for the main idea.

CHECKLIST FOR INFORMATIVE WRITING   2

- ■ Is its major focus the subject being discussed?
- ■ Is its primary purpose to inform rather than persuade?
- ■ Is its information complete and accurate?
- ■ Can its information be verified?
- ■ Is its information arranged for clarity?

---

3 **Writing to persuade a reader**

Persuasive writing seeks to convince the reader about a matter of opinion. This writing is sometimes called **argumentative** because it argues a position. (Because the techniques of written argument can be especially demanding on a writer, this handbook devotes all of Chapter 6 to them.)

Persuasive writing focuses mainly on the reader, whom the writer wants to influence. When you write to persuade, you deal with the debatable, that which has other sides to it. Persuasive writing seeks to change the reader's mind or at least to bring the reader's point of view closer to the writer's. Even the writer who feels sure that the reader's position on the subject will never change is expected to argue as convincingly as possible.

To be persuasive, you cannot merely state an opinion. Your reader expects you to offer convincing support for your point of view. Such support often relies upon information that explains and defends a point of view. Persuasive writing, therefore, often calls for informative writing (see 1b-2) to provide the evidence that lends strength to an argument. Examples of persuasive writing include editorials, letters to the editor, reviews, sermons, business or research proposals, opinion essays in magazines, and books that argue a point of view. For example, consider this passage that aims to persuade the reader.

> The search for some biological basis for math ability or disability is fraught with logical and experimental difficulties. Since not all math under-achievers are women, and not all women are mathematics-avoidant, poor performance in math is unlikely to be due to some genetic or hormonal difference between the sexes. Moreover, no amount of research so far has unearthed a "mathematical competency" in some tangible, measurable substance in the body. Since "masculinity" cannot be injected into women to test whether or not it improves their mathematics, the theories that attribute such ability to genes or hormones must depend for their proof on circumstantial evidence. So long as about seven percent of the Ph.D.'s in mathematics are earned by women, we have to conclude either that these women have genes, hormones, and brain organization different from those of the rest of us, or that certain positive experiences in their lives have largely undone the negative fact that they are female, or both.
>
> —SHEILA TOBIAS, *Overcoming Math Anxiety*

CHECKLIST FOR PERSUASIVE WRITING　　　3

- ■ Is its major focus the reader?
- ■ Is its primary purpose to convince rather than inform?
- ■ Does it offer information or reasons to support its point of view?
- ■ Is its point of view based on sound reasoning and logic?
- ■ Are the points of its argument arranged for clarity?
- ■ Does it evoke an intended reaction from the reader?

This passage is successful because it sends a *message* (about math ability and disability) to a *reader* (a person who might become or already is interested in the subject) for a *purpose* (to persuade a reader that math ability or disability is not related to gender). The writer's first sentence summarizes the point of view that she argues in the rest of the paragraph. The other sentences support the writer's assertion.

EXERCISE 1-1

For each paragraph, decide if the dominant purpose is *informative* or *persuasive*. Then, answer the questions in Chart 2 or Chart 3 in relation to the paragraph, and explain your answers.

A.   Trees are living archives, carrying within their structure a record not only of their age but also of precipitation and temperature for each year in which a ring was formed. The record might also include the marks of forest fires, early frosts and, incorporated into the wood itself, chemical elements the tree removed from its environment. Thus, if we only knew how to unlock its secrets, a tree could tell us a great deal about what was happening in its neighborhood from the time of its beginning. Trees can tell us what was happening before written records became available. They also have a great deal to tell us about our future. The records of past climate that they contain can help us to understand the natural forces that produce our weather, and this, in turn, can help us plan.

—JAMES S. TREFIL, "Concentric Clues from Growth Rings Unlock the Past"

B.   Noisy invasion of public spaces by yahoos is hardly a new problem, but unless my experience has been atypical, it seems to be nearing epidemic proportions. And the brutes are branching out. No longer content merely to destroy the sweet holy silence of the movie theatres, like nasty malignant cells, they're now everywhere—and they're out for blood. I see them on subway platforms, where their infernal amplified radios bring demented stares to other passengers' faces but never seem to arouse the offenders from their somnambulant stupor. I've pulled up beside roving packs of them at red lights, where they stare like zombies, blithely unaware that the decibel level of their tape decks is precipitating anxiety attacks in passers-by for miles. I've come face to face with them as close to home as a campsite in Algonquin Park and as far away as a surf-washed beach in Bali; recently I've even encountered them at live theatre. All of which convinces me there's something awry in the land.

—WENDY DENNIS, "A Tongue-Lashing for Deaf Ears"

C. Although Littleman, my eleven-year-old poodle, has never been separated from his thirteen-year-old mother, Simone, they are remarkably different. Simone weighs in at about five kilograms with very delicate, sophisticated features and coarse, curly hair. Slightly shorter, Littleman tops the scale at no more than three kilograms and is quite handsome with his teddy-bear features and soft wavy hair. Simone was the first dog in the family and is a pedigreed poodle. In many ways she is the picture of a thoroughbred, with her snobby attitude and nonchalant manners. On the other hand, Littleman came into the family a year later with four other puppies of pure breeding, but they were never registered. Unlike his mother, Littleman is very friendly, almost to the point of being pesty at times.

—LINDA NEAL, student

D. Over a period of several days we map and describe nine new ruins. The process is somewhat mechanical, but we each take pleasure in the simple tasks. As the Anasazi had a complicated culture, so have we. We are takers of notes, measurers of stone, examiners of fragments in the dust. We search for order in chaos wherever we go. We worry over what is lost. In our best moments we remember to ask ourselves what it is we are doing, whom we are benefiting by these acts. One of the great dreams of man must be to find some place between the extremes of nature and civilization where it is possible to live without regret.

—BARRY LOPEZ, "Searching for Ancestors"

EXERCISE 1-2

In one issue of a newspaper or a magazine, find an informative article and a persuasive article. Consulting section 1b, explain why you identify them as you do. Next, for each article, go back to Chart 2 or Chart 3, whichever is appropriate for the purpose you have identified, and answer the questions. Explain each answer.

EXERCISE 1-3

Consulting section 1b, assume that you have to write on each of these topics twice, once to inform and once to persuade your reader. Be prepared to discuss how your two treatments of each topic would differ.

1. diets
2. Canadian film
3. garbage
4. sense of humour
5. rap music
6. VCRs

1c Understanding audiences for writing

Good writing is often judged by its ability to reach its intended **audience.** To be effective, informative and persuasive writing (see 1b) need to be geared to the fact that someone is "out there" to receive the communication. If you write without considering your reader, you risk communicating only with yourself.

As a writer for one or more readers, you need to consider who your audience is, especially concerning background. For example, in writing meant to persuade people to vote for a particular candidate, if you imply disrespect for people who stay home and raise children, you risk losing votes of many homemakers and their spouses. Or, if you want to persuade Members of Parliament that homemakers should be eligible for a day-care subsidy, you would need to address some of the MPs' practical concerns, such as the impact of your proposal on the federal budget.

Also, as you write, you need to think about what you can assume an audience already knows. For example, a sales report filled with technical language assumes that its readers know the specialized vocabulary. The general reading public would have trouble understanding such a report. But if the material were rewritten without technical terms, general readers could understand it.

If you know or can reasonably assume even a few of the characteristics listed in Chart 4, your chances of reaching your audience

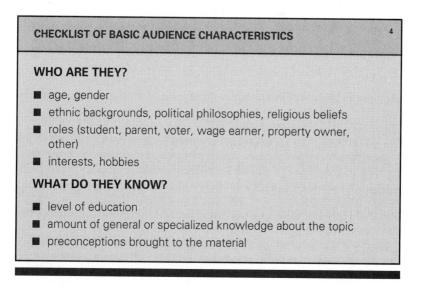

CHECKLIST OF BASIC AUDIENCE CHARACTERISTICS　　　　4

WHO ARE THEY?

- age, gender
- ethnic backgrounds, political philosophies, religious beliefs
- roles (student, parent, voter, wage earner, property owner, other)
- interests, hobbies

WHAT DO THEY KNOW?

- level of education
- amount of general or specialized knowledge about the topic
- preconceptions brought to the material

improve. The more explicit your information about your audience, the better able you are to reach it. Often, of course, you can only guess at the details. Chart 4 can help you get started.

1 Understanding the general reading public

The **general reading public** is composed of educated, experienced readers, people who frequently read newspapers, magazines, and books. These readers often have some general information about the subject you are dealing with, but they enjoy learning something new or seeing something from a different perspective. The general reading public expects material to be clear and to be free of advanced technical information.

2 Understanding your instructor as a reader

When you write for a class assignment, your audience will almost certainly be your **instructor.** Sometimes, especially when you are planning or revising your work, your instructor might want other students in your class to collaborate as an audience. In most cases, however, your final audience remains your instructor.

Your instructor is a member of the general reading public and also someone who recognizes that you are an apprentice. Your instructor knows that few students are experienced writers or complete experts on their subjects. Still, your instructor always expects your writing to reflect that you took time to learn the material thoroughly and to write about it well. In part, therefore, an instructor is a *judge,* someone to whom you must demonstrate that you are doing your best. Instructors are very experienced readers who can quickly recognize a minimal effort or a negative attitude (as when a paper carries a tone that suggests "Tell me what you want and I'll give it to you").

Think of your instructor as a representative reader typical of the audience you want to reach. *Inexperienced writers sometimes wrongly assume that instructors will fill in mentally what is missing on the page.* Instructors expect what they read to include everything that the writer wants to say or imply. Do not leave out material. Even if you write immediately after your instructor has heard you give an oral report on the same subject, write as if no one is aware of what you know.

Your instructor is also an *academic,* a member of a group whose professional life centres on intellectual endeavours. You must, therefore, write within the constraints of academic writing. For example, if you are told to write on a topic of your choice, you definitely do not have total freedom to choose. Your topic must have some intrinsic intellectual interest. For example, an essay should not merely give directions on how to cut a wedding cake or use an eraser.

3 Understanding specialists as readers

Specialists are members of the general reading public who have expert knowledge on specific subjects. In writing for specialists, you are expected to know the specialty and also to realize that your readers have advanced expertise.

Specialized readers often share not only knowledge but also assumptions, interests, and beliefs. For example, they may be members of a club that concentrates on a hobby, such as amateur astronomy or orchid raising. They may have similar backgrounds, such as having immigrated from another country or having worked at a similar job. They may have similar views on matters related to religion and politics. When you write for readers who share specialized knowledge, you have to balance the necessity to be thorough with the demand not to go into too much detail about technical terms and special references.

1d Understanding the effect of tone

The **tone** of your writing is established by *what you say* and *how you say it.* Tone underlies much of written communication. This section gives a brief overview of tone, with references to longer discussions that you can consult elsewhere in this handbook.

The tone in your writing needs to be shaped to your purpose for writing (see 1b) and awareness of your audience (see 1c). Your tone reveals your attitude both toward the material about which you are writing and toward anyone you expect to read your writing. For example, if your tone implies that you feel superior to your readers, your material will be condescending and distasteful. Similarly, if your tone hints that you are uninformed or unsure, your readers will quickly lose confidence in what you are saying.

In your academic writing, you want to achieve a reasonable tone, both in the content of your material and in your choice of words. For example, readers might think a writer unreasonable who distorts information or tries to manipulate emotions unfairly by using slanted language (see 21a-4). Choose evenhanded or neutral words ("the politician being investigated for taking bribes") rather than biased ones ("the corrupt, deceitful politician"). Also, readers can infer from sexist language (see 21b) that a writer is insensitive to gender issues in word choice. Choose gender-neutral terms and language that represents both men and women fairly ("police officer," "the doctors and their spouses") rather than sexist language ("policeman," "the doctors and their wives"). Similarly, pretentious language (see 21e-1) reflects negatively on a writer because it can obscure the message. Choose straightforward words ("the concert") rather than overblown words ("the orchestral event").

As important, when you move from writing privately for yourself to writing for an audience, the level of formality (see 21a-1) in your writing should reflect your goal. Although readers enjoy lively language, they can be jarred by an overly informal tone being injected into a serious discussion. Readers of academic writing expect to be treated respectfully. A medium level of formality is most effective. For example, in a newspaper report about the results of an election, you would not refer to the loser or winner as *guy* or *gal*, no matter how relaxed the candidate appears.

EXERCISE 1-4

Each of these passages was written for a general reading audience. Consulting sections 1c and 1d, read each paragraph and decide (1) if its tone is appropriate for academic writing and (2) if the choice of words assumes knowledge that only a specialist would have.

A.   Pernicious anemia, a uniformly fatal disease, was spectacularly reversed by liver extract (much later found to be due to the presence of vitamin B_{12} in the extracts). Diabetes mellitus could be treated—at least to the extent of reducing the elevated blood sugar and correcting the acidosis that otherwise led to diabetic coma and death—by the insulin preparation isolated by Banting and Best. Pellagra, a common cause of death among the impoverished rural populations in the South, had become curable with Goldberger's discovery of the vitamin B complex and the subsequent identification of nicotinic acid. Diphtheria could be prevented by immunization against the toxin of diphtheria bacilli and, when it occurred, treated more or less effectively with diphtheria antitoxin.

—LEWIS THOMAS, "1933 Medicine"

B.   Forty-five minutes south of the capital city by train, in the small suburb of Myorenji, near Yokohama, 13-year-old Naoko Masuo returns from school, slips quietly into her family's two-story house and settles into her homework. She is wearing a plaid skirt and blue blazer, the uniform of the Shoe-ei Girls School, where she is a seventh-grader. "I made it," her smile seems to say. For three years, when she was in fourth through sixth grades in public school, Naoko's schedule was high-pressure: she would rush home from school, study for a short time and then leave again to attend *juku,* or cram school, three hours a day, three times a week. Her goal was to enter a good private school, and the exam would be tough.

—CAROL SIMONS, "Kyoiku Mamas"

C.　　Without mucus, a slug would quickly be invaded by a host of microbial denizens and die. It would also be immobile, for slugs require mucus underfoot on which to crawl. Secreted from the pedal gland, located just beneath the head, the mucus flows down to the slug's single muscular foot. Like a miniature asphalt machine, the slug first lays its road and then, with wavelike motions of its foot, moves over it. As the mucus "road" dries, it becomes a silvery map of a slug's travels.

—SCOTT MCCREDIE,
"They're Still Slimy, But Naked Snails Are Finding New Friends"

D.　　My husband and I constantly marvel at the fact that our two sons, born of the same parents and only two years apart in age, are such completely opposite human beings. The most obvious differences became apparent at their births. Our first born, Mark, was big and bold—his intense, already wise eyes, broad shoulders, huge and heavy hands, and powerful, chunky legs gave us the impression that he could have walked out of the delivery room on his own. Our second son, Wayne, was delightfully different. Rather than have the football physique that Mark was born with, Wayne came into the world with a long, slim, wiry body more suited to running, jumping, and contorting. Wayne's eyes, rather than being intense like Mark's, were impish and innocent. When Mark was delivered, he cried only momentarily, then seemed to settle into a state of intense concentration, as if trying to absorb everything he could about the strange, new environment he found himself in. Conversely, Wayne screamed from the moment he first appeared until the nurse took him to the nursery. There was nothing helpless or pathetic about his cry either— he was damned angry!

—ROSEANNE LABONTE, student

1e Using sources for writing

You are your first **source** for writing. To write, you can always draw on the general fund of your prior knowledge—what you already know. Other sources for writing can be what you add to your prior knowledge by reading an article or book, watching television or movies, listening to lectures or speeches, or engaging in any other activity from which you can learn something.

Writing based on your prior knowledge is something you have been doing ever since you started putting pencil to paper. Whatever ideas and details you include in your writing you have had to learn previously, with the possible exception of wholly personal writing about your own emotions experienced at the moment you are writing.

Some college and university writing assignments call for you to use only your prior knowledge. In those cases, do not consult sources for any kind of new information. (If you are not sure whether you can draw on outside sources for a specific assignment, ask your instructor before you use any.) To stimulate yourself to think of ideas and details you already know but perhaps have not thought about recently, use the techniques described in sections 2d through 2i.

For other writing assignments, you will consult sources—sometimes referred to as *outside sources,* meaning outside of what you already know. In such cases, you have a few very important obligations, which are listed in Chart 5.

GUIDELINES FOR USING SOURCES IN WRITING

5

- Be sure to represent a source accurately. For guidance in quoting, paraphrasing, or summarizing source material, see Chapter 31.

- Synthesize source material, do not merely report it. Make connections for your reader between the ideas and details in the source and your own ideas as stimulated by the source. For guidance in synthesizing sources, see 5f.

- Credit your source by naming it clearly and completely. Ask your instructor what method to use to give credit to the sources you use. Four widely used systems for communicating to a reader that you are giving credit to (documenting) sources are described in Chapter 33.

- For guidance on giving credit to only a single source that you refer to throughout an essay, see section 5f.

- Remember that using a source without informing readers of that use is plagiarism. For help in avoiding plagiarism, see Chapter 31.

---

2 Planning and Shaping

Understanding the writing process

Many people assume that a real writer can pick up a pen or sit at a computer and magically write a finished product, word by perfect word. Experienced writers know better. They know that **writing is a process,** a series of activities that start the moment they begin thinking about a subject and end when they complete a final draft. Experienced writers know, also, that good writing is rewriting. Their drafts are filled with additions, deletions, rearrangements, and rewordings.

For example, on the next page you can see how the paragraph you just read was reworked into final form. Notice that two sentences were dropped, two sentences were combined, one sentence was added, and various words were dropped, changed, or added. Such activities are typical of writing.

Writing is an ongoing process of considering alternatives and making choices. The better you understand the writing process, the better you will write and the more you can enjoy writing. For the sake of explanation, the parts of the writing process are discussed separately in this chapter. In real life, the steps overlap, looping back and forth as each piece of writing evolves.

Understanding writing as a multistage process allows you to work efficiently, concentrating on one activity at a time rather than trying to juggle all of the facets of a writing project simultaneously. Chart 6 summarizes the steps in the writing process. If you are a writer who likes to visualize a process, see the diagram on page 17. A straight line would not be adequate because it would exclude the recursive nature of writing. The arrows on the diagram imply movement. Planning is not over when drafting begins, drafting is not necessarily over merely because the major activity shifts to revision, and editing sometimes

~~Chapter One discusses what writing is.~~ ~~This chapter~~

~~explains how writing happens.~~ Many people assume that a real

Pick up a pen

writer can ~~put pen to paper~~ or sit at ~~the keyboard of~~

magically a

a computer and write (finished product*,* *word by perfect word.*)

Experienced writers ~~all~~ know better. They know that writing

is a process, ~~Writing is~~ a series of activities that start

they begin

the moment thinking about a subject ~~begins~~ and end when they

Complete the a

final draft*.* ~~is complete.~~ Experienced writers know, also,

that good writing is rewriting. *Their drafts are filled with additions, deletions, rearrangements, and rewordings.*

Draft and Revision of Opening Paragraph in Chapter 2 by Lynn Troyka

---

AN OVERVIEW OF THE WRITING PROCESS 6

Planning calls for you to gather ideas and think about a focus.

Shaping calls for you to consider ways to organize your material.

Drafting calls for you to write your ideas in sentences and paragraphs.

Revising calls for you to evaluate your draft and, based on your decisions, rewrite it by adding, cutting, replacing, moving—and often totally recasting material.

Editing calls for you to check the technical correctness of your grammar, spelling, punctuation, and mechanics.

Proofreading calls for you to read your final copy for typing errors or handwriting legibility.

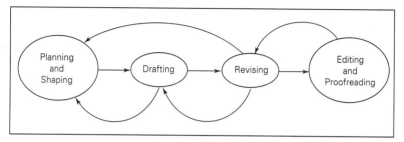

Visualizing the Writing Process

inspires writers to see the need for additional revising—and perhaps some new planning.

As you work with the writing process, rest assured that there is no *one* way to write. When you start, allow yourself to move through each stage of the writing process and see what is involved. Then as you gain experience, begin to observe what works best for you. Once you have a general sense of the pattern of *your* writing process, you can adapt the process to suit each new situation that you encounter as a writer.

Most writers struggle some of the time with ideas that are difficult to express, sentences that will not take shape, and words that are not precise. Do not be impatient with yourself, and do not get discouraged. Writing takes time. The more you write, the easier it will be, but remember that experienced writers know that writing never happens magically.

An aside about the words used to discuss writing: Instructors refer to written products in different ways. Often the words are used interchangeably, but sometimes they have specific meanings for specific instructors. Listen closely and ask if you are unsure of what you hear. For example, the words *essay, theme,* and *composition* usually—but not always—refer to writing that runs from about 500 to 1,000 words. This handbook uses *essay.* The word *paper* can mean anything from a few paragraphs to a long and detailed report or a complex research project. This handbook uses *paper* to refer to longer writing projects, such as research papers, that draw on many outside sources.

2b Adjusting for each writing situation

Writing begins with thinking about each **writing situation.** Your thinking involves answering the questions in Chart 7. Then you adjust your writing process (see 2a) to accommodate each particular writing situation.

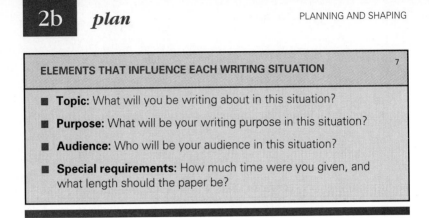

The **topic** underlies all aspects of the writing situation. If you must choose your own topic or narrow an assigned topic, keep in mind the constraints of academic writing (see 2c). If the topic is assigned, you must not go "off the topic." Whatever the topic, *you* are the starting place for your writing. Draw upon yourself as a source. Whatever you have seen, heard, read, and even dreamed contributes to your fund of ideas and knowledge. Keep in mind the need to marshal specific support for the points you make about your topic.

The **purpose** of your college or university writing is usually *to inform* or *to persuade* (see 1b). Effective writing reflects a clear sense of purpose. Some writing assignments include or clearly imply a statement of purpose. For example, your purpose is informative if you are writing about the dangers of smoking. Conversely, your purpose is persuasive if you are writing an argument against smoking. Other assignments do not stipulate the writing purpose, which means you must choose either an informative or persuasive purpose based on the topic, what you want to say about it (often referred to as the *focus*), and how you develop what you want to say.

Your **audience,** for college or university writing (see 1c) is often primarily, though not exclusively, your instructor. Your instructor is both a member of the general reading public and an academic. Some writing assignments name a specialized audience, which means your readers have more technical knowledge than does the general reading public. You have to write to their level. Sometimes an assignment stipulates that the writing will be read by other students in the class. In such situations, students serve as surrogate instructors, so you are expected to write with the same tone and level of information as you would for your instructor alone.

plan **2b**

Special requirements influence every writing situation. These include the time allotted for the assignment, the expected length of the writing, and other practical constraints. If an assignment is due in one week, you have to expect that your instructor wants writing that shows more than one day's work. If the paper is due overnight, it has to be written more hastily, though never carelessly. If research is required, you have to build time for it into your schedule.

Your assignment is a major resource for you as you write. Refer to it often. Ideally, your instructor writes the assignment on the board or distributes it on paper. Some instructors, however, only announce an assignment, in which case you are expected to write it down. Try to record every word spoken, always ask questions if you need clarifications, and write down the answers you get or any given in response to other students' questions.

To give you examples of the writing process in progress, this chapter shows you the work of two actual students—Carol Moreno and Daniel Casey—as they plan and shape their essays. Then in Chapter 3, Carol Moreno's essay is discussed as it evolves through three drafts (shown in section 3f). Daniel Casey's essay is developed in Chapter 6, and its final draft appears in section 6i. Here is the written statement of the assignment that each student received.

Carol Moreno was given this assignment: Write an essay of 700 to 800 words in which you discuss a challenge you faced and tried to meet. Your writing purpose can be informative or persuasive. Expect to write three drafts. Your first draft (in rough form, showing your comments to yourself and changes you made) and your second (cleanly typed) draft are due in one week. I will read your second draft as an "essay in progress" and will make comments to help you toward a third, final draft. That third, final draft (cleanly typed) is due one week after I hand back your second draft with my comments.

Daniel Casey was given this assignment: Write an essay of 500 to 700 words that argues about whether holidays have become too commercialized in North America. Your final draft is due in one week. Bring your earlier drafts to class for possible discussion.

Moreno read her assignment with an eye toward analyzing the elements of her writing situation. The *topic* was a challenge she faced and tried to meet, a subject that Moreno realized she would have to narrow considerably (for her process of narrowing the topic, see 2c–2). For a writing *purpose,* Moreno tentatively chose an informative purpose, knowing that as she got further into her planning, she might change her mind. She saw that her instructor was to be her *audience* and that the *special requirements* of length and time were given in the assignment.

Casey read his assignment to analyze his writing situation. He saw immediately that most elements were stated. The *topic* was commercialization of holidays in North America, and the *purpose* persuasive because students were expected to adopt and argue a position about the topic. The *audience* was the instructor, though Casey realized that the class might hear or see earlier drafts once the final draft was finished. The *special requirements* of length and time were given in the assignment.

EXERCISE 2-1

Consulting section 2b, for each assignment listed below, answer these questions: (a) Is its purpose to inform or to persuade? (b) Is the audience the general reading public or specialists? (c) What special requirements of length and time are stated or implied?

1. *English:* Write a 500- to 700-word essay arguing for or against doubling the size of your school's student body. This assignment is due in one week.

2. *Journalism:* Write a 300-word editorial for the student newspaper (to be published next week) praising or criticizing your school's policy on selling parking stickers to students and faculty. Draw on your personal experience, if any.

3. *Art:* You have twenty minutes in class to compare and contrast Greek and Roman styles of architecture.

4. *Biology:* Write a one-paragraph description of the process of hydration.

5. *Economics:* Write a 1000-word essay on the broad impact of capitalism since 1989 on the former communist nations of Eastern Europe. Draw on your reading. This assignment is due in two weeks.

2c Choosing a topic for writing

Choosing a topic calls for making sound decisions. Experienced writers know that the quality of their writing depends on how they handle a topic. Always think through a topic before you rush in and get too deeply involved to pull out within the time allotted.

Of course, some assignments leave no room for making choices about the topic. You may be given very specific instructions such as "Explain how oxygen is absorbed from the lungs," or you may be asked to describe the view from your classroom window. Your job with such assignments is to do precisely what is asked and not wander off the topic.

1 Selecting a topic on your own

Some instructors ask students to choose their own topic. In such situations, do not assume that all subjects are suitable for academic writing. Academic settings call for topics that can reflect your ability to think ideas through. For example, the old reliable essay about a summer vacation is probably not safe territory for a college or university essay if you have nothing extraordinary to report. Your essays need to dive into issues and concepts, and they should demonstrate that you can use specific, concrete details to support what you want to say.

When you choose a topic on your own, avoid topics so narrow that they give you little to say. For example, you would probably reach a dead end if you tried to write a 2500-word essay about what your sleeping cat looks like.

2 Narrowing an assigned topic

The real challenge in dealing with topics comes when you have a very broad subject. You have to *narrow the subject*. Narrowing means thinking of subdivisions of the subject, of different areas within the subject. Most very broad subjects can be broken down in hundreds of ways, but you need not think of all of them. When one seems possible, think it through at the start so that you can decide whether you can develop it well in writing. **What separates most good writing from bad is the writer's ability to move back and forth between general statements and specific details.**

For example, if the subject is marriage, you might decide to talk about what makes marriages successful. But you cannot depend merely on generalizations such as "In successful marriages husbands and wives learn to accept each other's faults." You need to explain why accepting faults is important, and you need to give concrete illustrations of what you are talking about.

As you narrow a broad subject to obtain a writing topic, keep in mind the writing situation (see 2b) of each assignment. Think about what topics are possible and which of these you can handle well.

SUBJECT	*Music*
WRITING SITUATION	first-year composition class informative purpose instructor as audience 500 words, one week
POSSIBLE TOPICS	the moods music creates classical music of the Renaissance country and western music as big business
SUBJECT	*Cities*
WRITING SITUATION	sociology course persuasive purpose students and then instructor as audience 500 to 700 words, one week
POSSIBLE TOPICS	comforts of city living discomforts of city living why city planning is important
SUBJECT	*Mythology*
WRITING SITUATION	humanities course informative purpose instructor as audience, someone who is a specialist in mythology 1000 words, two weeks
POSSIBLE TOPICS	the purpose of myths comparison of Ojibway and Roman myths explaining why seasons change

Carol Moreno narrowed the topic of her assignment (see pages 19-20) because "a challenge you faced and tried to meet" was too vague and general. To stimulate her thinking, Moreno used some of the techniques for gathering ideas presented in the rest of this chapter. She used an entry from her journal (shown in 2e), freewriting (in 2f), and mapping (in 2i). As a result, Moreno decided to write about her need to build up her strength and stamina. Her essay is discussed in Chapter 3 as it evolves through three drafts, all of which are shown in section 3f.

Daniel Casey did not have to narrow his topic because it was stated in his assignment (see page 19): the commercialization of holidays in North America. He did, however, have to choose a position to argue on the topic. What helped him the most were brainstorming (see his work in 2g), asking the "journalist's questions" (see his work in 2h), and using a subject tree (see his work in 2l). The development of Casey's essay is discussed in Chapter 6, and his final draft appears in section 6i.

✦ COMPUTER TIPS: Using a computer, you can record your thoughts as they occur to you. Try freewriting (2f) or brainstorming (2g). Also, consider using invisible writing by dimming the screen so that you cannot see what you are writing. This helps you avoid the temptation to edit while you are getting your ideas down. After a while, brighten the screen to look at what you wrote. ✦

As you use idea-gathering techniques, do not delete material. You never know what you might want later. A computer can save everything for you and then retrieve it when you are ready to decide which material to use and in what order.

EXERCISE 2-2

Consulting section 2c, for five of these general topics, think of three narrowed topics that would be suitable for a 500- to 700-word essay in a writing course. Assume that each essay is due in one week and that the audience is the general reading public, as represented by the course's instructor. List your three narrowed topics and explain briefly why each is suitable for the writing situation. Then repeat the exercise using an interesting topic not on this list.

1. clichés
2. television violence
3. music
4. ethnic identity
5. daydreaming
6. Valentine's Day
7. the Internet
8. self-improvement
9. cost of textbooks
10. humour

2d Gathering ideas for writing

Techniques for gathering ideas, sometimes called *prewriting strategies* or *invention techniques,* can help you discover how much you know about a topic before you decide to write about it. Chart 8 lists various ways to gather ideas for writing and refers you to the sections in this handbook where you can learn more about each technique.

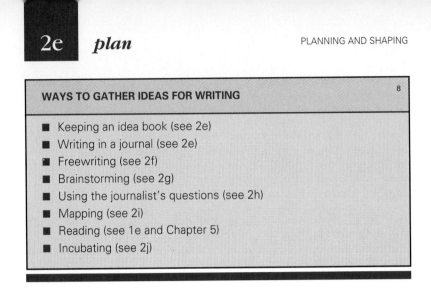

WAYS TO GATHER IDEAS FOR WRITING   8

- Keeping an idea book (see 2e)
- Writing in a journal (see 2e)
- Freewriting (see 2f)
- Brainstorming (see 2g)
- Using the journalist's questions (see 2h)
- Mapping (see 2i)
- Reading (see 1e and Chapter 5)
- Incubating (see 2j)

Students sometimes worry that they have nothing to write about. Often, however, students know far more than they give themselves credit for. The challenge is to uncover what is there but seems not to be. As you use these various techniques for gathering ideas, find out which work best for *you* and *your* style of thinking.

No one technique of generating ideas always works for all topics. Experiment. If one method does not provide enough useful material, try another. Also, even if one strategy produces some good material, try another to turn up additional possibilities.

2e Keeping an idea book and writing in a journal

Your ease with writing will grow as you develop the habits of mind that typify writers. Professional writers are always on the lookout for ideas to write about and for details to develop their ideas. They listen, watch, talk with people, and generally keep their minds open. For this reason, many writers always carry an **idea book**—a pocketsize notebook—to jot down ideas that spring to mind. Good ideas can melt away like snowflakes. Use an idea book throughout your college or university years, and watch your powers of observation increase.

Many writers, both amateur and professional, write in a **journal.** Keeping a journal gives you the chance to have a "conversation on paper" with yourself. Fifteen minutes a day can be enough—before going to bed, between classes, on a bus. *You* are your audience, so the content and tone can be as personal and informal as you wish.

Unlike a diary, a journal is not merely for listing what you did that day. A journal is for your thoughts. You can draw on your reading, your observations, your dreams. You can respond to quotations, react to movies or plays, or think through your opinions, beliefs, and tastes. Writing is a way of discovering, of allowing thoughts to emerge as the physical act of writing moves along.

Keeping a journal can help you in three ways. First, writing every day gives you the habit of productivity. The more you write, the more you get used to the feeling of words pouring out of you onto paper, the easier it will become for you to write in all situations. Second, a journal instils the habit of close observation and thinking. Third, a journal serves as an excellent source of ideas when you need to write in response to an assignment.

Here is an excerpt of a journal entry Carol Moreno had written before she got the assignment to write an essay about facing a challenge (see page 19). When reading through her journal for ideas for her essay, Moreno realized that she had faced the challenge of needing to develop more strength and stamina.

September 30   I got to add 5 more reps today and it's only the sixth weight lifting class. I wasn't really surprised— I can tell I'm stronger. I wonder if I'm strong enough yet to lift Gran into the wheelchair alone. I was so scared last summer when I almost dropped her. Besides being terrified of hurting her, I thought that somehow the admissions committee would find out and tell me I was too weak to be accepted into nursing school. What if I hadn't noticed the weight-lifting course for P.E. credit!?! Weight lifting is the best exercise I've ever done and I'm not getting beefy looking either.

Excerpt from Carol Moreno's Journal

2f Freewriting

Freewriting is writing nonstop. It means writing down whatever comes into your mind without stopping to worry about whether the ideas are good or the spelling is correct. When you freewrite, do nothing to interrupt the flow. Do not censor any thoughts or flashes of insight. Do not go back and review. Do not cross out. Some days your freewriting might seem mindless, but other days it can reveal interesting ideas to you.

Freewriting helps get you used to the "feel" of pen moving across paper or of fingers in constant motion at a computer. Freewriting works best if you set a goal: perhaps writing for 15 minutes or filling one or two pages. Keep going until you reach that goal, even if you have to write one word over and over until a new word comes to mind.

If you write on a computer, you can avoid the temptation to stop and criticize your writing by doing "invisible writing." Dim the screen so you cannot see your writing. The computer will still be recording your ideas, but you will not be able to see them until you brighten the screen again. To create the same effect writing by hand, use a worn-out ballpoint pen and a piece of carbon paper between two sheets of paper.

Focused freewriting means starting with a set topic. You can focus your freewriting in any way you like—perhaps with a phrase from your journal or a quotation you like. Using the focus as a starting point, write until you meet the time or page limit you have set as a goal. Again, do not censor what you say. Keep moving forward.

Like journals, freewriting can be a source for ideas and details to write about. Carol Moreno wanted to explore the topic of her experience in learning to lift weights. She felt it had potential for her essay assignment (on page 19). Here is an excerpt from her focused freewriting on "pumping iron."

Pumping iron — what the steroid jocks call it and exactly what I DO NOT want to be — a muscle cube. Great that Prof. Moore told us women's muscles don't bulk up much unless a weight lifting program is really intense.— they just get longer. No bulk for me PLEASE. Just want upper body strength —oh, and the aerobic stuff from swimming, which makes me feel great. Lift, sweat, swim, lift, sweat, swim, lift, sweat, swim.

Excerpt from Carol Moreno's Freewriting

EXERCISE 2-3

Consulting section 2f, freewrite for five minutes on one of these topics. Then think of one topic that interests you and is not on this list, and freewrite on that topic.

1. pizza
2. procrastinating
3. a dream vacation
4. meeting deadlines
5. playing a sport
6. telling jokes
7. libraries
8. chocolate
9. falling in love
10. world peace

2g Brainstorming

Brainstorming means listing all the ideas that come to mind associated with a topic. The ideas can be listed as words, phrases, or even random sentences. Let your mind range freely, generating quantities of ideas before eliminating some.

You can brainstorm in one concentrated session or over several days, depending on how much time is available for the assignment. In courses that permit collaborative work, brainstorming in groups can work especially well because one person's ideas bounce off the next person's, and collectively more ideas get listed.

Brainstorming is done in two steps: First, you make a list, and then you try to find patterns in the list and ways to group the ideas into categories. Set aside any items that do not fit into groups. If an area interests you but its list is thin, brainstorm on that area alone. If you run out of ideas, ask yourself questions to stimulate your thinking. You might try exploratory questions about the topic, such as: What is it? What is it the same as? How is it different? Why or how does it happen? How is it done? What caused it or results from it? What does it look, smell, sound, feel, or taste like?

Daniel Casey's essay, discussed in Chapter 6, develops an argument concerning the benefits of the commercialization of holidays. For Casey's final draft, see section 6i. Realizing that his position was open to debate, Casey used the technique of brainstorming to help himself think through his opinion. On the next page is an excerpt from the ideas as they came to Casey at random. The items followed by an asterisk (*) are those Casey chose for the fourth paragraph—about the spirit of the holidays—of his essay, shown in section 6i.

Excerpt from Daniel Casey's Brainstormed List
people feel cheerful*
the economy is stimulated
people give to charities
strangers exchange friendly greetings*
everyone gives and gets gifts
children love visiting Santa (and the Easter Bunny)*
festive atmosphere in stores*
sending greeting cards helps friends stay in touch*
arouses positive sentimental feelings
stimulates good will

EXERCISE 2-4

Here is a brainstormed list for an assignment in a business class on ways to get the public to go see a new movie. Consulting section 2g, look over the list, and then group ideas. Some ideas may not fit into any group.

coming attractions	suspense
TV ads	book the movie was based on
provocative movie reviews	locations
how movie was made	rating
sneak previews	adventure
word of mouth	newspaper ads
director	stars
topical subject	dialogue
special effects	excitement
personal interviews	photography

EXERCISE 2-5

Consulting section 2g, brainstorm on a subject that interests you. First make a random list, and then group ideas within the list. If you cannot think of a subject, use one from Exercise 2-2 or Exercise 2-3.

2h Using the journalist's questions

Journalist's questions ask *Who? What? When? Why? Where? How?* Asking these questions forces you to approach a topic from several different perspectives.

plan **2i**

Daniel Casey used the journalist's questions to explore and expand his thinking about specific benefits of the commercialization of holidays in North America. His answers to the questions helped him decide that he had enough details to write an effective essay (for his final draft, see section 6i).

WHO	Who specifically benefits from the commercial aspects of holidays?
WHAT	What specific benefits result from commercialization of holidays?
WHEN	When specifically do beneficial holidays fall?
WHY	Why specifically do some people object to the commercial aspects of holidays?
WHERE	Where specifically can evidence of benefits be seen or felt?
HOW	How do specific commercial aspects of holidays create benefits?

EXERCISE 2-6

Consulting section 2h, ask the journalist's questions about one of these subjects: day-care centres, watching soap operas, eating junk food, or shoplifting. Then think of an interesting topic not on this list, and ask the journalist's questions about that topic.

2i **Mapping**

Mapping, also called *clustering* or *webbing,* is much like brainstorming (see 2g), but it is more visual and less linear. Many writers find that mapping frees them to think more creatively by associating ideas more easily.

To map, start with your topic circled in the middle of a sheet of unlined paper. Next, draw a line radiating out from the centre and label it with the name of a major subdivision of your topic. Circle it and from that circle radiate out to more specific subdivisions. When you finish with one major subdivision of your subject, go back to the centre and start again with another major division. As you go along, add anything that occurs to you for any section of the map. Continue the process until you run out of ideas. The technique of mapping, by the way, also can be used the same way as using a subject tree (see 2l): to lay out the logical relationships of ideas to each other. But many writers seem to prefer to use mapping for discovering ideas already known but not remembered, as Carol Moreno did. You use the techniques as they suit you best.

Here is Carol Moreno's mapping for ideas to use in her essay about women lifting weights (for the three drafts of her essay, see section 3f). After Moreno finished mapping, she was satisfied that she had enough information to use in her essay.

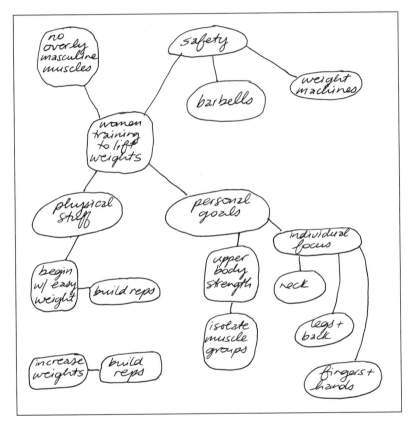

Carol Moreno's Mapping

EXERCISE 2-7

For a topic you have some information about, use mapping to chart what you know. Write the topic in the middle of a blank page, and work out from there.

2j Using incubation

When you allow your ideas to **incubate,** you give them time to grow and develop. Incubation works especially well when you need to solve a problem in your writing (for example, if material is too thin and needs expansion, if material covers too much and needs pruning, or if connections among your ideas are not clear for your reader). Time is a key element for successful incubation. Arrange your time to make sure that you will not be interrupted. You need time to think, to allow your mind to wander, and then to come back and focus on the writing. Sometimes incubating an idea overnight permits sleep to help you discover or clarify an idea.

One helpful strategy is to turn attention to something entirely different from your writing problem. Concentrate *very hard* on that entirely different matter so that your conscious mind is totally distracted from the writing problem. After a while, relax and guide your mind back to the writing problem you want to solve.

Another strategy is to allow your mind to relax and wander, without concentrating on anything special. Open your mind to random thoughts, but do not dwell on any one thought very long. After a while, guide your mind back to the writing problem you are trying to solve. When you come back to the writing problem, you might see solutions that did not occur to you before.

2k Shaping ideas

Shaping activities are related to the idea that writing is often called *composing,* the putting together of ideas to create a *composition,* one of the synonyms for *essay.* To shape the ideas that you have gathered, you need to group them (see 2l) and sequence them (see 2m).

As you shape ideas, keep in mind that the form of an essay is related to the classical notion of a story having a beginning, a middle, and an end. An academic essay always has an introduction, a body, and a conclusion. The length of each paragraph is in proportion to the overall length of the essay. Introductory and concluding paragraphs are generally shorter than body paragraphs, and no body paragraph should overpower the others by its length. (Types of paragraphs useful for academic writing are discussed in Chapter 4.)

21 Grouping ideas

When you group ideas, you make connections and find patterns. To do this, put each batch of related ideas into its own group. As you create groups, use the concept of **levels of generality** to help you make decisions: One idea is more general than another if it falls into a larger, less specific category than the other. Remember that generality is a relative term. Each idea exists in the context of a whole relationship of ideas. An idea may be general in relationship to one set of ideas but specific in relation to another set.

For example, "bank account" is more general than "chequing account." In turn, "chequing account" is more general than "business chequing account" or "regular chequing account." And those terms are more general than "account 221222 at the EZ-Come-EZ-Go Bank."

To identify groups of ideas, review the material you accumulated while gathering ideas (see 2e through 2j). Look for general ideas. Then, group less general ideas under them. If your notes contain only general ideas, or only very specific details, return to techniques for gathering ideas to supply what you need. A standard tool for grouping ideas is to make a "subject tree" to see whether you have enough content to write about. A subject tree resembles a map (see 2i): It shows ideas and details in order from most general at the top to most specific at the bottom.

Daniel Casey used a subject tree while shaping his essay that takes the position that benefits result from the commercialization of holidays in North America (for his final draft, see section 6i). He used the subject tree to lay out the ideas in his third paragraph according to their relative levels of generality. You can write out a subject tree for single paragraphs and for checking the interrelationships of the ideas in a whole essay. You use the techniques as they suit you best.

2m Sequencing ideas for writing

When you sequence ideas for writing, you decide what you want your readers to encounter first, second, and on until the last. When readers can follow your line of reasoning, they are more likely to understand the message that you want your material to deliver.

Within paragraphs, you can present ideas in any of the many ways explained in Chapter 4. Within an essay, the sequence in which you put those paragraphs reveals to your reader your evolving material. No one sequence or structure fits all academic essays, but certain elements are usually present. For the major elements in essays

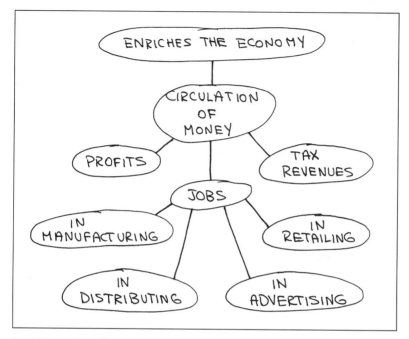

Daniel Casey's Subject Tree

with persuasive purpose, see Chart 43 in section 6g. When you write essays with an informative purpose, be sure to include the elements in Chart 9. (Carol Moreno's essay in section 3f includes the elements in Chart 9.)

2n Shaping writing with a thesis statement

A **thesis statement** is the central message of an essay. It is evidence that you have something definite to say about the topic. An effective thesis statement prepares your reader for the essence of what you discuss in an essay. As the writer, you want to compose a thesis statement with care so that it accurately reflects the content of your essay. If you find a mismatch between your thesis statement and the rest of your essay, revise to coordinate them better. The basic requirements for a thesis statement appear in Chart 10.

Some instructors ask for more than the basic requirements. For example, you might be required to put your thesis statement at the end of your introductory paragraph. (For an example, see the final draft

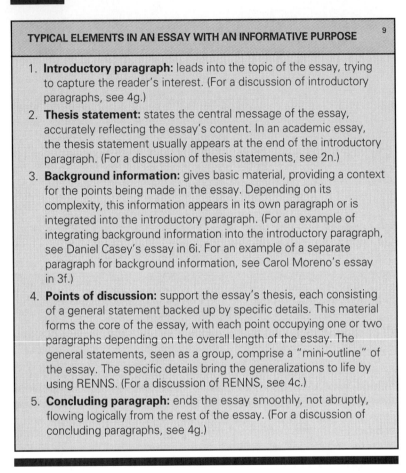

TYPICAL ELEMENTS IN AN ESSAY WITH AN INFORMATIVE PURPOSE   9

1. **Introductory paragraph:** leads into the topic of the essay, trying to capture the reader's interest. (For a discussion of introductory paragraphs, see 4g.)

2. **Thesis statement:** states the central message of the essay, accurately reflecting the essay's content. In an academic essay, the thesis statement usually appears at the end of the introductory paragraph. (For a discussion of thesis statements, see 2n.)

3. **Background information:** gives basic material, providing a context for the points being made in the essay. Depending on its complexity, this information appears in its own paragraph or is integrated into the introductory paragraph. (For an example of integrating background information into the introductory paragraph, see Daniel Casey's essay in 6i. For an example of a separate paragraph for background information, see Carol Moreno's essay in 3f.)

4. **Points of discussion:** support the essay's thesis, each consisting of a general statement backed up by specific details. This material forms the core of the essay, with each point occupying one or two paragraphs depending on the overall length of the essay. The general statements, seen as a group, comprise a "mini-outline" of the essay. The specific details bring the generalizations to life by using RENNS. (For a discussion of RENNS, see 4c.)

5. **Concluding paragraph:** ends the essay smoothly, not abruptly, flowing logically from the rest of the essay. (For a discussion of concluding paragraphs, see 4g.)

of Carol Moreno's essay in 3f.) Also, many instructors require that the thesis statement be contained in one sentence. Other instructors permit two sentences if the material to be covered warrants such length. All requirements, basic and additional, are designed to help you think in structured patterns that communicate clearly with readers. Be sure not to confuse a title (see 3c–2) with a thesis statement.

Until you have written one or more drafts, all parts of a thesis statement might not accurately reflect what you say in the essay. To begin, make an **assertion**—a sentence stating your topic and the point you want to make about it. The exact wording of this assertion probably will not appear in your final draft, but it serves as a focus for your

BASIC REQUIREMENTS FOR A THESIS STATEMENT	10

1. It states the essay's **subject**—the topic that you are discussing.
2. It reflects the essay's **purpose**—either to give your readers information or to persuade your readers to agree with you.
3. It includes a **focus**—your assertion that conveys your point of view.
4. It uses **specific language**—vague words are avoided.
5. It *may* briefly state the major subdivisions of the essay's topic.

thinking as you progress through a **preliminary thesis statement** toward a fully developed one.

To write her essay about women lifting weights, Carol Moreno used this progression from basic assertion to final thesis statement.

I think women can "pump iron" like men. [This assertion is a start.]

If she is trained well, any woman can "pump iron" well, just like a man. [This preliminary thesis is more developed because it mentions training, but the word *well* is used twice and is vague, and the word *any* is inaccurate.]

In spite of most people thinking only men can "pump iron," women can also do it successfully with the right training. [This draft is better because it is becoming more specific, but "most people thinking only men" is not an aspect of the topic Moreno intends to explore. Also, the concept of building strength, a major aspect of Moreno's final draft, is missing.]

With the right training, women can also "pump iron" successfully to build strength. [This is the final version of Moreno's thesis statement. *Also* is a transitional word connecting the thesis statement to the sentence that comes before it in Moreno's introductory paragraph.]

The final version fulfils the requirements for a thesis statement described in Chart 10.

Here are more examples of thesis statements written for 500- to 700-word essays with an **informative purpose** (see section 1b–2). The ineffective versions resemble assertions or preliminary thesis statements. The effective versions are final thesis statements written by students after they had gathered and grouped ideas. The good versions fulfil the requirements in Chart 10.

TOPIC	*classical music*
NO	Classical music combines many different sounds.
YES	Classical music can be played by groups of various sizes, ranging from chamber ensembles to full symphony orchestras.
TOPIC	*women artists*
NO	The paintings of women are getting more attention.
YES	During the past ten years the works of artists Mary Cassatt and Rosa Bonheur have finally gained widespread critical acclaim.

For a persuasive purpose, Daniel Casey wrote this thesis statement for his essay about the commercialization of holidays (see section 6i):

> After all, commercial uses of holidays benefit the economy and lift people's spirits.

Casey's thesis statement reveals that the *topic* is commercialization of holidays, the *purpose* is to persuade, and the *focus* is the benefits of holidays' commercial uses.

Here are ineffective and effective thesis statements written for 500- to 700-word essays with a **persuasive purpose.** The ineffective versions resemble some types of preliminary thesis statements. The effective versions are final thesis statements written by students after they had gathered and grouped ideas. For example, the material here on city living is built on one of the "possible topics" evolved from narrowing the large subject of cities (see 2c-2). The good versions fulfil the requirements in Chart 10.

TOPIC	*discomforts of city living*
NO	The discomforts of living in a modern city are many.
YES	Rising crime rates, increasingly overcrowded conditions, and growing expenses make living comfortably in a modern city difficult.
TOPIC	*deceptive advertising*
NO	Deceptive advertising can cause many problems for consumers.
YES	Deceptive advertising can cost consumers not only money but also their health.

The *No* examples of thesis statements shown above suffer from being too broad. They are so general that they offer no focus, and readers cannot predict the essay's thrust.

Another type of ineffective thesis statement results from an overly narrow focus. In such cases, the thesis statement is closer in scope to a topic sentence that begins a paragraph.

NO	The classical composer Béla Bartók was Hungarian.
YES	Although best known today as a composer, Béla Bartók was also an important ethnomusicologist who studied Hungarian folk music in his native country as well as at Columbia University in New York.
NO	Car thefts on Silver Avenue between First and Second Streets are intolerable.
YES	Because of increasing car thefts, people should take stronger security measures in the area of Silver Avenue between First and Second Streets.

EXERCISE 2-8

Each of the following sets of sentences offers several versions of a thesis statement. Within each set, the thesis statements progress from weak to strong. The fourth thesis statement in each set is the best. Based on the Basic Requirements listed in Chart 10, identify the characteristics of the fourth thesis statement in each set. Then explain why the other choices in each set are weak.

A. 1. Advertising is complex.
   2. Magazine advertisements appeal to readers.
   3. Magazine advertisements must be creative.
   4. To appeal to readers, magazine advertisements must skilfully use language, colour, and design.

B. 1. Tennis is excellent exercise.
   2. Playing tennis is fun.
   3. Tennis requires various skills.
   4. Playing tennis for fun and exercise requires agility, stamina, and strategy.

C. 1. *Hamlet* is a play about revenge.
   2. Hamlet must avenge his father's murder.
   3. Some characters in *Hamlet* want revenge.
   4. In *Hamlet*, Hamlet, Fortinbras, and Laertes all seek revenge.

D. 1. Maintaining friendships requires work.
   2. To have good friends, a person must learn how to be a good friend.
   3. To be a good friend, a person must value the meaning of friendship.
   4. Unless a person is sensitive to others and communicates with them honestly, that person will not be able to build strong friendships.

E. 1. Many people are uninterested in politics.
   2. Adults have become increasingly dissatisfied with the political process.
   3. Fewer adults than ever vote in local elections.

4. Fewer postsecondary students expressed a strong preference or voted in the most recent municipal election than in either of the last two elections.

EXERCISE 2-9

Here are writing assignments, narrowed topics, and tentative thesis statements. Evaluate each thesis statement according to the Basic Requirements in Chart 10.

1. **Marketing assignment:** 700- to 800-word persuasive report on the school's cafeteria. *Audience:* the instructor and the cafeteria's manager. *Topic:* cafeteria conditions. *Thesis:* The cafeteria could attract more students if it improved the quality of its food, its appearance, and the friendliness of its staff.

2. **Music assignment:** 300- to 500-word review of a performance. *Audience:* the instructor and other students in the class. *Topic:* the local symphony's final spring concert. *Thesis:* The "Basically Beethoven" program that ended the local symphony's spring season was pleasing.

3. **Chemistry assignment:** 800- to 1000-word informative report about the ozone layer. *Audience:* the instructor and visiting students and instructors attending a seminar. *Topic:* recent research on the ozone layer. *Thesis:* Canada should increase efforts to slow the destruction of the ozone layer.

4. **Journalism assignment:** 200- to 300-word article about campus crime. *Audience:* the instructor, the student body, and the administration. *Topic:* recent robberies. *Thesis:* During the fall term, campus robberies equalled the number of robberies that took place in the prior five years combined.

5. **Business writing assignment:** 400- to 500-word persuasive report about the career-counselling services available to you. *Audience:* students in their final year, career counsellors, and the instructor. *Topic:* job placement for graduates. *Thesis:* Liberal arts graduates are hired mainly by business and industry.

20   Knowing how to outline

Many writers find outlining a useful planning strategy. If you are working from an outline and make changes in organization as you write, be sure to revise your outline at the end if you are expected to submit it as part of an assignment. An outline helps pull together the results of gathering and ordering ideas and preparing a thesis statement. It also provides a visual guide and checklist. Some writers always use outlines; others prefer not to. Writers who do like outlines use them at various points in the writing process: for example, before drafting, to arrange material; during drafting, to keep track of evolving material; or while revising, to check the logic of an early draft's organization. Especially for academic writing, outlines can clearly reveal flaws: missing information, undesirable repetitions, digressions from the thesis. Some instructors require outlines because they want students to practise planning the arrangement and organization of a piece of writing.

An **informal outline** does not have to follow all the formal conventions of outlining. An informal outline is particularly useful for planning when the order within main ideas is still evolving or when topics imply their own arrangement, such as spatial arrangement for describing a room. An informal outline can also be considered a *working plan,* a layout of the major parts of the material intended for an essay. Here is part of an informal outline that served as a working plan for Carol Moreno when she was writing her essay on weight lifting for women. (For Moreno's techniques of gathering ideas for writing, see 2e, 2f, and 2i; for the three drafts of her essay, see 3f.) This excerpt includes the essay's thesis statement and fourth paragraph.

Thesis Statement: With the right training, women can also "pump iron" for increased strength and stamina.

> using weights
>   safety is vital
>   free weights
>   don't bend at waist
>   do align neck and back
>   do look straight ahead
>   weight machines—safety is easier

Sample Informal Outline

✚ COMPUTER TIP: You can informally outline an essay on a computer, especially after one draft. Read what you have written, and put a symbol near what seems most important. Then, look over the marked parts, and copy them to the bottom of your text so that you can see them grouped together. Shuffle them into several different orders. Does it matter which part comes first, second, and so on? Are the parts equally important, or do some seem subordinate to others? Try indenting the subordinate parts to make a rough outline. ✚

A **formal outline** follows conventions concerning content and format. The conventions are designed to display material so that relationships among ideas are clear and so that the content is orderly. A formal outline can be a *topic outline* or a *sentence outline.* Each item in a topic outline is a word or phrase; each item in a sentence outline is a complete sentence. Formal outlines never mix the two.

Many writers who use formal outlines find that a sentence outline brings them closer to drafting than a topic outline does. For example, a topic outline carries less information with the item "Gathering information" than does a sentence outline with the corresponding item "Gathering information is the first step to being well prepared."

Use Chart 11 for a summary of the conventions of formal outlining.

CONVENTIONS OF FORMAL OUTLINES   11

Formal Outline Pattern
Thesis Statement: . . . .
. . . .
I. First main idea . . . .
. . . .
   A. First subdivision of the main idea . . . .
. . . .
      1. First reason or example . . . .
. . . .
      2. Second reason or example . . . .
         a. First supporting detail . . . .
. . . .
         b. Second supporting detail . . . .
. . . .
   B. Second subdivision of the main idea . . . .
. . . .
II. Second main idea . . . .
. . . .

Formal Outline Guidelines
1. Numbers, letters, and indentations signal groupings and levels of importance.
2. Each level has more than one entry.
3. All subdivisions are at the same level of generality.
4. Headings do not overlap.
5. Entries are grammatically parallel (see Chapter 18).
6. Only the first word of each entry is capitalized. (All proper nouns are also capitalized, of course.)
7. Periods end each sentence in a *sentence outline* but not the items in a *topic outline.*
8. The introductory and concluding paragraphs are omitted, but the thesis statement is usually given above the outline itself (see examples at end of this chapter).

---

plan **20**

1. **Numbers, letters, and indentations.** All parts of a formal outline are systematically indented and numbered or lettered. Capital roman numerals (I, II, III) signal major subdivisions of the topic. Indented capital letters (A, B) signal the next level of generality. Further indented arabic numbers (1, 2, 3) show the third level of generality. Indented lowercase letters (a, b) show the fourth level, if there is one. The principle here is that within each major subdivision, each succeeding level of the outline shows more specific detail than the one before it. If an outline entry is longer than one line, the second line is indented as far as the first word of the preceding line.

2. **More than one entry at each level.** At all points on an outline, there is no I without a II, no A without a B, and so on. Unless a category has at least two parts, it cannot be divided. If a category has only one subdivision, you need to either eliminate that subdivision or expand the material to at least two subdivisions.

   NO   A. Free weights
                1. Safe lifting technique
             B. Weight machines

   YES   A. Free weights
             B. Weight machines

   YES   A. Free weights
                1. Unsafe lifting techniques
                2. Safe lifting techniques
             B. Weight machines

3. **Levels of generality.** All subdivisions are at the same level of generality. A main idea cannot be paired with a supporting detail.

   NO   A. Free weights
             B. Safe lifting techniques
             C. Weight machines

   YES   A. Free weights
             B. Weight machines

4. **Overlap.** Headings do not overlap. What is covered in subdivision 1, for example, must be quite distinct from what is covered in subdivision 2.

   NO   A. Free weights
                1. Unsafe lifting techniques
                2. Not aligning head and neck

   YES   A. Free weights
                1. Unsafe lifting techniques
                2. Safe lifting techniques

5. **Parallelism.** All entries within a level are parallel. For example, all might start with the *-ing* forms of verbs°*. (For more about parallelism in outlines, see 18h.)

   NO   A. Free weights
             B. Using weight machines
   YES   A. Free weights
             B. Weight machines
   YES   A. Using free weights
             B. Using weight machines

6. **Capitalization and punctuation.** Except for proper nouns°, only the first word of each entry is capitalized. In a sentence outline, end each sentence with a period. Do not punctuate the ends of entries in a topic outline.

7. **Introductory and concluding paragraphs.** The content of the introductory and concluding paragraphs is not part of a formal outline. The thesis statement comes before (above) the roman numeral I entry.

   Here is a topic outline of the final draft of Carol Moreno's essay on weight lifting for women (3f). A sentence outline starts on the opposite page so that you can compare the two types of outlines.

TOPIC OUTLINE

Thesis Statement: With the right training, women can also "pump iron" successfully for increased strength and stamina.

I. Avoiding massive muscle development
   A. Role of women's biology
      1. Not much muscle-bulking hormone
      2. Muscles get longer, not bulkier
   B. Role of combining exercise types
      1. Anaerobic (weight lifting)
      2. Aerobic (swimming)

II. Using weights safely
   A. Free weights
      1. Unsafe lifting technique
      2. Safe lifting technique
         a. Head alignment
         b. Neck and back alignment
   B. Weight machines (built-in safeguards)

---

*Throughout this book, a degree mark (°) indicates that you can find the definition of the word in the Glossary of Terms in this handbook.

III. Individualizing the program based on physical condition
   A. Role of resistance and reps
   B. Characteristics considered for personalizing the program
      1. Weight
      2. Age
      3. Physical condition
IV. Individualizing the program for other reasons
   A. Upper body strength
   B. Individual objectives
      1. Mine
      2. Car-crash victim's
      3. Physical therapist's

SENTENCE OUTLINE

Thesis Statement: With the right training, women can also "pump iron" successfully for increased strength and stamina.

I. The right training lets women who lift weights avoid developing massive muscles.
   A. Women's biology plays a role.
      1. Women don't produce much of a specific muscle-bulking hormone.
      2. Women's muscles tend to grow longer rather than bulkier.
   B. Combining exercise types plays a role.
      1. Anaerobic exercise, like weight lifting, builds muscle.
      2. Aerobic exercise, like swimming, builds endurance and stamina.

II. The right training shows women how to use weights safely to prevent injury.
   A. Free weights require special precautions.
      1. Bending at the waist and jerking a barbell up is unsafe.
      2. Squatting and using leg and back muscles to straighten up is safe.
         a. The head is held erect and faces forward.
         b. The neck and back are aligned and held straight.
   B. Weight machines make it easier to lift safely because they force proper body alignment.

III. The right training includes individualized programs based on a woman's physical condition.
   A. Progress comes from resistance and from repetitions tailored to individual capabilities.
   B. Programs consider a woman's physical characteristics.
      1. Her weight is considered.
      2. Her age is considered.
      3. Her physical conditioning is considered.
IV. The right training includes individualized programs based on a woman's personal goals.
   A. Certain muscle groups are targeted to increase women's upper body strength.
   B. Other muscle groups are targeted based on individual objectives.
      1. I wanted to strengthen muscles needed for lifting patients.
      2. An accident victim wanted to strengthen her neck muscles.
      3. A physical therapist wanted to strengthen her fingers and hands.

EXERCISE 2-10

Here is a sentence outline. Consulting section 2o, revise it into a topic outline. Then decide which form you would prefer as a guide to writing, and explain your decision.

> *Thesis Statement:* Common noise pollution, although it causes many problems in our society, can be reduced.

I. Noise pollution comes from many sources.
   A. Noise pollution occurs in many large cities.
      1. Traffic rumbles and screeches.
      2. Construction work blasts.
      3. Airplanes roar overhead.
   B. Noise pollution occurs in the workplace.
      1. Machines in factories boom.
      2. Machines used for outdoor construction thunder.
   C. Noise pollution occurs during leisure-time activities.
      1. Stereo headphones blare directly into eardrums.
      2. Film soundtracks bombard the ears.
      3. Music in discos assaults the ears.

plan 20

II. Noise pollution causes many problems.
   A. Excessive noise damages hearing.
   B. Excessive noise alters moods.
   C. Constant exposure to noise limits learning ability.
III. Reduction in noise pollution is possible.
   A. Pressure from community groups can support efforts to control excessive noise.
   B. Traffic regulations can help alleviate congestion and noise.
   C. Pressure from workers can force management to reduce noise.
   D. People can wear earplugs to avoid excessive noise.
   E. Reasonable sound levels for headphones, soundtracks, and discos can be required.

3 Drafting and Revising

In the writing process, drafting and revising follow from planning and shaping, discussed in Chapter 2. **Drafting** means getting ideas onto paper in sentences and paragraphs. In everyday conversation, people usually use the word *writing* when they talk about the activities involved in drafting. In discussing the writing process, however, the word *drafting* is more descriptive. It conveys the idea that the final product of the writing process is the result of a number of versions, each successively closer to what the writer intends and to what will communicate clearly to readers. **Revising** means taking a draft from its preliminary to its final version by evaluating, adding, cutting, moving material, editing, and proofreading.

3a Getting started

If ever you have trouble getting started when the time arrives for drafting (or any other part of the writing process), you are not alone. When experienced writers get stalled, they recognize what is happening and deal with it. If you run into a writing block, it may be the result of one of these common myths about writing.

MYTH	Writers are born, not made.
TRUTH	Everyone can write. Writers do not expect to "get it right" the first time. Being a good writer means being a patient rewriter.
MYTH	Writers have to be "in the mood" to write.
TRUTH	If writers always waited for "the mood" to descend, few would write at all. After all, news reporters and other professional writers often have to meet deadlines.
MYTH	Writers have to know how to spell every word and to recite the rules of grammar perfectly.

draft **3a**

TRUTH	Writers do not let spelling and grammar block them. They write and then check themselves. A good speller is someone who does not ignore the quiet inner voice that urges checking a dictionary. Similarly, writers use a handbook to check grammar rules.
MYTH	Writers do not have to revise.
TRUTH	Writers expect to revise. Once words are on paper, writers can see what readers see. This "re-vision" helps writers revise so that their writing delivers its intended message.
MYTH	Writing can be done at the last minute.
TRUTH	Drafting and revising take time. Ideas do not leap onto paper in final, polished form.

WAYS TO OVERCOME WRITER'S BLOCK 12

- **Avoid staring at a blank page.** Relax and move your hand across the page or keyboard. Write words, scribble, or draw while you think about your topic. The movement of filling the paper can help stimulate your mind to turn to actual drafting.

- **Visualize yourself writing.** Many professional writers say that they write more easily if they first picture themselves doing it. Before getting up in the morning, or when waiting for a bus, or walking to classes, summon a full visual image of yourself in the place where you usually write, with the materials you need, busy at work.

- **Picture an image or scene, or imagine a sound that relates to your topic.** Start writing by describing what you see or hear.

- **Write about your topic in a letter to a friend.** Relax and chat on paper to someone you like and feel comfortable with.

- **Try writing your material as if you were someone else.** Taking on a role may make you feel less inhibited about writing.

- **Start in the middle.** Begin with a body paragraph. Write from the centre of your essay out, instead of from beginning to end.

- **Use "focused freewriting"** (see 2f).

- **Switch your method of writing.** If you usually typewrite or use a computer, try writing by hand. If you usually use a pen, switch to a pencil. When you write by hand, try to treat yourself to good-quality paper. The pleasure of writing on smooth, strong paper helps many experienced writers want to keep going.

Once you realize the truths behind myths about writing, you can try the time-proven ways that experienced writers use to get started when they are blocked. As you use these strategies, suspend judgment; do not criticize yourself when trying to get underway. The time for evaluation comes during revision, but revising too soon can stall some writers. While the writing that results from these ideas is most certainly not a final draft, having something on paper is a comfort—and can serve as a springboard to drafting.

As you write, seek out places and times of the day that encourage you to write. You might write best in a quiet corner of the library; at 4:30 a.m. at the kitchen table before anyone else is awake; or outside when people are walking by. Most experienced writers find that they concentrate best when they are alone, working without the risk of interruption. But occasionally background noise—in a crowded cafeteria, for example—might be comforting. Be sure, however, not to mislead yourself: You will not write well or efficiently while you are talking to other people, stopping now and then to jot down a sentence or two. Also, do not mistake delaying tactics for preparation: You do need pencil and paper (or their equivalent) to write, but you do not need fifteen perfectly sharpened pencils sitting in a neat row.

✦ COMPUTER TIP: Some people write with a pen, some at a typewriter, and others at a computer. If you do not have a computer at your disposal, the usual methods of writing will continue to serve you well.

As much as possible, tailor your use of a computer to your personal needs. Some experienced writers prefer to use a computer only for preparing the final copy. Others like to plan and shape by hand and to write all drafts on a computer. Still other writers feel more comfortable writing out drafts by hand and then revising with a computer. Yet others like to use a computer throughout the writing process. See what works best for you in each writing situation. ✦

3b Knowing how to draft

Once you have your ideas planned and shaped for an essay, you are ready to **compose** them on paper. When you compose, you put together sentences and paragraphs into a unified whole. A *first draft* is a preliminary draft. Its purpose is to get your ideas onto paper, not to refine grammar and style (they come later, during revision). First drafts are not meant to be perfect; they are meant to give you something to revise. According to your personal preferences and each writing situation, you can use any of these ways (or your own ways) of writing a first draft.

✦ COMPUTER TIP: Make it a rule to save or back up your work every two pages or every ten to fifteen minutes. Also, some writers print out regularly. Printout, also called hard copy, gives you a record of your work, even if your disk develops problems. ✦

1. **Put aside all your notes from planning and shaping.** Write a "discovery draft." As you write, be open to discovering ideas and making connections that spring to mind during the physical act of writing. When you finish a discovery draft, you can decide to use it either as a first draft or as part of your notes when you write a structured first draft.

2. **Keep your notes from planning and shaping in front of you and use them as you write.** Write a structured first draft by arranging your notes in a preliminary sequence and working through them. Draft either the entire essay or blocks of one or two paragraphs at one time.

3. **Use a combination of approaches.** When you know the shape of your material, write according to that structure. When you feel "stuck" about what to say next, switch to writing as you would for a discovery draft.

The direction of drafting is forward: *keep pressing ahead*. If you are worried about the spelling of a word or a point in grammar, underline the material to check it later—and keep moving ahead. If you cannot think of an exact word, write an easy synonym and circle it to change later—and move on. If you are worried about your sentence style or the order in which you present the supporting details within a paragraph, write *Style?* or *Order?* in the margin and return to it later to revise—and press forward. If you begin to run dry, reread what you have written—but only to propel yourself to further writing, not to distract you into rewriting.

✦ COMPUTER TIP: Try to write a whole draft at one session, second-guessing and rewriting as little as possible. If you have questions, or think you may want to elaborate on something but cannot think how at the moment, insert a symbol that will alert you to "talk to yourself" later. When you finish the draft and begin revising, your symbols can help you focus on areas that need reworking. ✦

As you draft, use the essay's thesis statement (see 2n) as your springboard. A thesis statement has great organizing power, for it controls and limits what the essay will cover. Also, use your thesis statement as a connecting thread that unifies the essay. **Unity** is important for communicating clearly to an audience. You achieve unity when all parts of the essay relate to the thesis statement and to each other. An essay is unified when it meets two criteria: (1) the thesis statement clearly ties into all topic sentences: see 4b; and (2) the support for each topic sentence—the paragraph development—contains examples, reasons, facts, and details directly related to the topic and, in turn, to the thesis statement: see 4c.

Coherence is also important to communicate clearly to an audience. An essay is coherent when it supplies guideposts that communicate the relations among ideas. Coherence is achieved with transitional expressions, pronouns, repetition, and parallel structures. These techniques operate within paragraphs and to connect paragraphs (see 4d).

When you write, plan your practical arrangements. For example, try to work in a place where you are comfortable and will not be disturbed. If someone comes along and interrupts, you might lose a train of thought or an idea that has flashed into your mind. Also, keep enough paper at hand so that you use only one side of each sheet of paper. Later you will need to spread your full draft in front of you so that you can physically see how the parts relate to one another. As you write, leave large margins and plenty of room between lines so that you have space to enter changes later on.

To give you examples of the writing process used by college and university students, this chapter discusses the drafting and revising of two students—Carol Moreno and Daniel Casey, each of whom wrote in response to the assignments shown on page 19. You can see three complete drafts of Moreno's essay in this chapter (section 3f). Also, you can see the final draft of Daniel Casey's essay in section 6i. For examples of Moreno's and Casey's uses of the techniques of planning and shaping before they began drafting, see sections 2b through 2o.

3c Knowing how to revise

To **revise** you must evaluate. You assess your first (or subsequent) draft and decide where improvements are needed. Then you make the improvements and evaluate each on its own as well as in the context of the surrounding material. The revision process continues until you are satisfied that the essay is the best that you can make it in the time available. Keep in mind that academic writing, especially through the vehicle of revision, is an engaging intellectual endeavour that encourages students to stretch to the maximum.

To revise successfully you need first to *expect to revise*. Some people think that anyone who revises is not a good writer. The opposite is true. Writing is largely revising. Experienced writers know that the final draft of any writing project shows on paper only a fraction of the decisions made from draft to successive draft. Revision means "to see again," to look with fresh eyes. Good writers can truly *see* their drafts and rework them so that they evolve and improve.

To revise successfully you need also to distance yourself from each draft. You need to read your writing with objective eyes. A natural reaction of many writers is to want to hold onto their every word, especially if they had trouble getting started with a draft. If you ever have such feelings, resist them and work on distancing yourself from the material. Before revising, give yourself some time for that rosy glow of authorial pride to dim a bit. The classical writer Horace recommended waiting nine years. Given the hectic pace of modern life, you do not have that much time. But do try to wait a few hours before going back to look anew at your work.

If an objective perspective still eludes you, try reading your draft aloud; hearing the material can give you a fresh new sense of content and organization. Another useful method is to read the paragraphs in reverse order, starting with the conclusion; eventually, of course, you must read your essay from beginning to end, but to achieve distance you can temporarily depart from that sequence.

1 | Knowing the steps and activities of revision

Once you understand the attitudes that underlie the revision process, you are ready to move into actual revising.

To revise, you work to improve your draft at all levels: whole essay, paragraph, sentence, and word. A revised draft usually looks quite different from the preceding draft. To revise effectively you likely need to engage in all the activities in Chart 13 and Chart 14.

As you engage in each activity, keep in mind the whole picture. Changes affect more than the place revised. Check that your separate changes operate well in the context of the whole essay or a particular paragraph. As with drafting (see 3b), getting distance from your material allows you the chance to be more objective.

Revising is usually separate from editing (see 3d). Editing involves concentrating on important surface features such as correct spelling and punctuation. When revising, you pay attention to the meaning that you want your material to deliver effectively.

✚ COMPUTER TIP: Relieved of the sometimes tedious work of copying and recopying material, many writers feel more creative when they use a computer. Their ideas seem to flow more freely when each new thought does not lead to a recopying job. Nevertheless, do not let yourself be seduced by the wonders of a computer. It is only a machine. A neatly printed page might "look" like a final draft, even when it is a very rough draft. Resist the urge to think that neatness means completion. ✚

STEPS FOR REVISING   13

1. Shift mentally from suspending judgment (during idea gathering and drafting) to making judgments.
2. Read your draft critically to evaluate it. Be guided by the questions on the Revision Checklist in this chapter or by material supplied by your instructor.
3. Decide whether to write an entirely new draft or to revise the one you have. Do not be overly harsh. While some early drafts serve best as "discovery drafts" rather than first drafts, many early drafts provide sufficient raw material for the revision process to get underway.
4. Be systematic. Do not evaluate at random. You need to pay attention to many different elements of a draft, from overall organization to choice of words. Some writers prefer to consider all elements concurrently, but most writers work better when they concentrate on different elements sequentially during separate rounds of revision.

  | **Using the organizing power of your thesis statement and essay title during revision**

As you revise, pay special attention to your essay's thesis statement and title. Both features can help you stay on the track. Also, they orient your reader to what to expect, which helps you communicate your message as clearly as possible.

If your **thesis statement** (see 2n, especially Chart 10) does not match what you say in your essay, you need to revise either the thesis statement or the essay—and sometimes both. A thesis statement must present the topic of the essay, the writer's particular focus on that topic, and the writer's purpose for writing the essay. The first draft of a thesis statement is often merely an estimate of what will be covered in the essay. Early in the revision process, check the accuracy of your estimate. Then use the thesis statement's controlling power to bring it and your essay in line with each other.

Each writer's experience with revising a thesis statement varies from essay to essay. Carol Moreno wrote a number of versions of her thesis statement before she started drafting. After writing her first draft, Moreno checked the thesis statement and satisfied herself that it communicated what she wanted to say. But she decided to change parts of her essay to conform more closely to her thesis statement.

rev **3c**

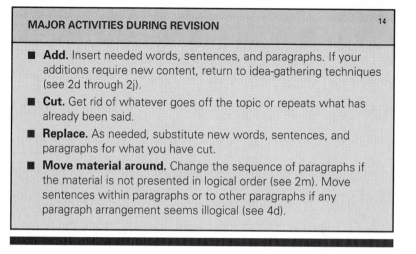

> **MAJOR ACTIVITIES DURING REVISION** 14
>
> - **Add.** Insert needed words, sentences, and paragraphs. If your additions require new content, return to idea-gathering techniques (see 2d through 2j).
> - **Cut.** Get rid of whatever goes off the topic or repeats what has already been said.
> - **Replace.** As needed, substitute new words, sentences, and paragraphs for what you have cut.
> - **Move material around.** Change the sequence of paragraphs if the material is not presented in logical order (see 2m). Move sentences within paragraphs or to other paragraphs if any paragraph arrangement seems illogical (see 4d).

(For an example of a thesis statement being revised for a research paper from the first through the final draft, see 32r).

The **title** of an essay also plays an important organizing role during revision. An effective title sets you on your course and tells your reader what to expect. (Some writers like to start a first draft with a title at the top of the page to focus their thinking. As they revise drafts, they revise the title as needed.) An effective title might not come to mind until you have drafted, revised, and edited your essay, by which time your thinking about your topic has crystallized. Remember that a title is never the same as a thesis statement.

Titles can be *direct* or *indirect*. A *direct title* tells exactly what the essay will be about. A direct title contains key words under which the essay would be catalogued in a library or other database system. The title of Carol Moreno's essay shown in 3f is direct: "Women Can Pump Iron, Too." Similarly, the title of Daniel Casey's essay in section 6i is direct: "Commercialism at Holiday Time Benefits Everyone." Each title is specific and prepares the reader for the topic of the essay.

A *direct title* should not be too broad. An overly broad title implies that the writer has not thought through the essay's content. An unsatisfactory title for Moreno's essay would be "Pumping Iron." Conversely, a direct title should not be too narrow. Equally unsatisfactory would be a title that is overly long—for example, by listing the topics of most of the essay's body paragraphs: "Women Pump Iron for Their Physical and Personal Objectives."

An *indirect title* is also acceptable in some situations, according to the writer's taste and instructor's requirements. An indirect title hints at the essay's topic. It presents a puzzle that can be solved by reading the essay.

This approach can be intriguing for the reader, but the writer has to make sure that the title is not too obscure. For example, for Carol Moreno's essay a satisfactory indirect title would be "The Meaning of Muscles," but an unsatisfactory, overly indirect title would be "Equal Play."

Whether direct or indirect, a title stands alone. For example, Carol Moreno (whose essay's good title is "Women Can Pump Iron, Too") would have been wrong had she written as her essay's first sentence: "They certainly can" or "I am proof of that." Chart 15 gives guidelines for titles.

GUIDELINES FOR ESSAY TITLES 15

- Do not wait until the last minute to tack on a title. You might write a title before you start to draft or while you are revising, but always check as you review your essay, to make sure that the title clearly relates to the content of the evolving essay.

- For a direct title, use key words relating to your topic, but do not reveal your entire essay.

- For an indirect title, be sure that it hints accurately and that its meaning will be clear once a reader finishes your essay.

- Do not use quotation marks or underlining with the title (*unless* your title includes another title; see section 30f).

- Do not refer to your essay title with words like *it* or *this,* as if the title were part of the first sentence in the essay.

---

3 Using revision checklists

Revision checklists can help you focus your attention as you evaluate your writing to revise it. Either use a checklist provided by your instructor, or compile your own based on the revision checklists in Chart 16 and Chart 17. The checklists here are comprehensive and detailed; do not let them overwhelm you. Feel free to adapt them to your writing assignments as well as to your personal weaknesses and strengths. Also, the checklists here move from the **larger elements** of the whole essay and paragraphs to the **smaller elements** of sentences and words. This progression for the sake of self-evaluation works well for many writers. (To see how Carol Moreno used these Revision Checklists, see section 3f.)

REVISION CHECKLIST: THE WHOLE ESSAY AND PARAGRAPHS   16

The answer to each question should be "yes." If it is not, you need to revise. The reference numbers in parentheses tell you what chapter or section of this handbook to consult.

1. Is your essay topic suitable and sufficiently narrow (2c)?
2. Does your thesis statement communicate your topic and focus (2n) and your purpose (1b)?
3. Does your essay reflect awareness of your audience (1c)?
4. Is your tone appropriate (1d)?
5. Is your essay logically organized (2m) and are your paragraphs logically arranged (4e)?
6. Have you cut material that goes off the topic?
7. Is your reasoning sound (5h-5j) and do you avoid logical fallacies (5k)?
8. Is your introduction related to the rest of your essay (4g)?
9. Does each body paragraph express its main idea in a topic sentence as needed (4b)? Are the main ideas clearly related to the thesis statement, and have you covered all that your thesis statement "promises" (2n)?
10. Are your body paragraphs sufficiently developed with concrete support for their main idea (4c)?
11. Have you used necessary transitions (4d-1, 4d-5)?
12. Do your paragraphs maintain coherence (4d)?
13. Does your conclusion provide a sense of completion (4g)?
14. Does your title reflect the content of the essay (3c-2)?

◆ ESL NOTE: If English is not your first language, you may want to consult Part Nine to check your use of verb–preposition combinations, articles, word order, verbals, and modal auxiliaries in addition to using the Revision Checklist. ◆

4   Knowing how to use criticism

When criticism is constructive, you can learn a great deal about your writing through the eyes of others. Still, you have much company

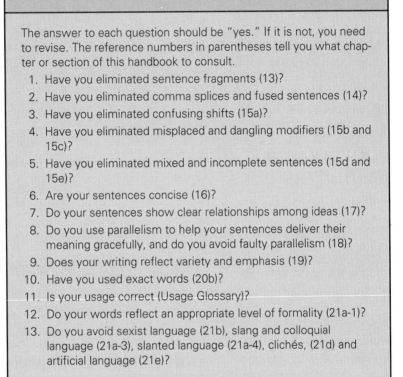

REVISION CHECKLIST: SENTENCES AND WORDS   17

The answer to each question should be "yes." If it is not, you need to revise. The reference numbers in parentheses tell you what chapter or section of this handbook to consult.

1. Have you eliminated sentence fragments (13)?
2. Have you eliminated comma splices and fused sentences (14)?
3. Have you eliminated confusing shifts (15a)?
4. Have you eliminated misplaced and dangling modifiers (15b and 15c)?
5. Have you eliminated mixed and incomplete sentences (15d and 15e)?
6. Are your sentences concise (16)?
7. Do your sentences show clear relationships among ideas (17)?
8. Do you use parallelism to help your sentences deliver their meaning gracefully, and do you avoid faulty parallelism (18)?
9. Does your writing reflect variety and emphasis (19)?
10. Have you used exact words (20b)?
11. Is your usage correct (Usage Glossary)?
12. Do your words reflect an appropriate level of formality (21a-1)?
13. Do you avoid sexist language (21b), slang and colloquial language (21a-3), slanted language (21a-4), clichés, (21d) and artificial language (21e)?

among writers if your initial reaction to criticism is defensive. Someone else's reactions to your writing can feel like an intrusion at first. Writing is a personal act, even when a writer is trying to communicate with a reader. The more you write, however, the more you will come to welcome constructive criticism.

The eyes of another person, someone who cares to help you improve, can give you an objective view of your material. Useful criticism helps you move your writing closer to what a reader needs to complete the act of communication. When working with comments, look at each one separately. First, make sure that you understand what the comment says. If you are unsure, ask. Next, be open-minded about the comment so that you do not miss good opportunities to improve. Finally, use the comments to revise according to what you think will improve your draft.

5   Knowing how to be a peer critic

Being a **peer critic** means using structured procedures to react to and make suggestions about another student's writing. Peer critiquing is an interactive communication process. It involves reading and thinking together, asking and explaining, talking and listening. As a student writer, be sure that your instructor wants you to use peer critiquing before you do so. There can be a fine line between giving opinions and doing others' work for them.

When you are a peer critic, you are part of a respected tradition of colleagues helping colleagues. Professional writers often seek to improve their rough drafts by asking other writers for comments. When you give comments as a student writer, know that you are not expected to be an expert. What you do offer can be quite valuable: opinions from the point of view of a writer who understands what his or her peer is going through. Try always to base your comments on an understanding of the writing process and of the features that characterize effective writing. The more concrete and specific your comments, the more helpful. The comment "this is good" might seem pleasant, but it says little. What makes the writing good: ideas? patterns of organization? sentences? words?

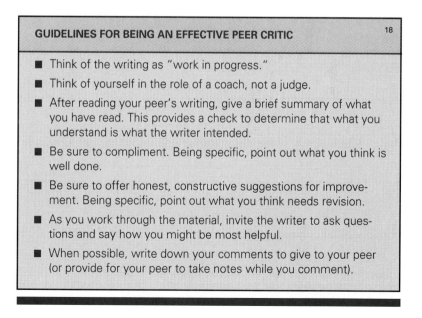

GUIDELINES FOR BEING AN EFFECTIVE PEER CRITIC   18

- Think of the writing as "work in progress."
- Think of yourself in the role of a coach, not a judge.
- After reading your peer's writing, give a brief summary of what you have read. This provides a check to determine that what you understand is what the writer intended.
- Be sure to compliment. Being specific, point out what you think is well done.
- Be sure to offer honest, constructive suggestions for improvement. Being specific, point out what you think needs revision.
- As you work through the material, invite the writer to ask questions and say how you might be most helpful.
- When possible, write down your comments to give to your peer (or provide for your peer to take notes while you comment).

When you receive comments from a peer critic, remain open-minded about what is said. Constructive criticism can help you read your writing in a fresh way that results in better revision. Encourage your peer to be honest. You, however, are the person who decides which comments to use, and which to ignore, when revising.

If your instructor distributes a list to guide peer discussion, follow it carefully. If you are expected to decide what to discuss with peers, you can use or adapt the revision checklists in this handbook section. Guidelines for being an effective peer critic are in Chart 18.

3d Knowing how to edit

When you **edit,** you are expected to check the technical correctness of your writing. You pay attention to surface features of your writing, such as grammar, spelling, and punctuation, and the correct use of capitals, numbers, italics, and abbreviations. Writers sometimes refer to editing as revising (see 3c). In this handbook, editing is discussed separately because editing focuses more on presentation than on meaning.

If you edit too soon in the writing process, you might distract yourself from checking to see if your material delivers its meaning effectively. You are ready to edit when you have a final draft that contains suitable content, organization, development, and sentence structure. Your job during editing is not to generate a new draft but to fine-tune the surface features of the draft you have. Once you have polished your work, you are ready to transcribe it into a final copy and proofread (see 3e) it.

EDITING CHECKLIST   19

The answer to each question should be "yes." If it is not, you need to edit. The reference numbers in parentheses tell you what chapter of this handbook to consult.

1. Is your grammar correct (7 to 14)?
2. Is your spelling correct, and are your hyphens correct (22)?
3. Have you correctly used commas (24)?
4. Have you correctly used all other punctuation (25 through 29)?
5. Have you correctly used capital letters, italics, abbreviations, and numbers (30)?

Editing is crucial in writing. No matter how much attention you have paid to planning, shaping, drafting, and revising, you must edit carefully. Slapdash editing will distract your readers and, in writing for assignments, lower your grade.

Editing takes patience. Inexperienced writers sometimes rush editing, especially if they have revised well and feel that they have prepared a good essay. When you edit, resist any impulse to hurry. Matters of grammar and punctuation take concentration—and frequently they take time to check by looking up rules and conventions in this handbook. As you edit, be systematic. Use a checklist supplied by your instructor or one that you compile from the editing checklist in Chart 19.

3e   Knowing how to proofread

When you **proofread,** you check a final version carefully before handing it in. To make sure that your work is an accurate and clean transcription of your final draft, proofread after you revise (see 3c) and edit (see 3d). If you try to proofread while you edit, one process might distract from the other.

Proofreading involves a careful, line-by-line reading of your writing. You may want to proofread with a ruler so that you can focus on one line at a time. Starting at the end also helps you avoid becoming distracted by the content of your paper. Another effective proofreading technique is to read your final draft aloud, to yourself or to a friend. This can help you hear and see errors that might have slipped past your notice.

✚ COMPUTER TIP: You can use the screen to help you proofread and edit. Highlight a five- or six-line section, and read each section slowly and carefully. This strategy allows you to work in small segments, which reduces the tendency to read too quickly and ignore errors.

You might try making your own "spell-and-style checker" by keeping a file of the mistakes that you have made in the past. (For example, the difference between *its* and *it's* may always escape you, or you may know that you tend to misuse the colon.) Call up your mistake file, and search your draft for those items. ✚

In proofreading, look for letters or words inadvertently left out. If you handwrite your material, write legibly. If you type, neatly correct any typing errors. If a page has numerous errors, retype the page. Do not expect your instructor to make allowances for crude typing; if you cannot type well, arrange to have your paper typed properly. No matter how hard you have worked on other parts of the writing process, if your final copy is inaccurate or messy, you will not reach your audience successfully.

✦ COMPUTER TIP: Get to know any special tools for writers that are included in the software programs for your computer. For example:

- Spell-check programs call attention to words that do not match their dictionaries. The programs are a big help for spotting typos, but they have limits. Suppose you intended to type "west" but instead typed "rest." Because "rest" appears as a correctly spelled word in the program's dictionary, the program will not call "west" to your attention. Always read your work carefully yourself.

- Thesaurus programs are no different from printed thesauruses. You must evaluate each suggested substitution for sense within the context of what you are writing.

- Style-check programs examine your file against grammar, usage, and punctuation rules, alerting you to writing in your paper that differs from a program's standards. Fixing what the program finds is still your job. Use style-check programs with caution. For example, if you are told some of your sentences are in the passive voice, change them to active voice only if you think the change is needed (see 8m and 8n).

- Tutorials like Blue Pencil, available with this handbook, offer you exercises to work on at your own pace. Blue Pencil closely resembles the editing process. It scores your answers and explains what is wrong with and how to fix any incorrect ones. It also refers you to the appropriate section in this handbook. ✦

3f   Case study: A student writing an essay

This section is a case study of a student, Carol Moreno, going through the process of writing an essay. As you examine her three drafts, refer back to her writing assignment on page 19. In addition, look at the discussion of how she shaped her ideas (see 2k) and wrote her thesis statement (see 2n). See 2o for sample outlines.

1   Writing and revising a first draft

Carol Moreno wrote about a challenge she faced and met. As a result of using planning techniques (see 2e, 2f, and 2i), she chose the topic of weight lifting for women who want to build up their strength. She decided that her writing purpose would be *to inform* (see 1b-2). She then wrote the first draft, expecting to revise it later.

As Moreno revised her first draft, she worked systematically through the larger elements of the whole essay and paragraphs, and then she turned to her sentences and words. As she did this, she referred to the Revision Checklists in Chart 16 and Chart 17. Here is Moreno's first draft, along with her notes to herself about revisions she wanted to make when she wrote her second draft.

What do I mean here?

I should say why she needed lifting

FIRST DRAFT, REVISED BY STUDENT

Pumping Iron

(It all) began when my grandmother broke her hip. I couldn't (lift) her alone when I was *she does not weigh much, but* helping take care of her. ∧I needed strength, *she was too much for me.* (and) I'm planning to be a nurse. Then I found

I need to clarify the connection but I could satisfy a physical ed requirement in college with a weight lifting course for women. (I) thought only big, macho men lift weights. But if she is trained well, any woman can "pump iron" well, just like a man.

Lots of I's — is this only about me!

I have to check when I revise whether this thesis statement fits the rest of my essay

Hoping for strength and endurance The first day of class we did not exercise. We talked about who we are and why we wanted to take the course. We heard about *can lead to* *unless lifters* how to avoid injury by learning the safe use *and weight machines. Free weights are* of free weights (barbells). To be safe, no *barbells.* matter how little the weight, lifters must never raise a barbell by bending at the *grasp* waist. Instead, they should squat, grab the barbell, and then straighten up into a *To avoid a that* *serious* standing position. Twists can lead to injury, *so* lifters must keep head erect, facing forward, back and neck aligned. Lifters use weight machines sitting down, which is a big advantage of the Nautilus and Universal.

Move: This should be my third ¶.

My second ¶ should give background.

I have to bring in more than myself to say who we are

I need to go into more detail here.

happy (I) was relieved that (I) won't develop overly masculine muscle mass. We learned

more up to be #2 (background)

→

that we can rely on women's biology. Our
bodies produce only very small amounts of
the hormones that enlarge muscles in men.
Normally women's grow longer rather than
bulkier. Weight lifting is a form of
anareobic exercise. It does not make people
breathe harder or their hearts beat faster.
Arobic exercise like swimming build
endurance, so I took up swimming.

After safety comes our needs for
physical strength. A well-planned,
progressive weight-training program.
begins with whatever weight you can lift
comfortably and then gradually adds What
builds muscle strength is the number of
"reps" we do, not necessarily an increase in
the amount of added weight. In my class, we
ranged from 18 to 43, scrawny to fat, and
lazy to superstar, and we each developed a
program that was OK for us. Some women
didn't listen to our instructor who urged us
not to do more reps or weight than our
programs called for even if it seemed too
easy. This turned out to be good advice
because those of us who didn't listen woke
up feeling as though our bodies had been
twisted by evil forces.

After meeting her physical
capabilities, a weight lifter needs to
design her personal goals. Most students in
my group wanted to improve their upper body
strength. Each student learned to use
specific exercises to isolate certain muscle
groups, for example we might work on our

[Handwritten annotations:]
I need to tie these together (check 4d)
With normal training,
sp (muscles)
sp
running, walking, and
My topic sentence needs work
Am I being too informal here?
You / It
a person
to the base weight as she gets stronger.
the lifter does,
resistance from adding
pudgy
couch potato
I'm not trying here
try
our first workouts
Start sentence here? Not sure.
the next morning
In addition to fitting to
I need specific examples of students

arms and (abdomen) *sp?* one day and our shoulders
and chest the next day. ~~My goal is nursing,~~
~~which I want to pursue. I want to help~~   *I'm off the topic*
~~others, but I'm also very interested in the~~
~~science I'll learn. I hear there is a lot~~
~~of memorization, which I'm pretty good at.~~
~~I also will have "clinical" assignments to~~
~~give us hands-on experience in hospitals.~~
Because I had had such trouble lifting my
grandmother, I added exercises to strengthen
my legs and back. Another student added neck
strengthening exercises. Someone else added
finger and hand exercises.

At the end of the course, we had to
evaluate our progress. When I started, I
could lift 10 pounds, ~~but~~ By the end I could   *over my head for 3 reps.*
lift 10 pounds for 20 reps and 18 pounds for   *over my head*
3 reps. I am so proud of my accomplishments
that I *still* work out three or four times a week   *I need a stronger ending.*
I am proof that any woman can become   *I forgot to talk about my swimming.*
stronger and have more stamina.

---

2 Revising a second draft

After Carol Moreno finished writing and entering notes to herself on her first draft (see 3f-1), she revised her work into a second
draft and typed a clean copy to give to her instructor. As stated in the
assignment (see page 19), Moreno's instructor considered the second
draft an "essay in progress," so that all comments by the instructor
were aimed at helping Moreno write an effective third, final draft.

Here is Moreno's second draft with two types of comments from
the instructor: *questions* to stimulate Moreno to clarify and expand on
ideas in the draft as well as section *codes*—the number-letter combinations—for Moreno to consult in this handbook.

SECOND DRAFT WITH INSTRUCTOR'S COMMENTS

this title is very broad—try again?

PUMPING IRON

When my grandmother fell and broke her
hip last summer, I wanted to help take care
of her. She was bedridden, but I couldn't   *interesting reaction—can you be more descriptive?*

I like this sentence—good balance.

lift her and I was shocked. My grandmother
doesn't weigh much, but she was too much for
me. I'm planning to be a nurse, so I need my   *can you explain why to help your readers understand your concerns?*

strength. When I realized that I could   *(see 30)*
satisfy one of my phys ed requirements by

This thesis statement says you'll discuss what most people think, but do you? (see 2n)

taking a weight-lifting course, I decided to
try it. In spite of most people thinking only
men "pump iron," women can also do it
successfully with the right training.

Women who lift weights, I was happy to
learn from my course, can easily avoid
overly masculine muscle mass. Women can   *To do what?*
rely on their biology. Women's bodies   *good for you! This information is instructive.*
produce only very small amounts of the
hormones that enlarge muscles in men. With

with what result?

normal weight training, women's muscles
grow longer rather than bulkier. Also,
women benefit most when they combine   *why use parentheses for key information?*
anaerobic exercise (weight lifting) with
aerobic exercise. Anaerobic exercise
strengthens and builds muscles, but it does

only for a few seconds or ??

not make people breathe harder or their
hearts beat faster. Aerobic exercise like
running, walking, and swimming builds   *why? how?*
endurance, not massive muscles. Thanks to
my instructor, I balanced my weight-lifting   *Is there a better word?*
workouts by swimming laps twice a week.

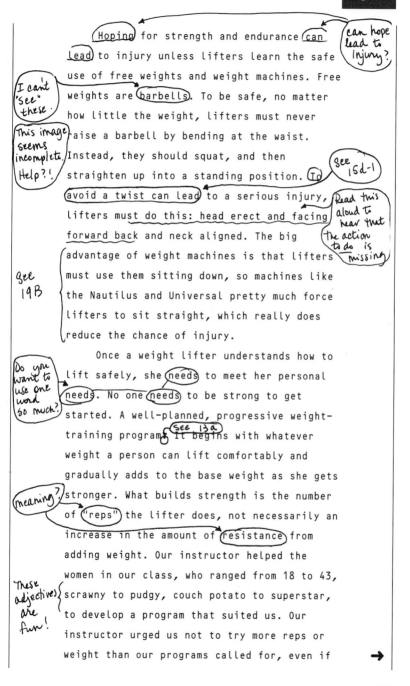

can hope lead to injury?

Hoping for strength and endurance can lead to injury unless lifters learn the safe use of free weights and weight machines. Free weights are barbells. To be safe, no matter how little the weight, lifters must never raise a barbell by bending at the waist. Instead, they should squat, and then straighten up into a standing position. To avoid a twist can lead to a serious injury, lifters must do this: head erect and facing forward back and neck aligned. The big advantage of weight machines is that lifters must use them sitting down, so machines like the Nautilus and Universal pretty much force lifters to sit straight, which really does reduce the chance of injury.

I can't "see" these.

This image seems incomplete. Help?!

see 15d-1

Read this aloud to hear that the action to do is missing

see 19B

Once a weight lifter understands how to lift safely, she needs to meet her personal needs. No one needs to be strong to get started. A well-planned, progressive weight-training program. It begins with whatever weight a person can lift comfortably and gradually adds to the base weight as she gets stronger. What builds strength is the number of "reps" the lifter does, not necessarily an increase in the amount of resistance from adding weight. Our instructor helped the women in our class, who ranged from 18 to 43, scrawny to pudgy, couch potato to superstar, to develop a program that suited us. Our instructor urged us not to try more reps or weight than our programs called for, even if

Do you want to use one word so much?

See 13a

meaning?

These adjectives are fun!

➡

our first workouts seemed too easy. This
turned out to be good advice because those of
us who did not listen woke up the next
morning feeling as though our bodies had been
twisted by evil forces.

Fun. again. Your voice (personality) comes through.

In addition to fitting a program to her
physical capabilities, a weight lifter needs
to design her personal goals. Most students in
my group wanted to improve their upper body
strength, so we focused on exercises to
strengthen our arms, shoulders, abdomen, and
chest. Each student learned to use specific
exercises to isolate certain muscle groups,
for example, we might work on our arms and
abdomen one day and our shoulders and chest
the next day. Because I had such trouble
lifting my grandmother, I added exercises to
strengthen my legs and back. Another student
added neck strengthening exercises. Someone
else, planning to be a physical therapist,
added finger and hand strengthening exercises.

Does one design a goal?

good details

why important?

See 14a and 14e

See 24b-1

excellent examples Carol!

Why did she choose this?

At the end of the course we had to
evaluate our progress. When I started, I
could lift 10 pounds over my head for 3 reps.
By the end, I could lift 10 pounds over my
head for 20 reps and 18 pounds for 3 reps.
Also, I could swim for 20 sustained minutes
instead of the 10 at first. I am so proud of
my accomplishments that I still work out
three or four times a week. I am proof that
any woman can benefit from "pumping iron."
Not only will she become stronger and have
more stamina, she will also feel very good.

How long was it?

See 24b-3

Can you communicate your enthusiasm to your reader more effectively?

Isn't this a bit flat?

rev **3f**

Dear Carol,

You have truly earned the right to feel proud of yourself. You've also inspired me to consider weight training myself!

As you revise for your final draft, I'd urge you to get more voice (your personality) into the essay. To do this, you don't have to become too informal; instead, find out how you felt about what you were doing and try to put that into words. Also, think about my questions and the codes that refer you to sections of the Troyka handbook. I will enjoy reading your final draft, I'm sure.

K.N.

3 Revising, editing, and proofreading a final draft

Moreno revised her essay in a third, final draft by working with the instructor's comments. Moreno started with the larger elements of the essay by thinking about the instructor's questions and suggestions. Next, Moreno used the codes—the number-letter combinations—that referred her to specific sections in this handbook concerning matters of word choice, style, grammar, and punctuation. She also referred to the Revision Checklists, Charts 16 and 17. Before typing a clean copy of her third, final draft, Moreno edited her writing by referring to the Editing Checklist in Chart 19. Here is the third, final draft of Moreno's essay. The labels in the margins are guideposts for you *only* in this handbook; do not use them on your final drafts.

THIRD, FINAL DRAFT BY STUDENT

title   Women Can Pump Iron, Too

When my grandmother fell and broke her hip last summer, I wanted to help take care of her. Because she was bedridden, she needed to be lifted at times, but I was shocked to discover that I could not lift her without my mother's or brother's help. My grandmother ➜

67

does not weigh much, but she was too much for
me. My pride was hurt, and even more
important, I began to worry about my plans to
be a nurse specializing in care of elderly
people. What if I were too weak to help my
patients get around? When I realized that I
could satisfy one of my Physical Education
requirements by taking a weight-lifting course
for women, I decided to try it. Many people
picture only big, macho men wanting to lift
weights, but times have changed. With the
right training, women can also "pump iron"
successfully to build strength.

Women who lift weights, I was happy to
learn from my course, can easily avoid
developing overly masculine muscle mass. Women
can rely on their biology to protect them.
Women's bodies produce only very small amounts
of the hormones that enlarge muscles in men.
With normal weight training, women's muscles
grow longer rather than bulkier. The result is
smoother, firmer muscles, not massive bulges.
Also, women benefit most when they combine
weight lifting, which is a form of anaerobic
exercise, with aerobic exercise. Anaerobic
exercise strengthens and builds muscles, but
it does not make people breathe harder or
their hearts beat faster for sustained
periods. In contrast, aerobic exercise like
running, walking, and swimming builds
endurance, but not massive muscles, because it
forces a person to take in more oxygen,

thesis
statement

background
information

which increases lung capacity, improves circulatory health, and tones the entire body. Encouraged by my instructor, I balanced my weight-lifting workouts by swimming laps twice a week.

support: first aspect of training

Striving for strength can end in injury unless weight lifters learn the safe use of free weights and weight machines. Free weights are barbells, the metal bars that round metal weights can be attached to at each end. To be safe, no matter how little the weight, lifters must never raise a barbell by bending at the waist, grabbing the barbell, and then straightening up. Instead, they should squat, grasp the barbell, and then use their leg muscles to straighten into a standing position. To avoid a twist that can lead to serious injury, lifters must use this posture: head erect and facing forward, back and neck aligned. The big advantage of weight machines, which use weighted handles and bars hooked to wires and pulleys, is that lifters must use them sitting down. Therefore, machines like the Nautilus and Universal actually force lifters to keep their bodies properly aligned, which drastically reduces the chance of injury.

support: second aspect of training

Once a weight lifter understands how to lift safely, she needs a weight-lifting regimen personalized to her specific physical needs. Because benefits come from "resistance," which is the stress that lifting any amount of →

weight puts on a muscle, no one has to be strong to get started. A well-planned, progressive weight-training program begins with whatever weight a person can lift comfortably and gradually adds to the base weight as she gets stronger. What builds muscle strength is the number of repetitions, or "reps," the lifter does, not necessarily an increase in the amount of resistance from adding weight. Our instructor helped the women in the class, who ranged from 18 to 43, scrawny to pudgy, and couch potato to superstar, develop a program that was right for our individual weights, ages, and overall level of conditioning. Everyone's program differed in how much weight to start out with and how many reps to do for each exercise. Our instructor urged us not to try more weight or reps than our programs called for, even if our first workouts seemed too easy. This turned out to be good advice because those of us who did not listen woke up the next day feeling as though our bodies had been twisted by evil forces.

support: third aspect of training

In addition to fitting a program to her physical capabilities, a weight lifter needs to design an individual routine to fit her personal goals. Most students in my group wanted to improve their upper body strength, so we focused on exercises to strengthen arms, shoulders, abdomen, and chest. Each student learned to use specific exercises to isolate certain muscle groups. Because muscles strengthen and grow when they are rested after a workout, our instructor taught us to work alternate muscle groups on different days. For example, a woman might work on her arms and abdomen one day and then her shoulders and chest the next day. Because I had had such trouble lifting my grandmother, I added exercises to strengthen my legs and back. Another student, who had hurt her neck in a car crash, added neck-strengthening exercises. Someone else, planning to be a physical therapist, added finger- and hand-strengthening exercises.

conclusion: outcome with call to action

At the end of our 10 weeks of weight training, we had to evaluate our progress. Was I impressed! I felt ready to lift the world. When I started, I could lift only 10 pounds over my head for 3 reps. By the end of the course, I could lift 10 pounds over my head for 20 reps, and I could lift 18 pounds for 3 reps. Also, I could swim laps for 20 sustained minutes instead of the 10 I had barely managed at first. I am so proud of my weight-training accomplishments that I still work out three or four times a week. I am proof that any woman can benefit from "pumping iron." Not only will she become stronger and have more stamina, she will also feel energetic and confident. After all, there is nothing to lose—except maybe some flab.

4 Rhetorical Strategies in Paragraphs

Rhetorical strategies in writing are techniques for presenting ideas so that a writer's intended message is delivered with clarity and impact. The rhetorical strategies available to you as a writer are sufficiently varied to let you choose many ways to make your writing effective. As you can see from the explanations and examples in this chapter, all rhetorical strategies reflect the typical patterns of thought that humans use quite naturally. As you try out these strategies, especially as they keep you aware of sequencing and arranging sentences, you can apply them to composing your paragraphs, and, in some situations, whole essays.

4a Understanding paragraphs

A **paragraph** is a group of sentences that work in concert to develop a unit of thought. Paragraphing permits you to subdivide material into manageable parts and, at the same time, to arrange those parts into a unified whole that effectively communicates its message.

Paragraphing is signalled by indentation. The first line is indented five spaces in a typewritten paper and one inch in a handwritten paper. (Business letters are sometimes typed in "block format," with paragraphs separated by a double space but no paragraph indentations. Generally block format is not appropriate for essays.)

The purpose of a paragraph helps to determine its structure. The most common purposes for academic writing are to inform and to persuade (see 1b). Some paragraphs introduce, conclude, or provide transitions. Most paragraphs, however, are **topical paragraphs,** also called *developmental paragraphs* or *body paragraphs.* They consist of a statement of a main idea, and specific, logical support for that main idea. Consider paragraph 1, a topical paragraph that seeks to inform. (To help discussion and reference in this chapter, a blue number appears at the left side of each sample paragraph.)

1 For most people, jellyfish are an ugly lump of stinging guck that washes up on the beach. But seeing them in action, you begin to understand why the world's 20 or so full-time jellyfish scientists view the creature as an elegantly beautiful specimen in which many mysteries of life might reside. "In a way, we're survivors of an earlier curiosity-driven group of naturalists—like those astronomers who used to count stars," says George Mackie, a University of Victoria–based zoologist who has been studying nerve function in the Portuguese man-of-war for 35 years and is invariably referred to as "the Grand Old Man of Jellies." "I'm doing this for the sheer love of it. Jellyfish are miracles of nature—so simple, yet they've survived for so long. They are seen as limp and ineffectual creatures; I don't think that's fair."

—Ric Dolphin, "Spineless Wonders"

Dolphin states his main idea in the second sentence. He then quotes an authority as support. This paragraph relates to the thesis° of the whole essay that although they seem simple, jellyfish are actually complex creatures that deserve close scientific attention.

Consider this topical paragraph that seeks to persuade. It, too, consists of a main idea and support.

2 Many people have expressed uneasiness about the advertising enterprise in our time. To put the matter abruptly, the advertising industry is a crude attempt to extend the principles of automation to every aspect of society. Ideally, advertising aims at the goal of a programmed harmony among all human impulses and aspirations and endeavors. Using handicraft methods, it stretches out toward the ultimate electronic goal of a collective consciousness. When all production and all consumption are brought into a pre-established harmony with all desire and all effort, then advertising will have liquidated itself by its own success.

—Marshall McLuhan, *Understanding Media*

McLuhan states his main idea in the second sentence. The rest of the paragraph demonstrates his point and expands upon it.

Dolphin's and McLuhan's paragraphs demonstrate the three major characteristics of an effective paragraph. They are shown in Chart 20.

Understanding paragraph structure can help you at various points during your writing process. Before drafting (see 3b), you might decide to subdivide your material into paragraphs and to develop each in an effective way. If you prefer to plan less at first and instead write a "discovery" or a rough draft that gets all your ideas down on paper, you can later sort out your material and arrange it into manageable paragraphs. When revising (see 3c), you might find that a particular paragraph is weak because it does not clearly state its main idea or it does not develop that idea well. Also, you might notice that although

73

> **MAJOR CHARACTERISTICS OF AN EFFECTIVE PARAGRAPH** 20
>
> ■ **Unity:** clear, logical relationship between the main idea of a paragraph and supporting evidence for that main idea (see 4b and 4c).
> ■ **Coherence:** smooth progression from one sentence to the next within a paragraph (see 4d).
> ■ **Development:** specific, concrete support for the main idea of the paragraph (see 4c).

each paragraph is well structured on its own, the paragraphs do not work together very well. This chapter offers you paragraphing options to consider as you plan, draft, and revise your writing.

4b Writing unified paragraphs.

A paragraph is **unified** when all its sentences clarify or help support the main idea. Unity is lost if a paragraph goes off the topic by including sentences unrelated to the main idea. Here is a paragraph about the novelist Jane Austen, which lacks unity because two *deliberately added* sentences go off the topic.

NO   An Austen novel is a *tour de force,* at least by modern standards. Of course, Jane Austen did not feel the need to sprinkle her text with foreign phrases. Nothing extraordinary happens—no murders, escapades, or disasters. Instead of adventure or melodrama we read about the prosaic daily comedy of family life. There is little complexity to the plots (compared to Dickens, say), and the suspense, such as it is, arises chiefly out of questions of love and marriage. Jane Austen single-handedly invented, and brought to perfection, what could be called the domestic genre of novel-writing, the literary equivalent to the seventeenth-century Dutch school of interior painting. In contrast, Rembrandt, the pre-eminent Dutch painter of that era, avoided domesticity for its own sake.

In the preceding paragraph, the second and last sentences wander away from the topic of Austin's literary achievement. As a result, unity is lost. A reader quickly loses patience with material that rambles and therefore fails to communicate a clear message. Paragraph 3 is the original version. It is unified because all its sentences relate to the central subject.

YES

3

An Austen novel is a *tour de force,* at least by modern standards. Nothing extraordinary happens—no murders, escapades, or disasters. Instead of adventure or melodrama we read about the prosaic daily comedy of family life. There is little complexity to the plots (compared to Dickens, say), and the suspense, such as it is, arises chiefly out of questions of love and marriage. Jane Austen single-handedly invented, and brought to perfection, what could be called the domestic genre of novel-writing, the literary equivalent to the seventeenth-century Dutch school of interior painting. Her books are, of course, much more than a faithful representation of the period, just as Vermeer's paintings were more than illustrations of young Dutch women at home. Like Vermeer, de Witte, and the other Dutch domestic painters, Austen chose to stay strictly within the limits of the everyday, not because her talent was small, but because her imagination did not require a broader canvas.

—Witold Rybczynski, *Home*

The sentence that contains the main idea of a paragraph is called the **topic sentence.** It shapes and controls the content of the rest of the paragraph.

Some paragraphs use two sentences to present a main idea. In such cases, the topic sentence is followed by a **limiting** or **clarifying sentence,** which serves to narrow the paragraph's focus. In paragraph 3, the first sentence is its topic sentence, and the second sentence is its limiting sentence. The rest of the sentences support the main idea.

Professional essay writers do not always use topic sentences, because these writers have the skill to carry the reader along without explicit signposts. Student writers are often advised to use topic sentences so that their essays will be clearly organized and their paragraphs will not stray from the controlling power of each main idea.

Topic sentence at the beginning of a paragraph

Most informative and persuasive paragraphs place the topic sentence first so that a reader knows immediately what to expect.

4

The clock, Lewis Mumford has pointed out, is the key machine of the machine age, both for its influence on technics and for its influence on the habits of men. Technically, the clock was the first really automatic machine that attained any importance in the life of men. Previous to its invention, the common machines were of such nature that their operation depended on some external and unreliable force, such as human or animal muscles, water, or wind. It is true that

4   the Greeks had invented a number of primitive automatic machines, but these were used, like Hero's steam engine, either for obtaining "supernatural" effects in the temples or for amusing the tyrants of Levantine cities. But the clock was the first automatic machine that attained public importance and a social function. Clock-making began the industry from which men learnt the elements of machine-making and gained the technical skill that was to produce the complicated machinery of the Industrial Revolution.

—GEORGE WOODCOCK, "The Tyranny of the Clock"

Sometimes the main idea in the topic sentence starts a paragraph and is then restated at the end of the paragraph.

5   *Every dream is a portrait of the dreamer.* You may think of your dream as a mirror that reflects your inner character—the aspects of your personality of which you are not fully aware. Once we understand this, we can also see that every trait portrayed in our dreams has to exist in us, somewhere, regardless of whether we are aware of it or admit it. *Whatever characteristics the dream figures have, whatever behavior they engage in, is also true of the dreamer in some way.*

—ROBERT A. JOHNSON, *Inner Work*

Topic sentence at the end of a paragraph

Some informative and persuasive paragraphs reveal the supporting details before the main idea. The topic sentence, therefore, comes at the end of a paragraph. This approach is particularly effective for building suspense and for dramatic effect. This arrangement forces readers to move through all the details before encountering the organizing effect of a main idea.

Paragraphs 6 and 7 end with a topic sentence. In paragraph 6, the main idea is fairly easy to predict as the specific suggestions accumulate. In paragraph 7, the main idea is less predictable, and it is thus more satisfying for some readers but more challenging for others.

6   Burnout is a potential problem for any hard working and persevering student. A preliminary step for preventing student burnout is for students to work in moderation. Students can concentrate on school every day, provided that they do not overtax themselves. One method students can use is to avoid concentrating on a single project for an extended period of time. For example, if students have to read two books for a midterm history test, they should do other assignments at intervals so that the two books will not get boring. Another means to moderate a workload is to regulate how many extracurricular projects to take on. *When a workload is manageable, a student's immunity to burnout is strengthened.*

—BRADLEY HOWARD, student

7 When I tell young softball players I played the game bare-handed, they regard me warily. Am I one of these geezers who's forever jawing about the fact that, in his day, you had to walk through six miles of snowdrifts just to get to school? Will I tediously lament the passing of the standing broad jump, and the glorious old days when the only football in the Maritimes was English rugger, and when hockey was an outdoor art rather than indoor mayhem, and at decent yacht clubs men were gentlemen and women were *personae non grata*? No, but I will tell today's softball players that—with their fancy uniforms, batters' helmets and, above all, gloves for every fielder—the game they play is more tarted-up and sissy that the one I knew.

—HARRY BRUCE, "The Softball Was Always Hard"

Topic sentence implied

Some paragraphs make a unified statement without the use of a topic sentence. Writers must construct such paragraphs carefully so that a reader can easily discern the main idea.

8 The Romans were entertained by puppets, as were the rulers of the Ottoman Empire with their favorite shadow puppet, Karaghoiz, teller of a thousand tales. In the Middle Ages, puppets were cast as devil and angel in religious mystery and morality plays until cast out entirely by the church. For centuries, there has been a rich puppetry heritage in India that matches that country's multilayered culture. The grace of Bali is reflected in its stylized, ceremonial rod and shadow puppets. The Bunraku puppets of Japan, unequaled for technique anywhere in the world, require a puppet master and two assistants to create one dramatic character on stage.

—DAN CODY, "Puppet Poetry"

Cody uses many examples to communicate the main idea that puppets have been popular in many cultures over time. A reader does not expect to puzzle over material, so implied topic sentences must be very clear, even though they are silent.

EXERCISE 4-1

Consulting sections 4a and 4b, identify all topic sentences, limiting sentences, and topic sentences repeated at the ends of paragraphs. If there is no topic sentence, compose an implied one.

A.

9 A good college program should stress the development of high-level reading, writing, and mathematical skills and should provide you with a broad historical, social, and cultural perspective, no matter what subject

you choose as your major. The program should teach you not only the most current knowledge in your field but also—just as important—prepare you to keep learning throughout your life. After all, you will

9 probably change jobs, and possibly even careers, at least six times, and you'll have other responsibilities, too—perhaps as a spouse and as a parent and certainly as a member of a community whose bounds extend beyond the workplace.

—FRANK T. RHODES, "Let the Student Decide"

B.   The once majestic oak tree crashes to the ground amid the destructive flames, as its panic-stricken inhabitants attempt to flee the fiery tomb. Undergrowth that formerly flourished smoulders in ashes. A family of deer darts furiously from one wall of flame to the other, with-

10 out an emergency exit. On the outskirts of the inferno, fire fighters try desperately to stop the destruction. Somewhere at the source of this chaos lies a former campsite containing the cause of this destruction—an untended campfire. This scene is one of many which illustrate how human apathy and carelessness destroy nature.

—ANNE BRYSON, student

C.   The dead cat in the Creeds bag is a classic example of an urban legend. Like a rumor, an urban legend is presented as the truth, contains a large number of corroborating facts, and is set in the recent past. Unlike a rumor, it has a developed plot that often results in an ironic twist. The bare-bones information of a snake biting a customer in a store (in Vancouver, it's a furrier; in Montreal, it's a sporting goods store) is a

11 rumor. If it is elaborated into the story of a friend of a neighbor who was rushed to hospital and now is slightly paralyzed because of the snakebite, it is becoming a legend. If the same story persists for a number of years (and the dead cat has been traced back to 1906), it has achieved legend status. Although they are generally believed to be true by the teller, the same tales are passed along by word of mouth simultaneously across North America—the state of the art of apocrypha now.

—IAN PEARSON, "The Cat in the Bag and Other Absolutely Untrue Tales from Our Urban Mythology"

D.   Peanuts contain no cholesterol and a lot of nutrition. A 3.5-ounce
12 package of unsalted peanuts contains more than half of your daily protein requirement. But peanuts are far from a health food. That same 3.5-ounce package also contains 564 calories.

—LOUISE KLEIN, "Peanut Gallery"

E.   Put in uniform at six or seven, by the time a boy reaches the NHL, he is a veteran of close to 1,000 games—30-minute games, later 32-, then
13 45-, finally 60-minute games, played more than twice a week, more than seventy times a year between late September and late March. It is more

games from a younger age, over a longer season than ever before. But it is less hockey than ever before. For, every time a twelve-year-old boy plays a thirty-minute game, sharing the ice with teammates, he plays only about ten minutes. And ten minutes a game, anticipated and pre-

13 pared for all day, travelled to and from, dressed and undressed for, means ten minutes of hockey a day, more than two days a week, more than seventy days a hockey season. And every day that a twelve-year-old plays only ten minutes, he doesn't play two hours on a backyard rink, or longer on school or playground rinks during weekends and holidays.

—KEN DRYDEN, "The Game"

4c Supporting the main idea of a paragraph

As a writer, when you know how to achieve effective **paragraph development,** your material is far more likely to deliver its message to your reader. Most successful topical paragraphs that seek to inform or persuade (see 1b) contain a generalization, which is communicated in the topic sentence of the paragraph (see 4b). But more is needed. In writing most topical paragraphs, you must be sure to *develop the paragraph*. Development is provided by specific, concrete details that support the generalization. Without development, a topical paragraph contains only the broad claim of the generalization. It goes around in circles because it merely repeats the generalization over and over. It therefore does little to inform or persuade the reader.

Here is a paragraph that is unsuccessful because it contains one generalization restated four times in different words. Compare it with paragraph 1, an example of a successful paragraph, early in this chapter.

NO   For most people, jellyfish are an ugly lump of sting-ing guck that washes up on the beach. The average observer finds jellyfish disgusting. People have always been afraid of jellyfish because of their strange appear-ance and their sting. They seem like a lower form of life.

This *No* paragraph is stalled. It goes nowhere. Such material does not hold the reader's interest because it neither informs nor persuades.

When you write a topical paragraph, remember that **what separates most good writing from bad is the writer's ability to move back and forth between generalizations and specific details.** A successful topical paragraph includes a generalization and specific, concrete supporting details.

Using detail is one of the keys to effective, successful development in topical paragraphs. Details bring generalizations to life by providing concrete, specific illustrations. "RENNS" is a memory device you can use to check whether you have included sufficient detail in a topical paragraph. Chart 21 explains RENNS. A well-supported paragraph usually has only a selection of RENNS, so do not expect your paragraphs to have all categories in the list. Also, RENNS does not mean that the supporting details must occur in the order of the letters in RENNS. To see RENNS in action, read the many sample paragraphs in this chapter with an eye for the details. Also, consider paragraphs 14, 15, and 16 especially.

USING "RENNS" TO CHECK FOR SPECIFIC, CONCRETE DETAILS   21

- **R**easons
- **E**xamples
- **N**ames
- **N**umbers
- **S**enses (sight, sound, smell, taste, touch)

Here is a paragraph that has three of the five types of RENNS. Locate as many RENNS as you can before you read the analysis that follows the paragraph.

14   A dramatic increase in the grizzly bear sightings in Alberta has touched off a heated dispute among wildlife experts that centres on a seemingly simple issue: Are there really more grizzlies or merely more observers? More than 400 sightings were reported in Alberta in 1992, almost 10 times the number reported 10 years ago. The province's Department of Environmental Protection now estimates that 800 to 850 grizzly bears live in Alberta and that their number will reach 1000 by the turn of the century. Wildlife-conservation groups say the jump in sightings is mainly fuelled by greater activity by recreational users in the remote backcountry where grizzlies live. "My guess is, there are only 300 to 400 bears, and more likely, it's closer to the lower end," says Brian Horejsi, a conservation biologist with the group Speak Up For Wildlife.

—TERRY BULLICK, "When Is a Grizzly Not a Grizzly?"

Paragraph 14 succeeds because it does more than merely repeat its topic sentence, which is its first sentence. It develops the topic sentence to support the claim that grizzlies have not actually increased in number. It uses Numbers to document the apparent increase in sightings of grizzlies, but it uses Reasons to discount the claim that the rise in numbers means more actual bears. It has Names, such as Speak Up For

Wildlife and the Department of Environmental Protection, which serve to support the claim.

Here is a paragraph that has four of the five types of RENNS. Locate as many RENNS as you can before you read the analysis of RENNS that follows the paragraph.

> Tennyson called it a "flying flame." Benjamin Franklin termed it a "sudden and terrible mischief." In Roman mythology, the god Jupiter used spiky thunderbolts as letters to the editor when he chose to show displeasure with the poor mortals below. By whatever name, lightning is a spectacular natural event. Captured in photographs, its grandeur and beauty are safely petrified in static portraits of primal energy. In reality, at 24,000 to 28,000 degrees C°, it is four times hotter than the surface of the sun. It can vaporize steel, plough up fields, shatter giant trees and scatter livid incendiary sparks over vast forests. Each day it kills 20 people.
>
> 15
>
> —MICHAEL CLUGSTON, "Twice Struck"

Paragraph 15 succeeds because it illustrates its topic sentence, which is the fourth sentence. The paragraph develops its topic sentence with specific, concrete facts about the nature of lightning. It has Names, like Franklin and Tennyson, to testify to the power of the natural phenomenon. It has Numbers, such as those describing the temperature of lightning and the statistic that each day lightning kills twenty people. These Senses of sight and touch are appealed to in images of flame, "spiky thunderbolts," and intense heat. It also uses Examples, such as lightning's power to do powerful damage to steel, fields, and trees.

Some well-developed paragraphs have a single extended example to support the topic sentence.

> He was one of the greatest scientists the world has ever known, yet if I had to convey the essence of Albert Einstein in a single word, I would choose *simplicity.* Perhaps an anecdote will help. Once, caught in a downpour, he took off his hat and held it under his coat.
>
> 16 Asked why, he explained, with admirable logic, that the rain would damage the hat, but his hair would be none the worse for its wetting. This knack of going instinctively to the heart of the matter was the secret of his major scientific discoveries—this and his extraordinary feeling for beauty.
>
> —BANESH HOFFMAN, "My Friend, Albert Einstein"

EXERCISE 4-2

Reread the paragraphs in Exercise 4-1 and identify the RENNS (consult 4c) in each paragraph.

EXERCISE 4-3

Using your own words to complete the thought, fill in the blanks with a word or phrase that is specific. Then choose one of the five as a topic sentence and write a well-developed paragraph. Use as many RENNS (consult 4c) as you need to give the topic sentence concrete, specific support.

1. The place where I feel most comfortable is _____ .
2. _____ can cause major problems for students.
3. Budgeting time is a skill I _____ .
4. The greatest Canadian asset is _____ .
5. Getting a good job depends largely on _____ .

4d   Writing coherent paragraphs

A paragraph is **coherent** when its sentences are related to each other, not only in content but also in grammatical structures and choice of words. To achieve coherence in your writing, write each sentence of a paragraph so that it flows sensibly from the one before. A coherent paragraph gives a reader a sense of continuity. Note in paragraphs 17 through 20 that each sentence continues from the previous sentence, by use of the techniques of coherence listed in Chart 22. As you draft and revise, monitor continuity in your paragraphs.

TECHNIQUES OF COHERENCE   22

- Use **transitional expressions** effectively (4d-1)
- Use **pronouns** effectively (4d-2)
- Use **deliberate repetition** effectively (4d-3)
- Use **parallel structures** effectively (4d-4)

---

1   Using transitional expressions

Transitional expressions are words and phrases that signal connections among ideas. By signalling how ideas relate to each other, you achieve coherence in your writing. Commonly used transitional expressions are listed in Chart 23. When you use them, be sure to vary your choices within each list to achieve variety in your writing. ❖ COMMA ALERT: Transitional expressions are usually set off with commas; see 24b-3. ❖ Here are some illustrations:

CONTINUITY BY ADDITION

Woodpeckers use their beaks to find food and to chisel out nests. **In addition,** they claim their territory and signal their desire to mate by drumming their beaks on trees.

CONTINUITY BY CONTRAST

Most birds communicate by singing. Woodpeckers, **however,** communicate by the duration and rhythm of the drumming of their beaks.

CONTINUITY BY RESULT

Woodpeckers communicate by drumming their beaks on dry branches or tree trunks. **As a result,** they can communicate across greater distances than songbirds can.

COMMON TRANSITIONAL EXPRESSIONS AND THE RELATIONSHIPS THEY SIGNAL	23

RELATIONSHIP	WORDS
ADDITION	also, in addition, too, moreover, and, besides, furthermore, equally important, then, finally,
EXAMPLE	for example, for instance, thus, as an illustration, namely, specifically,
CONTRAST	but, yet, however, on the other hand, nevertheless, nonetheless, conversely, in contrast, still, at the same time,
COMPARISON	similarly, likewise, in the same way,
CONCESSION	of course, to be sure, certainly, granted,
RESULT	therefore, thus, as a result, so, accordingly,
SUMMARY	hence, in short, in brief, in summary, in conclusion, finally,
TIME SEQUENCE	first, second, third, next, then, finally, afterwards, before, soon, later, meanwhile, subsequently, immediately, eventually, currently,
PLACE	in the front, in the foreground, in the back, in the background, at the side, adjacent, nearby, in the distance, here, there,

Consider how the transitional expressions (shown in boldface) help to make this paragraph coherent.

17 **In addition to** causing viewers to lose touch with society, television has had negative effects on viewers' imagination. Before the days of television, people were entertained by exciting radio shows such as *Superman, Batman,* and "War of the Worlds." **Of course,** the listener was required to pay careful attention to the story if all details were to be comprehended. **Better yet,** while listening to the stories, listeners would form their own images of the actions taking place. When the broadcaster would give brief descriptions of the Martian space ships invading earth, **for example,** every member of the audience would imagine a different space ship. **In contrast,** television's version of "War of the Worlds" will not stir the imagination at all, **for** everyone can clearly see the actions taking place. All viewers see the same space ship with the same features. Each aspect is clearly defined, and **therefore,** no one will imagine anything different from what is seen. **Thus,** television cannot be considered an effective tool for stimulating the imagination.

—Tom Paradis, "A Child's Other World"

2 Using pronouns

When you use pronouns that clearly refer to nouns or other pronouns (see Chapter 10), you help your reader follow the bridges you build from one sentence to the next. Consider how the pronouns, shown in boldface, help make the following paragraph coherent.

18 The funniest people I know are often unaware of just how ticked off **they** are about things until **they** start to kid around about them. Nature did not build **these** people to sputter or preach; instead, in response to the world's irritations, **they** create little plays in their minds—parodies, cartoons, fantasies. When **they** see how funny **their** creations are, **they** also understand how really sore **they** were at **their** sources. **Their** anger is a revelation, one that works backward in the minds of an audience: the audience starts out laughing and winds up fuming.

—Roger Rosenblatt, "What Brand of Laughter Do You Use?"

3 Using deliberate, selective repetition

You can achieve coherence by repeating key words in a paragraph. A key word is usually one related to the main idea in the topic sentence or to a major detail in one of the supporting sentences.

Repeating a key word now and then helps your reader follow your material. This technique must be used sparingly, however, because you risk being monotonous. The shorter a paragraph, the less likely that repeated words will be effective.

Consider how the careful reuse of key words (shown in bold-face) helps make this paragraph coherent.

19
Anthropologist Elena Padilla, author of *Up from Puerto Rico,* describing Puerto Rican **life** in a poor and squalid district of New York, tells **how** much people know about each other—**who** is to be trusted and **who** not, **who** is defiant of the law and **who** upholds it, **who** is competent and well informed and **who** is inept and ignorant—and **how** these things are known from the **public life** of the sidewalk and its associated enterprises. These are matters of **public** character. But she also tells **how** select are those permitted to drop into the kitchen for a cup of coffee, **how** strong are the ties, and **how** limited the number of a person's genuine confidants, those **who** share in a person's **private life** and **private affairs.** She tells **how** it is not considered **dignified** for everyone to know one's **affairs.** Nor is it considered **dignified** to snoop on others beyond the face presented in **public.** It does violence to a person's **privacy** and rights. In this, the people she describes are essentially the same as the people of the mixed, Americanized city street on which I **live,** and essentially the same as the people **who live** in high-income apartments or fine town houses, too.

—Jane Jacobs, *The Economy of Cities*

4 **Using parallel structures**

Parallel structures can help you achieve coherence in a para-graph. **Parallelism** is created when grammatically equivalent forms are used several times. The repeated tempos and sounds of parallel structures reinforce connections among ideas and create a dramatic effect. Be aware, however, that a thin line exists between effective parallelism (see Chapter 18) and lack of conciseness (see Chapter 16).

In paragraph 20, the authors use many parallel structures (shown in boldface) including a parallel series of words: *the sacred, the secu-lar, the scientific.* They also use parallel phrases°: *sometimes smiled at, sometimes frowned upon.* They end the paragraph with a group of six parallel clauses°, starting with *banish danger with a gesture.*

20
Superstitions are **sometimes smiled at** and **sometimes frowned upon** as observances characteristic of the old-fashioned, the unenlightened, children, peasants, servants, immigrants, foreigners

or backwoods people. Nevertheless, they give all of us ways of moving back and forth among the different worlds in which we live—**the sacred, the secular,** and **the scientific.** They allow us
20 to keep a private world also, where, smiling a little, we can **banish danger with a gesture** and **summon luck with a rhyme, make the sun shine in spite of storm clouds, force the stranger to do our bidding, keep an enemy at bay,** and **straighten the paths of those we love.**

—MARGARET MEAD AND RHODA METRAUX, "New Superstitions for Old"

5 | Showing relationships among paragraphs

Paragraphs in an essay do not stand in isolation. You can use the techniques of coherence discussed in this chapter to communicate relationships among paragraphs in an essay. Transitional expressions, pronouns, deliberate repetition, and parallel structures can all help you link ideas from paragraph to paragraph throughout an essay.

One excellent way to connect paragraphs is to start a new paragraph with a reference to the previous paragraph. Passage 21 uses this technique. Also, the student essays and research papers throughout this handbook make the connections among paragraphs that help to maintain coherence in longer pieces of writing.

Passage 21 shows two paragraphs and the start of a third paragraph from a book examining Canada's identity as a nation. Repeated words connecting these paragraphs include *nation, nationalism, history, historical,* and *Canadian(s)*. The "From that year on" sentence tightly links the first and second paragraphs: A reader does not know what year is meant or what important events made it a turning point without reading the first paragraph. The opening sentence of the third paragraph creates another strong link by repeating the term *nationalism,* the word that concludes the second paragraph. This concept, introduced in the first two paragraphs, is qualified and nuanced in the final paragraph.

As a nation, Canada was born again in 1957. The year lies across our history like a fault-line: Diefenbaker won his first election; Pearson won his Nobel Peace Prize; Walter Gordon brought down his report on foreign ownership; and the Canada Council was established.
21 These events, along with Quebec's Quiet Revolution, which began three years later, created the Canada of today, a society that seems to contain only a few trace elements of what Earle Birney called in the 1940s "a highschool land/deadset in adolescence."

From that year on, Canadian-American relations were redefined by a force for which there was no historical antecedent. This was the force, at first tentative and apologetic, then increasingly vocal, then rancorous, then celebratory, of Canadian nationalism.

21   This nationalism was always firmly rooted in pragmatism. Whenever times got tough or the price of flag-waving seemed likely to be too high, Canadians lowered their banners. This was predictable. Far more interesting was the way the minimum acceptable low-water mark of nationalism expression demanded by Canadians of their governments kept getting raised.

—RICHARD GWYN, *The 49th Paradox*

EXERCISE 4-4

Consulting section 4d, identify the techniques of coherence—words of transition, pronouns, deliberate repetition, and parallel structures—in each paragraph.

A.   Kathy sat with her legs dangling over the edge of the side of the hood. The band of her earphones held back strands of straight copper hair which had come loose from two thick braids that hung down her back. She swayed with the music that only she could hear, making circles in the warm air, her shoulders raised. Her arms reached out to her side; her opened hands reached for the air; her closed hands brought the air back to her. Her arms reached over her head; her opened hands reached for a cloud; her closed hands brought the cloud back to her. Her head moved from side to side; her eyes opened and closed to the tempo of the tunes. Kathy was motion.

22

—CLAIRE BURKE, student

B.   Newton's law may have wider application than just the physical world. In the social world, racism, once set into motion, will remain in motion unless acted upon by an outside force. The collective "we" must be the outside force. We must fight racism through education. We must make sure every school has the resources to do its job. We must present to our children a culturally diverse curriculum that reflects our pluralistic society. This can help students understand that prejudice is learned through contact with prejudiced people, rather than with the people toward whom the prejudice is directed.

23

—RANDOLPH H. MANNING, "Fighting Racism with Inclusion"

C.   Elephant shrews come into the world nose first, and "nose first" they go through the rest of their nervous lives. Ever alert for danger, these tiny mammals depend on their noses as we do our eyes, mapping their twilight world primarily by scent. Their long, flexible noses twitch constantly, probing, sniffing, and exploring every detail of their brushy, dry habitat.

24

—SUSAN LUMPKIN, "The Elephant Shrew—By a Nose!"

D.   The snow geese are first, rising off the ponds to breakfast in the sorghum fields up the river. Twenty thousand of them, perhaps more, great white birds with black wing tips rising out of the darkness into the rosy reflected light of dawn. They make a sweeping turn, a cloud of wings ris-
25 ing above the cottonwoods. But *cloud* is the wrong word. They do not form a disorderly blackbird rabble but a kaleidoscope of goose formations, always shifting, but always orderly. The light catches them—white against the tan velvet of the hills. Then they are overhead, line after line, layer above layer of formations, and the sky is filled with the clamor of an infinity of geese.

— Tony Hillerman, *Hillerman Country*

E.   A full-grown brown bear can weigh more than 1,000 pounds, stand 12 feet tall on its hind legs and outrun a horse for short distances. Technically, brown bears are the same species as the grizzly bear—the one known as *Ursus arctos.* There are some differences, however. Brown bears occupy the coastal rim of southern Alaska and parts of the
26 Yukon and British Columbia. Grizzlies are found farther inland, for the most part; their range also includes much of western Canada and some of Montana, Idaho, and Wyoming. Brownies tend to be larger; grizzlies tend to have a more dish-shaped face and a more pronounced hump. The main difference, however, is that brown bears have access to migrating salmon and grizzlies don't.

— Boyd Norton, "It's a Good Thing McNeil's Big Bears Get Plenty to Eat"

EXERCISE 4-5

Reread the paragraphs in Exercise 4-1, and then, consulting section 4d, identify all techniques of coherence—words of transition, pronouns, deliberate repetition, and parallel structures.

EXERCISE 4-6

Consulting sections 4c and 4d, develop three of the following topic sentences into paragraphs that are unified with RENNS and techniques of coherence. After you finish, list the RENNS and the techniques of coherence you have built into each paragraph.

1.   Newspaper comic strips reflect many current problems.
2.   What constitutes garbage in Canada says a great deal about Canadian culture.
3.   Children are taught to compete at too early an age.
4.   Learning to do laundry can be perilous to one's clothes.
5.   College athletics is big business.

4e Arranging a paragraph

Arranging a paragraph means putting its sentences into an order logical for communicating the message of the paragraph clearly and effectively. This section shows you the most common choices for arrangements of topical paragraphs. Choices include sequencing according to time and to location; moving from general to specific, from specific to general, and from least to most important; and progressing from problem to solution.

As you write, you might prefer to postpone your final decisions about the arrangement of your paragraphs until after you have written a first draft. As you revise, you can experiment to see how your sentences can be arranged for greatest impact.

According to time

A paragraph arranged according to time is put into a *chronological sequence*. It tells what happened or what is happening during a period of time.

27   Other visitors include schools of dolphin swimming with synchronized precision and the occasional humpback whale. Before 1950, these 14-meter marine mammals were a common sight in the waters of the Great Barrier Reef as they passed on their annual migration between Antarctic waters and the tropics, where their calves were born. Then in the 1950s whaling stations were set up on the New South Wales and Queensland coasts, and together with the long-established Antarctic hunts by the Soviet Union and America, whales were slaughtered in their thousands. By the time the whaling stations on the eastern Australian coast closed in the early 1960s, it was estimated that only two hundred remained in these waters. Today, their numbers are slowly increasing, but sightings are still rare.

—ALLAN MOULT, "Volcanic Peaks, Tropical Rainforest, and Mangrove Swamps"

According to location

A paragraph arranged according to location is put into a *spatial sequence*. It describes the position of objects relative to one another, often from a central point of reference. The topic sentence usually establishes a location that serves as the orientation for all other places mentioned. The other sentences in the paragraph often use transitional expressions (see Chart 23) that indicate *place*.

28 The old store, lighted only by three fifty-watt bulbs, smelled of coal oil and baking bread. In the middle of the rectangular room, where the oak floor sagged a little, stood an iron stove. To the right was a wooden table with an unfinished game of checkers and a stool made from an apple-tree stump. On shelves around the walls sat earthen jugs with corncob stoppers, a few canned goods, and some of the two thousand old clocks and clockworks Thurmond Watts owned. Only one was ticking; the others he just looked at.

—WILLIAM LEAST HEAT MOON, *Blue Highways*

From general to specific

An arrangement of sentences from the general to the specific is the most common organization for a paragraph. Seen in many of the examples earlier in this chapter, a general-to-specific arrangement begins with a topic sentence (and perhaps is followed by a limiting or clarifying sentence) and ends with specific details.

29 The search for water was a continuous one on the endless prairies. Certainly a good water supply was of prime importance to the homesteader. Frequently the first settler, filing on land in a new locality, would select a quarter-section near a lake or a large slough. Slough water, for drinking purposes, was fine in the early spring. But with the advent of warm weather, the bugs would have to be strained out of it. By summer, too, it would take on an amber colour. Many a homestead child arrived back with a pail of drinking water from a nearby slough to have his horrified mother discover a frog resting in the bottom of the pail. Occurrences such as these caused pioneer wives to agitate for the digging of a well.

—GEORGE SHEPHERD, *West of Yesterday*

From specific to general

A less common arrangement moves from the specific to the general. Like paragraphs 6 and 7 earlier in this chapter, a paragraph with such an arrangement ends with a topic sentence and begins with the details that support the topic sentence.

30 Replacing the spark plugs probably ranks number one on the troubleshooting list of most home auto mechanics. Too often this effort produces little or no improvement, as the problem lies elsewhere. Within the ignition system the plug wires, distributor unit, coil, and ignition control unit play just as vital a role as the spark plugs. However, performance problems are by no means limited to the ignition system. The fuel system and emissions control system also help determine engine performance, and each of these systems

30 contains several components which equal the spark plug in importance. The do-it-yourself mechanic who wants to provide basic care for a car should be able to do more than change the spark plugs.

—DANNY WITT, student

From least to most important

A sentence arrangement that moves from the least to the most important is known as *climactic order* because it saves the climax for the end. This arrangement can be effective in holding the reader's interest because the best part comes at the end. In informative and persuasive writing, this type of arrangement usually calls for the topic sentence at the beginning of the paragraph, although sometimes the topic sentence works well at the end. Here is a climactic paragraph that begins with a topic sentence. ("The Department" in the paragraph is Canada's Department of External Affairs.)

31 The significance of General de Gaulle's famous *"Vive le Québec libre"* spoken from a balcony in Montreal in 1967 was debated in the Department as it was throughout the country. Mr. Pearson declared the general's utterance to be unacceptable, and de Gaulle promptly left the country without completing his visit. Although there were some dissenting voices, particularly to the effect that the government had overreacted, there was general agreement that the General's statement was not a slip of the tongue. After General de Gaulle's visitation, the government could no longer assume that the influence of France would always be benign so far as Canada was concerned. Now one thing had become clear: Canada's relations with France had become a matter of prime concern not just within the Department, but all its diplomatic posts.

—ARTHUR ANDREW, *The Rise and Fall of a Middle Power*

From problem to solution

An effective arrangement can be to present a problem and move quickly to a suggested solution. The topic sentence presents the problem and the next sentence—the limiting or clarifying sentence—presents the main idea of the solution. The rest of the sentences give the specifics of the solution.

32 When I first met them, Sara and Michael were a two-career couple with a home of their own, and a large boat bought with a large loan. What interested them in a concept called voluntary simplicity was the birth of their daughter and a powerful desire to raise her themselves. Neither one of them, it turned out, was willing to restrict what they considered their "real life" into the brief time

before work and the tired hours afterward. "A lot of people think that as they have children and things get more expensive, the only answer is to work harder in order to earn more money. It's not the only answer," insists Michael. The couple's decision was to trade two full-time careers for two half-time careers, and to curtail consumption. They decided to spend their money only on things that contributed to their major goal, the construction of a world where family and friendship, work and play, were all of a piece, a world, moreover, which did not make wasteful use of the earth's resources.

—LINDA WELTNER, "Stripping Down to Bare Happiness"

EXERCISE 4-7

For each paragraph, arrange the sentences into a logical sequence. Begin by locating the topic sentence and placing it at the beginning of the paragraph. As you work, consult sections 4b and 4c.

PARAGRAPH A

1. Handel, through his use of a major key and a dynamic and melismatic melody in the Hallelujah Chorus of his *Messiah,* gives us a sense of hopeful elation.

2. Although defined as "the art of arranging sounds with reference to rhythm, pitch and tone quality" by Funk and Wagnall, music is, in reality, much, much more.

3. Chopin, on the other hand, through his use of the minor mode, bass register and slow tempo, conveys to us the feeling of sullen despair in the third movement of his Second Piano Sonata.

4. There is no doubt that we experience certain feelings when we fall under its hypnotic influence.

5. For example, music is surely the art of creating emotional responses through the skillful manipulation of sounds.

6. Examples of this power can be found among the works of any of the great composers.

—KEVIN KERWOOD, student

PARAGRAPH B

1. After a busy day, lens wearers often do not feel like taking time out to clean and disinfect their lenses, and many wearers skip the chore.

2. When buying a pair of glasses, a person deals with just the expense of the glasses themselves.

3. Although contact lenses make the wearer more attractive, glasses are easier and less expensive to care for.

4. However, in addition to the cost of the lenses themselves, contact lens wearers must shoulder the extra expense of cleaning supplies.
5. This inattention creates a danger of infection.
6. In contrast, contact lenses require daily cleaning and weekly enzyming that inconvenience lens wearers.
7. Glasses can be cleaned quickly with water and tissue at the wearer's convenience.

—Heather Martin, student

PARAGRAPH C

1. In the heat of a game, the skills come automatically.
2. The end result: The player attains a reflexive mastery of, say, the nuances of a slap shot or how to defend during a one-on-one rush.
3. Sports psychology assumes there is a physiological connection between an athlete's mental state and physical performance.
4. With repeated practice, control of these skills becomes imprinted in the lower brain centres (the cerebellum and brain stem) where involuntary motor activity is coordinated.
5. An athlete learning or practising a physical skill is, in a sense, training the higher brain centres, primarily the cerebral cortex, which governs conscious thought, perception and voluntary muscular activity.

—Robert Colapinto and Tim Falconer,
"The Confidence Game: Psychology on Ice"

EXERCISE 4-8

Consulting sections 4b and 4e, first identify all topic sentences. Then identify the arrangement or arrangements that organize the sentences in each paragraph. Choose from time, location, general to specific, specific to general, least to most important, and problem to solution.

A. A combination of cries from exotic animals and laughter and gasps from children fills the air along with the aroma of popcorn and peanuts. A hungry lion bellows for dinner, his roar breaking through the confusing chatter of other animals. Birds of all kinds chirp endlessly at curious children. Monkeys swing from limb to limb performing gymnastics for gawking onlookers. A comedy routine by orangutans employing old shoes and garments incites squeals of amusement. Reptiles sleep peacefully behind glass windows, yet they send shivers down the spines of those who remember the quick death many of these reptiles can induce. The sights and sounds and smells of the zoo inform and entertain children of all ages.

33

—Deborah Harris, student

B.   No one even agrees anymore on what "old" is. Not long ago, 30
34 was middle-aged and 60 was old. Now, more and more people are living
into their 70s, 80s and beyond—and many of them are living well, without any incapacitating mental or physical decline. Today, old age is defined
not simply by chronological years, but by degree of health and well being.
— CAROL TAVRIS, "Old Age Is Not What It Used to Be"

C.   There is something slightly inhuman and robotic about the reporters
who deliver the news to us on television. As a class they do not represent
humanity. TV newspeople are never ugly. They are never old and seldom
middle-aged. They are rarely overweight or bald and they do not wear
striking or ungainly clothing. They are never unhappy or ill at ease. They
are, without exception, middle class: no national TV reporter speaks with
35 a regional or working-class accent, or for that matter, a Rosedale honk
or a Westmount whine. Whatever eccentricities they may have are sup-
pressed. They are chosen not to reflect the audience but to reflect the way
producers believe—perhaps with good reason—that we want to see our
society represented. They appear to be picked as carefully as actors in a
play—except that directors of plays often look for striking or anomalous
characteristics and TV news producers never do.
— ROBERT FULFORD, "The Grand Illusion"

D.   Lately, bee researchers have been distracted by a new challenge
from abroad. It is, of course, the so-called "killer bee" that was imported
into Brazil from Africa in the mid-1950s and has been heading our way
ever since. The Africanized bee looks like the Italian bee but is more de-
36 fensive and more inclined to attack in force. It consumes much of the
honey that it produces, leaving relatively little for anyone who attempts
to work with it. It travels fast, competes with local bees and, worse,
mates with them. It has ruined the honey industry in Venezuela and now
the big question is: Will the same thing happen here?
— JIM DOHERTY, "The Hobby That Challenges You to Think Like a Bee"

E.   When children begin to play with other children and when they finally go to school, their names take on a public dimension. The child
with a "funny" name is usually in for trouble, but most kids are proud of
their names and want to write them on their books and pads and homework. There was a time when older children carved their names or initials
on trees. Now that there are so many people and so few trees, the spray
37 can has taken over from the jackknife, but the impulse to put one's identifying mark where all the world can see it is as strong as ever. The popularity of commercially produced name-on objects of every kind, from
teeshirts to miniature license plates, also attests to the importance
youngsters (and a lot of grown-ups too) place on claiming and proclaiming
their names.
— CASEY MILLER AND KATE SWIFT, "Women and Names"

EXERCISE 4-9

Often more than one arrangement can be effective for discussing a subject. Think through the topics listed here and consider what arrangement (one or more) might be effective for discussing the subject. Consulting section 4e, choose from general to specific, specific to general, least to most important, problem to solution, location, and time. Be ready to explain your choices. As long as you can give a convincing rationale, you will be correct.

1. ways to make friends
2. automobile accidents
3. how to combine work and postsecondary education
4. role of the Supreme Court of Canada
5. what parents of teenagers can learn from William Shakespeare's play *Romeo and Juliet*
6. the role of computers at home
7. travelling by bus
8. how to survive an earthquake
9. the problems with junk food
10. music favourites today

4f Knowing patterns for developing a paragraph

Patterns for **paragraph development** in informative and persuasive writing (see 1b) have evolved as writers have sought methods to express their ideas most effectively. When you know a variety of patterns for paragraph development, you have more choices when you are seeking ways to help your paragraphs deliver their meanings most effectively.

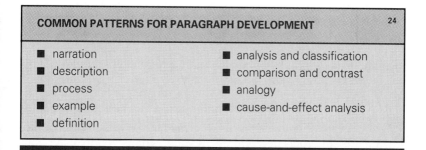

COMMON PATTERNS FOR PARAGRAPH DEVELOPMENT 24

- narration
- description
- process
- example
- definition

- analysis and classification
- comparison and contrast
- analogy
- cause-and-effect analysis

For the purpose of illustration, the patterns in this section are discussed separately. In essay writing, however, paragraph patterns often overlap. For example, narrative writing often contains descriptions; explanations of processes often include comparisons and contrasts; and so on. As you write paragraphs of various patterns, you will likely find that many patterns share characteristics. Your goal is to use paragraph patterns in the service of communicating meaning, not for their own sakes.

1 Using narration

Narrative writing tells about what is happening or what has happened. In informative and persuasive writing, narration is usually written in chronological sequence. Narrative paragraphs that illustrate other aspects of informative and persuasive writing include paragraphs 16, 31, and 54.

Here is another example of a narrative paragraph. Its main idea appears at the end of the first sentence, which begins to describe Eric the Red's exploits.

> 38 On good days, as one looked out from the west coast of Iceland, a faint line of mountains could be seen in the remote distance; and to Eric the Red, the violent son of a savage father, they offered both a way of escape and a promise of adventure. Thorwaldr, the father, outlawed from Norway for manslaughter, had fled to Iceland; Eric, outlawed in his turn for homicide, determined to find his refuge in the unknown country to the west. In 982 he sailed west, discovered a huge ice-covered island, and wintered on its farther shore. He could not return home for good, nor did he want to: instead, he decided to found a colony on the land of his discovery. He called it Greenland, a boldly fraudulent advertisement intended to attract prospective immigrants; and in 986, triumphantly leading a fleet of twenty-four ships, he set sail again, reached the west coast of his island once more in safety, and laid the basis of two settlements.
>
> —DONALD CREIGHTON, *Canada: The Heroic Beginnings*

2 Using description

Descriptive writing appeals to a reader's senses—sight, sound, smell, taste, and touch. Descriptive writing permits you to share your sensual impressions of a person, a place, or an object. Descriptive paragraphs that illustrate other aspects of informative and persuasive writing include paragraphs 17, 18, and 27. Here is another example of a descriptive paragraph.

39   Somewhere to the far north of Newfoundland, the St. Lawrence Seaway, Place Ville Marie, the Macdonald-Cartier Freeway, the bald-headed prairie and Stanley Park lies an unreal world, conceived in the mind's eye, born out of fantasy and cauled in myth. It is a weird and terrible land where nothing is as it may seem. Home of the iceworm and the igloo, of mad trappers and mushing Mounties, of pingos and polar bears, of the legions of the damned that were conjured into being by Robert Service, its voice is the baleful whisper of the aurora borealis, the eerie howl of Jack London's malemutes and the whining dirge of C.B.C.'s wind machines. It is a "white hell", "the ultimate desolation", a "howling wasteland", "the Land that God forgot" and "the Land God Gave to Cain." It is a region almost wholly of our contriving, and we have made of it so inimical a world that the truly alien moon, even as seen on television screens, seems to have more reality.

—FARLEY MOWAT, "The Nature of the North"

---

3 | Using process

Process is a term used for writing that describes a sequence of actions by which something is done or made. Usually a process description is developed in chronological order. For an example, see paragraph 40. To be effective, process writing must include all steps. The amount of detail depends on whether you want to instruct the reader about how to do something or you want to offer a general overview of the process. Here is a process description written to give the reader a general picture. A process description that gives directions appears in paragraph 41.

40   Making chocolate is not as simple as grinding a bag of beans. The machinery in a chocolate factory towers over you, rumbling and whirring. A huge cleaner first blows the beans away from their accompanying debris—sticks and stones, coins and even bullets can fall among cocoa beans being bagged. Then they go into another machine for roasting. Next comes separation in a winnower, shells sliding out one side, beans falling from the other. Grinding follows, resulting in chocolate liquor. Fermentation, roasting and "conching" all influence the flavor of chocolate. Chocolate is "conched"—rolled

over and over against itself like pebbles in the sea—in enormous circular machines named conches for the shells they once resembled.
40 Climbing a flight of steps to peer into this huge, slow-moving glacier, I was expecting something like molten mud but found myself forced to conclude it resembled nothing so much as chocolate.

—RUTH MEHRTENS GALVIN, "Sybaritic to Some, Sinful to Others"

Here is a process description that gives the reader specific, step-by-step instructions.

41 Carrying loads of equal weight like paint cans and toolboxes is easier if you carry one in each hand. Keep your shoulders back and down so that the weight is balanced on each side of your body, not suspended in front. With this method, you will be able to lift heavier loads and also to walk and stand erect. Your back will not be strained by being pulled to one side.

—JOHN WARDE, "Safe Lifting Techniques"

4 Using example

A paragraph developed by example uses illustrations to provide evidence in support of the main idea. Examples are highly effective for developing topical paragraphs. They supply a reader with concrete, specific information. Many of the sample paragraphs in this chapter are developed with examples, among them paragraphs 1, 5, 6, 14, and 29. Here is another paragraph with examples used to develop the topic sentence.

42 One major value of rain forests is biomedical. The plants and animals of rain forests are the source of many compounds used in today's medicines. A drug that helps treat Parkinson's disease is manufactured from a plant that grows only in South American rain forests. Some plants and insects found in rain forests contain rare chemicals that relieve certain mental disorders. Discoveries, however, have only begun. Scientists say that rain forests contain over a thousand plants that have great anticancer potential. To destroy life forms in these forests is to deprive the human race of further medical advances.

—GARY LEE HOUSEMAN, student

5 Using definition

A paragraph of definition develops a topic by explaining the meaning of a word or a concept. A paragraph of definition is an *extended definition*—it is more extensive than a dictionary denotation (although the paragraph may include a dictionary definition). An effective paragraph of definition does not use abstractions to explain abstractions. Here is a paragraph that offers an extended definition of tolerance.

43
The Latin root of the word "tolerance" refers to things that can be borne, endured, are supportable. The intrinsic meaning of "tolerance" is the capacity to sustain and endure, as of hardship. From this comes the inferential meaning of patients with the opinions and practices of those who differ. It is interesting that the word is used in connection with the coining of money and with machinery, to indicate the margin within which coins may deviate from the fixed standard, or dimensions or parts of machine from the norm.

—DOROTHY THOMPSON, "Concerning Tolerance"

6 Using analysis and classification

Analysis (sometimes called *division*) divides things up. Classification groups things together. A paragraph developed by analysis divides one subject into its component parts. Paragraphs of analysis written in this pattern usually start by identifying the one subject and continue by explaining that subject's distinct parts. For example, here is a paragraph that identifies a new type of zoo design and then analyzes changes in our world that have brought about that design.

44
The current revolution in zoo design—the landscape revolution—is driven by three kinds of change that have occurred during this century. First are great leaps in animal ecology, veterinary medicine, landscape design, and exhibit technology, making possible unprecedented realism in zoo exhibits. Second, and perhaps most important, is the progressive disappearance of wilderness—the very subject of zoos—from the earth. Third is knowledge derived from market research and from environmental psychology, making possible a sophisticated focus on the zoo-goer.

—MELISSA GREENE, "No Rms, Jungle Vu"

A paragraph developed by classification groups information according to some scheme. The separate groups must be *from the same class*—they must have some underlying characteristics in common. For example, different galaxies can be classified into three general groups based on their shape. Here is a paragraph that discusses the three types of galaxies.

45   There are three basic types of galaxies: spiral galaxies, like the Milky Way; spherical swarms of stars called elliptical galaxies; and loose collections of stars with no distinct structural form, called irregular galaxies. The Large and Small Magellanic Clouds, the Milky Way satellite galaxies, are irregulars. Two nearby ellipticals are companions of the Andromeda Galaxy and are easily seen in photographs. The smallest elliptical galaxies, called dwarf spheroidal systems, have only a few thousand stars. But giant ellipticals are the titans of the cosmos, with populations of up to 50 trillion stars. Spiral galaxies have a comparatively small size range. The upper limit is marked by NGC 6872 and UGC 2885, both roughly 10 times the number of the Milky Way, while NGC 3928 is only about one-quarter of our galaxy's diameter. Although spiral galaxies are outnumbered by ellipticals, they *appear* to be most common because a typical spiral is larger and brighter than an average elliptical. Irregular galaxies are less numerous than spirals or ellipticals, and most are quite small.

—Terrence Dickinson, "Galactic Encounters"

7   Using comparison and contrast

Comparison deals with similarities, while contrast deals with differences. Paragraphs using comparison and contrast can be structured in two ways. A *point-by-point structure* allows you to move back and forth between the two items being compared. A *block structure* allows you to discuss one item completely before discussing the other.

Here is a paragraph structured point-by-point for comparison and contrast.

46   In the business environment, tone is especially important. Business writing is not literary writing. Literary artists use unique styles to "express" themselves to a general audience. Business people write to particular persons in particular situations, not so much to express themselves as to accomplish particular purposes, "to get a job done." If a reader does not like a novelist's tone, nothing much can happen to the writer short of failing to sell some books. In the business situation, however, an offensive style may not only prevent

46   a sale but may also turn away a customer, work against a promotion, or even cost you a job.

—JOHN S. FIELDEN, "What Do You Mean, You Don't Like My Style!"

| PATTERNS FOR COMPARISON AND CONTRAST | 25 |

POINT-BY-POINT STRUCTURE

Student body: college A, college B
Curriculum: college A, college B
Location: college A, college B

BLOCK STRUCTURE

College A: student body, curriculum, location
College B: student body, curriculum, location

Here is a block-form comparison of games and business.

47   Games are of limited duration, take place on or in fixed and finite sites and are governed by openly promulgated rules that are enforced on the spot by neutral professionals. Moreover, they are performed by relatively evenly matched teams that are counseled and led through every move by seasoned hands. Scores are kept, and at the end of the game, a winner is declared. Business is usually a little different. In fact, if there is anyone out there who can say that the business is of limited duration, takes place on a fixed site, is governed by openly promulgated rules that are enforced on the spot by neutral professionals, competes only on relatively even terms, and performs in a way that can be measured in runs or points, then that person is either extraordinarily lucky or seriously deluded.

—WARREN BENNIS, "Time to Hang Up the Old Sports Clichés"

| **8** | **Using analogy** |

Analogy is a type of comparison. It compares objects or ideas from different classes—things not normally associated. For example, a fatal disease has certain points in common with war. Analogy is particularly effective when you want to explain the unfamiliar in terms of the familiar. Often a paragraph developed with analogy starts with

101

a simile or metaphor (see 21c) to introduce the comparison. Here is a paragraph developed by analogy that starts with a simile and then explains the effect of casual speech by comparing it to casual dress.

> Casual dress, like casual speech, tends to be loose, relaxed and colorful. It often contains what might be called "slang words": blue jeans, sneakers, baseball caps, aprons, flowered cotton house-dresses, and the like. These garments could not be worn on a formal occasion without causing disapproval, but in ordinary circumstances they pass without remark. "Vulgar words" in dress, on the other hand, give emphasis and get immediate attention in almost any circumstances, just as they do in speech. Only the skillful can employ them without some loss of face, and even then they must be used in the right way. A torn, unbuttoned shirt, or wildly uncombed hair can signify strong emotions: passion, grief, rage, despair. They are most effective if people already think of you as being neatly dressed, just as the curses of well-spoken persons count for more than those of the customarily foul-mouthed.
>
> —ALISON LURIE, *The Language of Clothes*

48

---

9   Using cause-and-effect analysis

Cause-and-effect analysis involves examining outcomes and reasons for those outcomes. Causes lead to an event or an effect, and effects result from causes. (Section 5i describes making reasonable connections between causes and effects.) Here is a paragraph developed through a discussion of how television (the cause) becomes in-dispensable (the effect) to parents of young children.

> Because television is so wonderfully available as child amuser and child defuser, capable of rendering a volatile three-year-old harmless at the flick of a switch, parents grow to depend upon it in the course of their daily lives. And as they continue to utilize television day after day, its importance in their children's lives increases. From a simple source of entertainment provided by parents when they need a break from child care, television gradually changes into a powerful and disruptive presence in family life. But despite their increasing resentment of television's intrusions into their family life, and despite their considerable guilt at not being able to control their children's viewing, parents do not take steps to extricate themselves from television's domination. They can no longer cope without it.
>
> —MARIE WINN, *The Plug-In Drug*

49

EXERCISE 4-10

Consulting section 4f, identify the pattern or patterns each paragraph illustrates. Choose from narration, description, process, example, definition, analysis, classification, comparison and contrast, analogy, and cause and effect.

A.   What was South Vietnam still seems like a different country from the North—more commercial, more casual, seemingly less wrapped up in political correctness. The main market in Hanoi had little to offer except local vegetables, a few plastic tools, and the incongruously colonial-looking green pith helmets that most northern men wear. (Hanoi's market also featured several tubs of live bullfrogs while we were there. Two market ladies chatted with each other while lopping the frogs' legs off with strokes of their cleavers.) In Saigon, there are rows of "shop-

50 houses," the tan-colored buildings with red-tile roofs and open store-fronts that are found throughout Southeast Asia, and stores selling paintings, lacquerware, and a few cheap imported calculators and digital watches. In Hanoi, there are virtually no private cars—the streets look the way China's must have looked fifteen or twenty years ago, dense with bicycle traffic but very quiet. In Saigon, there are lots of motorcycles and a few private cars, including original Mustangs and other veteran American models. Still, no place in Vietnam has anything like the bustle of a typical Southeast Asian trading center.

—JAMES FALLOWS, "No Hard Feelings?"

B.   I retain only one confused impression from my earliest years: it is all red, and black, and warm. Our apartment was red: the upholstery was of red moquette, the Renaissance dining-room was red, the fig-ured silk hangings over the stained-glass doors were red, and the velvet

51 curtains in Papa's study were red too. The furniture in this awful sanctum was made of black pear wood; I used to creep into the knee-hole under the desk and envelop myself in its dusty glooms; it was dark and warm, and the red of the carpet rejoiced my eyes. That is how I seem to have passed the early days of infancy. Safely ensconced, I watched, I touched, I took stock of the world.

—SIMONE DE BEAUVOIR, Memoirs of a Dutiful Daughter

C.   In the case of wool, very hot water can actually cause some struc-tural changes within the fiber, but the resulting shrinkage is minor. The

52 fundamental cause of shrinkage in wool is felting, in which the fibers scrunch together in a tighter bunch, and the yarn, fabric, and garment fol-low suit. Wool fibers are curly and rough-surfaced, and when squished together under the lubricating influence of water, the fibers wind around

52 each other, like two springs interlocking. Because of their rough surfaces, they stick together and cannot be pulled apart.

—JAMES GORMAN, "Gadgets"

D.   *Hard,* in terms of wood, really means *harder* to cut, but most hardwoods are also fine and even-grained. They are not apt to split, and they take polish well. For these reasons, they are generally better for small wood carving than the softwoods; most sculptors prefer to use hardwoods for large pieces, too. All the fruitwoods, like cherry, apple, pear, and orange, are hard, and so are oak, mahogany, walnut, birch, holly, and maple. Hardwoods range in color from the almost white of holly to the almost black of walnut. Oak and mahogany are the most open-grained, and therefore more apt to split. They are probably less good for small carvings than the other kinds.

53

—FLORENCE H. PETTIT, *How to Make Whirligigs and Whimmy Doodles*

E.   After our lunch, we drove to the Liverpool public library, where I was scheduled to read. By then, we were forty-five minutes late, and on arrival we saw five middle-aged white women heading away toward an old car across the street. When they recognized me, the women came over and apologized: They were really sorry, they said, but they had to leave or they'd get in trouble on the job. I looked at them. Every one of them was wearing an inexpensive, faded house-dress and, over that, a cheap and shapeless cardigan sweater. I felt honored by their open-mindedness in having wanted to come and listen to my poetry. I thought and I said that it was I who should apologize: I was late. It was I who felt, moreover, unprepared: What in my work, to date, deserves the open-minded attention of blue-collar white women terrified by the prospect of overstaying a union-guaranteed hour for lunch?

54

—JUNE JORDAN, "Waiting for a Taxi"

F.   In many ways, chopsticks are the culinary equivalent of the stick shift. They enhance the act of eating and make it more participatory, tactile, not to mention fun. They give a certain ceremony to consumption and force the calorie-conscious diner to focus on the ritual of gustation, and therefore on the amount of food being shoveled into the mouth at any time.

55

—DENA KLEIMAN, "Older than Forks, Safer than Knives"

G.   Lacking access to a year-round supermarket, the many species—from ants to wolves—that in the course of evolution have learned the advantages of hoarding must devote a lot of energy and ingenuity to protecting their stashes from marauders. Creatures like beavers and honeybees, for example, hoard food to get them through cold winters. Others, like desert rodents that face food scarcities throughout the year,

56

must take advantage of the short-lived harvests that follow occasional rains. For animals like burying beetles that dine on mice hundreds of times their size, a habit of biting off more than they can chew at the moment forces them to store their leftovers. Still others, like the male MacGregor's bowerbird, stockpile goodies during mating season so they can concentrate on wooing females and defending their arena de l'amour.

—JANE BRODY, "A Hoarder's Life: Filling the Cache—And Finding It"

EXERCISE 4-11

Consulting section 4f, write paragraphs for three of the following topics.

1. a classification of drivers
2. a personal definition of political freedom
3. a narrative of your first experience as an authority figure
4. a cause-and-effect analysis of the increase in crime in large cities
5. an analogy about learning to use a college or university library

4g Writing introductory, transitional, and concluding paragraphs

Introductory, transitional, and concluding paragraphs are generally shorter than the topical paragraphs with which they appear.

Introductory paragraphs

In informative and persuasive writing, an introductory paragraph sets the stage and prepares a reader for what lies ahead. An introduction provides a bridge from the reader's mind to yours. In so doing, it needs to arouse the reader's interest in your subject. An introduction must clearly relate to the rest of your essay. If it points in one direction and your essay goes off in another, your reader will be confused, even annoyed, and will likely stop reading.

For academic writing, many instructors require that an introductory paragraph include a statement of the thesis of the essay, so that the central idea of the essay is clearly available early on. Many instructors want students to demonstrate from the start that all parts of any essay are related. Professional writers do not necessarily include a thesis statement in their introductory paragraphs; with experience comes skill at maintaining a line of thought without overtly stating a central idea. Student writers, however, often need to practise explicitly and demonstrate openly external clues to essay organization. As you write successive drafts of an essay, expect to revise your introduction, in whole or part, so that it works well in concert with your other paragraphs.

When instructors require a thesis statement, they often want it to be in the last sentence or two of the introductory paragraph. Here is an example of an introductory paragraph with a thesis statement (shown in italics).

> Most sprinters live in a narrow corridor of space and time. Life rushes at them quickly, and success and failure are measured by
> 57 frustrating, tiny increments. Florence Griffith Joyner paints her running world in bold, colorful strokes. *For her, there's a lot of romance to running fast.*
>
>   —CRAIG A. MASBACK, "Siren of Speed"

You can see additional examples of introductory paragraphs with a thesis statement in the last sentence in the student essays in sections 3f and 6i.

An introductory paragraph often includes one or more **introductory devices** that serve to stimulate a reader's interest in the subject of the essay. Usually the introductory device precedes the thesis statement. As you write your introductory paragraphs, keep in mind the guidelines in Chart 26.

Here is an introduction that uses two anecdotes before its thesis statement (shown in italics).

> On seeing another child fall and hurt himself, Hope, just nine months old, stared, tears welling up in her eyes, and crawled to her mother to be comforted—as though she had been hurt, not her friend. When 15-month-old Michael saw his friend Paul crying, Michael fetched his own teddy bear and offered it to Paul; when
> 58 that didn't stop Paul's tears, Michael brought Paul's security blanket from another room. *Such small acts of sympathy and caring, observed in scientific studies, are leading researchers to trace the roots of empathy—the ability to share another's emotions—to infancy, contradicting a longstanding assumption that infants and toddlers were incapable of these feelings.*
>
>   —DANIEL GOLEMAN, "Researchers Trace Empathy's Roots to Infancy"

The key to the effectiveness of an introductory device is how well it relates to the essay's thesis and to the material in the topical paragraphs. An introductory device must be well integrated into the paragraph, not mechanically slotted in for its own sake. Note how smoothly the message of the quotation in the following introduction becomes a dramatic contrast that leads into the thesis statement (shown in italics).

INTRODUCTORY PARAGRAPHS 26

DEVICES TO TRY

- Providing relevant background information
- Relating a brief, interesting story or anecdote
- Giving a pertinent statistic or statistics
- Asking a provocative question or questions
- Using an appropriate quotation
- Making an analogy
- Defining a term used throughout the essay
- Identifying the situation

STRATEGIES TO AVOID

- Obvious statements that refer to what the essay is about or will accomplish, such as "I am going to discuss the causes of falling oil prices"
- Apologies, such as "I am not sure this is right, but this is my opinion"
- Overworked expressions such as "Haste really does make waste, as I recently discovered" or Love is grand"

---

59 "Alone one is never lonely," says May Sarton in her essay "The Rewards of Living a Solitary Life." Most people, however, do not share Sarton's opinion: They are terrified of living alone. They are used to living with others—children with parents, roommates with roommates, friends with friends, husbands with wives. When the statistics catch up with them, therefore, they are rarely prepared. *Chances are high that most adult men and women will need to know how to live alone, briefly or longer, at some time in their lives.*

—TARA FOSTER, student

In the following paragraph, the author uses a question and some dramatic description to arouse interest and to set the stage for his thesis statement (shown in italics).

60 What should you do? You are out riding your bike, playing golf, or in the middle of a long run when you look up and suddenly see a jagged streak of light shoot across the sky, followed by a deafening clap of thunder. *Unfortunately, most outdoor exercisers*

60 *do not know whether to stay put or make a dash for shelter when a thunderstorm approaches, and sometimes the consequences are tragic.*

—GERALD SECOR COUZENS, "If Lightning Strikes"

In the following paragraph, statistics and numbers help the author lead into his thesis statement (shown in italics).

61 According to General Douglas MacArthur's headquarters, there were 78,150 dead and 13,083 missing. The United States Atomic Bomb Casualty Commission claims there were 79,000 dead. Both sets of figures are probably far too low. There is reason to believe that at the time of the surrender Japanese authorities lied about the number of survivors, exaggerating it to get extra medical supplies. The Japanese welfare ministry's figures of 260,000 dead and 163,263 missing may well be too high. *But the very order of such discrepancies speaks volumes about the scale of the catastrophe.* The dead were literally uncountable.

—KILDARE DOBBS, *Reading the Time*

Transitional paragraphs

A transitional paragraph usually consists of one or two sentences that help you move from a few pages on one subtopic to the next large group of paragraphs on a second subtopic. Transitional paragraphs are uncommon in short essays. In longer papers written for college or university, transitional paragraphs sometimes recapitulate the thesis° in the context of what was just discussed and what will follow.

Here is a two-sentence transitional paragraph written as a bridge between a lengthy discussion of people's gestures and the coming long discussion of people's eating habits.

62 Like gestures, eating habits are personality indicators, and even food preferences and attitudes toward food reveal the inner self. Food plays an important role in the lives of most people beyond its obvious one as a necessity.

—JEAN ROSENBAUM, M.D., *Is Your Volkswagen a Sex Symbol?*

Concluding paragraphs

A concluding paragraph serves to bring your discussion to an end that logically follows from your thesis° and its discussion. A conclusion that is merely tacked onto an essay does not give the reader a sense of completion. An ending that flows gracefully and sensibly from what has come before it reinforces the writer's ideas and enhances an

---

CONCLUDING PARAGRAPHS	27

DEVICES TO TRY

- Using any device appropriate for introductory paragraphs (see Chart 26)—but avoid using the same one in both the introduction and conclusion
- Summarizing the main points of the essay—but avoid a summary if the essay is less than three pages long
- Asking for awareness, action, or a similar resolution from readers
- Looking ahead to the future

STRATEGIES TO AVOID

- Introducing new ideas or facts that belong in the body of the essay
- Rewording your introduction
- Announcing what you have done, as in "In this paper, I have explained the drop in oil prices"
- Making absolute claims, as in "I have proved that oil prices do not affect gasoline prices"
- Apologizing, as in "Even though I am not an expert, I feel my position is correct" or "I may not have convinced you, but there is good evidence for my position"

---

essay. A concluding paragraph often includes one or more **concluding devices.** As you write your concluding paragraphs, keep in mind the guidelines listed in Chart 27.

Here is a concluding paragraph that summarizes an essay that discusses pizza, including the many versions of pizzalike foods enjoyed by various cultures throughout time.

> For a food that is traced to Neolithic beginnings, like Mexico's tortillas, Armenia's lahmejoun, Scottish oatcakes, and even matzohs, pizza has remained fresh and vibrant. Whether it is galettes, the latest thin-crusted invasion from France with bacon and onion toppings, or a plain slice of a cheese pie, the varieties of pizza are clearly limited only by one's imagination.

63

> —LISA PRATT, "A Slice of History"

This paragraph concludes an essay that argues for the recognition of First Nations governments in Canada. It reinforces the essay's message with a call for justice and cooperation.

> What we are looking for is not just power to deal with the social problems we face but reconciliation with Canada. We are trying to find a way of creating harmony in the country. The way you achieve that is to produce justice; our people have to feel justice, not just think about it. We have to experience it before we can believe it. There is absolutely no way that First Nations governments can meet the needs of the First Nations peoples without the help of the provinces or the federal government. What we are asking is to become partners working towards the same future.
>
> —OVIDE MERCREDI, "Self-Government as a Way to Heal"

The following conclusion ends an essay that discusses the risks of genetic engineering. The author points to the future and calls for action.

> I am not advocating that we stop the development of the new biology. I believe that we can achieve wonderful and important results with it. But we do need to ensure that its application is both peaceful and safe. We have to learn from the history of nuclear physics and organic chemistry. Indeed, I believe we have no real choice. We cannot afford to develop the new biological technologies without controlling them.
>
> —SUSAN WRIGHT, "Genetic Engineering: The Risks"

EXERCISE 4-12

Consulting section 4g, write an introduction and conclusion for each essay informally outlined below. To gain additional experience, write an alternative introductory and concluding paragraph for one of the essays.

A. Reading for fun

   Thesis: People read many kinds of books for pleasure.

   Topical paragraph 1: murder mysteries and thrillers
   Topical paragraph 2: romances and westerns
   Topical paragraph 3: science fiction

B. Computer games

   Thesis: Interactive video games require players to exercise their skills of dexterity, intelligence, and imagination.

   Topical paragraph 1: manual dexterity
   Topical paragraph 2: intelligence
   Topical paragraph 3: imagination

C. Using credit cards

Thesis: Although credit cards can help people manage their finances wisely, they can also offer too much temptation.

Topical paragraph 1: convenience and safety
Topical paragraph 2: tracking purchases
Topical paragraph 3: overspending dangers

EXERCISE 4-13

Reread the paragraphs in Exercise 4-10 and do the following:

1. Consulting section 4b, identify all topic sentences, limiting sentences, and implied topic sentences.
2. Consulting section 4c, identify all RENNS.
3. Consulting section 4d, identify all techniques of coherence.
4. Consulting section 4e, identify paragraph arrangements.

5 Critical Thinking, Reading, and Writing

This chapter shows you how to participate actively in the ongoing exchanges of ideas and opinions that you encounter in college, university, and beyond. To participate, you need to understand **critical thinking** as a concept (see 5a) and as an activity (see 5b); **critical reading** as a concept (see 5c) and as an activity (see 5d through 5f); **writing critically** (see 5g); and **reasoning critically** (see 5h through 5k).

5a Understanding critical thinking

Thinking is not something you choose to do, any more than a fish "chooses" to live in water. To be human *is* to think. But while thinking may come naturally, awareness of *how* you think does not. Thinking about thinking is the key to **critical thinking.** When you think critically, you take control of your conscious thought processes. Without such control, you risk being controlled by the ideas of others. Indeed, critical thinking is at the heart of a liberal (from the Latin word for *free*) education.

The word **critical** here has a neutral meaning. It does not mean taking a negative view or finding fault, as when someone criticizes another person for doing something wrong. The essence of critical thinking is thinking beyond the obvious—beyond the flash of visual images on a television screen, the alluring promises of glossy advertisements, the evasive statements by some people in the news, the half-truths of some propaganda, the manipulations of slanted language and faulty reasoning.

Critical thinking is an attitude as much as an activity. If you face life with curiosity and a desire to dig beneath the surface, you are a critical thinker. If you do not believe everything you read or hear, you are a critical thinker. If you find pleasure in contemplating the puzzle of conflicting ideologies, theories, personalities, and facts, you are a critical thinker.

Activities of the mind and higher-order reasoning—the core of a college and university education—are processes of contemplation and deliberation. These processes take time. They contrast with the glorification of speed in today's culture: fast foods, instant mixes, self-developing film, short-spurt images in movies and videos. If you are among the people who assume that speed is a measure of intelligence, consider this true anecdote about Albert Einstein. The first time that Banesh Hoffman, a scientist, was expected to talk about his work to Albert Einstein, Hoffman was speechless and overawed. Einstein instantly put Hoffman at ease when he said: "Please go slowly. I don't understand things quickly."

5b Engaging in critical thinking

Critical thinking is a process that evolves from becoming fully aware of something to reflecting on it to reacting to it. You use this sequence often in your life, even if you have never called the process "critical thinking." You engage in it when you meet someone new and decide whether you like the person; when you read a book and form an opinion of it; when you learn a new job and then evaluate the job itself as well as your ability to do the work.

Applied in academic settings, the general process of critical thinking is described in Chart 28. That process holds not only for thinking critically but also for reading critically (see 5c and 5e) and writing critically (see 5g).

As with the writing process (see 2a), the steps of the critical thinking process are not rigidly in place. Each element is described separately in this handbook to help you understand its operation, but in reality the elements are intertwined. Expect, therefore, to sometimes combine steps, reverse their order, and return to parts of the process needed anew.

❖ ALERT: Summary (step 2 in Chart 28) and synthesis (step 4) are two different processes. Be careful not to think that your summary is a synthesis. For fuller discussion of the differences, see 5f. ❖

5c Understanding the reading process

If you understand **the reading process,** you can effectively come to "know," to compose meaning. Reading is not a passive activity. It involves more than looking for words. Reading is an active process—a dynamic, meaning-making encounter involving the interaction of the

	28
STEPS IN THE CRITICAL THINKING PROCESS	

1. **Analyze:** Consider the whole and then break it into component parts so that you can examine them separately. By seeing them as distinct units, you can come to understand how they interrelate.

2. **Summarize:** Extract and restate the material's main message or central point at the literal level (see 5d-1). (For a discussion of the differences between summary and synthesis, see 5f; for guidelines on writing a summary, see 31e.)

3. **Interpret:** Read "between the lines" to make inferences (see 5d-2) about the unstated assumptions implied by the material. Also, evaluate the material for its underlying currents as conveyed by tone, slant, and clarity of distinctions between fact and opinion (see 5d-3); by the quality of evidence (see 5h); and by the rigour of its reasoning (see 5i and j) and logic (see 5k).

4. **Synthesize:** Pull together what you have summarized, analyzed, and interpreted to connect it to what you already know (your prior knowledge) or what you are currently learning. Find links that help you grasp the new material to create a new whole, one that reflects your ability to see and explain relationships among ideas (see also 5f).

5. **Assess critically:** Judge the quality of the material on its own and as it holds up in your synthesis of it with related material.

page, eye, and brain. When you read, your mind actively makes connections between what you know already and what is new to you. By this process you comprehend and absorb new material.

Reading calls for **making predictions.** As you read, your mind is always involved in guessing what is coming next. Once it discovers what comes next, it either confirms or revises its prediction and moves on. For example, if you encountered a chapter title "The Heartbeat," your predictions could range from romance to how the heart pumps blood. As you read on, you would confirm or revise your prediction according to what you found—you would be in the realm of romance if you encountered a paragraph about lovers and roses, and you would be in the realm of biology if you encountered material that included diagrams of the physiology of the heart.

Predicting during reading happens at split-second speed without the reader's being aware of it. Without predictions, the mind would have to consider infinite possibilities for assimilating every new piece of information; with predictions, the mind can narrow its expectations to reasonable proportions.

Deciding on your **purpose for reading** before you begin to read can help your prediction process. Purposes for reading vary. Most reading in college and university is for the purpose of learning new information, appreciating literary works, or reviewing notes on classes or readings. These types of reading involve much *rereading;* one encounter with the material rarely suffices. According to the late Vladimir Nabokov, a respected novelist and teacher, "Curiously enough, one cannot *read* a book: one can only *reread* it. A good reader, a major reader, an active and creative reader, is a rereader."

Your purpose in reading determines the speed at which you can expect to read. When you are hunting for a particular fact in an almanac, you can skim the material until you come to what you want. When you read about a subject that you know well, your mind is familiar with the material, so you can move somewhat rapidly through most of it, slowing down when you come to new material. When you are unfamiliar with the subject, your mind needs time to absorb the new material, so you have to proceed slowly.

5d Engaging in the reading process

During the reading process, full meaning emerges on the three levels described in Chart 29. Be careful as a reader not to stop at the literal level. Only when you go to the next two levels is complete understanding possible.

1 Reading for literal meaning

Reading for literal meaning, sometimes called *reading "on" the line*, calls for you to understand what is said. It does not include impressions or opinions about the material. Depending on whether you are reading a text written for an informative, persuasive, or expressive purpose (see Chapter 1), the literal level has to do with (1) the key facts, the line of reasoning in an argument, or the central details of plot and character; and (2) the minor details that lend texture to the picture.

Whenever you encounter a complex writing style, take time to "unpack" the sentences. Try to break them down into shorter units or reword them into a simpler style. Do not assume that all writing is clear merely because it is in print. Authors write with a rich variety of styles, and not all are equally accessible on a first reading.

STEPS IN THE READING PROCESS 29

1. **Read for literal meaning:** Read "on" the lines to see what is stated (see 5d-1).
2. **Read to make inferences:** Read "between" the lines to see what is not stated but implied (see 5d-2).
3. **Read to evaluate:** Read "beyond" the lines to assess the soundness of the writer's reasoning, the accuracy of the writer's choice of words, and the fairness of the writer's treatment of the reader (see 5d-3).

When you find a concept that you need to think through, take the time to come to know the new idea. Although no student has unlimited time for reading and thinking, rushing through material to "cover" it rather than understand it costs more time in the long run.

Chart 30 offers suggestions that can help you comprehend most efficiently what you are reading.

2 Reading to make inferences

Reading to make inferences, sometimes called *reading "between" the lines,* means understanding what is implied but not stated. Often you have to infer information, or background, or the author's purpose. Consider this passage:

> How to tell the difference between modern art and junk puzzles many people although few are willing to admit it. The owner of an art gallery in Chicago had a prospective buyer for two sculptures made of discarded metal and put them outside his warehouse to clean them up. Unfortunately, some junk dealers, who apparently didn't recognize abstract expressionism when they saw it, hauled the two 300-pound pieces away.
>
> —ORA GYGI, "Things Are Seldom What They Seem"

The literal meaning is that many people cannot tell the difference between art and junk. A summary of the passage is that two abstract metal sculptures were carted away as junk when an art dealer left them outside a warehouse to clean them.

Now read the material inferentially. You can begin with the unexplained statement "few are willing to admit" they do not know

116

WAYS TO HELP YOUR READING COMPREHENSION 30

- When reading about an unfamiliar subject, associate the new material with what you already know. If necessary, build your store of prior knowledge by reading easier material on the subject in other sources. Then, return to the more difficult material; your way will be eased by having established a knowledge base.

- If your mind wanders, comprehension can elude you because your brain is busy with extraneous material. Be fiercely determined to concentrate, and resist the appeal of other thoughts. Do whatever it takes: Arrange for silence or music, for being alone or in a crowded library's reading room, for reading at your best time of day (some people concentrate better in the morning, others in the evening).

- Unless you have allotted sufficient time to work with new material, you cannot comprehend it. Students can be pulled in many different directions, so be sure to discipline yourself to balance classes, working, socializing, and participating in family activities with the unavoidable, time-consuming, yet totally engaging demands of reading, learning, and studying. Nothing prevents your success as much as lack of time.

- If you are unfamiliar with any key terms in your reading, you cannot fully understand the material. Take time to list them and their meanings. Try to figure meanings out using context clues (see 20c-2). Many textbooks have a list of important terms and their definitions (often called a "glossary") at the end of each chapter or at the back of the book (as in this handbook). Also, always have a good dictionary at hand (see 20a). As you accumulate new words, keep your list taped inside your book so that you can consult the information easily.

---

the difference between art and junk. Reading between the lines, you realize that people feel embarrassed *not* to know; they feel uneducated, or without good taste, or perhaps left out.

With this inference in mind, you can move to the last two sentences, in which the author offers not only the literal irony (see 21c) of the art's being carted away as junk, but also the implied irony that the people who carted it away are not among those who might feel embarrassed. This implied irony suggests that the people either do not care if they know the difference between art and junk (after all, they assumed it was junk and went on their way) or they "apparently" (a good word for inference making) want to give the impression that they do not know the difference. Thus, it is the art dealer who ends up being embarrassed, for it is he who created the problem by leaving the sculptures outdoors unattended.

The process of inferring adds texture and invaluable background to facilitate your interpretation of a passage. As you read to make inferences, consult Chart 31.

CHECKLIST FOR MAKING INFERENCES DURING READING 31

1. What is being said beyond the literal level?
2. What is implied rather than stated?
3. What words need to be read for their implied meanings (connotations) as well as for their stated meanings (denotations)? (For more about word meanings, see 20b-1.)
4. What information does the author expect me to have before I start to read the material?
5. What information does the author expect me to have about his or her background, philosophy, and the like?
6. What does the author seem to assume are my biases?
7. What do I need to be aware of concerning author bias?

---

3 Reading to evaluate

Evaluative reading, sometimes called *reading "beyond" the lines,* calls for many skills, including recognizing the impact of the author's tone, detecting prejudice, and differentiating fact from opinion.

Recognizing whether an author's tone is appropriate

Tone is communicated by all aspects of a piece of writing, from the writer's choice of words to the content of the message (see 1d). An author's tone should be appropriate to the author's purpose° and audience°. For example, most academic writing should not use language that is either informal or overly stiff and formal (see 21a-1).

Most authors use a serious tone, but sometimes they use humour to get their point across; if you read such material exclusively for its literal meaning, you will miss the point. In this passage, Stephen Leacock describes his reaction to a review of his writing. Although Leacock pretends to take the criticism seriously, his tone and language betray his amusement at attempts to reduce humorous writing to rhetorical formulas.

An English reviewer writing in a literary journal, the very name of which is enough to put contradiction to sleep, has said of my writing, "What is there, after all, in Professor Leacock's humour but a rather ingenious mixture of hyperbole and myosis?"

The man was right. How he stumbled upon this trade secret, I do not know. But I am willing to admit, since the truth is out, that it has long been my custom in preparing an article of a humorous nature to go down to the cellar and mix up half a gallon of myosis with a pint of hyperbole. If I want to give the article a decidedly literary character, I find it well to put in about half a pint of paresis. The whole thing is amazingly simple.

—STEPHEN LEACOCK, *Further Foolishness*

Most readers are wary of a highly emotional tone whose purpose is not to give information but to incite the reader.

NO   Urban renewal must be stopped! Urban redevelopment is ruining this country. Money-hungry capitalists are robbing treasures from law-abiding citizens! Corrupt politicians are murderers, caring nothing about people being thrown out of their homes into the streets.

Writers of such material do not respect their readers, for such writers assume that readers do not recognize screaming in print when they see it. Discerning readers instantly know the tone here is emotional and unreasonable. The exaggerations (robbing treasures, politicians as murderers) hint at the truth of some cases, but they are generalizations too extreme to be taken seriously.

On the other hand, if a writer's tone sounds reasonable and moderate, readers are more likely to pay attention.

YES   Urban renewal is revitalizing our cities, but it has caused some serious problems. While investors are trying to replace slums with decent housing, they must also remember that they are displacing people who do not want to leave their familiar neighbourhoods. Surely a cooperative effort between government and the private sector can lead to creative solutions.

Detecting prejudice

In writing, **prejudice** is revealed in negative opinions based on beliefs rather than on facts or evidence. Negative opinions might be expressed in positive language, but the underlying assumptions are negative.

119

Prejudicial statements are like these: *Poor people like living in crowded conditions because they are used to the surroundings; Women are not aggressive enough to succeed in business; Men make good soldiers because they enjoy killing.* Often writers imply their prejudices rather than state them outright. Detecting underlying negative opinions that distort information is important for critical reading, because discerning readers must call into question any argument that rests upon a weak foundation. (See also Hasty Generalization in 5k.)

Differentiating fact from opinion

Facts are statements that can be verified. A person may use experiment, research, and/or observation to verify facts. *Opinions* are statements of personal beliefs. Because they contain ideas that cannot be verified, opinions are open to debate.

An author sometimes intentionally blurs the difference between fact and opinion, and a discerning reader must be able to tell the difference. Sometimes that difference is quite obvious. Consider these statements:

A.   A woman can never make a good mathematician.

B.   Although fear of math is not purely a female phenomenon, girls tend to drop out of math sooner than boys, and adult women experience an aversion to math and math-related activity that is akin to anxiety.

Because of the word *never,* statement *A* is clearly an opinion. Statement *B* seems to be factual. Knowing who made these statements can sometimes help a reader distinguish between fact and opinion. Statement *A* is by a male Soviet mathematician living in Russia, as reported by David K. Shipler, a well-respected veteran reporter on Russian affairs for the *New York Times.* Statement *B* appears in a book called *Overcoming Math Anxiety* by Sheila Tobias, a university professor who has undertaken research studies to find out why many people dislike math. Tobias' research may confirm statement *B* as fact.

One aid in differentiating between fact and opinion is to *think beyond the obvious.* For example, is "Strenuous exercise is good for your health" a fact? Although the statement has the ring of truth, it is not a fact. People with severe arthritis or heart trouble could be harmed by some forms of exercise. Also, what does "strenuous" mean—a dozen pushups, jogging, aerobics, or playing tennis?

A second aid in differentiating between fact and opinion is to *remember that facts sometimes masquerade as opinions, and opinions sometimes try to pass for facts.* Evaluative reading demands concentration and a willingness to deal with matters that are relative and sometimes ambiguous. For example, in an essay for or against capital punishment, you would likely evaluate the argument differently if you knew that the author is currently on death row, or a disinterested party with a philosophy to discuss.

At times, however, the stance of the author is less clear. Consider these statements:

C. Common warts usually occur on the hands, especially on the backs of the fingers, but they may occur on any part of the skin. These dry, elevated lesions have numerous projections on the surface.

D. Warts are wonderful structures. They can appear overnight on any part of the skin, like mushrooms on a damp lawn, full grown and splendid in the complexity of their architecture.

Both statements are about warts. Judging only from the words— often all the evidence available—and without knowing who the authors are, we might say that *C* is fact and *D* is opinion.

If you have information about the authors, your judgments can be more subtle and therefore more reliable. Statement *C* is from a respected medical encyclopedia; thus it can be confirmed as fact. Statement *D* is by Lewis Thomas, a distinguished physician, hospital administrator, researcher, and writer who won the (U.S.) National Book Award for his popular essays revealing the intricacies of biology to laypeople. Given this information about Thomas, you would be justified in judging statement *D* to be factual—facts brought to life by drawing on metaphor (see 21c) to illustrate them in a new way and explain them inventively.

EXERCISE 5-1

Consulting section 5d, decide if each statement is a fact or an opinion. When the author and source are provided, explain how that information influences your judgment.

1. Jogging promotes good mental health.
2. Cotton clothing is more comfortable than polyester clothing.
3. "Every journey into the past is complicated by delusions, false memories, false namings of real events." (Adrienne Rich, poet, *Of Woman Born*)
4. Edmund Hillary performed two major feats: He not only led the first successful climb to the top of Mount Everest but also he led the first group to cross the Antarctic continent from sea to sea.
5. "History is the branch of knowledge that deals systematically with the past." (*Webster's New World Dictionary*, Third College Edition)

6. "Any peace is honourable." (Morley Safer, *Toronto Star*)
7. The earth's temperature is gradually rising.
8. Slaves in ancient Egypt were often killed when they finished building a pyramid so that they could not reveal the entrances to thieves who would loot the tombs.
9. "Our cities tend to be functional but nondescript, anchored against the wind, with nothing to please the eye. Quebec City is an exception." (Mordecai Richler, *Oh Canada! Oh Quebec!*)
10. "But since it opened to the public in 1982, Elvis's place in suburban Whitehaven, a 30-minute drive from downtown Memphis, has attracted more than 3 million visitors. That figure makes it one of the top house attractions in the U.S. This year alone, some 640,000 people will visit Graceland, and in the process they will spend more than $10 million on tickets, food, and souvenirs." (J. D. Reed, "The Mansion Music Made," *Time*)

EXERCISE 5-2

Consulting section 5d, after you read this passage, (1) list all literal information, (2) list all implied information, and (3) list the opinions stated.

EXAMPLE   The study found many complaints against the lawyers were not investigated, seemingly out of a "desire to avoid difficult cases."
                                                                      —NORMAN F. DACEY

Literal information: Few complaints against lawyers are investigated.
Implied information: The words "difficult cases" imply a coverup: lawyers, or others in power, hesitate to criticize lawyers for fear of being sued, or for fear of a public outcry if the truth about abuses and errors were revealed.
Opinions: None—all is factual because it refers to, and contains a quote from, a study.

A.   A number of authentic artifacts of Norse origin have come from the remains of villages occupied by ancestral Inuit in Arctic Canada. The widespread distribution of smelted iron, copper, and bronze in Canadian Arctic Inuit sites suggests that metal, even in small fragments, was a valuable trade commodity to the early Inuit, and was widely distributed through their trade routes. The Vinland sagas indicate that the Norse were willing to trade with the Skrælings, and it seems likely that trade with Inuit would have been beneficial too. The Greenland colonies depended on trade with Europe for many of their requirements—grain, metal, timber, and luxury goods, such as bishop's vestments. In addition, after 1261, they were required to pay fines and annual tribute to the Norwegian king, as well as tithes and crusade taxes to the Roman church. This tribute was paid in the materials of the country: walrus hides, polar bear skins (on at least one occasion a live polar bear), but primarily ivory from walrus tusks.
                                                                  —ROBERT McGHEE, "The Vikings"

B.   The kind of constitution and government Gandhi envisaged for an independent India was spelled out at the forty-fifth convention of the All-India Congress, which began at Karachi on March 27, 1931. It was a party political convention the like of which I had not seen before—nor seen since—with its ringing revolutionary proclamations acclaimed by some 350 leaders, men and women, just out of jail, squatting in the heat under a tent in a semicircle at Gandhi's feet, all of them, like Gandhi, spinning away like children playing with toys as they talked. They made up the so-called Subjects Committee, selected from the five thousand delegates to do the real work of the convention, though in reality, it was Gandhi alone who dominated the proceedings, writing most of the resolutions and moving their adoption with his customary eloquence and surprising firmness.

—WILLIAM L. SHIRER, *Gandhi: A Memoir*

5e   Engaging in critical reading

The concept of **critical reading** parallels that of critical thinking (see 5a and 5b). To read critically is to think about what you are reading while you are reading it. Do not let words merely drift by as your eyes scan the pages. Remain conscious of how the reading process operates, especially the roles of *prior knowledge* and *prediction* (see 5c); and get to know the material on all three levels of meaning—*the literal, the inferential,* and *the evaluative* (see 5d).

To help yourself along, use very specific approaches such as reading systematically (see 5e-1) and reading actively and closely (see 5e-2). As you use them, adapt them to your personal style of getting the most out of your reading.

1   Reading systematically

To **read systematically** is to use a structured plan for delving into the material. Your goal is to come to know and truly understand the material and—equally important—to be able to discuss it and even write about it. Guidelines for reading systematically start below and continue on the next page.

1. **Preview:** Before you start reading, look ahead. Glance over the pages you intend to read so that your mind can start making predictions (see 5c). Looking ahead "prepares" your mind for the material. As you look over the pages, ask yourself

questions that the material stimulates. Do not expect to answer all the questions at this point; their purpose is to focus your thoughts.

- To preview a textbook, first survey the whole book by reading chapter titles for an overview (book titles can be misleading). Next, survey the chapter you are assigned by reading all headings large and small; boldface words (in darker print); and all visuals and their captions, including photographs, drawings, tables, figures, and charts. If a glossary is at the end of the chapter, scan it for words you do and do not know.

- To preview material that has few or no headings, read and ask questions of the book and (if any) chapter titles; of the author's name and any introductory notes about the author, such as those that precede the essays in many books of collected essays; and of pivotal paragraphs, such as the first few paragraphs and (unless you are reading for suspense) the last pages or paragraphs. If a preface or introduction begins a book, skim it.

2. **Read:** Read the material actively and closely as explained in 5e-2. Seek the full meaning at all levels explained in 5d. Most of all, expect to reread. College- and university-level material can rarely be fully understood and absorbed in one reading. Budget your time so that you can make many passes through the material.

3. **Review:** Go back to the spots you looked at when you previewed the material. Look, too, at other pivotal places that you discovered. Ask yourself the same sort of questions, this time answering them as fully as possible. If you cannot, reread for the answers. For best success, review in chunks—small sections that you can capture comfortably. Do not try to cover too much at once.

- To stimulate your concentration during reading, keep in mind that you intend to review. This awareness will help you to stay alert. Also, the next day, and again about a week later, repeat your review—always adding new material that you have learned since the previous review. As much as time permits, re-review at intervals during a course. The more reinforcement, the better.

- Collaborative learning can help you reinforce what you learn from reading. Ask a friend or classmate who knows the material to discuss it with you, even test you.

Conversely, offer to teach the material to someone; you will quickly discover whether or not you have mastered it well enough to communicate it.

The steps for reading systematically closely parallel those in the **writing process** (see Chapters 2 and 3). Like *planning* in writing, *previewing* gets you ready and keeps you from plunging ahead inefficiently. Like *drafting* in writing, *reading* means moving through the material so that you come to "know" it and gain authority over it. Like *revising* in writing, *reviewing* involves going back over the material to clarify, fine-tune, and make it thoroughly your own.

2 Reading actively and closely

The secret to **reading actively and closely** is to annotate as you read. *Annotating* means writing notes to yourself in a book's margins, underlining or highlighting key passages, and using asterisks and other codes to alert you to special material. A well-annotated book is usually a well-read book.

Most readers annotate only after they have previewed the material and read it once, as explained in 5e-1. You might find, however, that you like to have a pencil in your hand from the moment you start to read. Experiment to find what works best for you.

Active reading calls for making annotations that relate to the content and meaning of the material. Restate major points "in a nutshell" in the margin. When you review, they will stand out. If you underline or highlight, be sure to jot in the margin key words or phrases that will jog your memory when you need to recall what is important. Extract meaning on the literal, inferential, and evaluative levels (see 5d). The excerpt on page 126 shows active-reading annotations in blue ink.

Close reading calls for making annotations that record the connections you make between the material and your prior knowledge and experience. Close reading can also elicit questions and opinions about the material. This is your chance to think on paper. It opens a conversation between you and the author. If this is a relatively new practice for you, do not lose your nerve or get discouraged. Let your mind range across ideas that you associate with what you are reading. Consider yourself a partner in the making of meaning, a full participant in the exchange of ideas, opinions, and experiences that typify a higher education. The excerpt on page 126 shows close-reading annotations in black ink.

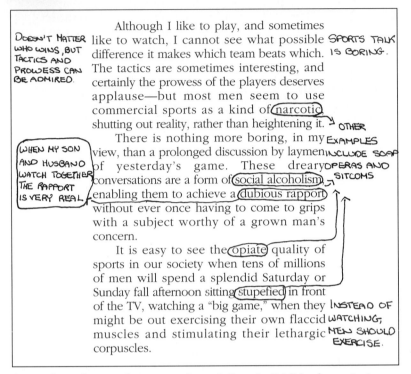

The annotated excerpt reads:

DOESN'T MATTER WHO WINS, BUT TACTICS AND PROWESS CAN BE ADMIRED.

Although I like to play, and sometimes like to watch, I cannot see what possible difference it makes which team beats which. SPORTS TALK IS BORING. The tactics are sometimes interesting, and certainly the prowess of the players deserves applause—but most men seem to use commercial sports as a kind of narcotic, shutting out reality, rather than heightening it.

OTHER EXAMPLES INCLUDE SOAP OPERAS AND SITCOMS

WHEN MY SON AND HUSBAND WATCH TOGETHER THE RAPPORT IS VERY REAL

There is nothing more boring, in my view, than a prolonged discussion by laymen of yesterday's game. These dreary conversations are a form of social alcoholism, enabling them to achieve a dubious rapport without ever once having to come to grips with a subject worthy of a grown man's concern.

It is easy to see the opiate quality of sports in our society when tens of millions of men will spend a splendid Saturday or Sunday fall afternoon sitting stupefied in front of the TV, watching a "big game," when they might be out exercising their own flaccid muscles and stimulating their lethargic corpuscles.

INSTEAD OF WATCHING, MEN SHOULD EXERCISE.

Annotations of excerpt from essay shown in Exercise 5-3 [blue for content (active reading) and black for synthesis (close reading)].

If you feel unable to write in a book—even though the practice of annotating texts dates back to the Middle Ages—try keeping a "double-entry notebook." On one side of each sheet of paper write "close-reading" notes on the content; on the other side, enter "active-reading" notes detailing the connections you make. Be sure to include information that identifies the passages referred to so that you can easily relocate them. On page 127 is a short example from a double-entry notebook (the symbol ¶ stands for "paragraph").

EXERCISE 5-3

Below and on the next two pages is the complete, brief essay from which the excerpt in the example above was taken. The essay was first published as an informal opinion in a newspaper column. Annotate the entire essay, with notes about content in one colour (such as blue) and your notes synthesizing the material in another (such as red).

S. HARRIS ESSAY. "SPORTS ONLY"

CONTENT	CONNECTIONS I MAKE
#1 H. LIKES SPORTS AND EXERCISE. HE EVEN BUILT A TENNIS COURT FOR HIS SUMMER HOME.	H. ISN'T "EVERYMAN." IT TAKES BIG BUCKS TO BUILD ONE'S OWN TENNIS COURT.
#2 H. THINKS THE AVERAGE NORTH AMERICAN MALE IS OBSESSED WITH SPORTS.	THAT "AVERAGE" (IF THERE IS SUCH A THING) MALE SOUNDS A LOT LIKE MY HUSBAND.
#3 ATHLETICS / SPORTS ARE ONE STRAND, NOT THE WEB, OF SOCIETY.	IT'S WORTH THINKING WHY SPORTS HAVE SUCH A MAJOR HOLD ON MEN. AND WHY NOT WOMEN, ON "AVERAGE"? (THIS MIGHT BE A TOPIC FOR A PAPER SOMEDAY.)

Double-entry notebook excerpt, based on first three paragraphs of the essay in Exercise 5-3 [left side for content (active reading) and right side for synthesis (close reading)].

Sports Only Exercise Our Eyes
Sydney J. Harris

Before I proceed a line further, let me make it clear that I enjoy physical exercise and sports as much as any man. I like to bat a baseball, dribble a basketball, kick a soccer ball and, most of all, swat a tennis ball. A man who scorned physical activity would hardly build a tennis court on his summer-house grounds, or use it every day.

Having made this obeisance, let me now confess that I am puzzled and upset—and have been for many years—by the almost obsessive interest in sports taken by the average North American male.

Athletics is one strand in life, and even the ancient Greek philosophers recognized its importance. But it is by no means the whole web, as it seems to be in our society. If North American men are not talking business, they are talking sports, or they are not talking at all.

This strikes me as an enormously adolescent, not to say retarded, attitude on the part of presumed adults. Especially when most of the passion and enthusiasm center around professional teams which bear no indigenous relation to the city they play for, and consist of mercenaries who will wear any town's insignia if the price is right.

Although I like to play, and sometimes like to watch, I cannot see what possible difference it makes which team beats which. The tactics are sometimes interesting, and certainly the prowess of the players deserves applause—but most men seem to use commercial sports as a kind of narcotic, shutting out reality, rather than heightening it.

There is nothing more boring, in my view, than a prolonged discussion by laymen of yesterday's game. These dreary conversations are a form of social alcoholism, enabling them to achieve a dubious rapport without ever once having to come to grips with a subject worthy of a grown man's concern.

It is easy to see the opiate quality of sports in our society when tens of millions of men will spend a splendid Saturday or Sunday fall afternoon sitting stupefied in front of the TV, watching a "big game," when they might be out exercising their own flaccid muscles and stimulating their lethargic corpuscles.

Ironically, our obsession with professional athletes not only makes us mentally limited and conversationally dull, it also keeps us physically inert—thus violating the very reason men began engaging in athletic competitions. It is tempting to call this malaise of "spectatoritis" childish—except that children have more sense, and would rather run out and play themselves.

5f Distinguishing between summary and synthesis

A crucial distinction in critical thinking, critical reading, and critical writing resides in the **differences between summary and synthesis.**

Summary comes before synthesis (see Chart 28 in 5c). To summarize is to extract the main message or central point of a passage. A summary does not include supporting evidence or details. It is the gist, the hub, the seed of what the author is saying, it is not your reaction to it. You summarize informally in a conversation and more formally in a speech. When you write a summary, use the guidelines in Chart 132 in section 31e. They apply generally to the kind of summarizing you do in content annotations (see 5e-2), in writing an essay that draws on only one source (see 5g), and in a research paper based on multiple sources (see Chapters 31, 34, and 35).

Synthesis comes after analysis, summary, and interpretation (see Chart 28 in 5c). To synthesize is to weave together ideas from more than one source; to connect ideas from one or more sources to what you already know from your having read, listened, and experienced life; to create a new whole that is your own as a result of your thinking about diverse yet related ideas. Unsynthesized ideas and information are like separate spools of thread, neatly lined up, possibly coordinated, but not integrated. Synthesized ideas and information become threads woven into a tapestry that creates a new whole. Synthesis is the evidence of your ability to tie ideas together in the tapestry of what you learn and know and experience.

Many techniques can help that thinking along. When you synthesize unconsciously, your mind connects ideas by thought processes mirrored in the rhetorical strategies discussed in section 4f. To synthesize, consciously apply these strategies. For example, compare ideas in sources; contrast ideas in sources; create definitions that combine and extend definitions in individual sources; apply examples or descriptions from one source to illustrate ideas in another; find causes and/or effects described in one source that explain another.

❖ ALERT: "Synthesis by summary"—a mere listing of who said what about a topic—is not true synthesism. It does not create new connections among ideas. ❖

Here is an example of synthesis connecting the essay in Exercise 5-3 to the excerpt below by Robert Lipsyte. (Lipsyte, a sports columnist for the *New York Times*, published his long essay in the spring of 1995 at the end of a nine-month-long major-league baseball strike. He asserts that sports have become too commercialized and no longer inspire loyalty, teach good sportsmanship, or provide young people with admirable role models.)

> Baseball has done us a favor. It's about time we understood that staged competitive sports events—and baseball can stand for all the games—are no longer the testing ground of our country's manhood and the theater of its once seemingly limitless energy and power.

As a mirror of our culture, sports now show us spoiled fools as role models, cities and colleges held hostage and games that exist only to hawk products. The pathetic posturing of in-your-face macho has replaced a once self-confident masculinity.

—ROBERT LIPSYTE, "The Emasculation of Sports"

SYNTHESIS BY COMPARISON AND CONTRAST

Both Harris and Lipsyte criticize professional sports, but their reasons differ. In part, Harris thinks that people who passively watch sports on TV and rarely exercise are destroying their physical health. Lipsyte sees something less obvious, but potentially more sinister: the destruction of traditional values in sports. No longer are athletes heroes who inspire; they are puppets of sports as "big business."

SYNTHESIS BY DEFINITION

The omission of women from each writer's discussion seems a very loud silence. Considered together, these essays define sports as a male preoccupation and undertaking. Harris condemns only men for their inability to think and talk beyond sports and business, an insulting and exaggerated description made even less valid by the absence of women. Lipsyte, even in the 1995 atmosphere of women excelling in many team and individual sports, claims that we have lost a "once self-confident masculinity." An extended definition would include women, even though they might prefer to avoid the negative portraits of Harris and Lipsyte.

A synthesis belongs to the person who made the connections; someone else might make entirely different connections. Still, any synthesis needs to be sensibly reasoned and informed by an individual intelligence.

Try these techniques for stimulating your mind to recall prior knowledge and work toward creating a synthesis. (The critical response essay by a student, Anna Lozanov, in 5g, is an excellent example of making connections between reading and one's personal experience.)

■ Use the technique of mapping (see 2i) to lay out and discover relationships between elements in the material and between the material and other ideas that come to mind.

■ Use your powers of play. Mentally toss ideas around, even if you make connections that seem outrageous. Try opposites (for example, read about athletes and think about the most unathletic person you know). Try turning an idea upside down (for example, read about the value of being a good sport and list the benefits of being a bad sport). Try visualizing what you are reading about, and then tinker with the mental picture (for example, picture two people playing tennis and substitute dogs playing frisbee or seals playing ping pong). The possibilities are endless—make word associations, think up song lyrics, draft a TV advertisement. The goal is always to jump-start your thinking so that you see ideas in new ways.

■ Discuss your reading with someone else. Summarize its content and elicit the other person's opinion or ideas. Deliberately debate that opinion or challenge those ideas. Discussions and debates can get your mind moving.

EXERCISE 5-4

Here is an excerpt from an essay by Robert Lipsyte. (Another excerpt from this essay is show on pages 129–130.) The words in brackets are added in this handbook to supply background information some readers might need.

> We have come to see that [basketball star Michael] Jordan, [football star] Troy Aikman, and [baseball star] Ken Griffey have nothing to offer us beyond the gorgeous, breathtaking mechanics of what they do. And it's not enough, now that there is no longer a dependable emotional return beyond the sensation of the moment itself. The changes in sports—the moving of franchises, free agency—have made it impossible to count on a player, a team, an entire league still being around for next year's comeback. The connection between player and fan has been irrevocably destabilized, for love and loyalty demand a future. Along the way, those many virtues of self-discipline, responsibility, altruism and dedication seem to have been deleted from the athletic contract with America.
>
> —ROBERT LIPSYTE, "The Emasculation of Sports"

Consulting sections 5e-2 and 5f, do this:

1. Summarize the excerpt here.
2. Annotate it for its content and for the connections you make to its content.
3. Draft a synthesis connecting this essay and the essay by Sydney J. Harris reprinted in Exercise 5-3.

5g Writing a critical response

A **critical response** essay has two missions: first, to summarize a source's central point or main idea; second, to respond to the source's main idea with your reactions based on your synthesis (see 5b and 5f).

GUIDELINES FOR WRITING A CRITICAL RESPONSE 32

- Write a summary of the main idea or central point of what you are responding to [whether you are responding to part or all of a source).

- Write a smooth transition between that summary and your response. Although a statement bridging the two parts of a critical response paper need not observe all the formal requirements of a thesis statement (see 2n), it should at least subtly signal the beginning of your response.

- Respond to the source, basing your reaction on the influences of your own experience, your prior knowledge, and your opinions.

- Fulfil all documentation requirements. See Chapter 33 for coverage of four widely used documentation systems (MLA, APA, CM, and CBE), and ask your instructor which to use.

A well-written critical response accomplishes these two missions with grace and style. That is, it does not say "My summary is…" and "Now, here's what I think…." Your goal is to write a well-integrated essay. Its length and whether you respond to a single passage or to an entire work vary with the assignment. Chart 32 gives general guidelines for writing a critical response.

Here is a critical response essay written by Anna Lozanov, a university student. The assignment was to read and respond to the brief essay "Sports Only Exercise Our Eyes" by Sydney J. Harris shown in Exercise 5-3. Lozanov's bridge statement comes at the beginning of the third paragraph: "Just this weekend, however, I had an occasion to reconsider the value of sports." The Work Cited at the end of the essay uses MLA documentation style (see 33c) to identify the source. The numbers in parentheses in the essay indicate the pages in the cited work where the quoted words can be found.

Critical Response by Anna Lozanov

to "Sports Only Exercise Our Eyes" by Sydney J. Harris

Except for a brief period in high school when I was

wild about a certain basketball player, I never gave

sports much thought. I went to games because my friends

went, not because I cared about football or baseball or

track. I certainly never expected to defend sports, and

---

when I first read Sydney Harris's essay "Sports Only Exercise Our Eyes," I thoroughly agreed with him. Like Harris, I believed that men who live and breathe sports are "mentally limited and conversationally dull" (111).

For the entire thirteen years of my marriage I have complained about the amount of time my husband, John, spends watching televised sports. Of course, I've tried to get him to take an interest in something else. There was the time as a newlywed when I flamboyantly interrupted the sixth game of the World Series--wearing only a transparent nightie. Then, in 1978, I had the further audacity to go into labour with our first child-- right in the middle of the Grey Cup. Even the child tried to help me cure my husband of what Harris calls an "obsession" (111). Some months after the fateful game, the kid thoroughly soaked his father, who was concentrating so intently on the Tigers' struggle for the American League pennant that he didn't even notice! Only a commercial brought the dazed sports fan back into the living room from Tiger Stadium.

Just this weekend, however, I had an occasion to reconsider the value of sports. Having just read the Harris essay, I found myself paying closer attention to my husband and sons' Saturday afternoon television routine. I was surprised to discover that they didn't just "vegetate" in front of the TV; during the course of the afternoon, they actually discussed ethics, priorities, commitments, and the consequences of abusing one's body. When one of the commentators raised issues like point shaving and using steroids, John and the kids talked about cheating and using drugs. When another commentator brought up the issue of skipping one's final year to go straight to the pros, John explained the →

importance of a university education and discussed the
short career of most professional football players.

Then, I started to think about all the times I've
gone to the basement and found my husband and sons
performing exercise routines as they watched a game on
TV. Even our seven year old, who loathes exercise, pedals
vigorously on the exercise bike while the others do sit-
ups and curls. Believe it or not, there are times when
they're all exercising more than just their eyes.

I still agree with Harris that many people spend too
much time watching televised sports, but after this
weekend, I certainly can't say that all of that time is
wasted--at least not at my house. Anything that can turn
my couch potatoes into thinking, talking, active human
beings can't be all bad. Next weekend, instead of putting
on a nightie, I think I'll join my family on the couch.

Work Cited

Harris, Sydney J. "Sports Only Exercise Our Eyes." The
Best of Sydney J. Harris. Boston: Houghton, 1975. 111-12.

5h Assessing evidence critically

The cornerstone of all reasoning is evidence. Readers expect writers to provide solid evidence for any assertion made or conclusion
reached. Writers who successfully communicate their messages use
evidence well to support their assertions or conclusions. Evidence consists of facts, statistical information, examples, and opinions of experts.

1 Evaluating evidence

Chart 33 lists guidelines for evaluating evidence that you read
and for deciding what evidence to include in your writing. Each guideline is discussed after the chart.

gr **5h**

| GUIDELINES FOR USING EVIDENCE EFFECTIVELY | 33 |

- Is the evidence sufficient?
- Is the evidence representative?
- Is the evidence relevant?
- Is the evidence accurate, whether from primary or secondary sources?
- Are the claims qualified fairly based on the evidence?

- **Is the evidence sufficient?** A general rule for both readers and writers is the more evidence, the better. As a reader, you can usually have more confidence in the results of a survey that draws on a hundred respondents than in a survey involving only ten. As a writer, you may convince your reader that violence is a serious problem in high schools on the basis of two specific examples, but you will be more convincing if you can give five examples—or, better still, statistics for a school district, a city, or a nation.

- **Is the evidence representative?** As a reader, assess objectivity and fairness; do not assume them because words are in print. Do not trust a claim or conclusion about a group based on only a few members rather than on a truly representative or typical sample. A pollster surveying national political views would not get representative evidence by asking questions of the first 1500 people to walk by a street corner in Calgary because that group would not truly represent the varied regional, racial, political, and ethnic makeup of the electorate. As a writer, make sure the evidence you offer represents your claim fairly; do not base your point on exceptions.

- **Is the evidence relevant?** Determining relevance can demand subtle thinking. Suppose you read evidence that one hundred students who had watched television for more than two hours a day throughout high school earned significantly lower scores on a college entrance exam than one hundred students who had not. Would you conclude that students who watch less television perform better on college entrance exams? Perhaps, closer examination of the evidence might reveal other differences between the two groups—differences in geographical region, family background, socioeconomic group, quality of schools attended. Therefore, the evidence would not be relevant to that conclusion about TV watching and college entrance exams.

- **Is the evidence accurate?** Without accuracy, evidence is useless. Evidence must come from reliable sources, whether they are *primary sources* or *secondary sources* (see 5h-2). Equally important, reliable evidence must be presented carefully so that it does not misrepresent or distort information.

- **Is the evidence qualified?** Evidence rarely justifies claims that use words such as *all, certainly, always,* or *never.* Conclusions are more reasonable when qualified with words such as *some, many, a few, probably, possibly, perhaps, may, usually,* and *often.* Remember that today's "facts" may be revised as time passes, information changes, and knowledge grows.

| 2 | **Understanding differences between primary and secondary sources as evidence** |

Primary sources present first-hand evidence based on your own or someone else's original work or direct observation. First-hand evidence has the greatest impact on a reader. Consider this eyewitness account:

> Poverty is dirt.... Let me explain about housekeeping with no money. For breakfast I give my children grits with no oleo or cornbread without eggs and oleo. This does not use up many dishes. What dishes there are, I wash in cold water and with no soap. Even the cheapest soap has to be saved for the baby's diapers. Look at my hands, so cracked and red. Once I saved for two months to buy a jar of Vaseline for my hands and the baby's diaper rash. When I had saved enough, I went to buy it and the price had gone up two cents. The baby and I suffered on. I have to decide every day if I can bear to put my cracked sore hands into the cold water and strong soap. But you ask, why not hot water? Fuel costs money. If you have a wood fire it costs money. If you burn electricity, it costs money. Hot water is a luxury. I do not have luxuries....
>
> —JO GOODWIN PARKER, in *America's Other Children*

As a reader and as a writer, remember that not all eyewitness accounts are equally reliable. What is it about Parker's account that makes you trust what she says? She is specific. She is also authoritative. It is doubtful that anyone would have invented the story about being two cents short of the price of a jar of Vaseline. As a writer of personal observations, you need to be as specific as possible—to prove that you truly saw what you say you saw. Use language that appeals to all five senses: describe sights, sounds, and experiences that could have been seen, heard, or experienced only by someone who was there. Show your readers *your* cracked, red hands.

As evidence, primary sources that meet the guidelines in Chart 33 provide invaluable reports of observations. Few will ever see the surface of the moon or the top of Mt. Everest. People rely, therefore, upon the first-hand reports of the astronauts and mountain climbers who have been there. Indeed, much of history depends heavily on letters, diaries, and journals—the reports of eyewitnesses who saw events unfold.

Surveys, polls, and experiments are some of the means by which people extend their powers of observation beyond what can be "seen" in the everyday sense of the word. Jo Parker could look at her hands. Who can see, however, the attitude of the public toward marriage, toward a political candidate, toward inflation? For evidence on such matters, polls or surveys are necessary. They constitute primary evidence and must be carefully controlled—through weighing, measuring, or quantifying information that would otherwise not be available.

Secondary sources report, describe, comment on, or analyze the experiences or the work of others. As evidence, a secondary source is at least once removed from the primary source. It reports *about* the original work, the direct observation, or the first-hand experience. Still, such evidence can have great value and enormous impact. Consider this second-hand, reported observation.

> The immediate causes of death from nuclear attack are the blast wave, which can flatten heavily reinforced buildings many kilometers away, the firestorm, the gamma rays and the neutrons, which effectively fry the insides of passersby. A school girl who survived the American nuclear attack on Hiroshima, the event that ended the Second World War, wrote this first-hand account:

> > Through a darkness like the bottom of hell, I could hear the voices of the other students calling for their mothers. And at the base of the bridge, inside a big cistern that had been dug out there, was a mother weeping, holding above her head a naked baby that was burned bright red all over its body…. But every single person who passed was wounded, all of them, and there was no one, there was no one to turn to for help. And the singed hair on the heads of the people was frizzled and whitish and covered with dust. They did not appear to be human, not creatures of this world.

> —CARL SAGAN, *Cosmos*

As with Parker's eyewitness account, the strength or value of a second-hand account hinges on the reliability of the reporter. That reliability is a function of how specific, accurate, and authoritative the observations are. Here the standard maxim "consider the source" becomes crucial. An expert's reputation must stem from some special experience (as the parents of many children could be "experts" on child reading) or training (as an accountant could be an expert on taxes). Because the author of the example paragraph, Carl Sagan, is a respected scientist, scholar, and writer, his report of the schoolgirl's eyewitness account is likely to be reliable, authoritative, worthwhile secondary evidence.

Sagan is a secondary source because although readers can feel quite confident that Sagan is fully and fairly representing what the schoolgirl said, *no one* can be sure of that without seeing her original account. If you were to use Sagan's version of her account as evidence, it would be third-hand evidence: one person (you) further removed from another (Sagan) and yet further from the original source (the schoolgirl). In college or university, you must often depend on secondary sources (for example, most textbooks), but sometimes you are expected to use primary sources (for example, a published diary, scientists' journal articles reporting their research, works of literature). Chart 34 gives guidelines for evaluating a secondary source.

❖ ALERT: You can use the guidelines in Chart 34 to evaluate electronic sources as well as conventional print sources. Be skeptical about any electronically accessed source that cannot be verified according to these guidelines. ❖

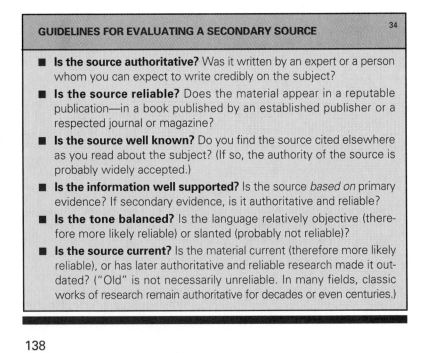

GUIDELINES FOR EVALUATING A SECONDARY SOURCE	34

- **Is the source authoritative?** Was it written by an expert or a person whom you can expect to write credibly on the subject?

- **Is the source reliable?** Does the material appear in a reputable publication—in a book published by an established publisher or a respected journal or magazine?

- **Is the source well known?** Do you find the source cited elsewhere as you read about the subject? (If so, the authority of the source is probably widely accepted.)

- **Is the information well supported?** Is the source *based on* primary evidence? If secondary evidence, is it authoritative and reliable?

- **Is the tone balanced?** Is the language relatively objective (therefore more likely reliable) or slanted (probably not reliable)?

- **Is the source current?** Is the material current (therefore more likely reliable), or has later authoritative and reliable research made it outdated? ("Old" is not necessarily unreliable. In many fields, classic works of research remain authoritative for decades or even centuries.)

EXERCISE 5-5

Consulting section 5h, decide the following: (a) Would each passage constitute primary or secondary evidence? (b) Is the evidence acceptable? Why or why not?

1.   I went one morning to a place along the banks of the Madeira River where the railroad ran, alongside rapids impassable to river traffic, and I searched for any marks it may have left on the land. But there was nothing except a clearing where swarms of insects hovered over the dead black hen and other items spread out on a red cloth as an offering to the gods of macumba, or black magic. This strain of African origins in Brazil's ethnic character is strong in the Northwest Region.

—WILLIAM S. ELLIS, "Brazil's Imperiled Rain Forest"

2.   Most climatologists believe that the world will eventually slip back into an ice age in 10,000 to 20,000 years. The Earth has been unusually cold for the last two to three million years, and we are just lucky to be living during one of the warm spells. But the concern of most weather watchers looking at the next century is with fire rather than ice. By burning fossil fuels and chopping down forests, humans have measurably increased the amount of carbon dioxide in the atmosphere. From somewhere around 300 parts per million at the turn of the century, this level has risen to 340 parts per million today. If the use of fossil fuels continues to increase, carbon dioxide could reach 600 parts per million during the next century.

—STEVE OLSON, "Computing Climate"

5i Assessing cause and effect critically

Cause and effect is a mode of thinking that seeks to establish some relationship, or link, between two or more specific pieces of evidence. Regardless of whether you begin with a cause or an effect, you are working with this basic pattern:

BASIC PATTERN FOR CAUSE AND EFFECT

Cause A ⟶ produces ⟶ effect B

You may seek to understand the effects of a known cause (for example, studying two more hours each night):

More studying ⟶ produces ⟶ ?

Or you may attempt to determine the cause or causes of a known effect (for example, recurrent headaches):

? ⟶ produces ⟶ recurrent headaches

139

If you want to use reasoning based on a relationship of cause and effect, evaluate the connections carefully. As you evaluate cause-and-effect relationships, keep in mind the guidelines in Chart 35. Each guideline is discussed after the chart.

GUIDELINES FOR ASSESSING CAUSE AND EFFECT 35

- Is there a clear relationship between events?
- If the events recur, are they always in the same sequence?
- Are there multiple causes and/or effects?

- **Is there a clear relationship between events?** When you read or write about causes and effects, carefully think through the reasoning. Related causes and effects happen in sequence: A cause exists or occurs before an effect. *First* the wind blows; *then* a door slams; *then* a pane of glass in the door breaks. But just because the order of events implies a cause-and-effect relationship, that relationship does not necessarily exist. Perhaps someone slammed the door shut. Perhaps someone threw a baseball through the glass pane. A cause-and-effect relationship must be linked by more than chronological sequence. The fact that *B* happens after *A* does not prove that *A* causes *B*.

- **Is there a pattern of repetition?** To establish that *A* causes *B*, there must be proof that every time *A* is present, *B* occurs—or that *B* never occurs unless *A* is present. The need for a pattern of repetition explains why Health and Welfare Canada performs many tests before declaring a new food or medicine safe for human consumption.

- **Are there multiple causes and effects?** Avoid oversimplification. The basic pattern of cause and effect—single cause, single effect (*A* causes *B*)—rarely represents the full picture.

It is oversimplifying to assume that the disaster at Chernobyl is the only cause of recent global warming trends. There may be a number of other possible causes, such as the depletion of the ozone layer, the destruction of the rainforests, or the eruption of Mount St. Helens. Similarly, one cause can produce **multiple effects:**

Oversimplification of effects usually involves focusing on one effect and ignoring others. For example, advertisements about a liquid diet drink focus on its most appealing effect: rapid weight loss. But they ignore other less desirable effects such as loss of nutrients and vulnerability to rapidly regaining the weight.

5j   Assessing reasoning processes critically

To think critically you need to be able to understand reasoning processes so that you can recognize and evaluate them in your reading and use them correctly in your writing. **Induction** and **deduction** are reasoning processes. They are natural thought patterns that people use every day to think through ideas and to make decisions. The differences between the two processes are summarized in Chart 36.

COMPARISON OF INDUCTIVE AND DEDUCTIVE REASONING		36
	INDUCTIVE REASONING	**DEDUCTIVE REASONING**
ARGUMENT BEGINS	with specific evidence	with a general claim
ARGUMENT CONCLUDES	with a general claim	with a specific statement
CONCLUSION IS	reliable or unreliable	true or false
REASONING IS USED	to discover something new	to apply what is known

1 — Recognizing and using inductive reasoning

Induction is the process of arriving at general principles from particular facts or instances, as summarized in Chart 37. Suppose that you go to the local Motor Vehicle Licence Agency to renew your driver's licence, and you have to stand in line for two hours until you get the document. Then a few months later, when you return to the Agency for new licence plates, a clerk gives you the wrong advice, and you have to stand in two different lines for three hours. Another time you go there in response to a letter asking for information, and you discover that you should have brought your car registration form, although the letter failed to mention that fact. You conclude that the Agency is inefficient and seems not to care about the convenience of its patrons. You have arrived at this conclusion by means of induction.

SUMMARY OF INDUCTIVE REASONING 37

1. **Inductive reasoning moves from the specific to the general.** It begins with the evidence of specific facts, observations, or experiences and moves to a general conclusion.
2. Inductive conclusions are considered *reliable* or *unreliable,* not true or false. An inductive conclusion indicates probability, the degree to which the conclusion is likely to be true. Frustrating though it may be for those who seek certainty, inductive thinking is, of necessity, based only on a sampling of the facts.
3. An inductive conclusion is held to be reliable or unreliable in relation to the quantity and quality of the evidence (see 5e) supporting it.
4. Induction leads to new "truths." Induction can support statements about the unknown on the basis of what is known.

---

2 — Recognizing and using deductive reasoning

Deduction is the process of reasoning from general claims to a specific instance. If several unproductive visits to the Motor Vehicle Licence Agency have convinced you that the Agency cares little about the convenience of its patrons (as the experiences described in 5j-1 suggest), you will not be happy the next time you must return. Your reasoning might go something like this:

> The Agency wastes people's time.
> I have to go to the Agency tomorrow.
> Therefore, tomorrow my time will be wasted.

You reached the conclusion—"therefore, tomorrow my time will be wasted"—by means of deduction.

Deductive arguments have three parts: two **premises** and a **conclusion.** This three-part structure is known as a **syllogism.** The first premise of a deductive argument may be a fact or an assumption. The second premise may also be a fact or an assumption.

Whether or not an argument is **valid** has to do with the argument's form or structure. Here the word *valid* is not the general term people use in conversation to mean "acceptable" or "well grounded." In the context of reading and writing logical arguments, the word *valid* has a very specific meaning. A deductive argument is *valid* when the conclusion logically follows from the premises. The following argument is valid.

VALID

PREMISE 1	When it snows, the streets get wet. [fact]
PREMISE 2	It is snowing. [fact]
CONCLUSION	Therefore, the streets are wet.

The following argument is invalid.

INVALID

PREMISE 1	When it snows, the streets get wet. [fact]
PREMISE 2	The streets are wet. [fact]
CONCLUSION	Therefore, it is snowing.

The invalid argument has acceptable premises because the premises are facts. The argument's conclusion, however, is wrong. It ignores other reasons for why the streets may be wet. The street could be wet from rain, from street-cleaning trucks that spray water, or from people using hoses to cool off the pavement or to wash their cars. Because the conclusion does not follow logically from the premises, the argument is invalid.

The following argument is also invalid. The conclusion does not flow from the premises (the car may not start for many reasons other than a dead battery).

INVALID

PREMISE **1**	When the battery is dead, a car will not start. [fact]
PREMISE **2**	My car will not start. [fact]
CONCLUSION	My battery is dead.

When a premise is an assumption, the premise must be able to be defended with evidence. The following argument is valid. Its conclusion flows logically from the premises. An argument's validity, however, is independent of its truth. Is premise 1 true? Different economists will offer different opinions. *Only if both premises are true is an argument true.* This argument may be true or false depending on whether the first premise is true or false. The writer must support the claim that is the first premise.

VALID (AND POSSIBLY TRUE)

PREMISE **1**	When the unemployment rate rises, an economic recession occurs. [assumption: the writer must present evidence in support of this statement]
PREMISE **2**	The unemployment rate has risen. [fact]
CONCLUSION	An economic recession will occur.

The following argument is valid. Its conclusion follows from its premises. Is the argument, however, true? Because the argument contains an assumption in its first premise, the argument can be true only if the premise is proved true. Such proof is not possible. Therefore, although the argument is valid, it is not true.

VALID (BUT NOT TRUE)

PREMISE **1**	If you buy a Supermacho 357 sports car, you will achieve instant popularity. [assumption]
PREMISE **2**	Kim just bought a Supermacho 357 sports car. [fact]
CONCLUSION	Kim will achieve instant popularity.

In any deductive argument, beware of premises that are implied but not stated—called **unstated assumptions.** Remember that an argument can be logically valid even though it is based on wrong assumptions. The response to such an argument is to attack the assumptions, not the conclusion. Often the assumptions are wrong. For example, suppose a corporation argued that it should not be required to install pollution control devices because the cost would cut into its profits. This argument rests on the unstated assumption that no corporation should do something that would lower its profits. That assumption is wrong, and so is the argument. But it can be shown to be wrong only when the assumptions are challenged. Similarly, if someone says that certain information has to be correct because it was printed in a newspaper, the person's deductive reasoning is flawed. Here the unstated assumption is that everything in a newspaper is correct—which is not true. Whenever there is an unstated assumption, supply it and then check to make sure it is true. Deductive reasoning is summarized in Chart 38.

SUMMARY OF DEDUCTIVE REASONING   38

1. **Deductive reasoning moves from the general to the specific**. The three-part structure that makes up a deductive argument includes two premises and a conclusion drawn from them.

2. A deductive argument is valid if the conclusion logically follows from the premises.

3. A deductive conclusion may be judged true or false. If both premises are true, the conclusion is true. If the argument contains an assumption, the writer must prove the truth of the assumption to establish the truth of the argument.

4. Deductive reasoning applies what the writer already knows. Though it does not yield anything new, it builds stronger arguments than does inductive reasoning because it offers the certainty of a conclusion's being true or false.

EXERCISE 5-6

Consulting section 5j-2, ignore for the moment whether the premises seem to you to be true, but determine if each conclusion is valid. Explain your answer.

1. Faddish clothes are expensive.
   This shirt is expensive.
   This shirt must be part of a fad.

2. When a storm is threatening, small-craft warnings are issued.
   A storm is threatening.
   Small-craft warnings will be issued.

3. The Governor General's Awards are given to outstanding literary works.
   Margaret Atwood's *The Robber Bride* did not win the Governor General's Award for Fiction.
   The Robber Bride is not an outstanding literary work.

4. All provinces send representatives to federal–provincial conferences.
   The Northwest Territories sends representatives to federal–provincial conferences.
   The Northwest Territories is a province.
5. All risks are frightening.
   Changing to a new job is a risk.
   The change to a new job is frightening.
6. Before an occupancy permit can be issued, a new home must be inspected.
   Our new home has been issued an occupancy permit.
   Our new home has been inspected.
7. Most weekly news magazines give only superficial coverage of world affairs.
   This is a weekly news magazine.
   This will give only superficial coverage of world affairs.
8. Science fiction novels are usually violent.
   This is a science fiction novel.
   This novel is obviously violent.
9. All Members of Parliament are entitled to subsidized haircuts.
   Elaine Laurendeau is a Member of Parliament.
   Elaine Laurendeau is entitled to subsidized haircuts.
10. All great chefs are men.
    Madame Benoît was a great chef.
    Madame Benoît was a man.

5k ## Recognizing and avoiding logical fallacies

Logical fallacies are flaws in reasoning that lead to illogical statements. They tend to occur most often when ideas are being argued, although they can be found in all types of writing. Most logical fallacies masquerade as reasonable statements, but they are in fact attempts to manipulate readers by reaching their emotions instead of their intellects, their hearts rather than their heads. Most logical fallacies are known by labels; each indicates a way that thinking has gone wrong during the reasoning process.

Hasty generalization

A **hasty generalization** occurs when someone generalizes from inadequate evidence. If the statement "My hometown is the best place in the province to live" is supported with only two examples of why it is pleasant, the generalization is hasty. **Stereotyping** is a type of hasty generalization that occurs when someone makes prejudiced, sweeping claims about all of the members of a particular religious, ethnic, racial, or political group: "Everyone from country X is dishonest." **Sexism** occurs when someone discriminates against people on the basis of sex. (See 11q and 21b for advice on how to avoid sexist language, a form of sexism, in your writing.) One often-heard combination of stereotyping and sexism occurs when a car driven by a woman has hit a car driven by a man, and the man says, "That's just like a woman."

False analogy

A **false analogy** is a comparison in which the differences outweigh the similarities, or the similarities are irrelevant to the claim the analogy is intended to support. "Old Joe Smith would never make a good prime minister because an old dog cannot learn new tricks." Homespun analogies like this often seem to have an air of wisdom about them, but just as often they fall apart when examined closely. Learning the role of the prime minister is hardly comparable to a dog's learning new tricks.

Begging the question

An argument that **begs the question** states a claim, but the support is based on the claim, so the reasoning is circular. Sometimes, the support simply restates the claim: "Wrestling is a dangerous sport because it is unsafe." "Unsafe" conveys the same idea as "dangerous"; it does not provide evidence to support the claim that wrestling is dangerous. Another question-begging argument offers a second statement as support, but the support for the second statement is the argument in the first statement: "Wrestling is a dangerous sport because wrestlers get injured. Anyone as big and strong as a wrestler would not get injured if the sport were safe." Begging the question also occurs in statements such as "Wrestlers love danger." There is an unstated assumption that wrestling is dangerous as well as an assumption that no proof is called for because the audience shares the opinion that wrestling is dangerous.

Irrelevant argument

An **irrelevant argument** is called *non sequitur* in Latin, which translates as "it does not follow." This flaw occurs when a conclusion does not follow from the premises: "Marie Trudel is a forceful speaker, so she will make a good mayor." It does not follow that someone's ability to be a forceful speaker means that person would be a good mayor.

False cause

The fallacy of **false cause** is called *post hoc, ergo propter hoc* in Latin—which means "after this, therefore because of this." This fallacy results when someone assumes that because two events are related in time, the first one *causes* the second one. This cause-and-effect fallacy is very common. "A new weather satellite was launched last week, and it has been raining ever since" implies—illogically—that the rain (the second event) is a result of the satellite launch (the first event).

Self-contradiction

Self-contradiction occurs when two premises are used that cannot simultaneously be true: "Only when nuclear weapons have finally destroyed us will we be convinced of the need to control them." This statement is self-contradictory in that no one would be around to be convinced if everyone had been destroyed.

Red herring

A **red herring,** sometimes referred to as **ignoring the question,** sidetracks an issue by bringing up a totally unrelated issue: "Why worry about pandas becoming extinct when we should be concerned about the plight of the homeless?" Someone who introduces an irrelevant issue hopes to distract the audience as a red herring might distract bloodhounds from a scent.

Argument to the person

An **argument to the person,** also known as *ad hominem,* attacks a person's appearance, personal habits, or character instead of dealing with the merits of the individual's arguments, ideas, or opinions. "We could take her position in favour of jailing child abusers seriously if she were not so nasty to the children who live next door to her" is one type of *ad hominem* attack. It seems so reasonable to belittle suggestions about dealing with child abusers from someone who may (or may not) be nasty to the children next door. In truth, however, the suggestions, not the person who makes them, must be dealt with. The person who argues is *not* the argument.

Guilt by association

Guilt by association is a kind of *ad hominem* attack implying that an individual's arguments, ideas, or opinions lack merit because of that person's activities, interests, or associates. The claim that because Jack belongs to the International Hill Climbers Association, which declared bankruptcy last month, he is unfit to be mayor uses guilt by association.

Bandwagon

Bandwagon, also known as **going along with the crowd** or *ad populum,* implies that something is right because everyone is doing it, that truth is determined by majority vote: "Smoking is not bad for people because millions of people smoke."

False or irrelevant authority

Using **false or irrelevant authority,** sometimes called *ad verecundiam,* means citing the opinion of an "expert" who has no claim to expertise about the subject at hand. This fallacy attempts to transfer prestige from one area to another. Many television commercials rely on this tactic—a famous tennis player praising a brand of motor oil or a popular movie star lauding a brand of cheese.

Card-stacking

Card-stacking, also known as **special pleading,** ignores evidence on the other side of a question. From all the available facts, the person arguing selects only those that will build the best (or worst) possible case. Many television commercials use this strategy. When three slim, happy consumers rave about a new diet plan, they do not mention that (a) the plan does not work for everyone and that (b) other plans work better for some people. The makers of the commercial select evidence that helps their cause and ignore any that does not.

The either-or fallacy

The either-or fallacy, also known as **false dilemma,** offers only two alternatives when more exist. Such fallacies often touch on emotional issues and can therefore seem accurate at first. When people reflect, however, they quickly come to realize that more alternatives are available. Here is a typical example of an either-or fallacy: "Either go to university or forget about getting a job." This statement implies that a university education is a prerequisite for all jobs, which is not true.

Taking something out of context

Taking something out of context separates an idea or fact from the material surrounding it, thus distorting it for special purposes. Suppose a critic writes about a movie saying, "The plot was predictable and boring but the music was sparkling." Then an advertisement for the movie says, "Critic calls this movie 'sparkling.' "The critic's words have been taken out of context—and distorted.

SUMMARY OF LOGICAL FALLACIES	39

- **Hasty generalization:** generalizing from inadequate evidence (stereotyping is hasty generalization using prejudiced claims about a group of people)
- **False analogy:** using a comparison in which the differences outweigh the similarities, or in which the similarities are irrelevant to the claim the analogy is intended to support
- **Begging the question:** circular reasoning that offers as proof of an argument a version of the argument itself or uses a (presumably) shared assumption to stand for proof
- **Irrelevant argument:** reaching a conclusion that does not follow from the premises
- **False cause:** assuming that because two events are related in time, the first caused the second
- **Self-contradiction:** using two premises that cannot both be true
- **Red herring:** sidetracking the issue by raising a second, unrelated issue
- **Argument to the person:** attacking the person making the argument rather than the argument itself
- **Guilt by association:** attacking a person's ideas because of that person's interests or associates
- **Bandwagon:** implying that something is right or is permissible because "everyone" does it
- **False or irrelevant authority:** citing the opinion of a person who has no expertise about the subject
- **Card-stacking:** ignoring evidence on the other side of a question
- **The either-or fallacy:** offering only two alternatives when more exist
- **Taking something out of context:** distorting an idea or fact by separating it from the material surrounding it
- **Appeal to ignorance:** assuming that an argument is valid simply because there is no evidence on the other side of the issue
- **Ambiguity and equivocation:** using expressions that are not clear because they have more than one meaning

Appeal to ignorance

Appeal to ignorance assumes that an argument is valid simply because it has not been shown to be false. Conversely, something is not false simply because it has not been shown to be true. Appeals to ignorance can be very persuasive because they prey on people's superstitions or lack of knowledge. Here is a typical example of such flawed reasoning: "Since no one has proven that depression does not cause cancer, we can assume that it does." The absence of opposing evidence proves nothing.

Ambiguity and equivocation

Ambiguity and **equivocation** describe expressions that are not clear because they have more than one meaning. An ambiguous expression may be taken either way by the reader. A statement such as "They were entertaining guests" is ambiguous. Were the guests amusing to be with or were people giving hospitality to guests? An equivocal expression, by contrast, is one used in two or more ways within a single argument. If someone argued that the prime minister *played a role* in constitutional negotiations and then, two sentences later, said that the prime minister was *playing a role* when he called himself a supporter of the "distinct society" clause to satisfy Quebec, the person would be equivocating.

EXERCISE 5-7

Consulting section 5k, identify and explain the fallacy in each item. If the item does not contain a logical flaw, circle its number.

EXAMPLE   Seat belts are the only hope for reducing the death rate from automobile accidents. [This is an *either-or fallacy* because it assumes that nothing but seat belts can reduce the number of fatalities from car accidents.]

1. Joanna Hayes should write a book about international espionage. She has starred in three films that show the inner workings of foreign spy rings.
2. It is ridiculous to have spent thousands of dollars to rescue those two whales from being trapped in the Arctic ice. Why, look at all of the people trapped in jobs that they don't like.
3. Every time my roommate has a math test, she becomes extremely nervous. Clearly, she is not good at math.
4. Plagiarism is deceitful because it is dishonest.
5. The local political coalition to protect the environment would get my support and that of many other people if its leaders did not drive cars that get poor gasoline mileage.

6. UFOs must exist because no reputable studies have proven conclusively that they do not.

7. Water fluoridation affects the brain. Citywide, students' test scores began to drop five months after fluoridation began.

8. Learning to manage a corporation is exactly like learning to ride a bicycle: Once you learn the skills, you never forget how, and you never fall.

9. Medicare is free; the government pays for it from taxes.

10. Reading good literature is the one way to appreciate culture.

6 Writing Argument

When writing **argument** for your college or university courses, you seek to convince a reader to agree with you concerning a topic open to debate. A written argument states and supports one position about the debatable topic. Support for that position depends on evidence, reasons, and examples chosen for their direct relation to the point being argued. One section of the written argument might present and attempt to refute other positions on the topic, but the central thrust of the essay is to argue for one point of view.

Taking and defending a position in a written argument is an engaging intellectual process, especially when it involves a topic of substance about which universal agreement is unlikely. The ability to think critically by analyzing, synthesizing, and assessing (see Chart 28 in section 5c) is challenged by the activity of examining all sides of a topic, choosing one side to defend, and marshalling convincing support for that one side.

If you are among the people who find any type of arguing distasteful, you are not alone. But rest assured that written argument differs drastically from everyday, informal arguing. Informal arguing sometimes originates in anger and might involve bursts of temper or unpleasant emotional confrontations. Written argument, in contrast, can always be a constructive activity. When you write an argument, you can disagree without being disagreeable. An effective written argument sets forth its position calmly, respectfully, and logically. Any passion that underlies a writer's position is evident not from angry words but from the force of a balanced, well-developed, clearly written discussion.

The ability to argue reasonably and effectively is an important skill that people need not only in their studies but throughout their lives—in family relationships, with friends, and in the business world. People engage in debates (perhaps more often in speaking than in writing) that call for an exchange of solidly supported views. Once you become adept at the techniques of written argument, you can use them equally effectively for oral argument.

Much of the material in the earlier chapters of this handbook can help you compose a written argument. A list of useful sections is given in Chart 40. This chapter concentrates on the special demands of writing argument. The writing of two student essays is discussed in this chapter, and the final draft of each essay appears in section 6i.

MATERIAL FROM EARLIER CHAPTERS IN THIS HANDBOOK TO USE 40
WHEN WRITING AN ARGUMENT

- Checklist for persuasive writing (1b-3)
- Audiences for writing (1c)
- Establishing a suitable tone (1d)
- Choosing a topic (2c)
- The writing process: planning and shaping (Chapter 2)
- The writing process: drafting and revising (Chapter 3)
- Writing paragraphs (Chapter 4)
- Reading and thinking critically (Chapter 5)
- Using evidence to think critically (5h)
- Analyzing cause and effect (5i)
- Using inductive and deductive reasoning (5j)
- Avoiding logical fallacies (5k)

The terms *persuasive writing* and *argumentative writing* often are used interchangeably. When a distinction is made between them, persuasive writing is the broader term. It includes advertisements, letters to editors, emotional pleas in speeches or writing, and formal written arguments. The focus of this chapter is formal written argument as usually assigned in college and university courses.

6a Choosing a topic for a written argument

When you choose a topic for written argument, be sure that it is open to debate. Be careful not to confuse matters of information with matters of debate. Facts are matters of information, not debate. An essay becomes an argument when it takes a position concerning the fact or other piece of information.

FACT	Students at this college **are required** to take physical education.
POSITION OPEN TO DEBATE	Students at this college **should not be required** to take physical education.
OPPOSITE POSITION OPEN TO DEBATE	Students at this college **should be required** to take physical education.

A written argument could take one of these opposing positions and defend it. The essay could not argue for two or more sides, though it might mention other points of view and attempt to refute them.

When you are assigned a written argument, be sure to read and think through the assignment carefully. Instructors construct assignments for written argument in a number of ways. You might be given both the topic and the position to take on that topic. In such cases, you are expected to fulfil the assignment whether or not you agree personally with the given point of view. You are judged on your ability to marshal a defence of the assigned position and to reason logically about it. Another type of assignment is unstructured, requiring you to choose the debatable topic and the position to defend. In such cases, the topic that you choose should be **suitable for postsecondary writing** (see 2c-1), not trivial (for example, not the best way to chew gum). The topic should be **narrowed sufficiently** (see 2c-2) to fit the writing situation. You are judged on your ability to think of a debatable topic of substance, to narrow the topic so that your essay can include general statements and specific details, to choose a defensible position about that topic, and to present and support your position convincingly. If you cannot decide what position you agree with personally because all sides of a debatable topic have merit, do not get blocked. You need not make a lifetime commitment to your position. Rather, concentrate on the merits of one position, and present that position as effectively as possible.

The two sample essays at the end of this chapter were written in response to the assignment shown in the box below. This assignment states the topic but asks students to take a position about it.

Lindsey Black and Daniel Casey were given this assignment: Write an essay of 500 to 700 words that argues about whether holidays have become too commercialized in North America. Your final draft is due in one week. Bring your earlier drafts to class for possible sharing and discussion.

Black and Casey analyzed the four aspects of the **writing situation** (see 2b) reflected in the assignment. The essay *topic* is stated (whether holidays have become too commercialized in North America). The essay's *purpose* is persuasive, but students are free to choose the position to argue for (the student can choose to argue that the holidays have become too commercialized *or* that they have not become too commercialized). The *audience* for the essay is not specified and is therefore assumed to be the instructor and, perhaps, other members of the class. The *special requirements* include the essay's length (between 500 and 700 words) and the time for getting the essay into final draft (one week).

6b Developing an assertion and a thesis statement for written argument

An **assertion** is a statement that gives a position about a debatable topic and that can be supported by evidence, reasons, and examples (including facts, statistics, names, experiences, and experts). The thinking process that moves you from a topic to a defensible position calls, first, for you to make an assertion about the topic. The exact wording of the assertion often does not find its way into the essay, but the assertion serves as a focus for your thinking and your writing.

TOPIC	*The commercialization of holidays*
ASSERTION	Holidays have become too commercialized.
ASSERTION	Holidays have not become too commercialized.

Before you decide on an assertion—the position that you want to argue—you need to explore the topic. Do not rush into deciding on your assertion. Try to wait until you have as full a picture as possible. Consider all sides. Remember that **what mainly separates most good writing from bad is the writer's ability to move back and forth between general statements and specific details.** Try to avoid a position that limits you to *only* general statements or to *only* specific details. In deciding on your assertion, use the memory device of RENNS (see 4c) to see whether you can marshall sufficient details to support your generalizations.

Even if you know immediately what assertion you want to argue for, do not stop there. The more you think through all sides of the topic, the broader will be the perspective that you bring to your writing. Also, as you think through your position and consider alternative points of view, be open to changing your mind and taking an opposite position.

Before too long, however, do settle on a position; switching positions at the last minute lessens your chances of writing an effective essay.

To stimulate your thinking about the topic and your assertion about it, use the techniques for gathering ideas explained and illustrated in sections 2e through 2k. Jot down your thoughts as they develop. Do not lose the unique opportunity that the act of writing gives you to discover new ideas and fresh insights. Writers of effective arguments often list for themselves the various points that come to mind, using two columns to represent visually two contrasting points of view. (Head the columns with labels that emphasize contrast: for example, *agree* and *disagree* or *for* and *against*.) The lists can then supply ideas during drafting and revising.

Whenever possible, use outside resources for developing an assertion. These include talking with other people and conducting research. Getting points of view from other people helps you explore a debatable topic. As you talk with people, interview them rather than argue with them. Your goal is to come to know opposing points of view, so resist any temptation to "win" a verbal argument; people sometimes hesitate to offer their ideas fully and openly when their listener is hostile. If your assignment permits you to use the library, do so. Written argument can be particularly enhanced when your position is supported with facts and reference to experts. (See 1e, 5h, and Chapters 31–35.)

Next, using your assertion as a base, you compose a thesis statement (see 2n) to use in the essay. It states the position that you present and support in the essay. To write this essay about holiday commercialism shown in 6i, Daniel Casey used this progression from basic assertion to final thesis statement.

I think holiday commercialism is a good thing. [This assertion is a start.]

All commercial uses of holidays are very good for our economy and people's spirits. [This preliminary thesis is more developed because it gives a reason—economic and emotional benefits—but the word *all* is misleading and the vocabulary level of *very good* needs work.]

In spite of what some people think, commercial uses of holidays benefit the economy and people's spirits. [This draft is better, but "what some people think" was not an aspect of the topic Casey intended to explore. Also, *benefit spirits* needs revision.]

Such commercial uses of holidays benefit the economy and lift people's spirits. [This is the final version of Casey's thesis statement; *Such* is a transitional word connecting the thesis statement to sentences in the introductory paragraph that describe several holiday activities.]

The final version meets the requirements listed in Chart 10 in section 2n.

EXERCISE 6-1

Develop an assertion and a thesis statement for a written argument on each of the following topics. You may choose any defensible position.

EXAMPLE **Topic:** *Book censorship in high school*
Assertion: *Books should not be censored in high school.*
Thesis statement: *When books are taken off high school library shelves and are dropped from high school curricula, students are denied exposure to an open exchange of ideas.*

1. television
2. prisons
3. drugs and athletics
4. diets for weight loss
5. grades

6c Considering the audience for written argument

The purpose of written argument is to convince a reader—the audience—of a matter of opinion. Key factors in considering audience are discussed in 1c. When you write argument, consider one additional factor about audience: the degree of agreement expected from the reader.

When a topic is emotionally charged, chances are high that any position being argued will elicit either strong agreement or strong disagreement. For example, topics such as abortion, capital punishment, and gun control arouse very strong emotions in many people. Such topics are emotionally loaded because they touch on matters of personal beliefs, including religion and individual rights. A topic such as the commercialization of holidays (see the two essays in section 6i) is somewhat less emotionally loaded. Even less emotionally loaded, yet still open to debate, are topics such as whether everyone needs a postsecondary education or whether Computer X is better than Computer Y.

The degree to which a reader might be friendly or hostile can influence what strategies you use to try to convince that reader. For example, when you anticipate that many readers will not agree with you, consider using techniques of **Rogerian argument.** Rogerian argument has been adapted from the principles of communication developed by psychologist Carl Rogers. Communication, according to Rogers, is eased when people find common ground in their points of view. The common ground in a debate over capital punishment might be that both sides find crime to be a growing problem today. Once both sides agree about the problem, they might have more tolerance for the divergence of opinion concerning whether capital punishment is a deterrent to crime.

6d Using the classical pattern for written argument

No one structure fits all written argument. For college and university courses, most written arguments include certain elements. Lindsey Black's essay in section 6i uses a structure based on the **classical pattern of argument** developed by the ancient Greeks and Romans and still highly respected today. Daniel Casey's essay in section 6i uses a modified form of that structure. Chart 41 will help you recognize the elements in a written argument.

ELEMENTS IN THE CLASSICAL PATTERN FOR WRITTEN ARGUMENT 41

1. **Introductory paragraph:** sets the context for the position that is argued in the essay. (For a discussion of introductory paragraphs, see 4g.)

2. **Thesis statement:** states the position being argued. In a short essay, the thesis statement often appears at the end of the introductory paragraph. (For a discussion of thesis statements, see 2n.)

3. **Background information:** gives the reader basic information needed for understanding the position being argued. This information can be part of the introductory paragraph (as in Daniel Casey's essay in section 6i) or can appear in its own paragraph (as in Lindsey Black's essay in section 6i).

4. **Reasons or evidence:** supports the position being argued. This material is the core of the essay. If the support consists of evidence, consult the discussion in 5h. Also, be sure that your reasoning is logical (see 5k). Each type of evidence or reason usually consists of a general statement backed up with specific details or examples. Depending on the length of the essay, one or two paragraphs are devoted to each reason or type of evidence. ➜

ELEMENTS IN THE CLASSICAL PATTERN FOR WRITTEN ARGUMENT 41
(cont'd.)

The best sequence for presenting the complete set of reasons and types of evidence depends on the impact you want to achieve. Moving from evidence most familiar to the reader to evidence least familiar helps the reader move from the known to the unknown. This order might catch the reader's interest early on. Moving from evidence least important to evidence most important might build the reader's suspense. (For more about various types of paragraph arrangement, see 4e.)

5. **Anticipation of likely objections and responses to them:** mentions positions opposed to the one being argued and rebuts them briefly. In classical argument, this "refutation" appears in its own paragraph, immediately before the concluding paragraph (as in Lindsey Black's essay). An alternative placement is immediately after the introductory paragraph, as a bridge to the rest of the essay; in such arrangements the essay's thesis statement falls either at the end of the introductory paragraph or at the end of the "refutation" paragraph (as in Daniel Casey's essay in section 6i). In still another arrangement, each paragraph that presents a type of evidence or reason (item 4 on this list) also mentions and responds to the opposing position.

6. **Concluding paragraph:** brings the essay to an end that flows logically and gracefully from the rest of the essay. It does not cut off the reader abruptly. (For a discussion of concluding paragraphs, see 4g.)

6e Using the Toulmin model for argument

The Toulmin model for argument has recently gained popularity among teachers and students because it clarifies the major elements in an effective argument. The terms used in the Toulmin model may seem unfamiliar, even intimidating, at first. But worry not. The concepts that the terms describe are ones you have encountered before. What is new is placing those concepts into the vocabulary and structure of the Toulmin model.

The essential elements of the Toulmin model are presented in Chart 42.

ELEMENTS IN THE TOULMIN MODEL OF ARGUMENT	42
TOULMIN'S TERM	**MORE FAMILIAR TERMS**
the claim	the main point or central message, usually disclosed in the thesis statement
the support	data or other evidence, from broad reasons to specific details
the warrant	underlying assumptions, usually not stated but clearly implied; readers infer assumptions

The elements in Chart 42 can be identified in Daniel Casey's written argument shown in 6i:

- Casey's claim: Commercial uses of holidays benefit the economy and lift people's spirits.

- Casey's support: (1) Economic prosperity creates circulation of money which in turn creates jobs. (2) Holidays are festive times that cheer people up with decorations, costumes, gift-giving, and a friendly atmosphere. (3) Successful businesses improve everyone's quality of life by sponsoring charitable causes, parades, fireworks displays, and cultural events.

- Casey's warrants: (1) Benefiting the economy is an important objective from which everyone gains. (2) Even the spiritual aspects of the holidays are not paramount.

The concept of a warrant may seem difficult to understand. It can help to think of warrants as related to the concept of reading to make inferences, a key part of reading critically (see 5d). Like inferences, which are implications you must find "between the lines," warrants are implied assumptions you must infer from the stated argument.

To help you figure out the warrant that underlies an argument you are writing or reading, try placing it into one of Toulmin's three broad categories for warrants: (1) A warrant based on **authority** rests on respect for the credibility and trustworthiness of the person; (2) a warrant based on **substance** rests on the reliability of factual evidence; (3) a warrant based on **motivation** rests on the values and beliefs of the audience and the writer. Daniel Casey's warrant listed above is a motivational warrant because it is not based on authority or factual evidence—it is based on the writer's valuing of economic prosperity over spiritual considerations.

The concepts in the Toulmin model can help you read arguments with a critical eye. The concepts are equally useful for you as a writer. As you draft and revise your written argument, evaluate what you are saying by checking whether you can analyze it for the elements in the Toulmin model. If you can't your argument needs work.

6f Defining terms in written argument

When you **define terms,** you explain what you mean by key words that you use. Words are key words when they are central to the message that you want to communicate. The meaning of some key words is readily evident. Key words open to interpretation, however, should be made specific enough to be clear.

NO   Commercialism at holiday time is **bad.**

YES   Commercialism at holiday time is **ruining the spirit of the holidays.**

YES   Commercialism at holiday time **tempts too many people to spend more money than they can afford.**

Some key words might vary with the context of a discussion and should be explained in an essay. Abstract words such as *love, freedom,* and *democracy* have to be explained because they have different meanings in different contexts. In his paper (see 6i), Daniel Casey uses *economy,* a word with many meanings, in the topic sentence of the third paragraph of his essay. He explains *economy* as the *ongoing circulation of money,* and he uses the rest of the paragraph to explain how that circulation operates. In this way, Casey makes clear that he is not referring to any of the other meanings of *economy:* the management of finances, the avoidance of waste, or the efficient use of resources.

Other key terms might be unfamiliar to the reader even though they are known words. For example, Casey opens his essay with the words *signs of commercialism.* Although each word by itself is familiar, the term is not. Casey therefore gives examples to illustrate the concept. In so doing, he creates an effective introduction to his essay by bringing the reader to a quick understanding of his topic.

Many students ask whether they should use actual dictionary definitions in an essay. Looking words up in a dictionary to understand precise meanings is a very important activity for writers. Quoting a dictionary definition, however, is not always wise. Dictionary definitions tend to be overused in student writing, and they are often seen as the "easy way out." Using an **extended definition** is usually a more effective approach, which is what Casey did for *economy* in the third paragraph of his essay. (For another example of extended definition, of *tolerance,* see paragraph 43 in 4f-5.) If you do use a dictionary definition in your writing, be sure to work it into your material gracefully. Do not simply tack it on abruptly to what you are saying. In general, do not rely on it for your opening sentence. Also, be aware that references to a dictionary must be complete. Do not simply refer to "Gage," which is far too general. Each dictionary has its own name, such as the *Gage Canadian Dictionary.*

6g Reasoning effectively in written argument

When you reason effectively, you increase your chances of persuading your reader to agree with you. In many instances, of course, you cannot expect actually to change your reader's mind. The basis for a debatable position is often personal opinion or belief, neither of which can be expected to change as the result of one written argument. Nevertheless, you still have an important goal: to convince your reader that your point of view has merit. People often "agree to disagree," in the best spirit of intellectual exchange. Round-table discussions among various experts heard on the CBC or PBS are conducted in such a spirit.

The opposite positions taken by Lindsey Black and Daniel Casey (see 6i) concerning commercialism at holiday time stem from their personal beliefs and perceptions of the world. Black feels that commercialism is ruining the holidays. Casey recognizes the existence of commercialism, but he sees it as beneficial. The chance of either person convincing the other is slight. What can happen, however, is that each person can respect the quality of the other's argument.

An argument of good quality relies on three types of appeals to reason: the logical, the emotional, and the ethical. Chart 43 gives a summary of how to use the three appeals.

GUIDELINES FOR REASONING EFFECTIVELY IN WRITTEN ARGUMENT 43

- **Be logical:** Use sound reasoning.
- **Enlist the emotions of the reader:** Enlist the values and beliefs of the reader, usually by arousing "the better self" of the reader.
- **Establish credibility:** Show that you as the writer can be relied upon as a knowledgeable person with good sense.

The most widely used appeal in written argument is the **logical appeal,** called *logos* by the ancient Greeks. Logical reasoning is sound reasoning. This type of reasoning is important in all thinking and writing. Chapter 5 of this handbook, therefore, is a close companion to this chapter. Logical reasoning calls for using evidence well, as explained in 5h. Logical reasoning also means analyzing cause and effect correctly, as explained in 5i. A sound argument uses patterns of inductive reasoning and deductive reasoning, as explained in 5j. A sound argument also clearly distinguishes between fact and opinion, as explained in 5d-3. Finally, sound reasoning means avoiding logical fallacies, as explained in 5k.

Written argument for college and university courses relies heavily on logic. Both Lindsey Black and Daniel Casey (see 6i) used logical reasoning throughout their essays. While the reader might not agree with the reasons or types of evidence presented, the reader can respect the logic of their arguments.

The **emotional appeal,** called *pathos* by the ancient Greeks, can be effective when used in conjunction with logical appeals. The word *emotional* has a specific meaning in this context. It means arousing and enlisting the emotions of the reader. Often it arouses the "better self" of the reader by eliciting sympathy, civic pride, and other feelings based on values and beliefs. Effective emotional appeals use description and examples to stir emotions, but they leave the actual stirring to the reader. Restraint is more effective than excessive sentimentality.

Both Casey and Black (see 6i) use emotional appeals in their essays, but always in conjunction with a logical presentation of material. Casey appeals to the emotions when in his fifth paragraph he mentions stores giving toys to children in hospitals. But he does not overdo it. He does not say that anyone who disagrees with him hates children and feels no pity for their suffering from dreadful illnesses that ravage their tiny bodies. If he had indulged in such excesses, the reader would resent being manipulated and therefore would probably reject his argument. Black appeals to the emotions when she writes in her second paragraph about the origins of the holiday spirit. With restraint, she mentions the meaning of each holiday. She does not attempt to tell the reader how to feel; she simply points out facts that support the logic of her argument and that might also stir the reader's pride in country and heritage.

The **ethical appeal,** called *ethos* by the ancient Greeks, means establishing the ethics and credibility of the writer. Credibility is gained if the writer uses correct facts, undistorted evidence, and accurate interpretations of events. Readers do not trust a writer who states opinions as fact or who makes a claim that cannot possibly be supported. The statement "A child who does not get gifts for Christmas suffers a trauma from which recovery is impossible" is an opinion as well as an exaggeration. It has no place in written argument.

Ethical appeals cannot take the place of logical appeals, but the two types of appeals work well together. One effective way to make an ethical appeal is to draw on personal experience. (Some college and university instructors do not want students to write in the first person, so ask your instructor before you use it.) If you use personal experience, always be sure that it relates directly to a generalization that you are supporting. Also, be aware that a personal experience can say as much about the writer as about the experience. For example, if Casey had been a volunteer at a hospital when gifts from a local business were distributed, the story of the experience not only would have supported his claim in his fifth paragraph, but also would have illustrated his good character.

6h Establishing a reasonable tone in written argument

To be reasonable, you have to be fair. By anticipating opposing positions and responding to them (see 6c), you have a particularly good chance to show that you are fair. When you alert your reader to other ways of thinking about the issue, you demonstrate that you have not ignored other positions. Doing this implies respect for the other side, which in turn makes the tone (see 1d) of the essay more reasonable.

To achieve a reasonable tone, choose your words carefully. Avoid words that exaggerate. Use figurative language, such as similes and metaphors (see 21c), to enhance your point rather than distort it. No matter how strongly you disagree with opposing arguments, never insult the other side. Name-calling is impolite, shows poor self-control, and demonstrates poor judgment. The more emotionally loaded a topic (for example, abortion, capital punishment, and gun control), the more might be the temptation to use angry words. Words such as *stupid* or *pigheaded,* however, say more about the writer than about the issue.

Artificial language (see 21e) also ruins a reasonable tone. The *Yes* example that follows is used by Daniel Casey as the first sentence in his essay in section 6i. Compare its impact with what would happen if Casey had used the *No* example.

NO   Emblems of commercial enterprise are ubiquitously visible as the populace prepares for the celebration of festivals and commemorations throughout the continent.

YES   Signs of commercialism at holiday time are easy to see in North America.

165

6i Writing and revising a written argument

Lindsey Black chose the position that holidays have become too commercialized. Daniel Casey, on the other hand, chose the position that the commercialization of holidays has advantages. The final draft of each essay appears at the end of this chapter. The labels identify the structural elements of written argument discussed in 6d.

In an early draft of her essay, Black wrote an introduction that included the background information on the holidays, now in her second paragraph. When she revised, she moved the information to a separate paragraph because she saw that the introductory paragraph was too long and the thesis statement was being overshadowed. Also, she felt that a separate paragraph giving background information had the additional advantage of giving her the space to use an emotional appeal (see 6g). An early draft of Black's third paragraph consisted only of the topic sentence and the last three sentences of the final draft. When she revised, Black saw that she needed more examples to support the generalization in her topic sentence. She added the material about greeting cards and about time and stress.

REVISION CHECKLIST FOR WRITTEN ARGUMENT 44

1. Does the thesis statement concern a debatable topic (see 6b)?
2. Is the material structured well for a written argument (see 6d)?
3. Do the reasons or evidence support the thesis statement? Are the generalizations supported by specific details (see 6d)?
4. Are opposing positions mentioned and responded to (see 6d)?
5. Are terms defined (see 6f)?
6. Are the appeals to reason used correctly and well (see 6g)?
7. Is the tone reasonable (see 6h)?

Daniel Casey wrote a discovery draft (see 3b) to explore further the ideas that he evolved while planning his essay: for his brainstorming, see section 2g; for his use of the journalist's questions, see section 2h; for the sequencing of his ideas, see section 2m. As he wrote his draft, he discovered, for example, that he needed to define the term *signs of commercialism* by giving specific examples. He also found that he had two reasons he could develop in support of his thesis: an enriched economy and an enhanced spirit. He wanted a third reason, so he interviewed some friends who worked in a shopping mall, and they mentioned what some of the stores do for the community at holiday time. The second paragraph of Casey's essay was the next-to-last paragraph in an early draft. He moved it when he revised because he decided that it built an effective bridge to his thesis statement.

As both Black and Casey revised, they consulted the Revision Checklists in 3c to remind them of general principles of writing, and they looked over the checklist in Chart 44.

EXERCISE 6-2

Choose a topic below, and write an essay that argues for a debatable position about the topic. Apply all the principles you have learned in this chapter.

1. animal experimentation
2. nuclear power
3. value of the space program
4. celebrity endorsements
5. day-care centres

6. surrogate mothers
7. gun control
8. school prayer
9. optimism
10. highway speed limits

Lindsey Black

Professor Gregory

English 101

April 10, 19XX

Commercialism Is Ruining the Holidays

introduction: identification of the situation

Holidays should be special occasions that have religious, historical, and cultural significance. Increasingly, however, holidays in North America are turning into little more than business opportunities. From coast to coast, the jingles and beeps of cash registers drown out the traditional sounds of holiday observance.

thesis statement

The spirit of the holidays is being destroyed by commercialism. →

---

background:
origins and
significance

The origins of the holiday spirit are varied in Canada and the United States. Thanksgiving reminds us to be grateful for our blessings, and holidays like Canada Day or the Fourth of July stimulate pride in the founding of the country. Labour Day is a tribute to workers. Remembrance Day in Canada and Memorial Day in the United States honour soldiers who died in defence of their country. Christmas and Easter have great religious significance to Christians. Holidays used to be occasions for people to come together and celebrate their heritages. Today, however, the overriding message of the holidays is "spend money."

evidence: one
type

The most visible evidence that commercialism now dominates holidays is the unfortunate emphasis on spending money in preparation for religious holidays. For example, buying and mailing Christmas cards has become standard practice for individuals, families, and industry. How many people can ignore the social and the business pressures to mail cards? The commitment of money and time for this activity is not small. The gift situation is equally stressful. Although exchanging gifts on Christmas or Hanukkah was always part of the celebration, the thought behind the present used to be the point. Today, however, advertising-- particularly on television--sets a high standard of expectations. Can home-baked cookies compare to a microwave oven? Can hand-drawn, handwritten

cards be as impressive as elaborate greeting
cards that play music?

evidence:
another type

Other evidence that commercialism is
ruining holidays is the emphasis on shopping for
bargains rather than on activities related to
cultural history. Huge sales held before
holidays, and often on the holiday itself, are
advertised heavily in newspapers, on television,
and on radio. The emphasis on shopping before
Christmas and then on Boxing Day sales tends to
overshadow the true spirit of the season. The
image of the family gathering on Thanksgiving
Day is being replaced with the image of the
family shopping the day after Thanksgiving. Some
special days, in fact, seem to have been created
with the sole purpose of making money--for
instance, Valentine's Day, Mother's and Father's
Day, and the more recent Grandparents' Day.
While these are not technically holidays, such
occasions illustrate how business seizes on an
opportunity to make a profit.

major likely
objections and
responses to
them

In spite of all this, not all people are
troubled by the spirit of commercialism on
holidays. Many people enjoy the festivity of
exchanging cards and gifts. Some people feel
that the chance to buy at sales helps them stay
within their budgets and therefore enjoy life
more. What these people do not realize is that
the festive spirit of giving can quickly turn
sour when large amounts of money are suddenly
not available for necessities. Also, these

➜

people do not realize that holiday sales
tend to lure shoppers into spending more money
than they had planned, often for things that
they did not think they needed until they saw
them "on sale."

conclusion:
call for
awareness

Holiday celebrations in North America
today have more to do with the wallet than the
spirit. Some people refuse to participate in the
frenzy of a commercial interpretation of
holidays, of course. But for too many people,
holidays are becoming stressful rather than
joyful, and upsetting rather than uplifting.

Daniel Casey

Professor Gregory

English 101

April 10, 19XX

Commercialism at Holiday Time Benefits Everyone

introduction:
gives back-
ground

Signs of commercialism at holiday time are
easy to see in North America. Christmas
decorations begin their call to consumers in
October. Labour Day reminds shoppers to prepare
for the seasonal change in clothing fashions.
Halloween and Easter mean children can expect
treats from the Great Pumpkin or the Easter
Bunny.

presentation
and refutation
of opposite
view

Some people disapprove of these commercial
uses of holidays in North America. These people
feel that the meaning of a holiday gets lost

when television is blaring news of the latest
holiday sale or expensive gift item. Many people
also feel that the proliferation of gifts and
greeting cards creates stressful pressure on
budgets and ruins any pleasure derived from
giving and receiving. No one, however, has to
forget the meaning of a holiday simply because
commerce is involved. In fact, commercialism can
increase people's enjoyment of the holidays.

thesis statement After all, commercial uses of holidays benefit
the economy and lift people's spirits.

reason: one effect Commerce at holiday time in North America
enriches the economy. Prosperity is based on the
ongoing circulation of money, which holidays
encourage. When people spend money on gifts and
holiday products, jobs are created. The jobs are
in many sectors of the economy: manufacturing,
distribution, advertising, and retailing. Jobs
help people support their families. Profits help
business and industry grow. Salaries and profits
bring about tax revenues that support schools,
police, hospitals, and other government services.

reason: second effect In addition to economic benefits,
commercial activity enhances the spirit of
holidays. Most people feel more cheerful at
holiday time. Everyone takes part in one big
party. Advertising related to holidays, along
with stores filled with holiday products,
creates an atmosphere of festivity across the
nation. Being able to say "Happy Thanksgiving"
or "Merry Christmas" to strangers while shopping
breaks down barriers and helps everyone feel ➡

part of one big family. The festivity on the streets, in malls, and in stores is infectious. Giving and getting gifts and greeting cards helps people stay in touch with each other and express their feelings. Children look forward all year to wearing a store-bought costume for Halloween, sitting on Santa's lap in a department store, and talking to the Easter Bunny at the local shopping mall.

reason: third effect

The holiday activities that help businesses prosper also inspire many businesses to improve everyone's quality of life. Many companies, for example, organize collections of clothing and preparation of hot meals for needy people at holiday time. Toy stores often give away toys for Christmas and Hanukkah to children in hospitals and in caretaking homes. Santa Claus parades in virtually every city annually delight people of all ages. In small towns and large cities, many businesses sponsor fireworks, mounted and displayed safely by professionals, to celebrate Canada Day. Good will and good business go together to everyone's benefit at holiday time.

conclusion: summary of main points

While commercialism can detract from the true meaning of a holiday, it does not have to. People can discipline themselves to balance the spiritual with the commercial. People should recognize that the advantages of a stimulated economy and a collective festive spirit are worth the effort of such self-discipline.

PART

II Understanding Grammar

When you understand grammar, you have one tool to help you think about and discuss the ways that your sentences deliver their meaning to your readers. Part Two describes the elements of language and explains the standard rules for using those elements. As you use Chapters 7 through 12, remember that grammar is only a tool. Other parts of this handbook offer you additional perspectives on writing and the choices that writers can make.

7 Parts of Speech and Structures of the Sentence

PARTS OF SPEECH

Knowing **parts of speech** gives you a basic vocabulary for identifying words and understanding how language works. Sections 7a through 7i explain the **noun, pronoun, verb, adjective, adverb, preposition, conjunction,** and **interjection.** As you use this material, be aware that no part of speech exists in a vacuum. To identify a word's part of speech correctly, see how the word functions in the sentence you are analyzing. Often, the same word functions differently in different sentences.

> We ate **fish.** [*Fish* is a noun. It names a thing.]
>
> We **fish** on weekends. [*Fish* is a verb. It names an action.]

7a Recognizing nouns

A **noun** names a person, place, thing, or idea: student, school, textbook, education. For a list of types of nouns, see Chart 45. Nouns function as subjects°,* objects°, and complements°.

❖ ALERT: Words that often appear with nouns tell how much or many, whose, which one, and similar information. These words include **articles** (*a, an, the*) and other **determiners** or **limiting adjectives.** For more about these words, see 7e and Chapter 42ESL. ❖

---

*Throughout this book, a degree mark (°) indicates that you can find the definition of the word in the Glossary of Terms in this handbook.

NOUNS		45
PROPER	names specific people, places, or things (first letter is always capitalized)	**John Lennon, Paris, Buick**
COMMON	names general groups, places, people, or things	**singer, automobile**
CONCRETE	names things experienced through the senses: sight, hearing, taste, smell, and touch	**landscape, pizza, thunder**
ABSTRACT	names things not knowable through the senses	**freedom, shyness**
COLLECTIVE	names groups	**family, team**
NONCOUNT OR MASS	names uncountable things	**water, time**
COUNT	names countable items	**lake, minutes**

◆ ESL NOTE: Sometimes a **suffix** (a word ending) can help you identify the part of speech. Usually, words with these suffixes are nouns: *-ness, -ence, -ance, -ty,* and *-ment.* For more on suffixes, see 20c-1 and 22. ◆

7b **Recognizing pronouns**

A **pronoun** takes the place of a noun°. The word (or words) a pronoun replaces is called its **antecedent.** Pronouns have three different forms, known as **cases:** subjective case, objective case, and possessive case. For more details about pronoun case, see Chapter 9. For types of pronouns, see Chart 46.

David is an accountant. [noun]

He is an accountant. [pronoun]

The finance committee needs to consult **him**. [The pronoun *him* refers to its antecedent, *David*.]

PRONOUNS

PERSONAL *I, you, they, her, its, ours,* and others	refers to people or things	**I** saw **her** take your book to **them.**
RELATIVE *who, which, that*	introduces certain noun clauses° and adjective clauses°	The book **that** I lost was valuable.
INTERROGATIVE *who, whose, what, which,* and others	introduces a question	**Who** called?
DEMONSTRATIVE *this, these, that, those*	points out the antecedent°	Whose books are **these**?
REFLEXIVE; INTENSIVE *myself, themselves,* and other *-self* or *-selves* words	reflects back to the antecedent; intensifies the antecedent	They claim to support **themselves.** I **myself** doubt it.
RECIPROCAL *each other, one another*	refers to individual parts of a plural antecedent	We respect **each other.**
INDEFINITE *all, anyone, each,* and others	refers to nonspecific persons or things	**Everyone** is welcome here.

EXERCISE 7-1

Consulting sections 7a and 7b, underline and label all nouns (N) and pronouns (P). Circle all articles.

>   N   N   N   N
> EXAMPLE   Treadmills can be a way to fitness and rehabilitation.

1. Not only humans use them.
2. Scientists conduct experiments by placing lobsters on treadmills.
3. Scientists can study a lobster when it is fitted with a small mask.
4. The lobster may reach speeds up to a kilometre an hour.
5. Through the mask, researchers can monitor the heartbeat of the crustacean that they are studying.

7c   Recognizing verbs

Main verbs express action, occurrence, or state of being.

I **dance.** [action]

The audience **became** silent. [occurrence]

Your dancing **was** excellent. [state of being]

❖ ALERT: If you are not sure whether a word is a verb, try putting the word into a different tense°. If the sentence still makes sense, the word is a verb. (For an explanation of verb tense, see 8g.)

NO   He is a **changed** man. He is a **will change** man. [The sentence does not make sense when the verb *will change* is substituted, so *changed* is not functioning as a verb.]

YES   The store **changed** owners. The store **will change** owners. [Because the sentence still makes sense when the verb *will change* is substituted, *changed* is functioning as a verb.] ❖

For a detailed discussion of all verb types and the information that they convey, see Chapter 8.

EXERCISE 7-2

Consulting section 7c, underline all verbs.

EXAMPLE   A famous holiday poem <u>was published</u> only because of a good-hearted thief.

1. Clement C. Moore wrote the poem for his three daughters.
2. Moore intended it as a private gift, not for publication.
3. He called the poem "An Account of a Visit from St. Nicholas."
4. Mysteriously and fortunately, the poem was mailed to a newspaper editor.
5. Today we know that poem as "The Night Before Christmas."

7d   Recognizing verbals

Verbals are verb parts functioning as nouns°, adjectives°, or adverbs°. For types of verbals, see Chart 47.

◆ ESL NOTE: For information about using gerunds and infinitives, see Chapter 45ESL. ◆

7e

VERBALS AND THEIR FUNCTIONS   47

INFINITIVE *to* + simple form° of verb	1. noun° 2. adjective° or adverb°	**To eat** now is inconvenient. Still, we have far **to** **go.**
GERUND *-ing* form of verb	noun°	**Eating** in roadside restaurants can be an adventure.
PAST PARTICIPLE *-ed* form of regular verb° or equivalent in irregular verb°	adjective°	**Boiled, filtered** water is usually safe to drink.
PRESENT PARTICIPLE *-ing* form of verb	1. adjective° 2. noun°	**Running** water may not be safe. **Running** is a popular sport.

7e Recognizing adjectives

Adjectives modify—that is, they describe or limit—nouns°, pronouns°, and word groups that function as nouns. For a detailed discussion of adjectives, see Chapter 12.

> I saw a **green** tree. [*Green* modifies the noun *tree.*]
>
> It was **leafy.** [*Leafy* modifies the pronoun *it.*]
>
> The flowering trees were **beautiful.** [*Beautiful* modifies the noun phrase *the flowering trees.*]

Descriptive adjectives, like *leafy* and *green,* can show levels of intensity: *green, greener, greenest; leafy, more leafy, most leafy.* **Proper adjectives** are formed from proper nouns°: *American, Victorian.*

◆ ESL NOTE: Usually, words with these suffixes are adjectives: *-ful, -ish, -less,* and *-like.* For more about suffixes, see 20c-1 and 22d. ◆

Determiners are sometimes called **limiting adjectives.** They "limit" nouns by conveying information such as whether a noun is general (***a*** *tree*) or specific (***the*** *tree*). They also tell which one (***this*** *tree*), how many (***twelve*** *trees*), whose (***our*** *tree*), and similar information.

The determiners, *a, an,* and *the* are also called **articles.** *The* is a
definite article. Before a noun, *the* conveys that the noun refers to a
specific item (*the plan*). *A* and *an* are **indefinite articles.** They convey that a noun refers to an item in a nonspecific or general way (*a
plan*). When you choose between *a* and *an,* remember to use *a* when
the word following it starts with a consonant sound: *a carrot, a broken
egg, a hip;* use *an* when the word following it starts with a vowel
sound: *an egg, an old carrot, an honour.* For more on articles, see
Chapter 42ESL. Chart 48 lists determiners. Some words in the chart
also function as pronouns. To identify a word's part of speech, see
how it functions in a sentence.

That car belongs to Harold. [*that* = demonstrative adjective]

That is Harold's car. [*that* = demonstrative pronoun]

DETERMINERS (LIMITING ADJECTIVES)   48

ARTICLES *a, an, the*	**A** reporter working on **an** assignment is using **the** telephone.
DEMONSTRATIVE *this, these, that, those*	**Those** students rent **that** house.
INDEFINITE *any, each, few, other, some,* and others	**Few** films today have complex plots.
INTERROGATIVE *what, which, whose*	**What** answer did you give?
NUMERICAL *one, first, two, second,* and others	The **fifth** question was tricky.
POSSESSIVE *my, your, their,* and others	**My** violin is older than **your** cello.
RELATIVE *what, which, whose, whatever,* and others	We don't know **which** road to take.

7f Recognizing adverbs

An **adverb** modifies—that is, describes or limits—verbs°, adjectives°, other adverbs, and entire sentences. For a detailed discussion of
adverbs, see Chapter 12.

Chefs plan meals **carefully.** [*Carefully* modifies the verb *plan.*]

Vegetables provide **very** important vitamins. [*Very* modifies the adjective *important.*]

Those potato chips are **too** heavily salted. [*Too* modifies the adverb *heavily.*]

Fortunately, people are learning that salt can be harmful. [*Fortunately* modifies the entire sentence.]

Many adverbs are easy to recognize because they are formed by adding *-ly* to adjectives: *sadly, loudly, normally.* Some adjectives, however, end in *-ly: brotherly, lovely.* Also, many adverbs do not end in *-ly: very, much, always, not, yesterday, so,* and *well* are a few that do not.

Descriptive adverbs can show levels of intensity, usually by adding *more* (or *less*) and *most* (or *least*): *more happily, least clearly.*

Conjunctive adverbs modify by creating logical connections in meaning, as shown in Chart 49. Conjunctive adverbs can appear in the first position of a sentence, in the middle of a sentence, or in the last position of a sentence.

Therefore, we consider Isaac Newton an important scientist.

We consider Isaac Newton, **therefore,** an important scientist.

We consider Isaac Newton an important scientist, **therefore.**

Relative adverbs are words such as *where* and *when* used to introduce adjective clauses°; see 7o-2.

CONJUNCTIVE ADVERBS AND THE RELATIONSHIPS THEY EXPRESS	49

RELATIONSHIP	WORDS
ADDITION	*also, furthermore, moreover, besides,*
CONTRAST	*however, still, nevertheless, conversely, nonetheless, instead, otherwise,*
COMPARISON	*similarly, likewise,*
RESULT OR SUMMARY	*therefore, thus, consequently, accordingly, hence, then,*
TIME	*next, then, meanwhile, finally, subsequently,*
EMPHASIS	*indeed, certainly,*

EXERCISE 7-3

Consulting 7d, 7e, and 7f, underline and label all adjectives (ADJ) and adverbs (ADV).

                     ADJ   ADJ

EXAMPLE   Do you believe the <u>common</u> claim that <u>one</u> person

            ADV   ADJ

           can <u>really</u> make a <u>big</u> difference?

1. A determined woman in Fredericton fought successfully to save three very old oaks from being cut down.
2. Eventually, she founded a civic group, which works closely with local businesspeople, to plant only native trees in the open places in Fredericton.
3. A second individual carefully mapped the recycling sites in his town and then widely distributed the unusual map.
4. New residents gratefully consult this map to learn where to take discarded newspapers, glass bottles, and aluminum cans for mandatory recycling.
5. A third person spoke so passionately about the beautiful tall grass of her Saskatchewan homeland that the city turned those grassy plans into a popular park.

7g   Recognizing prepositions

Prepositions include common words such as *in, under, by, after, to, on, over,* and *since.* Prepositions function with other words in **prepositional phrases.** Prepositional phrases often set out relationships in time or space: *in April, under the orange umbrella.*

In the fall, we will hear a concert **by our favourite tenor.**

After the concert, he will fly **to Paris.**

Some words that function as prepositions also function as other parts of speech. To check whether a word is a preposition, see how it functions in its sentence.

The mountain climbers have not radioed in **since** yesterday. [preposition]

Since they have left the base camp, the mountain climbers can communicate with us only by radio. [subordinating conjunction: see 7h]

At first I was not worried, but I have **since** changed my mind. [adverb: see 7f]

◆ ESL NOTE: For a list of prepositions and the idioms they involve, see Chapter 44ESL. ◆

7h Recognizing conjunctions

A **conjunction** connects words, phrases°, or clauses°. **Coordinating conjunctions** join two or more grammatically equivalent structures.

We hike **and** camp every summer. [*And* joins two words.]

I love the outdoors, **but** my family does not. [*But* joins two sentences.]

Correlative conjunctions function in pairs to join equivalent grammatical structures. They include *both...and, either...or, neither...nor, not only...but (also), whether...or,* and *not...so much as.*

Both English **and** French are spoken in many homes in Canada.

Not only students **but also** business people should study a second language.

COORDINATING CONJUNCTIONS AND THE RELATIONSHIPS THEY EXPRESS		50
RELATIONSHIP	**WORDS**	
ADDITION	*and*	
CONTRAST	*but, yet*	
RESULT OR EFFECT	*so*	
RESULT OR CAUSE	*for*	
CHOICE	*or*	
NEGATIVE CHOICE	*nor*	

SUBORDINATING CONJUNCTIONS AND THE RELATIONSHIPS THEY EXPRESS		51
RELATIONSHIP	**WORDS**	
TIME	*after, before, once, since, until, when, whenever, while*	
REASON OR CAUSE	*as, because, since*	
RESULT OR EFFECT	*in order that, so, so that, that*	
CONDITION	*if, even if, provided that, unless*	
CONTRAST	*although, even though, though, whereas*	
LOCATION	*where, wherever*	
CHOICE	*rather than, than, whether*	

Subordinating conjunctions introduce dependent clauses°, which are structures that are grammatically less important than those in an independent clause° within the same sentence. Subordinating conjunctions are listed in Chart 51.

Many people were happy **after** they heard the news.

Because it snowed, school was cancelled.

7i   Recognizing interjections

An **interjection** is a word or expression that conveys surprise or another strong emotion. Alone, an interjection is usually punctuated with an exclamation point(*!*). As part of a sentence, an interjection is set off with a comma (or commas). In academic writing, use interjections sparingly, if at all.

Hooray! I got the promotion.

Oh, they are late.

EXERCISE 7-4

Consulting sections 7a through 7i, identify the part of speech of each numbered and underlined word. Choose from noun, pronoun, verb, adjective, adverb, preposition, coordinating conjunction, correlative conjunction, and subordinating conjunction.

Some <u>people</u> have had <u>tantalizing</u> clues to the possibility of life <u>after</u> death.
      1   **2**   **3**

Near-death experiences <u>have</u> been reported by more than eight million peo-
                  4

ple <u>in</u> many cultures. Today, researchers <u>are</u> studying these <u>strange</u> experiences.
   5   **6**   **7**

Some people report that their thought <u>processes</u> were <u>extraordinarily</u> fast and
                        8   **9**

clear. <u>Others</u> describe <u>intense</u> feelings of peace <u>and</u> <u>joy</u>, accompanied <u>by</u> brilliant
    10   **11**   **12** **13**   **14**

light. Still others <u>mention</u> <u>enhanced</u> vision <u>or</u> hearing. <u>Furthermore</u>, they seemed
       15   **16**   **17**   **18**

to be watching <u>themselves</u> from a <u>distance</u>. Researchers <u>believe</u> <u>that</u> these
          19   **20**   **21** **22**

experiences are <u>both</u> too numerous <u>and</u> <u>too</u> <u>similar</u> to ignore.
         23   **23** **24** **25**

STRUCTURES OF THE SENTENCE

When you know how sentences are formed, you have one tool for understanding the art of writing.

7j Defining the sentence

The sentence has several definitions, each of which views it from a different perspective. On its most mechanical level, a sentence starts with a capital letter and finishes with a period, question mark, or exclamation point. A sentence can be defined according to its purpose. **Declarative sentences** make a statement: *Sky diving is dangerous.* **Interrogative sentences** ask a question: *Is sky diving dangerous?* **Imperative sentences** give a command: *Be careful when you skydive.* **Exclamatory sentences** begin with *What* or *How* and express strong feeling: *How I love sky diving!* Grammatically, a sentence contains an **independent clause** (a group of words that can stand alone as an independent unit): *Sky diving is dangerous.* Sometimes a sentence is described as a "complete thought," but the concept of "complete" is too subjective to be reliable.

An infinite variety of sentences can be composed, but all sentences share a common foundation. Sections 7k through 7o present the basic structures of sentences.

7k Recognizing subjects and predicates

A sentence consists of two basic parts: a **subject** and a **predicate.**
The **simple subject** is the word or group of words that acts, is described, or is acted upon.

The **telephone** rang. [Simple subject, *telephone*, acts.]

The **telephone** is red. [Simple subject, *telephone*, is described.]

The **telephone** was being connected. [Simple subject, *telephone*, is acted upon.]

The **complete subject** is the simple subject and its modifiers (all the words that describe or limit it): ***The red telephone*** *rang.*

A **compound subject** consists of two or more nouns° or pronouns° and their modifiers: ***The telephone and the doorbell*** *rang.*

The **predicate** is the part of the sentence that contains the verb. The predicate tells what the subject is doing or experiencing or what is being done to the subject.

The telephone **rang.** [*Rang* tells us what the subject, *telephone*, did.]

The telephone **is** red. [*Is* tells what the subject, *telephone*, experiences.]

The telephone **was being connected.** [*Was being connected* tells what was being done to the subject, *telephone*.]

A **simple predicate** contains only the verb: *The lawyer listened.* A **complete predicate** contains the verb and its modifiers°: *The lawyer listened carefully.* A **compound predicate** contains two or more verbs: *The lawyer listened and waited.*

❖ ALERT: In sentences that make a statement, the subject usually comes before the predicate. (One exception is inverted sentences°; see 19f.) In sentences that ask a question, part of the predicate usually comes before the subject. For more about word order, see Chapter 43ESL. ❖

SENTENCE PATTERNS: GROUP I   52

■ COMPLETE SUBJECT   +   COMPLETE PREDICATE
  The red telephone   rang loudly.
        ↑   ↑
   SIMPLE SUBJECT   SIMPLE PREDICATE (VERB)

■ COMPLETE SUBJECT   +   COMPLETE PREDICATE
  The telephone and the doorbell   rang loudly.
        ↖   ↗
   COMPOUND SUBJECT

■ COMPLETE SUBJECT   +   COMPLETE PREDICATE
  The red telephone   rang and startled everyone in the room.
                              ↖   ↗
                         COMPOUND PREDICATE

◆ ESL NOTE: Avoid repeating a subject with a personal pronoun in the same clause.

NO	My grandfather, **he** lived to be eighty-seven.
YES	My grandfather lived to be eighty-seven.
NO	Winter storms that bring ice, sleet, and snow **they** can cause traffic problems.
YES	Winter storms that bring ice, sleet, and snow can cause traffic problems. ◆

EXERCISE 7-5

Consulting section 7k, separate the complete subject from the complete predicate with a slash.

EXAMPLE   One of the most devastating natural disasters of recorded history / began on April 5, 1815.

1. Mount Tambora, located in present-day Indonesia, erupted.
2. The eruption exploded the top 1200 metres of the mountain.
3. The blast was heard over 1400 kilometres away.
4. A thick cloud of volcanic ash circled the globe and reached North America the following summer.
5. The sun could not penetrate the cloud throughout the entire summer.

---

71 **Recognizing direct and indirect objects**

Direct objects and **indirect objects** occur in the predicate° of a sentence.

A **direct object** receives the action—it completes the meaning—of a transitive verb°. To find a direct object, make up a *whom?* or *what?* question about the verb.

An **indirect object** answers a *to whom? for whom? to what?* or *for what?* question about the verb. Chart 53 shows the relationships of direct and indirect objects in sentences.

◆ ESL NOTES: (1) In sentences with indirect objects that follow the word *to* or *for*, always put the direct object before the indirect object.

NO   Will you please give **to John** this letter?

YES   Will you please give this letter **to John**?

(2) When a pronoun is used as an indirect object, always use *to* or *for* before the pronoun.

NO   Please explain **me** the rule.

YES   Please explain the rule to **me**. ◆

EXERCISE 7-6

Consulting section 7l, draw a single line under all direct objects and a double line under all indirect objects.

EXAMPLE   Television-watching guarantees <u>injury</u> <u>to people</u> by the thousands every year, a British survey claims.

SENTENCE PATTERNS: GROUP II

53

- COMPLETE SUBJECT + COMPLETE PREDICATE
  The caller   offered   money.
                                        ↑   ↑
                                      VERB   DIRECT OBJECT

- COMPLETE SUBJECT + COMPLETE PREDICATE
  The caller   offered the lawyer money.
                                ↑   ↑   ↑
                              VERB   INDIRECT   DIRECT
                                      OBJECT   OBJECT

---

1. Gory scenes on television give some people such a severe fright that they faint.
2. Others are injured when they try ironing or perhaps painting while they give the television screen their full attention.
3. Last month, the survey reports, one person threw a glass at the screen and sprained his wrist.
4. Another person gave her knee a bad twist while dancing along with a music video.
5. Also, an enthusiastic sports fan jumped for joy and banged his head on a chandelier.

7m Recognizing complements, modifiers, and appositives

1 Recognizing complements

A **complement** occurs in the predicate° of a sentence. It renames or describes a subject° or an object°.

A **subject complement** is a noun°, pronoun°, or adjective° that follows a linking verb° (for an explanation of linking verbs, see 8a, especially Chart 58). Some systems of grammar use the term **predicate nominative** for a noun used as a subject complement and the term **predicate adjective** for an adjective used as a subject complement.

187

SENTENCE PATTERNS: GROUP III		54

■ COMPLETE SUBJECT   +   COMPLETE PREDICATE
The caller   was   a   student.

              LINKING   SUBJECT
              VERB   COMPLEMENT

■ COMPLETE SUBJECT   +   COMPLETE PREDICATE
The student   called   himself   a   victim.

           VERB   DIRECT   OBJECT
                  OBJECT   COMPLEMENT

An **object complement** is a noun° or an adjective° that follows a direct object° (see section 7l) and either describes or renames it. Chart 54 shows the relationships of subject complements and object complements in sentences.

EXERCISE 7-7

Consulting section 7m-1, underline all complements and identify each as a subject complement (SUB) or an object complement (OB).

EXAMPLE   Most Canadians rate their water supply <u>acceptable</u>.

1. Industrial waste and pesticides can make water hazardous to drink, however.
2. The purity of river water is often suspect.
3. Water that looks, smells, or tastes peculiar should be tested for pollutants.
4. Even clean-looking water may be contaminated.
5. Home filter systems can make water safe.

2 | **Recognizing modifiers**

A **modifier** is a word or group of words that functions as an adjective° or adverb°. Modifiers can appear in the subject° or the predicate° of a sentence.

The **large red** telephone rang. [Adjectives *large* and *red* modify the noun *telephone*.]

The lawyer answered **quickly.** [The adverb *quickly* modifes the verb *answered*.]

The person **on the telephone** was **extremely** upset. [The prepositional phrase° *on the telephone* modifes the noun *person*; the adverb *extremely* modifies the adjective *upset*.]

Therefore, the lawyer spoke **gently.** [The adverb° *therefore* modifies the independent clause° *the lawyer spoke gently*; the adverb *gently* modifies the verb *spoke*.]

Because the lawyer's voice was calm, the caller felt reassured. [The adverb clause° *because the lawyer's voice was calm* modifies the independent clause *the caller felt reassured*.]

3   Recognizing appositives

An **appositive** is a word or group of words that renames the noun° or pronoun° preceding it.

The student's story, **a tale of broken promises,** was complicated. [*A tale of broken promises* is an appositive that renames the noun *story*.]

The lawyer consulted an expert, **her law professor.** [*Her law professor* is an appositive that renames the noun *expert*.]

The student, **Jamil Amin,** asked to speak to his lawyer. [*Jamil Amin* is an appositive that renames the noun *student*.]

❖ PUNCTUATION ALERT: When an appositive is not essential for identifying the noun or pronoun it renames (that is, when an appositive is nonrestrictive), use a comma or commas to set it off from whatever it renames and any words following it (see 24e-2). ❖

7n   Recognizing phrases

A **phrase** is a group of related words that does not contain both a subject° and a predicate°. A phrase cannot stand alone as an independent unit. Phrases function as parts of speech. A **noun phrase** functions as a noun° in a sentence.

The **modern population census** dates back to the **seventeenth century.**

A **verb phrase** functions as a verb° in a sentence.

Two military censuses **are mentioned** in the Bible.

The Romans **had been conducting** censuses every five years to establish tax liabilities.

A **prepositional phrase** always starts with a preposition° and functions as a modifier°.

After the collapse **of Rome,** censuses were discontinued **until modern times.** [*After the collapse, of Rome,* and *until modern times* are all prepositional phrases.]

William the Conqueror conducted a census **of landowners in newly conquered England in 1086.** [three prepositional phrases in a row beginning with *of, in, in*]

An **absolute phrase** usually contains a noun or pronoun and a participle°. It modifies the entire sentence to which it is attached.

Censuses being the fashion, Quebec and Nova Scotia took sixteen counts between 1665 and 1754.

Eighteenth-century Sweden and Denmark had complete records of their populations, **each adult and child having been accounted for.**

A **verbal phrase** is a word group that contains a verbal. Verbals are infinitives°, present participles°, and past participles°. **Infinitive phrases** function as nouns° or modifiers°. (An infinitive is the simple form° of a verb, usually preceded by the word *to;* see 8b.) **Participial phrases** function as adjectives°. Participial phrases can be formed from a verb's present participle (its *-ing* form) and from its past participle (the *-ed* form of a regular verb or the irregular form; see 8d).

In 1624, Virginia began **to count its citizens** in a census. [infinitive phrase = direct object]

Going from door to door, census takers interview millions of people. [participial phrase = adjective modifying *census takers*]

Amazed by some people's answers, the census takers always listen carefully. [participial phrase = adjective modifying *census takers*]

Gerund phrases function as nouns°. Telling the difference between a gerund phrase and a participial phrase using a present participle can be tricky because both use the *-ing* verb form. The key is to determine how the verbal phrase is functioning: a gerund phrase functions only as a noun°, and a participial phrase functions only as a modifier°.

Including each person in the census was important. [gerund phrase = noun used as the subject]

Including each person in the census, Abby spent many hours on the crowded city block. [participial phrase = modifier used as adjective describing *Abby*]

EXERCISE 7-8

Consulting section 7n, combine each set of sentences into a single sentence, converting one sentence in each set into a phrase. Choose from among noun phrases, verb phrases, prepositional phrases, participial phrases, and gerund phrases. You can omit, add, or change words. Most sets can be combined in several equally correct ways, but be sure to check that your combined sentence makes sense.

EXAMPLE   North American pioneer literature is filled with many supposedly authentic accounts of wolves attacking humans. It does not, however, provide definite evidence that a wolf has ever killed a human in North America.

North American pioneer literature, filled with many supposedly authentic accounts of wolves attacking humans, does not, however, provide definite evidence that a wolf has ever killed a human in North America. [verbal (participial) phrase]

1. Wolves possess speed, stamina, and strength. They have rich vocal communication and body language and a highly developed sense of smell.

2. In Canada, wolves number about 60 000. They inhabit 90 percent of the country.

3. Many wolves live in Algonquin Park. This wilderness area is in the Canadian Shield. It was established as a protected area in 1893.

4. Some people have an image of Canada as a wilderness country. Less than 6 percent of Canada's land is actually legally protected as wilderness.

5. People often believe that travelling alone in wolf country is hazardous. They have read too much Jack London.

6. Wolves are wandering, secretive hunters. Their biology and behaviour are thus difficult to study.

7. Wolves do much of their hunting in winter. They prey on moose and deer. They prey on these animals so that they can survive in this time of stress.

8. Wolves exhibit many cooperative characteristics. They mate for life and raise their young together.

9. Wolves can be playful with their pups. They rank second only to humans in their social bonding and care-giving skills.

10. Hunting or trapping of wolves goes on in fully 65 percent of Canadian wilderness areas. This fact is rarely acknowledged.

7o   Recognizing clauses

A **clause** is a group of words that contains a subject° and a predicate°. Clauses are divided into two categories: **independent clauses** (also known as **main clauses**) and **dependent clauses** (also known as **subordinate clauses**).

1   Recognizing independent clauses

An **independent clause** contains a subject° and a predicate°. It can stand alone as a sentence because it is an independent grammatical unit (see 7j). Chart 55 shows the basic pattern.

2   Recognizing dependent clauses

A **dependent clause** contains a subject° and a predicate° but cannot stand alone as a sentence. A dependent clause must be joined to an independent clause (see 7o-1).

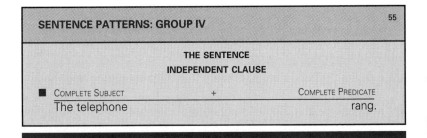

SENTENCE PATTERNS: GROUP IV		55
THE SENTENCE		
INDEPENDENT CLAUSE		
■ COMPLETE SUBJECT	+	COMPLETE PREDICATE
The telephone		rang.

Some dependent clauses start with subordinating conjunctions such as *although, because, when, until*. A subordinating conjunction expresses a relationship between the meaning in the dependent clause and the meaning in the independent clause (see Chart 51). Clauses that start with subordinating conjunctions function as adverbs° and so are called **adverb clauses** (or sometimes **subordinate clauses**).

Adverb clauses usually answer some question about the independent clause: *how? why? when? under what circumstances?* Adverb clauses modify verbs°, adjectives°, other adverbs, and entire independent clauses.

✤ PUNCTUATION ALERT: When an adverb clause comes before its independent clause, the clauses are usually separated by a comma (see 24b-1). ✤

If the vote passes, the city will install sewers. [The adverb clause modifies the verb *install;* the clause explains "under what conditions."]

They are drawing up plans **as quickly as they can.** [The adverb clause modifies the verb *drawing up;* it explains "how."]

The homeowners feel happier **because they know the flooding will soon be better controlled.** [The adverb clause modifies the entire independent clause; it explains "why."]

Adjective clauses (also called *relative clauses*) start with relative pronouns°, the most common of which are *who, which,* and *that,* or relative adverbs° such as *when* or *where.* An adjective clause modifies the noun° or pronoun° that it follows.

The car **that Jack bought** is practical. [The adjective clause describes the noun *car; that* refers to *car.*]

The day **when I can buy my own car** is getting closer. [The adjective clause modifies the noun *day; when* refers to *day.*]

Chart 56 shows common sentence patterns for adverb and adjective clauses.

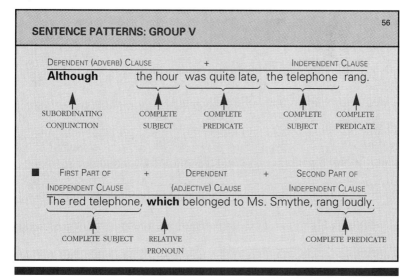

SENTENCE PATTERNS: GROUP V 56

DEPENDENT (ADVERB) CLAUSE	+		INDEPENDENT CLAUSE	
Although	the hour	was quite late,	the telephone	rang.
↑	↑	↑	↑	↑
SUBORDINATING CONJUNCTION	COMPLETE SUBJECT	COMPLETE PREDICATE	COMPLETE SUBJECT	COMPLETE PREDICATE

■ FIRST PART OF INDEPENDENT CLAUSE	+	DEPENDENT (ADJECTIVE) CLAUSE	+	SECOND PART OF INDEPENDENT CLAUSE
The red telephone,	**which**	belonged to Ms. Smythe,		rang loudly.
↑	↑			↑
COMPLETE SUBJECT	RELATIVE PRONOUN			COMPLETE PREDICATE

When you write adjective clauses, use *who, whom, whoever, whomever,* and *whose* when the antecedent° is a person or an animal with a name.

> The di Pietros, **who collect cars,** are wealthy.

> Their dog Bowser, **who is quite large,** is spoiled.

When you write adjective clauses, use *which* or *that* if the antecedent° is a thing or an animal. Either *which* or *that* begins restrictive° adjective clauses, and *which* begins nonrestrictive° ones.

❖ PUNCTUATION ALERT: When an adjective clause is nonrestrictive, use commas to separate it from the independent clause°. (A restrictive clause is essential to limit meaning; a nonrestrictive clause is non-essential; see 24e.)

> The car **that I want to buy** has a cassette player.

> The car **which I want to buy** has a cassette player. [The adjective clause is restrictive, and so either *that* or *which* may be used.]

> My current car, **which I bought used,** needs major repairs. [The adjective clause is nonrestrictive, so it begins with *which* and is set off with commas.] ❖

Sometimes, *that* can be omitted from a sentence. For purposes of grammatical analysis, however, the omitted *that* is considered to be implied and therefore present.

> The car [that] I buy will have to get good mileage.

❖ ALERT: Omitting the word *that* can make a sentence harder to understand. Be sure to use *that* when it makes your writing clearer.

> **NO**   I know Dale Smythe, who won a car in a raffle, is selling it.

> **YES**   I know **that** Dale Smythe, who won a car in a raffle, is selling it. ❖

EXERCISE 7-9

Consulting section 7o-2, underline the dependent clauses. Write ADJ at the end of adjective clauses and ADV at the end of adverb clauses.

EXAMPLE   *When cooks on São Miguel island in the Azores decide to prepare their favourite stew,* they dig a hole on the shores of Lake Furnas.

1. Although São Miguel's Furnas volcano erupted thousands of years ago, the collapsed mountain top formed a lake bed that is still hot.

2. The ground around Lake Furnas acts as a natural oven because its temperature is more than 93°C.

3. To prepare the famous stew, which is called *cozido*, cooks assemble chicken, beef, sausage, and vegetables in a pan.

4. After the pan is tied in a cloth bag, it is buried in the hole.

5. The *cozido* simmers for about six hours, a cooking time that brings it to tasty perfection.

Noun clauses often begin with many of the same words as adjective clauses: *that, who, which,* and their derivatives, as well as *when, where, whether, why,* or *how.* Noun clauses, however, do not modify; they replace nouns.

Promises are not always dependable. [noun]

What politicians promise is not always dependable. [noun clause]

The electorate often cannot figure out the **truth.** [noun]

The electorate often cannot know **that the truth is being manipulated.** [noun clause]

Because they start with similar words, noun clauses and adjective clauses are sometimes confused with each other. A noun clause *is* a subject°, object°, or complement°. An adjective clause *modifies* a subject, object, or complement. The word starting an adjective clause has an antecedent° in the sentence. The word starting a noun clause does not.

Politicians understand **whom they must please.** [Noun clause is an object; *whom* does not need an antecedent here.]

Politicians **who make promises** sometimes fail to keep them. [Adjective clause modifies *politicians*, which is the antecedent of *who*.]

◆ ESL NOTE: Noun clauses in indirect questions are phrased as statements, not questions: *Kara asked why we needed the purple dye.* Avoid such sentences as *Kara asked why did* [or *do*] *we need the purple dye?* Tense, pronoun, and other changes may be necessary when a direct question is rephrased as an indirect question; see 15a-4. ◆

Elliptical clauses are grammatically incomplete for the deliberate purpose of concise prose (see Chapter 16). The term *elliptical* comes from the word *ellipsis,* meaning "omission." An elliptical clause delivers its meaning only if the context makes clear what the missing elements are. Common are *that* or *which* in adjective clauses, *that* in some noun clauses, subject and verb in adverb clauses, and the second half of comparisons.

Engineering is one of the majors **[that] she considered.** [relative pronoun omitted from adjective clause]

She decided **[that] she would prefer to major in management**. [relative pronoun omitted from noun clause]

After [he takes] a refresher course, he will be eligible for a raise. [subject and verb omitted from adverb clause]

Broiled fish tastes better **than boiled fish [tastes]**. [second half of the comparison omitted]

Sometimes an omission, although grammatically acceptable, interferes with the ability of a sentence to deliver its meaning, so omit nothing that helps to establish clarity.

EXERCISE 7-10

Consulting section 7o, use some of the subordinating conjunctions and relative pronouns from this list to combine each of the following pairs of sentences. Some pairs may be combined in a variety of ways. Create at least one elliptical construction. Subordinators may be used more than once, but try to use as many different ones as possible.

EXAMPLE   Famine occurs. Insects or rodents destroy crops or stored food.

> *When insects or rodents destroy crops or stored food, famine occurs.*

which	because	of which	since	if
while	as	how	that	although

1. Destruction of crops has been a problem for ages. The human race has an equally long history of trying to eliminate pests.
2. The earliest pesticides were not very effective. The earliest pesticides included sulphur, lead, mercury, and arsenic.
3. We now realize something. These original pesticides are poisonous.
4. They accumulate in the soil. They can limit or stop plant growth.
5. Some pests develop immunity to the chemicals. The pests are never completely destroyed.
6. The surviving pests reproduce quickly, passing on resistant genes. A new generation of resistant pests takes the place of those killed.
7. New pesticides are manufactured organic chemicals. The most famous is DDT, dichlorodiphenyltrichloroethane.
8. No one thought about something. DDT would contaminate and threaten the entire planet.
9. Some birds have trouble forming eggs. DDT accumulates in them.
10. In 1971 a special committee began reviewing pollutants. DDT was one.

7p   Recognizing sentence types

Sentences can be **simple, compound, complex,** and **compound-complex.**

A **simple sentence** is composed of a single independent clause° with no dependent clauses°.

Charlie Chaplin was born in London on April 16, 1889.

A mime, he became famous for his character the Little Tramp.

A **compound sentence** is composed of two or more independent clauses. These clauses may be connected by a coordinating conjunction (*and, but, for, or, nor, yet,* or *so*) or by a semicolon alone or with a conjunctive adverb.

✣ PUNCTUATION ALERT: Use a comma before a coordinating conjunction connecting two independent clauses; see 24a.

His father died early, **and** his mother spent time in mental hospitals.

Many people enjoy Chaplin films; others do not.

Many people enjoy Chaplin films; **however,** others do not. ✣

A **complex sentence** is composed of one independent clause and one or more dependent clauses.

✣ PUNCTUATION ALERT: When a dependent clause comes before its independent clause, the clauses are usually separated by a comma (see 24b-1).

When times were bad, Chaplin lived in the streets. [dependent clause starting *When;* independent clause starting *Chaplin*]

When Chaplin was performing with a troupe that was touring the United States, he was hired by Mack Sennett, **who owned the Keystone Comedies.** [dependent clause starting *When;* dependent clause starting *that;* independent clause starting *he;* dependent clause starting *who*] ✣

A **compound-complex sentence** joins a compound sentence and a complex sentence. It contains two or more independent clauses and one or more dependent clauses.

Chaplin's comedies were immediately successful, **and** his salaries were huge **because of the enormous popularity of his tramp character, who was famous for his tiny mustache, baggy trousers, big shoes, and trick derby.** [independent clause starting *Chaplin's;* independent clause starting *his salaries;* dependent clause starting *because;* dependent clause starting *who*]

197

Once studios could no longer afford him, Chaplin co-founded United Artists, **and** then he was able to produce and distribute his own films. [dependent clause starting *Once;* independent clause starting *Chaplin;* independent clause starting *then he was able*]

EXERCISE 7-11

Consulting section 7p, identify each sentence as simple, compound, complex, or compound-complex.

EXAMPLE   On his expedition to Newfoundland in 1583, Sir Humphrey Gilbert included a group of musicians and entertainers among his crew. *(simple)*

1. The first recorded performance of a play in French Canada took place at Port Royal on November 14, 1606.

2. The play, which was called *Théâtre de Neptune en la Nouvelle-France,* is the first recorded dramatic performance in North America.

3. The British also brought their tradition of theatre when they arrived in Canada, for as early as 1773 soldiers of the garrison in Halifax performed Benjamin Hoadly's comedy *The Suspicious Husband.*

4. The first plays to be written in English in Canada followed foreign models, and these included *Ponteach, or, The Savages of America; The New Gentle Shepherd;* and *Acadius, or, Love in a Calm.*

5. Garrison theatre is often cited as the origin for the development of Canadian drama, but civilian amateur and professional theatre also existed in the eighteenth and early nineteenth centuries.

6. During the French regime in Quebec, many dramatic performances were given, yet the opposition of the church and the widely dispersed population of the colony prevented the establishment of a powerful theatrical tradition.

7. In the nineteenth century, the church continued to condemn touring performers who visited Quebec as godless and immoral, and even Sarah Bernhardt was denounced from the pulpit when she first appeared in Quebec in 1880.

8. From the first days of the colonies, drama was used as the vehicle for political satire, not only on stage but also in pamphlets and newspapers.

9. By the 1850s most towns had a theatre or "opera house," and the larger centres could support resident companies on a long-time basis and provide lavishly decorated and well-equipped facilities.

10. Toward the end of the nineteenth century, the theatre had established itself successfully in Canada; about forty theatres across the country could provide seating for a thousand patrons, and in some years as many as three hundred troupes toured and performed.

8. Verbs

8a Understanding verbs

Verbs convey information about what is happening, what has happened, and what will happen. In English, a verb tells of an action, an occurrence, or a state of being.

> Many people **overeat** on Thanksgiving. [action]
>
> Mother's Day **fell** early this year. [occurrence]
>
> New Year's Day **is** tomorrow. [state of being]

To understand more about the information verbs convey and the various types of verbs, see Chart 57.

OVERVIEW OF VERBS	57

INFORMATION VERBS CONVEY

PERSON	Who or what acts or experiences an action—**first person** (the one speaking), **second person** (the one being spoken to), or **third person** (the person or thing being spoken about).
NUMBER	How many subjects act or experience an action—**singular** (one) or **plural** (more than one).
TENSE	When an action occurs—in the **past, present,** or **future;** see 8g–8k.
MOOD	What attitude is expressed toward the action—**indicative, imperative,** or **subjunctive;** see 8l–8m.
VOICE	Whether the subject acts or is acted upon—**active voice** or **passive voice;** see 8n–8o. ➜

| OVERVIEW OF VERBS *(continued)* | 57 |

TYPES OF VERBS

MAIN VERB — A verb expressing action, occurrence, or state of being.
She **talked** to the group.

LINKING VERB — A main verb that conveys a state of being (*is*), relates to the senses (*taste*), or indicates a condition (*grow*) and that joins a subject to a word or words that rename or describe it. (More about linking verbs follows this chart.)
She **was** happy about speaking.

AUXILIARY VERB — A verb that combines with a main verb to convey information about tense, mood, or voice.
She **has** talked to them before.
Modal auxiliary verbs° include *can, could, may, might, should, would, must*, and others that add shades of meaning such as ability or possibility to verbs (see 8e and Chapter 46ESL).

TRANSITIVE VERB — A verb that must be followed by a direct object°—a noun° or pronoun° that completes the verb's message (see 8f).
She **spoke** *French* to them.

INTRANSITIVE VERB — A verb that does not have a direct object completing its message (see 8f).
She **talked** slowly.

Linking verbs are main verbs that indicate a state of being or a condition. They link a subject with a **subject complement**—a word (or words) that renames or describes the subject.

Some systems of grammar use the term **predicate nominative** for a subject complement that is a noun° or pronoun° renaming the subject and the term **predicate adjective** for a subject complement that is an adjective° describing the subject.

Some people consider a linking verb as an equal sign between a subject and its complement. Chart 58 presents an overview of linking verbs.

LINKING VERBS   58

- Linking verbs may be forms of the verb *to be* (*am, is, was, were*; see 8e for a complete list).

  Pierre Trudeau   **was**   prime minister.
  ‾‾‾‾‾‾‾‾‾‾‾‾   ‾‾‾   ‾‾‾‾‾‾‾‾‾‾‾‾
  SUBJECT   LINKING VERB   COMPLEMENT (PREDICATE
                                          NOMINATIVE: RENAMES SUBJECT)

- Linking verbs may deal with the senses (*look, smell, taste, sound,* and *feel*).

  Pierre Trudeau   **sounded**   confident.
  ‾‾‾‾‾‾‾‾‾‾‾‾   ‾‾‾‾‾‾‾   ‾‾‾‾‾‾‾‾‾
  SUBJECT   LINKING VERB   COMPLEMENT (PREDICATE
                                          ADJECTIVE: DESCRIBES SUBJECT)

- Certain other verbs that convey a sense of existing or becoming— *appear, seem, become, get, grow, turn, remain, stay,* and *prove,* for example—can be linking verbs.

  Pierre Trudeau   **grew**   old.
  ‾‾‾‾‾‾‾‾‾‾‾‾   ‾‾‾‾   ‾‾‾
  SUBJECT   LINKING VERB   COMPLEMENT (PREDICATE
                                          ADJECTIVE: DESCRIBES SUBJECT)

- To test whether a verb other than a form of *to be* is functioning as a linking verb, substitute *was* (for a singular subject) or *were* (for a plural subject) for the original verb. If the sentence makes sense, the original verb is functioning as a linking verb.

  NO   Pierre Trudeau **grew** a beard → Pierre Trudeau **was** a beard. [*Grew* is not functioning as a linking verb.]

  YES   Pierre Trudeau **grew** old → Pierre Trudeau **was** old. [*Grew* is functioning as a linking verb.]

VERB FORMS

8b ### Recognizing the forms of main verbs

A **main verb** names an action (*people **dance***), an occurrence (*Mother's Day **fell** early this year*), or a state of being (*New Year's Day **is** tomorrow*). Every main verb has five forms.

- The **simple form** conveys an action, occurrence, or state of being taking place in the present (*I **laugh***) or, with an auxiliary verb°, in the future (*I **will laugh***).

201

■ The **past-tense form** is the basis for conveying an action, occurrence, or state completed in the past (*I **laughed***). Regular verbs° add *-ed* or *-d* to the simple form. Irregular verbs° vary; see Chart 59.

■ The **past-participle form** in regular verbs uses the same form as the past tense. Irregular verbs vary; see Chart 59. To function as a verb, a past participle must combine with a subject° and one or more auxiliary verbs: *I **have laughed***. Otherwise, past participles function as adjectives°: ***crumbled cookies.***

■ The **present-participle form** adds *-ing* to the simple form (*laughing*). To function as a verb, a present participle combines with a subject and one or more auxiliary verbs (*I **was laughing***). Otherwise, present participles function as adjectives (*my **laughing** friends*) or as nouns° (***laughing** is healthy*).

■ The **infinitive** uses the simple form, usually but not always following to (*I started **to laugh***). The infinitive functions as a noun or an adjective, not a verb.

◆ ESL NOTE: When they function as parts of speech other than verbs, verb forms are called verbals° (see 7d). Present participles functioning as nouns are called gerunds°. For information about using gerunds and infinitives as objects after certain verbs, see Chapter 45ESL. ◆

8c   Using the *-s* form of verbs

The *-s* form of a verb occurs in the third-person singular in the present tense°. The *-s* ending is added to a verb's simple form: *smell, smells.*

The bread **smells** delicious.

The verbs *be* and *have* are irregular verbs. For the third-person singular, present tense, *be* uses **is** and *have* uses **has.**

The cheesecake **is** popular.

The eclair **has** chocolate on top.

Even if you tend to drop the *-s* or *-es* ending when you speak, do not forget to use it when you write. Proofread carefully for the correct use of the *-s* form. (For an explanation of the *-s* form of verbs in subject–verb agreement, see 11b.)

EXERCISE 8-1

Consulting sections 8b and 8c, rewrite each sentence, changing the subject to the word given in parentheses. Change the form of the italicized verb to match this new subject. Keep all sentences in the present tense.

EXAMPLE   Often in literature, a colourful figure *suggests* particular feelings or special characteristics. (colourful figures)

Often in literature, *colourful figures suggest* particular feelings or special characteristics.

1. A green figure *appears* in ancient folklore. (Green figures)
2. These characters *represent* nature, fertility, and growing things. (This character)
3. This fertility symbol *takes* part in dances and other celebrations of spring's return. (These fertility symbols)
4. In many cultures, any signs of spring *trigger* festivals that *emphasize* the colour green. (any sign of spring) (a festival)
5. Today, a person who *has* a talent for gardening *is* said to have a green thumb, and green giants *adorn* one company's cans of vegetables. (people who) (a green giant)

8d Using regular and irregular verbs

A **regular verb** forms its past tense and past participle by adding -*ed* or -*d* to the simple form. Most verbs in English are regular. Some English verbs are **irregular.** They form the past tense and past participle in various ways. For a list of the most common irregular verbs, see Chart 59.

❖ SPELLING ALERT: For information about when to change a *y* to an *i* when adding the -*ed* ending, see 22c. For information about when to double a final consonant before the -*ed* ending, see 22c. ❖

Speakers sometimes skip over the -*ed* sound, hitting the sound lightly or not at all. Even if you are not used to hearing or pronouncing this sound, do not forget to add it when you write. Proofread carefully for -*ed* endings.

NO   The cake was **suppose** to be tasty.

YES   The cake was **supposed** to be tasty.

About two hundred verbs in English are **irregular.** Unfortunately, a verb's simple form does not provide a clue about whether the verb is irregular or regular. Irregular verbs do not consistently add *-ed* or *-d* to form the past tense and past participle. Some irregular verbs change an internal vowel to make past tense and past participle: *sing, sang, sung.* Some change an internal vowel and add an ending other than *-ed* or *-d: grow, grew, grown.* Some use the simple form throughout: *cost, cost, cost.*

Although you can always look up the principal parts of any verb, memorizing any you do not know is much more efficient in the long run. The most frequently used irregular verbs are listed in Chart 59.

COMMON IRREGULAR VERBS   59

SIMPLE FORM	PAST TENSE	PAST PARTICIPLE
arise	arose	arisen
awake	awoke *or* awaked	awaked *or* awoken
be (is, am, are)	was, were	been
bear	bore	borne *or* born
beat	beat	beaten
become	became	become
begin	began	begun
bend	bent	bent
bet	bet	bet
bid (offer)	bid	bid
bid (command)	bade	bidden
bind	bound	bound
bite	bit	bitten *or* bit
blow	blew	blown
break	broke	broken
bring	brought	brought
build	built	built
burst	burst	burst
buy	bought	bought
cast	cast	cast
catch	caught	caught
choose	chose	chosen
cling	clung	clung
come	came	come

COMMON IRREGULAR VERBS *(continued)*

SIMPLE FORM	PAST TENSE	PAST PARTICIPLE
cost	cost	cost
creep	crept	crept
cut	cut	cut
deal	dealt	dealt
dig	dug	dug
dive	dived *or* dove	dived
do	did	done
draw	drew	drawn
drink	drank	drunk
drive	drove	driven
eat	ate	eaten
fall	fell	fallen
feed	fed	fed
feel	felt	felt
fight	fought	fought
find	found	found
flee	fled	fled
fling	flung	flung
fly	flew	flown
forbid	forbade *or* forbad	forbidden
forget	forgot	forgotten *or* forgot
forgive	forgave	forgiven
forsake	forsook	forsaken
freeze	froze	frozen
get	got	got *or* gotten
give	gave	given
go	went	gone
grow	grew	grown
hang (suspend)*	hung	hung
have	had	had

*When it means to execute by hanging, hang is a regular verb: "In wartime, armies routinely hanged deserters."

➔

COMMON IRREGULAR VERBS *(continued)*

SIMPLE FORM	PAST TENSE	PAST PARTICIPLE
hear	heard	heard
hide	hid	hidden
hit	hit	hit
hurt	hurt	hurt
keep	kept	kept
know	knew	known
lay	laid	laid
lead	led	led
leave	left	left
lend	lent	lent
let	let	let
lie	lay	lain
light	lighted *or* lit	lighted *or* lit
lose	lost	lost
make	made	made
mean	meant	meant
pay	paid	paid
prove	proved	proved *or* proven
quit	quit	quit
read	read	read
rid	rid	rid
ride	rode	ridden
ring	rang	rung
rise	rose	risen
run	ran	run
say	said	said
see	saw	seen
seek	sought	sought
send	sent	sent
set	set	set
shake	shook	shaken
shine (glow)[*]	shone	shone
shoot	shot	shot

[*]When it means to polish, shine is a regular verb: "We shined our shoes."

COMMON IRREGULAR VERBS *(continued)*

SIMPLE FORM	PAST TENSE	PAST PARTICIPLE
show	showed	shown *or* showed
shrink	shrank	shrunk
sing	sang	sung
sink	sank *or* sunk	sunk
sit	sat	sat
slay	slew	slain
sleep	slept	slept
sling	slung	slung
speak	spoke	spoken
spend	spent	spent
spin	spun	spun
spring	sprang *or* sprung	sprung
stand	stood	stood
steal	stole	stolen
sting	stung	stung
stink	stank *or* stunk	stunk
stride	strode	stridden
strike	struck	struck
strive	strove	striven
swear	swore	sworn
sweep	swept	swept
swim	swam	swum
swing	swung	swung
take	took	taken
teach	taught	taught
tear	tore	torn
tell	told	told
think	thought	thought
throw	threw	thrown
understand	understood	understood
wake	woke *or* waked	waked *or* woken
wear	wore	worn
wring	wrung	wrung
write	wrote	written

EXERCISE 8-2

Consulting section 8d, in each blank write the correct past-tense form of the regular verb (simple form) in parentheses.

EXAMPLE   Rising annual temperatures over the last ten years (cause) **caused** many scientists to predict climate changes.

(1) The 1980s (contain) _____ six of the warmest years ever recorded. (2) Some scientists (believe) _____ that rises and falls in annual temperatures (occur) _____ naturally over time. (3) Others (fear) _____ that human behaviour (contribute) _____ to a warming climate. (4) They (point) _____ out that fossil fuels (release) _____ gases that (act) _____ like a layer of insulation around the earth. (5) This layer (absorb) _____ heat and (warm) _____ the earth's atmosphere.

EXERCISE 8-3

Consulting section 8d, in each blank write the correct past-tense form of the irregular verb (simple form) in parentheses. Use the list of irregular verbs in Chart 59.

EXAMPLE   The colourful butterflies (begin) **began** to arrive a few at a time in November.

(1) As the month of November (wear) _____ on, millions of black, white, and orange flocks of monarch butterflies (fly) _____ through the sky. (2) Scientists (know) _____ that the monarch butterfly (have) _____ been migrating between Canada and Mexico for more than ten thousand years. (3) Zoologists (rise) _____ early to observe the migration of these butterflies. (4) In 1975, the scientists (find) _____ evidence suggesting that monarch butterflies might be threatened by the destruction of the Mexican forests for farmland. (5) A group concerned about the monarchs (seek) _____ help from the Mexican government, which in 1980 (take) _____ legal steps to protect the butterflies. (6) Laws were passed that (make) _____ it illegal to establish agricultural development in or around the monarch retreats. (7) The laws also (forbid) _____ logging, an industry essential to many local residents. (8) Conservation groups (understand) _____ the peasants' concerns and (begin) _____ looking for ways to help these people. (9) For example, scientists (seek) _____ ways to improve production of crops that (grow) _____ on existing farmland. (10) Also, residents of the area (lead) _____ tours of sightseers through the regions.

8e Using auxiliary verbs

Auxiliary verbs, also called **helping verbs,** combine with main verbs° to make verb phrases°.

AUXILIARY VERB · MAIN VERB

■ I **am** **shopping** for new shoes.

VERB PHRASE

AUXILIARY VERB · MAIN VERB

■ Clothing prices **have** **soared** recently.

VERB PHRASE

AUXILIARY VERB · MAIN VERB

■ Leather shoes **might** **cost** hundreds of dollars.

VERB PHRASE

Auxiliary verbs deserve special attention because they occur very frequently in English. Also, the forms of the three most common auxiliaries—*be, do,* and *have*—vary more than usual; see Charts 60 and 61.

THE FORMS OF THE VERB *BE*			60
SIMPLE FORM	be	-*S* FORM	is
PAST TENSE	was, were	PRESENT PARTICIPLE	being
PAST PARTICIPLE	been		

PERSON	PRESENT TENSE	PAST TENSE
I	am	was
you (singular)	are	were
he, she, it	is	was
we	are	were
you (plural)	are	were
they	are	were

❖ ALERT: The verb *be*, along with its various forms, can also function as a *linking verb* (see Chart 58). In joining a subject° to a subject complement°, it acts as a main verb° rather than an auxiliary verb. Academic writing requires standard forms and uses of the verb *be* as a main verb and as an auxiliary verb.

> The gym **is** [not *be*] a busy place. [*Gym* is the subject; *is* is the linking verb, which acts as a main verb; *busy place* is the subject complement.]

> The gym **is** [not *be*] filling with spectators. [*Gym* is the subject; *is* is the auxiliary verb and *filling* is the main verb; together *is filling* is a verb phrase.] ❖

THE FORMS OF THE VERBS *DO* AND *HAVE*

61

SIMPLE FORM	do	**SIMPLE FORM**	have
PAST TENSE	did	**PAST TENSE**	had
PAST PARTICIPLE	done	**PAST PARTICIPLE**	had
-S FORM	does	**-S FORM**	has
PRESENT PARTICIPLE	doing	**PRESENT PARTICIPLE**	having

◆ ESL NOTE: When an auxiliary verb is used with a main verb, the auxiliary may change form to agree with a third-person singular subject, but the main verb does not change.

NO	**Does** the library **closes** at 6:00?
YES	**Does** the library **close** at 6:00? ◆

The verbs *can, could, may, might, must, shall, should, will,* and *would* are **modal auxiliary verbs.** Modal auxiliaries work in concert with the simple form° of main verbs to communicate a meaning of ability, permission, obligation, advisability, necessity, or possibility.

> Exercise **can lengthen** lives. [possibility]

> The exercise **must occur** regularly. [necessity, obligation]

> People **should protect** their bodies. [advisability]

> **May** I **exercise?** [permission]

> She **can jog** for five miles. [ability]

◆ ESL NOTE: For more about modal auxiliary verbs and the meanings they communicate, see Chapter 46ESL. ◆

EXERCISE 8-4

Consulting section 8e, use auxiliary verbs from the list below to fill in the blanks. Use each auxiliary verb only once.

~~might~~   can   was   will   have   would

EXAMPLE   A shy person or one who is nervous about making conversation just **might** find help at Ireland's Blarney Castle.

(1) The block of limestone known as the Blarney Stone _____ set in a tower in 1446 at Blarney Castle. (2) According to legend, when the king of the castle saved an old woman from drowning, she promised the king that if he kissed the stone, he _____ be able to speak sweetly and convincingly. (3) Since then, Irish people claim that anyone who kisses the Blarney Stone _____ receive the gift of eloquence. (4) Today, a person who _____ speak witty words of flattery is said to have "the gift of blarney." (5) Tourists who _____ heard the legend travel to the castle near Cork, Ireland, hoping that the Blarney Stone will work its magic on their words.

EXERCISE 8-5

Consulting section 8e, use each of the auxiliary verbs listed below to fill in the blanks. For some sentences, more than one correct answer is possible, but use each auxiliary verb only once.

must   should   will   can   ~~are~~   do

EXAMPLE   After years of being ignored by car dealers, women **are** finally being recognized as intelligent customers.

(1) In the next few years, women _____ buy about half the cars sold in North America. (2) To be effective, car salespeople _____ pay attention to the woman buyer. (3) The old ideas that women are interested only in style and colour _____ change. (4) Salespeople now realize that women _____ understand technical information about a car's performance. (5) A salesperson _____ expect both men and women buyers to evaluate factors like dependability, value, safety, and comfort.

8f   Using intransitive and transitive verbs

A verb is **intransitive** when an object° is not required to complete its meaning: *I **sing** loudly.* A verb is **transitive** when an object is necessary to complete its meaning: *I **need** a guitar.* Some verbs are transitive only (for example, *need, have, like, owe, remember*).

Many verbs have both transitive and intransitive meanings. Other verbs are transitive only. Dictionaries usually label verbs as transitive (vt) or intransitive (vi). Chart 62 shows how transitive and intransitive verbs function.

COMPARISON OF INTRANSITIVE AND TRANSITIVE VERBS   62

INTRANSITIVE (OBJECT NOT NEEDED)

They **sat** together quietly. [*Together* and *quietly* are not direct objects°; they are modifiers°.]

The cat **sees** in the dark. [*In the dark* is not a direct object; it is a modifier.]

I can **hear** well. [*Well* is not a direct object; it is a modifier.]

TRANSITIVE (OBJECT NEEDED)

They **sent** a birthday card to me. [*a birthday card* = direct object]

The cat **sees** the dog [*dog* = direct object]

I can **hear** you. [*you* = direct object]

The verbs *lie* and *lay* are particularly confusing. *Lie* is intransitive (it cannot be followed by an object). *Lay* is transitive (it must be followed by an object). Some of their forms, however, are similar. Get to know these forms so that you can use them with ease.

	LIE	LAY
SIMPLE FORM	lie	lay
PAST TENSE	lay	laid
PAST PARTICIPLE	lain	laid
-*s* FORM	lies	lays
PRESENT PARTICIPLE	lying	laying

To *lie* means to recline, to place oneself down, or to remain; to *lay* means to place something down. Note from the examples that the word *lay* is both the past tense of *lie* and the present-tense simple form of *lay*.

INTRANSITIVE

PRESENT TENSE   The hikers **lie** down to rest.
PAST TENSE   The hikers **lay** down to rest.

TRANSITIVE

PRESENT TENSE	The hikers **lay** their backpacks on a rock. [*Backpacks* is an object.]
PAST TENSE	The hikers **laid** their backpacks on a rock. [*Backpacks* is an object.]

EXERCISE 8-6

Consulting section 8f, in each blank write the correct word from each pair in parentheses.

EXAMPLE   Memory of last year's outdoor camping trip (lies, lays) **lies** heavy
            on my mind.

(1) Planning on two days and a night in the woods, we left early and were soon (lying, laying) _____ our supplies in the shade of an old oak tree. (2) We were sure the supplies could safely (lay, lie) _____ in that spot all afternoon. (3) When the sun rose higher in the sky, the shade moved so that each bundle of food (lay, laid) _____ in the sun for hours. (4) As the spot where our gear was (laying, lying) _____ heated up, our food over-heated and spoiled. (5) While we (lay, laid) _____ hungry in our tent that night, we vowed not to go camping again.

VERB TENSE

8g Understanding verb tense

Verbs use **tense** to express time. They do this by changing form. English has six verb tenses, divided into simple and perfect groups. The three **simple tenses** divide time into present, past, and future. The **present tense** describes what is happening, what is true at the moment, and what is consistently true: *Rick **wants** to speak Spanish fluently.* The **past tense** tells of an action completed or a condition ended: *Rick **wanted** to improve rapidly.* The **future tense** indicates action yet to be taken or a condition not yet experienced: *Rick **will want** to progress even further next year.*

The three **perfect tenses** also divide time into present, past, and future. They show more complex time relationships than do the simple tenses, as explained in 8i.

The three simple tenses and the three perfect tenses also have **progressive forms.** These forms show an ongoing or a continuing dimension to whatever the verb describes, as explained in 8j. Chart 63 summarizes verb tenses and progressive forms.

SUMMARY OF TENSES—INCLUDING PROGRESSIVE FORMS			63

SIMPLE TENSES

	REGULAR VERB	IRREGULAR VERB	PROGRESSIVE FORM
PRESENT	I talk	I eat	I am talking; I am eating
PAST	I talked	I ate	I was talking; I was eating
FUTURE	I will talk	I will eat	I will be talking; I will be eating

PERFECT TENSES

	REGULAR VERB	IRREGULAR VERB	PROGRESSIVE FORM
PRESENT PERFECT	I have talked	I have eaten	I have been talking; I have been eating
PAST PERFECT	I had talked	I had eaten	I had been talking; I had been eating
FUTURE PERFECT	I will have talked	I will have eaten	I will have been talking; I will have been eating

◆ ESL NOTE: Chart 63 shows that most verb tenses are formed by combining one or more auxiliary verbs° with the simple form°, the present participle°, or the past participle° of a main verb°. Auxiliary verbs are important in the formation of most tenses, so be sure not to omit them.

NO	**I talking** to you.
YES	**I am talking** to you. ◆

8h Using the simple present tense

The **simple present tense** uses the simple form of the verb (see 8b). It describes what happens regularly, what takes place in the present, and what is generally or consistently true. Also, it can express a future occurrence with verbs like *start, stop, begin, end, arrive,* and *depart.*

Calculus class **meets** every morning. [regularly occurring action]

Mastering calculus **takes** time. [general truth]

The course **ends** in eight weeks. [future event with end]

❖ VERB ALERT FOR WRITING ABOUT LITERATURE: Use the present tense to describe or discuss action in a work of literature, no matter how old the work; see 37b-2.

> In Shakespeare's *Romeo and Juliet,* Juliet's father **wants** her to marry Paris, but Juliet **loves** Romeo. ❖

For action prior to or after the action you are describing or discussing, use the correct sequence of tenses as explained in 8k.

8i Forming and using the perfect tenses

The **perfect tenses** generally describe actions or occurrences completed, or to be completed, before a more recent point in time. They use the past participle (see 8b) together with auxiliary verbs° to form verb phrases°. For the present perfect, use *has* for third-person° singular subjects° and *have* for all other subjects, along with the past participle.

PRESENT PERFECT	Our government **has offered** to help. [action completed but condition still in effect]
PRESENT PERFECT	The drought **has created** terrible hardship. [condition completed and still prevailing]
PRESENT PERFECT	We **have always believed** in freedom of speech. [condition true once and still true]

For the past perfect, use *had* with the past participle. For the future perfect, use *will have* with the past participle.

PAST PERFECT	As soon as the tornado **had passed**, the heavy rain started. [Both events occurred in the past; the earlier event, the tornado's passing, was completed before the later event, the rain's starting, took place, so the earlier event uses *had*.]
FUTURE PERFECT	Our chickens' egg production **will have reached** 500 per day by next year. [The event will be complete before a specified or predictable time.]

8j Forming and using progressive forms

Progressive forms show an ongoing action or condition. They also express habitual or recurring actions or conditions. They use the present participle° (the *-ing* form) of the verb together with the appropriate form of the verb *be* as an auxiliary verb°. (See Chart 63.)

For the present progressive, use the form of *be* that fits with the subject in person° and number°, plus the present participle: ***I am** thinking*, ***you are** thinking*, ***she is** thinking*. For the past progressive, use *was* or *were* to fit with the subject in person and number, plus the present participle: ***I was** thinking*, ***you were** thinking*, ***she was** thinking*. For the present perfect progressive, use *have been* or *has been* to fit with the subject. In all other progressive tenses, the auxiliary verbs do not change form to show person and number.

PRESENT PROGRESSIVE	The smog **is stinging** everyone's eyes. [event taking place now]
PAST PROGRESSIVE	Eye drops **were selling** well last week. [event ongoing in the past within stated limits]
FUTURE PROGRESSIVE	We **will be ordering** more eye drops than usual this month. [recurring event that will take place in the future]
PRESENT PERFECT PROGRESSIVE	Scientists **have been warning** us about air pollution for years. [recurring event that took place in the past and may still take place]
PAST PERFECT PROGRESSIVE	We **had been ordering** three cases of eye drops a month until the smog worsened. [recurring past event that has now ended]
FUTURE PERFECT PROGRESSIVE	In May, we **will have owned** this pharmacy for five years. [ongoing condition to be completed at a specific time in the future]

EXERCISE 8-7

Consulting sections 8g through 8j, select the verb in parentheses that best suits the meaning. If more than one answer is possible, be prepared to explain the differences in meaning between the choices.

EXAMPLE   Before 1960, astronomers (have not spotted, had not spotted) stars that send out both light and sound waves.

Before 1960, astronomers *had not spotted* stars that send out both light and sound waves.

1.   In 1960, two astronomers at Mount Palomar Observatory (had discovered, discovered) a starlike object at the edge of the universe.

2.   The astronomers were astounded to discover that this object (emits, was emitting) as much light as 1000 galaxies.

3.   Today, we (use, are using) the name *quasar*, which (stands for, stood for) *quasistellar*. *Quasistellar* (meant, means) "starlike object."

4.   Up to now, more than 300 quasars (had been found, have been found) in space.

5. Although astronomers today generally (had agreed, agree) that quasars are powerful, fast-moving energy sources, they (will contradict, contradict) each other's theories about the origin of quasars.

6. One group currently (has been believing, believes) that quasars (consisted, consist) of giant, swirling masses of gas.

7. These astronomers (say, said) that the gas (collapsed, is collapsing) on itself all the time, so that quasars (had generated, are generating) and releasing tremendous energy.

8. Other scientists (were asserting, assert) that quasars (develop, have been developing) from explosions of matter and antimatter, just as science fiction writers (predict, have been predicting) for many years.

9. When scientists (had conducted, conduct) experiments that (brought, bring) matter and antimatter together, an explosion (will occur, occurs).

10. Until we (understand, understood) more about the birth and death of galaxies, we probably (will not discover, have not discovered) the real story behind quasars.

8k   Using accurate tense sequence

When you want your sentences to deliver messages about actions, occurrences, or states that occur over time, you must depend on verb tenses in sequences. These sequences often include more than one verb. Using **accurate tense sequences**—that is, showing the relationships correctly—is important for clear communication (see Chart 64).

SUMMARY OF SEQUENCE OF TENSES   64

WHEN INDEPENDENT-CLAUSE VERB IS IN THE SIMPLE PRESENT TENSE, FOR THE DEPENDENT-CLAUSE VERB:

- Use the present tense° to show same-time action.

    The director **says** that the movie **is** a tribute to Chaplin.

    I **avoid** shellfish because I **am** allergic to it.

- Use the past tense° to show earlier action.

    I **am** sure that I **deposited** the cheque.

- Use the present perfect tense° to show (1) a period of time extending from some point in the past to the present—often accompanied by *for* or *since*—or (2) an indefinite past time.

    They **say** that they **have lived** in Canada since 1979.   ➔

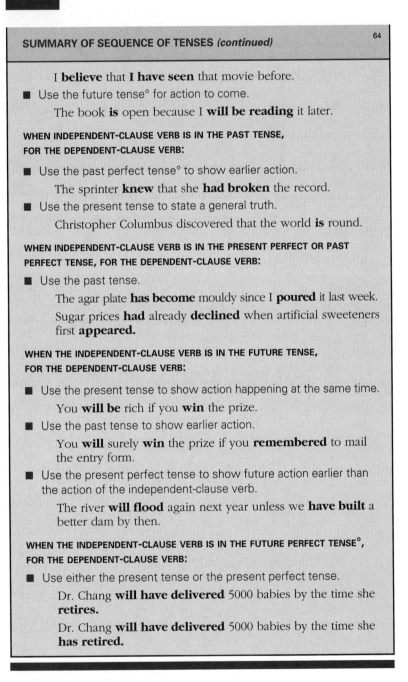

SUMMARY OF SEQUENCE OF TENSES *(continued)* 64

I **believe** that **I have seen** that movie before.

■ Use the future tense° for action to come.

The book **is** open because I **will be reading** it later.

**WHEN INDEPENDENT-CLAUSE VERB IS IN THE PAST TENSE,
FOR THE DEPENDENT-CLAUSE VERB:**

■ Use the past perfect tense° to show earlier action.

The sprinter **knew** that she **had broken** the record.

■ Use the present tense to state a general truth.

Christopher Columbus discovered that the world **is** round.

**WHEN INDEPENDENT-CLAUSE VERB IS IN THE PRESENT PERFECT OR PAST
PERFECT TENSE, FOR THE DEPENDENT-CLAUSE VERB:**

■ Use the past tense.

The agar plate **has become** mouldy since I **poured** it last week.

Sugar prices **had** already **declined** when artificial sweeteners
first **appeared.**

**WHEN THE INDEPENDENT-CLAUSE VERB IS IN THE FUTURE TENSE,
FOR THE DEPENDENT-CLAUSE VERB:**

■ Use the present tense to show action happening at the same time.

You **will be** rich if you **win** the prize.

■ Use the past tense to show earlier action.

You **will** surely **win** the prize if you **remembered** to mail
the entry form.

■ Use the present perfect tense to show future action earlier than
the action of the independent-clause verb.

The river **will flood** again next year unless we **have built** a
better dam by then.

**WHEN THE INDEPENDENT-CLAUSE VERB IS IN THE FUTURE PERFECT TENSE°,
FOR THE DEPENDENT-CLAUSE VERB:**

■ Use either the present tense or the present perfect tense.

Dr. Chang **will have delivered** 5000 babies by the time she
retires.

Dr. Chang **will have delivered** 5000 babies by the time she
has retired.

❖ ALERT: When an independent-clause verb is in the future tense, do not use a future tense in the dependent clause.

NO	The river **will flood** again next year unless we **will build** a better dam.
YES	The river **will flood** again next year unless we **build** a better dam. [Dependent-clause verb *build* is in the present tense.]
YES	The river **will flood** again next year unless we **have built** a better dam by then. [Dependent-clause verb *have built* is in the present perfect tense.] ❖

Tense sequences that include infinitives° or participles° must be correct. The **present infinitive** can name or describe an activity or occurrence coming either at the same time or after the time expressed in the main verb°.

I **hope to buy** a used car. [*To buy* comes at a future time. *Hope* is the main verb, and its action is now.]

I **hoped to buy** a used car. [*Hoped* is the main verb, and its action is over.]

I **had hoped to buy** a used car. [*Had hoped* is the main verb, and its action is over.]

The **present participle** (a verb's -*ing* form) can describe action happening at the same time.

Driving his new car, the man **smiled.** [The driving and the smiling happened at the same time.]

To describe an action that occurs before the action in the main verb°, use the perfect infinitive° (*to have gone, to have smiled*); the past participle°; or the present perfect participle° (*having gone, having smiled*).

Candida **claimed to have written** fifty short stories in college. [First Candida wrote; then she claimed.]

Pleased with the short story, Candida **mailed** it to several magazines. [First Candida was pleased; then she mailed.]

Having sold one short story, Candida **invested** in a word processor. [First Candida sold a story; then she bought a word processor.]

EXERCISE 8-8

Consulting section 8k, select the verb form in parentheses that best suits the sequence of tenses. Be ready to explain your choices.

EXAMPLE   When he (is, was) seven years old, Yo Yo Ma, possibly the world's greatest living cellist, (moves, moved) to the United States with his family.

When he *was* seven years old, Yo Yo Ma, possibly the world's greatest living cellist, *moved* to the United States with his family.

1. Yo Yo Ma, who (had been born, was born) in France to Chinese parents, (lived, lives) in Boston, Massachusetts, today and (toured, tours) as one of the world's greatest cellists.

2. By the time his next concert tour ends, Mr. Ma (will be, will have been) away from home more than half the year.

3. Mr. Ma's older sister, Dr. Yeou-Cheng Ma, was nearly the person with the concert career. She had been training to become a concert violinist until her brother's musical genius (began, had begun) to be noticed.

4. Even though Dr. Ma eventually (becomes, became) a physician, she still (had been playing, plays) the violin.

5. The family interest in music (continues, was continuing), for Mr. Ma's children (take, had taken) piano lessons.

6. Although most people today (knew, know) Mr. Ma as a brilliant cellist, he (was making, has made) films as well.

7. Last year, while he (had been travelling, was travelling) in the Kalahari Desert, he (was filming, filmed) dances of southern Africa's Bush people.

8. Mr. Ma first (becomes, became) interested in the Kalahari people when he (had studied, studied) anthropology 20 years ago at Harvard University.

9. Living near Harvard University now, Mr. Ma has been known to point out to visitors the university library where, he claims, he (fell asleep, was falling asleep) in the stacks when he (had been, was) a student.

10. Indicating another building, Mr. Ma admits that in one of its classrooms he almost (failed, had failed) German.

EXERCISE 8-9

The verbs in each of the following sentences are in correct sequence. For each sentence, change the main verb as directed in the parentheses. Then, consulting section 8k, adjust dependent verbs, infinitives, or participles if necessary to maintain correct verb sequence. Some sentences may have several correct answers.

EXAMPLE   If people exercise regularly, their physical fitness improves almost daily. (Change *exercise* to *would exercise*.)

If people *would exercise* regularly, their physical fitness *would improve* almost daily.

1. As research studies show, regular exercise boosts oxygen in the blood and increases physical endurance. (Change *show* to *showed.*)
2. Another effect of exercise was that it caused the body to produce substances linked to feelings of well-being. (Change *was* to *is.*)
3. People who exercise regularly for several months sometimes find that exercise makes them more creative because it helps them to think clearly and concentrate well. (Change *makes* to *can make.*)
4. After several months, exercisers also had a better sense of their own capabilities and exhibited signs of greater self-esteem. (Change *had* to *will have.*)
5. Because effective exercise required that a person make and observe a consistent routine, regular exercisers became efficient time managers. (Change *required* to *requires.*)

MOOD

81 Understanding mood

Mood refers to the ability of verbs to convey a writer's attitude toward a statement. The most common mood in English is the **indicative mood.** It is used for statements about real things, or highly likely ones, and for questions about fact.

> **INDICATIVE**   The door to the tutoring centre opened.
> She seemed to be looking for someone.
> Do you want to see a tutor?

The **imperative mood** expresses commands and direct requests. When the subject is omitted in an imperative sentence—and it often is—the subject is implied to be either *you* or the indefinite pronoun *anybody, somebody,* or *everybody.*

❖ PUNCTUATION ALERT: A strong command is followed by an exclamation point; a mild command or a request is followed by a period (see 23a and 23e).

> **IMPERATIVE**   Please shut the door.
> Watch out, that hinge is broken! ❖

The **subjunctive mood** can express speculations and other unreal conditions, conjectures, wishes, recommendations, indirect requests, and demands. Subjunctive verb forms are used much less often in English than they once were. Still, they are common for expressing unreal conditions or conjectures in *if* clauses° and in such phrases° as *far be it from me* and *come what may.*

> **SUBJUNCTIVE**   If **I were** you, I would ask for a tutor.

8m Using correct subjunctive forms

For the **present subjunctive,** use the simple form of the verb (see 8b) for all persons° and numbers°.

> The prosecutor asks that **she testify** [not *testifies*] again.

> It is important that **they be** [not *are*] allowed to testify.

For the **past subjunctive,** use the same form as the simple past tense: *I wish that **I had** a car.* The one exception is for the past subjunctive of *be:* use *were* for all persons and numbers.

> I wish that **I were** [not *was*] leaving on vacation today.

> They asked if **she were** [not *was*] leaving on vacation today.

1 Using the subjunctive in *if, as if, as though,* and *unless* clauses

In dependent clauses introduced by *if* and sometimes by *unless,* the subjunctive is often used to describe speculations or conditions contrary to fact.

> If **it were** [not *was*] to rain, attendance at the race would be disappointing. [speculation]

In an *unless* clause, the subjunctive signals that what the clause says is highly unlikely.

> Unless **rain were** [not *was*] to create floods, the race will be held this Sunday. [Floods are highly unlikely.]

> The runner looked as if **he were** [not *was*] winded.

✤ ALERT: Not every clause introduced by *if* requires the subjunctive. Use the subjunctive only when an *if* clause describes a speculation or condition contrary to fact.

> **INDICATIVE**   If **she is** going to leave late, **I will** drive her to the race. [Her leaving late is highly likely.]

> **SUBJUNCTIVE**   If **she were** going to leave late, **I would** drive her to the race. [Her leaving late is speculative.] ✤

2	Using the subjunctive in *that* clauses for wishes, indirect requests, recommendations, and demands

When *that* clauses describe wishes, requests, demands, or recommendations, the subjunctive can convey the message.

I wish that this **race were** [not *was*] over. [wish about something happening now]

He wishes that **he had seen** [not *saw*] the race. [wish about something that is past]

The judges are demanding that the **doctor examine** [not *examines*] the runners. [demand for something that would happen in the future]

❖ ALERT: Modal auxiliary verbs like *would, could, might,* and *should* can convey speculations and conditions contrary to fact: *If the **runner were** [not *was*] faster, we **would** see a better race.* When the independent clause expresses a conditional statement with a modal auxiliary, be sure to use the appropriate subjunctive form, not another modal auxiliary, in the dependent clause.

NO   If **I would have** trained for the race, **I might have** won.

YES   If **I had** trained for the race, **I might have** won. ❖

EXERCISE 8-10

Consulting section 8l and 9m, fill in the blanks with the appropriate subjunctive form of the verb in parentheses.

EXAMPLE Imagining the possibility of brain transplants requires that we (to be) **be** open minded, as it (to be) **were**.

(1) If almost any organ other than the brain (to be) _____ the candidate for a swap, we would probably give our consent. (2) If the brain (to be) _____ to hold whatever impulses form our personalities, few people would want to risk a transplant. (3) Many popular movies have asked that we (to suspend) _____ disbelief and imagine the consequences should a personality actually (to be) _____ transferred to another body. (4) In real life, however, the complexities of a successful brain transplant require that not-yet-developed surgical techniques (to be) _____ used. (5) For example, it would be essential that during the actual transplant each one of the 500 trillion nerve connections within the brain (to continue) _____ to function as though the brain (to be) _____ lying undisturbed in a living human body.

VOICE

8n Understanding voice

Voice refers to verbs' ability to show whether a subject° acts or receives the action named by the verb. English has two voices: active and passive. In the **active voice,** the subject performs the action.

> Most clams live in salt water. [The subject *clams* does the acting; clams *live.*]

> They **burrow** into the sandy bottoms of shallow waters. [The subject *they* does the acting; they *burrow.*]

In the **passive voice,** the subject is acted upon, and the person or thing doing the acting often appears as the object° of the preposition° *by.* Verbs in the passive voice add forms of *be* and *have,* as well as *will,* as auxiliaries to the past participle° of the main verb°.

> Clams **are considered** a delicacy by many people. [The subject *clams* is acted upon by *people,* the object of the preposition *by.*]

> They **are** also **admired** by crabs and starfish. [The subject *they* is acted upon by *crabs and starfish,* the objects of the preposition *by.*]

When you write, your decisions about audience° and purpose° should influence the voice that you choose for a sentence. Misusing voice usually creates problems of writing style rather than problems of incorrect grammar. To make your writing clear, use voice consistently in sentences on the same topic. For ways to identify and correct confusing shifts in voice, see 15a-2.

8o Writing in the active voice, not the passive voice, except to convey special types of emphasis

Because the active voice emphasizes the doer of an action, active constructions are more direct and dramatic. Active constructions also use fewer words than passive constructions (see 16a-2). Most sentences in the passive voice can easily be converted to the active voice.

PASSIVE   African tribal masks are often imitated by Western sculptors.

ACTIVE   Western sculptors often imitate African tribal masks.

The passive voice, however, does have some uses. If you learn what they are, you can use the passive to advantage.

---

1 | Using the passive voice when the doer of the action is unknown or unimportant

When no one knows who or what did something, the passive voice is useful.

The lock **was broken** sometime after four o'clock. [Who broke the lock is unknown.]

When the doer of an action is unimportant, writers often use the passive voice.

In 1899, the year I was born, **a peace conference was held** at The Hague. [The doers of the action—holders of the conference— are unimportant to White's point.]

—E. B. WHITE, "Unity"

---

2 | Using the passive voice to focus attention on the action rather than on the doer of the action

The passive voice emphasizes the action, while the active voice focuses on the doer of the action. In a passage about important contributions to the history of science, you might want to emphasize a doer by using the active voice.

ACTIVE   **Joseph Priestley discovered** oxygen in 1774.

But in a passage summarizing what is known about oxygen, you may want to make oxygen, rather than Priestley, the sentence subject. Doing so requires a passive-voice verb.

PASSIVE   **Oxygen was discovered** in 1774 by Joseph Priestley.

PASSIVE   The unsigned letter **was sent** before it **could be retrieved** from the mailroom. [Emphasis on events, not on the doers of the action.]

ACTIVE   **The postal clerk sent** the unsigned letter before **I could retrieve** it from the mail room. [Emphasis is on the people rather than the actions.]

3 | Using active or passive voice in the social and natural sciences

Many writers in scientific disciplines (see Chapter 38) overuse the passive voice. Yet style manuals for scientific disciplines agree with the advice given in this section: Prefer the active voice. "Verbs are vigorous, direct communicators," point out the editors of the *Publication Manual of the American Psychological Association* (the APA). "Use the active rather than the passive voice."[*]

EXERCISE 8-11

Consulting sections 8n and 8o, determine first whether each of these sentences is in the active or the passive voice. Second, rewrite the sentence in the other voice. Then decide which voice best suits the meaning, and be ready to explain your choice.

EXAMPLE In the West African country of Ghana, a few wood carvers are creating coffins that reflect their occupants' special interests. (*Active; change to passive.*)

In the West African country of Ghana, coffins that reflect their occupants' special interests *are being created* by a few wood carvers.

1. A coffin in the shape of a green onion was chosen by a farmer.
2. A hunter's family buried him in a wooden coffin shaped like a leopard.
3. A dead chief was carried through his fishing village by friends and relatives bearing his body in a large, pink, wooden replica of a fish.
4. Wood carver Paa Joe can turn out about ten coffins a year.
5. A few of these fantasy coffins have been displayed in museums, although most of them end up buried in the ground.

[*]American Psychological Association, *Publication Manual of the American Psychological Association,* 4th ed. (Washington: APA), 32.

Focus on Revising

REVISING YOUR WRITING

If you have trouble with your verbs when you write, including unnecessary use of the passive voice, go back to your writing and locate the problems. Using this chapter as a resource, revise your writing to correct these kinds of problems: -*s* endings (see 8c); -*ed* endings (see 8d); auxiliary verbs (see 8e); transitive and intransitive verbs, including lie and lay (see 8f); tenses (see 8g–8j); tense sequences (see 8k); the subjunctive mood (see 8l–8m); active versus passive voice (see 8n–8o).

CASE STUDY: REVISING TO ELIMINATE VERB ERRORS

In these case studies, you can observe a student writer revising. Then, you have the chance to revise other student writing on your own.

Observation

A student wrote the following draft for a course called Popular Culture. The assignment called for choosing a popular cultural event in Canada and then writing about it. While this paragraph is well organized and offers good examples to support its topic, the draft's effectiveness is diminished by the presence of errors in verb forms and verb tense, and by the unnecessary use of the passive.

Read through the draft. The verb errors are highlighted and explained. Before you look at the student's revision, revise the material yourself. Then compare your revision with the student's.

The Calgary Stampede was an example of the persistence of a popular cultural event over a long period of time. The Stampede, actually a combination of exhibition and stampede, is held annually in much its present form since 1923, beginning with a parade and involving a rodeo and other events over the course of ten days.

simple past used; need present tense: 8h

present tense used; need present perfect progressive: 8j

→

The first exhibition, billed the "Greatest Outdoor Show on Earth," had taken place in 1886. It was accompany by the world-famous Stampede rodeo in 1912. The latter event was begun by Guy Weadick, an American trick roper who decided Calgary was a fit place for a big rodeo. Although initially a success, the event was not repeat until 1919 as a "Great Victory Stampede" marking the end of World War I. If Guy Weadick was to return, he would find that the Stampede still includes the traditional tests of cowboy versus animal. The chuckwagon races still are a popular spectator event.

With its many events, including bareback bronc riding, steer wrestling, and calf roping, the Stampede is one of the largest rodeos in the world with approximately $500 000 prize money. About 1 million visitors come to the Stampede every year, among them once the Queen and the Duke of Edinburgh, who attended many events and took part in square dancing. Just like Anne of Green Gables, the landscapes of Tom Thomson, or the RCMP Musical Ride, the Calgary Stampede had become a quintessential icon of Canadian identity.

Margin annotations:
- past perfect used; need simple past: 8i
- *-ed* missing: 8d
- unneeded passive voice: 8n
- *-ed* missing: 8d
- subjunctive needed for *if* clause: 8m-1
- past perfect used; need present perfect: 8i

Here is how the student revised the material to eliminate the verb errors. In revising from the unneeded passive voice to the active voice, the student had alternatives in word choice. Your revisions into the active voice might differ in wording from the student's.

The Calgary Stampede is an example of the persistence of a popular cultural event over a long period of time. The Stampede, actually a combination of exhibition and stampede, has been held annually in much its present form since 1923, beginning with a parade and involving a rodeo and other events over the course of ten days.

The first exhibition, billed the "Greatest Outdoor Show on Earth," took place in 1886. It was accompanied by the world-famous Stampede rodeo in 1912. Guy Weadick, an American trick roper, began the latter event when he decided Calgary was a fit place for a big rodeo. Although initially a success, the event was not repeated until 1919 as a "Great Victory Stampede" marking the end of World War I. If Guy Weadick were to return, he would find that the Stampede still includes the traditional tests of cowboy versus animal. The chuckwagon races still are a popular spectator event.

With its many events including bareback bronc riding, steer wrestling, and calf roping, the Stampede is one of the largest rodeos in the world with approximately $500 000 prize money. About 1 million visitors come to the Stampede every year, among them once the Queen and the Duke of Edinburgh, who attended many events and took part in square dancing. Just like Anne of Green Gables, the landscapes of Tom Thomson, or the RCMP Musical Ride, the Calgary Stampede has become a quintessential icon of Canadian identity.

Participation

A student wrote the following draft for a course called Introduction to Environmental Studies. The assignment was to write about an environmental problem created by developments in technology. The material is concise and logical, but the draft's effectiveness is diminished by errors in verb forms and verb tense and by the unnecessary use of the passive voice.

Read through the draft. Then revise it to eliminate the errors. Also, make any additional revisions you think would improve the content, organization, and style of the material.

Toronto's CN Tower had become the world's tallest free-standing bird killer. The tower, along with Toronto's many other skyscrapers, has prove a fascinating but fatal attraction for birds of all kinds. The birds dash to their deaths against the fully lit tower or flutter disoriented until falling exhausted to the earth. ➔

The CN Tower, when under construction, was worrying bird watchers because of its great size. The morning after the tower's completion, there were two hundred dead and injured birds laying around the tower's base. Officials at the tower agree to dim decorative lights and to shut off lights at eleven o'clock instead of two o'clock in the morning. Deaths have been reduced by this action, but the problem still is remaining.

More than forty buildings in Toronto are identified as notable bird killers. The Toronto-Dominion Centre, Commerce Court, and the Imperial Oil Building are well known for causing high mortality rates. Casualties were reduced, however, by dimming lights during spring and fall migrations.

Not only tall buildings kill birds. Many birds are falling prey to large picture windows on buildings in Toronto's Eglinton Park. Picture windows in office buildings like Hydro Place on University Avenue posed threats to birds that mistake reflections for reality. That building's mirrored surfaces threaten birds that migrated by day. Many robins and blue jays are also flying into the building's glass walls that reflect Queen's Park. Ironically, many birds fall as a result of human safety features; for instance, tall buildings frequently had lights to ward off low-flying airplanes.

As bird killers, man-made obstacles still rank small beside natural threats to migrators flying thousands of miles during the spring and fall. A sudden storm, for example, can wipe out thousands of birds. But, as more tall buildings rose in Toronto, the toll of birds is being looked at with grave concern. The hazard of tall buildings, combined with reduction in habitats and other human interference, may make the situation even worse.

9 Case of Nouns and Pronouns

9a Understanding case

Case refers to the different forms that nouns° and pronouns° take to deliver information. Case communicates how the noun or pronoun relates to other words in a sentence.

Nouns "show" case only in the possessive, by the use of the apostrophe (see Chapter 27) or by an *of* construction. Pronouns have three cases: subjective case°, objective case, and possessive case°.

Personal pronouns, the most common type of pronouns, have a full range of cases that show changes in **person** (first, second, and third person) and **number** (singular and plural). (See Chart 65.) For more about the concepts of person and number, see Chart 72 in section 11a.

CASES OF PERSONAL PRONOUNS						65
	SUBJECTIVE		**OBJECTIVE**		**POSSESSIVE**	
PERSON	SING. PLUR.		SING. PLUR.		SING.	PLUR.
FIRST	I	we	me	us	my/mine	our/ours
SECOND	you	you	you	you	your/yours	/your/yours
THIRD	he	they	him	them	his	their/theirs
	she		her		her/hers	
	it		it		its	

A pronoun in the **subjective case** functions as a subject°.

We were going to get married. [*We* is the subject.]

John and **I** wanted an inexpensive band to play at our wedding. [*I* is part of the compound subject *John and I.*]

He and **I** found an affordable one-person band. [*He* and *I* are compound subjects.]

A pronoun in the **objective case** functions as a direct object°, an indirect object°, or the object of a preposition°.

We saw **him** perform in a public park. [*Him* is the direct object.]

We showed **him** our budget. [*Him* is the indirect object.]

He wrote down what we wanted and shook hands with **us**. [*Us* is the object of the preposition *with.*]

A pronoun in the **possessive case** indicates possession or ownership. For a discussion of the possessive case before gerunds, see 9h.

The **musician's** contract was in the mail the next day. [*Musician's,* a noun in the possessive case, indicates ownership.]

The first signature on the contract was **mine**. [*Mine,* a pronoun in the possessive case, indicates ownership and refers to the noun *signature.*]

My fiancé signed **his** name next to **mine**. [*His* and *mine,* pronouns in the possessive case, indicate ownership and refer to the noun *name.*]

❖ PUNCTUATION ALERT: Do not use an apostrophe for a personal pronoun in the possessive case (see 27b). ❖

The pronouns *who* and *whoever* also change form for case changes, as explained in 9e.

9b Using the same cases for pronouns in compound constructions as in single constructions

A compound construction contains more than one subject° or object°.

He saw the eclipse of the sun. [single subject]

He and I saw the eclipse of the sun. [compound subject]

That eclipse astonished **us**. [single object]

That eclipse astonished **him and me**. [compound object]

A compound construction has no effect on the choice of pronoun case. A compound subject uses the subjective case, and a compound object uses the objective case. Sometimes, however, people make the mistake of switching cases for compounds. If you are unsure which case to use, try the "drop test." Temporarily drop all of the compound elements *except* the pronoun in question, as explained in Chart 66.

TEST FOR COMPOUND SUBJECTS   66

~~Janet and~~ me ⟩ learned about the moon.

~~Janet and~~ I

After dropping **Janet and**, only **I learned about the moon** is correct; therefore, **Janet and I** is the right choice.

This "drop test" also works when a compound subject contains only pronouns: **She and I** [not **Her and me, She and me,** or **Her and I**] *learned about the moon.*

TEST FOR COMPOUND OBJECTS   67

The instructor told ~~Janet and~~ I ⟩ about the moon's phases.

The instructor told ~~Janet and~~ me

After dropping **Janet and**, only **The instructor told me** is correct; therefore, **Janet and me** is the right choice.

The "drop test" in Chart 67 works for compound objects. Also, this test works when a compound object contains only pronouns: *The instructor told **her and me*** [not ***she and I, her and I,*** or ***she and me***] *about the moon's phases.*

These principles apply to all sequences of pronouns (for example, the rules that govern *her and me* apply also to *me and her*). Also, when you write compound constructions that contain pronouns, do not mix pronouns in the subjective case with pronouns in the objective case: For example, do not use the combinations *him and I* (objective and subjective) or *she and me* (subjective and objective).

When pronouns in a prepositional phrase° are compound, do not allow the pronouns to slip into the wrong case. A prepositional phrase always has an object°, so any pronouns that follow words such as *to, with, from,* and *for* must be in the objective case.

> **NO**   The instructor gave an assignment **to Sam and I.** [*To* is a preposition; *I* is in the subjective case and cannot follow a preposition.]
>
> **YES**   The instructor gave an assignment **to Sam and me.** [*To* is a preposition; *me* is in the objective case, so it is correct.]
>
> **NO**   The instructor spoke **with he and I.** [*With* is a preposition; both *he* and *I* are in the subjective case and cannot follow a preposition.]
>
> **NO**   The instructor spoke **with him and I.** [*With* is a preposition; *him* is in the objective case, so it is correct. *I* is in the subjective case and cannot follow a preposition.]
>
> **YES**   The instructor spoke **with him and me.** [*With* is a preposition; *him* and *me* are both in the objective case, so this construction is correct.]

Between is a preposition that frequently leads people to pronoun error. A pronoun after *between,* like those after other prepositions, must always be in the objective case.

> **NO**   The instructor divided the work **between Sam and I.** [*Between* is a preposition; *I* is in the subjective case and cannot follow a preposition.]
>
> **YES**   The instructor divided the work **between Sam and me.** [*Between* is a preposition; *me* is in the objective case, so it is correct.]

When you are in doubt about pronoun case in prepositional phrases, use the "drop test" for compound objects in Chart 67.

EXERCISE 9-1

Consulting section 9b, select the correct pronoun from each pair in parentheses and write it in the blank.

EXAMPLE   "Just between you and (I, me) **me**," said my workout partner, "I could stand to lose a few pounds."

I suggested that [1](us, we) _____ both consider going on a low-fat diet. Consulting a doctor first seemed like the right plan for Al and [2](I, me) _____ , and so I made appointments for [3](he and I, him and me) _____ with Mary Standish, my own physician. [4](We, Us) _____ both were seen the next evening. After examining us separately, Dr. Standish told Al and [5](I, me) _____ that between [6](he and I, him and me) _____ [7](we, us) _____ should lose twelve kilograms. Dr. Standish gave a list of desirable and undesirable foods to [8](we, us) _____ two. Naturally, the desirable list seemed undesirable and the undesirable delicious, agreed Al and [9](I, me) _____. Al had a different problem. Because the diet was now the same goal for both [10](he and I, him and me) _____ , he dreaded the competition between [11](we, us) _____ two. "Don't worry," I told Al. "It's not a matter of you versus [12](me, I) _____ , because the big loser is the real winner!"

9c Matching noun and pronoun cases in appositives

The case rules hold when pronouns are renamed by appositives° and when they are appositive themselves. The pronouns and nouns must be in the same case. To check, temporarily drop the noun to see whether subjective or objective pronouns read correctly.

We ~~tennis players~~
Us ~~tennis players~~
> practise hard.

After dropping *tennis players*, only *we* is correct; therefore, *We practised hard* is the right choice.

This test also works when the pronouns function as the appositive, coming after the noun: *The winners, **she** and **I*** [not *her* and *me*], *advanced to the finals.* Because they rename *winners*, which is the subject, the pronouns must be in the subjective case.

This test also works when the nouns and pronouns are in the objective case: *The coach tells **us*** [not *we*] *tennis players to practise hard. The crowd cheered the winners, **her** and **me*** [not *she* and *I*].

9d Avoiding the objective case after linking verbs

A **linking verb** connects a subject° to a word that renames it. Linking verbs indicate a state of being *(am, is, are, was, were, etc.)*, relate to the senses *(look, smell, taste, sound, feel)*, or indicate a condition *(appear, seem, become, grow, turn, remain,* and *prove)*.

Because a pronoun coming after any linking verb renames the subject, the pronoun must be in the subjective case.

The contest winner was **I.** [*I* renames *the contest winner,* the subject, so the subjective case is correct.]

The ones who will benefit are **they** and **I.** [*They* and *I* rename *the ones who will benefit,* the subject, so the subjective case is correct.]

Who is there? It is **I.** [*I* renames *it,* the subject, so the subjective case is correct.]

Although in speech and informal writing, the objective case is sometimes substituted in the constructions shown in the last two examples above, always use the subjective case in academic writing.

EXERCISE 9-2

Consulting sections 9a through 9d, select the correct pronoun of each pair in parentheses and write it in the blank.

EXAMPLE   The two of you have suggested that (we, us) **we** roommates all have sausage and mushroom pizza for dinner tonight.

After much discussion, Kari and ¹(I, me) _____ have reached a decision. We thought carefully about what you and Saroya have asked Kari and ²(I, me) _____ to do, because it is ³(we, us) _____ who have to live with ⁴(you and she, you and her) _____ for the rest of the semester. Because Kari hates mushrooms and I hate sausage, this proposal has no appeal whatsoever for either ⁵(she, her) _____ or ⁶(I, me) _____ . We have now thought of a compromise that should satisfy you two as well as ⁷(we, us) _____ . Tell Saroya that tonight's pizza eaters can certainly be you and ⁸(she, her) _____ , but hamburgers are on the menu for Kari and ⁹(I, me) _____ .

9e Using *who, whoever, whom,* and *whomever*

The pronouns *who* and *whoever* are in the subjective case. The pronouns *whom* and *whomever* are in the objective case. (See Chart 68.) They do not change form.

CASES OF RELATIVE AND INTERROGATIVE PRONOUNS		68
SUBJECTIVE	**OBJECTIVE**	**POSSESSIVE**
who	whom	whose
whoever	whomever	———

1	Using *who, whoever, whom,* and *whomever* in dependent clauses

Pronouns such as *who, whoever, whom,* and *whomever* start many **dependent clauses°**. To determine what pronoun case is correct in a dependent clause, you need to find out whether the pronoun is functioning as a subject° or an object° in its own clause. Informal spoken English tends to blur distinctions between *who* and *whom,* so you may not want to rely entirely on what sounds right.

To check your use of *who* and *whom,* adapt the "drop test" introduced in section 9b. As Chart 69 shows, temporarily drop everything in the sentence up to the pronoun in question, and then make substitutions. Remember that *he, she, they, who,* and *whoever* are subjects, and *him, her, them, whom,* and *whomever* (the -*m* forms and *her*) are objects.

TEST FOR *WHO/WHOM* IN SUBJECTIVE CASE		69
EXAMPLE	I wondered **(who, whom)** would vote.	
DROP	I wondered	
TEST	Temporarily substitute *he* and *him* (or *she* and *her*): **"He** would vote" or **"Him** would vote."	
ANSWER	**He.** Therefore, because *he* is subjective, *who,* which is also the subjective, is correct: "I wondered **who** would vote."	

The subjective case is used even if words such as *I think* or *he says* come between the subject and verb. Ignore these expressions in determining the correct pronoun: *She is the candidate who [I think] will get my vote.* The "drop test" in Chart 70 also works for *whoever:*

> Voter enumeration attempts to locate **whoever** is eligible to vote. ["**He** (not *him*) is eligible to vote" proves that the subjective case of **whoever** is needed.]

		70
TEST FOR *WHO/WHOM* IN OBJECTIVE CASE		

EXAMPLE	Often, a second pair of enumerators comes by to register residents (**who, whom**) the first enumeration missed.
DROP	Often, a second pair of enumerators comes by to register residents.
TEST	Try *they* and *them* in the resulting sentence: "The first enumeration missed **they**" or "The first enumeration missed **them**."
ANSWER	**Them.** Therefore, because *them* is objective, *whom*, which is also objective, is correct: "Often, a second pair of enumerators comes by to register residents **whom** the first enumeration missed."

The "drop test" in Chart 70 also works for *whomever:*

> All voters can vote for **whomever** they wish. ["All voters can vote for **him** (not *he*)" proves that the objective case of **whomever** is needed.]

2   **Using *who* and *whom* in questions**

At the beginning of questions, use *who* if the question is about the subject° and *whom* if the question is about the object°. To determine case, recast the question into a statement using *he* or *him* (or *she* or *her*).

> **Who** watched the space shuttle lift off? ["**He** (not *Him*) watched the space shuttle lift off" uses the subjective case, so *Who* is correct.]
>
> Ann admires **whom**? ["Ann admires **him** (not *he*)" uses the objective case, so *whom* is correct.]
>
> **Whom** does Ann admire? ["Ann admires **him** (not *he*)" uses the objective case, so *whom* is correct.]

EXERCISE 9-3

Consulting section 9e, select the correct pronoun of each pair in parentheses and write it in the blank.

EXAMPLE   Is there an age group of children (who, whom) **who** do not tell lies?

If the word *liar* means [1](whoever, whomever) _____ makes false statements with the intent to deceive, then even three- and four-year-olds fit the definition. Studies show that young children will lie to [2](whoever, whomever) _____ they think might be angered by the truth. Because young children may not define lying the way adults do, [3](whoever, whomever) _____ the child considers to have given false information may be considered a liar. For example, a parent [4](who, whom) _____ changes plans because of bad weather may be accused of lying by a young child. To the child [5](who, whom) _____ the change affects, the original statements were false and therefore the person [6](who, whom) _____ made them is a liar.

9f Using the appropriate pronoun after *than* or *as*

A sentence of comparison often can be clear even though some of the words following *than* or *as* are implied rather than directly stated. For example, the word *are* does not have to be expressed at the end of this sentence: *My two-month-old Saint Bernard is larger **than** most full-grown dogs [are].*

When a pronoun follows *than* or *as,* the pronoun case carries essential information about what is being said. For example, these two sentences convey two very different messages, simply because of the choice between the words *me* and *I* after *than.*

1. My sister loved that dog more **than me.**
2. My sister loved that dog more **than I.**

Because the pronoun *me* functions as a subject, sentence 1 means "My sister loved that dog more *than she loved me.*" On the other hand, sentence 2 means "My sister loved that dog more *than I loved it.*" To make sure that any sentence of comparison delivers its message clearly, either mentally fill in the words to check that you have chosen the correct pronoun case, or write in all the words after *than* or *as.*

9g Using pronouns with infinitives

An **infinitive** is the simple form° of a verb usually, but not always, following *to: to laugh.* Objective-case pronouns serve as both subjects° and objects° of infinitives.

> Our tennis coach expects **me to serve.** [The word *me* is the subject of the infinitive *to serve,* and so it is in the objective case.]

> Our tennis coach expects **him to beat me.** [The word *him* is the subject of the infinitive *to beat,* and *me* is the object of the infinitive; so both are in the objective case.]

9h Using pronouns with *-ing* words

A **gerund** is a verb's *-ing* form functioning as a noun°. (***Brisk walking** is excellent exercise.*) When a noun or pronoun precedes a gerund, the possessive case is called for. (***Kim's brisk walking** built up his stamina. **His brisk walking** built up his stamina.*) In contrast, a present participle—a form that also ends in *-ing*—functions as a modifier. It does not take the possessive case. (*Kim, **walking briskly**, caught up to me.*)

The possessive case, therefore, communicates important information. Consider these two sentences, which convey two different messages, entirely as a result of the possessive:

1. The detective noticed the **man staggering.**
2. The detective noticed the **man's staggering.**

Sentence 1 means that the detective noticed the man; sentence 2 means that the detective noticed the staggering. The same distinction applies to pronouns:

1. The detective noticed **him staggering.**
2. The detective noticed **his staggering.**

In conversation, such a distinction is often ignored, but readers of academic writing expect that information will be precise. Consider the difference in the following two examples:

(AS SUBJECT) GERUND   The **premier's calling for a tax increase** surprised her supporters.

(AS MODIFIER) PARTICIPLE   The premier, **calling for a tax increase,** surprised her supporters.

EXERCISE 9-4

Consulting sections 9f, 9g, and 9h, select the correct pronoun of each pair in parentheses and write it in the blank.

EXAMPLE   When executives at the Hewlett Packard Company decided not to manufacture a personal computer brought to them by its designer, young Steve Wozniak, the rejection motivated (him, his) **his** founding the Apple Computer Company.

Few people in Steve Wozniak's world of personal computers have had careers as rewarding as [1](he, him) _____ and his friend Steve Jobs. Their story begins with [2](them, their) _____ selling a van and a calculator to get [3](they, them) _____ enough cash to make a prototype computer. Many people with an idea like Wozniak and Jobs's are less willing than [4](them, they) _____ to take risks. Apple's spectacular success as a company came from [5](it, its) _____ creating computers easy for individuals to own and use. Because their idea made both Wozniak and Jobs multimillionaires before age thirty, the notion of [6](them, their) _____ leaving the business world seemed to interest [7](they, them) _____. Wozniak went back to college but eventually returned to Apple, which continued to want [8](his, him) _____ conceptualizing, designing, and engineering computers for them. Jobs started a new computer company, NExt, but [9](it, its) _____ repeating Apple's success is still only a dream.

9i   Using -*self* pronouns

Reflexive pronouns° reflect back on the subject° or object°: *The detective disguised **himself**. He relied on **himself** to solve the mystery.*

Do not use reflexive pronouns to substitute for personal pronouns° as subjects or objects: *The detective and **I** [not myself] had a long talk. He wanted my partner and **me** [not myself] to help him.*

Intensive pronouns provide emphasis by making another word more intense in meaning: *The detective felt that his career **itself** was at stake.*

❖ USAGE ALERT: Avoid nonstandard forms of reflexive and intensive pronouns. Use *himself*, never *hisself*; use *themselves*, never *their self, theirselves, themself,* or *themselfs.* ❖

10

Pronoun Reference

A pronoun° always refers to a noun° or another pronoun, which is called the pronoun's **antecedent.** The term **pronoun reference** refers to this pronoun–antecedent relationship. For writing to communicate a clear message, each pronoun must relate directly to an antecedent.

Consider these sentences and lines in poetry in which each pronoun has a clear referent.

> **Facts** do not cease to exist just because **they** are ignored.
>
> —ALDOUS HUXLEY

> Whatever **women** do **they** must do twice as well as men to be thought half so good . . . luckily, it's not difficult.
>
> —CHARLOTTE WHITTON

> **I** knew a woman, lovely in **her** bones,
> When small birds sighed, **she** would sigh back at **them;**
>
> —THEODORE ROETHKE, "I Knew a Woman"

HOW TO CORRECT FAULTY PRONOUN REFERENCE	71

- Make a pronoun refer clearly to a single nearby antecedent (see 10a).
- Place pronouns close to their antecedents (see 10b).
- Make a pronoun refer to a definite antecedent (see 10c).
- Do not overuse *it* (see 10d), and reserve *you* only for direct address° (see 10e).
- Use *who, which,* and *that* correctly (see 10f).

10a Making a pronoun refer clearly to a single antecedent

When pronoun reference is unclear, the meaning gets muddled. Be sure that each pronoun that you use refers clearly to a single, nearby antecedent. If you find that you need the same pronoun to refer to more than one antecedent, revise the passage by replacing some pronouns with nouns° so that all the remaining pronouns clearly refer to a single antecedent.

NO   In 1911, **Roald Amundsen** reached the South Pole just thirty-five days before **Robert F. Scott** arrived. **He** [who? Amundsen or Scott?] had told people that **he** was going to sail for the Arctic but then **he** turned south for the Antarctic. On the journey home, **he** [who? Amundsen or Scott?] and **his** party froze to death just a few miles from safety.

YES   In 1911, **Roald Amundsen** reached the South Pole just thirty-five days before **Robert F. Scott** arrived. **Amundsen** had told people that **he** was going to sail for the Arctic but then **he** turned south for the Antarctic. On the journey home, **Scott** and **his** party froze to death just a few miles from safety.

When you use more than one pronoun in a sentence, be sure that each has a clear antecedent.

Robert F. Scott used **horses** for **his** trip to the Pole, but **they** perished quickly because **they** were not suited for travel over ice and snow.

Said and *told,* when used with pronouns that refer to more than one person, are particularly likely to create confusion for readers. Quotation marks and slight rewording can clarify meaning.

NO   Her mother told her she was going to visit the Yukon.

YES   Her mother told her, "You are going to visit the Yukon."

YES   Her mother told her, "I am going to visit the Yukon."

10b Placing pronouns close to their antecedents for clarity

If too much material comes between a pronoun and its antecedent, even though they may be logically related, unclear pronoun reference results. Readers lose track of the meaning of a passage if they have to trace back too far to find the antecedent of a pronoun.

NO   **Alfred Wegener,** a highly trained German meteorologist and professor of geophysics and meteorology at the University of Graz in Austria, was the first person to suggest that all the continents on earth were originally part of one large land mass. According to this theory, the supercontinent broke up long ago and the fragments drifted apart. **He** named this supercontinent Pangaea. [Although *he* can refer only to *Wegener,* too much material intervenes between the pronoun and its antecedent.]

YES   **Alfred Wegener,** a highly trained German meteorologist and professor of geophysics and meteorology at the University of Graz in Austria, was the first person to suggest that all the continents on earth were originally part of one large land mass. According to this theory, the supercontinent broke up long ago and the fragments drifted apart. **Wegener** named this supercontinent Pangaea.

At the beginning of a new paragraph within an essay, many writers avoid using a pronoun to refer to a name in a prior paragraph. They prefer to repeat the name instead, particularly when the prior paragraph is long or when the subject matter is complex. Your repeating the name can help your reader follow more easily the message that you want your material to deliver.

◆ ESL NOTE: Many languages omit a pronoun as a subject° because the verb° delivers the needed information. English, however, requires the use of the pronoun as a subject.

NO   Political science is an important academic subject; **is** studied all over the world.

YES   Political science is an important academic subject; **it is** studied all over the world. ◆

EXERCISE 10-1

Consulting sections 10a and 10b, revise so that each pronoun refers clearly to its antecedent. Either replace pronouns with nouns or restructure the material to clarify pronoun reference.

EXAMPLE   When Ludwig II became king of Bavaria in 1864, he was a passionate admirer of composer Richard Wagner. He had first heard one of his operas a few years earlier and had fallen in love with the exciting world of German legend that he portrayed.

Here is one acceptable revision: *When Ludwig II became king of Bavaria in 1864, he was a passionate admirer of composer Richard Wagner. Ludwig had first heard one of Wagner's operas a few years earlier and had fallen in love with the exciting world of German legend that Wagner portrayed.*

At the time he was crowned king, Wagner had gone into hiding to escape his many creditors. He sent his secretary to find him and offer him the protection that only a royal patron could provide. The secretary delivered this message, telling him to go at once to the royal court at Munich, where all his debts would be paid. Moreover, he would provide him with everything he needed so that he could continue his composing free of material cares.

Thus began an intense friendship. Wagner enjoyed Ludwig's company, playing hard with him but also working hard. He spent his money freely—too freely, many Bavarians believed. When he began to try to influence Bavarian politics, the people became restless.

Finally, his advisors told him to choose between this friendship and his royal obligations. Regretfully, he chose to honour his responsibilities as king and told him to leave the court. His devotion to him continued, however, until his death. He himself met a bizarre end. Declared insane and forced to give up the monarchy, he was found drowned. The mystery of his death—murder, suicide, accident—was never solved.

10c   Making a pronoun refer to a definite antecedent

1   Not using a pronoun to refer to a noun's possessive form

A noun's possessive form cannot be the antecedent° to a pronoun, unless the pronoun is also in the possessive case.

NO   The **geologist's** discovery brought **him** fame. [The pronoun *him* is not possessive and therefore cannot refer to the possessive *geologist's*.]

YES   The **geologist** became famous because of **his** discovery.

YES   The **geologist's** discovery was **his** alone.

2

Not using a pronoun to refer to an adjective

An adjective° cannot be an antecedent. A pronoun, therefore, cannot refer to an adjective.

NO   Avery likes to study **geological** records. **That** will be her major. [*That* cannot refer to the adjective *geological.*]

YES   Avery likes to study **geological** records. **Geology** will be her major.

3

Making *it, that, this,* and *which* refer to only one antecedent

When you use *it, that, this,* and *which,* check to see that the referent of these pronouns can be determined easily by your readers.

NO   Comets usually fly by the earth at 160 000 km/h, whereas asteroids sometimes collide with the earth. **This** interests scientists. [Does *this* refer to the speed of the comets, comets flying by the earth, or asteroids colliding with the earth?]

YES   Comets usually fly by the earth at 160 000 km/h, whereas asteroids sometimes collide with the earth. **This difference** interests scientists. [Adding a noun after *this* or *that* is an effective way to make your meaning clear.]

NO   A fireball, caused by the impact of either a comet or an asteroid, rose nineteen kilometres somewhere above central Siberia in 1908, but **it** is still unknown. [Does *it* refer to the cause of the fireball or its size and location?]

YES   A fireball, caused by the impact of either a comet or an asteroid, rose nineteen kilometres above central Siberia in 1908, but **the source of the explosion** is still unknown.

NO   I told my friends that I was going to major in geology, **which** annoyed my parents. [What does *which* refer to?]

YES   My parents were annoyed because I discussed my major with my friends.

YES   My parents were annoyed because I chose to major in geology.

246

---

4 Using *they* and *it* precisely

The expression *they say* cannot take the place of stating precisely who is doing the saying. Your reader is entitled to more than a *they* to provide authority for a statement.

NO   **They** say that earthquakes are becoming more frequent.

YES   **Seismologists** say that earthquakes are becoming more frequent.

In speech, a common statement is *It said on the radio.* Because such expressions are inexact and wordy, they should be avoided in academic writing: ***The newspaper reports*** [not *It said in the newspaper*] *that minor earthquakes occur almost daily in California.*

---

5 Not using a pronoun in the first sentence of a work to refer to the work's title

When referring to a title, repeat or reword whatever part of the title you want to use.

TITLE   Geophysics as a Major

FIRST SENTENCE

NO   This subject unites the sciences of physics, biology, and ancient life.

YES   Geophysics unites the sciences of physics, biology, and ancient life.

10d Not overusing *it*

It has three different uses in English.

1. *It* is a personal pronoun: *Kumar wants to visit the Canadian observatory where a supernova was discovered in 1987, but **it** is located in Chile.*
2. *It* is an expletive, a word that postpones the subject: ***It** is interesting to observe the stars.*
3. *It* is part of idiomatic expressions of weather, time, or distance: ***It** is sunny.* ***It** is midnight.* ***It** is not far to the hotel.*

All of these uses are acceptable, but combining them in the same sentence can create confusion.

NO	Because our car was overheating, **it** came as no surprise that **it** broke down just as **it** began to rain. [*It* is overused here even though all three uses—2, 1, and 3 above, respectively—are acceptable.]
YES	**It** came as no surprise that our overheating car broke down just as the rain began to fall.

See section 16a-1 for advice about revising wordy sentences that use expletive structures, and see section 11f for advice about using singular verbs with *it* expletives.

◆ ESL NOTE: Be careful not to omit *it* from an expletive (also called a *subject filler*).

NO	**Is** a lovely day.
YES	**It is** a lovely day. ◆

10e Using *you* only for direct address

In academic writing, *you* is not a suitable substitute for specific words that refer to people, situations, and occurrences. Exact language is always preferable. Also, *you* used for other than direct address tends to lead to wordiness. This handbook uses *you* to address you directly as the reader; it never uses *you* to refer to people in general.

NO	Uprisings in prison often occur when **you allow** overcrowded conditions to continue. [Are you, the reader of this handbook, allowing the conditions to continue?]
YES	Uprisings in prison often occur when **the authorities allow** overcrowded conditions to occur.
NO	In many provinces, **you have your prisons** with few rehabilitation programs. [Do you, the reader, have few programs? Also, are the prisons yours?]
YES	In many provinces, **prisons have** few rehabilitation programs.
NO	In Russia **you** usually have to stand in long lines to buy groceries. [Are you, the reader, planning to do your grocery shopping in Russia?]
YES	**Russian consumers** usually have to stand in long lines to buy groceries.

EXERCISE 10-2

Consulting sections 10a to 10e, rewrite each sentence so that all pronoun references are clear. If you consider a passage correct as written, circle its number.

EXAMPLE   In a research study, it says that romantic love is a chemical process.

> *A research study claims that romantic love is a chemical process.* [Revision avoids imprecise use of *it says*.]

1. Scientific evidence supports lovers' claims that they feel swept away.
2. When you fall in love, you are flooded with substances that your body manufactures.
3. It is surprising that love owes its "natural high" to phenylethylamine (PEA), a chemical cousin of the amphetamines, as well as to emotion.
4. As the body builds up a tolerance for PEA, it is necessary to produce more and more of it to create the euphoria of romantic love.
5. Although chocolate is high in PEA, gobbling it will not revive your wilting love affair.
6. Infatuation based on PEA lasts no longer than four years. This is when most divorces take place.
7. Chemicals called endorphins are good news for romantics. They promote long-term intimate attachments.
8. Endorphins' special effects on lovers allow them to exert a soothing, not an exciting, influence.
9. Oxytocin is called the "cuddle chemical" because it seems that it encourages mothers to nuzzle their babies.
10. Romantic love also owes a debt to this, for it promotes similar feelings in adult lovers.

10f   Using *who*, *which*, and *that* correctly

Who refers to people or to animals with names or special talents.

John Polanyi, who was awarded the Nobel Prize in chemistry, speaks passionately in support of nuclear disarmament.

Lassie, who was known for her intelligence and courage, was actually played by a series of male collie dogs.

Which and *that* refer to animals, things, and sometimes anonymous or collective groups of people. Some writers use *which* both for restrictive clauses (clauses that add essential information to a sentence) and for nonrestrictive clauses (clauses that could be omitted from a sentence without changing the essential meaning). Other writers reserve *which* for nonrestrictive clauses and *that* for restrictive clauses. You can follow either practice as long as you are consistent in each piece of writing. For help in distinguishing between restrictive and nonrestrictive clauses, see 24e.

> The zoos **that most delight children** display newborn animals as well as animals that can be touched safely. [*That* introduces information essential for understanding which zoos are being referred to.]

> Zoos, **which delight most children,** have been attracting fewer visitors each year. [*Which* introduces information that could be dropped from the sentence without changing the essential message.]

Who can be used for restrictive and nonrestrictive clauses alike.

❖ COMMA ALERT: Set off nonrestrictive clauses with commas. Do not set off restrictive clauses with commas (see 24e). ❖

EXERCISE 10-3

Consulting section 10f, fill in the blanks with *who, which,* or *that.*

EXAMPLE   Psychologists have found that most people **who** believe that the moon influences behaviour actually believe that others, not they themselves, are affected by the moon.

1. Does the moon really affect human behaviour? Ancient people believed the power _____ came from the moon was divine.

2. The word *lunatic,* _____ is derived from the Latin *luna,* suggests that people _____ are exposed to the moon become mad.

3. The moon, _____ has been credited by some researchers with influencing the stock market, is also thought by some experts to affect agricultural yields.

4. Some nurses _____ work in hospital delivery rooms claim it is the moon _____ stimulates labour pains to begin.

5. The moon may also affect certain groups of people, _____ include sleepwalkers and those _____ suffer from migraine headaches.

11 Agreement

The concept of *agreement* in human affairs implies the aligning or matching of ideas. Grammatical agreement also is based on matching. Applying the rules governing grammatical agreement can be tricky, so almost everyone consults a handbook now and then to check one or another rule.

This chapter discusses agreement between subjects and verbs (see 11a through 11l) and between pronouns and antecedents (see 11m through 11r).

SUBJECT–VERB AGREEMENT

11a Understanding subject–verb agreement

Subject–verb agreement means that subjects° and verbs° in clauses must "match" in form. To agree grammatically, subjects and verbs must match in number (singular or plural) and in person (first, second, or third person). The major concepts in grammatical agreement are explained in Chart 72.

The **firefly glows** with luminescent light. [*firefly* = singular subject in the third person; *glows* = singular verb in the third person]

Fireflies glow with luminescent light. [*fireflies* = plural subject in the third person; *glow* = plural verb in the third person]

This **insect is** nocturnal. [*insect* = singular subject in the third person; *is* = singular verb in the third person]

These **insects are** nocturnal. [*insects* = plural subject in the third person; *are* = plural verb in the third person]

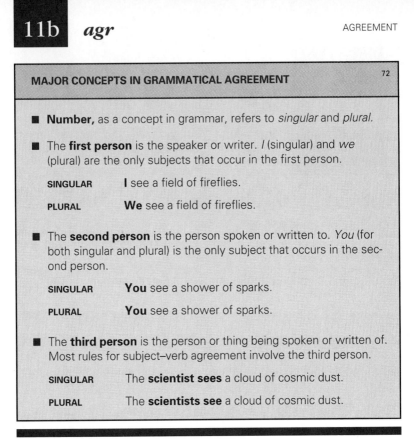

MAJOR CONCEPTS IN GRAMMATICAL AGREEMENT

- **Number,** as a concept in grammar, refers to *singular* and *plural.*

- The **first person** is the speaker or writer. *I* (singular) and *we* (plural) are the only subjects that occur in the first person.

    SINGULAR   **I** see a field of fireflies.

    PLURAL   **We** see a field of fireflies.

- The **second person** is the person spoken or written to. *You* (for both singular and plural) is the only subject that occurs in the second person.

    SINGULAR   **You** see a shower of sparks.

    PLURAL   **You** see a shower of sparks.

- The **third person** is the person or thing being spoken or written of. Most rules for subject–verb agreement involve the third person.

    SINGULAR   The **scientist sees** a cloud of cosmic dust.

    PLURAL   The **scientists see** a cloud of cosmic dust.

11b   Using the final *-s* or *-es* either for plural subjects or for singular verbs

Subject–verb agreement often involves one letter: *s*. The basic pattern for agreement is shown in Chart 73. Keep in mind that the *-s* added to subjects and the *-s* added to verbs serve very different functions.

Most **plural subjects** are formed by adding an *-s* or *-es: lip* becomes *lips; princess* becomes *princesses.* Exceptions include most pronouns (*they, it*) and a few nouns that for singular and plural either do not change (*deer, deer*) or change internally (*mouse, mice; child, children*).

Singular verbs in the present tense of the third person are formed by adding *-s* or *-es* to the simple form of the verb: *laugh, laughs; kiss, kisses.* Even the exceptions—the verbs *be (is)* and *have (has)*—end in *s*.

agr **11b**

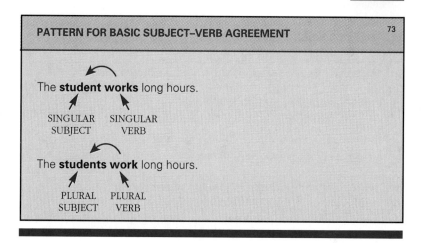

PATTERN FOR BASIC SUBJECT–VERB AGREEMENT ⁣73

The **student works** long hours.

SINGULAR SINGULAR
SUBJECT VERB

The **students work** long hours.

PLURAL PLURAL
SUBJECT VERB

The **student disagrees** that **students watch** too much television.

Most part-time **jobs involve** ten or twenty hours a week.

Studying requires all remaining time.

Here is a memory device to help you visualize how, in most cases, the *s* works in agreement. The -*s* (or -*es*) can take only one path at a time, going either to the top or to the bottom.

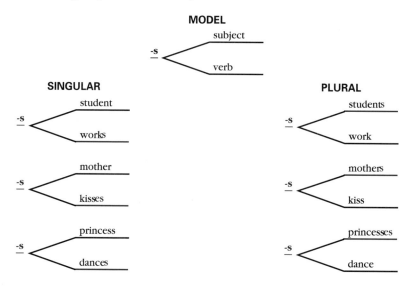

MODEL

-s < subject / verb

SINGULAR

-s < student / works

-s < mother / kisses

-s < princess / dances

PLURAL

-s < students / work

-s < mothers / kiss

-s < princesses / dance

253

The principle of the memory device holds, even for the exceptions discussed earlier in this section: *It* [singular pronoun] *is late; the* **mice** (plural with internal change) *are sleeping.*

♣ ESL ALERT: Do not add *-s* to a main verb used with an auxiliary verb (a helping verb such as *be, do, can, might, must, would;* see 8e): *The coach* **can walk** [not **can walks**] *to campus.* ♣

EXERCISE 11-1

Consulting sections 11a and 11b, use the subject and verb in each set to write two complete sentences—one with the subject as a singular and one with the subject as a plural. Keep all verbs in the present tense.

1. child laugh	2. theory state	3. match might light	4. committee vote
5. man smile	6. it change	7. bus speed	8. parade celebrate

11c For agreement, ignoring words between a subject and verb

Words that separate the subject° from the verb° do not affect what the verb should agree with. The pattern is shown in Chart 74. Such intervening material often appears as a prepositional phrase°. Eliminate all prepositional phrases from consideration when you look for the subject of a clause.

NO **Winners** of the regional contest **goes** to the national finals. [*Winners* is the subject. The verb must agree with it; *of the regional contest* is a prepositional phrase.]

YES **Winners** of the regional contest **go** to the national finals.

Be especially careful with a construction that starts *one of the.* This construction takes a singular verb, to agree with the word *one.* Do not be distracted by the plural noun that comes after *of the.*

NO **One** of the problems **are** broken equipment.

NO **One** of the problem **is** broken equipment.

YES **One** of the problems **is** broken equipment.

Similarly, to locate the subject of a sentence, eliminate any phrases that start with *including, together with, along with, accompanied by, in*

PATTERN WHEN WORDS SEPARATE A SUBJECT AND VERB   74

The **student** < ~~in my class~~ / ~~in my classes~~ > **works** long hours.

↑ SINGULAR SUBJECT   ↑ INTERVENING WORDS   ↑ SINGULAR VERB

The **students** < ~~in my class~~ / ~~in my classes~~ > **work** long hours.

↑ PLURAL SUBJECT   ↑ INTERVENING WORDS   ↑ PLURAL VERB

---

addition to, except, and *as well as.* Be sure that the verb agrees with the subject, not with the intervening material.

NO   **The moon,** as well as Venus, **are** visible in the night sky. [*The moon* is the subject. The verb must agree with it. Ignore *as well as Venus.*]

YES   **The moon,** as well as Venus, **is** visible in the night sky.

NO   **The Big Dipper,** along with many other constellations, **are** easy to learn to find. [*The Big Dipper* is the subject. The verb must agree with it. Ignore *along with many other constellations.*]

YES   **The Big Dipper,** along with many other constellations, **is** easy to learn to find.

11d Using verbs with subjects connected with *and*

When subjects are connected with *and,* they comprise a compound subject° (see 7k) and require a plural verb. Chart 75 shows this pattern.

PATTERN WHEN TWO SUBJECTS ARE JOINED BY *AND*   75

The student and the instructor **work** long hours.

COMPOUND
SUBJECT
(USES *AND*)

PLURAL
VERB

The Cascade Diner *and* the Wayside Diner *have* [not *has*] fried halibut today.

An exception occurs when *and* joins parts that combine to form a single thing or person.

My ***best friend and neighbour* makes** [not *make*] excellent chili. [The best friend is the same person as the neighbour. If two different people were involved, *makes* would become *make*.]

***Macaroni and cheese* contains** [not *contain*] pasta, protein, and many calories.

each, every

The words *each* and *every* remain singular even when they modify° a compound subject. Therefore, when *each* or *every* precedes a compound subject, the verb that follows it must be singular, not plural. (For information about verb agreement for *each* or *every* used alone, not as a modifier, see 11g.)

***Each* human hand and foot makes** [not *make*] a distinctive print.

To identify lawbreakers, ***every* police chief, detective, and RCMP officer depends** [not *depend*] on such prints.

❖ USAGE ALERT: Use either *each* or *every*, not both together, to single out something: ***Each*** (not *each and every*) *robber has been caught.*❖

11e **Making the verb agree with the nearest subject**

When subjects are joined with *or, nor, either ... or, neither ... nor,* or *not only ... but (also),* make the verb agree with the subject closest to it. For subject–verb agreement, ignore everything before the final subject.

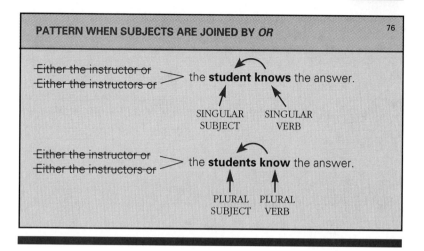

PATTERN WHEN SUBJECTS ARE JOINED BY *OR*   76

~~Either the instructor or~~
~~Either the instructors or~~ > the **student knows** the answer.

SINGULAR   SINGULAR
SUBJECT   VERB

~~Either the instructor or~~
~~Either the instructors or~~ > the **students know** the answer.

PLURAL   PLURAL
SUBJECT   VERB

~~Not only the spider but also~~ **all other arachnids have** four pairs of legs.

~~Neither spiders nor~~ **flies tempt** my appetite.

~~Six clam fritters, four blue crabs, or~~ **one steamed lobster tempts** my appetite. [For less awkward wording, rearrange the items to place the plural subject next to the verb: *One steamed lobster, four blue crabs, or six clam fritters tempt my appetite.*]

11f Using verbs in inverted word order

In English, the subject of a sentence normally precedes its verb: *Astronomy is interesting.* Inverted word order means a change in the usual order. Most questions use inverted word order. Be sure to look *after* the verb, not before it, to check that the subject and verb agree.

Is astronomy interesting?

What **are** the **requirements** for the major?

Do ~~Ravi and Mary~~ study astronomy?

If you occasionally choose to write a sentence in inverted word order to convey emphasis (see 19f), be sure to locate the subject and then make the verb agree with it.

Into deep space **shoot** probing **satellites.** [The plural verb *shoot* agrees with the inverted plural subject *satellites.*]

On the television screen **appears** an **image** of Saturn. [The singular verb *appears* agrees with the inverted singular subject *image.*]

Expletive constructions use inverted word order. With the use of *there* or *it,* they postpone the subject. Check ahead in such sentences to identify the subject, and then make sure that the verb agrees with the subject. For advice on being concise by eliminating some expletives, see 16a-1.

> **There are** nine **planets** in our solar system. [The verb *are* agrees with the subject *planets.*]

> **There is** probably no **life** on eight of them. [The verb *is* agrees with the subject *life.*]

It plus a singular form of the verb *be* can be an expletive construction as well: ***It is*** *astronomers who want new telescopes.*

EXERCISE 11-2

Consulting sections 11e and 11f, supply the correct present-tense form of the verb in parentheses.

EXAMPLE   Either sales and marketing or finance (to provide) **provides** the basic training for most top corporate executives.

1.   To an outsider, the chief executive officer (CEO) of a company or conglomerate of companies (to seem) _____ to be an independent decision-maker.

2.   Neither the economic climate nor a business's social responsibilities (to permit) _____ independence today, however.

3.   There (to be) _____ many conflicting demands to reconcile from both shareholders and consumers.

4.   Not only daily operations but also the public image of the corporation (to set) _____ the environment for a CEO.

5.   It (to be) _____ up to the finance people to set the corporation's short-term goals.

11g Using verbs with indefinite pronouns

Many **indefinite pronouns** refer to unknown persons, things, quantities, or ideas—thus the label "indefinite." In context in a sentence, even indefinite pronouns that do not have a specific antecedent° can take on clear meaning. Most indefinite pronouns are singular and require a singular verb for agreement. Two indefinite pronouns, *both* and *many*, are always plural and require a plural verb. A few indefinite pronouns can be singular or plural. See Chart 77 for a list of indefinite pronouns and their numbers. (For advice on avoiding sexist language with indefinite pronouns, see 11q and 21b.)

COMMON INDEFINITE PRONOUNS		77
ALWAYS PLURAL		
both	many	
ALWAYS SINGULAR		
another	every	no one
anybody	everybody	nothing
anyone	everyone	one
anything	everything	somebody
each	neither	someone
either	nobody	something
SINGULAR OR PLURAL DEPENDING ON CONTEXT		
all	more	none
any	most	some

SINGULAR INDEFINITE PRONOUNS

Everything about that intersection **is** dangerous.

But whenever **anyone says** anything, **nothing is** done.

Each of us **has** [not *have*] to shovel snow; **each is** [not *are*] expected to help.

Every snowstorm of the past two years **has** [not *have*] been severe; **every** one of them **has** [not *have*] caused massive traffic jams.

SINGULAR OR PLURAL INDEFINITE PRONOUNS

Some of our streams **are** polluted. [*Some* refers to the plural *streams*, so the plural verb *are* is correct.]

Some pollution **is** reversible, but **all** pollution **is** a threat to the balance of nature. [*Some* and *all* refer to the singular *pollution,* so the singular verb *is* is correct in both cases.]

All that environmentalists ask **is** to give nature a chance. [*All* has the meaning here of "the entire thing" or "the only thing," so the singular verb *is* is correct.]

Winter has driven the birds south; **all are** gone. [*All* refers to *birds,* so the plural verb *are* is correct.]

❖ USAGE ALERT: Do not mix singular and plural when indefinite pronouns function as adjectives°, as in constructions such as *this kind, this type, these kinds,* and *these types. This* is singular, as are *kind* and *type; these* is plural, as are *kinds* and *types: **This kind** of weather **makes** me shiver. **These kinds** of sweaters **keep** me warm.*❖

11h Using verbs in context for collective nouns

A **collective noun** names a group of people or things: *family, group, audience, class, number, committee, team,* and the like. When the group acts as one unit, use a singular verb. When the members of the group act individually, thus creating more than one action, use a plural verb.

The senior class nervously **awaits** final exams. [*Class* is acting as a single unit, so the verb is singular.]

The senior class were fitted for their graduation robes today. [Each member was fitted individually, so because there was more than one fitting the verb is plural.]

The couple in blue **is** engaged. [*Couple* refers to a single unit, so the verb is singular.]

The couple say their vows tomorrow. [Each of the two people will take a separate action, so because there is more than one action, the verb is plural.]

11i Making a linking verb agree with the subject—not the subject complement

Linking verbs indicate a state of being or a condition. They connect the subject to its **complement,** which is a word that renames or describes the subject. You can think of a linking verb as an equal sign between a subject and its complement, called the **subject complement.**

> The car **looks** new. [*The car = new; the car* is the subject, *looks* is the linking verb, and *new* is the subject complement.]

When you write a sentence that contains a subject complement, remember that the verb always agrees with the subject. For the purposes of agreement, ignore the subject complement.

NO	**The worst part** of owning a car **are** the bills. [The subject is *the worst part,* with which the verb *are* does not agree; the subject complement is *the bills.*]
YES	**The worst part** of owning a car **is** the bills. [The subject *the worst part* agrees with the verb *is;* the subject complement is *the bills.*]

When the wording of a sentence is revised so that the word or words that were the subject complement become the subject, the same rule applies: the verb always agrees with the subject. For the purposes of agreement, ignore the subject complement.

NO	**Bills is** the worst part of owning a car.
YES	**Bills are** the worst part of owning a car.

11j Using verbs that agree with the antecedents of *who, which,* and *that*

The pronouns *who, which,* and *that* have the same form in singular and plural. Before deciding whether the verb° should be singular or plural, find the pronoun's antecedents°.

> The scientist will share the income from her new patent with the graduate **students who work** with her. [*Who* refers to *students,* so the plural verb *work* is used.]

> George Jones is **the student who works** in the science lab. [*Who* refers to *student,* so the singular verb *works* is used.]

Be especially careful when you use *one of the* or *the only one of the* in a sentence before *who, which,* or *that.* If the pronoun refers to *one,* use a singular verb. If the pronoun refers to what comes after *one of the,* use a plural verb.

> Tracy is one of the students **who talk** in class. [*Who* refers to *students,* so *talk* is plural.]

> Jim is the only one of the students **who talks** in class. [*Who* refers to only *one,* so *talks* is singular.]

261

EXERCISE 11-3

Consulting sections 11g through 11j, supply the correct present-tense form of the verb in parentheses.

EXAMPLE Everyone (to know) **knows** that a good laugh (to make) _____ most people feel better.

1. Now a group of humour consultants (to work) _____ to introduce laughter to North American businesses.
2. They believe that the best introduction for a speech (to be) _____ jokes and humorous observations.
3. C. W. Metcalf has developed one of the programs that (to encourage) _____ people to laugh at their own problems.
4. A large number of personnel officers (to say) _____ they prefer to hire workers who (to have) _____ a sense of humour.
5. Sales representatives find that almost anyone (to listen) _____ more attentively to a person who (to make) _____ an amusing comment.

11k Using singular verbs with subjects that specify amounts and with singular subjects that are in plural form

Subjects that refer to sums of money, distance, or measurement are considered singular and take singular verbs.

Two hours is not enough time to finish that project.

Three hundred dollars is what we must pay.

Three-quarters of an inch is needed for a perfect fit.

Five kilometres is a short sprint for some serious joggers.

Many words that end in -s or -ics are singular in meaning and so need singular verbs, despite their plural appearance. These words include *news, ethics,* and *measles.* They also include *economics, mathematics, physics,* and *statistics* when these words refer to courses of study. Also, *the United States of America* is singular (see also 41c).

The **news gets** better each day. [*News* is singular, so the singular verb *gets* is correct.]

Statistics is required of science majors. [*Statistics* is a course of study, so the singular verb *is* is correct.]

Statistics show that a teacher shortage is coming. [*Statistics* refers to separate pieces of information, so the plural verb *show* is correct.]

Some nouns are singular in some contexts and plural in others. They include *politics* and *sports*. Such words agree with singular or plural verbs, depending on the meaning of the sentence.

Sports is a good way to build physical stamina.

Three **sports are** offered at the recreation centre.

Some words require a plural verb even though they refer to one thing: *jeans, pants, scissors, clippers, tweezers, eyeglasses, thanks,* and *riches.* If, however, the word *pair* is used in conjunction with *jeans, pants, scissors, clippers, tweezers,* or *eyeglasses,* a singular verb is required to agree with *pair.*

My slacks need pressing.

My pair of slacks needs pressing.

Series and *means* have the same form in singular and plural, so the meaning determines whether the verb is singular or plural.

Six new television series are beginning this week.

A series of disasters is plaguing our production.

111 Using singular verbs for titles of written works, companies, and words as terms

Even when plural° and compound nouns° occur in a title, the title itself indicates one work or entity. Therefore, titles of written works are singular and require singular verbs.

Breathing Lessons by Anne Tyler **is** a prize-winning novel.

If a word that is plural is referred to as a term, it requires a singular verb.

***We* implies** that I am included.

I've come to think that ***scattered showers* is** a meteorologist's euphemism for *drenching thunderstorms.*

EXERCISE 11-4

Consulting sections 11k and 11l, supply the correct present-tense form of the verb in parentheses.

EXAMPLE   Although it names awards as desirable as Oscars, the term *Louies* rarely (to gain) **gains** instant recognition.

1.   One of the highlights of the greeting-card industry (to be) _____ its annual international meeting, at which Louies are awarded to the year's outstanding cards.

2. Thirty (to be) _____ an astonishing number of categories for greeting cards, including graduation, get well, religious holidays, other holidays, and special effects.

3. The category *special effects* (to include) _____ cards with pop-up, musical, and even lighted messages, which flash out their greetings.

4. Each birth announcement card from one publisher (to come) _____ with two envelopes, one pink and one blue.

5. Of all the many greetings sent through the mail, the number-one bestseller (to remain) _____ Christmas cards.

PRONOUN–ANTECEDENT AGREEMENT

11m Understanding pronoun–antecedent agreement

Pronoun–antecedent agreement means that pronouns (such as *it, they, their;* see 7b) must "match" in form with their **antecedents**— the nouns°, noun phrases°, or other pronouns to which they refer. To agree grammatically, pronouns must match in number (singular or plural) and in person (first, second, or third person); Chart 78 shows these relationships. For explanations of major concepts in grammatical agreement, consult Chart 72 in section 11a.

PATTERN FOR BASIC PRONOUN–ANTECEDENT AGREEMENT   78

Loud music has **its** harmful side effects.

THIRD-PERSON SINGULAR ANTECEDENT   THIRD-PERSON SINGULAR PRONOUN

The **musicians** damaged **their** hearing.

THIRD-PERSON PLURAL ANTECEDENT   THIRD-PERSON PLURAL PRONOUN

Agreement between pronouns and antecedents must be clear so that readers are not distracted by having to figure out the intended meaning of a sentence. (For related material on subjects and verbs, see section 11a. Also, for advice about staying consistent in person and number, see section 15a-1.)

The **firefly** glows with luminescent light when **it** emerges from **its** nest at dusk. [The singular pronouns *it* and *its* match their singular antecedent *firefly*.]

Fireflies glow with luminescent light when **they** emerge from **their** nests at dusk. [The plural pronouns *they* and *their* match their plural antecedent *fireflies*.]

11n Using pronouns with antecedents connected with *and*

When two or more antecedents are connected with *and,* they require a plural pronoun, even if the separate antecedents are singular. (For related material on subjects and verbs, see 11d.)

The Cascade Diner *and* the Wayside Diner closed for New Year's Eve to give **their** [not *its*] employees the night off. [separate diners]

An exception occurs when *and* joins singular nouns that combine to form a single thing or person.

My **best friend and neighbour** makes **his** [not *their*] excellent chili every Saturday. [The best friend is the same person as the neighbour. If two different people were involved, *his* would become *their*—and *makes* would become *make*.]

each, every

The words *each* and *every* are singular. When *each* or *every* precedes antecedents joined by *and,* the pronoun must be singular. (For related material on subjects and verbs, see 11d. Also, for advice about pronoun agreement for *each* or *every* used alone, see 11p.)

Each human hand and foot leaves **its** [not *their*] distinctive footprint.

The same rule holds when the construction *one of the* follows *each* or *every: **Each one of the robbers** left **his** [not *their*] fingerprints at the scene.*

11o Making the pronoun agree with the nearest antecedent

Antecedents joined by *or, nor,* or correlative conjunctions (such as *either ... or, not only ... but [also];* for a list, see 7h) often mix singular and plural. For the purposes of agreement, ignore everything before the final antecedent. (For related material on subject–verb agreement, see 11e.) The pattern in Chart 79 illustrates this principle.

PATTERN WHEN ANTECEDENTS ARE JOINED BY *OR*   79

Either the loudspeakers or **the microphone** needs **its** electric cord repaired.

SINGULAR ANTECEDENT   SINGULAR PRONOUN

Either the microphone or **loudspeakers** need **their** electric cords repaired.

PLURAL ANTECEDENT   PLURAL PRONOUN

Each night after the restaurant closes, either the resident mice or **the owner's cat** manages to get **itself** a good meal of leftovers.

Each night after the restaurant closes, either the owner's cat or **the resident mice** manage to get **themselves** a good meal of leftovers.

11p Using pronouns with indefinite-pronoun antecedents

Many indefinite pronouns refer to unknown persons, things, quantities, or ideas—thus the label "indefinite." In context within a sentence, even indefinite pronouns that do not have a specific antecedent take on clear meaning. Most indefinite pronouns are singular. Two indefinite pronouns, *both* and *many*, are plural and thus function as plurals when they are antecedents. A few indefinite pronouns can be singular or plural, depending on the meaning of the sentence. (For a list of indefinite pronouns grouped by number, see Chart 77 in section 11g. For advice on avoiding sexist language with indefinite pronouns, see 11q and 21b.)

SINGULAR INDEFINITE PRONOUNS

Everyone taking this course hopes to get **his or her** [not *their*] degree within a year.

Anybody wanting to wear a cap and gown at graduation must have **his or her** [not *their*] measurements taken.

Each student **is** [not *are*] hoping for a passing grade.

Each of the students handed in **his or her** [not *their*] final term paper.

Every student **needs** [not *need*] encouragement now and then.

Every student in my classes **is** [not *are*] studying hard.

SINGULAR OR PLURAL INDEFINITE PRONOUNS

When winter break arrives for students, **most** leave **their** dormitories for the comforts of home. [*Most* refers to students, so the plural pronoun *their* is correct.]

As for the luggage, **most** is already on **its** way to the airport. [*Most* refers to *luggage*, so the singular pronoun *its* is correct.]

None fear that **they** will fail. [The entire group does not expect to fail, so a plural noun is correct.]

None fears that **he or she** will fail. [No one individual expects to fail, so a singular pronoun is correct; note that *he or she* always functions as a singular pronoun (see Chart 80).]

11q Avoiding sexist pronoun use

In the past, grammatical convention specified using masculine pronouns to refer to indefinite pronouns: "*Everyone* open *his* book." Today, people are more conscious that the pronouns *he, his, him,* and *himself* exclude women, who comprise over half the population. Many experienced writers try to avoid using masculine pronouns to refer to the entire population. Chart 80 shows three ways to avoid using masculine pronouns when referring to males and females together. (For advice on how to avoid other types of sexist language, see 21b.)

WAYS TO AVOID USING ONLY THE MASCULINE PRONOUN TO REFER TO MALES AND FEMALES TOGETHER   80

Solution 1: Use a pair of pronouns—but try to avoid a pair more than once in a sentence or in many sentences in a row. When you use a *he or she* construction, remember that it acts as a singular pronoun.

> **Everyone** hopes that **he or she** wins the scholarship.

> With the explosion of medical information, a **doctor** usually has time to read in only **his or her** specialty.

Solution 2: Revise into the plural.

> **Many people** hope that **they** win the scholarship.

> With the explosion of medical information, few **doctors** have time to read outside **their** specialties.

Solution 3: Recast the sentence.

> Everyone hopes to win the scholarship.

> With the explosion of medical information, few specialists have time for general reading.

11r Using pronouns with collective-noun antecedents

A **collective noun** names a group of people or things, such as *family, group, audience, class, number, committee,* and *team.* When the group acts as one unit, use a singular pronoun to refer to it. When the members of the group act individually, thus performing more than one action, use a plural pronoun.

> **The audience** was cheering as **it** stood to applaud the performers. [The audience was acting as one unit, so the singular pronoun *it* is correct.]

> **The audience** put on **their** coats and walked out. [Here the members of the audience were acting as individuals, so all the actions are counted as many individual actions. Therefore the plural pronoun *their* is correct.]

The family is spending **its** vacation in the Laurentians. [All the family members went to one place together.]

The family are spending **their** vacations in the Laurentians, the Rockies, and the Swiss Alps. [Each family member went to a different place.]

EXERCISE 11-5

Consulting sections 11p through 11r, choose the proper pronoun to agree with its antecedent.

EXAMPLE   Many people wonder what gives certain leaders (his or her, their) **their** spark and magnetic personal appeal.

1. The cluster of personal traits that produces star quality is called *charisma*, a state that bestows special power on (its, their) _____ bearers.

2. Charisma is the quality that allows an individual to empower (himself, herself, himself or herself, themselves) _____ and others.

3. Power and authority alone do not guarantee charisma; to produce it, (it, they) _____ must be combined with passion and strong purpose.

4. A charismatic leader has the ability to draw other people into (his, her, his or her, their) _____ dream or vision.

5. (He, She, He or she, They) _____ inspires followers to believe that the leader's goals are the same as (his, her, his or her, their) _____ own.

6. Not all leaders who possess charisma enjoy having this ability to attract and influence (his, his or her, their) _____ followers.

7. Charismatic leaders are often creative, especially in (his, his or her, their) _____ capacity for solving problems in original ways.

8. Today, a number of major corporations offer (its, their) _____ employees charisma-training courses to enhance leadership qualities.

9. Usually, it is not the quiet, low-profile manager but rather the charismatic manager with strong leadership qualities who convinces others that (his, her, his or her, their) _____ best interests are served by the course of action (he, she, he or she, they) _____ is proposing.

10. Charisma trainers advise would-be leaders to start by bringing order to (his, her, his or her, their) _____ activities; in stressful times, anyone who appears to have some part of (his, her, his or her, their) _____ life under control makes others relax and perform (his, her, his or her, their) _____ responsibilities better.

Focus on Revising

REVISING YOUR WRITING

If you make errors in agreement when you write, go back to your writing and locate the errors. Using this chapter as a resource, revise your writing to correct the problems. Sections 11a through 11l discuss subject–verb agreement. Sections 11m through 11r discuss pronoun–antecedent agreement.

CASE STUDY: REVISING FOR AGREEMENT

In these case studies, you can observe a student writer revising. Then you have the chance to revise other student writing on your own.

Observation

A student wrote the following draft for a course in training rehabilitation therapists. The assignment was to discuss the main idea of a film about handicapped athletes. The material offers a good summary of the film, but the draft's effectiveness is diminished by errors in subject–verb agreement and in pronoun–antecedent agreement.

Read through the draft. The errors are highlighted and explained. Before you look at the student's revision, revise the material yourself. Then compare your revision with the student's.

> Last week, students training as physical therapists saw a film about severely handicapped people participating actively in sports. The class know now that doing the impossible is becoming normal for many handicapped people.
> General fitness and eagerness to compete is among the reasons that a handicapped person might want to develop their skill in sports. All that is

singular verb needed for this collective noun: 11h

verb should be plural for subjects joined by *and*: 11d

singular pronoun needed: 11m

needed is a minimum of mobility and the will to train very hard. Either artificial limbs—called *prostheses*—or a wheelchair allow many severely handicapped people to become athletes. Advances in design and material have led to better athletic equipment for the handicapped.

Barriers are broken daily. Rafting, rock climbing, and basketball have found enthusiasts among the handicapped. Marathon racing, along with skiing and cycling, also have great appeal. Many have tried their skill at these sports. One competitive event for the handicapped was the eighth Paralympic Games, which was held in Seoul, South Korea, the site of the 1988 Olympics. Every disabled athlete needs to train somewhat differently to accommodate their particular handicap. One of today's most versatile athletes compete in a triathlon event by wearing one kind of prosthesis for cycling, another for running, and none for swimming.

Annotations (left margin):
- the linking verb should agree with the subject: 11i
- verb should agree with subject, not with words between subject and verb: 11c
- singular verb needed to agree with *one:* 11c

Annotations (right margin):
- verb should agree with subject closer to it: 11e
- plural verb needed to agree with this use of *which:* 11j
- singular pronoun needed: 11p

Here is how the student revised the paragraph to correct the agreement errors. Your revision might not match this one exactly. Your revision should, however, deal with each error highlighted on the draft.

Last week, students training as physical therapists saw a film about severely handicapped people participating actively in sports. The class knows now that doing the impossible is becoming normal for many handicapped people.

General fitness and eagerness to compete are among the reasons that a handicapped person might want to develop his or ➔

her skill in sports. All that is needed are a minimum of mobility and the will to train very hard. Either artificial limbs—called *prostheses*—or a wheelchair allows many severely handicapped people to become athletes. Advances in design and material have led to better athletic equipment for the handicapped.

Barriers are broken daily. Rafting, rock climbing, and basketball have found enthusiasts among the handicapped. Marathon racing, along with skiing and cycling, also has great appeal. Many have tried their skill at these sports. One competitive event for the handicapped was the eighth Paralympic Games, which were held in Seoul, South Korea, the site of the 1988 Olympics.

Every disabled athlete needs to train somewhat differently to accommodate his or her particular handicap. One of today's most versatile athletes competes in a triathlon event by wearing one kind of prosthesis for cycling, another for running, and none for swimming.

Participation

A student wrote the following draft for a course called Introduction to Health Sciences. The assignment was to write about a function of the body. The material is concisely written and explains the material clearly, but the draft's effectiveness is diminished by pronoun–antecedent agreement errors and by subject-verb agreement errors.

Read through the draft. Then revise it to eliminate the errors. Also, make any additional revisions you think would improve the content, organization, and style of the material.

Without kidney function, the body's ability to regulate fluids, blood pressure, red-cell production, protein levels, and blood chemistry are destroyed. If the kidneys no longer function, the standard prescription are dialysis treatments. Two or three times a week are the norm for the treatments, which sometimes continues for months or even years. Dialysis, though, does not do everything that healthy kidneys does.

Regulating the amount of water in the blood and tissues are the best-known function of the kidney. Therefore, someone without functioning kidneys must be careful to keep their fluid intake within limits set by the doctor. Dialysis help to remove excess fluid. Reducing salt and controlling fluid intake also helps.

Neither medical procedures nor diet are effective, however, without cooperation from the patient.

The whole family are affected, so it is important for the medical team to discuss the functions of a healthy kidney with the patient and the family so that he better understand the problems involved. Once the team makes their treatment recommendations known, everyone can work together with greater patience and understanding.

12 Using Adjectives and Adverbs

Distinguishing between adjectives and adverbs

Both **adjectives** and **adverbs** are modifiers—words or groups of words that describe other words.

> **ADJECTIVE** The **brisk** *wind* blew. [Adjective *brisk* modifies noun *wind*.]

> **ADVERB** The wind *blew* **briskly.** [Adverb *briskly* modifies verb *blew*.]

SUMMARY OF DIFFERENCES BETWEEN ADJECTIVES AND ADVERBS 81	
WHAT ADJECTIVES MODIFY	**EXAMPLE**
nouns	The **busy** *lawyer* took a **quick** *look* at the members of the jury.
pronouns	*She* felt **triumphant**, for *they* were **attentive**.
WHAT ADVERBS MODIFY	**EXAMPLE**
verbs	The lawyer *spoke* **quickly** and **well**.
adverbs	The lawyer spoke **very** *quickly*.
adjectives	The lawyer was **extremely** *busy*.
independent clauses	**Therefore**, the *lawyer* rested.

The key to distinguishing between adjectives and adverbs is understanding that they modify different words or groups of words. As Chart 81 demonstrates, if you want to modify a noun° or pronoun°, use an adjective. If you want to modify a verb°, an adjective, or another adverb, use an adverb.

Inexperienced writers sometimes interchange adjectives and adverbs because of the *-ly* ending. Even though many adverbs do end in *-ly* (eat *swiftly,* eat *frequently,* eat *hungrily*), some do not (eat *fast,* eat *often,* eat *seldom*). To complicate matters further, some adjectives end in *-ly* (*lovely* flower, *friendly* dog). The *-ly* ending, therefore, is not a reliable way to identify adverbs.

EXERCISE 12-1

Consulting section 12a, first underline and label all adjectives (ADJ) and adverbs (ADV). Then go back and draw an arrow from each adjective and adverb to the word or words it modifies.

1. Before the Industrial Revolution, mortality rates were high, extremely variable, and dependent upon crop conditions and rapidly spreading epidemics.
2. A 1990 survey indicates that more seniors are living independently; for this age group, life has improved dramatically because of pensions, increased mobility, and improved general health.
3. Alarmingly, the suicide rate among young Canadian men has risen greatly over the past twenty years and it is notably higher than the suicide rate for women.
4. Age-specific mortality rates for the native population are higher than those for the Canadian population in almost all age categories; consequently, life expectancy for natives is less than for the population as a whole.
5. Today, we are hardly able to appreciate that children four generations ago could reasonably expect to be orphaned before reaching maturity, or that parents often lost one or more of their children.

12b Using adverbs—not adjectives—to modify verbs, adjectives, and other adverbs

Do not use adjectives as adverbs. Always use adverbs to modify verbs, adjectives, and other adverbs.

NO	The candidate inspired us **great.** [Adjective *great* cannot modify verb *inspired.*]
YES	The candidate inspired us **greatly.** [Adverb *greatly* can modify verb *inspired.*]
NO	The candidate felt **unusual** energetic. [Adjective *unusual* cannot modify adjective *energetic.*]
YES	The candidate felt **unusually energetic.** [Adverb *unusually* can modify adjective *energetic.*]
NO	The candidate spoke **exceptional forcefully.** [Adjective *exceptional* cannot modify adverb *forcefully.*]
YES	The candidate spoke **exceptionally forcefully.** [Adverb *exceptionally* modifies adverb *forcefully.*]

12c Not using double negatives

A **double negative** is a statement with two negative modifiers, the second of which repeats the message of the first. (This form, nonstandard today, was standard in the days of Chaucer and Shakespeare.) Negative modifiers include *no, never, not, none, nothing, hardly, scarcely,* and *barely.*

NO	The factory workers will **never** vote for **no** strike.
YES	The factory workers will **never** vote for **a** strike.

The words *not, no,* and *nothing* are particularly common in double negatives.

NO	The union members did **not** have **no** money in reserve.
YES	The union members did **not** have **any** money in reserve.
YES	The union members had **no** money in reserve.

If you use contractions, which many writers prefer to avoid in their academic writing, be especially careful not to use double negatives. When the word *not* is used in a contraction (such as *isn't, don't, didn't,* or *haven't*), the negative message carried by the contracted *not* applies to the entire statement. Do not let the *not* slip by your notice; do not add a second negative.

NO	He did**n't** hear **nothing.**
YES	He did**n't** hear **anything.**
NO	They have**n't** had **no** meeting.
YES	They have**n't** had **any** meeting.

12d Using adjectives—not adverbs—as complements after linking verbs

Linking verbs indicate a state of being or a condition. They include *be (am, is, are, was, were);* verbs related to the senses, including *look, smell, taste, sound,* and *feel;* and verbs such as *appear, seem, become, grow, turn, remain,* and *prove.* Linking verbs connect the subject° to a complement—a word that renames or describes the subject (see 7m-1). You can think of a linking verb as an equal sign between a subject and its complement.

The guests looked **happy.** [subject *guests* = adjective *happy*]

Problems can arise with verbs that function sometimes as linking verbs and sometimes as action verbs, depending on the structure of the sentence. As linking verbs, these verbs use adjectives in complements. As action verbs, these verbs use adverbs.

Zora **looks happy.** [*looks* = linking verb; *happy* = adjective]

Zora **looks happily** at the sunset. [*looks* = action verb; *happily* = adverb]

Bad—Badly

The words *bad* (adjective) and *badly* (adverb) are particularly prone to misuse with linking verbs such as *feel, grow, smell, sound, taste.* Only the adjective *bad* is correct when a verb is functioning as a linking verb. (When a verb functions as an action verb, *badly* is fine: *Zora played the piano badly.*)

FOR DESCRIBING A FEELING

| NO | The student felt **badly.** |
| YES | The student felt **bad.** |

FOR DESCRIBING A SMELL

NO   The food smelled **badly.**

YES   The food smelled **bad.**

Good—Well

Well functions both as an adverb and as an adjective. As a modifier°, *good* is always an adjective: *He wore his **good** suit. Well* is an adjective referring to good health, but it is an adverb in all other contexts.

You look **well** = You look to be in good health. [*well* = adjective]

You write **well** = You write skilfully. [*well* = adverb]

Except when *well* is an adjective referring to health, use *good* only as an adjective and *well* only as an adverb.

NO   She sings **good.** [*sings* = action verb; adverb, not adjective, required; *good* is an adjective]

YES   She sings **well.** [*well* = adverb]

EXERCISE 12-2

Consulting sections 12b, 12c, and 12d, choose the correct uses of negatives and of adjectives and adverbs.

EXAMPLE   If Halloween and horror stories are a (good, well) **good** indicator, most people never want (nothing, anything) **anything** to do with bats.

1.   Myths have labelled bats as (aggressively, aggressive) _____ and short-tempered, but biologists who (frequent, frequently) _____ handle bats call them (extreme, extremely) _____ shy and (gently, gentle) _____ .

2.   These researchers who feel (bad, badly) _____ about the bats' terrifying reputation report that bats don't (never, ever) _____ act like the fearsome creatures in legends.

3.   Bats (actual, actually) _____ (greedily, greedy) _____ eat insects by the millions, a fact that might make some people begin to feel (well, good) _____ about bats.

4.   Varying (wide, widely) _____ in size and weight, some bats have a (terrifyingly, terrifying) _____ 180-cm wingspan, while others weigh less than a penny.

5.   Many people think bats come in nothing but neutral colours like mouse grey or brown, but some bats are (bright, brightly) _____ red or yellow.

Using correct comparative and superlative forms of adjectives and adverbs

When comparisons are made, descriptive adjectives and adverbs often carry the message. Adjectives and adverbs, therefore, have forms that communicate relative degrees of intensity.

1 | Using correct forms of comparison for regular adjectives and adverbs

Most adjectives and adverbs show degrees of intensity by adding *-er* and *-est* endings or by combining with the words *more, less, least* (see Chart 82). A few adjectives and adverbs are irregular, as explained in 12e-2.

FORMS OF COMPARISON FOR REGULAR ADJECTIVES AND ADVERBS   82

FORM	FUNCTION
■ Positive	Used when nothing is being compared
■ Comparative	Used when two things are being compared, with *-er* ending or *more/less*
■ Superlative	Used when three or more things are being compared, with *-est* ending or *most/least*

POSITIVE	COMPARATIVE	SUPERLATIVE
green	greener	greenest
happy	happier	happiest
selfish	less selfish	least selfish
beautiful	more beautiful	most beautiful

Her tree is **green.**

Her tree is **greener** than his tree.

Her tree is the **greenest** tree on the block.

The choice of whether to use *-er, -est* or *more, most, less, least* depends largely on the number of syllables in the adjective or adverb.

- With **one-syllable words,** the *-er* and *-est* endings are most common: *large, larger, largest* (adjective); *far, farther, farthest* (adverb).

- With **three-syllable words,** *more, most, less, least* are used.

- With **adverbs of two or more syllables,** *more, most, less, least* are used: *easily, more easily, most easily.*

- With **adjectives of two syllables,** practice varies: some take the *-er, -est* endings; others combine with *more* and *most.*

One general rule covers two-syllable adjectives ending in *-y:* use the *-er, -est* endings after changing the *-y* to *i: pretty, prettier, prettiest.* For other two-syllable adjectives, form comparatives and superlatives intuitively, based on what you have heard or read for a particular adjective.

Be careful not to use a **double comparative** or **double superlative.** The words *more, most, less, least* cannot be used if the *-er* or *-est* ending has been used.

He was **younger** [not *more younger*] than his brother.

Her music was the **snappiest** [not *more snappiest*] on the radio.

People danced **more easily** [not *more easier*] to her music.

| 2 | **Using correct forms of comparison for irregular adjectives and adverbs** |

A few comparative and superlative forms are irregular. They are listed in Chart 83. Memorize them so that they always spring easily to mind.

The Perkinses saw a **good** movie.

The Perkinses saw a **better** movie than the Smiths did.

The Perkinses saw **the best** movie that they had ever seen.

The Changs had **little** trouble finding jobs.

The Changs had **less** trouble finding jobs than the Smiths did.

The Changs had **the least** trouble finding jobs of everyone.

❖ USAGE ALERT: Do not use *less* and *fewer* interchangeably. Use *less* with noncountable items or values that form one whole. Use *fewer* with numbers or anything that can be counted: *They consumed **fewer** calories; the sugar substitute had **less aftertaste.*** ❖

IRREGULAR COMPARATIVES AND SUPERLATIVES		83
POSITIVE [1]	**COMPARATIVE [2]**	**SUPERLATIVE [3+]**
good (adjective)	better	best
well (adjective and adverb)	better	best
bad (adjective)	worse	worst
badly (adverb)	worse	worst
many	more	most
much	more	most
POSITIVE [1]	**COMPARATIVE [2]**	**SUPERLATIVE [3+]**
some	more	most
little	less	least

EXERCISE 12-3

Consulting section 12e, do two things: First, complete this chart. Next, write sentences that set a context for each word in the completed chart.

EXAMPLE   *little:* Towering redwoods dwarfed the little Douglas fir.

POSITIVE [1]	COMPARATIVE [2]	SUPERLATIVE [3+]
little		
	greedier	
		most complete
gladly		
		fewest
	thicker	
some		

12f Avoiding too many nouns as modifiers

Sometimes nouns—words that name a person, place, thing, or idea—function as modifiers° of other nouns: *truck driver, train track, security system.* These very familiar terms create no problems. However, when nouns pile up in a sequence of modifiers, the reader has difficulty figuring out which nouns are being modified and which nouns are doing the modifying. As you revise such sentences, you can use any of several routes to clarify your material.

Sentence Rewritten

NO I asked my advisor to write **two college recommendation** letters for me.

YES I asked my advisor to write **letters of recommendation** to **two colleges** for me.

One Noun Changed to Possessive Case and Another to Adjective Form

NO The **university biology lab facilities** are available to students doing advanced **biology research projects**.

YES The **university's** biology lab facilities are available to students doing advanced **biological** research projects.

Noun Changed to Prepositional Phrase

NO Our **student advisor training program** has won awards for excellence.

YES Our training program **for student advisors** has won awards for excellence. [Notice that this change requires the plural *advisors*.]

EXERCISE 12-4

Consulting all sections of this chapter, select the better choice from each set of words in parentheses so that these sentences are suitable for academic writing.

EXAMPLE   Stunt work is a visual art that (frequent, frequently) **frequently** involves physical risk to the performer.

1. The first stunt performers were (most likely, likeliest) _____ the Roman gladiators, trained to entertain the crowds with their great skill in chariot driving and sword play.

2. Actors in the early silent movies sustained (many, more) _____ injuries during filming because they used no doubles for their stunts.

3. In a 1916 movie about the American Civil War, no (fewer, less) _____ than sixty-seven extras suffered injuries during the filming of one scene.

4. Today, more than two hundred (high, highly) _____ trained stunt performers, ranging in age from ten to eighty-two, work (regular, regularly) _____ in Hollywood movies.

5. In a single year, stunt performer Harry Madsen was beaten, knifed, shot, set on fire, and thrown out of a fourth-floor window. He was paid (good, well) _____ and had a (good, well) _____ time, too.

PART

III

Writing Correct Sentences

When you write correct sentences, you increase your chances of communicating clearly with your readers. Part Three offers you practical advice about how to avoid the most common sentence errors that interfere with the delivery of meaning. As you use Chapters 13 through 15, keep in mind that correct sentences give you a foundation on which you can build an effective, graceful, and memorable writing style.

Sentence Fragments

A sentence fragment occurs when a portion of a sentence is punctuated as a complete sentence. This chapter shows you how to distinguish between sentence fragments and complete sentences.

FRAGMENT	The telephone with redial capacity. [no verb°*]
REVISED	The telephone has redial capacity.
FRAGMENT	Rang loudly for ten minutes. [no subject°]
REVISED	The telephone rang loudly for ten minutes.
FRAGMENT	At midnight. [no verb° or subject°]
REVISED	The telephone rang at midnight.
FRAGMENT	**Because** the telephone rang loudly. [dependent clause° with subordinating conjunction°]
REVISED	Because the telephone rang loudly, the family was awakened in the middle of the night.
FRAGMENT	The telephone call **that** woke the family. [dependent clause° with relative pronoun°]
REVISED	The telephone call that woke the family was a wrong number.

Sentence fragments distract readers by intruding on the clarity of the message that you want your material to deliver.

NO	The lawyer was angry. When she returned from court. She found the key witness waiting in her office. [Was the lawyer angry when she returned from court or when she found the witness in her office?]

*Throughout this book, a degree mark (°) indicates that you can find the definition of the word in the Glossary of Terms in this handbook.

frag **13a**

YES	The lawyer was angry when she returned from court. She found the key witness waiting in her office.
YES	The lawyer was angry. When she returned from court, she found the key witness waiting in her office.

Wait until the revising° and editing° stages of your writing process to check for sentence fragments. While you are drafting°, if you suspect a sentence fragment, quickly underline or highlight the material. Then, you can easily find and check it later.

13a Testing for sentence completeness

If you write sentence fragments frequently, you need a system to check that your sentences are complete. Here is a test you can use.

TEST FOR SENTENCE COMPLETENESS 84

Question 1: **Is there a verb°?** If no, there is a fragment. To revise, see 13c.

NO Thousands of whales in the Arctic Ocean because of an early winter. [a fragment]

Question 2: **Is there a subject°?** If no, there is a fragment. To revise, see 13c.

NO Raced to reach the whales. [a fragment]

Question 3: **Does the word group include a subordinating word° and lack an independent clause°?** If yes, there is a fragment. To revise, see 13b.

NO Because the ship intended to cut a path through the ice. [a fragment]

QUESTION 1: Is there a verb?

If there is no verb, you are looking at a sentence fragment. Verbs convey information about what is happening, what has happened, or what will happen. In testing for sentence completeness, find a verb that can change form to communicate a change in time.

Yesterday, the telephone **rang.**

Now the telephone **rings.**

Verbals° do not function as verbs. Verbals are gerunds° (-*ing* forms as nouns°), present participles° (-*ing* forms as modifiers°), past participles° (-*ed* or irregular past forms as modifiers), and infinitives° (*to* forms).

FRAGMENT	Yesterday, the students registering for classes.
REVISED	Yesterday, the students **were** registering for classes.
FRAGMENT	Now the students registering for classes.
REVISED	Now the students **are** registering for classes.
FRAGMENT	Told about an excellent teacher.
REVISED	**They had been** told about an excellent teacher.
FRAGMENT	Now the students to register for classes.
REVISED	Now the students **want** to register for classes.

QUESTION 2: Is there a subject?

If there is no subject, you are looking at a sentence fragment. To find a subject, ask the verb "who?" or "what?"

FRAGMENT	Studied hard for class. [Who studied? unknown]
REVISED	The students studied hard for class. [Who studied? students]
FRAGMENT	Contained some difficult questions. [What contained? unknown]
REVISED	The test contained some difficult questions. [What contained? the test]

Every sentence must have its own subject. A sentence fragment without a subject often occurs when the missing subject is the same as the subject in the preceding sentence.

NO	The students formed a study group to prepare for the midterm exam. **Decided** to study together for the rest of the course.
YES	The students formed a study group to prepare for the midterm exam. **They decided** to study together for the rest of the course.
YES	The students formed a study group to prepare for the midterm exam, **and they decided** to study together for the rest of the course.

Imperative statements—commands and some requests—are an exception. They are not sentence fragments. Imperative statements imply the word "you" as the subject.

Run! = (You) run!

Study hard. = (You) study hard.

Please return my books. = (You) please return my books.

QUESTION 3: Do the subject and verb start with a subordinating word and lack an independent clause to complete the thought?

If the answer to Question 3 is "yes," you are looking at a sentence fragment. Subordinating words begin **dependent clauses.** A dependent clause cannot stand alone as an independent unit; it must be joined to an independent clause to be part of a complete sentence.

One type of subordinating word is a **subordinating conjunction.** A subordinating conjunction comes at the beginning of a dependent clause. Here are frequently used subordinating conjunctions. (For a more complete list that also tells the relationship each word expresses, see Chart 51 in section 7h.)

after	because	since	when
although	before	unless	whenever
as	if	until	where

FRAGMENT	**Because** she returned my books.
REVISED	**Because** she returned my books, I can study.
FRAGMENT	**When** I study.
REVISED	I have to concentrate **when** I study.

❖ PUNCTUATION ALERT: When a dependent clause starting with a subordinating conjunction (an adverb clause) comes before an independent clause, a comma usually separates the clauses (see 24b-1).❖

Another type of subordinating word is a **relative pronoun.** The most common relative pronouns are *who, which,* and *that.*

FRAGMENT	The test **that** we studied for.
REVISED	The test **that** we studied for was cancelled.
FRAGMENT	The professor **who** taught the course.
REVISED	The professor **who** taught the course was ill.

Questions can begin with words such as *when, where, who,* and *which* without being sentence fragments: *When do you want to study? Where is the library? Who is your professor? Which class are you taking?*

Chart 85 summarizes information on correcting a sentence fragment once you have identified its grammatical structure.

HOW TO CORRECT SENTENCE FRAGMENTS   85

REVISION STRATEGY

- If the sentence fragment is a dependent clause°, join it to an adjacent independent clause° (see 13b).
- If the sentence fragment is a dependent clause, revise it into an independent clause (see 13b).
- If the sentence fragment is a phrase°, join it to an adjacent independent clause (see 13c).
- If the sentence fragment is a phrase, revise it into an independent clause (see 13c).

EXERCISE 13-1

Using the Test for Sentence Completeness in Chart 84, check each word group. If a word group is a sentence fragment, explain what makes it incomplete. If a word group is a complete sentence, circle its number.

EXAMPLE   In 1972, a mummy discovered in a Chinese tomb. [No verb; Question 1 in Chart 84]

1. Researchers unwrapping the mummy containing carefully preserved body of a woman in an ancient tomb.
2. Which had been wound in twenty layers of silk.
3. Turned out to be a Chinese aristocrat named Lady Dai.
4. She was embalmed in a bath of mercury salts.
5. When she died around 168 B.C.
6. Bamboo matting and five tonnes of charcoal.
7. Absorbed excess water in the tomb and kept the body dry.
8. The body of another Chinese princess had been buried in a magnificent jade suit.
9. Because jade was also believed to preserve bodies.
10. Had decayed, unlike Lady Dai's.

13b Revising dependent clauses punctuated as sentences

A **dependent clause** contains both a subject° and a verb° but also contains a subordinating word° (see Question 3 in Chart 84). It cannot stand on its own as a sentence.

To correct a dependent clause punctuated as a sentence, you can either (1) join the dependent clause to an independent clause that comes directly before or after, or (2) drop the subordinating word. Whichever strategy you use, if necessary, add words to create an independent clause that makes sense.

FRAGMENT	Many people over twenty-five years of age are deciding to get university degrees. **Because they want the benefits of an advanced education.**
REVISED	Many people over twenty-five years of age are deciding to get university degrees because they want the benefits of an advanced education. [joined into one sentence]
REVISED	Many people over twenty-five years of age are deciding to get university degrees. They want the benefits of an advanced education. [subordinating conjunction° dropped to create an independent clause]
FRAGMENT	University attracts many older students. **Who could not attend upon graduation from high school.**
REVISED	University attracts many older students who could not attend upon graduation from high school. [joined into one sentence]
REVISED	University attracts many older students. They could not attend upon graduation from high school. [relative pronoun dropped and *they* added to create an independent clause]

❖ USAGE ALERT: When trying to identify dependent clauses, be especially careful with words that indicate time—such as *after, before, since,* and *until.* In some sentences, they function as subordinating conjunctions, but in other sentences they function as adverbs° and prepositions°. Do not automatically assume when you see these words that you are looking at a dependent clause.

Before, the class was never full. Now it is overfilled. [These are two complete sentences. In the first sentence, *before* is an adverb° modifying the independent clause° *the class was never full.*]

291

Before this semester, the class was never full. [This is a complete sentence. *Before* is the preposition° in the prepositional phrase° *before this semester.*]

Before the professor arrived. [This is a dependent clause° punctuated as a sentence, so it is a sentence fragment. *Before* is a subordinating conjunction°.]

Before the professor arrived, the room was empty. [This is a complete sentence. The dependent clause precedes an independent clause.]✤

EXERCISE 13-2

Consulting sections 13a and 13b, find and correct any sentence fragments. If a sentence is correct, circle its number.

EXAMPLE   Mordecai Richler is a novelist and essayist. Who was born in Montreal in 1931.

Mordecai Richler is a novelist and essayist who was born in Montreal in 1931.

1.   Richler made his reputation with the satirical novel *The Apprenticeship of Duddy Kravitz*. Which is a hard-edged portrait of a young entrepreneur and hustler from Montreal's Jewish quarter.

2.   Still, Richler must have warm feelings for his old St. Urbain neighbourhood and the remarkable characters who inhabit it. Because mingled with the satire are sympathy and even nostalgia.

3.   Unless people can be convinced otherwise. They will continue to believe that there is much of Richler himself in his funny, pathetic, yet engaging anti-heroes. Who try to make their way in an unsympathetic world.

4.   Even though much of Richler's wit is aimed at people striving to escape their modest backgrounds. Satires like *Solomon Gursky Was Here* have not spared the Canadian elite, whom Richler shows with feet of clay and closets full of embarrassing secrets.

5.   In a series of essays, Richler has turned his pen against nationalist intellectuals in Quebec. If Richler insists. That his essay *Oh Canada! Oh Quebec!* with its sad subtitle *Requiem for a Divided Country* is serious political analysis. Why does his publisher catalogue it as "humour"?

13c Revising phrases punctuated as sentences

A **phrase** is a group of words that lacks a subject°, a verb°, or both. A phrase cannot stand on its own as a sentence. To revise a phrase punctuated as a sentence, you may choose to (1) rewrite it to become an independent clause°, or (2) join it to an independent clause that comes directly before or after.

A phrase containing only a verbal (an infinitive°, a past participle°, or a present participle°) but no verb is a fragment, not a sentence.

FRAGMENT	The mayor called a news conference last week. **To announce new programs for crime prevention and care for the homeless.** [*To announce* starts an infinitive phrase, not a sentence.]
REVISED	The mayor called a news conference last week to announce new programs for crime prevention and care for the homeless. [joined into one sentence]
REVISED	The mayor called a news conference last week. She wanted to announce new programs for crime prevention and care for the homeless. [rewritten]
FRAGMENT	**Introduced by her assistant.** The mayor began with an opening statement. [*Introduced* starts a participial phrase, not a sentence.]
REVISED	Introduced by her assistant, the mayor began with an opening statement. [joined into one sentence]
REVISED	The mayor was introduced by her assistant. She began with an opening statement. [rewritten]
FRAGMENT	**Hoping for strong public support.** She gave many examples of problems everywhere in the city. [*Hoping* starts a participle phrase, not a sentence.]
REVISED	Hoping for strong public support, she gave many examples of problems everywhere in the city. [joined into one sentence]
REVISED	She was hoping for strong public support. She gave many examples of problems everywhere in the city. [rewritten]

A **prepositional phrase** starts with a preposition°. It is not a sentence.

FRAGMENT	Cigarette smoke made the conference room seem airless. **During the long news conference.** [*During* starts a prepositional phrase, not a sentence.]
REVISED	Cigarette smoke made the conference room seem airless during the long news conference. [joined into one sentence]
REVISED	Cigarette smoke made the conference room seem airless. It was hard to breathe during the long news conference. [rewritten]

An **appositive** is one or more words that renames a noun°. It is not a sentence.

FRAGMENT	Most people respected the mayor. **A politician with fresh ideas and practical solutions.** [*A politician* starts an appositive, not a sentence.]
REVISED	Most people respected the mayor, a politician with fresh ideas and practical solutions. [joined into one sentence]
REVISED	Most people respected the mayor. She seemed to be a politician with fresh ideas and practical solutions. [rewritten]

A **compound predicate** contains two or more verbs°. To be part of a complete sentence, a predicate must have a subject. When the second half of a compound predicate is punctuated as a separate sentence, it is not a sentence.

FRAGMENT	The reporters asked the mayor many questions about the details of her program. **And then discussed her answers among themselves.** [*And then discussed* is the start of a compound predicate, not a sentence.]
REVISED	The reporters asked the mayor many questions about the details of her program and then discussed her answers among themselves. [joined into one sentence]
REVISED	The reporters asked the mayor many questions about the details of her program. Then the reporters discussed her answers among themselves. [rewritten]

EXERCISE 13-3

Go back to Exercise 13-1 and revise any sentence fragments into complete sentences. In some cases you may be able to combine two fragments into one complete sentence.

EXERCISE 13-4

Consulting sections 13a, 13b, and 13c, revise this paragraph to eliminate any sentence fragments. In some cases, you can combine word groups to create complete sentences; in other cases, you must supply missing elements to revise word groups. Some sentences may not require revision. In your final version, check not only the individual sentences but also the clarity of the whole paragraph.

(1) The technological accomplishments of the first North Americans are overlooked by modern textbooks on the history of science. (2) And have often been underestimated. (3) One example being the great earthen mounds constructed by the Adena Mound Builders along the shore of the Mississippi River and its tributaries in the United States. (4) More than 100 000 of such temple, burial, and dwelling sites left today. (5) The average mound involving some 3 million hours of human labour. (6) The great mound at Cahokia is not as high as the pyramid of Pharaoh Cheops in Egypt, but it is much larger at its base. (7) Representing a greater achievement than the Egyptian pyramid. (8) Another example on a far smaller scale being the domed snow house known as the igloo. (9) Built by the Inuit people of the Far North. (10) This construction, called a technological masterpiece. (11) Classical Greece did not have the dome. (12) In its architectural vocabulary. (13) In early Europe, only the Romans, gifted engineers, learned to use it.

13d   Recognizing intentional fragments

Professional writers sometimes intentionally use fragments for emphasis and effect.

> But in the main I feel like a brown bag of miscellany propped against a wall. Pour out the contents, and there is discovered a jumble of small things priceless and worthless. **A first-water diamond, an empty spool, bits of broken glass, lengths of string, a key to a door long since crumbled away, a rusty knife-blade, old shoes saved for a road that never was and never will be, a nail bent under the weight of things too heavy for any nail, a dried flower or two still a little fragrant.**
>
> —Zora Neale Hurston, *How It Feels to Be Colored Me*

The ability to judge the difference between an acceptable and unacceptable sentence fragment comes from much exposure to reading the work of skilled writers. Many instructors, therefore, do not accept sentence fragments in student writing until a student can demonstrate the consistent ability to write well-constructed complete sentences.

EXERCISE 13-5

Consulting sections 13a, 13b, and 13c, revise this paragraph to eliminate any sentence fragments. In some cases, you can combine word groups to create complete sentences; in other cases, you must supply missing elements to revise word groups. In your final version, check not only the individual sentences but also the clarity of the whole paragraph.

(1) Some of the most magnificent Easter eggs in the world. (2) Created by Peter Carl Fabergé. (3) A master Russian goldsmith. (4) In 1884, Czar Alexander III, wanting a special Easter gift for his wife, the Czarina. (5) Although Fabergé's first Imperial Easter Egg appeared to be an ordinary hen's egg. (6) The outer shell made of gold that had been enamelled to the off-white colour of a hen's egg. (7) Opening to reveal a yolk, also of gold, which contained a tiny chicken, elaborately crafted of several shades of gold. (8) Hidden inside the chicken was a surprise. (9) An intricate jewelled model of the imperial crown. (10) Which opened to reveal a tiny ruby egg. (11) Because the Czar was so delighted. (12) He commissioned Fabergé to create a new egg each Easter. (13) And gave the goldsmith one other instruction. (14) To include a surprise in each egg. (15) Which, of course, Fabergé wisely did.

EXERCISE 13-6

Consulting sections 13a, 13b, and 13c, revise this paragraph to eliminate any sentence fragments. In some cases, you can join word groups to create complete sentences; in other cases, you have to revise the word groups into complete sentences. In your final version, check not only the individual sentences but also the clarity of the whole paragraph.

(1) Students looking for jobs need more than the "Help Wanted" section of a newspaper. (2) One major tool, a carefully written résumé. (3) A résumé should be written in a standard form. (4) And proofread carefully to eliminate errors in spelling, punctuation, or grammar. (5) For the content of the résumé. (6) Students should analyze all types of experiences. (7) A résumé including not only paid jobs but also volunteer positions and extracurricular activities. (8) Students have a better chance of getting a job. (9) If they have supervised other people, handled money, or taken on highly responsible tasks. (10) Such as participating in political campaigns or chairing major committees at school. (11) Many employers will consider student résumés. (12) Especially when the résumés include names of the students' supervisors.

Focus on Revising

REVISING YOUR WRITING

If you write sentence fragments, go back to your writing and locate them. Then figure out why each is a sentence fragment by using the Test for Sentence Completeness in 13a. Next, revise each sentence fragment into a complete sentence, referring to 13a, 13b, and 13c.

CASE STUDIES: REVISING TO AVOID SENTENCE FRAGMENTS

In these case studies, you can observe a student writer revising. Then you have the chance to revise other student writing on your own.

Observation

A student wrote the following draft for a course called Introduction to the Novel. The assignment was to compose a paragraph about the childhood of a major novelist. This material is well organized as a narrative and tells an interesting story, but the draft's effectiveness is diminished by the presence of sentence fragments.

Read through the draft. The sentence fragments are highlighted. Before you look at the student's revision, revise the material yourself. Then compare your revision with the student's.

The creative imagination of Victorian novelist Charlotte Brontë got an early start. When she was a child. Her father brought her brother, Branwell, a set of wooden soldiers. Her father who was a clergyman and who wrote poetry and a novel as well as sermons. After he gave Branwell the set. He told Charlotte and her sisters, Emily and Anne, each to pick one of

dependent clause punctuated as a sentence: 13b

dependent clause punctuated as a sentence: 13b

the toy soldiers. And give it a   —phrase—part of
name. Each sister then made up   compound
a history of her soldier. Soon   predicate—
creating tales of heroism.   punctuated as a
                                  sentence: 13c

phrase—with *-ing*   Inspired by the pleasure of   ┐
form of verb—   telling stories. Charlotte, together   phrase—with
punctuated as a   with her brother, invented an   past participle
sentence: 13c   imaginary kingdom. With Angria   of verb—
                     as its name. Because she   punctuated as a
                                                 sentence: 13c
prepositional phrase   treasured her fantasies and   ┐
punctuated as a   wanted to remember them.   dependent
sentence: 13c   Charlotte began to write them in   clause
                       notebooks. Wanting them to   punctuated as a
                                                     sentence: 13b
phrase—using *-ing*   look like miniature editions of
form of verb—   books. She printed in a tiny,
punctuated as a   almost microscopically small
sentence: 13c   handwriting. Those notebooks
                      stand as a reminder of how early
                      in life Charlotte Brontë
                      expressed her creativity.

Here is how the student revised the paragraph to eliminate the sentence fragments. In many places, the student could correct the error in more than one way. Your revision, therefore, might not be exactly like this one, but it should not contain any sentence fragments.

The creative imagination of Victorian novelist Charlotte Brontë got an early start. When she was a child, her father brought her brother, Branwell, a set of wooden soldiers. Her father was a clergyman who wrote poetry and a novel as well as sermons. After he gave Branwell the set, he told Charlotte and her sisters, Emily and Anne, each to pick one of the toy soldiers and give it a name. Each sister then made up a history of her soldier, and each soon was creating tales of heroism. Inspired by the pleasure of telling stories, Charlotte, together with her brother, invented an imaginary kingdom with Angria as its name. Because she treasured her fantasies and wanted to remember them, Charlotte began to write them in notebooks. Wanting her notebooks to look like miniature editions of books, she printed in a tiny, almost microscopically small handwriting. Those notebooks stand as a reminder of how early in life Charlotte Brontë expressed her creativity.

frag **13**

Participation

A student wrote the following draft for a course called European History. The assignment was to discuss the political atmosphere of a European nation during the seventeenth century. This material is effectively organized for chronological presentation of information, and it uses specific details well. The draft's effectiveness, however, is diminished by the presence of sentence fragments.

Read through the draft. Then revise it to eliminate the sentence fragments. Also, make any additional revisions that you think would improve the content, organization, and style of the material.

In seventeenth-century England, from the death of Elizabeth I in 1603 to William of Orange's ascension to the throne in 1689. The monarchy of England was the cause of unrest and uncertainty.

Queen Elizabeth I died single and childless in 1603. Because she did not have a direct descendant. The throne passed to the Queen's cousin. Who was crowned James I. Discord over the relative power of Parliament and the crown emerged under James I. And erupted during the reign of James's son, Charles I. Incapable of resolving the conflicts, Charles I lost both the throne and his head to Oliver Cromwell's Puritan Revolution in 1649.

Holding fast to his anti-monarchy sentiments and refusing a crown. Oliver Cromwell did not establish a new line of English monarchs. Instead, he became Lord Protector of England. When Cromwell died, his son Richard lacked the charisma and political astuteness to hold on to power. As a result, the son of Charles I was recalled from France. Where he had fled to live in safety. He was crowned Charles II in 1660. And had very limited power, according to new laws passed by Parliament. Charles II sired no legitimate heirs, so the succession passed to his brother, James. An apparently able man with one serious political handicap in seventeenth-century England. He was Catholic, at a time when the English feared that the Pope was plotting to reclaim England and rule it from Rome. When the second wife of James baptized her newborn son Catholic. Unease over James's rule escalated rapidly. To ensure the safety of his wife and new son. James sent them to France and followed soon after. James's Protestant daughter Mary took the throne. With her husband William of Orange. A Dutchman who was a staunch supporter of Protestantism. Their union was so popular with the English that William continued to rule after Mary's death in 1694. Thus, the century that saw much upheaval and instability in England ended in relative calm.

14 Comma Splices and Fused Sentences

A **comma splice** (or **comma fault**) is an error that occurs when a comma by itself joins independent clauses°. A comma is correct between two independent clauses only when it is followed by a coordinating conjunction (*and, but, for, or, nor, yet,* and *so*). The word *splice* means "to fasten ends together." The end of one independent clause and the beginning of another should not be fastened together with a comma alone.

COMMA SPLICE   The iceberg broke off from the glacier, it drifted into the sea.

A **fused sentence** is an error that occurs when two independent clauses° are not joined by a comma with a coordinating conjunction (*and, but, for, or nor, yet,* and *so*) or by other punctuation. The word *fused* means "united as if by melting together." Two independent clauses cannot be united as if melted together. A fused sentence is also known as a *run-on sentence* or a *run-together sentence.*

FUSED SENTENCE   The iceberg broke off from the glacier it drifted into the sea.

Comma splices and fused sentences are two versions of the same problem: incorrect joining of two independent clauses. Both comma splices and fused sentences distract readers from understanding the meaning you want your material to deliver.

If you tend to write comma splices and fused sentences, you might have trouble recognizing them, because they can seem to blend with surrounding sentences. Expect, therefore, to analyze your sentences individually. Wait until the revising° and editing° stages of your writing process to check for comma splices and fused sentences. While you are drafting°, if you suspect an error, quickly underline or highlight the material and keep drafting. Then, you can easily find and check it later.

Chart 86 shows you how to correct these errors and refers you to sections in this chapter for fuller explanations.

HOW TO FIND AND CORRECT COMMA SPLICES AND FUSED SENTENCES [86]

FINDING COMMA SPLICES AND FUSED SENTENCES

- Look for a pronoun° starting the second independent clause.

  NO The physicist Marie Curie discovered radium, **she** won two Nobel prizes.

- Look for a conjunctive adverb° (Chart 49 in 7f) or transitional expression° starting the second independent clause°.

  NO Marie Curie and her husband, Pierre, worked together at first, **however**, he died at age 47.

- Look for a second independent clause that explains/amplifies contrasts with, or gives an example of information in the first independent clause.

  NO Radium can cause cancer **radium is used to cure cancer.**

FIXING COMMA SPLICES AND FUSED SENTENCES

- Use a period (14b) or a semicolon (14e) between independent clauses.

  YES The physicist Marie Curie discovered radium. **She** won two Nobel Prizes.

- Use a comma + coordinating conjunction° between the clauses (14c).

  YES The physicist Marie Curie discovered radium, **and** she won two Nobel Prizes.

- Use a semicolon + conjunctive adverb or transitional expression between the clauses (14e).

  YES Marie Curie and her husband, Pierre, worked together at first; **however** he died at age 47.

- Revise one independent clause into a dependent clause° (14d).

  YES Radium, **which can cause cancer,** is also used to cure cancer.

14a Recognizing comma splices and fused sentences

To recognize comma splices and fused sentences, you need to be able to recognize an independent clause, a clause that contains a subject° and predicate°. An independent clause can stand alone as a sentence because it is an independent grammatical unit.

    SUBJECT   PREDICATE

Alexander Graham Bell   was a Canadian inventor.

If you tend to write comma splices, here is a useful technique for proofreading your work. Cover all the words on one side of the comma and see if the words remaining constitute an independent clause. If they do, cover that clause and uncover all the words on the other side of the comma. If the second side of the comma is also an independent clause, you have written a comma splice. Also, to help yourself avoid writing comma splices, become familiar with correct uses for commas, explained in Chapter 24.

Experienced writers sometimes use a comma to join very brief parallel independent clauses, especially if a negative sentence is followed by a positive sentence. *Mosquitoes do not bite, they stab.* Many instructors consider this form an error in student writing; you will never be wrong if you use a semicolon or period.

14b Using a period or semicolon to correct comma splices and fused sentences

You can use a period or semicolon to correct comma splices and fused sentences. For the sake of sentence variety and emphasis, however, do not always choose punctuation to correct this type of error. (Other methods are discussed in 14c and 14d.) Strings of too many short sentences rarely establish relationships and levels of importance among ideas.

A **period** can separate the independent clauses in a comma splice or fused sentence.

COMMA SPLICE	A shark is all cartilage, it does not have a bone in its body.
FUSED SENTENCE	A shark is all cartilage it does not have a bone in its body.
CORRECTED	A shark is all cartilage. It does not have a bone in its body.

A **semicolon** can separate the independent clauses° in a comma splice or fused sentence. Choose a semicolon only when the separate sentences are closely related in meaning. (See also 25a.)

COMMA SPLICE	Sharks can smell blood from 400 metres away, they swim toward the source like a guided missile.
FUSED SENTENCE	Sharks can smell blood from 400 metres away they swim toward the source like a guided missile.
CORRECTED	Sharks can smell blood from 400 metres away; they swim toward the source like a guided missile.

14c Using coordinating conjunctions to correct comma splices and fused sentences

When ideas in independent clauses° are closely related and grammatically equivalent, you can connect them with a coordinating conjunction (*and, but, or, nor, for, so,* and *yet*). If you are correcting a comma splice, keep the comma and insert a coordinating conjunction after it. If you are correcting a fused sentence, insert a comma followed by a coordinating conjunction.

❖ PUNCTUATION ALERT: Use a comma before a coordinating conjunction that links independent clauses° (see 24a).❖

❖ USAGE ALERT: When using a coordinating conjunction, be sure that it fits the meaning of the material. *And* signals addition, *but* and *yet* signal contrast, *for* and *so* signal cause, and *or* and *nor* signal alternatives.❖

COMMA SPLICE	Every living creature gives off a weak electrical charge in the water, special pores on a shark's skin can detect these signals.
FUSED SENTENCE	Every living creature gives off a weak electrical charge in the water special pores on a shark's skin can detect these signals.
CORRECTED	Every living creature gives off a weak electrical field in the water, and special pores on a shark's skin can detect these signals.
COMMA SPLICE	The great white shark supposedly eats humans, however most white sharks spit them out after the first bite.

303

FUSED SENTENCE	The great white shark supposedly eats humans however most white sharks spit them out after the first bite.
CORRECTED	The great white shark supposedly eats humans, but most white sharks spit them out after the first bite.

EXERCISE 14-1

Consulting sections 14a, 14b, and 14c, revise any comma splices or fused sentences by using a period, a semicolon, or a coordinating conjunction and comma.

EXAMPLE   Emily Carr was born in Victoria, British Columbia, in 1871, she died there in 1945.

Emily Carr was born in Victoria, British Columbia, in 1871; she died there in 1945.

1. Carr grew up in a disciplined, conventional household in a small and conservative city, however she went off to study art in San Francisco in 1891, after the death of her parents.
2. When she came home two years later, Carr set up a studio of her own, she roamed the beaches and forests of British Columbia sketching Indian totem poles and longhouses in their natural setting.
3. In 1910, Carr began her most important voyage she travelled to France where she developed the vivid postimpressionist style of painting for which she became known.
4. After her return to Canada, Carr's work showed new vigour clearly, her French experience had taught her how to interpret the powerful rhythms of Northwest Coast Indian art and the majesty of the region's mountains and forests.
5. Carr worked in obscurity until she was fifty-seven, she displayed her work that year in a national exhibition and, with the help of Lawren Harris and other members of the Group of Seven, she began to win wider recognition.

14d   Revising an independent clause into a dependent clause to correct a comma splice or fused sentence

You can revise a comma splice or fused sentence by changing one of two independent clauses° into a dependent clause°. This method is suitable when one idea can logically be subordinated to the other.

One way to create a dependent clause is to insert a subordinating conjunction (such as *because* and *although*; for a complete list, see Chart 51 in section 7h.) When using a subordinating conjunction, be sure that it fits the meaning of the material: for example, *as* and *because* signal reason, *although* signals contrast, *if* signals condition, and *when* signals time. This type of dependent clause is called an **adverb clause.**

❖ PUNCTUATION ALERTS: (1) If you put a period after a dependent clause that is not attached to an independent clause, you will create the error called a *sentence fragment;* see Chapter 13. (2) Generally, use a comma after an introductory dependent clause that starts with a subordinating conjunction; see 24b-1.❖

COMMA SPLICE	Homer and Langley Collyer had packed their house from top to bottom with junk, police could not open the front door to investigate a missing-persons report on the brothers.
FUSED SENTENCE	Homer and Langley Collyer had packed their house from top to bottom with junk police could not open the front door to investigate a missing-persons report on the brothers.
CORRECTED	**Because Homer and Langley Collyer had packed their house from top to bottom with junk,** police could not open the front door to investigate a missing-persons report on the brothers.
COMMA SPLICE	Old newspapers, toys, car parts, and books filled every room to the ceiling, enough space remained for fourteen pianos.
FUSED SENTENCE	Old newspapers, toys, car parts, and books filled every room to the ceiling enough space remained for fourteen pianos.
CORRECTED	**Although old newspapers, toys, car parts, and books filled every room to the ceiling,** enough space remained for fourteen pianos.

Another way to create a dependent clause is to use a **relative pronoun** (*that, which, who*). This type of dependent clause is called an **adjective clause.**

❖ PUNCTUATION ALERT: To determine whether you need commas to set off an adjective clause, check whether it is nonrestrictive (nonessential) or restrictive° (essential), as explained in 24e.❖

COMMA SPLICE	The Collyers had been crushed under a pile of newspapers, the newspapers had toppled onto the brothers.
FUSED SENTENCE	The Collyers had been crushed under a pile of newspapers the newspapers had toppled onto the brothers.
CORRECTED	The Collyers had been crushed under a pile of newspapers **that had toppled onto the brothers.**

EXERCISE 14-2

Consulting sections 14a through 14d, revise any comma splices or fused sentences.

(1) Because millions of North Americans are now cruising the information superhighway, traffic pileups and confrontations are more likely. (2) The Internet connects thousands of on-line computer networks around the world it has created a new form of personal communication that requires new rules. (3) Just as on a real highway, not all users of the information highway observe "netiquette," the rules governing on-line courtesy. (4) Sometimes the faceless communication gives timid on-liners confidence to speak their minds, however, at other times some users have less pleasant experiences. (5) A flame, for example, is an insulting message it is the on-line equivalent of a poison pen letter. (6) The quick response time of electronic mail encourages hasty people to react hastily instant anger can be thoughtlessly expressed. (7) Flamers cannot always be identified, their real names are concealed by passwords.

(8) Another prank is to impersonate another user by adopting his or her on-line name, as a result, there is no way to identify the person sending a fake message. (9) Internet lurkers are undesirable too they read other people's messages in the public spaces but are too fearful of being flamed to send their own messages.

14e Using a semicolon or a period before a conjunctive adverb or other transitional expression between independent clauses

Conjunctive adverbs and other transitional expressions link ideas between sentences. When these words fall between sentences, a period or semicolon must immediately precede them.

Conjunctive adverbs include such words as *however, therefore, also, next, then, thus, furthermore,* and *nevertheless* (for a complete list, see Chart 49 in section 7f). Remember that these words are *not* coordinating conjunctions, which work in concert with commas to join independent clauses (see 14c).

❖ PUNCTUATION ALERT: A conjunctive adverb at the beginning of a sentence is usually followed by a comma (see 24b-3).❖

COMMA SPLICE	Buying or leasing a car is a matter of individual preference, **however,** it is wise to consider several points before making a decision.
FUSED SENTENCE	Buying or leasing a car is a matter of individual preference **however,** it is wise to consider several points before making a decision.
CORRECTED	Buying or leasing a car is a matter of individual preference; **however,** it is wise to consider several points before making a decision.

Transitional expressions include *for example, for instance, in addition, in fact, of course,* and *on the other hand* (see Chart 23 in section 4d-1 for a complete list).

❖ PUNCTUATION ALERT: A transitional expression at the beginning of a sentence is usually followed by a comma (see 24b-3).❖

COMMA SPLICE	Car leasing requires a smaller down payment, **for example,** in many cases you need only $1000 or $2000 and the first monthly payment.
FUSED SENTENCE	Car leasing requires a smaller down payment **for example,** in many cases you need only $1000 or $2000 and the first monthly payment.
CORRECTED	Car leasing requires a smaller down payment. **For example,** in many cases you need only $1000 or $2000 and the first monthly payment.

A conjunctive adverb or other transitional expression can appear in more than one location within an independent clause°. In contrast, a coordinating conjunction (*and, but, or, nor, for, so,* and *yet*) can appear only between independent clauses that it joins.

> Car leasing grows more popular every year. **However,** leasers have nothing to show for their money when the lease ends.
> [conjunctive adverb]

Car leasing grows more popular every year. Leasers, **however,** have nothing to show for their money when the lease ends. [conjunctive adverb]

Car leasing grows more popular every year. Leasers have nothing to show for their money, **however,** when the lease ends. [conjunctive adverb]

Car leasing grows more popular every year. Leasers have nothing to show for their money when the lease ends, **however**. [conjunctive adverb]

Car leasing grows more popular every year, **but** leasers have nothing to show for their money when the lease ends. [coordinating conjunction]

EXERCISE 14-3

Consulting section 14e, revise any comma splices or fused sentences caused by a conjunctive adverb or other transitional expression. If an item is correct, circle its number.

EXAMPLE   The horror stories of the New England writer H. P. Lovecraft were little known during his lifetime however they gained a following of enthusiastic readers after his death in 1937.

The horror stories of the New England writer H. P. Lovecraft were little known during his lifetime. However, they gained a following of enthusiastic readers after his death in 1937.

1. Lovecraft wrote vividly of monsters from beyond space and time however, he insisted that he did not believe in the supernatural.

2. "The Shadow over Innsmouth" is Lovecraft's famous tale about the strange inhabitants of a New England port, specifically, they are part fish and part human.

3. Lovecraft wanted his invented historical backgrounds to sound factual so he often cited impressive-sounding reference works; of course, he simply made most of them up.

4. Many of Lovecraft's stories mention a volume of secret lore called the *Neocronomicon*, however, it was entirely a product of his imagination.

5. No such book exists nevertheless libraries still receive call slips for the *Neocronomicon* filled out by gullible Lovecraft readers.

EXERCISE 14-4

Consulting all sections in this chapter, revise all comma splices, using a different method of correction for each one. If an item is correct, circle its number.

EXAMPLE   People hold strong but erroneous beliefs about animal behaviour, for example, it is commonly thought that ostriches bury their heads in the sand.

People hold strong but erroneous beliefs about animal behaviour. For example, it is commonly thought that ostriches bury their heads in the sand.

1. Ostriches are said to bury their heads in the sand so that their enemies will not notice them this, naturalists maintain, is a myth.
2. A South African naturalist examined eighty years of records from ostrich farms where more than 200 000 of the birds were reared, he found that no one reported a single case of an ostrich burying its head.
3. Ostriches do listen intently for chirps, cries, and approaching footsteps with their heads near the ground, sometimes, they even lower their heads just to rest their neck muscles.
4. They also poke their heads into bushes because they are curious animals.
5. They never bury their heads in sand, they would probably suffocate if they did.

EXERCISE 14-5

Consulting all sections in this chapter, revise any fused sentences, using as many different methods explained in this chapter as you can.

(1) During the nineteenth century, a number of fearless women travelled long distances from their homes they visited places far more exotic than their native France or England. (2) Isabella Bird, for example, a British clergyman's daughter, began travelling and writing when she was in her forties she often wrote by the light of a portable oil lamp and with a gun in her pocket. (3) In 1896, she celebrated her sixty-fourth birthday that same year she crossed northwest China she hoped to reach Tibet. (4) While she was travelling, her guides collapsed with fever then her rice supply ran dangerously low. (5) Only when tribal warfare broke out, however, and the bridges were torn down did she turn around. (6) Like Isabella Bird, Flora Tristan, a native of France, proved her adventurous spirit she sailed from France to Peru, a trip that inspired her to write a book. (7) The book was published in 1838 however, its title, *Peregrinations of a Pariah,* meaning "travels of an outcast," suggests that not everyone admired its courageous author.

EXERCISE 14-6

Consulting all sections in this chapter, revise all comma splices or fused sentences, using as many different methods of correction as you can. If a sentence is correct, circle its number. After you have corrected the comma splices and fused sentences, check not only the correctness of the individual sentences but also the clarity of the entire paragraph.

(1) Archaeologists are studying modern Australia to learn how humans lived on this planet thousands of years ago many customs of the Stone Age are still practised by some Australian Aborigines today. (2) French archaeologist and painter Michel Lorblanchet spent four years in Northern Australia studying painting techniques. (3) Lorblanchet watched the Aboriginal painters work, these artists create dramatic images by spitting red ochre pain on sandstone walls in caves. (4) The artists put a mixture of red ochre and water in their mouths, as a result saliva becomes the third ingredient, which gives the paint the right consistency so that it adheres to the wall. (5) To create the mixture, they chew for several minutes their lips and teeth turn brick-red. (6) Next, they place their left hands against the wall and spit rapidly around their hands. (7) The imprint of an artist's hand is unique indeed it acts as an identifying marker. (8) Spit-painting is spiritually significant it is an act that unites painter and painting. (9) Spit is the product of human breath, it is believed to imprint images of the artist's soul on the cave wall. (1) Similar hand prints were found in an 18 000-year-old cave painting in France therefore Lorblanchet believes they were painted the same way.

Focus on Revising

REVISING YOUR WRITING

If you write comma splices or fused sentences, go back to your writing and locate them. Then figure out why each is an error by using Chart 86 above section 14a on How to Find and Correct Comma Splices and Fused Sentences. Next, using the explanations in 14b through 14e, revise your writing to eliminate the errors.

CASE STUDIES: REVISING TO AVOID COMMA SPLICES AND FUSED SENTENCES

In these case studies, you can observe a student writer revising. Then you have the chance to revise other student writing on your own.

Observation

A student wrote the following draft for a course called Introduction to Sociology in Canada. The assignment was to discuss a community organization. This material is well organized and presents its information clearly and fully. However, the draft's effectiveness is diminished by comma splices and fused sentences.

Read through the draft. The errors are highlighted and explained. Before you look at the student's revision, revise the material yourself. Then compare your revision with the student's.

> Did you know that Girl Guides of Canada, often called "Guiding," provides young women with experiences that enhance their lives by teaching them to "look wide" and "find life's gleams," while having fun? Guiding's aims, objectives, and programs are geared toward helping young women grow the three major areas of concentration are personal

fused sentence with amplification in second independent clause: 14a

development, service, and
sisterhood.

Girl Guides of Canada was
started in 1910, it is the largest
organization of young women in
Canada. Today its membership
includes 215 000 girls between
the ages of five and seventeen
in addition, 54 000 adults
eighteen years of age and above
serve as volunteer leaders. The
movement welcomes every
woman and girl without
distinction of creed, race, class,
or nationality. Guides are
divided into five age groups,
Sparks are for five-year-olds,
Brownies for six- to nine-year-
olds, *Guides* for nine- to twelve-
year-olds, *Pathfinders* for
twelve- to fifteen-year-olds, and
Senior Branches for fifteen- to
eighteen-year-olds. They can
join Guiding at any age, they are
welcome as long as they are
committed to the organization's
goals.

By exposing its members to
varied activities, Guiding helps
young women become
responsible citizens, able to offer
leadership and service to the
community, whether local,
national, or global. To acheive
such goals, Guiding has
developed extensive programs,
they include nature study, hiking,
camping, crafts, group songs
and games, and mental and
physical challenges that stimulate
members' imaginations and teach
them self-confidence.

comma splice with pronoun it: 14a

fused sentence with transitional expression: 14a

fused sentence with transitional expression: 14a

comma splice with examples in second independent clause; 14a

comma splice with pronoun they: 14a

comma splice with pronoun they: 14a

comma splice with pronoun they: 14a

Here is how the student revised the draft to correct comma splices and fused sentences. In many places, the student could correct the errors in more than one way. Your revision, therefore, might not be exactly like this one, but it should deal with each error highlighted on the draft.

Did you know that Girl Guides of Canada, often called "Guiding," provides young women with experiences that enhance their lives by teaching them to "look wide" and "find life's gleams," while having fun? Guiding's aims, objectives, and programs are geared toward helping young women grow; the three major areas of concentration are personal development, service, and sisterhood.

Girl Guides of Canada was started in 1910. It is the largest organization of young women in Canada. Today its membership includes 215 000 girls between the ages of five and seventeen. In addition, 54 000 adults eighteen years of age and above serve as volunteer leaders. The movement welcomes every woman and girl without distinction of creed, race, class, or nationality. Guides are divided into five age groups. _Sparks_ are for five-year-olds, _Brownies_ for six- to nine-year-olds, _Guides_ for nine- to twelve-year-olds, _Pathfinders_ for twelve- to fifteen-year-olds, and _Senior Branches_ for fifteen- to eighteen-year-olds. They can join Guiding at any age; they are welcome as long as they are committed to the organization's goals.

By exposing its members to varied activities, Guiding helps young women become responsible citizens, able to offer leadership and service to the community, whether local, national, or global. To achieve such goals, Guiding has developed extensive programs. They include nature study, hiking, camping, crafts, group songs and games, and mental and physical challenges that stimulate members' imaginations and teach them self-confidence.

Participation

A student wrote the following draft for a course called Introduction to Fashion Design. The assignment was to describe characteristics of fabric. This material is well organized and uses specific examples well, but the draft's effectiveness is diminished by comma splices and fused sentences.

Read through the draft. Then revise it to eliminate the comma splices and fused sentences. Also, make any additional revisions that you think would improve the content, organization, and style of the material.

As consumers, when we buy clothes, we often make choices on the basis of the fabric of an article of clothing, therefore, fashion designers always pay attention to matters of composition and design in fabrics.

Fabric is composed of natural fibres, synthetic fibres, and blends of the two. Natural fibres include cotton, linen, and wool, they offer the advantages of durability and absorbency. Synthetic fibres include rayon, polyester, acrylic, or combinations of them and other synthetic fibres they resist wrinkling and retain their colour well. Fibre blends combine natural and synthetic fibres to create combinations such as cotton and polyester, which offer the advantages of each but have their own problems, such as retaining stains.

The design of fabric is affected by the way that the fabric is produced, for example, a fabric can be produced on a loom to create woven fabrics such as crepe and denim, conversely, a fabric can be produced on a knitting machine to create fabrics such as jersey and velour. Once the basic fabric is being produced, special patterns can be woven or knit into it, for instance, diagonal patterns can be woven into cotton fabrics for a geometric effect, and vertical patterns can be woven into a cable-stitched fabric for a thicker look and feel. Various finishes can further alter a fabric's appearance stone washing, for example, gives denim a worn look, and brushing gives flannel a softer look. Puckers or wrinkles can be set into a fabric, these features characterize fabrics such as seersucker and crinkle gauze.

These many options, and others, in fabrics permit fashion designers to satisfy the needs of many different types of people, some consumers care more about being in style than building a long-lasting wardrobe, while others place a high priority on ease of care or on comfortable fit.

Sentences that Send Unclear Messages

A sentence can seem structurally correct at first glance, as if no grammatical principles of English had been violated, but can still have internal flaws that keep it from delivering a sensible message. Wait until the revising° and editing° stages of your writing process to check your sentences for the problems listed in Chart 87. While you are drafting°, if you suspect that you have made one of these errors, quickly underline or highlight the material and continue drafting. Then, you can easily find and check it later.

WAYS THAT SENTENCES SEND UNCLEAR MESSAGES	87
PROBLEM	**SEE SECTION**
■ Unnecessary shifts	
Person° and number°	15a-1
Subject° and voice°	15a-2
Tense° and mood°	15a-3
Direct discourse° and indirect discourse°	15a-4
■ Misplaced modifiers°	15b
■ Dangling modifiers°	15c
■ Mixed sentences	
Mixed constructions	15d-1
Faulty predication	15d-2
■ Incomplete sentences	15e

Many sentence flaws that send unclear messages can be hard to spot because of the way the human brain works. When writers know what they mean to say, they sometimes misread what is on the paper for what they intend. The mind unconsciously adjusts an error or fills in missing material. Readers, on the other hand, see only what is on the paper. For suggestions to help you see such flaws, see Chart 88.

NO	Heated for 30 seconds, you get bubbles on the surface of the mixture. [This sentence says *you* are heated for 30 seconds.]
YES	After the mixture is heated for 30 seconds, bubbles form on the surface.
NO	After you boil the mixture for two minutes, it is cooled in a test tube. [This sentence shifts from *you* to *it* and from the active voice° to the passive voice°.]
YES	After the mixture is boiled for two minutes, it is cooled in a test tube.
YES	After boiling the mixture for two minutes, cool it in a test tube.
NO	The chemical reaction taking place rapidly creates a salt. [*Rapidly* could refer to the speed of the reaction or to the speed at which the salt is created; readers cannot know.]
YES	The chemical reaction takes place rapidly and creates a salt.
YES	The chemical reaction rapidly creates a salt.

PROOFREADING TO FIND SENTENCE FLAWS   88

- Finish your revision in enough time so you can put it aside and go back to it with fresh eyes that can spot flaws more easily.

- Work backwards, from your last sentence to your first, so that you can see each sentence as a separate unit free of a context that might lure you to overlook flaws.

- Ask an experienced reader to check your writing for sentence flaws. If you make an error discussed in this chapter, you likely make that error repeatedly. Once you become aware of it, you will have made a major step toward eliminating that type of error.

- Proofread an extra time exclusively for any error that you tend to make more than any other.

shift **15a**

15a Avoiding unnecessary shifts

Shift is a term for an abrupt, unneeded change of person°, number°, subject°, voice°, tense°, mood°, or kind of discourse (direct° or indirect°). Unnecessary shifts blur meaning. Readers expect to stay on the track that you as the writer start them on. If you switch tracks, your readers become confused.

1 Staying consistent in person and number

Person in English consists of the *first person (I, we),* words that designate the speaker or writer; *second person (you),* the word that designates the one being spoken or written to; and *third person (he, she, it, they),* words that designate the person or thing spoken or written about. All common nouns° are third-person words. (For more about person, see Chart 72 in section 11a.)

NO   **They** enjoy feeling productive, but when a job is unsatisfying, **you** usually become depressed. [*They* shifts to *you.*]

YES   **They** enjoy feeling productive, but when a job is unsatisfying, **they** usually become depressed.

Number refers to *singular* (one) or *plural* (more than one). Do not start to write in one number and then shift for no reason to the other number. Such shifting gives your sentences an unstable quality, and your message becomes fuzzy.

NO   Because most **people** are living longer, an **employee** in the twenty-first century will retire later. [The plural *people* shifts to the singular *employee.*]

YES   Because most **people** are living longer, **employees** in the twenty-first century will retire later.

A common cause of inconsistency in person and number is shifts to *you* (second person) from *I* (first person) or from a noun (third person) such as *person, the public,* or *people.* In academic writing, reserve *you* for sentences that address the reader directly; use the third person for general statements.

NO   **I** enjoy reading forecasts of the future, but **you** wonder which will turn out to be correct. [*I,* which is first person, shifts to *you,* which is second person.]

317

YES   I enjoy reading forecasts of the future, but **I** wonder which will turn out to be correct.

NO   By the year 2000, **North Americans** will pay twice today's price for a car, and **you** will get twice the gas mileage. [*North Americans*, which is third person, shifts to *you*, which is second person.]

YES   By the year 2000, **North Americans** will pay twice today's price for a car, and **they** will get twice the gas mileage.

Another common cause of inconsistency in number is a shift from singular to plural in the third person. A plural pronoun (for example, *they*) should not be used to refer to a singular noun (for example, *employee*) or a singular third-person pronoun (for example, *someone*). Use *he* or *she* (or *he or she*, which acts as a singular pronoun) or *it* to refer to a singular noun. When you use words such as *employee* or *someone* in a general sense, without any specific "employee" or "someone" in mind, you might think that a "he" or "she" is not involved. Still, you have to choose a singular pronoun. Another choice is to change to the plural *employees*, in which case the plural pronoun *they* would be correct. A third possibility is revising so that personal pronouns are unneeded.

NO   When an **employee** is treated with respect, **they** usually feel highly motivated.

YES   When an **employee** is treated with respect, **he or she** usually feels highly motivated.

YES   When **employees** are treated with respect, **they** usually feel highly motivated.

YES   **Employees** who are treated with respect usually feel highly motivated.

YES   An **employee** who is treated with respect usually feels highly motivated.

Try to avoid sexist language when you use indefinite pronouns (such as *someone* or *everyone;* for a complete list, see Chart 77 in 11g); see 11q and especially 21b for advice about nonsexist language.

❖ VERB ALERT: After you have revised person or number based on the advice here, check the verbs in the sentence to see whether any verb needs a change in number as well (see 8c). In the examples just shown, all Yes choices contain verb changes.❖

EXERCISE 15-1

Consulting section 15a-1, eliminate shifts in person and number. Be alert to shifts between, as well as within, sentences. Some sentences may not need revision.

(1) According to some experts, snobbery is measured by your mental attitude, not the extent of your worldly goods. (2) Because a snob is unsure of his or her social position, snobs are driven by what others think of them. (3) You tend to be too dependent on buying status symbols to define your place in the world, and snobs look down on others. (4) The origin of this word can be traced to the British Isles. (5) When commoners were first allowed to enter England's Cambridge University in the 1700s, each student was required to identify their social position. (6) The commoner had to use the Latin words *sine nobilitate*, meaning "without nobility." (7) Eventually, the students shortened this phrase to "s.nob," and the word came to signify persons aspiring to a higher social level.

---

2 | **Staying consistent in subject and voice**

The **subject** of a sentence is the word or group of words that acts, is acted upon, or is described: ***People** laugh, **people** were entertained, **people** are nice.*

Some subject shifts are justified by the meaning of a passage: ***People** look forward to the future, but **the future** holds many secrets.*

Shift in subject is rarely justified when it is accompanied by a shift in **voice.** The voice of a sentence is either *active (People expect changes)* or *passive (Changes are expected).* (For information about active and passive voice, see 8n–8o.) Unnecessary shifts in subject and voice cause a sentence or longer stretch of writing to drift out of focus.

NO	Most **people expect** major improvements in the future, but some **hardships are also anticipated.** [The subject shifts from *people* to *hardships,* and the voice shifts from active to passive.]
YES	Most **people expect** major improvements in the future, but **they also anticipate** some hardships.
YES	Most people expect major improvements in the future but also anticipate some hardships.

3 Staying consistent in tense and mood

Tense refers to the ability of verbs to show time. Tense changes are required to describe time changes: We *will go to the movies after we finish dinner.* If a tense shift within or between sentences is illogical, clarity suffers. (For information about correct sequences of tenses, see section 8k.)

NO The campaign to clean up the movies **began** in the 1920s as civic and religious groups **try** to ban sex and violence from the screen. [The tense shifts from the past *began* to the present *try*.]

YES The campaign to clean up the movies **began** in the 1920s as civic and religious groups **tried** to ban sex and violence from the screen.

NO Producers and distributors **created** a film Production Code in the 1930s. At first, violating its guidelines **carried** no penalty. Eventually, however, films that **fail** to get the board's Seal of Approval **do not receive** wide distribution. [This shift occurs between sentences: the past tense *created* and *carried* shift to the present tense *fail* and *do not receive*.]

YES Producers and distributors **created** a film Production Code in the 1930s. At first, violating its guidelines **carried** no penalty. Eventually, however, films that **failed** to get the board's Seal of Approval **did not receive** wide distribution.

Mood refers to whether a sentence is a statement or question (*indicative mood*), a command or request (*imperative mood*), or a conditional or other-than-real statement (*subjunctive mood*); see section 8l. A shift between moods may blur the message of a passage.

NO The Production Code included two guidelines about violence. **Do not show** the details of brutal killings, and **movies should not be** explicit about how to commit crimes. [The verbs shift from the imperative mood *do not show* to the indicative mood *movies should not be*.]

YES The Production Code included two guidelines about violence: **Do not show** the details of brutal killings, and **do not show** explicitly how to commit crimes. [This revision uses the imperative mood for both guidelines.]

YES The Production Code included two guidelines about violence. **Movies were not to show** the details of brutal killings or explicit ways to commit crimes.

NO   The Code writers worried that if a crime **were to be accurately depicted** in a movie, copycat crimes **will follow.** [The sentence shifts from the subjunctive mood *if a crime were to be depicted* to the indicative mood *copycat crimes will follow.*]

YES   The Code writers worried that if a crime **were to be accurately depicted** in a movie, copycat crimes **would follow.**

4   Avoiding unmarked shifts between indirect and direct discourse within the same sentence

Indirect discourse reports speech or conversation and is not enclosed in quotation marks. **Direct discourse** repeats speech or conversation exactly and encloses the spoken words in quotation marks (see 24g). Sentences that merge indirect and direct discourse without quotation marks and without other necessary changes that mark words as either reported or quoted distort the intended message.

NO   A critic said that board members were acting as censors and **what you are doing is dictatorial.** [The first clause is indirect discourse; the second clause shifts into unmarked direct discourse, garbling the message.]

YES   A critic said that board members were acting as censors and **that what they were doing was dictatorial.** [This revision consistently uses indirect discourse.]

YES   A critic said that board members were acting as censors and added, **"What you are doing is dictatorial."** [This revision uses indirect and direct discourse correctly, with quotation marks and other changes to distinguish reported words from spoken words.]

Changing a message from a direct-discourse version to an indirect-discourse version usually requires a change of verb tense° and other grammatical features. Simply removing the quotation marks is not enough.

NO   He asked **did we enjoy** the movie? [This version has the verb form needed for direct discourse, but the pronoun *we* is wrong and quotation punctuation is missing.]

YES   He asked **whether we enjoyed** the movie. [This version is entirely indirect discourse, and the verb has changed from *enjoy* to *enjoyed*.]

YES He asked, **"Did you enjoy** the movie?" [This version is direct discourse. It repeats the original speech exactly, with correct quotation punctuation.]

EXERCISE 15-2

Consulting section 15a, revise these sentences to eliminate all incorrect shifts. Some sentences can be revised several ways.

EXAMPLE During the Victorian era, all gentlemen worthy of the name are obliged to raise their hats to ladies.

During the Victorian era, all gentlemen worthy of the name *were* obliged to raise their hats to ladies.

1. The Victorian male's custom of tipping his hat had serious drawbacks, though; for instance, if you were carrying parcels you would have to set them down first.
2. In 1896, an inventor named James Boyle developed a self-tipping hat that solves the problem.
3. If a man nodded while wearing Boyle's invention, they activated a lifting mechanism concealed in the hat's crown.
4. Boyle claimed that since the novelty of the moving hat would attract attention, advertising also can be one of its uses.
5. He said that companies could place signs on the hats and you will be able to advertise any product innovatively and inexpensively.

EXERCISE 15-3

Consulting section 15a, revise this paragraph to eliminate incorrect shifts between, as well as within, sentences.

(1) The robots of today can perform many more tasks than its earlier counterpart. (2) Twenty years ago, a robot remained stationary and welded a car body or lifted heavy steel bars. (3) Today's robot, on the other hand, performs work that included cleaning offices, guarding a hotel room, and inspecting automobiles. (4) A doctor has performed brain surgery using a robot arm that allows them to drill into a person's skull and reach your brain more accurately. (5) A robot recently joined the police force in Dallas, Texas, and a suspect was forced into surrendering by the robot. (6) When the robot broke a window, the suspect shouted "Help," and asked what is that? (7) Many people do not realize that service robots often prepare your fast food or sort the packages you brought to the post office. (8) In the near future, robots selling for about $20 000 will work without human assistance, and you will be able to buy a robot costing $50 000 that will do household chores.

15b Avoiding misplaced modifiers

A **modifier** is a word, phrase°, or clause° that describes other words, phrases, or clauses. A **misplaced modifier** is a describer that is positioned incorrectly in a sentence, thus distorting meaning. As you write and revise, always check to see that your modifiers are placed as close as possible to what they describe so that your reader will be able to follow your intended meaning.

1 Avoiding ambiguous placements

With **ambiguous placement,** a modifier is confusing to a reader because it can refer to two or more words in a sentence.

Limiting words (such as *only, not only, just, not just, almost hardly, nearly, even, exactly, merely, scarcely, simply*) can change meaning according to where they are placed. When you use such words, position them precisely. Consider how different placements of *only* change the meaning of this sentence: *Professional coaches say that high salaries motivate players.*

Only professional coaches say that high salaries motivate players. [No one else says this.]

Professional coaches **only** say that high salaries motivate players. [The coaches probably do not mean what they say.]

Professional coaches say **only** that high salaries motivate players. [The coaches say nothing else.]

Professional coaches say that **only** high salaries motivate players. [Nothing except high salaries motivates players.]

Professional coaches say that high salaries **only** motivate players. [High salaries do nothing other than motivate players.]

Professional coaches say that high salaries motivate **only** players. [No others on the team, such as coaches and managers, are motivated by high salaries.]

Squinting modifiers are ambiguous because they can describe both what precedes and what follows them. Since a modifier cannot do double duty, the reader must make a choice and may make the one that the writer did not intend. For clarity, revise the sentence, making sure that the modifier is positioned where its meaning is precise.

NO   The football player being recruited **fervently** believed each successive offer would be better. [What was **fervent**, the recruitment or the player's belief?]

YES	The football player being recruited believed **fervently** that each successive offer would be better.
YES	The **fervently** recruited football player believed that each successive offer would be better.

2 Avoiding awkward placements

Awkward placements are interruptions that seriously break the flow of a message and thereby distract your reader from understanding your material. A **split infinitive** is one type of awkward placement. An **infinitive** is a verb form that starts with *to: to convince, to create.* When material comes between the *to* and its verb, it can interrupt meaning.

NO	Orson Welles's radio drama "War of the Worlds" managed **to,** in October 1938, **convince** listeners that they were hearing an invasion by Martians.
YES	In October 1938, Orson Welles's radio drama "War of the Worlds" managed **to convince** listeners that they were hearing an invasion by Martians.

Often the intervening word that splits an infinitive is an adverb ending in *-ly.* Many such adverbs sound awkward unless they are placed either before or after the infinitive.

NO	People feared they would no longer be able **to happily live** in peace.
YES	People feared they would no longer be able **to live happily** in peace.

Nevertheless, sometimes an adverb° seems awkward in any position except between *to* and the verb°. Many readers, therefore, are not distracted by split infinitives like this one:

Welles wanted **to realistically portray** a Martian invasion for the radio audience.

If you think your readers prefer that infinitives never be split, you can usually revise the sentence to avoid the split:

Welles wanted his "Martian invasion" **to sound** realistic for the radio audience.

Interruptions of subjects° and verbs, verb phrases°, and verbs and objects° can disturb the smooth flow of a sentence.

NO	The **announcer**, because the script, which Welles himself wrote, called for perfect imitations of emergency

announcements, **opened** with a warning that included a description of the "invasion." [subject–verb interrupted]

YES   Because the script, which Welles himself wrote, called for perfect imitations of emergency announcements, **the announcer opened** with a warning that included a description of the "invasion."

NO   Police switchboards **were,** not surprisingly, **jammed** with frantic phone calls. [verb phrase interrupted]

YES   Not surprisingly, police switchboards **were jammed** with frantic phone calls.

NO   Many churches **held** for their frightened communities **"end of the world" prayer services.** [verb–direct object interrupted]

YES   Many churches **held "end of the world" prayer services** for their frightened communities.

EXERCISE 15-4

Consulting section 15b, revise these sentences to correct any ambiguous or awkward placements. If a sentence is correct, circle its number.

EXAMPLE   The invention of the first car took place in 1885, one of the greatest accomplishments in history.

> The invention of the first car, *one of the greatest accomplishments in history,* took place in 1885.

1. The origins of the automobile can, if we look back in history, be found in 1769 in France.
2. The Frenchman Nicholas Cugnot, because of his determination to travel without the assistance of animals, built the first self-propelled vehicle.
3. Cugnot's invention only was powered by steam.
4. During a trial drive, the vehicle, which was run by a huge steam boiler that hung in front of its single front wheel and which was difficult to steer and hard to stop, knocked over a rock wall.
5. The invention of various types of gas-combustion engines, beginning in 1860, provided an alternative to clumsy steam power.
6. Two other inventors, Karl Benz and Gottlieb Daimler, were, in Germany, trying to invent a gas-driven vehicle.
7. Only they lived about 100 kilometres apart, but they did not know each other.
8. Benz is finally the man who produced the first car and was given credit for the invention of the automobile.

9. The first car rolled, after the finishing touches had been added, out of a workshop in a small German town.

10. It rattled and banged down the street to loudly and dramatically announce a revolution in transportation.

EXERCISE 15-5

Consulting section 15b, combine each list of word groups to create all the possible logical sentences (each list offers more than one possibility). Insert commas as needed. Use a slash to indicate where each word or group of words ends. Explain differences in meaning, if any, among the alternatives you create.

EXAMPLE   runners
          than couch potatoes do
          have lower blood pressure
          for the most part

A. For the most part, / runners / have lower blood pressure / than couch potatoes do. /

B. Runners / have lower blood pressure, / for the most part, / than couch potatoes do. /

C. Runners, / for the most part, / have lower blood pressure / than couch potatoes do. /

D. Runners / have lower blood pressure / than couch potatoes do, / for the most part. /

1. studied
    an entertainment lawyer
    corporate and copyright law
    the student
    to become
    intensively

2. introduced the
    happily
    muscular artist
    the matchmaker
    to the
    wrestler

3. the computer hacker used
    broke into
    only
    one simple password
    the company files

4. need
    love
    that
    know
    pediatricians
    not just
    children

5. have more patience
    as a rule
    bus drivers
    than the average citizen

15c   Avoiding dangling modifiers

A **dangling modifier** describes or limits a word or words that are not stated in a sentence. Because a reader will "attach" the information in the dangling modifier to a noun° or pronoun° that *does* appear in the sentence, the writer's intended meaning is lost.

Dangling modifiers can be hard for a writer to spot. Aware of the intended meaning, the writer unconsciously supplies the missing material, but the reader usually sees only the error and realizes that the meaning is flawed.

The first *No* example below says that the story's ending is doing the reading. The implied subject of the modifier is *we,* but nowhere is that subject stated—thus the modifier dangles. You can correct a dangling modifier by revising the sentence so that the intended subject° is stated.

NO	**Reading Faulkner's short story "A Rose for Emily,"** the ending surprised us.
YES	**Having read Faulkner's short story "A Rose for Emily," we** were surprised by the ending.
YES	We read Faulkner's short story "A Rose for Emily" and were surprised by the ending.
NO	**When courting Emily, the townspeople** gossiped about her. [*The townspeople* were not courting Emily.]
YES	**When Emily was being courted by Homer Barron, the townspeople** gossiped about her.

Dangling modifiers are sometimes caused by unnecessary use of the passive voice° (see 8n–8o).

NO	**To earn money, china-painting lessons** were offered by Emily to wealthy young women. [*China-painting lessons* cannot earn money.]
YES	**To earn money, Emily** offered china-painting lessons to wealthy young women.

EXERCISE 15-6

Consulting section 15c, identify and correct any dangling modifiers in these sentences. If a sentence is correct, circle its number.

EXAMPLE   Assigned to interview an unfriendly person, the experience can be instructive to a student journalist.

Assigned to interview an unfriendly person, *a student journalist can find the experience instructive.*

1. To be successful, careful plans must be made by the student journalist.
2. Being tense, the interview might begin on the wrong note for an inexperienced journalist.
3. Until relaxed, questions should mention only neutral topics.
4. After the journalist is more at ease, the person being interviewed might also relax.
5. With a list of questions, the interview process goes more smoothly for everyone involved.
6. Although easy to answer, mistakes are sometimes made on factual questions by a hostile interviewee.
7. By being analytic and evaluative, those mistakes can reveal a great deal to an experienced journalist.
8. Knowing how to pace an interview, the hard questions are more likely to be answered honestly after the interviewee has been caught off guard.
9. Until an interview is complete, the seasoned journalist always remains alert.
10. Essential information might be revealed when leaving.

15d Avoiding mixed sentences

A **mixed sentence** consists of parts that do not make sense together because the writer has lost track of the beginning of a sentence while writing the end. Careful proofreading, including reading aloud, can help a writer avoid this error.

1 Revising mixed constructions

A **mixed construction** starts out taking one grammatical form and then changes, derailing the meaning of the sentence.

NO   Because television's first transmissions in the 1920s included news programs quickly became popular with the public. [The opening dependent clause° starts off on one track, but the independent clause° goes off in another direction. What does the writer want to emphasize—the first transmissions or the popularity of news programs?]

YES   Television's first transmissions in the 1920s included news programs, which quickly became popular with the public. [The idea of the first transmissions is emphasized.]

YES	Because television's first transmissions in the 1920s included news programs, television quickly became popular with the public. [The idea of the popularity of the news programs is now emphasized.]
NO	By doubling the time allotment for network news to thirty minutes increased the prestige of network news programs. [A prepositional phrase°, such as *by doubling,* cannot be the subject of a sentence.]
YES	Doubling the time allotment for network news to thirty minutes increased the prestige of network news programs. [Dropping the preposition *by* clears up the problem.]
YES	By doubling the time allotment for network news to thirty minutes, the network executives increased the prestige of network news programs. [Inserting a logical subject, *the network executives,* clears up the problem; an independent clause° is now preceded by a modifying prepositional phrase°.]

The phrase *the fact that* is sometimes the cause of a mixed sentence.

NO	The fact that quiz show scandals in the 1950s prompted the networks to produce even more news shows.
YES	The fact is that quiz show scandals in the 1950s prompted the networks to produce even more news shows. [The added *is* clarifies the meaning.]
YES	Quiz show scandals in the 1950s prompted the networks to produce even more news shows. [Dropping *the fact that* clarifies the meaning.]

2 Revising faulty predication

Faulty predication, sometimes called *illogical predication,* occurs when a subject° and its predicate° do not make sense together.

NO	The **purpose** of television **was invented** to entertain people.
YES	The **purpose** of television was to entertain people.
YES	**Television was invented** to entertain people.

One key cause of illogical predication is a breakdown in the connection between a subject and its complement°. (A subject complement can be a noun°, a pronoun°, a noun clause° renaming a sentence subject, or an adjective° describing a sentence subject; see 7m-1.)

329

In the following *No* example, the subject complement *credible* could logically describe Lloyd Robertson, but *Lloyd Robertson* is not the subject. The subject is *characteristic,* so the meaning calls for a subject complement that renames some characteristic of Lloyd Robertson as a newscaster: thus, *credibility* instead of *credible.*

NO	Lloyd Robertson's outstanding **characteristic is credible** as a newscaster.
YES	Lloyd Robertson's outstanding **characteristic is credibility** as a newscaster. [The noun *credibility* renames *characteristic.*]
YES	**Lloyd Robertson is credible** as a newscaster. [The adjective *credible* describes the subject *Lloyd Robertson.*]

Illogical predication is a problem in many constructions that include *is when* or *is where.* Avoid these phrases in academic writing.

NO	A disaster **is when** television news shows get some of their highest ratings.
YES	Television news shows get some of their highest ratings during a disaster.

Also, avoid *reason … is because* constructions. Use *reason … is that* instead. Remember that *because* means "for the reason that," so *reason … is because* literally means "reason … is for the reason that," which is repetitious.

NO	One **reason** television news captured widespread attention **is because** it covered the Vietnam War thoroughly.
YES	One **reason** television news captured widespread attention **is that** it covered the Vietnam War thoroughly.
YES	Television news captured widespread attention **because** it covered the Vietnam War thoroughly.

EXERCISE 15-7

Consulting section 15d, revise the mixed sentences below so that the beginning of each sentence fits logically with its end. If a sentence is correct, circle its number.

EXAMPLE   In 1937, under the sponsorship of Lord Tweedsmuir, who was the Governor General at the time, sponsored the launching of the Governer General's Literary Awards.

In 1937, Lord Tweedsmuir, who was the Governor General at the time, sponsored the launching of the Governor General's Literary Awards.

1. The reason that Governor General Lord Tweedsmuir is better known in some quarters as John Buchan is because under that name he wrote *The Thirty-Nine Steps,* a spy novel that was filmed by Alfred Hitchcock.
2. The Governor General's Awards that he helped establish have become the greatest desirability of any literary awards in Canada, and as a result, the categories of works for which they are awarded have undergone frequent expansion and revision.
3. The fact that at first, only books in English were eligible for the awards, a situation that many believed to be a serious oversight.
4. The solution to this problem was remedied in 1959, when the Canada Council began to administer the awards and established an identical set of Governor General's Awards for works in French.
5. A controversial episode was when the refusal of an award in 1968, when Leonard Cohen declined the prize for his *Selected Poems, 1956-1968* and said, "Much in me strives for this honour, but the poems themselves forbid it absolutely."
6. About the same time, a less enigmatic explanation for refusing the award was given by several nationalistic Quebec writers announced they were rejecting it for political reasons.
7. However, in 1992 Cohen accepted the newly instituted Governor General's Performing Arts Award, so apparently his songs, unlike his poems, did permit it.
8. Although the judgment and taste of the awards' juries have sometimes been questioned, but we can note in their favour that recipients have included important writers such as Margaret Atwood, Northrop Frye, Alice Munro, Mavis Gallant, and Robertson Davies.
9. As further confirmation of the worth of the Governor General's Awards, since Michael Ondaatje's novel *The English Patient,* which won in 1992, also received Britain's prestigious Booker Prize, and the following year, Carol Shields's novel *The Stone Diairies* won the Governor General's Award and then the U.S. Pulitzer Prize.
10. Every year, a gala ceremony is where the current Governor General presents the literary prizes first awarded by Lord Tweedsmuir, the writer of suspense stories who became the monarch's representative in Canada.

15e Avoiding incomplete sentences

An **incomplete sentence** is missing words, phrases°, or clauses° necessary for grammatical correctness or sensible meaning. Such omissions blur your meaning, and your reader has to work hard to understand your message.

1   Using elliptical constructions carefully

An **elliptical construction** deliberately leaves out, rather than repeats, one or more words that appear elsewhere in the sentence. *I have my book and Joan's,* for example, is an acceptable way to express *I have my book and Joan's book.* An elliptical construction is correct only if the sentence contains the *exact* word or words omitted from the elliptical construction. Thus, *I have my book and Joan's* cannot be used to express the thought that Joan, for example, has many *books.*

NO	During the 1920s in Chicago, the cornetist Manuel Perez **was leading** one outstanding jazz group, Tommy and Jimmy Dorsey another. [The words *was leading* cannot take the place of *were leading,* which the subject *Tommy and Jimmy Dorsey* requires.]
YES	During the 1920s in Chicago, the cornetist Manuel Perez **was leading** one outstanding jazz group; Tommy and Jimmy Dorsey **were leading** another.
YES	During the 1920s in Chicago, the cornetist Manuel Perez **led** one outstanding jazz group, Tommy and Jimmy Dorsey another. [The verb *led* is correct both with *Manuel Perez* and with *Tommy and Jimmy Dorsey* and thus can be omitted after *Dorsey.*]
NO	The period of the big jazz dance bands **began** and **lasted through** World War II. [This sentence implies *through* after *began,* but *began* requires *in,* not *through.*]
YES	The period of the big jazz band **began in** and **lasted through** World War II.

2   Making comparisons complete, unambiguous, and logical

In writing a comparison, be sure to include all words needed to make clear the relationship between the items or ideas being compared.

NO	Individuals with high concern for achievement make **better** business executives. [*Better* implies a comparison, but none is stated.]

YES	Individuals with high concern for achievement make **better** business executives **than** do people with little interest in personal accomplishments.
NO	Most personnel officers value high achievers more than risk takers. [Unclear: more than risk takers value high achievers, or more than personnel officers value risk takers?]
YES	Most personnel officers value high achievers more than they value risk takers.
YES	Most personnel officers value high achievers more than risk takers do.
NO	A risk taker's chance of success is very different. [Different from what?]
YES	A risk taker's chance of success is very different **from a high achiever's.**
NO	Achievers value success **as much,** if not more than, a high salary. [Comparisons using *as ... as* require the second *as*.]
YES	Achievers value success **as much as,** if not more than, a high salary.

In speech, sentences such as *That was such a difficult exam, You're so smart,* or *I'm too upset* are common. These constructions using *so, too,* and *such* as intensifiers imply that a completing thought has been omitted, and listeners can simply ask for more information if they need it. In academic writing, however, be sure to supply the completing information or take out the intensifier.

NO	Risk takers are often **such** innovative people.
YES	Risk takers are often **such** innovative people that some businesses seek them out as employees.
YES	Risk takers are often innovative people.

3	**Proofreading for inadvertently omitted articles, pronouns, conjunctions, and prepositions**

Small words—articles°, pronouns°, conjunctions°, and prepositions°—needed to make sentences complete tend to drop out when a writer is rushing or is distracted. If you tend to omit small words, proofread your work an extra time exclusively to discover the missing words.

NO	On May 2, 1808, citizens Madrid rioted against French soldiers.
YES	On May 2, 1808, **the** citizens **of** Madrid rioted against French soldiers.
NO	On following day, captured rioters were taken into country and shot.
YES	On **the** following day, captured rioters were taken into **the** country and shot.
NO	The Spanish painter Francisco Goya recorded both the riot the execution in a pair of pictures painted 1814.
YES	The Spanish painter Francisco Goya recorded both the riot **and** the execution in a pair of pictures painted **in** 1814.

EXERCISE 15-8

Consulting section 15e, revise this paragraph to create correct elliptical constructions, to complete comparisons, and to insert any missing words.

(1) A Japanese tradition holds that anyone folds one thousand paper cranes will have good health and long life. (2) Sadako Sasaki was not yet two years old when an atomic bomb exploded over Hiroshima August 6, 1945. (3) Although she was not injured by the bomb blast, her health, like many other children of Hiroshima, was damaged by the radiation unleashed in the explosion. (4) From hospital bed where she lay ill with leukemia, Sadako at age twelve set out to fold a thousand paper cranes, devoting so much energy to the task. (5) Her efforts to fold the paper cranes became as difficult as her condition deteriorated, and at the time of death in 1956 she had completed only 644. (6) In Hiroshima's Peace Park stands a statue of a young girl commemorates the victims of the bombing, and May 5 each year it covered with paper cranes brought by children from all over Japan. (7) People around world regard Sadako's cranes as a symbol and a memorial to the enduring hope for peace as much as Anne Frank's diary.

Focus on Revising

REVISING YOUR WRITING

If you write sentences that send unclear messages, go back to your writing and locate the errors. Using this chapter as a resource, revise your writing to eliminate unnecessary shifts (15a), misplaced modifiers (15b), dangling modifiers (15c), mixed sentences (15d), and incomplete sentences (15e).

CASE STUDIES: REVISING TO CORRECT SENTENCES THAT SEND UNCLEAR MESSAGES

In these case studies, you can observe a student writer revising. Then you have the chance to revise other student writing on your own.

Observation

A student wrote the following draft for a course called Freshman Composition. The assignment was to compose a narrative of a personal experience with which other students in the class might sympathize. This narrative explains the experience clearly, uses specific examples well to illustrate the story, and draws on the writer's voice effectively. The draft's effectiveness is diminished, however, by the presence of sentences that send unclear messages by unnecessary shifts, misplaced modifiers, dangling modifiers, mixed sentences, and incomplete sentences.

Read through the draft. The unclear messages are highlighted and explained. Before you look at the student's revision, revise the material yourself. Then compare what you and the student did.

> Moving to a different part of Canada was one of the most difficult experiences of my life. Looking forward to my final year in high school, my father's company informed him that he had been transferred to northern Ontario, and would we be ready to move in a month? I liked

dangling modifier: 15c

shift from direct to indirect discourse: 15a-4

ambiguous comparison: 15e-2

incorrect elliptical construction: 15e-1

omitted word: 15e-3

unnecessary shift in person and number: 15a-1

unnecessary shift in tense: 15a-3

mixed construction: 15d-1

misplaced modifier; ambiguous placement: 15b-1

dangling modifier: 15c

omitted word: 15e-3

omitted word: 15e-3

misplaced modifier; ambiguous placement: 15b-1

Toronto much better than my father, so I was less than thrilled about having to leave. But after days of arguing and talking to my parents, I knew that the decision was final.

When our family arrived in northern Ontario, I was depressed. Our house was comfortable, about twice the size of our Toronto apartment, but you had the feeling that it was in the middle of nowhere. Living in the country, I couldn't go anywhere without car. In Toronto, all I have to do is hop on the subway to go anywhere in the city.

Also, by discovering that the ways people passed their time were different than in Toronto was the place that I wanted to be. Now that I lived in northern Ontario, I participated in winter activities, like cross-country skiing and winter camping, when not at work or in school only reluctantly. It was so cold! When living in Toronto, sports were not so common and participation in outdoor winter activities was often replaced by cozy spectator sports. Watching hockey games was as close my friends and I got to winter sport.

Slowly, however, I began to realize that in northern Ontario even there are movies, fast-food restaurants, and shopping malls. Mostly, the people made the big difference for me. It didn't happily take

long for me to get to know some
students in my high school, and

┌──────── to, much to my surprise, find that

misplaced
modifier;
awkward
placement: 15b-2

most were eager to make me feel
at home. They even got me
interested in skiing and winter
camping. By now, I can't imagine
a better place to live than
northern Ontario.

Here is how the student revised the draft to correct the errors.
In a few places, the student could correct the errors in more than
one way. Your revision, therefore, might not be exactly like this
one, but it should deal with each error highlighted on the draft.

Moving to a different part of Canada was one of the most
difficult experiences of my life. At the time that I was looking
forward to my final year in high school, my father's company
informed him that he had been transferred to northern Ontario, and
we would need to be ready to move in a month. I liked Toronto
much better than my father did, so I was less than thrilled about
having to leave. But after days of arguing with and talking to my
parents, I knew that the decision was final.

When our family arrived in northern Ontario, I was depressed.
Our house was comfortable, about twice the size of our Toronto
apartment, but I had the feeling that it was in the middle of nowhere.
Living in the country, I couldn't go anywhere without a car. In Toronto,
all I have to do is hop on the subway to go anywhere in the city.

Also, when I discovered that the ways people passed their time
were different, Toronto was the place that I wanted to be. Now that
I lived in northern Ontario, I participated only reluctantly in winter
activities, like cross-country skiing and winter camping, when not at
work or in school. It was so cold! When I was living in Toronto,
sports were not so common and participation in outdoor winter
activities was often replaced by cozy spectator sports. Watching
hockey games was as close as my friends and I got to winter sport.

Slowly, however, I began to realize that even in northern
Ontario there are movies, fast-food restaurants, and shopping
malls. Mostly, the people made the big difference for me. Happily,
it didn't take long for me to get to know some students in my
high school, and to find, much to my surprise, that most were
eager to make me feel at home. They even got me interested in
skiing and winter camping. By now, I can't imagine a better place
to live than northern Ontario.

Participation

A student working in the school peer counselling program for job hunters wrote the following draft for an article in the campus newspaper. This material shows a very good awareness of audience, and it contains well-organized, useful information. The draft's effectiveness is diminished, however, by the presence of sentences that send unclear messages because of unnecessary shifts, misplaced modifiers, dangling modifiers, mixed sentences, and incomplete sentences.

Read through the draft. Then revise it to eliminate the errors. Also, make any additional revisions that you think would improve the content, organization, and style of the material.

Most job hunters enter business world through a door labelled "Job Interviews." Regardless of training and experience the interview is the occasion when an employer gets an impression of the candidate. What can a person do so that you perform successfully at what is likely to be a fifteen-minute interview?

By understanding the objectives of the interview will help an applicant prepare. An applicant who knows the company's needs is better equipped. Most businesses with a position to fill interview with three basic questions in mind: Is this applicant qualified to do the job? Will this applicant perform if hired? Will you fit into the work environment?

A job applicant can use a well-prepared résumé to present information about experience and training. At the interview, applicants should be prepared to talk about courses taken, jobs held, and capabilities demonstrated. Probing for specific details, the applicant's abilities will be judged by the employer. Job applicants should be aware that personal questions about marital status or plans to have children are considered intrusive; however, such matters might be raised by some interviewers anyway. By preparing an answer like "Those areas of my life are personal," or "I make it a rule never to let my personal life interfere with business" will help an applicant's confidence.

A major concern of an interviewer is focused on whether the applicant would fit into the company. An applicant who plays merely a role to impress an interviewer is making a mistake, particularly if you are offered a job that you are not suited for. Present a natural image. Use the interview to find out how well the company's work environment will fit your personal style.

PART

IV Writing Effective Sentences

When you write effective sentences, you move beyond correctness to writing characterized by style and grace. Part Four shows you various techniques of writing style that can enhance the delivery of your message. As you use Chapters 16 through 19, remember that writers can make choices to help form and content work together to create memorable prose.

16 Conciseness

Conciseness describes writing that is direct and to the point. Wordy writing is not concise. Wordiness irritates readers, who must clear away excess words before sentences can deliver their messages. Concise writing can be achieved by eliminating wordy sentence structures (see 16a); dropping unneeded words (see 16b); and omitting redundancies (see 16c).

16a Eliminating wordy sentence structures

Wordy sentence structures make writing seem abstract and uninteresting. Whenever possible, revise to achieve conciseness.

1 Revising unnecessary expletive constructions

An **expletive construction** consists of *it* or *there* along with a form of the verb°* *be* placed before the subject° in a sentence. In some contexts, an expletive construction can create anticipation and provide emphasis, but usually expletive constructions are merely wordy. Removing the expletive and revising slightly eliminates wordy sentence structures.

NO	**It was** on Friday that we missed class.
YES	On Friday, we missed class.
YES	We missed class on Friday.
NO	**There was** a new teacher waiting for us.
YES	A new teacher was waiting for us.

*Throughout this book, a degree mark (°) indicates that you can find the definition of the word in the Glossary of Terms in this handbook.

◆ ESL NOTE: The *it* in an expletive construction is not a pronoun° referring to a specific antecedent°. The *it* is an "empty" word that fills the subject° position in a sentence but does not function as the actual subject. The actual subject appears after the expletive construction: *It was the **teacher** who answered the question.* (A more concise version is *The **teacher** answered the question.*)◆

◆ ESL NOTE: The *there* in an expletive construction does not designate a place. The *there* indicates merely that something exists. Expletive constructions with *there* shift the sequence of the subject and verb in a sentence, so that the actual subject appears after the expletive construction: ***There** are many **teachers** who can answer the question.* (A more concise version is *Many **teachers** can answer the question.*)◆

Revising unnecessary passive constructions

In the **active voice,** the subject of a sentence *does* the action named by the verb°.

ACTIVE   **Professor Higgins teaches** public speaking.
[*Professor Higgins* is the subject, and he does the action: he *teaches*.]

In the **passive voice,** the subject of a sentence *receives* the action named by the verb.

PASSIVE   **Public speaking is taught** by Professor Higgins.
[*Public speaking* is the subject, which receives the action *taught*.]

The active voice adds liveliness as well as conciseness, so it is usually preferable. The simplest way to revise from the passive voice to the active voice is to make the doer of the action the subject of the sentence. (In a passive construction, the doer of an action is usually identified in a phrase starting with *by*.) When you want to switch from passive to active, turn the noun° or pronoun° in the *by* phrase into the sentence subject.

NO   Volunteer work **was done by the students** for extra credit in sociology. [The students are doers of the action, but they are not the subject of the sentence.]

YES   The **students did** volunteer work for extra credit in sociology.

NO   The church basement **was decorated by the choir** for the party. [The choir is the doer of the action, but it is not the subject of the sentence.]

YES   The **choir decorated** the church basement for the party.

Sometimes you can revise a sentence from passive voice to active voice by using a new verb. This method works especially well when you want to keep the same subject.

PASSIVE	**The Central Powers were defeated** in World War I.
ACTIVE	**The Central Powers lost** World War I.
PASSIVE	Many **soldiers were stricken** with influenza.
ACTIVE	Many **soldiers caught** influenza.

Writers may sometimes have no choice but to use the passive voice, as when the doer of an action is unknown or when naming the doer would disrupt the focus of a sentence (see 8n–8o).

Writers sometimes, however, deliberately use the passive voice in sentence after sentence in the mistaken belief that it sounds "mature" or "academic."

NO	One very important quality developed by an individual during a first job is self-reliance. This strength was gained by me when I was allowed by my supervisor to set up and conduct my own survey project.
YES	During their first job, many individuals develop the very important quality of self-reliance. I gained this strength when my supervisor allowed me to set up and conduct my own survey project.
YES	During a first job, many people develop self-reliance, as I did when my supervisor let me set up and conduct my own survey project.

Be particularly alert for the passive voice that misleads readers because it hides information about who acts: *Cracks in the foundation of the structure had been found, but they were not considered serious.* The sentence leaves out important information telling who found cracks and who decided that they were not serious.

3 | Combining sentences and reducing clauses and phrases

As you revise, check your writing for conciseness. To counter-act wordiness, you can often combine sentences and reduce clauses° and phrases°.

Combining sentences

Look carefully at sets of sentences in your writing. You may be able to fit the information in one sentence into another sentence.

TWO SENTENCES

The *Titanic* was discovered seventy-three years after being sunk by an iceberg. The wreck was located in the Atlantic by a team of French and American scientists.

COMBINED SENTENCE

Seventy-three years after being sunk by an iceberg, the *Titanic* was located in the Atlantic by a team of French and American scientists.

TWO SENTENCES

The stern of the ship was missing and there was some external damage to the hull. Otherwise, the *Titanic* seemed to be in excellent condition.

COMBINED SENTENCE

Aside from its missing stern and external damage to its hull, the *Titanic* seemed to be in excellent condition.

For more advice about combining sentences, see Chapter 17.

Reducing clauses

You can sometimes reduce an adjective clause° simply by dropping the opening relative pronoun° and verb°.

The *Titanic,* **which was a huge ocean liner,** sank in 1912.

The *Titanic,* **a huge ocean liner,** sank in 1912.

Sometimes you can reduce a clause to a single word.

The scientists held a memorial service for the passengers and crew members **who had died.**

The scientists held a memorial service for the **dead** passengers and crew members.

You can create elliptical constructions° to reduce clauses. Be sure to omit only those words that are clearly implied (see 15e-1).

When they were confronted with disaster, some passengers behaved heroically, **while others behaved selfishly.**

Confronted with disaster, some passengers behaved heroically, **others selfishly.**

Keep your meaning clear when you reduce clauses. Making your writing concise should never get in the way of clarity.

Reducing phrases

Sometimes you can reduce phrases° to shorter phrases or to single words.

More than fifteen hundred **travellers on that voyage** died in the shipwreck.

More than fifteen hundred **passengers** died in the shipwreck.

Objects found inside the ship **included unbroken** bottles of wine and expensive **undamaged** china.

Found undamaged inside the ship were bottles of wine and expensive china.

4 Using strong verbs and avoiding nouns formed from verbs

Your writing will have more impact when you choose verbs° that are strong because they directly convey an action. *Be* and *have* are not strong verbs. Also, they tend to create wordy structures. When you revise weak verbs to strong ones, often you can reduce the number of words in your sentences.

WEAK VERB

The proposal before the city council **has to do with** locating the sewage treatment plant outside city limits.

STRONGER VERBS

The proposal before the city council **suggests** locating the sewage treatment plant outside city limits.

The proposal before the city council **argues against** locating the sewage treatment plant outside city limits.

WEAK VERBS

The board members **were of the opinion** that the revisions in the code **were not** changes they could accept.

STRONGER VERBS

The board members **said** that they **could not accept** the revisions in the code.

❖ ALERT: When you revise, look carefully at verbs with the pattern *be* + adjective° + *of* (*be aware of, be capable of, be fearful of*). Many of these phrases can be replaced with one-word verbs: ***I envy*** [not *am envious of*] *the council president's ability to speak in public.* Always avoid certain of these phrases: for example, always use ***appreciate*** [not *be appreciative of*], ***illustrate*** [not *be illustrative of*], and ***support*** [not *be supportive of*].

NO   The council president **was supportive of** the council's attempts to lower property taxes.

YES   The council president **supported** the council's attempts to lower property taxes. ✤

When you look for weak verbs to revise, look also for nominals (nouns derived from verbs, usually by added suffixes° such as *-ance, -ment,* or *-tion*). Turning a nominal back into a verb reduces words and increases impact.

NO   We **oversaw the establishment of** a student advisory committee.

YES   We **established** a student advisory committee.

NO   The building **had the appearance of** having been renovated.

YES   The building **appeared** to have been renovated.

5   **Using pronouns for conciseness**

Replacing nouns° with pronouns° can reduce wordiness. When changing nouns to pronouns, be sure that each pronoun's antecedent is unambiguous (see 10a–10c) and that each pronoun agrees with its antecedents (see 11m–11p).

NO   Queen Elizabeth II served as a driver and mechanic in World War II. **Elizabeth** joined the Auxiliary Territorial Service in 1944, while **the future queen** was still a princess. Although **Princess Elizabeth** did not know how to drive, she quickly learned how to strip and repair many kinds of engines.

YES   Queen Elizabeth II served as a driver and mechanic in World War II. **She** joined the Auxiliary Territorial Service in 1944, while **she** was still a princess. Although **she** did not know how to drive, she quickly learned how to strip and repair many kinds of engines.

EXERCISE 16-1

Consulting section 16a, combine each set of sentences to eliminate wordy constructions.

EXAMPLE   A creative idea, says psychologist Robert Epstein, can be like a rabbit. The rabbit runs by fast. We glimpse only the rabbit's ears or tail.

A creative idea, says psychologist Robert Epstein, can be like a rabbit that runs by so fast we glimpse only its ears or tail.

1. There is evidence that suggests that there is only one difference between creative people and the rest of us. It is creative people who are always poised to capture the new ideas we might not catch right away.

2. Creative thinking has to do with seizing opportunities. Creative thinking has to do with staying alert. Creative thinking has to do with seeking challenges and pushing boundaries.

3. The goal is that the idea be caught first and that the idea be evaluated later. A fleeting thought is captured by the alert person by writing it down at once. The goal is not to worry whether the thought will have eventual value.

4. There is an important part of creativity, and that is daydreaming, which is an activity allowing thoughts to bubble up spontaneously. These creative thoughts surprise us with their freshness.

5. Creativity can be unlocked in us by our trying something different. It is possible to turn pictures sideways or upside down to see them in new ways. We can mould clay while we think about a writing problem that is difficult.

6. It is stressed by the psychologist Robert Epstein that there are many exciting advances in everything. The advances are in fields from astrophysics to car design to dance. The advances creatively combine ideas that are from widely different sources.

7. Epstein gave his students the assignment of a problem. The problem called for the retrieval of a ping-pong ball. It was located at the bottom of a vertical drainpipe that was sealed at the bottom.

8. Some of the tools that the students had been given by Epstein were too short to reach the ball. Other tools that the students had been given were too wide to fit into the pipe.

9. The students were stumped at first. The students tried unsuccessfully to capture the ball with the tools. Then the students stepped back from the immediate situation. The students saw the big picture and began thinking creatively.

10. Water was poured down the drainpipe by the students. The ball achieved flotation and rose to the top. The ball was retrieved by the students there.

16b Eliminating unneeded words

To achieve conciseness, eliminate unneeded words that clutter sentences. Also, revise imprecise language so that six inexact words do not take the place of one precise word.

When a writer tries to write very formally or tries to reach an assigned word limit, **padding** usually results. Sentences loaded with **deadwood** contain empty words and phrases that increase the word count but lack meaning. If you find deadwood, clear it away.

PADDED

~~In fact,~~ the television station ~~which is situated in the local area~~ has won a great many awards ~~as a result of its having been involved in the~~ coverage of ~~all kinds of~~ controversial issues.

CONCISE

The local television station has won many awards for its coverage of controversial issues.

PADDED

The bookstore ~~entered the order for~~ the books ~~that the instructor has said will be utilized~~ in the course ~~sequence.~~

CONCISE

The bookstore ordered the books for the course.

Chart 89 lists typical empty words that are among the worst offenders. The chart also offers revised versions. Apply the principles found here to similar items not listed.

GUIDE FOR ELIMINATING EMPTY WORDS AND PHRASES		89
EMPTY WORD OR PHRASE	**WORDY EXAMPLE**	**REVISION**
as a matter of fact	*As a matter of fact,* statistics show that many marriages end in divorce.	Statistics show that many marriages end in divorce.
due to the fact that	Mary Stuart did not say the monarch's oath when she became queen of Scotland *due to the fact that* she was just six days old.	Mary Stuart did not say the monarch's oath when she became queen of Scotland because she was just six days old.
in a very real sense	*In a very real sense,* the drainage problems caused the house to collapse.	The drainage problems caused the house to collapse.

➔

GUIDE FOR ELIMINATING EMPTY WORDS AND PHRASES (*continued*)

factor	The project's final cost was an essential *factor* to consider.	The project's final cost was essential to consider.
manner	The child touched the snake in a reluctant *manner*.	The child touched the snake reluctantly.
nature	His comment was of an offensive *nature*.	His comment was offensive.
type of	Gordon took a relaxing *type of* vacation.	Gordon took a relaxing vacation.
seems	It *seems* that the union called a strike over health benefits.	The union called a strike over health benefits.
tendency	The team had a *tendency* to lose home games.	The team often lost home games.
in the process of	We are *in the process of* reviewing the proposal.	We are reviewing the proposal.
exist	The crime rate that *exists* is unacceptable.	The crime rate is unacceptable.
in light of the fact that	*In light of the fact that* jobs are scarce, I am going back to school.	Because jobs are scarce, I am going back to school.
for the purpose of	Work crews were dispatched *for the purpose of* fixing the potholes.	Work crews were dispatched to fix the potholes.
in the case of	*In the case of* the proposed water tax, residents were very angry.	Residents were very angry about the proposed water tax.

in the event that	*In the event that* you are late, I will leave.	If you are late, I will leave.
the point I am trying to make	*The point I am trying to make* is that news reporters should not invade people's privacy.	News reporters should not invade people's privacy.

EXERCISE 16-2

Consulting section 16b, eliminate unnecessary words or phrases. Be especially alert for empty words that add nothing to meaning.

EXAMPLE   Folk wisdom has a tendency to be untrue.

> *Folk wisdom is often untrue.*

(1) As a matter of fact, it seems as though a great many folk beliefs that are popular are, in a very real sense, dead wrong. (2) For example, ophthalmologists make the statement that reading in the dark will not have the effect of ruining a person's eyes. (3) In the case of spicy foods, specialists have proven that foods of this sort are not necessarily bad for the stomach, even for people who have been treated as ulcer patients. (4) What about our mothers' warning that exists about catching colds when we are in the process of becoming chilled? (5) It is certainly quite true that more people have a tendency to get sick in winter than people do in summer. (6) It seems that lower temperatures are not a factor that deserves the blame, however. (7) In view of the fact that cold weather often has a tendency to drive people indoors and to bring people together inside, this factor has the appearance of increasing our odds of infecting one another. (8) Finally, there has been a long-standing tradition that states that the full moon has the effect on people of making them crazy. (9) Investigations that were made by researchers who were tireless and careful came to the ultimate conclusion that there is no such relationship in existence.

16c   Revising redundancies

Planned repetition can create a powerful rhythmic effect (see 19g). The dull drone of unplanned repetition, however, can bore a reader and prevent the delivery of your message. Unplanned repetition is called **redundancy.**

Certain redundant word pairs are very common. Avoid expressions like *each and every, null and void, forever and ever,* and *final and conclusive.* Other common redundancies are *perfectly clear, few* (or *many*) *in number, consensus of opinion,* and *reason is because.*

NO Bringing the project to **final completion** three weeks early, the new manager earned our **respectful regard** when **the project was completed.**

YES **Completing** the project three weeks early, the new manager earned our **respect.**

YES The new manager earned our **respect** for **completing** the project three weeks early.

NO **Astonished,** the architect **circled around** the building in **amazement.**

YES **Astonished,** the architect **circled** the building.

YES The architect **walked around** the building **in amazement.**

Notice how redundancies deaden a sentence's impact.

NO The council members **proposed a discussion** of the amendment, but that **proposal for a discussion** was voted down after they had **discussed** it for a while.

YES The council members' proposal to discuss the amendment was eventually voted down.

NO The **consensus of opinion** among those of us who saw it is that the carton was **huge in size.**

YES Most of us who saw the carton agree that it was huge.

◆ ESL NOTE: In all languages, words often carry an unspoken message—an *implied meaning*—that is assumed by native speakers of the language. Implied meaning can cause redundancy in writing. For example, *I sent a letter by mail* is redundant; in English, *to send a letter* implies *by mail.* A good dictionary gives information about implied meaning of words (see the list of dictionaries in 20a). *Webster's New World Dictionary,* Third College Edition, for example, defines the verb *send* this way: "to dispatch, convey, or transmit (a letter, message, etc.) by mail, radio, etc." ◆

EXERCISE 16-3

Consulting section 16c, eliminate redundant words and phrases. Then revise the paragraph so that it is concise.

EXAMPLE   Oral history is an important legacy that can be handed down to future generations who come later.

Oral history is an important legacy for future generations.

(1) Now is the time to interview and talk to each and every family elder about the events and happenings of their lives. (2) The reason for the urgency is because the aging process of growing older can interrupt our dialogue with elderly relatives faster and more rapidly than we could or should be able to imagine. (3) To give just one example, in the 1980s, Ellen Miller, a woman in her forties, started to begin audiotaping her mother's memories and reminiscences of Berlin during the era of the early 1900s. (4) Before Miller had the change to videotape some sessions, however, Alzheimer's disease had robbed her mother of her speech and memory. (5) Upon her mother's death at the age of eighty-eight years, Miller sat down, listened again and heard once more the familiar gentle voice telling stories and tales of far-off days on another continent that vividly evoked those times. (6) Then and there Miller decided on the spot to make a film that would bring together these audiotapes combined with family photographs, her own narration, and her mother's favourite Beethoven piano sonata. (7) Ellen Miller advises those who want to capture and preserve their family history on tape to bring family heirlooms and photographs when the recording sessions are being held. (8) The interviewer should ask questions that are specific and particular and not vague, and the interviewer should keep his or her own comments to a minimum.

Focus on Revising

REVISING YOUR WRITING

If you need to write more concisely, go back to your writing and locate wordy material. Using this chapter as a resource, revise your writing to eliminate wordiness in sentences (see 16a) and to avoid unneeded words (see 16b) and redundancy (see 16c).

CASE STUDY: REVISING FOR CONCISENESS

In these case studies, you can observe a student writer revising. Then you have the chance to revise other student writing on your own.

Observation

A student wrote the following draft for a course called Business Management. The assignment was to write a summary of a research study related to the course. This material summarizes the source material thoroughly, but the draft's effectiveness is diminished by a lack of conciseness.

Read through the draft. The wordy material is highlighted and explained. Before you look at the student's revision, revise the material yourself. Then compare your work to the student's.

Researchers in business management interviewed and talked to over two hundred people who have experienced important, major career defeats. The study was undertaken by the researchers for the purpose of discovering why some smart people fail at their careers while there are others who generally do not fail. The results show that in a very real sense many people lack the recognition that most careers involve getting along

redundant: 16c

unnecessary passive construction: 16a-2

unneeded words: 16b

noun formed from verb: 16a-4

unneeded words: 16b

clause can be reduced to phrase: 16a-3

well with other people. It is often claimed by many employees who fail that "office politics" was the cause of the problems. In point of fact, however, those employees often have no ability to listen to others sensitively and to give and take criticism constructively. The researchers also found that some people fail to have success because they have an absence of commitment to their work. Sometimes the underlying reason is a fear. That fear is the fear of failure, which has the manifestation of being a lack of motivation. When people do not attempt to try to succeed, they do not expose themselves to the risk of failure. Finally, it was discovered by the researchers that the fact of the matter is that luck sometimes has a role, as when a change in management means that the new people bring in their own team.

Annotations (left):
- unnecessary expletive construction: 16a-1; and clause can be reduced to word: 16a-3
- unneeded words: 16b
- noun formed from verb: 16a-4
- weak verb: 16a-4
- redundant: 16c
- unnecessary passive construction: 16a-2

Annotations (right):
- weak verb: 16a-4
- redundant: 16c
- weak verb: 16a-4
- sentences can be combined: 16a-3
- noun formed from verb: 16a-4
- unneeded words: 16b
- weak verb: 16a-4

Here is how the student revised the paragraph to achieve conciseness. In a few places, the student could correct the error in more than one way. Your revision, therefore, might not be exactly like this one, but it should eliminate the wordy material highlighted on the draft.

Researchers in business management interviewed over two hundred people who have experienced major career defeats. The researchers wanted to discover why some smart people fail at their careers while others do not. The results show that many people do not recognize that most careers involve getting along well with other people. Many employees who fail claim that "office politics" caused the problems. However, those employees often do not listen to others sensitively and do not give and take criticism constructively. The researchers also found that some people fail because they are not committed to their work. Sometimes the underlying reason is a fear of failure, which manifests itself as a lack of motivation. When people do not try to succeed, they do not risk failure. Finally, the researchers discovered that luck sometimes plays a role, as when a change in management means that the new people bring in their own team.

Participation

A student wrote the following draft for a journalism class called Feature Writing. The material is logically presented and informative, but the draft's effectiveness is diminished by wordy constructions, padding, and redundancies.

Read through the draft. Then revise it to eliminate the errors. Also, make any additional revisions you think would improve the content, organization, and style of the material.

Postsecondary students seeking alternatives to dormitories, young adults moving out on their own, and newcomers to an area often rent apartments or houses. All of these potential renters should keep in mind that renting or leasing involves a legal agreement between landlord and tenant. It is recommended that anyone preparing to rent conduct careful and extensive evaluations of the entire situation before making any decisions. One major area to investigate is the evaluation of the type of landlord. It is also recommended that renters carefully examine the condition and nature of the premises before any lease is signed by them.

An initial step in the rent process is the investigation of the landlord. A list of current and former tenants of the facility can be requested from the landlord. Renters should not hesitate to contact a reasonable number of parties on the list. Renters should ask all of those with whom they come in contact whether the management of the property, in particular the landlord, is easy to contact if problems should arise and whether the landlord is willing to handle such problems without delay. If anyone is of the opinion that the landlord has a poor reputation for handling problems properly, it is better to find out before signing a lease or deposit cheque.

Also, for the purpose of being protected in the event of future disagreements, it is recommended that renters inspect the premises carefully. If there is any type of damage in the apartment, the details should be written down in a written inventory by the renters, and it should be signed and dated by the renters and the landlord. If any damages are to be repaired by the landlord, those promises should also be put in writing. In the event that any damage is present when renters leave the property, it is the renters who will probably be held legally liable for repairs since the landlord would be able to claim that the damage was done during the term of the renters' lease.

In short, only after careful consideration should the renter even consider signing a lease or leaving a deposit or signing anything that might be legally binding.

17 Coordination and Subordination

You can include **coordination** and **subordination** in your writing style to help you communicate relationships between two or more ideas. These techniques help your stylistic choices work in concert with the meaning that you want your sentences to deliver. While you are drafting°, concentrate on getting your ideas onto paper. When you are revising°, you can explore the full potential of coordination and subordination for enriching your writing style.

TWO IDEAS	The sky turned dark grey. The wind died suddenly.
COORDINATED VERSION	The sky turned dark grey, and the wind died suddenly.
SUBORDINATED VERSION	As the sky turned dark grey, the wind died suddenly. [The *wind* is the focus.]
SUBORDINATED VERSION	As the wind died suddenly, the sky turned dark grey. [The *sky* is the focus.]

COORDINATION

17a Understanding coordination

Coordination can produce harmony by bringing together related but separate elements to function smoothly in unison. Sections 17a through 17d explain coordination of independent clauses°. Coordinate sentences communicate balance in, or sequence of, the ideas that they contain. You can apply these same principles to the coordination of words, phrases°, and dependent clauses° (see also the explanation of parallelism, Chapter 18).

356

Patterns for coordinate sentences, also known as *compound sentences,* are shown in Chart 90. When you choose to coordinate sentences in your writing, keep these principles in mind:

- A coordinate sentence consists of two grammatically equivalent independent clauses.

- Coordinating independent clauses must be justified by the meaning that you want your sentence to communicate.

- The independent clauses must be joined either by a coordinating conjunction (see Chart 90) or by a semicolon (see 25a and 25b).

- The coordinating conjunction must accurately express the relationship (see Chart 91) between the ideas in the independent clauses.

- If you are tempted to coordinate more than two independent clauses, do so with much care (see 17d-1 and 19b-2).

✤ CONJUNCTION ALERT: Do not confuse coordinating conjunctions with conjunctive adverbs such as *also, however,* and *therefore* (for a complete list, see Chart 49 in section 7f). When conjunctive adverbs connect independent clauses, they function as explained in 7f and 14e.✤

✤ PUNCTUATION ALERT: You will never be wrong if you use a comma before a coordinating conjunction that joins two independent clauses (see 24a).

The sky turned dark grey, **and** the wind died suddenly.
The November morning had just begun, **but** it looked like dusk.✤

PATTERNS FOR COORDINATE (COMPOUND) SENTENCES		90
Independent clause ⟨	, and , but , for , nor , or , so , yet ; ⟩	independent clause

COORDINATING CONJUNCTIONS AND THE RELATIONSHIPS THEY EXPRESS   91

RELATIONSHIPS	WORDS
addition	*and*
contrast	*but, yet*
result or effect	*so*
reason or choice	*for*
choice	*or*
negative choice	*nor*

17b Using coordinate sentences to show relationships

You can choose to use a string of short sentences for the impact that such style creates. In most cases, however, a series of short sentences does not communicate well the relationships among the ideas. In such situations, coordination can help you avoid writing a series of short sentences that have unclear relationships.

UNCLEAR RELATIONSHIPS

We decided not to go to class. We planned to get the notes. Everyone else had the same plan. Most of us ended up failing the quiz.

CLEAR RELATIONSHIPS

We decided not to go to class, **but** we planned to get the notes. Everyone else had the same plan, **so** most of us ended up failing the quiz.

Overuse of coordination, however, can bore a reader with its unbroken rhythm (see 17d-2). For another technique to help you avoid an unwanted series of short sentences, see the discussion of subordination in 17e through 17h.

17c   Using coordinate sentences for effect

Coordinate sentences can help you communicate an unfolding of events, a sequence, or a list.

> There is Ontario patriotism, Quebec patriotism, or Western patriotism, each based on the hope that it may swallow up the others, **but** there is no Canadian patriotism, **and** we can have no Canadian nation when we have no Canadian patriotism.
>
> —Henri Bourassa, *The Nationalist Movement in Quebec*

In this passage, coordination underlines the contrasts that are drawn.

> What sets a canoeing expedition apart is that it purifies you more rapidly and inescapably than any other. Travel a thousand miles by train **and** you are a brute; pedal five hundred on a bicycle **and** you remain basically a bourgeois; paddle a hundred in a canoe **and** you are already a child of nature.
>
> —Pierre Elliott Trudeau, "The Ascetic in a Canoe"

17d   Avoiding the misuse of coordination

1   Avoiding illogical coordination

Coordination is illogical when ideas in the compounded independent clauses° are not related. Your reader expects one part of a coordinate construction to lead logically to the other.

NO   Computers came into common use in the 1970s, and they sometimes make costly errors.

The statement in each independent clause is true, but the ideas are not related closely enough. The date computers became commonly used is unrelated to their making errors. The two ideas should not be coordinated. Here are ideas that do coordinate logically.

YES   Computers came into common use in the 1970s, and they are now indispensible for conducting business.

YES   Modern computer systems are often very complex, and they sometimes make costly errors.

2

Avoiding the overuse of coordination

Overused coordination creates writing that reads as if it were whatever came into the writer's head. Readers become impatient with "babble" and quickly lose interest. When you are revising°, be sure to check that your intended meaning justifies the use of coordination.

NO   Dinosaurs could have disappeared for many reasons, and one theory holds that the climate suddenly became cold, and another theory suggests that a sudden shower of meteors and asteroids hit the earth, so the impact created a huge dust cloud that caused a false winter. The winter lasted for years, and the dinosaurs died, for most of the vegetation they lived on died out.

YES   Dinosaurs could have disappeared for many reasons. One theory holds that the climate suddenly became cold, and another suggests that a sudden shower of meteors and asteroids hit the earth. The impact created a huge dust cloud that caused a false winter. The winter lasted for years, killing most of the vegetation that dinosaurs used for food.

In the revised version, the sentences deliver their meanings clearly.

Writers also overuse coordination if they fail to feature some ideas more prominently than others. Such writing tends to drone on monotonously.

NO   Laughter seems to help healing, so many doctors are prescribing humour for their patients, and some hospitals are doing the same. Comedians have donated their time to several California hospitals, and the nurses in one large hospital in Texas have been trained to tell each patient a joke a day.

YES   Laughter seems to help healing. Many doctors and hospitals are prescribing humour for their patients. Comedians have donated their time to several California hospitals, and the nurses in one large hospital in Texas have been asked to tell each patient a joke a day.

In the revised version, some ideas are kept separate and some are put into a coordinate sentence. (For another way to revise overused coordination, see the discussion of subordination, 17e through 17h.)

◆ ESL NOTE: If your instructor tells you that your sentences are too long and complex, practise limiting them. When you write your next paper, follow the advice of many ESL teachers: Revise any sentence containing a combination of more than three independent and dependent clauses.◆

EXERCISE 17-1

Consulting sections 17a through 17d, revise these sentences to eliminate illogical or overused coordination. If you think a sentence needs no revision, circle its number.

EXAMPLE   Anthropologists can tell the age of a skeleton by analyzing its structure and chemical makeup, and most people know this, but many do not know that skeletons can tell us much more.

Most people know that anthropologists can tell the age of a skeleton by analyzing its structure and chemical makeup, but many do not know that skeletons can tell us much more.

1. The life that a person leads often leaves marks on the bones, so anthropologists study stress marks on bones, and they often can figure out the life habits of a person, and they often can guess a person's occupation.
2. For example, the forearm bone is usually enlarged in baseball pitchers, and a similar enlargement appears in the skeletons of spear-throwing hunters from prehistoric times.
3. Also, women who always carry their babies on their backs have stress marks at the base of the spine, but a professional clarinet player usually has an irregular lower jaw.
4. Professor Kenneth A. R. Kennedy has compiled a list of over 140 skeletal marks that indicate occupation, and he teaches anthropology at Cornell University.
5. Professor Kennedy's work has great legal value, and it is also very practical, for it is another tool to help investigators identify accident and murder victims, and the information can provide clues about the identities of missing people, and it can help with identifying war casualties.

EXERCISE 17-2

Consulting sections 17a through 17d, revise this paragraph. Choose which ideas seem to have equal weight and could therefore be contained in compound sentences. Your final version should have no more than two compound sentences—all other sentences should be left as they are.

Bicycle couriers represent the newest flourishing of urban subculture. They are a cosmopolitan phenomenon. They swarm the downtowns of big cities from Berlin to Vancouver. European bicycle couriers favour a streamlined, high-tech look, all vinyl and Spandex and severe haircuts. The North American branches of the tribe prefer a neo-primitive look. They are likely to sport nose rings, jangling handmade accessories, and flying dreadlocks. As often as not, couriers assemble the jewellery they wear from a bicycle repair kit. This subculture has transformed the bicycle helmet into a fashion statement. Once this practical piece of headgear was disparaged as "uncool."

SUBORDINATION

17e Understanding subordination

Subordination expresses the relative importance of ideas in a sentence by making a less important idea grammatically less prominent than a more important one. Sections 17e through 17h explain subordination of dependent° and independent clauses°: The more important idea appears in the independent clause—a group of words that can stand alone as a grammatical unit; the subordinated idea appears in the dependent clause—a group of words that cannot stand alone as a grammatical unit. What information you choose to subordinate depends on the meaning that you want a sentence to deliver.

Major patterns of subordination with dependent clauses are shown in Chart 92. Two types of dependent clauses are adverb clauses and adjective clauses (see Chart 92). An **adverb clause** is a dependent clause that starts with a subordinating conjunction°. Each subordinating conjunction has a specific meaning that expresses a relationship between the dependent clause and the independent clause, as shown in Chart 93.

An **adjective clause** is a dependent clause that can start with a relative pronoun (*who, which, that*), a relative adverb° (such as *where*), or a preposition° before a "relative" word (for example, *to whom, above which*).

PATTERNS OF SUBORDINATION WITH DEPENDENT CLAUSES   92

SENTENCES WITH ADVERB CLAUSES

- **Adverb clause,** independent clause.
  After the sky grew dark, the wind died suddenly.

- Independent clause, **adverb clause.**
  Birds stopped singing, **as they do during an eclipse.**

- Independent clause **adverb clause.**
  The shops closed **before the storm began.**

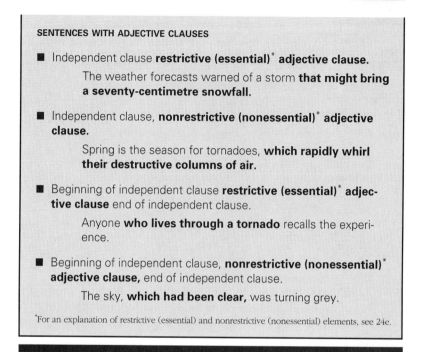

SENTENCES WITH ADJECTIVE CLAUSES

■ Independent clause **restrictive (essential)[*] adjective clause.**

The weather forecasts warned of a storm **that might bring a seventy-centimetre snowfall.**

■ Independent clause, **nonrestrictive (nonessential)[*] adjective clause.**

Spring is the season for tornadoes, **which rapidly whirl their destructive columns of air.**

■ Beginning of independent clause **restrictive (essential)[*] adjective clause** end of independent clause.

Anyone **who lives through a tornado** recalls the experience.

■ Beginning of independent clause, **nonrestrictive (nonessential)[*] adjective clause,** end of independent clause.

The sky, **which had been clear,** was turning grey.

[*]For an explanation of restrictive (essential) and nonrestrictive (nonessential) elements, see 24e.

SUBORDINATING CONJUNCTIONS AND THE RELATIONSHIPS THEY EXPRESS   93

RELATIONSHIPS	WORDS
time	*after, before, once, since, until, when, whenever, while*
reason or cause	*as, because, since*
purpose or result	*in order that, so, so that, that*
condition	*even if, if, provided that, unless*
contrast	*although, even though, though, whereas*
location	*where, wherever*
choice	*rather than, whether*

17f Choosing the subordinate conjunction appropriate to your meaning

Subordinating conjunctions express the relationship between major and minor ideas in sentences (see Chart 93). Consider the influence of the subordinating conjunction in each of the following sentences.

After you have handed it in, you cannot make any changes in your report. [time]

Because you have handed it in, you cannot make any changes in your report. [reason]

Unless you have handed it in, you cannot make any changes in your report. [condition]

Although you have handed it in, you can make changes in your report. [contrast]

I want to read your report **so that I can evaluate it.** [purpose]

Since you handed in your report, three more people have handed in theirs. [time]

Since I have seen the report, I can comment on it. [cause]

17g Using subordination to show relationships

Subordination directs your reader's attention to the idea in the independent clause° while at the same time using the idea in the dependent clause° to provide context and support. Consider these examples (dependent clauses are in boldface).

As soon as I saw the elephant, I knew with perfect certainty that I ought not to shoot it.

—GEORGE ORWELL, "Shooting an Elephant"

If they are very lucky, the passengers may catch a glimpse of dolphins playfully breaking water near the ship.

—ELIZABETH GRAY, student

Subordination usually communicates relationships among ideas more effectively than does a group of separate sentences, although you may occasionally use a string of short sentences for impact.

UNCLEAR RELATIONSHIPS

In 1910, my grandfather and his hired hand got caught in a dangerous snowstorm on the prairies. They were looking for cattle. They were lost and thought they were going to freeze to death. Suddenly they saw a light through the snow. Survival then seemed certain.

CLEAR RELATIONSHIPS

In 1910, my grandfather and his hired hand got caught in a dangerous snowstorm on the prairies **while they were looking for cattle.** They were lost and thought they were going to freeze to death **when suddenly they saw a light through the snow**. Survival then seemed certain.

In the clear version, the first four short sentences have been combined into two complex sentences°. The last sentence is left short.

EXERCISE 17-3

Consulting sections 17e through 17g, combine each pair of sentences, using an adverb clause to subordinate one idea. Then revise each sentence so that the adverb clause becomes the independent clause. Refer to the list of subordinating conjunctions in Chart 92.

EXAMPLE   Shoes can be colourful, glamorous, or even witty. They are meant to protect the foot from some of the dangers of walking.

> a: *Although shoes can be colourful, glamorous, or even witty, they are meant to protect the foot from some of the dangers of walking.*

> b: *Although they are meant to protect the foot from some of the dangers of walking, shoes can be colourful, glamorous, or even witty.*

1. Sandals are worn primarily to protect the sole of the foot. They are also worn for comfort and style.
2. Ornamentation was added to sandals worn by ancient peoples. Footwear became a stylish article of clothing.
3. Sandalmakers were constrained by certain requirements in ancient Egyptian society. They had to cater to their clients' fashion whims.
4. For example, the nobility demanded sandals with turned-up toes. Peasants were expected to wear sandals with rounded or pointed toes.
5. Clothing had to be made from available materials. Ancient Egyptian sandals were made of leather, woven palm leaves, or papyrus stalks.

EXERCISE 17-4

Consulting sections 17e through 17g, combine each pair of sentences, using an adjective clause to make one idea subordinate to the other. Then revise each sentence so that the adjective clause becomes the independent clause. Use the relative pronoun given in parentheses.

EXAMPLE   The artist Pablo Picasso died in 1973 at the age of 92. He is best known for creating the Cubist style in art. (who)

> *a:* *Pablo Picasso, who died in 1973 at the age of 92, is best known for creating the Cubist style in art.*
>
> *b:* *Pablo Picasso, who is best known for creating the Cubist style in art, died in 1973 at the age of 92.*

1. Pablo Picasso had mastered all the traditional art techniques at a young age. He quickly became interested in experimenting with different styles. (who)
2. Picasso's style is characterized by designs that depart from strict reality. It is heavily influenced by the primitive art of Africa. (which)
3. Picasso created shapes. The shapes seemed to some people to be grotesque distortions of reality. (that)
4. An art critic enjoyed Picasso's use of geometric shapes to present multiple viewpoints of an object on one canvas. The art was nicknamed "Cubism" by the art critic. (who)
5. Experts agree that the entire body of Picasso's art is not solely in any one style. The entire body of Picasso's art is amazingly varied. (which)

17h   Avoiding the misuse of subordination

1   Avoiding illogical subordination

Subordination is illogical when the subordinating conjunction does not make clear the relationship between the independent and dependent clause (see Chart 93).

> **NO**   Because Beethoven was deaf when he wrote his final symphonies, they are musical masterpieces.

The above sentence is illogical because it was not Beethoven's deafness that led to his writing symphonic masterpieces. Revising from *because* to *although* creates logical subordination:

> **YES**   Although Beethoven was deaf when he wrote his final symphonies, they are musical masterpieces.

| **2** | **Avoiding the overuse of subordination** |

Overused subordination occurs when too many images or ideas crowd together, making your reader lose track of your intended message. If you have used more than two subordinating conjunctions or relative pronouns° in a sentence, be skeptical about whether your meaning is clear.

NO   A new technique for eye surgery, which is supposed to correct nearsightedness, which previously could be corrected only by glasses, has been developed, although many doctors do not approve of it because it can create unstable eyesight.

YES   A new technique for eye surgery, which is supposed to correct nearsightedness, has been developed. Previously, nearsightedness could be corrected only by glasses. Because it can create unstable eyesight, many doctors do not approve of it, however.

In the revised version the first sentence has a relative clause°, the second is a simple sentence°, and the third has a dependent clause starting with *Because*. Some words have been moved to new positions. The revision communicates its message more clearly because it provides a variety of sentence structures (see 19a) while avoiding the clutter of overused subordination.

EXERCISE 17-5

Consulting section 17h, correct illogical or excessive subordination in this paragraph. As you revise, use not only some short sentences but also some correctly constructed adverb clauses. Also, apply the principles of coordination discussed in 17a through 17d, if you wish.

Because too many young ape mothers in zoos were rejecting or abusing their infants, zoo keepers decided to stop their usual practice of separating mother and infant from the rest of the ape community which was done so that the infant would supposedly be safe from harm from other apes. In the new arrangement, group settings were established that included older, experienced loving ape mothers as well as other infants and young mothers so that the abusive mothers could learn from good role models how to love and care for their infants and so that each mother would have childrearing support from the equivalent of aunts and cousins. The experiment was successful, and some pediatricians, who are doctors who specialize in child care, tried a similar program for abusive human mothers, which worked well even though the human mothers took far longer than the ape mothers to learn and use good mothering techniques.

17i Balancing subordination and coordination

Coordination and subordination can sometimes be used in concert with each other.

When Laura Secord overheard the American plans for attack, she realized she had to warn the British **and,** with only her lantern, she set out to walk the thirty kilometres from Queenston to Beaver Dams.

Varying sentence types can improve your ability to emphasize key points in your writing. Consider the following paragraph, which demonstrates a good balance in the use of coordination and subordination. It contains compound sentences (see 17a–17d), sentences that consist of dependent and independent clauses (see 17e–17h), and simple sentences°.

When I was growing up, I lived on a farm just across the field from my grandmother. My parents were busy trying to raise six children and to establish their struggling dairy farm. It was nice to have Grandma so close. **While my parents were providing the necessities of life,** my patient grandmother gave her time to her shy, young granddaughter. I always enjoyed going with Grandma and collecting the eggs that her chickens had just laid. Usually she knew which chickens would peck, **and** she was careful to let me gather the eggs from the less hostile ones.

—Patricia Mapes, student

Avoid using both a coordinating *and* a subordinating conjunction to express one relationship.

NO	**Although** the story was well written, **but** it was too unbelievable.
YES	Although the story was well written, it was too unbelievable.
YES	The story was well written, but it was too unbelievable.

EXERCISE 17-6

Consulting all sections of this chapter, use subordination and coordination to combine these sets of short, choppy sentences.

EXAMPLE   Owls cannot digest the bones and fur of the mice and birds they eat. They cough up a furry pellet every day.

Because owls cannot digest the bones and fur of the mice and birds they eat, they cough up a furry pellet every day.

1. Owl pellets are the latest teaching tool in biology classrooms. The pellets provide an alternative to dissecting frogs and other animals.
2. Inside the pellet are the remains of the owl's nightly meal. They include beautifully cleaned hummingbirds skulls, rat skeletons, and lots of bird feathers.
3. The owl pellet market has been cornered by companies in New York, California, and Washington. These companies distribute pellets to thousands of biology classrooms all over the world.
4. Company workers scour barns and the ground under trees where owls nest to pick up the pellets. The pellets sell for $1 each.
5. The owl pellet business may have a short future. The rural areas of North America are vanishing. Old barns are being bulldozed. All the barns are torn down. The owls will be gone, too.

EXERCISE 17-7

Using topics you choose, imitate the style of three different examples shown in this chapter. Select from the quotations by Bourassa, Trudeau, Orwell, Gray, and Mapes.

EXERCISE 17-8

Consulting all sections of this chapter, revise this passage by using coordination and subordination.

Harlequin Enterprises sells more than 700 million books a year. It markets them throughout the world. The company is a Canadian success story. It claims to have made "the language of love universal, crossing social, cultural and geographical borders with an ease unrivalled by any other publisher." Harlequin's success lies in its ability to market a formula. The heroines and heroes of all the books fulfil certain criteria of age, appearance, and profession. The romances follow a prescribed pattern. Fans of Harlequin's books do not care. They buy the new titles faithfully each month.

18 Parallelism

This chapter advises you how to avoid **faulty parallelism** (18b through 18e) and how to use the grace and power of **parallelism** to strengthen your writing (18f and 18g). It also explains parallelism in outlines and lists (18h).

Many writers attend to parallelism when they revise°. If while you are drafting° you think that your parallelism is faulty or that you can enhance your writing style by using parallelism, underline or highlight the material and keep your focus on getting ideas onto paper. When you revise, you can work on the places that you marked.

18a Understanding parallelism

Parallelism in writing, related to the concept of parallel lines in geometry, calls for the use of equivalent grammatical forms to express ideas of equal importance. An **equivalent grammatical form** is a word or group of words that matches—is parallel to—the structure of a corresponding word or group of words, as explained in Chart 94.

Also, when you are expressing ideas of equal weight in your writing, parallel sentence structures can echo that fact and offer you a writing style that uses balance and rhythm to help deliver your meaning.

> **They come like foxes** through the woods. **They attack like lions. They take flight like birds,** disappearing before they have really appeared.
>
> —Jérôme Lalemant, in *The Jesuit Relations*

The Jesuit missionary and martyr conveys the sense of stealth, courage, and speed of the Iroquois by using similes from the natural world. He sets out his images in parallel structure.

PARALLEL STRUCTURES   94

PARALLEL WORDS

Recommended exercise includes **running, swimming,** and **cycling.**
[The *-ing* words are parallel in structure and equal in importance.]

PARALLEL PHRASES

Exercise helps people **to maintain healthy bodies** and

to handle mental pressure. [The *to* phrases are parallel in structure
and equal in importance.]

PARALLEL CLAUSES

People exercise **because they want to look healthy,**

because they need to have stamina, or **because they hope to live**

longer. [The *because* clauses are parallel in structure and equal in
importance.]

18b Using words in parallel forms

To avoid faulty parallelism, be sure that words in parallel structures
occur in the same grammatical form.

> **NO**   The strikers had tried **pleading, threats,** and **shouting.**
>
> **YES**   The strikers had tried **pleading, threatening,** and
>   **shouting.**
>
> **YES**   The strikers had tried **pleas, threats,** and **shouts.**

Using words in parallel form can also enhance the impact of the meaning that you want your material to deliver (see 18f and 18g).

18c Using phrases and clauses in parallel forms

To avoid faulty parallelism, be sure that phrases° and clauses° in parallel structures occur in the same grammatical form.

NO   The committee members **read the petition, discussed its major points,** and **the unanimous decision was to ignore it.**

YES   The committee members **read the petition, discussed its major points,** and **unanimously decided to ignore it.** [revised to parallel phrases]

NO   **The signers heard that their petition had not been granted, they became very upset,** and then **staged a protest demonstration.**

YES   **The signers heard that their petition had not been granted, they became very upset,** and then **they staged a protest demonstration.** [revised to parallel clauses]

YES   **The signers heard that their petition had not been granted, became very upset,** and then **staged a protest demonstration.** [revised to parallel phrases]

Using phrases and clauses in parallel form can also enhance the impact of the meaning that you want your material to deliver (see 18f and 18g).

18d Using parallel structures with coordinating and correlative conjunctions and with *than* and *as*

1 Using parallel forms with coordinating conjunctions

The coordinating conjunctions are *and, but, or, nor, for, yet,* and *so* (for the relationship each expresses, see Chart 91 in section 17a). To avoid faulty parallelism, be sure that elements joined by coordinating conjunctions are parallel in grammatical form.

NO   **Love and being married** go together.

YES   **Love and marriage** go together.

YES   **Being in love and being married** go together.

2 | Using parallel forms with paired words (correlative conjunctions)

The correlative conjunctions are pairs of words that work in unison, such as *not only ... but (also), either ... or,* and *both ... and* (for more, see 7h). To avoid faulty parallelism, be sure that elements joined by correlative conjunctions are parallel in grammatical form. As you check your writing, pay particular attention to the correct placement of each half of the pair.

NO   Differing expectations for marriage **not only** can lead to disappointment **but also** to anger. [The words *can lead* apply to *disappointment* and to *anger,* so they belong before *not only.*]

YES   Differing expectations for marriage can lead **not only** to disappointment **but also** to anger.

—Norman DuBois, student

3 | Using parallel forms with *than* and *as*

To avoid faulty parallelism when you use *than* and *as* for comparisons, be sure that elements are parallel in grammatical form. Also, make sure that these comparisons are complete (see 15e-2).

NO   **Having a solid marriage** can be more satisfying **than** the **acquisition of wealth.**

YES   **Having a solid marriage** can be more satisfying **than acquiring wealth.**

YES   **A solid marriage** can be more satisfying **than wealth.**

—Eunice Fernandez, student

18e Repeating function words in parallel elements

In a series of two or more parallel elements, be consistent in the second and subsequent elements about repeating or omitting function words. These include articles (*the, a, an*); the *to* of the infinitive° (for example, *to* love) and prepositions (for example, *of, in, about.* If you think that repeating such words clarifies your meaning or might help your reader catch the parallelism that you intend, use them.

NO   **To assign** unanswered letters their proper weight, **free us** from the expectations of others, **to give us** back to ourselves—here lies **the great, the singular** power of self-respect.

YES   **To assign** unanswered letters their proper weight, **to free us** from the expectations of others, **to give us** back to ourselves—here lies **the great, the singular** power of self-respect.

—JOAN DIDION, "On Self-Respect"

To avoid faulty parallelism when you use *who, which,* or *that* to start a series of clauses°, be sure to repeat or omit the words consistently in subsequent clauses.

I have in my own life a precious friend, a woman of 65 **who has** lived very hard, **who is** wise, **who listens** well, **who has** been where I am and can help me understand it; **and who represents** not only an ultimate ideal mother to me but also the person I'd like to be when I grow up.

—JUDITH VIORST, "Friends, Good Friends—and Such Good Friends"

We looked into the bus, **which was** painted blue with orange daisies, **had** picnic benches instead of seats, and **showed** yellow curtains billowing out its windows.

—KERRIE FALK, student

18f Using parallel, balanced structures for impact

Parallel structures characterized by balance serve to emphasize the meaning that sentences deliver. Balanced, parallel structures can be words, phrases, clauses, or sentences.

Deliberate, rhythmic repetition of parallel, balanced word forms and word groups reinforces the impact of a message. (For information about misused repetition, see 16c.) Consider the impact of this passage:

It is a good country for the honest, industrious artisan. **It is a fine country for the** poor labourer who, after a few years of hard toil, can sit down in his own log-house and look abroad on his own land and see his children well settled in life as independent freeholders. **It is a good country for** the rich speculator who can afford to lay out a large sum in purchasing land in eligible situations; for if he has any judgement he will make a hundred per cent as interest for his money after waiting a few years. But **it is a hard**

country for the poor gentleman whose habits have rendered him unfit for manual labour.

—Catherine Parr Traill, *The Backwoods of Canada*

If Traill had expressed the same idea with only minimal parallelism, her message would have been weaker. Her structures reinforce the power of her message, and give her final sentence more weight because it is a slight variation on the parallel form. An ordinary structure would not have been as effective: "It is a good country for the honest, industrious artisan. The poor labourer ... will also do well. If a rich speculator can afford to lay out a large sum, ... he will make a hundred per cent as interest for his money after waiting a few years. The poor gentleman whose habits have rendered him unfit for manual labour will probably not become rich here."

A **balanced sentence** has two parallel structures, usually potential sentences in their own right, with contrasting content. A balanced sentence is a coordinate sentence (see 17a), characterized by opposition in the meaning of the two structures, sometimes with one cast in the negative: *Mosquitoes do not bite, they stab.* Consider the impact of this sentence:

> By night, the litter and desperation disappeared as the city's glittering lights came on; by day, the filth and despair reappeared as the sun rose.

—Jennifer Kirk, student

Similarly, consider the impact of this famous sentence, which adds unusual word order (*ask not,* instead of *do not ask*) to its parallelism and balance.

> Ask not what your country can do for you, ask what you can do for your country.

—John F. Kennedy

❧ COMMA ALERT: Authorities differ about using a comma or semicolon between the parts of a balanced sentence. In your academic writing, to avoid seeming to make the error of a comma splice (see Chapter 14), you are safer if you use a semicolon (or revise in other ways).❧

18g Using parallel sentences in longer passages for impact

Parallel, balanced sentences in longer passages can create a dramatic unity through carefully controlled repetition of words and word forms. Consider this rich passage of repeated words, concepts, and rhythms.

You ask me what is **poverty? Listen** to me. Here I am, dirty, **smelly,** and with no "proper" underwear on and with the **stench** of my rotting teeth near you. I will tell you. **Listen** to me. **Listen** without pity. I cannot use your pity. **Listen** with understanding. Put yourself in my dirty, worn-out, ill-fitting shoes, and hear me.

Poverty is getting up every morning from a dirt- and illness-stained mattress. The sheets have long since been used for diapers. **Poverty** is living in a **smell** that never leaves. **This is a smell** of urine, sour milk, and spoiling food sometimes joined with the strong **smell** of long-cooked onions. Onions are cheap. If you have **smelled** this **smell,** you did not know how it came. **It is the smell** of the outdoor privy. **It is the smell** of young children who cannot walk the long dark way in the night. **It is the smell** of the mattresses where years of "accidents" have happened. **It is the smell** of the milk which has gone sour because the refrigerator long has not worked, and it costs money to get it fixed. **It is the smell** of rotting garbage. I could bury it, but where is the shovel? Shovels cost money.

—Jo Goodwin Parker, "What Is Poverty?"

EXERCISE 18-1

Reread the Jo Goodwin Parker passage above. Then, consulting sections 18a through 18e, discover all parallel elements in addition to those shown in boldface.

EXERCISE 18-2

Using topics you choose, imitate the writing style of three different passages shown in this chapter. Select from the quotations from Lalemant, Didion, Viorst, Traill, Kennedy, or Parker.

EXERCISE 18-3

Consulting sections 18a through 18e, revise these sentences to eliminate errors in parallel structure.

EXAMPLE   Difficult bosses not only affect their employees' performance but their private lives are affected as well.

Difficult bosses affect *not only their employees' performances but their private lives as well.*

1. According to psychologist Harry Levinson, the five main types of bad boss are the workaholic, the kind of person you would describe as bullying, a person who communicates badly, the jellyfish type, and someone who insists on perfection.

2. As a way of getting ahead, to keep their self-respect, and for simple survival, wise employees handle problem bosses with a variety of strategies.

3. To cope with a bad-tempered employer, workers can both stand up for themselves and reasoning with a bullying boss.
4. Often bad bosses communicate poorly or fail to calculate the impact of their personality on others; being a careful listener and to be sensitive to others' responses are qualities that good bosses possess.
5. Employees who take the trouble to understand what makes their boss tick, engage in some self-analysis, and staying flexible are better prepared to cope with a difficult job environment than suffering in silence like some employees.

EXERCISE 18-4

Consulting sections 18a through 18e, combine the sentences in each numbered item, using techniques of parallelism.

EXAMPLE Philippine rain forests provide shelter for plants. They also protect animals. A Stone Age tribe called the Tasaday lives in a Philippine rain forest.

Philippine rain forests shelter plants, protect animals, and provide a home for a Stone Age tribe called the Tasaday.

1. The Tasaday had not developed even the most primitive forms of agriculture. They did not know how to weave. Making pottery was unknown to them.
2. Animals and plants provided their food. They used leaves as clothes. They lived in caves.
3. The Tasaday were unaware of modern conveniences. Also, they showed no evidence of modern anxieties either.
4. The Philippine government decided to protect the tribe's Stone Age culture. Also, the Tasaday's safety was ensured when the government declared the forest a national preserve.
5. Throughout the ages, the Tasaday have never had a war. This fact amazes anthropologists. The lack of war also inspires peace-loving people everywhere.

18h Using parallelism in outlines and lists

Items in formal outlines and lists must be parallel in grammar and structure. (For information about other issues of outline format and about how to develop an outline, see 2o.)

FORMAL OUTLINE NOT IN PARALLEL FORM

Reducing Traffic Fatalities

I. Stricter laws
   A. Top speed should be 80 km/h on highways.
   B. Higher fines
   C. Requiring jail sentences for repeat offenders
II. The use of safety devices should be mandated by law.

FORMAL OUTLINE IN PARALLEL FORM

Reducing Traffic Fatalities

I. **Passing** stricter speed laws
   A. **Making** 80 km/h the top speed on highways
   B. **Raising** fines for speeding
   C. **Requiring** jail sentences for repeat offenders
II. **Mandating** by law the use of safety devices

Although a nonparallel outline might serve as an informal, scratch outline for a writer's private purposes in the early stages of the writing process, only a parallel outline is acceptable as a final draft.

FORMAL LIST NOT IN PARALLEL FORM

Workaholics share these characteristics:

1. They are intense and driven.
2. Strong self-doubters
3. Labour is preferred to leisure by workaholics.

FORMAL LIST IN PARALLEL FORM

Workaholics share these characteristics:

1. **They are** intense and driven.
2. **They have** strong self-doubts.
3. **They prefer** labour to leisure.

EXERCISE 18-5

Consulting section 18h, revise this outline into parallel form.

Reducing Traffic Fatalities

I. Stricter laws
   A. Top speed on any highway should be 80 km/h.
   B. Higher fines
   C. Repeat offenders sentenced to jail

II. Legislating installation of safety devices
   A. All automobiles should be required to have safety belts in both front and back seats.

B. Making seat belt use mandatory for all drivers.

C. We should force auto manufacturers to offer airbags as an option in all cars.

EXERCISE 18-6

Find the parallel elements in the following examples. Next, using your own topics, imitate the style of two of the examples.

1. The time will come when that national spirit which has been spoken of will be truly felt among us, when we shall realize that we are four million Britons who are not free, when we shall be ready to take up that freedom, and to ask what the late prime minister of England assured us we should not be denied—our share of national rights.

> —EDWARD BLAKE, *A National Sentiment!*

2. It was the 18th of October, 1830, in the morning, when my feet first touched the Canadian shore. I threw myself on the ground, rolled in the sand, seized handfuls of it and kissed them, and danced around, till, in the eyes of several who were present, I passed for a madman.

> —JOSIAH HENSON (an escaped slave and the model for
> Harriet Beecher Stowe's Uncle Tom), *An Autobiography*

3. It was Sunday morning at 11 o'clock and David Suzuki was on the radio, warning of the environmental catastrophe looming around his listeners. A generation ago most of us would have been in church at this time; and here we were in church again. Dr. Suzuki's programme, with its visions of Armageddon and its call to repentance and conversion, was surely a sermon.

> —DAVID CAYLEY, "The Beer Can or the Highway?"

4. This stone bears witness to the common purpose of two nations, whose frontiers are the frontiers of friendship, whose ways are the ways of freedom, and whose works are the works of peace.

> —Inscription on the International Friendship Memorial erected to mark
> the opening of the St. Lawrence Seaway and Power Project,
> June 26, 1959

5. Each afternoon around three-thirty, as some of the workers were about to go home to prepare their early dinners, Uncle Kwok slowly and deliberately ambled in through the Wong front door, dragging his feet heavily, and gripping in one hand the small black satchel from which he was never separated.

> —JADE SNOW WONG, "Fifth Chinese Daughter"

19 Variety and Emphasis

19a Understanding variety and emphasis

Your writing style has **variety** when your sentence lengths and patterns vary; see 19b and 19c. Your writing style is characterized by **emphasis** when your sentencs are constructed to communicate the relative importance of their ideas. Strategies include choosing the subject of a sentence to highlight meaning (see 19d); adding modifiers° to basic sentences (see 19e); inverting standard word order (see 19f); and repeating important words or ideas (see 19g).

Consider the following passage, which successfully employs key techniques of variety and emphasis. The authors vary their sentence length (see 19b), include a variety of structures (see 19c), and use different kinds of modifiers in various positions (see 19e).

> Henri Poincaré, a famous mathematician who lived in the nineteenth century, devised an exercise in imagination to help people understand the relativity of measures. Imagine that one night while you were asleep everything in the universe became a thousand times larger than before. Remember this would include electrons, planets, all living creatures, your own body, and all the rulers and other measuring devices in the world. When you awoke, could you tell that anything had changed? Is there any experiment you could make to prove that some change had occurred? According to Poincaré there is no such experiment.
>
> —JUDITH AND HERBERT KOHL, *The View from the Oak*

The techniques of variety and emphasis can move your writing beyond being correct to having style and grace. Rarely do variety and emphasis emerge during drafting°. Until you are a very experienced writer, you might not be able to apply the principles in this chapter until you are revising°.

19b   Varying sentence length

When you use a variety of sentence lengths, you communicate clear distinctions among ideas. Such a style can help your readers understand the focus of your material. Also, such a style avoids the unbroken rhythm of monotonous sentence length, which can lull your reader into inattention.

1   Revising strings of too many short sentences

Strings of too many short sentences rarely establish relationships and levels of importance among ideas. Readers cannot easily make distinctions between major and minor points. Such strings, unless deliberately planned in a longer piece of writing for occasional impact (see 19b-3), suggest that the writer has not thought through the material and decided what to emphasize. The style tends to read like that of young children.

NO   Soto and his like invaded North America. They invaded from the south. Other invaders began to probe the continent's colder latitudes. In 1534, a middle-aged Breton named Jacques Cartier sailed up the St. Lawrence. He kidnapped two boys. They had gone out fishing from a distant Iroquoian town. The boys spent a winter in France. Then they led Cartier farther west. They came to where tides cease and the St. Lawrence narrows below a tall bluff. Here was their home, Stadacona, where Quebec City now stands.

YES   While Soto and his like were invading North America from the south, others began to probe its colder latitudes. In 1534, a middle-aged Breton named Jacques Cartier sailed up the St. Lawrence and kidnapped two boys out fishing from a distant Iroquoian town. After a winter in France, the boys led Cartier farther west, to where tides cease and the St. Lawrence narrows below a tall bluff. Here was their home, Stadacona, where Quebec City now stands.

—Ronald Wright, *Stolen Continents*

In the revised version, the sentence structures permit key ideas to be featured. The two versions use the same short last sentence, but because the revised version leads up to it with longer sentences, the message in the last sentence is emphasized. In the revised version, ten sentences reduce to four and 86 words (excluding the date, 1534) reduce to 77. (See also the explanation of conciseness, Chapter 16.)

2   Revising a string of too many compound sentences

A **compound sentence** consists of two or more independent clauses° that are grammatically equivalent and that communicate balance or sequence in the ideas that they contain (see 17a). Too often, compound sentences are short sentences only strung together with *and* or *but,* without consideration of the relationships among the ideas.

NO   Science fiction writers are often thinkers, and they are often dreamers, so they let their imaginations wander. Jules Verne was such a writer, and he predicted space ships and atomic submarines, but most people did not believe airplanes were possible.

YES   Science fiction writers are often thinkers and dreamers who let their imaginations wander. Jules Verne was one such writer. He predicted space ships and atomic submarines before most people believed airplanes were possible.

In the revised version, the relationships among the ideas are clear and key ideas are featured. In the last sentence a particularly obscure connection is clarified. For conciseness, one independent clause is reduced to a word, *dreamers;* another is reduced to a relative clause°, *who let their imaginations wander;* another starts a new sentence, *He predicted ...;* and another is reduced to a subordinate clause°, *before most people ... possible.*

3   Revising for a suitable mix of sentence lengths

To emphasize one idea among many others, you can express it in a sentence noticeably different in length or structure from the sentences surrounding it. Consider this passage, which carries its emphasis in one short sentence among longer ones:

> Today is one of those excellent January partly cloudies in which light chooses an unexpected landscape to trick out in gilt, and then shadow sweeps it away. **You know you are alive.** You take huge steps, trying to feel the planet's roundness arc between your feet. Kazantzakis says that when he was young he had a canary and a globe. When he freed the canary, it would perch on the globe and sing. All his life, wandering the earth, he felt as though he had a canary on top of his mind, singing.
>
> —Annie Dillard, *Pilgrim at Tinker Creek*

A long sentence among shorter ones is equally effective.

> Mistakes are not believed to be part of the normal behavior of a good machine. **If things go wrong, it must be a personal, human error, the result of fingering, tampering, a button getting stuck, someone hitting the wrong key.** The computer, at its normal best, is infallible. I wonder whether this can be true.
>
> —LEWIS THOMAS, "To Err Is Human"

EXERCISE 19-1

Consulting sections 19a and 19b, revise these sets of sentences to vary the sentence lengths effectively.

1. Horror tales are not new. *Frankenstein* was written in the nineteenth century. It was written by Mary Shelley. She was the wife of the poet Percy Bysshe Shelley. *Frankenstein* tells the story of a scientist. He makes a monster. He makes it from a human corpse.

2. Another famous horror tale of the nineteenth century is "The Monkey's Paw," by W. W. Jacobs, and it tells about an old English couple with a teenage son, and they get a monkey's paw. It has the power to grant three wishes, so the father wishes for 200 pounds, but the money comes because their son is killed in an accident at work. The mother uses the second wish to bring her son back, and soon there is a knocking at their door, and the mother rushes to unbolt it, but the father is terrified of seeing a walking, rotting corpse, so he uses the last wish, and the knocking stops.

3. After radios became common, horror programs broadcast their tales of terror into the living rooms of North America which were filled with families that included children of all ages who were grouped around the radio while they listened for the latest story of monsters and strange events. The many programs, which included *The Inner Sanctum,* which featured a creaking door, and *The Fat Man* who had a madman's laugh, scared and delighted the audience who came from different parts of the continent, from different occupations, and from different economic and social groups.

19c Using an occasional question, mild command, or exclamation

To vary your sentence structure and to emphasize material, you can call on four basic sentence types. The most common English sentence is **declarative.** A declarative sentence makes a statement—it declares something. Declarative sentences offer an almost infinite variety of structures and patterns.

A sentence that asks a question is called **interrogative.** Occasional questions can help you involve your reader. A sentence that issues a mild or strong command is called **imperative.** Occasional mild commands are particularly helpful for gently urging your reader to think along with you. A sentence that makes an exclamation is called **exclamatory.**

❖ PUNCTUATION ALERT: A mild command ends with a period. A strong command or an exclamation ends with an exclamation mark (see 23e).❖

Consider the following paragraph, which uses the three basic sentence types found most frequently in academic writing: declarative, interrogative, and imperative.

> Imagine what people ate during the winter as little as seventy-five years ago. They ate food that was local, long-lasting, and dull, like acorn squash, turnips, and cabbage. Walk into an American supermarket in February and the world lies before you: grapes, melons, artichokes, fennel, lettuce, peppers, pistachios, dates, even strawberries, to say nothing of ice cream. Have you ever considered what a triumph of civilization it is to be able to buy a pound of chicken livers? If you lived on a farm and had to kill a chicken when you wanted to eat one, you wouldn't ever accumulate a pound of chicken livers.

—PHYLLIS ROSE, "Shopping and Other Spiritual Adventures in America Today"

EXERCISE 19-2

The paragraph below effectively varies sentence lengths and uses a question and a command. The result emphasizes the key points. Write an imitation of this paragraph, closely following all aspects except the topic. Choose your own topic.

EXAMPLE   If your topic were gardens, your first sentence might be: *Why do most people plant tomatoes in their gardens when they know they will harvest many more tomatoes than the average family wants to eat in a whole year?*

Why do most North Americans spend $95 a year to operate their clothes dryers when Nature provides free energy for the same task? Consider the humble clothesline and clothespins. They cost about $30 for a lifetime and solar power is free, unlike an electric dryer, which can cost as much as $500. In an increasingly mechanized indoor life, people who hang their clothes on the line are obliged to notice the weather. Today is a perfect morning for drying, they think. Or: Will it rain this afternoon? Another line in the basement or spare room works well in rainy weather and in winter. Indoor drying has the further benefit of humidifying the house; ten kilos of wet wash contributes about four litres of water to the air.

19d Choosing the subject of a sentence according to your intended emphasis

The subject° of a sentence establishes the focus for that sentence. The subject you choose should correspond to the emphasis that you want to communicate to your reader.

Each of the following sentences, all of which are correct grammatically, contains the same information. Consider, however, how changes of the subject (and its verb°) influence meaning and impact.

Our study showed that 25 percent of undergraduates' time is spent eating or sleeping. [Focus is on the study.]

Undergraduates eat or sleep 25 percent of the time, according to our study. [Focus is on the undergraduates.]

Eating or sleeping occupies 25 percent of undergraduates' time, according to our study. [Focus is on eating and sleeping.]

Twenty-five percent of undergraduates' time **is spent** eating or sleeping, according to our study. [Focus is on the percentage of time.]

19e Adding modifiers to basic sentences for variety and emphasis

Adding modifiers° to basic sentences can provide you with a rich variety of sentence patterns.

1 Expanding basic sentences with modifiers

Sentences that consist only of a subject and verb usually seem very thin. You might use a very short sentence for its dramatic effect in emphasizing an idea (see 19b-3). When you want to avoid a very short sentence, however, you can expand the basic sentence as illustrated in Chart 95. Your decision to expand a basic sentence will depend on the focus of each sentence and how it works in concert with its surrounding sentences.

WAYS TO EXPAND A BASIC SENTENCE	95
BASIC SENTENCE	The river rose.
ADJECTIVE	The **swollen** river rose. ➔

WAYS TO EXPAND A BASIC SENTENCE *(continued)*	
ADVERB	The river rose **dangerously.**
PREPOSITIONAL PHRASE	**In April,** the river rose **above its banks.**
PARTICIPIAL PHRASES	**Swollen by melting snow,** the river rose, **flooding the farmland.**
ABSOLUTE PHRASE	**Trees swirling away in the current,** the river rose.
ADVERB CLAUSE	**Because the snows had been heavy that winter,** the river rose.
ADJECTIVE CLAUSE	The river, **which runs through vital farmland,** rose.

EXERCISE 19-3

Consulting section 19e-1, expand each sentence by adding (a) an adjective°, (b) an adverb°, (c) a prepositional phrase°, (d) a participial phrase°, (e) an absolute phrase°, (f) an adverb clause°, and (g) an adjective clause°.

1. We went to the fair.
2. The ride was full.
3. I won a basketball.
4. Rain poured from the sky.
5. Both of us got our clothes wet.

2   Positioning modifiers to create variety and emphasis

Research on learning suggests that readers are more likely to retain the message that is at the very beginning or the very end of a sentence. Although you do not have unlimited choices about where to place modifiers, you do have some. Try to place them according to the emphasis that you want to achieve. At the same time, be sure to place your modifiers precisely within sentences so that you avoid the error of misplaced modifiers (see 15b).

A sentence that starts with a subject° and verb° and then provides additional information with modifiers that appear after the subject and verb is called a **cumulative sentence.** The cumulative sentence is the most common sentence structure in English; it is called "cumulative" because information accumulates. Sometimes the cumulative sentence is referred to as a **loose sentence** because it lacks the tightly planned structure of other sentence varieties. Such sentences, easy to read because they reflect how humans receive and pass on information, often do not provide impact, however.

In contrast, a **periodic sentence,** also called a *climactic sentence,* is highly emphatic. It builds up to the period, reserving the main idea for the end of the sentence. It draws the reader in as it builds to its climax. Periodic sentences can be very effective, but if they are overused they lose their punch.

PERIODIC

If we had not felt that, after coming to this conclusion, we were bound to set aside our private opinions on matters of detail, if we had not felt ourselves bound to look at what was practicable, not obstinately rejecting the opinions of others nor adhering to our own; if we had not met, I say, in a spirit of conciliation, and with an anxious, overruling desire to form one people under one government, **we never would have succeeded.**

—John A. Macdonald, 1868

CUMULATIVE

We never would have succeeded if we had not felt that, after coming to this conclusion, we were bound to set aside our private opinions on matters of detail, if we had not felt ourselves bound to look at what was practicable, not obstinately rejecting the opinions of others nor adhering to our own; if we had not met, I say, in a spirit of conciliation, and with an anxious, overruling desire to form one people under one government.

Another way to vary sentence structures is to start sentences with introductory words, phrases°, or clauses°. (For a discussion of commas with introductory material, see 24b.)

WORD

Fortunately, I taught myself to read before I had to face boring reading drills in school.

—Andrew Furman, student

PHRASE

Along with cereal boxes and ketchup labels, comic books were the primers that taught me how to read.

—Gloria Steinem

CLAUSE   **Long before I wrote stories,** I listened for stories.

—EUDORA WELTY, *One Writer's Beginnings*

Often, modifiers may appear in several different positions within a sentence. Positioning modifiers offers you a chance to enhance your writing style with variety and emphasis. Here are sentences with the same modifiers in various positions. If you use this technique, be very careful to avoid placing modifiers in positions that create ambiguous meaning (see 15b-1).

> **Angrily** the physician slammed down the chart, **sternly** speaking to the patient.

> The physician slammed down the chart **angrily,** speaking **sternly** to the patient.

> The physician **angrily** slammed down the chart, speaking to the patient **sternly.**

EXERCISE 19-4

Consulting section 19e, combine each set of sentences by changing one sentence to a clause, phrase, or word that will modify the other sentence.

EXAMPLE The ancestor of our pencil was the penicillum. The penicillum was a brush made of animal hairs that the Romans used for writing and drawing.

> *The ancestor of our pencil was the penicillum,* a brush made of animal hairs that the Romans used for writing and drawing. *[sentence changed to phrase]*

1. These early writing implements were made of boar bristles, the hair of camels, badgers, and squirrels, and the down feathers of swans. This is according to the 1771 edition of the *Encyclopaedia Britannica.*

2. Graphite, a form of the element carbon, was to become a component of pencil lead. It would be the main component.

3. Cabinetmakers were producing the first version of the modern pencil by encasing strips of graphite in wood. This happened in the late 1600s.

4. They followed the sandwich-making principle. They sliced a strip of wood, cut a groove down the middle, glued the lead into the groove, then glued the two halves together.

5. At one time the ingredients of a fine pencil came from the geographically diverse areas of Siberia and Florida. Siberia is where the purest graphite was mined. Florida is where the best red cedar was grown.

6. When an acute shortage of southern red cedar developed in the United States during the early 1900s, pencil manufacturers bought old cedar fence posts. They were desperate.

7. The pencil makers had to substitute another kind of cedar. They dyed and perfumed it to match people's expectations of how a pencil should look and smell.

8. Pencils have had some unlikely promoters, such as the naturalist and writer Henry David Thoreau. He helped his father produce the highest-quality pencils in America during the 1840s.

9. The inventor Thomas Edison engaged a pencil factory to produce specially made stubby pencils just for him. He preferred short pencils.

10. The Scottish poet Robert Burns once lacked a pencil. He used his diamond ring to scratch verses on a windowpane.

19f Inverting standard word order

Standard word order in the English sentence places the subject° before the verb°. Because this pattern is so common, it is set in people's minds, so any variation creates emphasis. Inverted word order places the verb before the subject. Used too often, inverted word order can be distracting; but used sparingly, it can be very effective.

STANDARD	**The mayor walked** in. **The premier walked** out.
INVERTED	In **walked the mayor.** Out **walked the premier.**
STANDARD	**Responsibilities begin** in dreams.
INVERTED	In dreams **begin responsibilities.**

—DELMORE SCHWARTZ

19g Repeating important words or ideas to achieve emphasis

You can repeat some words to help emphasize meaning, but choose the words carefully. Repeat only those words that contain a main idea or that use rhythm to focus attention on a main idea. Consider this passage, which uses deliberate repetition to deliver its meaning.

> The **knowledge** that you can have is inexhaustible, and what is inexhaustible is benevolent. The **knowledge** that you cannot have is of the riddles of birth and death, of our future destiny and the purposes of God. Here there is no **knowledge,** but illusions that restrict freedom and limit hope. Accept the mystery behind **knowledge.** It is not darkness but shadow.

—NORTHROP FRYE, Convocation Address, 1988

389

Frye repeats the word *knowledge* in different contexts to distinguish between the kinds of knowledge available to humans and to show the importance of respecting the limits of our knowledge. His repetition of *inexhaustible,* his use of the parallel phrases *The knowledge that you can have ... The knowledge that you cannot have,* and his linking of important concepts with the conjunctions *and* and *but* set up a series of rhythms that give this passage an almost prophetic power, in keeping with its subject matter.

Be sure to use deliberate repetition sparingly, with central words, and only when your meaning justifies such a technique. Consider this passage, which is the result of limited vocabulary and a dull, unvaried style. Although few synonyms exist for the words *an insurance agent, car,* and *model,* some do. Also, the sentence structure has no variety.

NO   **An insurance agent** can be an excellent advisor when you want to buy a **car. An insurance agent** has records on most **cars. An insurance agent** knows which **models** tend to have most accidents. **An insurance agent** can tell you which **models** are the most expensive to repair if they are in a collision. **An insurance agent** can tell you which **models** are most likely to be stolen.

YES   If you are thinking of buying a new car, an insurance agent can be an excellent advisor. An insurance broker has complete records on most automobiles. For example, he or she knows which models are accident prone. Did you know that some car designs suffer more damage than others in a collision? If you want to know which automobiles crumple more than others and which are least expensive to repair, ask an insurance agent. Similarly, some models are more likely to be stolen, so find out from the person who specializes in dealing with claims.

EXERCISE 19-5

Consulting all sections of this chapter, revise this paragraph to achieve emphasis through varied sentence length and deliberate repetition. You can reduce or increase the number of sentences, and you can drop words to reduce unneeded repetition. Each writer's revision will vary somewhat, but try to include at least one revision to a question or exclamation (19c) and one revision to an inverted word order (19f).

The chimney is one of civilization's great technological innovations. The chimney represents a major step up from a hole in the roof or a slit in the wall. The heating of houses was not an urgent problem in the warm climates of ancient Egypt and Mesopotamia. Scholars believed this until a palace was uncovered during a recent excavation of the great lost city of Mari on the upper

Euphrates River in ancient Iraq. The palace, which was 4000 years old, was peppered with chimneys. Two thousand years later the Romans came along. The Romans were engineering geniuses. The Romans developed elaborate chimneys as part of their hot-air heating systems. The Roman empire declined in the fourth century A.D., and after then no one from the former colonies knew how to make chimneys. For four centuries western Europe had no chimneys. So the simple question has always been how chimneys finally got to western Europe. Nobody is quite sure, but here is what a current theory holds. Around A.D. 800, chimneys were brought by Syrian and Egyptian traders. They were from the East.

EXERCISE 19-6

Consulting all sections of this chapter, use techniques of variety and emphasis to revise the following paragraph.

French educator Louis Braille was born in 1809. He became blind at three years of age. He was enrolled at the Institute for the Blind when he was ten. The Institute was in Paris. Braille devised a writing system for blind people consisting of raised dots on paper. Braille's accomplishment was of enormous benefit to many people. At the time, he was only twenty years old. Braille's system used 43 configurations of raised dots. Some symbols represented individual letters of the alphabet. Other symbols stood for some combinations of letters. Still other symbols stood for some punctuation marks. A modified version is still used today. Few people know that Louis Braille was also a distinguished musician. He was so talented that as an adult he played the cello and the organ to great acclaim. He was known throughout Paris for his playing. Sadly, Braille died when only 43 years of age.

EXERCISE 19-7

Using topics you choose, imitate the variety and emphasis of two different passages shown in this chapter. Select from the quotations from the Kohls, Dillard, Thomas, or Frye.

PART

V Using Effective Words

When you use words effectively, you choose words that communicate your message precisely. Part Five alerts you to the meanings that reside in words and the effect that words have on your readers. As you use Chapters 20 through 22, keep in mind that words work in concert with effective sentence structures and paragraphs to create good writing.

20 Understanding the Meaning of Words

North American English, evolving over centuries into a rich language, reflects the contributions of many cultures. The earliest varieties of North American English can be traced from sixteenth-century Elizabethan English—the language of Shakespeare. As the New World expanded, so did the English spoken there. Changes from Elizabethan forms occurred in vocabulary, spelling, and syntactic patterns. Distinctly North American words originated colloquially—in spoken language— and words from all the cultures settling on this continent became part of the language. Food names, for example, show how other languages and cultures loaned words to English. Africans brought the words *okra* and *gumbo;* Spanish and Latin American peoples contributed *tortilla, taco,* and *enchilada.* From German we got *hamburger, wiener,* and *pretzel;* Italian supplied *spaghetti, pizza,* and *antipasto;* and Yiddish is responsible for *gefilte fish, tsimmes,* and *bagel.* North American English creates a truly international *smorgasbord,* a Scandinavian word meaning "a wide variety of appetizers and other tasty foods."

French language and culture have especially influenced the Canadian variety of North American English. This influence perhaps is felt less in the language of cuisine (itself a loan word from French) than in terms dealing with the environment, outdoor activities, and political or social institutions. Many English-speaking Canadians are familiar with French-Canadian dishes such as *poutine* and *tourtière,* and the expressions *café au lait* and *crêpes* have been adopted into English in Canada and elsewhere. Nevertheless, the most characteristic borrowings from French used in Canadian English are words such as *portage, voyageur, lacrosse, francophone, Métis,* and *concession* road. The languages of the aboriginal peoples of Canada have also enriched the English spoken here with words such as *kayak, pemmican, chinook,* and *caribou.*

Etymology is the study of the origins and historical development of words, including changes in form and meaning. For example, *alphabet* originates from the names of the first two letters in Greek: *a* = *alpha*, *b* = *beta*. The meanings of some words change with time. For example, W. Nelson Francis points out in *The English Language,* the word *nice* "has been used at one time or another in its 700-year history to mean ... foolish, wanton, strange, lazy, coy, modest, fastidious, refined, precise, subtle, slender, critical, attentive, minutely accurate, dainty, appetizing, agreeable."

To use English well, you want to be aware of the kinds of information that dictionaries offer (20a), to know how to choose exact words (20b), and to use strategies that actively build your vocabulary (20c).

20a Using dictionaries

Good dictionaries show how language has been used and is currently being used. Each dictionary entry gives the meaning of the word and much additional important information. Many dictionaries also include essays on the history and use of language.

1 Understanding all parts of a dictionary entry

A dictionary entry usually includes items 1 through 11, and sometimes 12 and 13, discussed below. As you use the list, consult the entry shown here for *celebrate,* taken from *Webster's New World Dictionary,* Third College Edition.

Dictionary Entry for *Celebrate*

Spelling and syllabication

Pronunciation

Part of speech

Grammatical forms

Etymology

Meanings

Related words

Synonyms

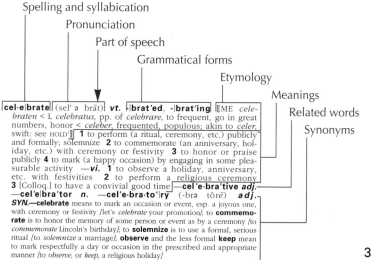

cel·e·brate (sel′ ə brāt) *vt.* **-|brat′ed, -|brat′ing** [ME *cele-braten* < L *celebratus,* pp. of *celebrare,* to frequent, go in great numbers, honor < *celeber,* frequented, populous; akin to *celer,* swift: see HOLD¹] **1** to perform (a ritual, ceremony, etc.) publicly and formally; solemnize **2** to commemorate (an anniversary, holiday, etc.) with ceremony or festivity **3** to honor or praise publicly **4** to mark (a happy occasion) by engaging in some pleasurable activity —*vi.* **1** to observe a holiday, anniversary, etc. with festivities **2** to perform a religious ceremony **3** [Colloq.] to have a convivial good time —**cel′e·bra′tive** *adj.* —**cel′e·bra′tor** *n.* —**cel′e·bra·to′|ry** (-brə tôr̄ē) *adj.* **SYN.—celebrate** means to mark an occasion or event, esp. a joyous one, with ceremony or festivity /let's *celebrate* your promotion/; to **commemorate** is to honor the memory of some person or event as by a ceremony /to *commemorate* Lincoln's birthday/; to **solemnize** is to use a formal, serious ritual /to *solemnize* a marriage/; **observe** and the less formal **keep** mean to mark respectfully a day or occasion in the prescribed and appropriate manner /to *observe,* or *keep,* a religious holiday/

395

1. **Spelling.** If more than one spelling is shown, the first is the most commonly used, and the others are acceptable.

Celebrate has only one spelling.

2. **Word Division.** Dots (or bars, in some dictionaries) separate the syllables of a word. Writers can hyphenate at syllables as long as the rules in section 22d are not violated. To help writers, *Webster's New World Dictionary,* Third College Edition, uses a hairline (a thin vertical line) to indicate any syllable that should not be used for hyphenating.

Cel•el brate has three syllables: *cel, e,* and *brate.* This dictionary recommends hyphenating the word *cel-ebrate* but not *cele-brate.*

3. **Pronunciation.** The symbols in parentheses show pronunciation. If more than one pronunciation is given, the first is the most common, and the others are acceptable. A guide to the pronunciation of the symbols appears in the front of most dictionaries, and some dictionaries provide a brief guide to the most common symbols at the bottom of pages.

Celebrate is pronounced *sel'ə brāt.* The accent mark after the *l* means that the stressed syllable is *sel.* The unusual looking symbol ə, called a *schwa,* is pronounced "uh," as in *a go.* The line over the *a* indicates the long *a* sound, as in *a te.*

4. **Part of Speech Labels.** Abbreviations, explained in the front of the dictionary, indicate parts of speech. Many words can function as more than one part of speech.

Celebrate is a transitive verb°* **(vt.),** for which four definitions are given; also, it is an intransitive verb° **(vi.),** for which three definitions are given.

5. **Grammatical Forms.** This information tells of variations in grammar: for a verb°, its principal parts and form variations; for a noun°, its plural if formed other than by adding only -*s;* for an adjective° or adverb°, its comparative and superlative forms°.

The principal parts of the verb *celebrate* are *celebrated* and *celebrating.*

6. **Etymology.** This information traces the way that the word has evolved through other languages over the years to become the word and meaning in current use.

Celebrate comes from a Middle English (ME) word that is derived from the Latin (L). The meaning evolved from the idea of "going in great numbers, honouring," a meaning reflected by the first definition in the entry.

7. **Definitions.** If a word has more than one meaning, the definitions are numbered in most dictionaries from the oldest

to the newest meaning. A few dictionaries start with the most common use.

The oldest meaning of *celebrate* is given first, and its most recent use is given last (item 4 in the **vt.** list and item 3 in the **vi.** list).

8. **Usage Labels.** If the use of a word is special, a usage label explains how the word should be used. Chart 96 explains the most common usage labels in dictionaries.

The most recent meaning of *celebrate* as an intransitive verb **(vi.)** is *colloquial.* Therefore, such use is informal (and probably should be avoided in academic writing).

9. **Field Labels.** When a word applies to a specialized area of study, such as chemistry or law, an abbreviation alerts a reader to the specialized meaning. For example, along with its everyday meanings, the word *centre* has specialized meanings in these fields: sports, mechanics, the military, and politics.

10. **Related Words.** Words based on the defined word appear, with their part of speech, at the end of the definitions.

Words related to *celebrate* are *celebrative* (adjective), *celebrator* (noun), and *celebratory* (adjective).

11. **Synonyms and Antonyms,** if any. Synonyms are words that are close in meaning. They are listed with their subtle differences explained. Also, for each word in the list of synonyms, a cross-reference appears at that word's entry so that the reader can tell where to find the complete list. For example, at the entry *commemorate,* this information appears: *SYN.* CELEBRATE. It means that synonyms for *commemorate* can be found at the entry for *celebrate.* Antonyms are words that are opposite in meaning to the word defined. Any antonyms are listed after any synonyms.

Celebrate and four of its synonyms are listed and explained; it has no antonyms.

12. **Idioms,** if any. When the defined word is an idiom, either in itself or when combined with other words, it has a meaning that differs from its usual meaning. For example, in *Webster's New World Dictionary,* the entry for *ceiling* lists and defines the idiom *hit the ceiling.* If an idiom is considered slang or colloquial, a usage label (see item 8 above and section 20a-2) alerts the reader.

13. **Examples.** Some definitions provide an example sentence that illustrates the defined word in use.

2 Understanding usage labels

Usage refers to the customary manner of using particular words or phrases. As a writer, you can refer to the **usage labels** in a dictionary to help you decide when a word is appropriate for use. For example, a word labelled *slang* usually is not suitable for academic writing, unless you are writing about the word itself. A word labelled *poetic* is likely to be found in poetry, not in prose.

The concept of usage also applies to the customary manner of using certain words (for example, *among* versus *between*). For a list and explanation of such words, see the Usage Glossary toward the back of this handbook.

USAGE LABELS		96
LABEL	**DEFINITION**	**EXAMPLE**
COLLOQUIAL	Characteristic of conversation and informal writing	**pa** [father] **ma** [mother]
SLANG	Not considered part of standard language, but sometimes used in informal conversation	**whirlybird** [helicopter]
OBSOLETE	No longer used; occurred in earlier writing	**betimes** [promptly, quickly]
POETIC	Found in poetry or poetic prose	**o'er** [for *over*]
DIALECT	Used only in some geographical areas	**tickle** [Newfoundland: a narrow channel or entrance to a harbour]

EXERCISE 20-1

Consulting sections 20a-1 and 20a-2, use a dictionary with entries that include a list of synonyms and some labels, as in the entry for *celebrate* on page 395. Then, write an explanation of each part, assuming that your audience is a student unfamiliar with such entries.

3 | Using unabridged dictionaries

Unabridged means "not shortened." Of the various kinds of dictionaries, unabridged dictionaries have the most in-depth, accurate, complete, and scholarly entries. They give many examples of current uses and changes in meanings of the word over time. They include infrequently used words that abridged dictionaries (see 20a-4) often omit.

The most comprehensive, authoritative unabridged dictionary of English is the *Oxford English Dictionary (OED)*. Its second edition has twenty volumes defining more than 616 500 words and terms. The *OED* traces each word's history, using quotations to illustrate changes in meaning and spelling over the life of the word. The second edition consists of three parts: (1) the first edition of the *OED,* largely unchanged; (2) the contents of the four supplements that accompanied the first edition; and (3) approximately 5000 words or terms new in the second edition.

Its comprehensive historical information and examples about English words make the *OED* a specialized dictionary (20a-5) as well as an unabridged dictionary. The following small excerpt from the second edition's entry for *celebrate* shows the kinds of information that you can get from the *OED*. Compare this material and format with the entry for *celebrate*, shown on page 395, which is reprinted from *Webster's New World Dictionary,* Third College Edition. In addition to the usual dictionary features, the *OED* offers a complete history of the word (*celebrate*'s first recorded use was in 1656). Note the historical examples of *celebrate* following its third meaning.

Sample OED Entry

celebrate ('sɔlibreit), *v.* [f. prec., or on analogy of vbs. so formed. See -ATE³.]

(**1656** BLOUNT *Glossogr., Celebrate,* to frequent, to solemnize with an Assembly of men, to make famous, also to keep a festival day or other time with great solemnity.)

3. To observe with solemn rites (a day, festival, season); to honour with religious ceremonies, festivities, or other observances (an event, occasion). Also *absol.* (see quot. 1937).

   1560 BIBLE (Genev.) *Lev.* xxiii. 32 From euen to euen shall ye celebrate [WYCL. halowe, COVERD. kepe] your Sabbath. **1591** SHAKS. I *Hen. VI*, I. VI. 14 Feast and banquet in the open streets, To celebrate the joy that God hath given us. **1672** DRYDEN *Conq. Granada* 1. i, with Pomp and Sports my Love I celebrate. **1697—** *Virg. Georg.* I. 466 Celebrate the mighty Mother's Day. **1737** L. CLARKE *Hist. Bible* IX. (1840) I. 376 The Feast of Tabernacles being then celebrating. **1841** Lane *Arab. Nts.* I. 71 The Minor Festival . . is celebrated with more rejoicing than the other. **1929** *Randolph Enterprise* (Elkins, W. Va.) 26 Sept. 3/2 [He] came over. . Sunday night to celebrate a little. **1937** PARTRIDGE *Dict. Slang* 136/1 *Celebrate*, v.i., to drink in honour of an event or a person; hence, to drink joyously. **1963** J.T. STORY *Something for Nothing* i. 40 It's Treasure's wedding day. Somebody's got to celebrate.

For most college and university students, *Webster's Third New International Dictionary of the English Language* provides any needed information. This highly respected, one-volume work has more than 470 000 entries and is especially strong in new scientific and technical terms. It uses quotations to show various meanings, and its definitions are given in order of their appearance in the language.

4 Using abridged dictionaries

Abridged means "shortened." Abridged dictionaries contain the most commonly used words. They are convenient in size and economical to buy, and they serve as practical reference books for writers and readers. Many good abridged dictionaries are referred to as "college" editions because they serve the needs of most college and university students.

The best Canadian abridged dictionary is the *Gage Canadian Dictionary.* It is slightly less inclusive than the dictionaries that follow, but it records usage in Canada as none of the other dictionaries do. Although still substantially American in content, the Canadian edition of the *Funk & Wagnalls Standard College Dictionary* is also worthy of consideration. The standard student reference book and spelling arbiter in Canada is the *Concise Oxford Dictionary.*

Among American dictionaries, *Webster's New World Dictionary of American English,* Revised College Edition, has more than 170 000 entries and gives detailed etymologies. Names of people, places, abbreviations, and foreign expressions appear in the main body of the work (rather than in appendixes). Definitions appear in chronological order of their acceptance into the language. *Webster's New World Dictionary* has a contemporary American emphasis. It uses a star symbol (★) for Americanisms—words that first became part of the language in the United States. It gives the origins of American place names (cities, states, rivers, and so on). There are also some Canadian entries. It supplies usage labels for many words and gives synonyms, often in lists that explain distinctions among closely related words. An appendix covers punctuation, italics, numbers, capitalization, abbreviations, and source documentation. Its introductory material includes essays on the English language and etymology. *Webster's New World Compact School and Office Dictionary* is based on *Webster's New World Dictionary,* Third College Edition. More complete than a "pocket" dictionary, it has 56 000 entries.

◆ ESL NOTE: A useful dictionary for students who speak English as a second language is the *Dictionary of Contemporary English* published by Longman. For a list of specialized dictionaries, see 20a-5. ◆

5 Using specialized dictionaries of English

A specialized dictionary focuses on a single area, such as slang, word origins, synonyms, antonyms, usage, or almost any other aspect of language. Most college and university libraries include all or some of the volumes listed here:

SPECIALIZED DICTIONARIES

SYNONYMS

New Roget's Thesaurus of the English Language in Dictionary Form

SLANG AND COLLOQUIALISMS

Dictionary of Slang and Unconventional English, ed. Eric Partridge

Dictionary of American Slang, ed. Harold Wentworth and Stuart Berg Flexner [out of print, but available in many libraries]

The Thesaurus of Slang, by Esther Lewin and Albert E. Lewin

NTC's Dictionary of American Slang and Colloquial Expressions, by Richard A. Spears

ETYMOLOGIES

Dictionary of Word and Phrase Origins, ed. William Morris and Mary Morris

Origins: A Short Etymological Dictionary of Modern English, ed. Eric Partridge [out of print, but available in many libraries]

CANADIANISMS

Dictionary of Canadianisms on Historical Principles, ed. Walter Avis et al.

USAGE

Modern American Usage, ed. Jacques Barzun

REGIONALISMS

Dictionary of American Regional English, ed. Frederic Cassidy

IDIOMS

A Dictionary of American Idioms, by Adam Makkai

Dictionary of English Idioms, published by Longman Inc.

Several major dictionaries are available on CD-ROM disks, including *The Merriman Webster Collegiate Dictionary, The Random House College Dictionary, The American Heritage Dictionary* (in a "talking edition"), and the second edition of *The Oxford English Dictionary* (the *OED*).

20b   Choosing exact words

The English language offers a wealth of words to choose among as a writer. **Diction,** the term for choice of words, affects the clarity and impact of the message that you want your sentences to deliver. As a writer, you want to use words that exactly fit the particular context of each piece of writing.

1   Understanding denotation and connotation

When you look up a word in the dictionary to find out what it means, you are looking for its **denotation.** For example, the denotation of the word *semester* is "a period of time of about eighteen weeks that makes up part of a school or college year."

Readers expect words to be used according to their established meanings for their established functions. Exactness is essential. When you use a thesaurus or dictionary of synonyms, be aware that subtle shades of meaning create distinctions among words that have the same general definition. These small differences in meaning allow you to be very precise in choosing just the right word, but they also oblige you to make sure that you know what precise meanings your words convey. For instance, describing a person famous for praiseworthy achievements in public life as *notorious* would be wrong. Although *notorious* means "well-known" and "publicly discussed"—which famous people are likely to be—*notorious* also carries the meaning "unfavourably known or talked about." Wilfrid Laurier is *famous,* not *notorious.* The Donnellys, on the other hand, are *notorious.*

Here is another example. *Obdurate* means "not easily moved to pity or sympathy," and its synonyms include "inflexible, obstinate, stubborn, hardened." The synonym *hardened* for *obdurate,* however, might prompt someone unfamiliar with *obdurate* to use the word incorrectly.

NO   Footprints showed in the *obdurate* concrete.

Here are two correct uses of *obdurate:*

YES   The supervisor remained *obdurate* in refusing to accept excuses.

YES   My *obdurate* roomates will not let my pet boa constrictor live in the bathtub.

❖ COMPUTER ALERT: Be especially careful about using a software program's thesaurus. Recent versions of sophisticated programs have thesauruses that offer synonyms for many words and that make substitutions easy. However, unless you know the exact meaning of an offered synonym, as well as its part of speech, you may introduce a grammatical error or a "wrong word" error into your writing. For example, one word-processing program's thesaurus offers the choices *low, below, beneath,* and *subterranean* as synonyms for *deep* with the sense of low (down, inside). None of these words, however, could replace *deep* in many sentences, including this one: *Mine shaft #4 is too deep* [not too *low, below, beneath,* or *subterranean*] *to be filled with sand or rocks.* ❖

Connotation refers to ideas implied, but not directly indicated, by a word. Connotations convey associations as emotional overtones beyond the direct, explicit definition of a word. For example, the word *home* usually evokes more emotion than does its denotation "a dwelling place" or its synonym *house. Home* may have very pleasant connotations of warmth, security, the love of family. Or *home* may have unpleasant connotations of an institution for elderly or sick people. As a student writer, be aware of the potential of connotation to help your words deliver their meaning. Connotations are never completely fixed, for they can vary with different contexts for a word. Still, people can communicate effectively because most words have relatively stable connotations and denotations in most contexts.

Being sensitive to the differences between the denotation and connotation of a word is essential for critical thinking. Critical thinkers must first consider material at its literal level (see 5d-1). Doing so calls for dealing with the denotation of words. Next, critical thinkers must move to the inferential level (see 5d-2)—to what is implied although not explicitly stated. Connotations of words often carry the inferential message, as illustrated in Chart 97.

COMPARING DENOTATION AND CONNOTATION		97
SAMPLE WORD	**DENOTATION**	**CONNOTATION**
ADDITIVE	an added substance	something unnatural, especially in food; perhaps perhaps harmful to health
CHEAP	inexpensive	of products, low quality; of people, stingy
NUCLEAR REACTOR MELTDOWN	melting of fuel rods in a nuclear reactor, releasing dangerous radiation	spectre of imminent death or eventual cancer; poisoning of food chain

EXERCISE 20-2

Consulting section 20b-1, separate the words in each set into one of three groups: *Neutral* if you think the word has no connotations; *Positive* if you think it has good connotations; *Negative* if you think it has bad connotations. If you think a word fits in more than one group, put it under each heading that applies, and be ready to explain your choices. If you are unsure of a word, consult your dictionary.

EXAMPLE   sensitive, touchy, tender, thin-skinned, impressionable

> *Neutral: impressionable; Positive: sensitive; Negative: touchy, thin-skinned*

1. carefree, exuberant, light-hearted, frivolous, rash, high-spirited, riotous, animated, reckless, joyful

2. thrifty, economical, frugal, stingy, tight-fisted, prudent, foresighted, penny-pinching, money-conscious

3. lawyer, attorney, shyster, learned counsel, ambulance chaser, advocate, legal practitioner, public defender, prosecutor

4. smell, odour, fragrance, stink, aroma, scent, stench, whiff, perfume, smoke, incense

5. flexible, yielding, wishy-washy, adaptable, tolerant, indulgent, undemanding, weak, submissive, imitative

6. loyal, dedicated, devoted, determined, stubborn, firm, unyielding

---

2 | Using specific and concrete language to bring life to general and abstract language

Specific words identify individual items in a group *(Oldsmobile, Honda, Ford)*. **General** words relate to an overall group *(car)*. **Concrete** words identify persons and things that can be perceived by the senses—seen, heard, tasted, felt, smelled (the *black padded vinyl dashboard* of my car). **Abstract** words denote qualities, concepts, relationships, acts, conditions, ideas *(transportation)*.

As a writer, you want to choose words suitable for your writing purpose° and your audience°. Usually, specific and concrete words bring life to general and abstract words. Whenever you choose general and abstract words, be sure to supply enough specific, concrete details and examples to illustrate effectively your generalizations and abstractions. Consider how sentences with general words come to life when they are revised with words that refer to specifics.

GENERAL	My car has a great deal of power, and it is very quick.
SPECIFIC	My Trans Am with 220 horsepower can go from zero to eighty in six seconds.
GENERAL	The car gets good gas mileage.
SPECIFIC	The Dodge Lancer uses about 7 litres of gas per 100 kilometres on the highway and 8 litres per 100 kilometres in the city.
GENERAL	Her car is comfortable and easy to drive.
SPECIFIC	When she drives her new Buick Regal on a five-hour trip, she arrives refreshed and does not need a long nap to recover, as she did when she drove her ten-year-old Upusho.

Specific language is not always preferable to general language, nor is concrete language always preferable to abstract language. Effective writing usually combines them. Consider the following from an effective essay comparing cars:

GENERAL AND SPECIFIC COMBINED

GENERAL   SPECIFIC   SPECIFIC   GENERAL
My car, a **220-horsepower Trans Am,** is **quick.** It accelerates

    SPECIFIC   SPECIFIC
from **0 to 80** kilometres per hour in **6 seconds**—but it uses

   SPECIFIC   SPECIFIC
13 litres of gas per 100 kilometre. The **Dodge Lancer,** on the

         GENERAL   GENERAL
other hand, gets **very good** gas **mileage:** It uses about

    SPECIFIC   GENERAL
7 litres per 100 kilometres in **highway driving** and

     SPECIFIC   GENERAL   SPECIFIC
8 litres per 100 kilometres when **traffic** is **bumper-to-bumper**

   GENERAL   SPECIFIC
or when **car trips** are **frequent and short.**

Do not overdo being specific and concrete. If you want to inform a nonspecialist reader about possible automobile fuels other than gasoline, *do* name the fuels and be very specific about their advantages and drawbacks. *Do not* go into a detailed, highly technical discussion of the chemical profiles of the fuels. Always base your choices on an awareness of your purpose for writing (see 1b) and your audience (see 1c).

EXERCISE 20-3

Consulting section 20b-2, revise the following paragraph by providing specific and concrete words and phrases to explain and enliven the ideas presented here in general and abstract language. As needed, you can revise these sentences to accommodate your changes in language.

The car was exactly what we were looking for. It was the right colour, size, and, best of all, price. It had nice seats, and it had many features we wanted. We were especially pleased by mileage it got on the highway. The dealer said that we could have it right away. The only problem was that he would not take our broken-down old car as a trade-in.

20c Increasing your vocabulary

The benefits of increasing your vocabulary are many. The more words you know, the more easily and the faster you can read. A large, rich vocabulary also helps you understand ideas and communicate them clearly and effectively in your writing. Use the techniques described in Chart 98.

TECHNIQUES FOR BUILDING YOUR VOCABULARY   98

TO FIND WORDS

- Use a highlighter pen to mark all unfamiliar words in textbooks and other reading material. Then define the words in the margin so you can study the meaning in context. Use context clues (see 20c-2) to figure out definitions, or look up the words in a dictionary. Write each word and its definitions on an index card or in a notebook.

- Listen carefully to learn how speakers use the language. Jot down new words to look up later. Write each word and its definitions on an index card or in a notebook.

TO STUDY WORDS

- Select some words that you intend to study each week. Put the date next to the word so that you can keep track of your goals. Whenever you look up a word in your dictionary, put a small checkmark next to it. When you accumulate three checkmarks next to a word, it is time to learn that word.

- Set aside time each day to study your selected words. Carry your cards or notebook to study in spare moments each day.

TECHNIQUES FOR BUILDING YOUR VOCABULARY *(continued)*

- Use mnemonics (see 22b) to help you memorize words. Set a goal of learning eight to ten new words a week. Use the words in your writing and, when possible, in conversation.
- Go back to words from previous weeks, whenever possible. List any words you have not learned well. Study them again, and *use* them.

---

1   Knowing prefixes and suffixes

Prefixes are syllables in front of a **root** word that modify its meaning. *Ante-* (before) placed before the root *diluvian* (an adjective formed from the Latin for *flood*) gives *antediluvian,* which means "before the flood." (The flood in question is the biblical Noah's Flood; in common usage, *antediluvian* simply means "very ancient.")

Suffixes are syllables added to the end of a root word that modify its meaning. For example, *excite* is formed by adding the prefix *ex-* (out) to the past participle of *ciere* (to set in motion). It has various forms when suffixes are added: *excited, exciting, excitedly, excitement.* The part of speech of a word is often signalled by the suffix.

Knowing common prefixes and suffixes is an excellent way to learn to decode unfamiliar words and increase your vocabulary.

PREFIXES

PREFIX	MEANING	EXAMPLE
ante-	before	*anteroom*
anti-	against	*antiballistic*
auto-	self	*autobiography*
contra-	against	*contradict*
dis-	not	*disagree*
extra-	more	*extraordinary*
hyper-	more	*hyperactive*
il-	not	*illegal*
im-	not	*immoral*
in-	not	*inadequate*
inter-	between	*interpersonal*
intra-	inside	*intravenous*
ir-	not	*irresponsible*
mal-	poor	*malnutrition* →

PREFIXES (*continued*)

mis-	wrongly, badly	*misunderstood*
mono-	one	*monopoly*
non-	not	*noninvolvement*
poly-	many	*polygamy*
post-	after	*postscript*
pre-	before	*prehistoric*
re-	back	*return*
retro-	back	*retroactive*
semi-	half	*semicircle*
sub-	under	*submissive*
super-	more	*supernatural*
trans-	across	*transportation*
ultra-	more	*ultraconservative*
un-	not	*unhappy*
uni-	one	*uniform*

SUFFIXES

NOUNS

SUFFIX	MEANING	EXAMPLE
-dom	state of	*freedom*
-hood	state of	*childhood*
-ness	state of	*kindness*
-ship	state of	*friendship*
-tion	act of	*integration*
-tude	state of	*solitude*

VERBS

SUFFIX	MEANING	EXAMPLE
-ate	to make	*integrate*
-ify	to make	*unify*
-ize	to make	*computerize*

ADJECTIVES

SUFFIX	MEANING	EXAMPLE
-able	able to be	*comfortable*
-ate	full of	*fortunate*
-ible	able to be	*compatible*
-ful	full of	*tactful*

Suffixes (*continued*)

-**less**	without	*penniless*
-**ous**	full of	*pompous*
-**y**	full of	*gloomy*

EXERCISE 20-4

Consulting section 20c-1, add a prefix to each italicized word to match the definition given. Use a dictionary if necessary.

EXAMPLE not a *citizen* = noncitizen

1. not *possible*
2. *examine* again
3. poor *function*
4. between *states*
5. not *reversible*

6. half *conscious*
7. *stated* incorrectly
8. not *believable*
9. *conceived* before
10. more *sensitive*

EXERCISE 20-5

Consulting section 20c-1, add a suffix to each italicized word to match the definition given. Notice that the form of the word should change to match the exact definition. Consult a dictionary to verify your spelling.

EXAMPLE act of *communicating* = communication

1. lacking *children*
2. to make *objective*
3. to make *beautiful*
4. to make *harmony*
5. state of being *kin*

6. able to be *touched*
7. without *care*
8. full of *mercy*
9. state of being a *bachelor*
10. full of *compassion*

2

Using context clues to figure out word meanings

The familiar words that surround an unknown word can give you hints about the meaning of the new word. Such **context clues** include four main types.

1. **Restatement context clue.** You can figure out an unknown word when a word you know repeats the meaning: *He jumped into the fray and enjoyed every minute of the fight. Fray* means "fight." Sometimes a restatement is set off by punctuation. For example, parentheses contain a definition in this sentence: *Fatty deposits on artery walls combine with calcium compounds to cause* arteriosclerosis (*hardening of the arteries*). Sometimes

a technical term is set off by punctuation after the definition of a term is given. For example, dashes set off a term after it is defined in this sentence: *The upper left part of the heart—the left atrium—receives blood returning from circulation.*

2. **Contrast context clue.** You can figure out an unknown word when an opposite or contrast is presented: *We feared that the new prime minister would be a* menace *to society, but she turned out to be a great peacemaker. Menace* means "threat"; the contrast that explains *menace* is *but she turned out to be a great peacemaker.* As you read, watch for words that express contrast (such as *but, however, nevertheless;* for a complete list see Chart 23 in 4d-1).

3. **Example context clue.** You can figure out an unfamiliar word when an example or illustration relating to the word is given: *They were* conscientious *workers, making sure that everything was done correctly and precisely.* A dictionary defines *conscientious* as "motivated by a desire to do what is right." The words "done correctly and precisely" are close to that meaning.

4. **General sense context clue.** You can use an entire passage to get a general sense of difficult words. For example, in *Nearly forty million North Americans are overweight; obesity has become an epidemic,* chances are good that *epidemic* refers to something happening to many people. Sometimes a "general sense context clue" will not make clear a word's exact denotation. For example, you might guess that *epidemic* indicates a widespread threat, but you might miss the connection of the word *epidemic* with the concept of disease. Interpreting the meaning of a word from the general sense carries the risk of allowing subtle variations that distinguish one word from another to slip by. You might want, therefore, to check the exact definition in a dictionary.

21 Understanding the Effect of Words

As words communicate meaning (see Chapter 20), they have an effect on the people reading or hearing them. As a writer, you want to choose words carefully. Sometimes the choices available to you are clearly either right or wrong, but often the choices are subtle. The guidelines discussed in this chapter can help you make good choices: using the right level of formality (see 21a-1); using edited Canadian English (see 21a-2); avoiding slang or inappropriate colloquial words or regional words (see 21a-3); avoiding slanted language (see 21a-4); avoiding sexist language (see 21b); using figurative language appropriately (see 21c); avoiding clichés (see 21d); and avoiding artificial language (see 21e).

21a Using appropriate language

As a writer, you need to pay special attention to **tone** (see 1d) and **diction** (see 20b). You want the words that you use to communicate your meaning as clearly and effectively as possible. Equally important, your choice of words should work in concert with the effectiveness of your sentence style (see Chapters 16–19) to create your individual style of writing.

1 Using appropriate levels of formality

Informal and highly formal levels of writing differ clearly in tone. They use different vocabulary and sentence structures. Tone in writing indicates the attitude of the writer toward the subject and toward the audience. Tone may be highly formal, informal, or somewhere in between.

Different tones are appropriate for different audiences°, different subjects, and different purposes°. An informal tone occurs in casual conversation or letters to friends. A highly formal tone, in contrast, occurs in sermons and proclamations.

Informal language, which creates an informal tone, may include slang, colloquialisms, and regionalisms (see 21a-3). In addition, informal writing often includes sentence fragments (see Chapter 13), contractions, and other forms that approximate casual speech. **Medium** language level uses general English: not too casual, not too scholarly. Unlike informal language, medium-level language is acceptable for academic writing. This level uses standard vocabulary (for example, *learn* instead of *wise up*), conventional sentence structure, and few or no contractions. A **highly formal** language level uses a polysyllabic Latinate vocabulary (*edify* instead of *learn*) and often stylistic flourishes such as extended or complex figures of speech. Academic writing, along with most writing for general audiences, should range from medium to somewhat formal levels of language.

INFORMAL	Ya know stars? They're a gas!
MEDIUM	Gas clouds slowly changed into stars.
FORMAL	The condensations of gas spun their slow gravitational pirouettes, slowly transmogrifying gas cloud into star.

—CARL SAGAN, "Starfolk: A Fable"

The informal example would be appropriate in a letter to a close friend or in a journal. The writer's attitude toward the subject is playful and humorous; the word choice and sentence structure assume great familiarity between writer and audience. The medium example would be appropriate in most academic and professional situations. The writer's attitude toward the subject is serious and straightforward. The formal example is addressed to an audience with considerable interest in and knowledge of scientific phenomena, such as readers of a science journal.

2   Using edited English for academic writing

The language standards that you are expected to use in academic writing are those of **edited English** as used in Canada: the accepted written language of a book like this handbook or a magazine like *Saturday Night* or *Equinox*. Such language conforms to widely established rules of grammar, sentence structure, punctuation, and spelling. Because advertising language and other language intended to reach and sway a large audience often ignore conventional usage, readers often encounter written English that varies from the standard. Do not let these published departures from edited English influence you into believing they are acceptable in academic writing.

Edited English is not a fancy dialect for the elite. It is a practical form of the language that educated people use. As a student writer, you might find that early drafts of your essays contain language that departs from edited English. When you use edited English in your academic writing, you will not risk distracting your readers from the message you want to communicate. Do not, however, revise° your words too early in the writing process°, or you will risk being distracted from getting your ideas onto paper.

| 3 | **Avoiding slang and colloquial or regional language for most academic writing** |

Slang consists of coined words and new meanings attached to established terms. Slang words and phrases usually pass out of use quickly, although occasionally they become accepted into standard usage. **Colloquial** language is characteristic of casual conversation and informal writing: *The student flunked chemistry* instead of *the student failed chemistry.*

Canadian slang has been influenced by that of the United States and Britain, but uniquely Canadian expressions do exist: *sodbuster, high muckymuck,* and from the world of hockey, *cream, deke,* and *rink rat.* At no time does slang communicate accurate meanings in academic or business writing.

Regional language (also called *dialectal language*) is specific to some geographic areas. *Coal oil* in one part of the country, for example, is *kerosene* in another. The *Saskatoon berry* is also known as the *shadberry,* the *juneberry,* or the *serviceberry.* Dialects are different from slang because dialectic differences reflect geographical regions and socioeconomic status. Using a dialect when writing for the general reading public tends to shut some people out of the communication. Except when dialect is the topic of the writing, academic writing rarely accommodates dialect well.

Although slang, colloquial words, and regional language are neither substandard nor illiterate, they are usually not appropriate for academic writing. Replacing them in your academic writing allows you to communicate clearly with the large number of people who speak and write in medium or somewhat formal levels of language (see 21a-1).

4 Avoiding slanted language

To communicate clearly, you will want to choose words that convince your audience of your fairness as a writer. When you are writing about a subject on which you hold strong opinions, it is easy to slip into biased or emotionally loaded language. Such **slanted language** usually does not persuade a careful reader to agree with your point. Instead, it makes the reader wary or hostile. For example, suppose you are arguing against the practice of scientific experimentation on animals. If you use language such as "laboratory Frankensteins" who "routinely and viciously maim helpless kittens and puppies," you are using slanted language. You want to use words that make your side of an issue the more convincing one. Once you start using slanted, biased language, readers feel manipulated rather than reasoned with.

21b Avoiding sexist language

Sexist language assigns roles or characteristics to people on the basis of gender. Most women *and* men today feel that sexist language unfairly discriminates against both sexes. Sexist language inaccurately assumes all nurses and homemakers are female (and therefore refers to them as "she") and all physicians and wage earners are male (and therefore refers to them as "he"). One of the most widespread occurrences of sexist language is the use of the pronoun *he* to refer to someone of unidentified sex. Although tradition holds that *he* is correct in such situations, using only masculine pronouns to represent the human species excludes women and thereby distorts reality.

If you want to avoid sexist language in your writing, follow the guidelines in Chart 99. Also, you can avoid sexism by avoiding demeaning, outdated stereotypes, such as *women are bad drivers* or *men are bad cooks*. Do not describe a woman by her looks, clothes, or age (unless you do the same for men). Do not use the first name of one spouse when you use a title (such as *Mr.* or *Mrs.*) and the last name for the other spouse: *Phil Miller* [not *Mr. Miller*] *and his wife, Jeannette, always travel on separate planes* or *Jeannette and Phil Miller live in Manitoba.*

HOW TO AVOID SEXIST LANGUAGE	99

■ Avoid using only the masculine pronoun to refer to males and females together. Use a pair of pronouns.

HOW TO AVOID SEXIST LANGUAGE *(continued)*   99

NO   A doctor has little time to read outside **his** specialty.

YES   A doctor has little time to read outside **his or her** specialty.

The "he or she" construction acts as a singular pronoun, and it therefore calls for a singular verb when it serves as the subject of a sentence. Try to avoid using the "he or she" construction, especially more than once in a sentence or in consecutive sentences. Revising into the plural may be a better solution.

NO   A successful doctor knows that **he** has to work long hours.

YES   Successful doctors know that **they** have to work long hours.

You may also recast a sentence to omit the gender-specific pronoun.

NO   Everyone hopes that **he** will win the scholarship.

YES   Everyone hopes to win the scholarship.

- Avoid the use of *man* when men and women are clearly intended in the meaning.

NO   **Man** is a social animal.

YES   **People** are social animals.

NO   Dogs are **man's** best friend.

YES   Dogs are **human's** best friends.

        Dogs are **people's** best friends.

        Dogs are **our** best friends.

- Avoid stereotyping jobs and roles by gender when men and women are included.

NO	YES
chairman	chair, chairperson
policeman	police officer
businessman	businessperson, business executive
statesman	diplomat, prime minister, statesperson

NO   teacher ... **she;** principal ... **he**

YES   teacher ... **they;** principals ... **they**

- Avoid expressions that exclude either sex.   ➜

HOW TO AVOID SEXIST LANGUAGE *(continued)*   99

NO	YES
mankind	humanity
the common man	the average person
man-sized sandwich	huge sandwich
old wives' tale	superstition

■ Avoid using demeaning and patronizing labels.

NO	YES
lady lawyer	lawyer
male nurse	nurse
gal Friday	assistant
coed	student

NO   My **girl** will send it.

YES   My **secretary** will send it.

       Ida Morea will send it.

EXERCISE 21-1

Consulting section 21b, revise the following sentences by changing sexist language to nonsexist language.

1. Man's sense of space and distance is variable.
2. Everyone establishes his own "personal space" by what he can do, not what he can see, in a given area.
3. A mother is usually seen standing very close to her children.
4. A lady politician, too, usually stands close to talk with one or two of her constituents but many feet away from large groups of people to whom she is talking.
5. The size of a person's "bubble" of personal space varies with his culture or ethnicity.
6. A German will go to great lengths to preserve his "private sphere" at home and at work.
7. An Englishman, however, is used to a common work space at the office.
8. For that reason, he is willing to exist close to his fellow workers.
9. Some U.S. and Canadian businessmen use the ladies who work in the office to help protect their personal bubbles.
10. They have the office girls announce all visitors and screen all phone calls.

21c Using figurative language

Figures of speech use words for more than their literal meanings, yet they are not merely decorative. **Figurative language** enhances meaning. It makes comparisons and connections that draw on one idea or image to explain another as shown in Chart 100.

TYPES OF FIGURATIVE LANGUAGE 100

■ **Analogy:** a comparison of similar traits between dissimilar things (The length of an analogy can range from one sentence to a paragraph to an entire essay; see 4f-8.)

> A cheetah sprinting across the dry plains after its prey, the base runner dashed for home plate.

■ **Irony:** the use of words to suggest the opposite of their usual sense

> Told that the car repair would cost $2000 and take at least two weeks, she said, "Oh, that would be wonderful!"

■ **Metaphor:** a comparison between otherwise dissimilar things without using the word *like* or *as* (Be alert to avoid the error of a mixed metaphor, explained in the text.)

> The rush-hour traffic bled out of all the city's major arteries.

■ **Overstatement** (also called *hyperbole*): deliberate exaggeration for emphasis

> Andrew Marvell says praising his love's eyes and forehead could take 100 years.

■ **Personification:** the assignment of a human trait to a nonhuman thing

> The book begged to be read.

■ **Simile:** a direct comparison between otherwise dissimilar things, using the word *like* or *as*

> Langston Hughes says that a deferred dream dries up like a raisin in the sun.

■ **Understatement:** deliberate restraint for emphasis

> It gets a little warm when the temperature reaches 35 degrees.

A mixed metaphor combines images that do not work well together. Consider this sentence, for example: *Milking the migrant workers for all they were worth, the supervisors barked orders at them.* Here the initial image is of taking milk from a cow, but the final image has supervisors barking, an action suggesting dogs. Avoid confusing your reader by combining two or more images that do not blend well.

EXERCISE 21-2

Consulting section 21c, identify each figure of speech. Also, revise any mixed metaphors.

1. In the 1990s we stand with one foot in the twentieth century while we set sail on the seas of a new era.
2. Having spent the whole day on the beach, he came home as red as a lobster.
3. If I eat one more bite of that chocolate cake, I'll explode.
4. What I love best about you is that you use all the hot water every time you take a shower.
5. The daisies nodded their heads in the hot sun.
6. Beginning to testify in the courtroom, the defendant was as nervous as a cat in a roomful of rocking chairs.
7. Think of the environment as a human body, where small problems in one part do not much affect other parts, any more than a paper cut causes most of us more than an instant's pain and a heartfelt "Ouch!" Problems throughout a system like the air or the oceans, however—say, pollution building up beyond the system's ability to cleanse itself—can kill the entire organism just as surely as cholesterol building up in arteries can kill you or me.
8. That actor displayed the entire range of human emotions from A to B.
9. My heart stopped when I opened the gift my parents gave me.
10. Our supervisor said that reorganizing the department according to our recommendations would be trading a headache for an upset stomach.

21d   Avoiding clichés

A **cliché** is a worn-out expression that has lost its capacity to communicate effectively. Many clichés are similes or metaphors, once clever, which have grown trite from overuse: *dead as a doornail, gentle as a lamb, straight as an arrow.* If you have heard words over and over again, so has your reader. If you cannot think of a way to rephrase a cliché, delete the phrase entirely.

English is full of frequently used word groups that are not clichés (for example, *up and down* and *in and out*). Common patterns are not clichés and need not be avoided.

EXERCISE 21-3

Consulting section 21d, revise these clichés. Use the idea in each cliché for a sentence of your own in plain English.

1. The bottom line is that Carl either raises his grade point average or finds himself in hot water.
2. Carl's grandfather says, "When the going gets tough, the tough get going."
3. Carl may not be the most brilliant engineering major who ever came down the pike, but he has plenty of get-up-and-go.
4. When they were handing out persistence, Carl was first in line.
5. The $64 000 question is: Will Carl make it safe and sound, or will the school drop him like a hot potato?

21e Avoiding artificial language

Sometimes student writers think that ornate words and complicated sentence structures make writing impressive. Experienced writers, however, work hard to communicate as clearly and directly as they can. As a student writer, avoid long, fancy words to explain a point. Try to make what you write as accessible as possible to your readers. Extremely complex ideas or subject areas may require complex terms or phrases to explain them, but in general the simpler the language, the more likely it will be understood.

1 Avoiding pretentious language

Pretentious language is too showy, calling undue attention to itself with complex sentences and polysyllabic words. Academic writing does not call for big words used for their own sake. Overblown words are likely to obscure your message.

As I alighted from my vehicle, my clothing was besmirched with filth. [*Translation:* My coat got dirty as I got out of my car.]

I hate it when he tries ostentatiously to flaunt his accoutrements recently acquired in the haberdashery shop. [*Translation:* I hate it when he tries to show off his new clothes.]

2 | Avoiding unnecessary jargon

Jargon is specialized vocabulary of a particular group. It consists of words that an outsider might not understand. As you write, consider your purpose° and audience° to decide whether a word is jargon in the context of your material. For example, a football fan easily understands a sportswriter's use of words such as *punt, sacked,* and *safety,* but they are jargon to people not familiar with football. Specialized language evolves in every field: professions, academic disciplines (see Chapters 36-38), business, and even hobbies. Avoid using jargon unnecessarily. When you must use jargon for a general audience, be sure to explain the specialized meanings.

This example, showing specialized language used appropriately, is from an undergraduate textbook. The writers assume students know or can decipher the meaning of *eutrophicates, terrestrial,* and *eutrophic.*

> As the lake eutrophicates, it gradually fills until the entire lake will be converted into a terrestrial community. Eutrophic change (or eutrophication) is the nutritional enrichment of the water, promoting the growth of aquatic plants.
>
> —DAVIS AND SOLOMON, *The World of Biology*

3 | Avoiding euphemisms

Euphemisms attempt to avoid the harsh reality of truth by using more pleasant-sounding, "tactful" words. The word *euphemism* comes from the Greek meaning "words of good omen" (*eu-,* "good" + *pheme,* "speaking").

Euphemisms are, of course, sometimes necessary for tact in social situations (using *passed away* instead of *died* when offering condolences, for example). In other situations, euphemisms drain meaning from truthful writing. Unnecessary euphemisms might describe socially unacceptable behaviour (for example, *Johnny has a wonderfully vivid imagination* instead of *Johnny lies*). Unnecessary euphemisms might try to hide unpleasant facts (*She is between assignments* instead of *She lost her job*).

4 | Avoiding "doublespeak"

Doublespeak is artificial, evasive language. It aims to distort and deceive. For example, many automobile dealerships today have renamed "used cars" as "pre-owned cars" or "previously distinguished cars." A major corporation has described its notice that laid off 5000 workers as a "career alternative enhancement package." The Pentagon has used "collateral damage" for unintended killing of innocent civilians.

To use doublespeak is to try to hide the truth, a highly unethical practice that seeks to control people's thoughts. So severe has the doublespeak problem become in our society that the National Council of Teachers of English in the United States yearly announces a Doublespeak Award to the "best" example of language that purposely misleads. A recent nominee for the award went to a foreign government for calling hostages "foreign guests" whose guards are "hosts." An award went to a U.S. Representative for saying the Congress "did not raise taxes," it "sought new revenues." Such misuses of language have devastating social and political consequences in a free society. As a writer, always avoid using doublespeak; use language truthfully.

5 | Avoiding bureaucratic language

Bureaucratic language is stuffy and overblown.

> You can include a page that also contains an Include instruction. The page including the Include instruction is included when you paginate the document but the included text referred to in its Include instruction is not included.

The irony in this example is that the writer seems to be trying to communicate very precisely. Bureaucratic language (or *bureaucratese*, the coined word to describe the style) is marked by unnecessary complexity. Always avoid such meaningless writing.

EXERCISE 21-4

Consulting section 21e, revise these examples of pretentious language, jargon, euphemism, "doublespeak," and bureaucratic language.

1. In-house employee interaction of a nonbusiness nature is disallowed.
2. An index card posted on the bulletin board advertised a gently worn bridal gown for sale.
3. Shortly after Mrs. Harriman went to her reward, Mr. Harriman moved to Prince Edward Island to be near his son, daughter-in-law, and their bundle of joy.
4. It is with grave misgivings that I undertake this endeavour to instruct myself in the intricacies of computer programming.
5. My male sibling concocted a tale that was entirely fallacious.

6. An individual's cognitive and affective domains are at the centre of his or her personality.

7. He told the police officer that the unanticipated collision occurred as the result of a sudden, involuntary explosive action from his nose and mouth that caused him to momentarily close his eyes, which prevented him from seeing the other motorist's automobile.

8. When the finalization of this negotiation comes through, it will clarify our position in a positive manner.

9. The refuse has accumulated because the sanitation engineers were on strike last month.

10. Employees who are employed by the company for no less than five years in a full-time capacity fulfil the eligibility requirements for participation in the company's savings program.

22 Spelling and Hyphenation

You might be surprised to know this about good spellers: They do not always remember how to spell every word they write, but they are very skilled at sensing when they should check the spelling of a word. Try, therefore, not to ignore your quiet inner voice that doubts a spelling; listen to it and look up the word. At the same time, do not allow spelling doubts to interrupt the flow of your writing during drafting (see 3b). Underline or circle words you want to check, and go back to them when you are editing (see 3d) your writing.

How do you look up a word in the dictionary if you do not know how to spell it? If you know the first few letters, find the general area for the word and browse for it. If you do not know how a word begins, try to find it listed in a thesaurus under an easy-to-spell synonym°. When you are writing on a computer, you can usually use a program that checks spelling. Be careful, though, to proofread for spelling errors that result when you substitute another correctly spelled word for the word that you intend (for example, *whole* if you mean *hole*).

As you spell, be aware that the various origins and ways English-speaking people pronounce words make it almost impossible to rely solely on pronunciation to spell a word. What you *can* rely on is using a system of proofreading and using spelling rules.

Note that Canadian spelling, because it is influenced by both British and American spellings, contains elements of both; however, the drift is toward American conventions because of the influence of the media. Both American and British spellings may occur in any given piece of writing. Here are some examples:

labor	*or*	labour	humor	*or*	humour
theater	*or*	theatre	catalog	*or*	catalogue
check	*or*	cheque	realize	*or*	realise
defense	*or*	defence	connection	*or*	connexion

Whatever spelling you choose, be consistent. If you use the spelling *labour* in a document, use *colour* as well; and if you spell *theatre*, use the spelling *centre*.

22a   Eliminating careless spelling errors

Many spelling errors are the result of illegible handwriting, slips of the pen, or typographical mistakes. Catching "typos" requires especially careful proofreading, using these techniques:

Techniques for Proofreading for Spelling

1. Slow down your reading speed so that you can concentrate on individual letters of words rather than on the meaning of the words.

2. Stay within your "visual span," the number of letters you can identify with a single glance (for most people, about six letters).

3. Put a ruler or large index card under each line as you proof-read, to focus your concentration and vision.

4. Read each paragraph *backwards,* from the last sentence to the first. This method helps to prevent your being distracted by the meaning of the material.

22b   Spelling homonyms and commonly confused words

Homonyms are words that sound exactly like others (*its, it's; morning, mourning*). There are also many words that sound so much alike that they are often confused with each other. A comprehensive list appears here (also, the most common sets are included in the Usage Glossary at the back of this handbook).

One source of confusion not covered by this list is "swallowed" pronunciation. For example, if a speaker fails to pronounce the letter -*d* at the end of words ("swallows" it), a writer may put down *use to, suppose to,* or *prejudice* when *used to, supposed to,* or *prejudiced* is required.

Another source of confusion is expressions that are always written as two words, not one: for example, *all right,* [not *alright*] and *a lot* [not *alot*].

The best way to remember how to distinguish between homonyms and between other commonly confused words is to use memory devices (mnemonics). For example, if you have trouble with the homonyms *stationary* and *stationery,* try this: *Stationary* means standing (*a* is in both) still while *stationery* is written on (*e* is in both).

HOMONYMS AND COMMONLY CONFUSED WORDS

☐	accept	to receive
	except	with the exclusion of
☐	advice	recommendation
	advise	to recommend
☐	affect	to produce an influence on (verb°); an emotional response (noun°)
	effect	result (noun); to bring about or cause (verb)
☐	aisle	space between rows
	isle	island
☐	allude	to make indirect reference to
	elude	to avoid
☐	allusion	indirect reference
	illusion	false idea, misleading appearance
☐	already	by this time
	all ready	fully prepared
☐	altar	sacred platform or place
	alter	to change
☐	altogether	thoroughly
	all together	everyone or everything in one place
☐	are	plural form of *to be*
	hour	sixty minutes
	our	plural form of *my*
☐	ascent	the act of rising or climbing
	assent	consent
☐	assistance	help
	assistants	helpers
☐	bare	nude, unadorned
	bear	to carry; an animal
☐	board	piece of wood
	bored	uninterested
☐	breath	air taken in
	breathe	to take in air
☐	brake	device for stopping
	break	destroy, make into pieces
☐	buy	to purchase
	by	next to, through the agency of
☐	capital	major city
	capitol	government building (U.S.)
☐	choose	to pick
	chose	past tense of *to choose*
☐	cite	to point out
	sight	vision
	site	a place

➔

425

HOMONYMS AND COMMONLY CONFUSED WORDS *(continued)*

clothes	garments
cloths	pieces of fabric
coarse	rough
course	path; series of lectures
complement	something that completes
compliment	praise, flattery
conscience	sense of morality
conscious	awake, aware
council	governing body
counsel	advice
dairy	place associated with milk production
diary	personal journal
descent	downward movement
dissent	disagreement
dessert	final, sweet course in a meal
desert	to abandon (verb); dry, sandy area (noun)
device	a plan; an implement
devise	to create
die	to lose life (verb) *(dying);* one of a pair of dice (noun)
dye	to change the colour of something *(dyeing)*
dominant	commanding, controlling
dominate	to control
elicit	to draw out
illicit	illegal
eminent	prominent
immanent	living within; inherent
imminent	about to happen
envelop	to surround
envelope	container for a letter or other papers
fair	light-skinned; just, honest
fare	money for transportation; food
formally	conventionally, with ceremony
formerly	previously
forth	forward
fourth	number four
gorilla	animal in ape family
guerrilla	soldier specializing in unconventional, surprise attacks
hear	to sense sound by ear
here	in this place
hole	opening
whole	complete; an entire thing
human	relating to the species *homo sapiens*
humane	compassionate

Homonyms and Commonly Confused Words *(continued)*

insure	buy or give insurance
ensure	guarantee, protect
its	possessive form of *it*
it's	contraction for *it is*
know	to comprehend
no	negative
later	after a time
latter	second one of two things
lead	heavy metal substance; to guide
led	past tense of *to lead*
lightning	storm-related electricity
lightening	making lighter
loose	unbound, not tightly fastened
lose	to misplace
maybe	perhaps
may be	might be
meat	animal flesh
meet	to encounter
miner	a person who works in a mine
minor	under age
moral	distinguishing right from wrong; the lesson of a fable, story, or event
morale	attitude or outlook, usually of a group
of	preposition indicating origin
off	away from
passed	past tense of *to pass*
past	at a previous time
patience	forbearance
patients	people under medical care
peace	absence of fighting
piece	part of a whole; musical arrangement
personal	intimate
personnel	employees
plain	simple, unadorned
plane	to shave wood; aircraft
precede	to come before
proceed	to continue
presence	being at hand; attendance at a place or in something
presents	gifts
principal	foremost (adjective°); school head (noun°)
principle	moral conviction, basic truth
quiet	silent, calm
quite	very

➜
427

Homonyms and Commonly Confused Words *(continued)*

rain	water drops falling to earth (noun); to fall like rain (verb)
reign	to rule
rein	strap to guide or control an animal (noun); to guide or control (verb)
raise	to lift up
raze	to tear down
respectfully	with respect
respectively	in that order
right	correct; opposite of *left*
rite	ritual
write	to put words on paper
road	path
rode	past tense of *to ride*
scene	place of an action; segment of a play
seen	viewed
sense	perception, understanding
since	measurement of past time; because
stationary	standing still
stationery	writing paper
than	in comparison with; besides
then	at that time; next; therefore
their	possessive form of *they*
there	in that place
they're	contraction for *they are*
through	finished; into and out of
threw	past tense of *to throw*
thorough	complete
to	toward
too	also; indicates degree *(too much)*
two	number following one
waist	midsection of the body
waste	discarded material (noun); to squander, to fail to use up (verb)
weak	not strong
week	seven days
weather	climatic condition
whether	if
where	in which place
were	past tense of *to be*
which	one of a group
witch	female sorcerer
whose	possessive form of *who*
who's	contraction for *who is*

your	possessive form of *you*
you're	contraction for *you are*
yore	long past

EXERCISE 22-1

Consulting section 22b, select the appropriate homonym from each group in parentheses.

According to the (Council, Counsel) on Aging, the North American population over 85 is growing faster (than, then) any other segment of society. The (council, counsel) (cites, sites) statistics indicating that elderly people who have access (to, too, two) good health care (are, our) likely to outlive (their, there, they're) parents. If elderly parents grow (to, too, two) (weak, week) to care for themselves, responsibility for them (maybe, may be) (passed, past) to children (know, no) longer young themselves. (Formally, Formerly) (use to, used to) (their, there) parents making independent decisions, adult children must now learn to (accept, except) that parents may need (assistance, assistants) with some decisions. Aging parents must be treated with courtesy and handled with (patience, patients). Frequent (personal, personnel) visits help to keep parents' (moral, morale) high or to (raise, raze) low spirits. In (principal, principle), adult children (all ready, already) (know, no) how to behave with aging parents; they must sometimes be prepared to reverse their (respectful, respective) roles.

22c
Using spelling rules for plurals, suffixes, and *ie, ei* words

Knowing the rules in Chart 101 will help you spell plurals, add suffixes, and spell words that contain *ie* or *ei* combinations.

SPELLING RULES FOR PLURALS, SUFFIXES, AND *IE, EI* WORDS   101

PLURALS

- **Adding -*s* or -*es*:** Most plurals are formed by adding -*s*, including words that end in "hard" -*ch* (sounding like *k*): *leg, legs; shoe, shoes; stomach, stomachs*. For words ending in -*s*, -*sh*, -*x*, -*z*, or "soft" -*ch* (as in *beach*), add -*es* to the singular: *beach, beaches; tax, taxes; coach, coaches*.

- **Words Ending in -*o*:** Add -*s* if the -*o* is preceded by a vowel (*radio, radios; cameo, cameos*). Add -*es* if the *o* is preceded by a ➡

429

SPELLING RULES FOR PLURALS, SUFFIXES, AND *IE, EI* WORDS *(cont.)*

consonant (*potato, potatoes*). A few words can be pluralized either way: *cargo, volcano, tornado, zero.*

- **Words Ending in *-f* or *-fe*:** Some *-f* and *-fe* words are made plural by adding *-s: belief, beliefs.* Others require changing *-f* or *-fe* to *-ves: life, lives; leaf, leaves.* Words ending in *-ff* or *-ffe* simply add *-s: staff, staffs; giraffe, giraffes.*

- **Compound Words:** For most compound words, add *-s* or *-es* at the end of the last word: *chequebooks, player-coaches.* For a few, the word to make plural is not the last one: *sister-in-law, sisters-in-law; kilometre per hour, kilometres per hour.* (For hyphenating compound words, see Chart 103 in 22d.)

- **Internal Changes and Endings Other Than *-s*:** A few words change internally or add endings other than *-s* to become plural: *foot, feet; man, men; mouse, mice; child, children.*

- **Foreign Words:** Plurals other than *-s* or *-es* are listed in good dictionaries. In general, for many Latin words ending in *-um*, form plurals by changing *-um* to *-a: curriculum, curricula; datum, data; medium, media; stratum, strata.* For Latin words that end in *-us*, the plural is often *-i: alumnus, alumni; syllabus, syllabi.* For Greek *-on* words, the plural is often *-a: criterion, criteria; phenomenon, phenomena.*

- **One-Form Words:** A few spellings are the same for the singular and plural: *deer, elk, quail.* The differences are conveyed by adding words, not endings: *one deer, nine deer; rice, bowls of rice.*

SUFFIXES

- ***-y* Words:** If the letter before the final *y* is a consonant, change the *y* to *i* unless the suffix begins with an *i* (for example, *-ing*): *fry, fried, frying.* If the letter before the *-y* is a vowel, keep the final *y: employ, employed, employing.* These rules do not apply to irregular verbs (see Chart 59 in section 8d).

- ***-e* Words:** Drop a final *e* when the suffix begins with a vowel unless doing so would cause confusion (for example, *be + ing* does not become *bing): require, requiring; like, liking.* Keep the final *e* when the suffix begins with a consonant: *require, requirement; like, likely.* Exceptions include *argument* and *truly.*

- **Words That Double a Final Letter:** If the final letter is a consonant, double it only if it passes these tests: (1) Its last two letters are a vowel followed by a consonant; and (2) the suffix begins with a vowel: *drop, dropped; forget, forgetful, forgettable.* (American

---

SPELLING RULES FOR PLURALS, SUFFIXES, AND *IE, EI* WORDS *(cont.)* 101

spelling adds a third test. The word must have one syllable or be accented on the last syllable: *begin* [accent on last syllable], *beginning* but *travel* [accent on last syllable], *traveling*. British spelling doubles the final consonant in many words even when the accent is not on the last syllable: *travel, travelling; worship, worshipper.*

■ ***-cede, -ceed, -sede* Words:** Only one word ends in *-sede: supersede.* Three words end in *-ceed: exceed, proceed, succeed.* All other words whose endings sound like "seed" end in *-cede: concede, intercede, precede.*

■ ***-ally* and *-ly* Words:** The suffixes *-ally* and *-ly* turn words into adverbs°. For words ending in *-ic*, add *-ally: logically, statistically.* Otherwise, add *-ly: quickly, sharply.*

■ ***-ance, -ence,* and *-ible, -able:*** No consistent rules govern words with these suffixes. The best advice is "When in doubt, look it up."

THE *IE, EI* RULE: The old rhyme for *ie* and *ei* is usually true:

"*I* before *e* [bel**ie**ve, f**ie**ld, gr**ie**f]
Except after *c* [c**ei**ling, conc**ei**t],
Or when sounded like *ay* [**ei**ght, v**ei**n],
As in n**ei**ghbour and w**ei**gh."

You may want to memorize these major exceptions:

ie	conscience	financier	science	species
ei	either	neither	leisure	seize
	counterfeit	foreign	forfeit	sleight
	weird			

EXERCISE 22-2

Consulting section 22c and Chart 101, form the plurals of these words.

1. scarf
2. species
3. rodeo
4. moose
5. leech
6. datum
7. log
8. brother-in-law
9. phenomenon
10. self
11. nacho
12. fungus
13. loaf
14. push-up

EXERCISE 22-3

Consulting section 22c, Chart 101, and a dictionary, follow the directions for each group of words.

1. Add *-able* or *-ible:* (a) profit; (b) reproduce; (c) control; (d) coerce; (e) recognize.

2. Add *-ance* or *-ence:* (a) luxuri _____; (b) prud _____; (c) devi _____; (d) resist _____; (e) independ _____.

3. Drop the final *e* as needed: (a) true + ly (b) joke + ing; (c) fortunate + ly; (d) appease + ing; (e) appease + ment.

4. Change the final *y* to *i* as needed: (a) happy + ness; (b) pry + ed; (c) pry + ing; (d) dry + ly; (e) beautify + ing.

5. Double the final consonant as needed: (a) commit + ed; (b) commit + ment; (c) drop + ed; (d) occur + ed; (e) regret + ful.

6. Insert *ie* or *ei* correctly: (a) rel _____ f; (b) ach _____ ve; (c) w _____ rd; (d) n _____ ce; (e) dec _____ ve.

22d Using hyphens correctly

1 Hyphenating at the end of a line

Unless the last word on a line would use up most of the right margin of your paper, do not divide it. If you must divide a word, try not to divide the last word on the first line of a paper, the last word in a paragraph, or the last word on a page. When you have to hyphenate, break the word only at a syllable, using the guidelines in Chart 102. If you are unsure of how to divide a word into syllables, consult a dictionary (see 20a).

GUIDELINES FOR END-OF-LINE HYPHENATION			102
■ **Do not divide very short words, one-syllable words, or words pronounced as one syllable.**			
NO	we-alth	en-vy	scream-ed
YES	wealth	envy	screamed

sp **22d**

GUIDELINES FOR END-OF-LINE HYPHENATION *(continued)*   102

- **Do not leave or carry over only one or two letters.**

NO	a-live	tax-i	he-licopter	helicopt-er
YES	alive	taxi	heli-copter	helicop-ter

- **Divide words only between syllables.**

NO	proc-ede
YES	pro-cede

- **Always follow rules for double consonants.**

NO	ful-lness	omitt-ing	asp-halt
YES	full-ness	omit-ting	as-phalt

- **Divide hyphenated words after the hyphen, if possible, rather than at any other syllable.**

NO	self-con-scious	good-look-ing report
YES	self-conscious	good-looking report

2	**Hyphenating prefixes, suffixes, compound words, and numbers**

Prefixes and **suffixes** are syllables attached to root words. **Compound words** use two or more words together to express one concept. Some prefixes and suffixes are hyphenated; others are not. Compound words can be written as separate words (*night shift*), hyphenated words (*tractor-trailer*), or one word (*handbook*). Chart 103 gives basic guidelines for word hyphenation.

HYPHENATING PREFIXES, SUFFIXES, COMPOUND WORDS, AND NUMBERS   103

- **Use hyphens after the prefixes *all-, ex-, quasi-,* and *self-.***

  all-inclusive   self-reliant   →

HYPHENATING PREFIXES, SUFFIXES, COMPOUND WORDS, AND NUMBERS *(continued)*   103

■ **Do not use a hyphen when *self* is a root word, not a prefix.**

NO	self-ishness	self-less
YES	selfishness	selfless

■ **Use a hyphen to avoid a distracting string of letters.**

NO	antiintellectual	belllike
YES	anti-intellectual	bell-like

■ **Use a hyphen before the suffix *-elect*.**

NO	presidentelect
YES	president-elect

■ **Use a hyphen when a prefix comes before a number or a word that starts with a capital letter.**

NO	post1950s	proAmerican
YES	post-1950s	pro-American

■ **Use a hyphen between a prefix and a compound word.**

NO	antigun control
YES	anti-gun control

■ **Use a hyphen to prevent confusion in meaning or pronunciation.**

YES	re-dress ("dress again")	redress ("set right")
	un-ionize ("remove the ions")	unionize ("form a union")

■ **Use a hyphen when two or more prefixes apply to one root word.**

YES	pre- and post-war eras.	two-, three-, or four-year program

COMPOUND WORDS

■ **Use a hyphen for most compound modifiers that precede the noun. Do not use a hyphen for most compound modifiers after the noun.**

YES	well-researched report	two-centimetre clearance

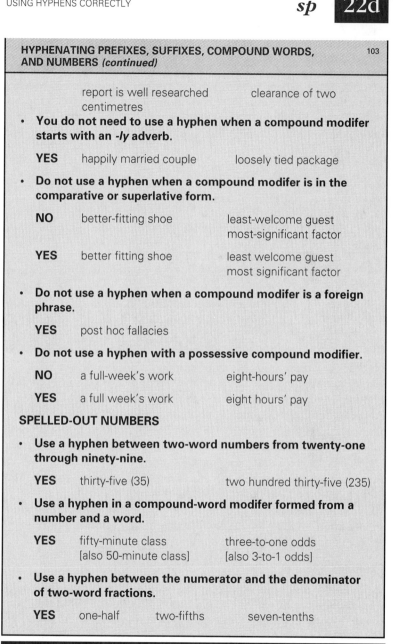

report is well researched   clearance of two
centimetres

- **You do not need to use a hyphen when a compound modifier starts with an *-ly* adverb.**

  YES   happily married couple   loosely tied package

- **Do not use a hyphen when a compound modifer is in the comparative or superlative form.**

  NO   better-fitting shoe   least-welcome guest
                                          most-significant factor

  YES   better fitting shoe   least welcome guest
                                          most significant factor

- **Do not use a hyphen when a compound modifer is a foreign phrase.**

  YES   post hoc fallacies

- **Do not use a hyphen with a possessive compound modifier.**

  NO   a full-week's work   eight-hours' pay

  YES   a full week's work   eight hours' pay

SPELLED-OUT NUMBERS

- **Use a hyphen between two-word numbers from twenty-one through ninety-nine.**

  YES   thirty-five (35)   two hundred thirty-five (235)

- **Use a hyphen in a compound-word modifer formed from a number and a word.**

  YES   fifty-minute class   three-to-one odds
              [also 50-minute class]   [also 3-to-1 odds]

- **Use a hyphen between the numerator and the denominator of two-word fractions.**

  YES   one-half   two-fifths   seven-tenths

❖ ALERT: Use figures rather than words for any fraction that needs more than two words to express. If you cannot use figures (for example, if you cannot rearrange a sentence that starts with a multiword fraction), use hyphens between the words of the numerator's number and the words of the denominator's number but not between the numerator and the denominator: two one-hundredths (2/100), thirty-three ten-thousandths (33/10 000). ❖

EXERCISE 22-4

Consulting section 22d, in the blanks write the correct form of the word in parentheses according to the way it is used in the sentence.

1. The tiger is (all powerful) _____ in the cat family.
2. (Comparison contrast) _____ studies of tigers and lions show that the tiger is the (more agile) _____ and powerful.
3. The tiger's body is a (boldly striped) _____ yellow, with a white (under body) _____.
4. The tiger's maximum length is about (3.3 metres) _____, about (one quarter) _____ of which is accounted for by its tail, and its maximum weight exceeds (two hundred) _____ kilograms.
5. The Bengal tiger, the largest of the family, is aggressive and (self confident) _____.
6. In India, where the Bengal is called a (village destroyer) _____, it has a reputation for going (in to) _____ villages to hunt for food.
7. Entire villages have been temporarily abandoned by (terror stricken) _____ people who have seen a Bengal tiger nearby.
8. Villagers seek to protect their homes by destroying tigers with traps, (spring loaded) _____ guns, and (poisoned arrows) _____.
9. Bengal tigers are also called (cattle killers) _____, although they attack domestic animals only when wild ones cannot be found.
10. Many people who do not live near a zoo get to see tigers only in (animal shows) _____, although (pro animal) _____ activists try to prevent tigers' being used this way.

EXERCISE 22-5

The following paragraph contains eleven misspelled words. Circle the words, correct them, and match them to a section in this chapter. If the error does not fall under any particular section, describe the cause of error in your own words.

An invitation arrived last week in a beautyful, crisp white envelop. I knew rite away it was a peace of important mail, unlike all the junk mail I usually receive. It seemed that the local chapter of the Falcon Club of Canada wanted to hear my thoughts on American car collecting. The prospect of giving a speech through me into a nervous frenzy as I tryed to prepare at the last minute—getting a haircut, memorizing my notes, practiseing in front of my freinds—all designed to insure that I would not humiliate myself publically. As it turned out, my heart-ache was pointless. The club really just wanted the opportunity to inspect my 1965 navy blue Ford Falcon.

PART

VI

Using Punctuation and Mechanics

 When you use punctuation and mechanics according to currently accepted practice, you avoid errors that interfere with the delivery of the meaning that you want to communicate. Part Six presents and explains the rules and conventions that readers have come to expect. As you use Chapters 23 through 30, remember that punctuation and mechanics are tools that help you deliver your message clearly to your readers.

23 The Period, Question Mark, and Exclamation Point

The period, question mark, and exclamation point are called **end punctuation** because they occur at the end of sentences.

I love you. Do you love me? I love you!

THE PERIOD

23a Using a period at the end of a statement, a mild command, or an indirect question

Unless a sentence asks a direct question°* (23c) or issues a strong command or emphatic declaration (23e), it ends with a period.

STATEMENT A journey of a thousand leagues begins with a single step.

—LAO-TSU

MILD COMMAND Put a gram of boldness into everything you do.

—BALTASAR GRACIAN

INDIRECT QUESTION I asked if they wanted to climb Mt. Everest. [A direct question would end with a question mark: I asked, *"Do you want to climb Mt. Everest?"*]

---

*Throughout this book, a degree mark (°) indicates that you can find the definition of the word in the Glossary of Terms in this handbook.

23b Using periods with most abbreviations

Most **abbreviations** call for periods, but some do not. Typical abbreviations with periods include *Mt., St., Dr., Mr., Ms., Mrs., Ph.D., M.D.,* and *R.N.* In general, the word *professor* is spelled out, not abbreviated. Also, *a.m.* and *p.m.* are appropriate with exact times (such as *2:15 p.m.*) but should not be used instead of the word *morning, evening,* or *night.* Abbreviations without periods include the names of some organizations and government agencies (such as *CBC* and *NFB*). For more information about abbreviations, see 30h and 30i.

Ms. Yuan, who works at the NFB, lectured to Dr. Benet's film class at 9:30 a.m.

❖ PUNCTUATION ALERT: When the period of an abbreviation falls at the end of a sentence, the period serves also to end the sentence.❖

THE QUESTION MARK

23c Using a question mark after a direct question

A **direct question** asks a question and ends with a question mark. In contrast, an **indirect question** reports a question and ends with a period (see 23a).

How many attempts have been made to climb Mt. Everest?
[An indirect question would be: *The tourists wanted to know how many attempts had been made to climb Mt. Everest.*]

❖ PUNCTUATION ALERT: Do not combine a question mark with a comma, a period, or an exclamation point.❖

NO   She asked, "How are you?."

YES   She asked, "How are you?"

Questions in a series are each followed by a question mark, whether or not each question is a complete sentence.

❖ CAPITALIZATION ALERT: When questions in a series are not complete sentences, you can choose whether or not to capitalize the first letter, as long as you are consistent in each piece of writing.❖

After the fierce storm had passed, the mountain climbers debated what to do next. Turn back? Move on? Rest for a while?

When a request is phrased as a question, it does not always require a question mark, especially when the request is phrased as a question to achieve a polite tone: *Would you please send me a copy.*

23d Using a question mark in parentheses

When a date or number is unknown or doubtful even after your very best research, you can use *(?).*

Mary Astell, an English author who wrote pamphlets on women's rights, was born in 1666 (?) and died in 1731.

The word *about* is often a graceful substitute for *(?)*: *Mary Astell was born about 1666.*

Do not use *(?)* to communicate that you are unsure of information: *It might rain* [not *will rain (?)] today.* Also, your choice of words, not (?), should communicate irony or sarcasm.

NO   Having the flu is a delightful (?) experience.

YES   Having the flu is as pleasant as almost drowning.

THE EXCLAMATION POINT

23e Using an exclamation point for a strong command or an emphatic declaration

An **exclamation point** can end a strong command or an emphatic declaration. A strong command gives a very firm order: *Look out behind you!* An emphatic declaration makes a shocking or surprising statement: *There's been an accident!*

❖ PUNCTUATION ALERT: Do not combine an exclamation point with a comma, a period, or a question mark.❖

NO   "There's been an accident!," cried my mother.

YES   "There's been an accident!" cried my mother.

23f Avoiding the overuse of exclamation points

In academic writing, your words, rather than exclamation points, should communicate the strength of your message. Reserve exclamation points for occasional emphatic dialogue. Use them only very rarely for a short emphatic declaration within a longer passage.

> When we were in Nepal, we tried each day to see Mt. Everest. But each day we failed to see it. Clouds defeated us! The summit never emerged from a heavy overcast.

If you use exclamation points too often in academic writing, your reader will think that your judgment of urgency is exaggerated.

NO Mountain climbing can be dangerous! You must learn correct procedures! You must have the proper equipment. Take rope! Wear spiked boots! Carry special picks designed for mountaineering.

YES Mountain climbing can be dangerous. Without knowing correct procedures, climbers quickly can turn an outing into a disaster. Required mountaineering gear includes rope, spiked boots, and special picks.

Your choice of words, not (!), should communicate amazement or sarcasm.

NO At 8882 metres (!), Mt. Everest is the world's highest mountain. I heard that Chris (!) wants to climb it.

YES At a majestically staggering 8882 metres, Mt. Everest is the world's highest mountain. Surely, Chris lacks the stamina to climb it.

EXERCISE 23-1

Consulting sections 23a-23f, insert any needed periods, question marks, and exclamation points. Also delete any unneeded ones.

EXAMPLE   The paintings of the great El Greco are associated with Spain, but he was actually born in 1541 on the island of Crete!

The paintings of the great El Greco are associated with Spain, but he was actually born in 1541 on the island of Crete.

443

1. After studying art in Crete, El Greco moved to Venice, Italy, before 1567 (?), apparently to study with the famous Venetian artist Titian.
2. Scholars wonder if Titian was referring to El Greco when Titian mentioned "a talented young pupil" in a letter to King Philip II?
3. El Greco later moved to Rome with a letter of introduction (dated Nov. 19, 1570) to a rich, influential art patron, Cardinal Alessandro Farnese.
4. Cardinal Farnese introduced El Greco to the outstanding (!) people of the city.
5. By 1572, El Greco had moved to the city of Toledo in Spain, where he spent the rest of his life!
6. Toledo was a rich, cultured, and intellectual city where El Greco worked as a sculptor, painter, and architect
7. Toward the end of his life, El Greco suffered from a mysterious (?) illness that reduced his capacity for work
8. "Was El Greco's eyesight affected by the illness" is a question that has been asked for centuries?
9. Visual problems might explain the elongated bodies in El Greco's portraits?
10. From time to time, physicians write articles diagnosing (?) El Greco's illness based on this artist's paintings!

EXERCISE 23-2

Insert needed periods, question marks, and exclamation points.

Did you know that every year more people are killed in Africa by crocodiles than by lions The crocodile is a large flesh-eating reptile that lives in and near tropical waterways A crocodile that weighs 50 kilograms can shut its jaws with a pressure of 700 kilograms In contrast, a human's jaws exert only 18 to 36 kilograms of pressure The largest crocodiles generally grow to be about 8 metres long, although rumours circulate of 10-metre crocodiles Crocodiles are cannibals They even eat their own young Although they may appear clumsy, crocodiles are very fast on land What is the best thing to do if you are chased by a crocodile Run in a zigzag pattern The crocodile cannot make sudden changes of direction.

24 The Comma

The comma is the most frequently used mark of punctuation, occurring twice as often as all other marks of punctuation combined. Rules for the comma are many: The comma *must* be used in certain places, it *must not* be used in other places, and it is *optional* in still other places. This chapter will help you sort through the various rules and uses of the comma: before a coordinating conjunction° linking independent clauses°, 24a; after an introductory clause°, phrase°, or word, 24b; to separate items in a series, 24c; to separate coordinate adjectives°, 24d; with nonrestrictive° (nonessential) elements, 24e; with parenthetical° and transitional expressions°, contrasts, words of direct address°, and tag sentences°, 24f; with quoted words, 24g; in names, dates, addresses, and numbers, 24h; to clarify meaning, 24i; to avoid misuse or overuse, 24j.

The role of the comma is to group and separate sentence parts, helping to create clarity for readers. Consider the clarity of the following paragraph, which contains all needed punctuation except commas.

NO   Among publishers typographical errors known as "typos" are an embarrassing fact of life. In spite of careful editing reviews and multiple readings few books are perfect upon publication. Soon after a book reaches the marketplace reports of errors embarrassments to authors and editors alike start to come in. Everyone laughed therefore although no one thought it was funny when an English textbook was published with this line: "Proofread your writing carefullly."

Here is the same paragraph with commas included.

YES   Among publishers, typographical errors, known as "typos," are an embarrassing fact of life. In spite of careful editing, reviews, and multiple readings, few books are perfect upon publication. Soon after a book reaches the marketplace, reports of errors, embarrassments to authors and editors alike, start to come in. Everyone laughed, therefore, although no one thought it was funny, when an English textbook was published with this line: "Proofread your writing carefullly."

In the *Yes* paragraph, the meaning is clear. Each comma in it is used for a specific reason according to a comma rule.

Avoid two practices that can get writers into trouble with commas: (1) As you are writing, do not insert a comma just because you happen to pause to think before moving on. (2) As you reread your writing, do not insert commas according to your personal habits of pausing. Although a comma alerts a reader to a slight pause (except in dates and other conventional material), pausing is not a reliable guide for writers, because people's breathing rhythms, accents, and thinking spans vary greatly.

24a   Using a comma before a coordinating conjunction that links independent clauses

When **coordinating conjunctions** (*and, but, or, nor, for, so, and yet*) link independent clauses°, they create **compound sentences°**. Use a comma before the coordinating conjunction.

PATTERN FOR COMMAS WHEN COORDINATING CONJUNCTIONS LINK INDEPENDENT CLAUSES   104

Independent clause, { and / but / for / or / nor / so / yet } independent clause.

The sky was dark grey, **and** the wind died suddenly.

The November morning had just begun, **but** it looked like dusk.

Shopkeepers closed their stores early, **for** they wanted to get home.

Soon high winds would start, **or** thick snow would begin silently.

Farmers had no time to continue harvesting, **nor** could they round up their animals in distant fields.

The firehouse whistle blew four times, **so** everyone knew a blizzard was closing in.

People on the road tried to reach safety, **yet** a few unlucky ones were stranded.

When the two independent clauses in a compound sentence are very short, some authorities omit the comma before the coordinating conjunction. However, you will never be wrong, and you avoid the risk of error, if you always use a comma in your academic writing.

❖ COMMA CAUTION: Do not put a comma after a coordinating conjunction that links independent clauses. ❖

NO   The sky was dark grey **and,** the wind died suddenly.

YES   The sky was dark grey, **and** the wind died suddenly.

❖ COMMA CAUTION: Do not use a comma when a coordinating conjunction links two words, phrases°, or dependent clauses° only. Use commas for a series of three or more items (see 24c).

NO   Learning a new language demands **time, and patience.**
       [Two words linked by *and* use no comma.]

YES   Learning a new language demands **time and patience.**

NO   Each language has **a beauty of its own, and forms of expression** which are duplicated nowhere else. [Two phrases linked by *and* use no comma.]

YES   Each language has **a beauty of its own and forms of expression** which are duplicated nowhere else.

                              —MARGARET MEAD, "Unispeak" ❖

❖ COMMA CAUTION: To avoid creating a comma splice, do not use a comma to separate independent clauses unless they are linked by a coordinating conjunction (see 14c).

NO   **Ten centimetres of snow fell in two hours, two centimetres of ice built up when the snow turned to freezing rain.** [The comma alone is insufficient. A coordinating conjunction must follow when the comma is used here.]

YES   Ten centimetres of snow fell in two hours, **and** two centimetres of ice built up when the snow turned to freezing rain. [The coordinating conjunction *and* links the two independent clauses.] ❖

YES   Ten centimetres of snow fell in two hours. Two centimetres of ice built up when the snow turned to freezing rain. [Independent clauses can become two separate sentences.] ♣

When independent clauses containing other commas are linked by a coordinating conjunction, you can choose to use a semicolon before the coordinating conjunction (see 25b). Base your decision on what would help your reader understand the material most easily.

Because temperatures remained low all winter, the snow could not melt until well into spring; **and** some people wondered when they would see grass again.

EXERCISE 24-1

Consulting section 24a, combine each pair of sentences using the coordinating conjunction shown in parentheses. When necessary, rearrange words. Insert commas before coordinating conjunctions that separate independent clauses.

EXAMPLE   William Lyon Mackenzie King was the grandson of the third prime minister of Canada, Alexander Mackenzie. He himself became the prime minister in 1921. (and)

William Lyon Mackenzie King was the grandson of the third prime minister of Canada, Alexander Mackenzie, and he himself became prime minister in 1921.

1. King studied law at the University of Toronto. He also attended the University of Chicago and Harvard University. (but)
2. King delivered a famous speech to the House of Commons in 1936 in which he said that some countries have too much history. We have too much geography. (but)
3. He was an ardent supporter of Canadian autonomy. He insisted that Canada be treated by its allies in World War II as an equal. (so)
4. Because of French-Canadian protests over Canada's support of Great Britain in the war, King promised that no conscripted soliders would be sent to fight. Later, he broke his promise and sent conscripts overseas. (but)
5. King is remembered for the wartime slogan "Conscription if necessary, but not necessarily conscription." His tenure as prime minister began long before World War II and continued long after it. (yet)
6. Despite his Canada-first policy, King kept up sentimental connections with England. He would not have had Lester Pearson send him fragments of buildings bombed out by the Blitz to decorate his garden. (or)
7. Although he was often accompanied by women on public occasions, King never married. He had no children. (nor)

8. In public, King was a colourless, pragmatic politician. His secret diaries reveal a man obsessed by strange fears and enthusiasms. (yet)
9. King suffered poor health in his last years. He died at Kingsmere, his estate in Quebec, in 1950. (and)
10. Since his death, King's reputation has suffered. His interest in séances and communing with his dead mother has drawn embarrassing attention to his private life. (for)

24b Using a comma after an introductory clause, phrase, or word

Use a comma to signal the end of an introductory element and the beginning of an independent clause.

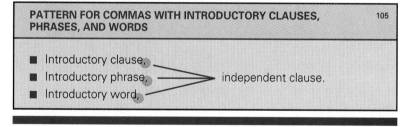

| PATTERN FOR COMMAS WITH INTRODUCTORY CLAUSES, PHRASES, AND WORDS | 105 |

■ Introductory clause,
■ Introductory phrase, ──────▷ independent clause.
■ Introductory word,

Some authorities omit the comma when an introductory element is very short and the sentence is clear without a comma. However, you will never be wrong if you use a comma after an introductory clause, phrase, or word in your academic writing.

1 | Using a comma after an introductory adverb clause

An **adverb clause** is a dependent clause (see 7o-2). It cannot stand alone as an independent unit because it starts with a subordinating conjunction (for example, *although, because, if;* for a complete list, see 7h). When an adverb clause precedes an independent clause, separate the clauses with a comma.

When it comes to eating, you can sometimes help yourself more by helping yourself less.

—Richard Armour

449

2 | Using a comma after an introductory phrase

A **phrase** is a group of words that cannot stand alone as an independent unit. It lacks a subject°, a predicate°, or both. Use a comma to set off a phrase that introduces an independent clause. (Types of phrases are explained in 7n.)

Between 1544 and 1689, sugar refineries appeared in London and New York. [prepositional phrase°]

Obtained mainly from sugar cane and sugar beets, sugar is also developed from the sap of maple trees. [past participle° phrase]

Beginning in infancy, we develop lifelong tastes for sweet and salty foods. [participial phrase°]

To satisfy a craving for ice cream, timid people sometimes brave midnight streets. [infinitive phrase°]

Eating being enjoyable, we tend to eat more than we need for fuel. [absolute phrase°]

3 | Using a comma after introductory words

Transitional expressions and **conjunctive adverbs** carry messages of a relationship between ideas in sentences and paragraphs. Transitional expressions include *for example* and *in addition* (for a complete list, see Chart 23 in section 4d-1). Conjunctive adverbs include *therefore* and *however* (for a complete list, see Chart 49 in section 7f). When these introductory words appear at the beginning of a sentence, most writers follow them with a comma.

For example, fructose is fruit sugar that is metabolized as a blood sugar.

Interjections are introductory words that convey surprise or other emotions. Use a comma after an interjection at the beginning of a sentence: ***Oh,** we did not realize that you are allergic to cats. **Yes,** your sneezing worries me.*

❖ PUNCTUATION ALERT: Use a comma before and a comma after a transitional expression, conjunctive adverb, or interjection that falls within a sentence. Use a comma before such words that fall at the end of a sentence.❖

EXERCISE 24-2

Consulting section 24b, insert commas where needed after introductory words, phrases, and clauses. If a sentence is correct, circle its number.

EXAMPLE   Although everyone values a car for transportation few people realize that a car can help them survive danger.

Although everyone values a car for transportation, few people realize that a car can help them survive danger.

(1) To protect your life in certain life-threatening circumstances you can use many resources from your car. (2) Surprisingly it contains many items that can help you survive. (3) For example a car's horn or its lights at night can alert rescuers well over a kilometre away. (4) However these strategies will eventually deplete the car's battery. (5) A reservoir of oil is available under the hood. (6) Burned in a hubcap a litre will spew a miniature cloud visible for kilometres. (7) While some people know that any hose in the car can be used as a siphon to get at gasoline few realize that windshield washer tubing can be used for a life-saving tourniquet. (8) When you need a fire that will not go out for three to four hours you can burn a tire. (9) In most situations your car can serve as a bunkhouse. (10) Yes survival experts know that giving people this information saves lives.

EXERCISE 24-3

Consulting section 24b, combine each set of sentences into one sentence that starts according to the directions in parentheses. You can add, delete, and rearrange words as needed. Be sure to use commas after introductory elements in the combined sentences.

EXAMPLE   Many important musicals have been produced in Toronto. The city has been called "the Broadway of the North." (clause beginning *because*)

Because important many musicals have been produced in Toronto, the city has been called "the Broadway of the North."

1. Theatre had always been part of the city's cultural life. The theatrical boom in Toronto began in the 1980s with the refurbishing of the Pantages and Elgin theatres. (clause beginning *although*)
2. The popularity of musicals has ensured financial success for revivals of Broadway classics. It has also sparked interest in new Canadian productions like *Napoleon* and *The House of Martin Guerre.* (phrase beginning *besides ensuring*)
3. Ed and David Mirvish built The Princess of Wales Theatre. They wanted a theatre to house a production of *Miss Saigon.* (phrase beginning *to house*)
4. The Canadian production of *Les Misérables* premiered at the Mirvishes' other theatre, the Royal Alexandra. It later toured Canada. (phrase beginning *premiering*)

5. The Tony Award–winning production of *Kiss of the Spider Woman* began its run at a Toronto theatre. It subsequently went on to London and New York. (begin with *similarly*)

6. Colm Wilkinson and Rebecca Caine starred in *The Phantom of the Opera* in Toronto. This musical has been staged all over the world. (phrase beginning *staged*)

7. Andrew Lloyd Webber's *Aspects of Love* was not a success on Broadway. A new production directed by Robin Phillips at the Elgin Theatre revitalized it. (clause beginning *although*)

8. The current interest in musicals has created many jobs for Canadian actors and musicians. Some people complain about importing American culture. (clause beginning *while*)

9. Garth Drabinsky announced that he was mounting a new production of the Kern-Hammerstein classic, *Showboat*. He made the announcement only to find that many people condemned the material as racist, and others criticized its American origins. (begin with *for example*)

10. *Showboat* was well received. Musical theatre once again showed that it is capable of dealing with controversial issues. (begin with *in the end*)

24c Using commas to separate items in a series

A **series** is a group of three or more elements—words, phrases°, or clauses°—that match in grammatical form as well as in importance in the same sentence.

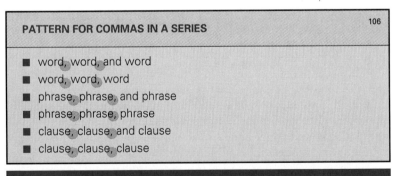

PATTERN FOR COMMAS IN A SERIES 106

- word, word, and word
- word, word, word
- phrase, phrase, and phrase
- phrase, phrase, phrase
- clause, clause, and clause
- clause, clause, clause

Marriage requires **sexual, financial, and emotional** discipline.
—Anne Roiphe, "Why Marriages Fail"

Culture is a way of **thinking, feeling, believing.**
—Clyde Kluckhorn, *Mirror for Man*

My love of flying goes back to those early days **of roller skates, of swings, of bicycles.**

—TERESA WIGGINS, student

The big world of action is both dangerous and mysterious; you'll never really understand it. **Stay out of it, sit still, don't try.**

—ELIZABETH JANEWAY, "Soaps, Cynicism, and Mind Control"

We have been taught **that children develop by ages and stages, that the steps are pretty much the same for everybody, and that to grow out of the limited behavior of childhood,** we must climb them all.

—GAIL SHEEHY, *Passages*

Some authorities omit the comma before the coordinating conjunction between the last two items of a series. This handbook does not recommend omitting this comma, for its absence can distort meaning and confuse a reader. If you never omit the comma in your academic writing, you will never be wrong.

When the items in a series contain commas or other punctuation, separate them with semicolons instead of commas (see 25d). This practice ensures that your sentence will deliver the meaning you intend.

If it's a bakery, they have to sell cake; if it's a photography shop, they have to develop film; **and** if it's a dry-goods store, they have to sell warm underwear.

—ART BUCHWALD, "Birth Control for Banks"

Numbered or lettered lists within a sentence are items in a series. Use commas (or semicolons if the items are long) to separate them when there are three or more items.

To file your insurance claim, please enclose (1) a letter requesting payment, (2) a police report about the robbery, and (3) proof of purchase of the items you say are missing.

❖ COMMA CAUTION: Do not use a comma before the first item or after the last item in a series unless a different rule makes it necessary.

NO   Many artists, writers, and composers, have indulged in daydreaming and reverie.

YES   Many artists, writers, and composers have indulged in daydreaming and reverie.

NO   Such dreamers include, Miró, Debussy, Dostoevsky, and Dickinson.

YES   Such dreamers include Miró, Debussy, Dostoevsky, and Dickinson.

YES Such dreamers include, of course, Miró, Debussy, Dostoevsky, and Dickinson. [The comma after *of course* is necessary to set off the phrase from the rest of the sentence.] ❖

EXERCISE 24-4

Consulting section 24c, insert commas to separate items in a series. If a sentence needs no commas, circle its number.

EXAMPLE   Recent studies show that people who watch television for more than a few straight hours are likely first to feel relaxed then to grow passive and eventually to develop self-contempt.

Recent studies show that people who watch television for more than a few straight hours are likely first to feel relaxed, then to grow passive, and eventually to develop self-contempt.

1. Viewers in the United States Canada West Germany and Italy aged 10 through 82 participated in a carefully designed study.
2. Participants agreed that for one week they would carry beepers listen for a signal about seven times a day and immediately fill in a form about their current mood and mental activity.
3. The participants were told to watch whatever amount of television they normally did and to do nothing special during the week of the study.
4. When viewing stretched on for hours, the viewers' responses showed that they lost their ability to concentrate that they felt increasingly unhappy and lonely and that they experienced guilt and anxiety.
5. A less expected problem was that after seeing so many beautiful competent captivating people on television the viewers felt inadequate and unable to compete.

24d Using a comma to separate coordinate adjectives

PATTERN FOR COMMAS WITH COORDINATE ADJECTIVES 107

coordinate adjective, coordinate adjective noun

Coordinate adjectives are two or more adjectives° that equally modify a noun°. Separate coordinate adjectives with commas (unless the coordinate adjectives are joined by a coordinating conjunction such as *and* or *but*).

COORDINATE ADJECTIVES

The **huge, restless** crowd waited for the concert to begin. [Both *huge* and *restless* modify *crowd*.]

The audience cheered happily when the **pulsating, rhythmic** music filled the stadium. [Both *pulsating* and *rhythmic* modify *music*.]

CUMULATIVE (NONCOORDINATE) ADJECTIVES

The concert featured **several new** bands. [*New* modifies *bands;* *several* modifies *new bands*.]

Each had a **distinctive musical** style. [*Musical* modifies *style; distinctive* modifies *musical style*.]

If you are not sure whether adjectives need a comma between them, use the "Tests for Coordinate Adjectives" in Chart 108.

TESTS FOR COORDINATE ADJECTIVES 108

If either test given here works, the adjectives are coordinate and need a comma between them.

- Can the order of the adjectives be reversed without changing the meaning or creating nonsense? If yes, use a comma.

  NO   The concert featured **new several** bands. (Only *several new* makes sense.)

  YES   The **huge, restless** (or *restless, huge*) crowd waited for the concert to begin.

  NO   Each had a **musical distinctive** style. (Only *distinctive musical* makes sense.)

  YES   The audience cheered happily as the **rhythmic, pulsating** (or *pulsating, rhythmic*) music filled the stadium.

- Can the word *and* be inserted between the adjectives? If yes, use a comma.

  NO   The concert featured **new and several** bands.

  YES   The **large and restless** crowd waited.

❖ COMMA CAUTION: (1) Do not put a comma after a final coordinate adjective and the noun it modifies. (2) Do not put a comma between adjectives that are not coordinate.❖

EXERCISE 24-5

Consulting section 24d, insert commas to separate coordinate adjectives. If a sentence needs no commas, circle its number.

EXAMPLE   The lively bright bird known as the parakeet was first imported to England from Australia in 1840.

The lively, bright bird known as the parakeet was first imported to England from Australia in 1840.

1. Small colourful parakeets were one of the best-loved pets of the nineteenth century.
2. No upper-class British parlour was considered fashionable without a cage of several singing parakeets.
3. Parakeets are small sturdy parrots who use their strong curved beaks for husking seeds.
4. Their feet have two toes pointing forward and two toes pointing backward, a highly unusual feature that makes for effortless efficient climbing—even in a cage.
5. Some parakeet owners report that their birds are able to speak a few short simple words after some persistent coaching.

24e Using commas to set off nonrestrictive (nonessential) elements; not setting off restrictive (essential) elements

Perhaps the most difficult comma decisions are those related to **restrictive (essential)** elements and **nonrestrictive (nonessential)** elements. The comma usage rules themselves are easy. The difficult part comes in understanding what *restrictive, essential, nonrestrictive,* and *nonessential* mean. Before trying to master the rules, use Chart 109 to become familiar with the meaning of these terms. Then apply the definitions as you closely reread your writing and analyze what you want your reader to understand from your sentences.

Here are additional examples of restrictive and nonrestrictive elements.

RESTRICTIVE ELEMENTS

Some people **in my neighbourhood** enjoy jogging. [The reader needs the information *in my neighbourhood* to know which people

DEFINITIONS OF "RESTRICTIVE" AND "NONRESTRICTIVE" 109

■ A **restrictive element** contains information **essential** for the reader to understand fully the meaning of the word or words that it modifies. It limits ("restricts") what it modifies.

Some provinces retest drivers **over age 65** to check their driving competency.

The prepositional phrase° *over age 65* limits the word *drivers* so that a reader understands which drivers are being retested (not all drivers, only those over age 65). Therefore, *over age 65* is restrictive.

■ A **nonrestrictive element** is **not essential** for a reader to understand fully the word or words that it modifies. It describes but does not limit (does not "restrict") what it modifies.

My parents, **who both are over age 65,** took a defensive driving course last year.

The relative clause° *who both are over age 65* describes *my parents,* but it is not essential to a reader's understanding which parents took a defensive driving course last year. Therefore, *who both are over age 65* is nonrestrictive.

enjoy jogging. The information is essential, so commas are not used.]

Some people **who are in excellent physical condition** enjoy jogging. [The reader needs the information *who are in excellent physical condition* to know which people enjoy jogging. The information is essential, so commas are not used.]

NONRESTRICTIVE ELEMENTS

An energetic person, Anna Hom enjoys jogging. [Without knowing that Anna Hom is energetic, the reader can understand that Anna Hom enjoys jogging. The information is not essential, so commas are used.]

Anna Hom, **who is in excellent physical condition,** enjoys jogging. [Without knowing that Anna Hom is in excellent physical condition, the reader can understand the information that Anna Hom enjoys jogging. The information is not essential, so commas are used.]

Anna Hom enjoys jogging, **which is also my favourite pastime.** [Without knowing about my favourite pastime, the reader can understand the information that Anna Hom enjoys jogging. The information is not essential, so commas are used.]

Once you understand the terms *restrictive, essential, nonrestrictive,* and *nonessential,* use Chart 110 to get to know the patterns for commas with nonrestrictive (nonessential) elements.

PATTERN FOR COMMAS WITH NONRESTRICTIVE ELEMENTS   110

- **Nonrestrictive element,** independent clause.
- Beginning of independent clause, **nonrestrictive element,** end of independent clause.
- Independent clause, **nonrestrictive element.**

✤ COMMA CAUTION: Remember, a restrictive element is essential. Do not set it off with commas (or any other punctuation) from the rest of the sentence.✤

---

1 | **Using commas to set off nonrestrictive (nonessential) clauses and phrases**

Adjective clauses usually begin with relative pronouns or relative adverbs, such as *who, whom, that, which,* and *where.* Set nonrestrictive (nonessential) adjective clauses off with commas.

NONRESTRICTIVE CLAUSES

Farming, **which is a major source of food production,** may not always be dependent on the weather. [*Farming* in this sentence is not meant to be restricted by *which is a major source of food production,* so the information is not essential and commas are used.]

Organic farmers, **who use only natural substances to produce food,** disapprove of the widespread use of chemicals in commercial agriculture. [*Organic farmers* in this sentence is not meant to be restricted by *who use only natural substances to produce food,* so the information is not essential and commas are used.]

RESTRICTIVE CLAUSES

Much food **that is canned or frozen** is grown by the same large companies **that process it for consumption.** [The first restrictive

458

clause limits the general word *food* to only food that is canned or frozen; the second one restricts the large companies to only those that process the food for consumption. The information in both cases is essential, and so commas are not used.]

❖ USAGE ALERT: In adjective clauses, use the relative pronoun *who* to refer to people. To refer to animals or things, some writers use the relative pronoun *which* both for restrictive and for nonrestrictive clauses. Other writers reserve *which* for nonrestrictive clauses and use *that* for restrictive clauses. You can follow either practice as long as you are consistent in each piece of writing.❖

A **phrase** is a group of related words without a subject°, a predicate°, or both. Set nonrestrictive (nonessential) phrases off with commas.

NONRESTRICTIVE PHRASES

Farmers, **wanting the best possible yields,** use many techniques to enhance their crops' growth. [*Farmers* in this sentence is not meant to be limited by the phrase *wanting the best possible yields,* so the information is not essential and commas are used.]

RESTRICTIVE PHRASES

Farmers **rejecting all pesticide use** are very hard to find. [*Farmers* in this sentence is meant to be narrowed to only those rejecting all pesticide use, so the information is essential and commas are not used.]

2 | Using commas to set off nonrestrictive appositives

An **appositive** is a word or group of words that renames the noun° or noun group preceding it. A **nonrestrictive appositive** is not essential for the identification of what it is renaming; it is set off by commas.

NONRESTRICTIVE APPOSITIVE

The agricultural scientist, **a new breed of farmer,** controls the farming environment. [The appositive *a new breed of farmer* is not essential in identifying who controls the farming environment, so the nonrestrictive appositive is set off with commas.]

Most appositives are nonrestrictive (nonessential). Once the name of something is given, words renaming it are not usually necessary to specify or limit it even more. In some cases, however, appositives are restrictive (essential) and are not set off with commas.

RESTRICTIVE APPOSITIVE

The agricultural scientist **Wendy Singh** has helped develop a new fertilization technique. [The appositive *Wendy Singh* is essential in identifying exactly which agricultural scientist has developed the new fertilization technique, so the restrictive appositive is not set off with commas.]

EXERCISE 24-6

Consulting section 24e and using your knowledge of restrictive and nonrestrictive clauses and phrases, insert commas as needed. If a sentence is correct, circle its number.

EXAMPLE   Elena Piscopia who began to study Aristotle at the age of seven took the examination for her doctoral degree.

Elena Piscopia, who began to study Aristotle at the age of seven, took the examination for her doctoral degree.

1. Elena Piscopia a resident of Venice was the first woman to receive a doctoral degree.
2. Many university officials reflecting the beliefs of their time opposed Elena's goal of higher education.
3. The doctoral examination of a woman a unique phenomenon in 1678 drew crowds of curious spectators.
4. Elena Piscopia who had prepared carefully for her questioners completed the examination easily.
5. Her replies which were given entirely in Latin amazed her examiners with their clarity and brilliance.
6. Elena Piscopia's father who was an exceptionally enlightened man for his time supported and encouraged his daughter's education.
7. Other women who lived in past centuries were not so lucky.
8. Christine de Pisane widowed at 25 turned to writing to support herself and her three children.
9. She found herself unprepared and taught herself a complete course of study that included Latin, history, philosophy, and literature.
10. She later wrote *The City of Ladies* a book about women leading creative lives.

24f Using commas to set off transitional and parenthetical expressions, contrasts, words of direct address, and tag sentences

Words, phrases°, or clauses° that interrupt a sentence but do not change its essential meaning should be set off, usually with commas. (Dashes or parentheses can also set material off; see sections 29a and 29b.)

Conjunctive adverbs such as *however* and *therefore* (for a complete list, see Chart 49 in section 7f) and **transitional expressions** such as *for example* and *in addition* (for a complete list, see Chart 23 in section 4d-1) can express connections within sentences. When they do, set them off with commas.

The Niagara Peninsula, **therefore,** is well suited to viticulture.

The Hillebrand and Inniskillen Wineries are located there, **for example.**

❖ COMMA CAUTION: Use a semicolon or a period—not a comma—before the conjunctive adverb or a transitional expression that falls between independent clauses. If you use a comma, you will create the error known as a comma splice (see Chapter 14).❖

Parenthetical expressions are "asides," additions to sentences that the writer thinks of as extra. Set them off with commas.

Sales of Canadian tobacco, **according to recent statistics,** have been steadily decreasing.

Canadian tobacco farmers, **sad to say,** must develop other means of support.

Expressions of contrast describe something by stating what it is not. Set them off with commas.

Feeding the world's population is a serious problem, **but not an intractable one.**

We must work against world hunger continuously, **not just when emergencies develop.**

Words of **direct address** indicate the person or group spoken to. Set them off by commas.

Join me, **brothers and sisters,** to end hunger.

Your contribution to the Relief Fund, **Steve,** will help us greatly.

Tag sentences consist of a verb°, a pronoun°, and often the word *not,* generally contracted. Set off tag sentences with commas. If the tag sentence is a question, end it with a question mark.

> Worldwide response to the Ethiopian famine was impressive, **wasn't it?**

> Response to future crises will be as generous, **I hope.**

EXERCISE 24-7

Consulting section 24f, add necessary commas to set off transitional, parenthetical, and contrasting elements, words of direct address, and tag sentences.

EXAMPLE   Writer's block it seems to me is a misunderstood phenomenon.

> *Writer's block, it seems to me, is a misunderstood phenomenon.*

1. Inability to write some say stems from lack of discipline and a tendency to procrastinate.

2. Therefore according to this thinking the only way to overcome writer's block is to exert more willpower.

3. But writer's block can be a complex psychological event that happens to conscientious and hard-working people not just the procrastinators.

4. Strange as it may seem such people are often unconsciously rebelling against their own self-tyranny and rigid standards of perfection.

5. If I told you my fellow writer that all it takes to start writing again is to quit punishing yourself you would think I was crazy wouldn't you.

24g   Using commas to set off quoted words from explanatory words

Use a comma to set off quoted words from short explanations in the same sentence. This rule holds whether the explanatory words come before, between, or after the quoted words.

PATTERNS FOR COMMAS WITH QUOTED WORDS   111

- Explanatory words, "Quoted words."
- "Quoted words," explanatory words.
- "Quoted words begin," explanatory words, "quoted words continue."

Speaking of ideal love, the poet William Blake wrote, "Love seeketh not itself to please."

"My love is a fever," said William Shakespeare about love's passion.

"I love no love," proclaimed poet Mary Coleridge, "but thee."

This use of commas is especially important in communicating conversations or other direct discourse. Explanatory words like *she said, they replied,* and *he answered* are called **speaker tags,** and they are always set off from immediately following words of direct discourse in the ways shown in the pattern chart.

Because explanatory words such as *that* or *as* create a different kind of grammatical setting (such as a noun clause° or a subject complement°) for the quoted words, do not separate the explanatory words from the quoted words with a comma. (For capitalization in quotations, see 30c.)

Shakespeare also wrote that "Love's not Time's fool."

The duke describes the duchess as being "too soon made glad."

Shaw's quip "Love is a gross exaggeration of the difference between one person and everybody else" delights me.

Sometimes words a person has spoken or written are conveyed through indirect discourse. The writer does not use direct quotation but instead paraphrases material. Do not use a comma after *that* in indirect discourse.

Shakespeare also wrote that people should be true to themselves.

❖ COMMA CAUTION: When quoted words end with a question mark or an exclamation point, keep that punctuation even if explanatory words follow.

QUOTED WORDS *"O Romeo! Romeo!"*

NO	"O Romeo! Romeo!," called Juliet as she stood at her window.
NO	"O Romeo! Romeo," called Juliet as she stood at her window.
YES	"O Romeo! Romeo!" called Juliet as she stood at her window.

QUOTED WORDS *"Wherefore art thou Romeo?"*

NO	"Wherefore art thou Romeo?," continued Juliet as she thought of her new-found love.
NO	"Wherefore art thou Romeo," continued Juliet as she thought of her new-found love.
YES	"Wherefore art thou Romeo?" continued Juliet as she thought of her new-found love.❖

EXERCISE 24-8

Consulting section 24g, punctuate the following dialogue correctly. If a sentence is correct, circle its number.

EXAMPLE   "Was anyone with the injured boy?," asked the admissions clerk.

"Was anyone with the injured boy?" asked the admissions clerk.

1. "His father" replied the ambulance driver "but he's unconscious."
2. "This boy looks like he needs surgery, but he is the son of the surgeon now on duty" said the clerk.
3. She explained in an agitated voice "Surgeons do not operate on their own family members."
4. "How can he be the surgeon's son when his father is still in the ambulance?" asked the driver.
5. With a disgusted look, the clerk told the driver "The surgeon is the boy's mother."

24h Using commas in dates, names, addresses, and numbers according to accepted practice

When you write dates, names, and numbers, be sure to use commas according to accepted practice.

RULES FOR COMMAS WITH DATES   112

- Use a comma between the date and the year: **July 20, 1969.**
- Use a comma between the day and the date: **Sunday,** July 20, 1969.
- Within a sentence, use a comma on both sides of the year in a full date.

Everyone wanted to be near a television set on **July 20, 1969,** to watch Armstrong emerge from the lunar landing module.

- Do not use a comma in a date that contains the month with only a day or the month with only a year. Also, do not use a comma in a date that contains only the season and year.

    The major news story during **July 1969** was the moon landing; news coverage was especially heavy on **July 21.**

RULES FOR COMMAS WITH DATES (*continued*)

■ An inverted date takes no commas: **20 July 1969.**

People stayed near their television sets on **20 July 1969** to watch the moon landing.

RULES FOR COMMAS WITH NAMES, PLACES, AND ADDRESSES 113

■ When an abbreviated title (Jr., M.D., Ph.D.) comes after a person's name, use a comma between the name and the title—**Rosa Gonzales**, M.D.—and also after the title if it is followed by the rest of the sentence:

The jury listened closely to the expert testimony of **Rosa Gonzales**, M.D., last week.

■ When you invert a person's name, use a comma to separate the last name from the first: **Whiteford**, Robert Karl.

■ Use a comma to separate the names of a city and province or territory: **Estevan, Saskatchewan**. If the city and province fall within a sentence, use a comma after the province as well, unless the province name ends the sentence and thus is followed by a period, question mark, or exclamation point.

Estevan, **Saskatchewan**, recorded the highest number of hours of sunshine in Canada in 1993.

■ When you write a complete address as part of a sentence, use a comma to separate all the items, with the exception of the postal code. The postal code follows the province after a double space but no comma. Also, do not follow the postal code with a comma.

I wrote to **Mr. U. Lern**, **10-01 Rule Road**, **Scarborough**, **Ontario M1P 2J7** for the instruction manual.

RULES FOR COMMAS WITH LETTERS 114

■ For the opening of an informal letter, use a comma:

Dear Betty,

For the opening of a business or formal letter, use a colon (:). ➜

465

RULES FOR COMMAS WITH LETTERS (*continued*)

- For the close of a letter, use a comma.

  Sincerely yours,   Best regards,
  Love,   Very truly yours,

RULES FOR COMMAS WITH NUMBERS   115

The SI—the international system of metric measurements used in Canada—does not use commas in large numbers. Instead, it uses spaces to separate sets of three digits. Nevertheless, the use of commas in numbers remains common in Canada. This chart lists rules for both number systems.

1. Rules for numbers in SI

- Counting from the right, put a space after every three digits in numbers with more than four digits: **72 867   156 567 066**

- A space is optional for most four-digit numbers. Use a consistent style within a given piece of writing.

  $ 1867 $ 1 867
  1867 km   1 867 km
  1867 potatoes   1 867 potatoes

  Always use a space in four-digit numbers when they are aligned in columns in a table or a chart.

- Do not use a space in four-digit years, in addresses, or in page numbers.

2. Rules for numbers in systems using commas

- Counting from the right, put a comma after every three digits in numbers with more than four digits: **72,867   156,567,066**

- A comma is optional for four-digit numbers. Use a consistent style within a given piece of writing.

  $ 1867 $ 1,867
  1867 km   1,867 km
  1867 potatoes   1,867 potatoes

- Do not use a comma for a four-digit year: **1990** (a year of five digits or more gets a comma: **25,000 B.C.**); in an address of four digits or more: **12161 Dean Drive;** or in a page number of four digits or more: **see page 1338**

RULES FOR COMMAS WITH NUMBERS (continued)
3 Use a comma to separate related measurements written as words: **five feet, four inches.** 4 Use a comma to separate a scene from an act in a play: **Act II, scene iv** 5 Use a comma to separate a reference to a page from a reference to a line: **page 10, line 6**

EXERCISE 24-9

Consulting section 24h, insert commas where they are needed. If a sentence is correct, circle its number.

EXAMPLE   The heaviest hailstone recorded in Canada fell on Cedoux Saskatchewan.

The heaviest hailstone recorded in Canada fell on Cedoux, Saskatchewan.

1. With a rainfall of 6655 mm, Henderson Lake British Columbia has the most annual precipitation in the country.
2. Burgeo Newfoundland has the second highest average annual precipitation with 1699.7 mm.
3. The warmest temperature in Canada—45 degrees Celsius—was recorded on July 5 1937 at Midale Saskatchewan.
4. Windsor Ontario with more than 200000 population holds the record for the highest average number of days per year with thunderstorms: 34 days.
5. Snag Yukon Territory has the record for the coldest temperature ever recorded in Canada; it was minus 63 degrees Celsius on February 3 1947.

24i Using commas to clarify meaning

Sometimes you will need to use a comma to clarify the meaning of a sentence, even though no other rule calls for one.

NO   Of the gymnastic team's twenty five were injured.

YES   Of the gymnastic team's twenty, five were injured.

NO	Those who can practise many hours a day.
YES	Those who can, practise many hours a day.
NO	George dressed and performed for the sellout crowd.
YES	George dressed, and performed for the sellout crowd.

EXERCISE 24-10

Consulting section 24i, insert commas to prevent misreading. If a sentence is correct, circle its number.

EXAMPLE   Though controversial subliminal learning appeals to many people.

Though controversial, subliminal learning appeals to many people.

1. Using specially prepared tape recorders communicate hidden messages to listeners.
2. Some people who want to learn supposedly without effort by listening to the tape.
3. To prevent shoplifting twenty major department stores started using subliminal tapes.
4. Of the twenty nine reported pilferage had decreased by about 37 percent.
5. Many people worry that governments or businesses might use subliminal learning to control people against their will.

 Avoiding misuse of the comma

Using commas correctly helps you deliver your meaning to your reader. As a writer, you frequently have to make decisions about whether a comma is needed. If as you are drafting° you are in doubt about a comma, insert and circle it clearly so that you can go back to it later when you are revising° and think through whether it is correct. Throughout this chapter, most sections that discuss a correct use of the comma include a comma caution to alert you to a related misuse of the comma. This section summarizes the most frequent misuses of the comma.

1 | **Avoiding misuse of a comma with coordinating conjunctions**

Section 24a discusses the correct use of commas with sentences joined by coordinating conjunctions°. Do not put a comma *after* a coordinating conjunction that joins two independent clauses° unless another rule makes it necessary. Also, do not use commas to separate two items joined with a coordinating conjunction.

NO	The sky was dark grey **and,** it looked like dusk.
YES	The sky was dark grey, and it looked like dusk.
NO	**The moon, and the stars** were shining last night.
YES	The moon and the stars were shining last night.

 Avoiding misuse of a comma with subordinating conjunctions and prepositions

Do not put a comma *after* a subordinating conjunction° or a preposition° unless another rule makes it necessary.

NO	**Although, the storm brought high winds,** it did no damage.
YES	**Although the storm brought high winds,** it did no damage.
NO	The storm did no damage **although, it brought high winds.**
YES	The storm did no damage **although it brought high winds.**
NO	People expected worse **between, the high winds and the heavy downpour.**
YES	People expected worse **between the high winds and the heavy downpour.**

---

3 **Avoiding misuse of commas to separate items**

Section 24c discusses the correct use of commas with items in a series. Do not use a comma *before* the first or *after* the last item in a series, unless another rule makes it necessary.

NO	The gymnasium was decorated with, **pictures of beavers, Mounties, and Canadian prime ministers** for Canada Day.
NO	The gymnasium was decorated with **pictures of beavers, Mounties, and Canadian prime ministers,** for Canada Day.

YES The gymnasium was decorated with **pictures of beavers, Mounties, and Canadian prime ministers** for Canada Day.

Section 24d discusses the correct use of commas with coordinate adjectives°. Do not put a comma after the final coordinate adjective and the noun it modifies. Also, do not use a comma between noncoordinate adjectives.

NO The **huge, restless,** crowd waited.

YES The **huge, restless** crowd waited.

NO The concert featured **several, new** bands.

YES The concert featured **several new** bands.

---

4 Avoiding misuse of commas with restrictive elements

Section 24e discusses the correct use of commas with restrictive (essential) elements° and nonrestrictive (nonessential) elements°. Do not use a comma to set off a restrictive (essential) element from the rest of a sentence.

NO Vegetables, **stir-fried in a wok,** are uniquely crisp and flavourful. [The information about being stir-fried in a wok is essential, so it is not set off with commas.]

YES Vegetables **stir-fried in a wok** are uniquely crisp and flavourful.

---

5 Avoiding misuse of commas with quotations

Section 24g discusses the correct use of commas with quoted material. Do not use a comma to set off indirect discourse° (often signalled by *that* or *as*).

NO Jon **said that, he likes stir-fried vegetables.**

YES Jon **said that he likes stir-fried vegetables.**

YES Jon **said, "I like stir-fried vegetables."**

| 6 | **Avoiding use of a comma to separate a subject from its verb, a verb from its object, a verb from its complement, and a preposition from its object** |

NO **Orville and Wilbur Wright, made** their first successful airplane flights on December 17, 1903. [As a rule, do not let a comma separate a subject° from its verb°.]

YES **Orville and Wilbur Wright made** their first successful airplane flights on December 17, 1903.

NO These inventors enthusiastically **tackled, the problems** of powered flight and aerodynamics. [As a rule, do not let a comma separate a verb from its object°.]

YES These inventors enthusiastically **tackled the problems** of powered flight and aerodynamics.

NO Flying has **become, both** an important industry and a popular hobby. [As a rule, do not let a comma separate a verb from its complement°.]

YES Flying has **become both** an important industry and a popular hobby.

NO Air Canada, which was founded in 1937 as Trans-Canada Airlines, today carries passengers **to, destinations worldwide.** [As a rule, do not let a comma separate a preposition° from its object.]

YES Air Canada, which was created in 1937 as Trans-Canada Airlines, today carries passengers **to destinations worldwide.**

Because the comma occurs so frequently, advice against overusing it sometimes clashes with a rule requiring it. In such cases, follow the rule that calls for the comma.

The circular design of Lester B. Pearson Airport, Mississauga, Ontario, was an experiment intended to improve passenger convenience. [Although the comma after *Ontario* separates the subject and verb, it is required because the place name is set off from the rest of the sentence; see 24h.]

EXERCISE 24-11

Some deliberately misused commas have been added in these sentences. Consulting 24j and the other sections in this chapter that are referred to in 24j, delete unneeded commas. If a sentence is correct, circle its number.

EXAMPLE Large North American cities experienced a cultural flowering during the 1920s, and nurtured a diversity of cultures.

Large North American cities experienced a cultural flowering during the 1920s and nurtured a diversity of cultures.

1. In the 1920s, the Harlem Renaissance, was not confined to New York City; Harlem was only one of several, African-American urban districts where the arts flourished during this decade.

2. Black urban singers began to attract a national audience and, Harlem surpassed Broadway in the originality of its musical revues, poetry, and fiction.

3. One of the leading poets of the Harlem Renaissance, was Claude McKay, who arrived in the United States from Jamaica in 1912 at the age of twenty-three.

4. He studied briefly at Booker T. Washington's, famous Tuskegee Institute in Alabama.

5. In 1917, he moved to Harlem, where he published his first poem.

6. McKay said that, poetry was his vehicle of protest, and he wrote his 1919 poem "If We Must Die" in response to, the race riots of that year.

7. In fact, Harlem was a neighbourhood seething in revolt, and racial pride.

8. Marcus Garvey, and his Universal Negro Improvement Association sought to transport blacks to, a new and better life in Africa.

9. Garvey, who was born in Jamaica like Claude McKay, was one of the first people, who taught African Americans that black is beautiful.

10. The Harlem Renaissance continued through 1945, when writers from Langston Hughes and Richard Wright to Zara Neale Hurston and Margaret Walker launched their great literary careers.

Focus on
Revising

REVISING YOUR WRITING

If you make comma errors when you write, go back to your writing and locate the errors. Using this chapter as a resource, revise your writing to correct the errors.

CASE STUDY: REVISING FOR CORRECT USE OF COMMAS

In these case studies, you can observe a student writer revising. Then you have the chance to revise other student writing on your own.

Observation

A student wrote the following draft for a course called Introduction to Geography. This material includes excellent specific details, but the draft's effectiveness is diminished by the presence of comma errors.

Read through the draft. The errors are highlighted and explained. Before you look at the student's revision, revise the material yourself. Then compare your version and the student's.

space or comma missing in a number of five digits: 24h

commas missing between items in a series: 24c

comma missing before coordinating conjunction linking independent clauses: 24a

commas missing between items in a series: 24c

In 1990, Canada produced 68331 tonnes of coal most of it from Alberta British Columbia Saskatchewan and Nova Scotia. Its worth was almost $2 billion, an indication of the continuing importance of this centuries-old industry. Such statistics do not however include the cost in terms of human life. Mining is frequently dangerous but coal mining is particularly hazardous because it exposes miners to deep tunnels soft rock dust explosives and vulnerable ventilation systems. In coal mines accidents and fatalities

comma missing to set off nonrestrictive appositive: 24e-2

commas missing to set off conjunctive adverb: 24f

comma missing after introductory phrase: 24b–2

→

occur more often than in other mines because the rock strata are usually weaker and methane gas may be present.

Springhill Nova Scotia famous as the birthplace of Anne Murray has been the site of numerous coal-mining disasters. In Springhill a town that once had the deepest mine in Canada 424 mine workers lost their lives from 1881 to 1969. In February 1891 125 miners died in an explosion and in November 1956 an accident killed 39 men, although the tragedy would have been worse if not for the rescue of 88 other trapped men. On October 23 1958 after a tunnel collapse crushed 74 miners 18 were rescued from nearly four kilometres down the deepest rescue operation ever carried out in Canada.

One of the survivors Douglas Jewkes who was rescued nine days after the tunnel caved in is reported to have said "I think this calls for a bottle of 7-Up." He explained that a vision of the soft drink had sustained him while he was trapped underground. Not surprisingly he was later hired by 7-Up. The event moved folk singers Ewan MacColl and Peggy Seeger to compose a ballad "The Springhill Mining Disaster" from which these lines are taken:

In the town of Springhill,
Nova Scotia,
Down in the dark of the

Margin annotations:

- commas missing with city and province names: 24h
- comma missing to set off nonrestrictive appositive: 24e-2
- commas missing to set off nonrestrictive clause: 24e-1
- commas missing with date: 24h
- comma missing to set off nonrestrictive appositive: 24e-2
- comma missing before quoted words: 24g
- comma missing after introductory words: 24b-3
- commas missing to set off nonrestrictive appositive: 24e-2
- commas missing to set off parenthetical expression: 24f
- comma missing to set off nonrestrictive appositive: 24e-2
- comma missing before coordinating conjunction linking independent clauses: 24a
- comma missing after introductory clause: 24b-1
- commas missing to set off nonrestrictive appositive: 24e-2
- comma missing to set off nonrestrictive clause: 24e-1

> Cumberland Mine,
> There's blood on the coal
> and the miners lie,
> In roads that never saw sun nor sky,
> Roads that never saw sun nor sky.

Here is how the student revised to correct the comma errors. Compare this version with your revision. Make sure that your revision has eliminated each of the errors highlighted in the draft.

In 1990, Canada produced 68331 tonnes of coal, most of it from Alberta, British Columbia, Saskatchewan, and Nova Scotia. Its worth was almost $2 billion, an indication of the continuing importance of this centuries-old industry. Such statistics do not, however, include the cost in terms of human life. Mining is frequently dangerous, but coal mining is particularly hazardous because it exposes miners to deep tunnels, soft rock, dust, explosives, and vulnerable ventilation systems. In coal mines, accidents and fatalities occur more often than in other mines because the rock strata are usually weaker and methane gas may be present.

Springhill, Nova Scotia, famous as the birthplace of Anne Murray, has been the site of numerous coal-mining disasters. In Springhill, a town that once had the deepest mine in Canada, 424 mine workers lost their lives from 1881 to 1969. In February 1891, 125 miners died in an explosion, and in November 1956, an accident killed 39 men, although the tragedy would have been worse if not for the rescue of 88 other trapped men. On October 23, 1958, after a tunnel collapse crushed 74 miners, 18 were rescued from nearly four kilometres down, the deepest rescue operation ever carried out in Canada.

One of the survivors, Douglas Jewkes, who was rescued nine days after the tunnel caved in, is reported to have said, "I think this calls for a bottle of 7-Up." He explained that a vision of the soft drink had sustained him while he was trapped underground. Not surprisingly, he was later hired by 7-Up. The event moved folk singers Ewan MacColl and Peggy Seeger to compose a ballad, "The Springhill Mining Disaster," from which these lines are taken:

> In the town of Springhill, Nova Scotia,
> Down in the dark of the Cumberland Mine,
> There's blood on the coal and the miners lie,
> In roads that never saw sun nor sky,
> Roads that never saw sun nor sky. →

Participation

A student wrote the following draft for a course called Introduction to Political Science. The assignment was to discuss an example of the power of consumers. The material is clear and logically presented, but the draft's effectiveness is diminished by comma errors.

Read through the draft. Then revise it to eliminate the errors. Also, make any additional revisions you think would improve the content, organization, and style of the material.

Consumers often feel that choosing a new car is a difficult time-consuming matter. Most automobile customers tend to concentrate on the price, the special features the look and the reputation of the car. Truly experienced informed car buyers however carefully investigate the car manufacturer's grievance procedures.

A common mistake that consumers make is to assume that the helpful friendly car salesperson will help resolve problems with the automobile after it is purchased. In fact the salesperson's job is essentially finished once the car is sold so a consumer with a complaint will usually hear "You'll have to talk to the service department."

If a car salesperson offers little or no help a consumer may feel cheated by the indifference. One reaction often felt by many people who end up with a lemon of a car is to write an angry letter to the chief executive officer of the automobile company. Before writing the consumer should realize that complaints to the manufacturers are referred back to the dealership. After all dealerships and manufacturers are not owned and managed by the same people.

In some cases consumers may benefit from legal advice. Different jurisdictions have varying "lemon laws" to help consumers who purchase defective cars. In some U.S. states for example the existence of a problem, that is unresolved, after six repair attempts by the dealership's service department can require a dealer to substitute a new vehicle. Chrysler Motors has the Customer Arbitration Board (CAB), which consists of a consumer advocate, a member of the general public, and an independent, technical expert. Any solution that the CAB proposes is binding on the dealer and Chrysler Motors.

It is comforting to know that a consumer, who buys a lemon of a car, is not always helpless isn't it? Sometimes a lemon can be made into lemonade, right?

25 The Semicolon

25a Using a semicolon between closely related independent clauses

When independent clauses° are clearly related in meaning, you can separate them with a semicolon instead of a period. The choice is yours in relation to the meaning you want your material to deliver. A period signals complete separation between independent clauses; a semicolon tells readers that the separation is softer.

SEMICOLON PATTERN I	116
Independent clause; independent clause.	

This is my husband's second marriage; it's the first for me.

—Ruth Sidel, "Marion Deluca"

A divorce is like an amputation; you survive, but there's less of you.

—Margaret Atwood

❖ COMMA CAUTION: Do not use only a comma between independent clauses, or you will create the error called a comma splice (see Chapter 14).❖

25b Using a semicolon before a coordinating conjunction joining independent clauses containing commas

When independent clauses° are linked by a coordinating conjunction (*and, but, or, nor, for, yet, so*), a comma should separate them (see 24a), but there is one exception. When one of the independent clauses contains a comma, you can use a semicolon before the coordinating conjunction. Choose according to what would be easier for your reader.

SEMICOLON PATTERN II 117

- Independent clause, one that contains a comma; coordinating conjunction independent clause.
- Independent clause; coordinating conjunction independent clause, one that contains a comma.
- Independent clause, one that contains commas; coordinating conjunction independent clause, one that contains a comma.

When the peacock has presented his back, the spectator will usually begin to walk around him to get a front view; but the peacock will continue to turn so that no front view is possible.

—FLANNERY O'CONNOR, "The King of the Birds"

For anything worth having, one must pay the price; and the price is always work, patience, love, self-sacrifice.

—JOHN BURROUGHS

25c Using a semicolon when conjunctive adverbs or other transitional expressions connect independent clauses

You can use a semicolon between two independent clauses when the second clause begins with a conjunctive adverb (*therefore, however;* for a complete list, see Chart 49 in 7f) or other transitional expression (*in fact, as a result;* for a complete list, see Chart 23 in 4d-1). Your other option is to use a period, creating two sentences.

SEMICOLON PATTERN III 118

- Independent clause; conjunctive adverb, independent clause..
- Independent clause; transitional expression, independent clause.

The average annual rainfall in the Okanagan Valley is less than 40 cm; **nevertheless,** it lies in the shadow of the rainy Cascade Mountains.

Irrigation came to the semidesert valley in the 1930s; **as a result,** it now produces much of British Columbia's—and even Canada's— fruit and wine.

❖ COMMA ALERTS: (1) Do not use *only* a comma between independent clauses connected by a conjunctive adverb or other words of transition, or you will create the error called a comma splice; see Chapter 14. (2) Usually use a comma *after* a conjunctive adverb or a transitional expression that begins an independent clause, although some writers omit the comma after short words, such as *then, next, soon.*❖

25d Using a semicolon between long or comma-containing items in a series

When a sentence contains a series of phrases° or clauses° that are long or that contain commas, use a semicolon, not a comma, to separate the items. This practice enables your reader to read without having to stop to figure out where one item in the series ends and the next begins. (For information on using commas in a series, see 24c.)

SEMICOLON PATTERN IV 119

Independent clause containing a series of items, any of which contain a comma; another item in the series; another item in the series.

Functioning as assistant chefs, the students chopped onions, green peppers, and parsley; sliced chicken and duck meat into strips; started a broth simmering; and filled a large, low, copper pan with oil before the head chef stepped to the stove.

25e Avoiding misuse of the semicolon

1 Not using a semicolon after an introductory phrase or between a dependent clause and an independent clause

NO   Once opened; the computer lab will be well used.

YES   Once opened, the computer lab will be well used.

NO   Although the new computers had arrived at the college; the computer lab was still being built.

YES   Although the new computers had arrived at the college, the computer lab was still being built.

2 Using a colon, not a semicolon, to introduce a list

NO   The newscast featured three major stories; the latest pictures of Uranus, a speech by the prime minister, and a series of prairie brush fires.

YES   The newscast featured three major stories: the latest pictures of Uranus, a speech by the prime minister, and a series of prairie brush fires.

EXERCISE 25-1

Consulting sections 25a-25e, insert semicolons where they are needed, and change any incorrectly used semicolons to correct punctuation. If a sentence is correct, circle its number.

EXAMPLE In the seventeenth century, the citizens of Holland became victims of tulip madness, this mania became so intense that regular businesses were neglected while people bought and sold tulips.

In the seventeenth century, the citizens of Holland became victims of tulip madness; this mania became so intense that regular businesses were neglected while people bought and sold tulips.

480

1. Tulips were first noted in Holland by Conrad Gesner in 1559, he saw them in the garden of Counsellor Herwart, a person famous for growing exotic plants.

2. Herwart had gotten the onionlike bulbs from a friend travelling in Turkey, where tulips were a favourite flower, in fact, the tulip's name comes from a Turkish word for *turban*.

3. Growing tulips quickly became popular throughout Dutch society, it became a mark of good taste to have a garden full of them.

4. Soon, merchants and shopkeepers were competing to find the rarest specimens, consequently, prices for these prized bulbs soared.

5. As tulip bulb prices reached preposterous heights, Dutch businesses of all kinds began to suffer because money needed for other goods was tied up in tulip purchases.

6. In 1635, a person might invest 100000 florins to buy forty bulbs, but four tuns of beer cost 32 florins, twelve sheep 120 florins, 450 kilograms of cheese 100 florins, and a silver cup 60 florins.

7. In Amsterdam, a very rare tulip was exchanged for the following items; 4600 florins, an expensive, gilded carriage, and two grey horses, complete with harnesses, bridles, and bells.

8. Brokers began to trade tulips on the stock exchanges, therefore, Dutch nobles, farmers, merchants, servants, and street-sweepers alike found themselves growing richer as prices rose.

9. One merchant discovered that a rare bulb was missing after a messenger had made a delivery, an hour later he found the messenger finishing lunch, which included the "onion" he had taken from the merchant's office.

10. Although Holland's tulip madness has calmed down considerably today; growing tulips is an important industry in that country.

EXERCISE 25-2

Combine each set of sentences into one sentence containing two independent clauses. Use a semicolon between the two clauses. You may add, omit, revise, and rearrange words. Try to use all the patterns in this chapter. More than one revision may be correct, so be ready to explain the reasoning behind your decisions.

EXAMPLE   Roller coasters have been around for a long time. Today's roller coasters barely resemble their ancestors. Today's roller coasters are scientifically designed.

Roller coasters have been around for a long time; however, today's scientifically designed roller coasters barely resemble their ancestors.

1. The first roller coaster in North America was installed in the late nineteenth century. It was installed as part of an amusement park. The park was in the Coney Island section of New York City. It was named the "Switchback Gravity Pleasure Railway."

2. The first roller coaster was extremely primitive. It was built of wood. It had only two inclines. It reached a downhill speed of a mere ten kilometres per hour.

3. Riders got on at the top of the first incline. Riders climbed out when the train reached the bottom. Then the riders walked up the hill to the top of the second incline. Once again they climbed in for the ride to the bottom.

4. Soon a chain drive for roller coasters was developed. The chain drive powered the train on the uphill parts. Higher inclines could be built. The higher inclines gave riders a greater thrill.

5. Major breakthroughs in roller-coaster design occurred in the 1970s. Roller coaster designers drew on advanced knowledge from physics, mathematics, and human physiology. The designers used computer simulations to check their work.

26 The Colon

26a Using a colon after an independent clause to introduce a list, an appositive, or a quotation

You can use a colon to introduce statements that summarize, re-state, or explain what is said in an independent clause°.

> **COLON PATTERN I** 120
>
> - Independent clauselist.
> - Independent clause appositive.
> - Independent clause "Quoted words."

A colon can introduce a list only when the words before the colon are an independent clause. After phrases such as *the following* or *as follows,* a colon is usually required. A colon is not called for with the words *such as* or *including* (see 26d).

LISTED ITEMS

If you really want to lose weight, you need give up only three things: breakfast, lunch, and dinner.

The students' demands included the following: an expanded menu in the cafeteria, improved janitorial services, and more up-to-date textbooks.

A colon can introduce an appositive—a word or words that rename a noun° or pronoun°—but only if the introductory words are an independent clause.

APPOSITIVE

The UBC Museum of Anthropology has one outstanding exhibit: its collection of remarkable Northwest Coast Indian artifacts. [*Collection of ... artifacts* renames *outstanding exhibit.*]

A colon can introduce a quotation, but only if the introductory words are an independent clause°. Use a comma, not a colon, if the introductory words are not an independent clause (see 24b).

QUOTATION

The little boy in *E.T.* did say something neat: "How do you explain school to a higher intelligence?"

—GEORGE F. WILL, "Well, *I* Don't Love You, E.T."

❖ QUOTATION ALERT: When a quotation is more than four lines, it must be *displayed* on lines indented ten spaces (see 28a).❖

26b Using a colon between two independent clauses

When the first independent clause° explains or summarizes the second independent clause, a colon can separate them.

COLON PATTERN II	121
Independent clause: Independent clause.	

❖ CAPITALIZATION ALERT: You can use a capital letter or a lower-case letter for the first word of an independent clause that follows a colon. Whichever you choose, be consistent in each piece of writing. This handbook uses a capital letter.

We will never forget the first time we made dinner at home together: He got stomach poisoning and for four days was too sick to go to work.

—LISA BALADENDRUM, student ❖

26c Using a colon to separate standard material

TITLE AND SUBTITLE
A Brief History of Time: From the Big Bang to Black Holes

HOURS, MINUTES, AND SECONDS
The plane took off at 7:15 p.m.
The track star passed the halfway point at 1:23:02.

In the military services, hours and minutes are written without colons (and always use four digits):

The staff meeting originally scheduled for Tuesday at 0930 will be held Tuesday at 1430 instead.

CHAPTERS AND VERSES OF THE BIBLE
Psalms 23:1–3   Luke 3:13

MEMO FORM
To: Dean Kristen Olivero
From: Professor Daniel Black
Re: Student Work-Study Program

SALUTATION OF FORMAL OR BUSINESS LETTER
Dear Ms. Morgan:

For the use of colons in documenting sources, see 33c–33d.

26d Avoiding misuse of the colon

A complete independent clause° must precede a colon, except with standard material (see 26c). When you have not written an independent clause, do not use a colon.

NO   The cook bought: eggs, milk, cheese, and bread.

YES   The cook bought eggs, milk, cheese, and bread.

The words *such as, including, like,* and *consists of* can be tricky: Do not let them lure you into using a colon incorrectly (see 26a).

NO   The health board discussed a number of problems, **such as:** poor water quality, an aging sewage treatment system, and the lack of an alternative water supply.

YES	The health board discussed a number of problems, **such as** poor water quality, an aging sewage treatment system, and the lack of an alternative water supply.
YES	The health board discussed a number of problems: poor water quality, an aging sewage treatment system, and the lack of an alternative water supply.

Do not use a colon to separate a phrase° or dependent clause° from an independent clause.

NO	Day after day: the drought dragged on.
YES	Day after day, the drought dragged on.
NO	After the drought ended: the farmers celebrated.
YES	After the drought ended, the farmers celebrated.

EXERCISE 26-1

Consulting sections 26a-26d, insert colons where they are needed and delete unnecessary ones. If a sentence is correct, circle its number.

EXAMPLE   Most runners ignore how slim their chances are of winning the New York Marathon, about 1 in 26000.

Most runners ignore how slim their chances are of winning the New York Marathon: about 1 in 26000.

1. Chefs in the most fashionable restaurants in large cities report a new dessert craze; chocolate cake with a melting chocolate centre.
2. The chefs describe two principal types of cake: (1) those with a solid chocolate layer that melts in the oven and (2) those that are underbaked so the centre stays semiliquid.
3. Although ingredients for the two versions of the cake vary, three are common in recipes for both, chocolate, sugar, and butter.
4. Unfortunately: lots of calories are common to both.
5. A book used in many business courses today is *Business Ethics; Concepts and Cases.*
6. Its author describes the primary aim of the book in these words "To introduce the reader to the ethical concepts that are relevant to resolving moral issues in business."
7. Among artists married to artists, two couples illustrate some interesting dynamics of fame, Lee Krasner and Jackson Pollock, both respected today, although Pollock is far more famous; and Georgia O'Keeffe and photographer Alfred Stieglitz, with O'Keeffe more famous than Stieglitz, at least in the last years of the twentieth century.

8. Insurance companies classify adventurous people such as: astronauts, drivers of hydroplanes, and auto race drivers, as bad risks.

9. Calling: "Max, Max," Belinda ran through the forest.

10. Cadets;
This year's graduation ceremony begins at 1400 hours, but tell your parents 200 p.m., so that no one will be confused.

11. On April 8, 1974, Babe Ruth's home-run record was finally broken. Henry Aaron became the new home-run king.

12. In the past century, vaccines have been developed for five diseases, diphtheria, measles, polio, typhoid fever, and whooping cough.

13. To;   All Employees
From;   Management
Re;   Vacation Schedules

14. In *Silent Spring,* the environmentalist Rachel Carson wrote these words about pollution, "The chemical barrage has been hurled against the fabric of life."

15. The city's budget crisis carries a message, How long can government continue to spend beyond its means?

The Apostrophe

The apostrophe plays three major roles: It helps to form the possessive of nouns and some pronouns; it stands for one or more omitted letters; and it helps to form the plurals of letters and numerals. It does *not* help form plurals of nouns or the possessive case of personal pronouns.

27a Using an apostrophe to form the possessive case of nouns and indefinite pronouns

The **possessive case** serves to communicate ownership or close relationship.

OWNERSHIP	The writer's pen
CLOSE RELATIONSHIP	The novel's plot

Possession in nouns° and certain indefinite pronouns° can be communicated by phrases beginning with *of (comments of the instructor, comments of Professor Montana)* or by an apostrophe in combination with an *s (instructor's comments)*.

1 Adding *'s* to show possession when nouns and indefinite pronouns do not end in *s*

The **dean's** duties included working closely with the resident assistants. [*dean* = singular noun° not ending in *s*]

In one more year I will receive my **bachelor's** degree.
[*bachelor* = singular noun not ending in *s*]

They care about their **children's** futures. [*children* = plural noun not ending in *s*]

An **indefinite pronoun** refers to nonspecific persons or things (for example, *any, few, someone, no one;* see 7b and 11g).

The accident was really **no one's** fault. [*no one* = indefinite pronoun not ending in *s*]

| **2** | Adding *'s* to show possession when singular nouns end in *s* |

Most academic writers today use *'s* to show possession when singular nouns end in *s,* although some writers prefer to use only the apostrophe. Be consistent in each piece of writing. This handbook uses *'s.*

That **business's** system for handling complaints is inefficient.

Chris's ordeal ended.

Lee **Jones's** insurance is expensive.

When adding *'s* could lead to tongue-twisting pronunciation, practice varies. All writers use the apostrophe. Some writers do not add the *s;* others do, for consistency with other practices.

Charles **Dickens's** story "A Christmas Carol" is a classic tale.

| **3** | Using only an apostrophe to show possession when a plural noun ends in *s* |

The **boys'** statements were recorded.

The newspapers have publicized several **medicines'** severe side effects recently.

Three **months'** maternity leave is in the **workers'** contract.

| **4** | Adding *'s* to the last word in singular compound words and phrases |

His **mother-in-law's** corporation just bought out a competitor.

The **tennis player's** strategy was brilliant.

They wanted to hear **somebody else's** interpretation of the rule.

5	Adding *'s* to only the last noun in joint or group possession

Olga and Joanne's books are valuable. [Olga and Joanne own the books together.]

Anne Gagnon and Charles Gagnon's article on solar heating interests me. [Anne Gagnon and Charles Gagnon wrote the article together.]

6	Adding *'s* to each noun in individual possession

Olga's and Joanne's books are valuable. [Olga and Joanne each own some of the valuable books, but they do not own the books together.]

After the fire, **the doctor's and the lawyer's** offices had to be rebuilt. [The doctor and the lawyer had separate offices.]

❖ APOSTROPHE CAUTION: Do not use an apostrophe to indicate the plural form of a noun. ❖

27b Not using an apostrophe with the possessive forms of personal pronouns

Some pronouns have specific possessive forms, which do not include an apostrophe. Contrast them with contractions, discussed in 27c.

PRONOUN	POSSESSIVE FORM(S)
he	his
she	her, hers
it	its
we	our, ours
you	your, yours
they	their, theirs
who	whose

Be especially alert to *it's* and *its,* as well as *who's* and *whose,* which are frequently confused. (*It's* stands for *it is; its* is a personal pronoun showing possession. *Who's* stands for *who is; whose* is a personal pronoun showing possession.)

NO	The government has to balance **it's** budget.
YES	The government has to balance **its** budget.

NO	The professor **who's** class was cancelled is at a meeting of bird watchers.
YES	The professor **whose** class was cancelled is at a meeting of bird watchers.

❖ APOSTROPHE CAUTION: The following forms are nonstandard, so do not use them: *its', his', hers', her's, yours', your's, theirs', their's, whos',* and *our's.*❖

27c Using an apostrophe to stand for omitted letters, numbers, or words in contractions

Contractions are words from which one or more letters have been intentionally omitted and in which apostrophes are inserted to signal the omission. Contractions are common in speaking and in informal writing, but many readers dislike them in academic writing. A major exception is *o'clock* (which stands for *of the clock*). To choose between a contraction and the full phrase, consider your audience and the level of formality you want. Here is a list of some common contractions.

SOME COMMON CONTRACTIONS

aren't = are not	*she's* = she is, she has
can't = cannot	*there's* = there is
didn't = did not	*they're* = they are
don't = do not	*wasn't* = was not
he's = he is, he has	*we're* = we are
it's = it is	*weren't* = were not
I'd = I would, I had	*we've* = we have
I'm = I am	*who's* = who is
isn't = is not	*won't* = will not
let's = let us	*you're* = you are

Contractions can help to show informal speech or dialect, especially in dramatic or fiction writing.

> Scout **yonder's** been **readin'** ever since she was born, and she **ain't** even started school yet. You look right puny for **goin'** on seven.
>
> —HARPER LEE, *To Kill a Mockingbird*

Apostrophes also indicate the omission of the first two numerals in years. Avoid this contraction in academic writing.

The class of **'50** is having a reunion this year.

They moved from Ottawa to Victoria after the blizzard of **'78**.

27d Using *'s* to form plurals of letters, numerals, symbols, and words when used as terms

Some writers use *'s* to form plurals of letters, numerals, years, symbols, and words used as terms. Others use *s* alone. Either style is acceptable as long as one style is used throughout a piece of writing.

WITH *'s*

Billie always has trouble printing ***W's***.

The address includes six ***6's***.

These trends should continue through the ***1990's***.

The ***for's*** in the paper were all misspelled as ***four's***.

When the keys jammed, a series of ***&'s*** showed on the screen.

WITH *s* ALONE

Billie always has trouble printing ***Ws***.

The address includes six ***6s***.

These trends should continue through the ***1990s***.

The ***fors*** in the paper were all misspelled as ***fours***.

When the keys jammed, a series of ***&s*** showed on the screen.

❖ UNDERLINING ALERT: Always underline (or use italic type for) letters, numbers, symbols and words referred to as in the examples above. For plurals, do not underline (or use italics for) the *'s* or *s*.

```
Many first-graders had trouble writing 8's and pronouncing

eight's phonetically.
```

Many first-graders had trouble writing *8*’s and pronouncing *eight*’s phonetically.❖

27e Avoiding misuse of the apostrophe

Do not overuse apostrophes by inserting them where they do not belong. Chart 122 lists ways of avoiding the main type of apostrophe errors. If you tend to make apostrophe errors, use Chart 122 to diagnose the causes of your problem; then stay conscious of them as you edit (see 3d) your writing.

GUIDELINES FOR AVOIDING APOSTROPHE ERRORS   122

1. Do not use an apostrophe with the present-tense verb form.
   NO   Cholesterol **plays'** an important role in how long we live.
   YES Cholesterol **plays** an important role in how long we live.

2. Do not add an apostrophe at the end of a nonpossessive noun ending in *s.*
   NO   Medical **studies'** reveal that cholesterol is the primary cause of coronary heart disease.
   YES Medical **studies** reveal that cholesterol is the primary cause of coronary heart disease.

3. Use an apostrophe after the *s* in the possessive plural of a noun.
   NO   The medical community is seeking more information from **doctor's** investigations into heart disease.
   YES The medical community is seeking more information from **doctors'** investigations into heart disease.

4. Do not use an apostrophe to form a nonpossessive plural.
   NO   **Team's** of doctors are trying to predict who might be most harmed by cholesterol.
   YES **Teams** of doctors are trying to predict who might be most harmed by cholesterol.

EXERCISE 27-1

Consulting sections 27a and 27e, rewrite these sentences to insert *'s* or an apostrophe alone to make the words in parentheses show possession. Delete the parentheses.

EXAMPLE   Born in 1732, Franz-Josef Haydn, one of (Austria) most notable musicians, sang in (St. Stephan) Choir until, at age 16, his voice changed.

Born in 1732, Franz-Josef Haydn, one of Austria's most notable musicians, sang in St. Stephan's choir until, at age 16, his voice changed.

1. (Haydn) music has delighted (music lovers) ears for more than two centuries.
2. The (composer) symphonies are still performed frequently, with the "Surprise Symphony" a favourite at (children) concerts.
3. Apart from recognizing (Haydn) music, however, (today) concertgoers would find little else familiar at an eighteenth-century (orchestra) performance.
4. Eighteenth-century (musicians) powdered wigs, satin breeches, and white stockings, colourful and elegant, were meant to be noticed.
5. Contemporary orchestral (musicians) black garb, usually (women) dresses and (men) tuxedos, is meant to keep (concertgoers) attention focused on (Brahms), (Beethoven), (Ives), or (Strauss) music, not on the people playing it.
6. Also, eighteenth-century (players) musical instruments differed from modern ones, in both appearance and sound.
7. In fact, 163 of the Austrian (singer-composer) compositions were written for the *baryton*, a now-obsolete instrument similar to a viola or cello.
8. In 1760, Prince Paul (Esterhazy) offer to hire Haydn as court musician freed him to pursue his (life) main purpose: composing.
9. After his (patron) death, Haydn left Austria to visit (London) musical world.
10. Although he died in 1809, this brilliant (music-maker) special legacy to Austria lives on because Haydn wrote his (homeland) national anthem.

EXERCISE 27-2

Consulting sections 27a, 27b, and 27e, rewrite these sentences so that each contains a possessive noun.

EXAMPLE   The Special Olympics is an international program promoting the physical fitness of mentally challenged children and adults.

> *The Special Olympics is an international program promoting mentally challenged children's and adults' physical fitness.*

1. Athletic competition is encouraged in accordance with the age and ability of the participants.
2. The training of these mentally challenged athletes takes place in schools and other institutions.

3. Handicaps of the participants do not prevent them from competing in sports from basketball to gymnastics and ice skating to wheelchair exercise.

4. The appeal of the competition for most athletes is the chance to participate in all the activities of their peers.

5. The perseverance of these competitors, in spite of major obstacles, is an inspiration to us all.

EXERCISE 27-3

Consulting all sections in this chapter, correct any errors in the use of apostrophes in the paragraph below.

(1) One of Albert Einsteins biographers tells about the famous physicists encounter with a little girl in his' neighbourhood. (2) The little girl stared at Einstein's soaking wet feet and said, "Mr. Einstein, youve come out without you'r boots again!" (3) Einstein laughed and, pulling up his trousers, replied, "Yes, and Ive forgotten my socks, too." (4) Most people arent as forgetful as Einstein, but sometimes our memories' let all of us down. (5) We may not be able to remember if our first job started in '81 or 82; we may forget whether our employers' husband spells his name with two ts or with one. (6) No one is absolutely sure how memory works. (7) Dr. Barbara Jones study of memory suggests that personality style's affect memory. (8) People with rigid personalities who's livelihoods depend on facts tend to have good memories. (9) Mr. Harry Lorayne and Dr. Laird Cermak's studies of memory each provide a different approach to improving that useful faculty. (10) Mr. Lorayne suggest's relating what you want to remember to something verbal or visual. (11) For instance, if you want to remember that your sister's-in-law's name is Rose, you would picture her wearing a rose corsage. (12) Dr. Cermaks suggestions include consideration of physiological factors. (13) He notes that doctors' are currently developing drugs that will prevent older people from losing the memories that are rightfully their's.

EXERCISE 27-4

Consulting all sections of this chapter, correct any errors in the use of apostrophes in the paragraph below.

(1) Many studies' have involved identical twins' who were separated at birth. (2) Identical twins come from a single fertilized egg that split's soon after conception, resulting in two fetuses' with identical genes. (3) Although identical twins may look like carbon copies of each other, theyre like snowflakes: no pair is exactly alike. (4) Every summer twins are the guests of

honour in Twinsburg, Ohio, which comes to life when over one thousand pair's of twins gather for the towns annual festival. (5) The conversation at the gathering usually involves twin's stories about tricking people by exchanging identities, about knowing each others thoughts, and about sharing secret's. (6) The stories' are entertaining, but many psychologists' find them informative as well.

28 Quotation Marks

Most commonly, quotation marks enclose **direct quotations**—spoken or written words from an outside source (see 28a). Quotation marks also set off some titles (see 28b), and they can call attention to words used in special senses (see 28c).

Always use quotation marks in pairs, and be especially careful not to omit the second (closing) quotation mark. **Double quotation marks** (" ") are standard. **Single quotation marks** (' ') are used only for quotation marks within quotation marks. (You may have noticed that in materials published in Great Britain, this convention is reversed.) In print, opening and closing quotation marks look slightly different from each other, but they look identical on a typewriter and many computer printers. Examples of both print and typewritten quotation marks are found in this chapter. For information about using brackets in quotations, see 29c; the ellipsis, see 29d; the slash, see 29e. For information about commas with quoted words, see 24g; for capitalizing letters with quotations, see 30c.

28a Using quotation marks to enclose direct quotations of not more than four lines

Direct quotations are exact words from a print or nonprint source. When you use a quotation, always check carefully that you have recorded it precisely as it appeared in the original (see also 31c-1).

1 Using double quotation marks to enclose short quotations

A quotation is considered "short" is it can be typed or handwritten to occupy no more than four lines on a page. Short quotations are enclosed in double quotation marks. Longer quotations are usually set off ("displayed") by indentation and line spacing, and they are not enclosed in quotation marks. The requirements for setting quotations off vary with different documentation styles. For advice about setting off quotations in specific documentation styles, see Chart 142 (MLA), Chart 143 (APA), Chart 144 (CM), and Chart 145 (CBE) in Chapter 33.

Whether a quotation is one or many lines, it must be documented; see Chapter 33. The examples in this chapter are in MLA parenthetical documentation.

Short Quotation

```
Hall explains the practicality of close conversational

distances: "If you are interested in something, your pupils

dilate; if I say something you don't like, they tend to

contract" (47).
```

```
Personal space "moves with us, expanding and contracting

according to the situation in which we find ourselves"

(Fisher, Bell, and Baum 149).
```

Any quotation marks that appear in the original source should also be used in a long (displayed) quotation.

Long Quotations (More Than Four Lines)

```
Robert Sommer, an environmental psychologist, uses literary

and personal analogies to describe personal space:

        Like the porcupines in Schopenhauer's fable, people

        like to be close enough to obtain warmth and

        comradeship but far enough away to avoid pricking one

        another. Personal space ... has been likened to a

        snail shell, a soap bubble, an aura, and "breathing

        room." (26)
```

❖ PUNCTUATION ALERT: In MLA documentation style, the period goes *after* the parenthetical reference for a short quotation (not displayed); the period goes *before* the parenthetical reference for a displayed quotation. ❖

2 | Using single quotation marks for quotations within quotations

When you quote four lines or less and the original words already contain quotation marks, use double quotations marks at the start and end of the directly quoted words. Then, substitute single quotation marks (' ') wherever there are double quotation marks in the original source.

ORIGINAL SOURCE

Personal space ... has been likened to a snail shell, a soap bubble, an aura, and "breathing room."

> —ROBERT SOMMER, *Personal Space: The Behavioral Bases of Design*, page 26

SINGLE QUOTATION MARKS WITHIN DOUBLE QUOTATION MARKS

Robert Sommer, an environmental psychologist, compares personal space to "a snail shell, a soap bubble, an aura, and 'breathing room'" (26).

3 | Using quotation marks correctly for short quotations of poetry and for direct discourse

A quotation of poetry is "short" if it is no more than three lines of the poem. As with short prose quotations, use double quotation marks to enclose the material. If you quote more than one line of poetry, use a slash with one space on each side to show the line divisions (see 29e).

> As Auden wittily defined personal space, "some thirty inches from my nose / The frontier of my person goes...."

❖ CAPITALIZATION ALERT: When you quote lines of poetry, follow the capitalization of your source. ❖

Quotation marks are also used to enclose speakers' words in **direct discourse°**. Whether you are reporting the exact words of a real speaker or making up dialogue in, for example, a short story, quotations marks let your readers know which words belong to the speaker and which words do not. Use double quotation marks at the beginning and end of a speaker's words, and start a new paragraph each time the speaker changes.

> Becky Tyde climbed up on Flo's counter, made room for herself beside an open tin of crumbly jam-filled cookies.
>
> "Are these any good?" she said to Flo, and boldly began to eat one. "When are you going to give us a job, Flo?"
>
> "You could go and work in the butcher shop," said Flo innocently. "You could go and work for your brother."
>
> "Roberta?" said Becky with a stagey sort of contempt. "You think I'd work for him?" Her brother who ran the butcher shop was named Robert but often called Roberta, because of his meek and nervous ways.
>
> —ALICE MUNRO, "Royal Beatings"

If one speaker's words require two or more paragraphs, use double quotation marks at the start of each paragraph *but* double quotations marks at the end of the last quoted paragraph *only*.

Indirect discourse reports what a speaker did. In contrast, direct discourse presents a speaker's exact words. Note that the difference between direct and indirect discourse is not only a matter of punctuation; usually the verb tenses differ. Do not enclose indirect discourse in quotation marks.

DIRECT DISCOURSE

The mayor said, "I intend to vote against that proposal."

INDIRECT DISCOURSE

The mayor said that he intended to vote against that proposal.

For advice on revising incorrect shifts between direct and indirect discourse, see 15a-4.

EXERCISE 28-1

Consulting section 28a, correct the use of double and single quotation marks. If a sentence is correct, circle its number.

EXAMPLE   As Margaret Laurence writes, "Freedom is more fragile than any of us in Canada would like to believe. I think again of F. R. Scott's words" "Freedom is a habit that must be kept alive by use.""

As Margaret Laurence writes, "Freedom is more fragile than any of us in Canada would like to believe. I think again of F. R Scott's words: 'Freedom is a habit that must be kept alive by use.'"

1. Canfield and Lebson write, No one understands the sleeping habits of these sharks.

2. In a poem written in 1628, Robert Hayman writes of Newfoundland, Where all are good, Fire, Water, Earth, and Aire, / What man made of these foure would not live there?

3. In his novel *Shoeless Joe*, which became the film *Field of Dreams*, W. P. Kinsella describes the moment of inspiration in the following way: There was silence in the room. Then a voice, stunning as thunder, clear and common as a train whistle—the voice of a ball-park announcer: "If you build it, he will come."

4. "Promises," said Hannah Arendt, are the uniquely human way of ordering the future.

5. According to Henry James, "Nothing ... will ever take the place of the good old fashion of "liking" a work of art or not liking it."

6. Pauline Kael, the movie critic, notes that "certain artists can, at moments in their lives, reach out and unify the audience" and in doing so give people the opportunity for a "shared response.

7. Don't let anyone convince you that you can't fulfil your ambitions, warned the speaker, or you surely won't.

8. Why have women passion, intellect, moral activity—these three—and a place in society where no one of the three can be exercised? asked Florence Nightingale in the 1850s.

9. "In seven cases, the report continued, outlets with the lowest prices had the highest percentages of defective merchandise.

10. Leslie Hanscom reports about the latest volume of the *Oxford English Dictionary*, Most of the new words are originating in the United States.

EXERCISE 28-2

Consulting section 28a, decide whether each sentence is direct or indirect discourse. Then rewrite each sentence in the other form. Be sure to make any changes needed for grammatical accuracy.

EXAMPLE   Clifton Fadiman once wrote that the playwright Charles MacArthur was having a hard time writing a visual joke for the movies. (indirect discourse)

"The playwright Charles MacArthur was having a hard time writing a visual joke for the movies," Clifton Fadiman once wrote.

1. Charlie Chaplin asked him what the problem was.

2. "How can I show a fat man slipping on a banana peel and still get a laugh? MacArthur asked.

3. MacArthur wondered if he should show the banana peel first, and then the man approaching and slipping on it. Or should he show the fat man first, the banana peel next, and then the man slipping on it?

4. Chaplin advised him against either one.

5. Chaplin told him, "Show the fat man approaching, then the banana peel. Next, show the fat man and the banana peel together. Then have the fat man step over the banana peel and disappear down a manhole."

28b Using quotation marks to enclose certain titles

When you refer to certain types of works by their titles, enclose the titles in quotation marks. Use quotation marks around the titles of short published works, like poems, short stories, essays, articles from periodicals, pamphlets, and brochures. Also use them around song titles and individual episodes of television or radio series.

Discuss the rhyme scheme of Andrew Marvell's "Delight in Disorder." [poem]

Have you read "Insecurity" by Neil Bissoondath? [short story]

One of the best sources I have found is "The Myth of Political Consultants." [magazine article]

"Shooting an Elephant" describes George Orwell's experience in Burma. [essay]

Underlining is used for titles of many other types of works, such as books and plays. A few titles are neither underlined or enclosed in quotation marks. (For useful lists showing how to present titles, see Chart 123 in 30e and Chart 124 in 30f).

❖ UNDERLINING ALERT: Underlining in typed or handwritten papers signals words that would appear in **italic type** if the paper were to be typeset. (Printed books, magazines, newspapers, and similar documents are "typeset.") If you use a computer and can produce italic type, you may choose either underlining or italics. Be consistent in each piece of writing. ❖

Do not put the title of your own paper in quotation marks when you place it on a title page or at the top of a page (see 28d).

EXERCISE 28-3

Consulting section 28b, correct any quotation mark errors. If a sentence is correct, circle its number.

1. Paulette Jiles, in her poem 'Paper Matches,' tartly observes the differences between the sexes.
2. On a *Twilight Zone* episode called Healer, the main character steals a magic artifact.
3. In her essay, The Harvest, The Kill, Jane Rule argues that vegetarianism is not a morally superior alternative to meat eating because 'harvesting and killing are the same activity, the interrupting of one life cycle for the sake of another.
4. Leonard Cohen's song Suzanne and Gordon Lightfoot's Canadian Railroad Trilogy were both written in 1967.
5. A snake gives Sherlock Holmes the clue he needs to solve a puzzling murder in the mystery story The Speckled Band.

28c   Using quotation marks for words used in special senses or for special purposes

Writers sometimes enclose in quotation marks words or phrases meant ironically or in some other nonliteral way.

> The proposed tax "reform" is actually a tax increase.

> The "wonderful companion for children" snarled menacingly.

Writers sometimes put technical terms in quotation marks and define them the first time they are used. No quotation marks are used once such terms have been introduced and defined.

> "Plagiarism"—the unacknowledged use of another person's words or ideas—can result in expulsion. Plagiarism is a serious offence.

The translation of a word or phrase can be enclosed in quotation marks. (Also underline any words or phrases that require translation.)

> My grandfather usually ended arguments with *de gustibus non disputandum est* ("there is no disputing about tastes").

Words being referred to as words can be either enclosed in quotation marks or underlined. Follow consistent practice throughout a paper.

NO	Many people confuse "affect" and *effect.*
YES	Many people confuse "affect" and "effect."
YES	Many people confuse *affect* and *effect.*

28d Avoiding the misuse of quotation marks

Writers sometimes enclose in quotation marks words they are uncomfortable about using, such as slang in formal writing or a cliché. Do not use quotation marks around language you sense is inappropriate to your audience or your purpose. Take the time to find accurate, appropriate, and fresh words instead.

> **NO**   They "eat like birds" in public, but they "stuff their faces" in private.
>
> **YES**   They eat very little in public, but they consume enormous amounts of food in private.

Do not enclose a word in quotation marks merely to call attention to it.

> **NO**   "Plagiarism" can result in expulsion.
>
> **YES**   Plagiarism can result in expulsion.

When you refer to published or performed works by title, you will often need quotation marks (see 28b) or underlining (see 30f) to set the title off. When you put your paper's title at the top of a page or on a title page, however, do not enclose it in quotation marks or underline it.

> **NO**   "The Elderly in Nursing Homes: A Case Study"
>
> **YES**   The Elderly in Nursing Homes: A Case Study

The only exception is if the title of *your* paper refers to another title or a word that requires setting off in quotation marks.

> **NO**   Character Development in Anne Hébert's Story The House on the Esplanade
>
> **YES**   Character Development in Anne Hébert's Story "The House on the Esplanade"

Do not put a nickname in quotation marks unless you are giving a nickname with a full name. When a person's nickname is widely known and used, for example, use *Joey Smallwood* or *J. R. Smallwood*, whichever is appropriate to your audience and purpose. You do not have to write *J. R. "Joey" Smallwood.*

EXERCISE 28-4

Consulting section 28d, correct any incorrect use of quotation marks. If a sentence is correct, circle its number.

EXAMPLE Many people confuse the spellings of "there," their, and they're.

> Many people confuse the spellings of "there," "their," and "they're."

1. "Accept" and *except* sound enough alike to confuse many listeners.
2. "Mickey" Mantle, "Yogi" Berra, and Whitey Ford helped make the Yankees champions in the 1950s.
3. Although the crown attorney thought it would be an "open and shut case," she found out that "life is full of surprises."
4. An "antigen" is any substance from outside the body that activates the body's immune system. Today scientists are focusing intensive research on "antigens."
5. *Valross*, whale-horse, is the Norwegian word from which we get *walrus*.

28e Following accepted practices for other punctuation with quotation marks

1 Placing commas and periods inside closing quotation marks

Because the class enjoyed Michel Tremblay's "The Thimble," they were looking forward to his longer works.

Ms. Rogers said, "Don't stand so close to me."

Edward T. Hall coined the word "proxemics."

For information about commas before quotations, see 24g.

2 Placing colons and semicolons outside closing quotation marks

We have to know "how close is close": We do not want to offend.

Some experts claim that the job market now offers "opportunities that never existed before"; others disagree.

3 Placing question marks, exclamation points, and dashes inside or outside closing quotation marks, according to the context

If a question mark, exclamation point, or dash belong with the words enclosed in quotation marks, put that punctuation mark inside the closing quotation mark.

505

"Did I Hear You Call My Name?" was the winning song.

"I've won the lottery!" he shouted.

"Who's there? Why don't you ans—"

If a question mark, exclamation point, or dash belongs with words that are *not* included in quotation marks, put the punctuation outside the closing quotation mark.

Have you read Al Purdy's poem "The Country North of Belleville"? If only I could write a story like Audrey Thomas's "Natural History"!

Weak excuses—a classic is "I have to visit my grandparents"— change little from year to year.

EXERCISE 28-5

Consulting section 28e, correct any errors in quotation marks and other punctuation with quotation marks. If a sentence is correct, circle its number.

1. One of the most famous passages in Shakespeare's plays is Hamlet's soliloquy, which begins with the question "To be, or not to be"?

2. "Take this script", Rudyard Kipling said to the nurse who had cared for his first-born child", and someday if you are in need of money you may be able to sell it at a handsome price."

3. Prime Minister Trudeau's claim that he used the expression fuddle-duddle, instead of a stronger four-letter word, led a Member of Parliament to quip, "Mr. Trudeau wants to be obscene but not heard".

4. After lulling the reader with a description of a beautiful dream palace in his poem Kubla Khan, Coleridge changes the mood abruptly: And 'mid this tumult Kubla heard from far / Ancestral voices prophesying war.

5. Gordie Howe was once asked how hockey players were coping with Canada's "language problem;" he replied, All pro athletes are bilingual. They speak English and profanity.

29 Other Marks of Punctuation

This chapter explains the uses of the dash (see 29a), parentheses (see 29b), brackets (see 29c), ellipsis (see 29d), and slash (see 29e).

THE DASH

29a Using the dash

The dash, or a pair of dashes, lets you interrupt a sentence's structure to add information. Such interruptions can fall in the middle or at the end of a sentence. Use dashes sparingly—if you do use them—so that their impact is not diluted by overexposure.

In typed papers, make a dash by hitting the hyphen key twice (--). Do not put a space before, between, or after the hyphens. In print, the dash is an unbroken line that is approximately the length of two hyphens joined together (—). In handwritten papers, make a dash slightly longer than a hyphen, using one unbroken line.

---

1 | **Using a dash or dashes to emphasize an example, a definition, an appositive, or a contrast**

EXAMPLE

Urban centres in Canada—Montreal, Toronto, and Winnipeg—Share problems of crime and prositution in core areas.

—LOVUS DEVINE, Student

DEFINITION

Our aboriginal peoples—Inuit, Indian, and Métis—challenge the model of two founding peoples that excludes them.

—WILLIAM THORSELL, "Let Us Compare Mythologies"

APPOSITIVE

And what of our national heroine—Laura Secord—our Paul Revere in drag. The fact is, that craggy face we all know from school books and chocolate boxes is not Laura Secord at all. It's a deception. The portrait was posed for by a grandniece and was painted over a portrait of Premier George Ross.

—BARRY CALLAGHAN, "Canadian Wry"

CONTRAST

Tampering with time brought most of the house tumbling down, and it was this that made Einstein's work so important—and controversial.

—BANESH HOFFMAN, "My Friend, Albert Einstein"

Always place the words that you set off in dashes next to or near the words they explain. Otherwise, the interruption will confuse your reader.

NO   The current argument **is—one that parents, faculty, students, and coaches all debate fiercely—whether** athletes should have to meet minimum academic standards to play their sports.

YES   The current **argument—one that parents, faculty, students, and coaches all debate fiercely—is whether** athletes should have to meet minimum academic standards to play their sports.

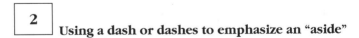

2 Using a dash or dashes to emphasize an "aside"

"Asides" are writers' comments within the structure of a sentence or a paragraph. In writing meant to seem objective, asides help writers convey their personal views. Consider your purpose° and audience° when deciding whether to insert an aside.

Another defining phrase is *distinct society.* French-speaking Quebecers—arguably hypersensitive, clearly insecure, but not necessarily separatist—have pleaded for this interpretation of themselves to be stitched into our constitution, but each time it has stuck in the craw of the rest of Canada.

—MORDECAI RICHLER, in *New York Times Magazine*

❖ PUNCTUATION ALERTS: (1) If the words within a pair of dashes would take a question mark or an exclamation point if they were a separate sentence, use that punctuation before the second dash: *A first date—do you remember?—stays in the memory forever.* (2) Do not use commas, semicolons, or periods next to dashes. When such a possibility comes up, revise the sentence to avoid it. (3) Do not enclose dashes in quotation marks except when the words require them. Correct form is as follows: *Many of George Orwell's essays—"A Hanging," for example—draw on his experiences as a civil servant. "Shooting an Elephant"—another Orwell essay—appears in many anthologies.* ❖

EXERCISE 29-1

Consulting section 29a, write a sentence about the italicized subject. In your sentence, use dashes to set off the contrast, appositive, aside, example, or definition called for.

EXAMPLE [*health,* definition] Anorexia nervosa—an eating disorder characterized by an aversion to eating and an obsession with losing weight—is extremely common among young female gymnasts and ballet dancers.

1. [*television program*, contrast]
2. [*politician*, appositive]
3. [*food*, aside]
4. [*music*, example]
5. [*recreational sport*, definition]

PARENTHESES

29b **Using parentheses**

Parentheses allow writers to interrupt a sentence's structure to add information of many kinds. Parentheses are like dashes in this function of setting off extra or interrupting words. Unlike dashes, which tend to make interruptions stand out, parentheses tend to de-emphasize what they enclose.

Use parentheses sparingly, because their overuse can be very distracting for readers.

1 Using parentheses to enclose interrupting words

EXPLANATION

After they've finished with the pantry, the medicine cabinet, and the attic, they will throw out the red geranium (too many leaves), sell the dog (too many fleas), and send the children off to boarding school (too many scuffmarks on the hardwood floors).

— SUZANNE BRITT, "Neat People vs. Sloppy People"

It's hard to explain to Americans what it feels like to be a Canadian. Pessimists among us would say that one has to translate the experience into their own terms and that this is necessary because Americans are incapable of thinking in any other terms—and this in itself is part of the problem. (Witness all those draft dodgers who went into shock when they discovered to their horror that Toronto was not Syracuse.)

— MARGARET ATWOOD, "Canadians: What Do They Want?"

EXAMPLE

Though other cities (Dresden, for instance) had been utterly destroyed in World War II, never before had a single weapon been responsible for such destruction.

— LAURENCE BEHRENS AND LEONARD J. ROSEN, *Writing and Reading Across the Curriculum*

ASIDE

When it tastes pungent and hot (remember that the pungency will be cut by the beans) stir in a large quantity of molasses. Most people don't put in enough molasses, and yet this is the essence of all good baked bean dishes.

— PIERRE BERTON, "Baked Beans"

The sheer decibel level of the noise around us is not enough to make us cranky, irritable, or aggressive. (It can, however, affect our mental and physical health, which is another matter.)

— CAROL TAVRIS, *Anger: The Misunderstood Emotion*

2

Using parentheses for certain numbers and letters of listed items

When you number listed items within a sentence, enclose the numbers (or letters) in parentheses.

❖ PUNCTUATION ALERTS: (1) Use a colon before a list only if the list is preceded by an independent clause; see 26b. (2) You can use commas or semicolons to separate items in a list that falls within a sentence, as long as you are consistent within a piece of writing. When any item itself contains punctuation, use a semicolon to separate the items so that your material is easily read.❖

> Four items are on the agenda for tonight's meeting: (1) current membership figures, (2) current treasury figures, (3) the budget for renovations, and (4) the campaign for soliciting additional public contributions.

In legal and some business writing, you can use parentheses to enclose a numeral that repeats a spelled-out number.

> The monthly rent is three hundred fifty dollars ($350).

> Your order of fifteen (15) gross was shipped today.

3

Using other punctuation with parentheses

Do not put a **comma** before an opening parenthesis even if what comes before the parenthetical material requires a comma.

NO   Although clearly different from my favourite film, (*The Wizard of Oz*) *Gone with the Wind* is an important film worth studying.

YES   Although clearly different from my favourite film (*The Wizard of Oz*), *Gone with the Wind* is an important film worth studying.

You can use a **question mark** or an **exclamation point** with parenthetical words that occur within the structure of a sentence.

> Looking for clues (what did we expect to find?) wasted four days.

A complete sentence enclosed in parentheses sometimes stands alone and sometimes falls within the structure of another sentence. Those that stand alone start with a capital and end with a period. Those that fall within the structure of another sentence do not start with a capital and do not end with a period.

NO	Looking for his car keys (he had left them at my sister's house.) wasted an entire hour.
YES	Looking for his car keys wasted an entire hour. (He had left them at my sister's house.)
YES	Looking for his car keys (he had left them at my sister's house) wasted an entire hour.

Place quotation marks to enclose words that require them, but do not use quotation marks around parentheses that come before or after those words.

NO	Alberta Hunter **"(Down Hearted Blues)"** is better known for her jazz singing than for her poetry.
YES	Alberta Hunter **("Down Hearted Blues")** is better known for her jazz singing than for her poetry.

EXERCISE 29-2

Consulting section 29b, supply needed or useful parentheses.

EXAMPLE   The world's largest and only? camel hospital was set up by the Israeli government in 1978.

The world's largest (and only?) camel hospital was set up by the Israeli government in 1978.

1. Railroad entrepreneur George Francis Train his real name dreamed of creating a chain of great cities connected by his Union Pacific Railroad.

2. Nowadays you can order almost anything clothing, toys, greeting cards, and even meat through mail-order catalogues.

3. W. C. Fields offered two pieces of advice on job hunting: 1 never show up for an interview in bare feet, and 2 do not read your prospective employer's mail while he is questioning you about your qualifications.

4. Patients who pretend to have ailments are known to doctors as "Munchausen" after Baron Karl Friedrich Hieronymus von Münchhausen; he was a German army officer who had a reputation for wild and unbelievable tales.

5. The questions raised by China's struggles to integrate capitalism with communism during the 1980s and 1990s Will the country disintegrate into civil war? Can the present economic boom be sustained? What will

emerge from the chaos? cannot yet be clearly answered, even by those who follow the country's progress closely.

BRACKETS

29c Using brackets

1 Using brackets to enclose words you insert into quotations

When you work quoted words into your own sentences (see 31c), you may have to change the form of a word or two to make the quoted words fit into the structure of your sentence. Enclose any changes you make in square brackets. (The examples with brackets in this section use MLA style° of parenthetical references; see 33c-1.)

ORIGINAL SOURCE

Surprisingly, this trend is almost reversed in Italy, where males interact closer and display significantly more contact than do male/female dyads and female couples.

—ROBERT SHUTER, "A Field Study of Nonverbal Communication in Germany, Italy, and the United States," page 305

QUOTATION WITH BRACKETS

Although German and American men stand farthest apart and touch each other the least, Shuter reported "this trend [to be] almost reversed in Italy" (305).

Enclose your words in brackets if you need to add explanations and clarifications to quoted material.

ORIGINAL SOURCE

This sort of information seems trivial, but it does affect international understanding. Imagine, for example, a business conference between an American and an Arab.

—CHARLES G. MORRIS, *Psychology: An Introduction,* page 516

QUOTATION WITH BRACKETS

"This sort of information [about personal space] seems trivial, but it does affect international understanding" (Morris 516).

Now and then you may find that an author or a typesetter has made a mistake in something you want to quote—a wrong date, a misspelled word, an error of fact. You cannot change another writer's words, but you want your readers to know that you did not make the error. To show that you see the error, insert the Latin word *sic* in brackets, right after the error. Meaning "so" or "thus," *sic* in brackets says to a reader, "It is thus in the original."

> The construction supervisor points out one unintended consequence of doubling the amount of floor space: "With that much extra room per person, the tennants [*sic*] would sublet."

 2 **Using brackets to enclose very brief parenthetical material inside parentheses**

> From that point on, Thomas Parker simply disappears. (His death [c. 1441] is unrecorded officially, but a gravestone marker is mentioned in a 1640 parish report.)

The abbreviation "c." means "about" when placed next to numerals that refer to time (see Chart 125 in section 30j).

THE ELLIPSIS

29d **Using the ellipsis**

An **ellipsis** is a set of three spaced dots (use the period key on a keyboard or a typewriter). Its most important function is to show that you have left out some of the original writer's words in material you are quoting.

ORIGINAL SOURCE

> Personal space is not necessarily spherical in shape, nor does it extend equally in all directions. (People are able to tolerate closer presence of a stranger at their sides than directly in front.) It has been likened to a snail shell, a soap bubble, an aura, and "breathing room."
>
> —ROBERT SOMMER, *Personal Space: The Behavioral Bases of Design,* page 26

Because ellipses signal readers that you have left out some of the source's words, you do not need an ellipsis to quote a single word. You can also quote a phrase without using an ellipsis as long as you do not omit any words between the first one and the last one that you quote.

Describing how personal space varies, Sommer says that it "is not necessarily spherical" for it does not "extend equally in all directions" (26).

If you do omit any of the original source's words between the first and the last word you quote, use an ellipsis at each omission.

Other descriptions of personal space include a "shell ... and 'breathing room' "(Sommer 26).

❖ PUNCTUATION ALERT: When you omit words from a source you are quoting, omit punctuation that accompanies the omitted words unless it correctly punctuates your sentence.

Other descriptions of personal space include a "shell ... and 'breathing room' " (Sommer 26). [comma omitted after *shell*]

Other descriptions of personal space include a "shell ... a ... bubble, ... and 'breathing room' " (Sommer 26). [commas kept after *shell* and *bubble* to separate three items in a series] ❖

In two situations, use a fourth dot—a sentence-ending period—along with an ellipsis.

1. When an ellipsis falls at the end of your sentence, add a sentence-ending period to the ellipsis.

Sommer goes on to say that people have described personal space as "a snail shell, a soap bubble, an aura...."

❖ DOCUMENTATION ALERT: In MLA documentation style, if a parenthetical reference is needed, put it after the ellipsis and closing quotation mark and before the sentence-ending period.

Sommer goes on to say that people have described personal space as "a snail shell, a soap bubble, an aura ..." (26).❖

2. When you omit a sentence or more from a source's words and the quoted words before and after the omission are independent clauses, add a fourth dot to the ellipsis.

Using similes to define its dimensions, Sommer explains that "personal space is not necessarily spherical in shape.... It has been likened to a snail shell, a soap bubble, an aura, and 'breathing room' " (26).

These rules apply to omissions of words from both prose and poetry. If you omit a line or more from poetry, however, use a full line of spaced dots.

Original Source

> Sing a song of sixpence,
> A pocket full of rye.
> Four and twenty blackbirds
> Baked in a pie.
> When the pie was opened,
> The birds began to sing.
> Wasn't that a pleasant dish
> To set before the king?

Poem with Omitted Lines

> Sing a song of sixpence,
> A pocket full of rye.
> Four and twenty blackbirds
> Baked in a pie
>
> . . . .
> Wasn't that a pleasant dish
> To set before the king?

THE SLASH

29e Using the slash

The **slash** (/) is a diagonal line also known as a *virgule* or *solidus*.

1 Using the slash to separate quoted lines of poetry

If you quote more than three lines of a poem in writing, set the poetry off with space and indentations as you would a prose quotation of more than four lines (see 28a). For three lines or less, use a sentence format and enclose the poetry lines in quotation marks, with a slash to divide one line from the next. Leave a space on each side of the slash.

> Consider the beginning of Anne Sexton's poem "Words": "Be careful of words, / even the miraculous ones."

Capitalize and punctuate each line as it is in the original, with this exception: End your sentence with a period if the quoted line of poetry does not have other end punctuation. If your quotation ends before the end of the line, use an ellipsis (see 29d).

---

2 Using the slash for numerical fractions in typed manuscripts

If you have to type numerical fractions, use the slash to separate numerator and denominator and a hyphen to tie a whole number to its fraction: *1/16, 1-2/3, 2/5, 3-7/8* (For advice on using spelled-out and numerical forms of numbers, see section 30l.)

---

3 Using the slash for *and/or*

Try not to use word combinations like *and/or* for writing in the humanities. In academic disciplines where use of such combinations is acceptable, separate the words with a slash. Leave no space before or after the slash. In the humanities, listing both alternatives in normal sentence structure is usually better than separating choices with a slash.

NO   The best quality of reproduction comes from 35mm slides/direct-positive films.

YES   The best quality of reproduction comes from 35mm slides or direct-positive films.

EXERCISE 29-3

Consulting all sections in this chapter, supply needed dashes, parentheses, brackets, ellipses, and slashes. If a sentence is correct as written, circle its number. In some sentences you can choose between dashes and parentheses; when you make your choice, be ready to explain it.

EXAMPLE   In Canada, there are almost four times as many managerial and administrative nonclerical workers as there are farmers.

> *In Canada, there are almost four times as many managerial and adminstrative (nonclerical) workers as there are farmers.*

1. In 1994, Neil Yerman a scribe and artist who writes with a turkey feather quill copied one letter at a time 304 805 of them, to be exact to create a Torah scroll.

2. The three longest rivers in Canada are 1 the Mackenzie 4241 km, 2 the Yukon 3185 km, and 3 the St. Lawrence 3058 km.

3. A series of resolutions was passed 11–0 with one council member abstaining calling on the mayor to improve safety conditions and step up law enforcement on the city buses.

4. Whatever it is you're doing writing, painting, or performing art should not be hard to understand. Art is communication.

5. Thunder is caused when the flash of lightning heats the air around it to temperatures up to 55 000°F (30 000°C).

6. I love Ogden Nash's limericks about animals, especially his lines about the many limbs of a certain sea creature: "I marvel at thee, Octopus; If I were thou, I'd call me Us."

7. After the internationally famous racehorse Dan Patch died suddenly from a weak heart, his devoted owner Will Savage died of the same condition a mere 32-1/2 hours later.

8. In his famous letter from the Birmingham jail on April 6, 1963, Martin Luther King, Jr., wrote: "You the eight clergymen who had urged him not to hold a protest deplore the demonstrations taking place in Birmingham."

9. Of his decision to resign as prime minister in 1984, Pierre Trudeau said, "I listened to my heart and saw if there were any signs of my destiny in the sky, and there were none there were just snowflakes."

10. Anyone in Canada who performs in public for private profit, of course a play, opera, or musical composition subject to copyright is liable to a fine of two hundred and fifty dollars $250.

EXERCISE 29-4

Follow the directions for each item. Consulting sections 29a, 29b, 29d, and 29e, use dashes, parentheses, ellipses, and slashes as needed.

EXAMPLE   Write a sentence using dashes that exclaims about getting something right.

> *I tried and failed, I tried and failed again—and then I did it!*

1. Write a sentence that quotes only three lines of the following sonnet by William Shakespeare:

    Let me not to the marriage of true minds
    Admit impediments. Love is not love
    Which alters when it alteration finds,
    Or bends with the remover to remove.
    O no, it is an ever-fixed mark
    That looks on tempests and is never shaken;

It is the star to every wand'ring bark
Whose worth's unknown, although his height be taken.
Love's not Time's fool, though rosy lips and cheeks
Within his bending sickle's compass come.
Love alters not with his brief hours and weeks,
But bears it out even to the edge of doom.
If this be error and upon me proved,
I never writ, nor no man ever loved.

2. Write a sentence in which you use parentheses to enclose a brief example.
3. Write a sentence in which you use dashes to set off a definition.
4. Write a sentence that includes a list of four numbered items.
5. Quote a few sentences from a source. Choose one from which you can omit a few words without losing meaning. Correctly indicate the omission. At the end, give the source of the quotation.

30 Capitals, Italics, Abbreviations, and Numbers

CAPITALS

30a Capitalizing the first word of a sentence

Always capitalize the first letter of the first word in a sentence: *Records show that 1.2 metres of snow fell last year.* Practice varies for using a capital letter to start each question in a series of questions. Whichever practice you choose, be consistent throughout a piece of writing. Of course, if the questions are complete sentences, start each with a capital letter.

YES   What facial feature would most people change if they could? Their eyes? Their ears? Their mouth?

YES   What facial feature would most people change if they could? their eyes? their ears? their mouth?

Practice varies for using a capital letter for a complete sentence following a colon (see 26b). Whichever practice you choose, be consistent throughout a piece of writing. This handbook uses a capital letter after the colon.

A complete sentence enclosed in parentheses sometimes stands alone and sometimes falls within the structure of another sentence. Those that stand alone start with a capital letter and end with a period. Those that fall within the structure of another sentence do not start with a capital letter and do not end with a period.

An implication of the above remarks, and it is intended, is that the accepted history of Canada begins with settlement. (A second implication today, and it is recognized here, is that agricultural settlement leads to urban foundations. That is, in fact, partly fallacious. A good case can be made that the urban foundations preceded settlement; that, in short, Canadian history was metropolitan from its beginnings.)

—W. L. MORTON, "The 'North' in Canadian Historiography"

The men had to get out and haul by ropes attached to bow and stern (two ropes were essential to prevent the canoe from yawing in against the shore), and this meant slithering over wet rocks slimy with vegetable growth, stumbling over the usual litter of fallen trees, and sometimes wading breast high in the stream.

—HUGH MACLENNAN, "The Rivers that Made a Nation"

30b Capitalizing listed items correctly

In a **run-in list,** the items are worked into the structure of a sentence or a paragraph rather than arranged with each item on a new line. When the items in a run-in list are complete sentences, capitalize the first letter of each item.

We found three reasons for the delay: (1) Bad weather held up delivery of raw materials. (2) Poor scheduling created confusion and slowdowns. (3) Lack of proper machine maintenance caused an equipment failure.

When the items in a run-in list are not complete sentences, begin each with a lower-case letter.

The reasons for the delay were (1) bad weather, (2) poor scheduling, and (3) equipment failure.

In a **displayed list,** the items are set up vertically, one below the other. If the items are sentences, capitalize the first letter. If the items are not sentences, you may start each with a capital letter or a lower-case letter. Whichever you choose, be consistent in each piece of writing.

❖ PARALLELISM ALERT: Make list items parallel in structure; for example, if one item is a sentence, use sentences for all the items (see 18h).❖

In a **formal outline,** each item must start with a capital letter (see 2o).

30c Capitalizing the first letter of an introduced quotation

If you have made quoted words part of the structure of your own sentence, do not capitalize the first quoted word.

Mme Paquette says that when students visit a country whose language they are trying to learn, they "absorb a good accent with the food."

If the words in your sentence serve only to introduce quoted words or if you are directly quoting speech, capitalize the first letter of the quoted words if it is capitalized in the original.

Mme Paquette says, "Students should always visit a country when they want to learn its language. They'll absorb a good accent with the food."

Do not capitalize the continuation of a one-sentence quotation within your sentence, and do not capitalize a partial quotation.

"Of course," she added, "the accent lasts longer than the food."

Smiling, she encouraged me to "travel—and eat—to learn to speak French."

30d Capitalizing *I* and *O*

Always capitalize the pronoun° *I,* no matter where it falls in a sentence or in a group of words or when it stands alone: *I love you, even though I do not want to marry you.* Always capitalize the interjection° *O: You are, O my fair love, a burning fever.* Do not capitalize the interjection *oh* unless it starts a sentence or is capitalized in material that you are quoting.

30e Capitalizing nouns and adjectives according to standard practice

Capitalize **proper nouns** (nouns° that name specific people, places, and things): *Mexico, Rome.* Also capitalize **proper adjectives** (adjectives° formed from proper nouns): *a Mexican entrepreneur, the Roman street.* Do not capitalize articles *(the, a, an)* accompanying proper nouns or proper adjectives.

cap 30e

A proper noun or adjective sometimes takes on a "common" meaning, losing its very specific "proper" associations. When this happens, the word loses its capital letter as well: *french fries, pasteurize.*

Many common nouns are capitalized when names or titles are added to them. For example, *lake* is not ordinarily capitalized, but when a specific name is added, it is: *Lake Erie.*

In your reading, expect sometimes to see capitalized words that this book says not to capitalize. How writers capitalize can sometimes depend on audience and purpose. For example, a corporation's written communications usually use *the Board of Directors* and *the Company,* not *the board of directors* and *the company.* Similarly, the administrators of your school might write *the Faculty* and *the College* or *the University,* words you would not capitalize in a paper. In specific contexts, adapt to the situation.

Chart 123 is a Capitalization Guide. Apply what you find in it to similar items not listed. Also, for information about using capital letters in addresses on envelopes, see section 39a.

CAPITALIZATION GUIDE		123
	CAPITALS	**LOWER-CASE LETTERS**
NAMES	Mother Teresa (*also, used as names: Mother, Dad, Mom, Pa, etc.*)	my mother (*relationship*)
	Doctor Who	the doctor (*role*)
TITLES	Prime Minister Campbell the Prime Minister (*now in office*)	a prime minister
	Liberal (*a party member*)	liberal (*a believer in liberal ideals*)
	Member of Parliament Sheila Copps	a member of parliament
	The Honourable Mr. Justice John Sopinka	the judge
	Queen Elizabeth II	the queen (*also* the Queen, referring to Canada's queen)
GROUPS OF HUMANITY	Caucasian (*race*) Native Canadian (*ethnic group*)	white (*also* White) →

CAPITALIZATION GUIDE *(continued)*

	CAPITALS	LOWER-CASE LETTERS
GROUPS OF HUMANITY (con't)	Jew, Catholic, Protestant, Buddhist *(religious affiliation)*	
ORGANIZATIONS	Parliament	parliamentary
	the Supreme Court of Canada	the court *(also* the Court)
	the Progressive Conservative Party	the party
	the Canadian Broadcasting Corporation	the corporation
PLACES	Whitehorse	the city
	the West *(a region)*	turn west *(a direction)*
	King Street	the street
	Atlantic Ocean [*also* the Atlantic]	the ocean
	the Rocky Mountains	the mountains
BUILDINGS	the House of Commons	the legislature *(but* the House; the Commons)
	Pauline Johnson High School	the high school
	China West Café	the restaurant
	St. Peter's Hospital	the hospital
SCIENTIFIC TERMS	Earth *(the planet)*	the earth *(where we live)*
	the Milky Way	the galaxy
		the moon, the sun
	Streptococcus aureus	a streptococcal infection
	Gresham's law	the theory of relativity
LANGUAGES, NATIONALITIES	Spanish Chinese	
SCHOOL COURSES	Chemistry 342	a chemistry course
	my English class	
NAMES OF THINGS	the *Calgary Herald*	the newspaper
	Canadian Living	the magazine
	Lakehead University	the university
	Canadian Club	whiskey

cap 30e

CAPITALIZATION GUIDE *(continued)*

	CAPITALS	LOWER-CASE LETTERS
	the Dodge Colt	the car
TIMES AND SEASONS	Friday August	spring, summer, fall, autumn, winter
HISTORICAL PERIODS	World War II the Great Depression (in the 1930s) the Reformation	the war the depression *(any economic depression)* an era, an age the eighteenth century fifth-century manuscripts
RELIGIOUS TERMS	God Buddhism the Torah the Koran the Bible	a god, a goddess a religion
LETTER PARTS	Dear Ms. Tauber: Sincerely, Yours truly,	
TITLES OF PUBLISHED AND RELEASED MATERIAL	"The Painted Door" *The Canadian Encyclopedia* *Waking Up the Neighbours*	[Capitalize the first letter of the first word and all other words except articles°, short prepositions°, and short conjunctions°]
COMPOUND WORDS	post-Victorian Indo-European	
ACRONYMS AND INITIALISMS	NATO NFB PACT ACTRA NAFTA IBM	
SOFTWARE	Microsoft Word DOS WordPerfect	[Capitalize software names as shown in the program documentation. Do not underline these names or enclose them in quotation marks.]

◆ ESL NOTE: When the subject of your paragraph or essay is a proper noun°, capitalize that word or those words.◆

EXERCISE 30-1

Consulting sections 30a through 30e, add capital letters as needed.

1. President Abraham Lincoln's secretary, whose name was Kennedy, and President John F. Kennedy's secretary, whose name was Lincoln, advised these ill-fated presidents not to go out just before their assassinations.
2. The first child of european parents to be born in north america was Snorro, whose mother was the widow of Leif Erickson's brother.
3. The ancient egyptians, the first to embalm their dead citizens, also embalmed their dead crocodiles.
4. Founded as the north-west mounted police in 1873, the rcmp holds contracts with every province except ontario and quebec to provide police services to communities that do not maintain their own law-enforcement agencies.
5. When Antonine Maillet was awarded france's prix goncourt in 1979, she said of the acadian people who are the subject of her prizewinning novel, "we don't have much to say. Just that we're alive."
6. An artificial hand invented in 1551 by a frenchman (his name was Ambroise Paré) had fingers that moved by cogs and levers, thus enabling a handless member of the cavalry to grasp the reins of his horse.
7. "Take care, o traitor," roared the hero, "Or your villainy will do you in!"
8. Researchers at the institute for policy studies of harvard university discovered that the following jobs are considered most boring by those who hold them: (1) assembly line worker, (2) elevator operator, (3) pool typist, (4) bank guard, (5) housewife.
9. What is the most common item in a family medicine chest? Is it aspirin? adhesive bandages? a thermometer? an antibacterial agent?
10. "I don't care what you do, my dear," the actress mrs. Patrick Campbell is supposed to have said, "as long as you don't do it in the street and frighten the horses!"
11. The letter announcing that the company was closing its doors and all employees were losing their jobs ended with the words "have a happy day."
12. The book that has sold the most copies of any book throughout the world is the bible.
13. I registered for biology 101 and history 121, but the courses I wanted in psychology and in art were filled by the time I got to registration.
14. The house of commons and the senate are located on parliament hill in ottawa.
15. The sun does not shine for 186 days at the north pole.

ITALICS (UNDERLINING)

In printed material, **roman type** is the standard; type that slants to the right is called **italic.** Words in italics indicate material that is underlined when typewritten or written by hand.

Shampoo Planet [roman]

Shampoo Planet [italic]

Shampoo Planet [underlined]

30f   Using standard practice for underlining titles and other words, letters, or numbers

Chart 124 provides a guide for making decisions about whether to underline. Apply what you find in it to similar items not listed.

GUIDE TO UNDERLINING	124

TITLES	
UNDERLINE	**DO NOT UNDERLINE**
Jane of Lantern Hill [a novel]	your own paper's title
Farther West [a play]	
Who Do You Think You Are? [a collection of short stories]	"Royal Beatings" [one story in the collection]
Simon & Schuster Handbook for Writers [a book]	"Writing Research" [one chapter in the book]
Active Voice: An Anthology of Canadian, American and Commonwealth Prose [a collection of essays]	"The Calgary Stampede" [one essay in the collection]
The Iliad [a long poem]	"Ark Anatomical" [a short poem]
The Lotus Eaters [a film]	
Equinox [a magazine]	"Nanook Passage" [an article in the magazine]
The Barber of Seville [title of an opera]	Concerto in B-flat Minor [identification of a musical work

➔

GUIDE TO UNDERLINING (continued)

TITLES

UNDERLINE

<u>Symphonie Fantastique</u> [title of a long musical work]

<u>The Road to Avonlea</u> [a television series]

<u>The Visit</u> [a record album, tape, or CD]

the <u>Brandon Sun</u> [a newspaper. Note: Even if *The* is part of the title printed on a newspaper, do not use a capital letter and do not underline it in your writing. In MLA and CM documentation°, omit the word *The*. In APA and CBE documentation, keep *The*.]

DO NOT UNDERLINE

by form, number, and key. Use neither quotation marks nor underlining.]

"After the Honeymoon" [an episode of a television series]

"Greensleeves" [a song or a single selection on an album or a tape]

Lotus 1-2-3 [software program names are neither underlined nor enclosed in quotation marks]

OTHER WORDS

the <u>Intrepid</u> [a ship; don't underline preceding initials like U.S.S. or H.M.S.]

<u>Voyager 2</u> [names of specific aircraft, spacecraft, and satellites]

<u>summa cum laude</u> [term in a language other than English]

What does <u>our</u> imply? [a word referred to as such]

the <u>abc</u>'s; confusing <u>3</u>'s and <u>8</u>'s [letters and numbers referred to as themselves]

aircraft carrier [a general class of ship]

Boeing 747 [general names shared by classes of aircraft, spacecraft, and satellites]

burrito, chutzpah [widely used and commonly understood words from languages other than English]

30g Underlining sparingly for special emphasis

Professional writers sometimes use italics to clarify a meaning or stress a point.

Many people we *think* are powerful turn out on closer examination to be merely frightened and anxious.

—MICHAEL KORDA, *Power!*

In your academic writing, rely on choice of words and sentence structures to convey emphasis.

EXERCISE 30-2

Consulting section 30f, eliminate unneeded underlining and quotation marks, and add needed underlining. Correct capitalization as necessary.

1. The first rule in an old book about <u>Rules of Etiquette</u> reads, "Do not eat in mittens."

2. Long before he became famous as <u>Captain Kirk</u> on "Star Trek," William Shatner got his start in theatre, acting, directing, and writing reviews at McGill university.

3. The Monitor and the Merrimac, the first iron-hulled ships to engage in battle, fought in the American Civil War.

4. According to one source, <u>Canada</u>'s name is derived from the Huron-Iroquois word <u>kanata</u>, meaning a village or settlement.

5. The legendary journalist Ma Murray infuriated powerful politicians with her editorials in The Bridge River–Lillooet News.

6. Judy Garland was the second-lowest-paid star in the film classic The Wizard of Oz; only the dog who portrayed <u>Toto</u> was paid less.

7. For distinguished accomplishments of people over age 70, we can look to Verdi, who composed the operas "Otello" at 74 and "Falstaff" at 80, and Tennyson, who wrote the short poem "Crossing the Bar" at age 80.

8. Handwriting experts say personality traits affect the way an individual dots an i and crosses a t.

9. The <u>Italian</u> word <u>ciao</u> is both a greeting and a farewell.

10. The students were asked to read the short story <u>The Village Inside</u> by Hugh Hood, from his collection "Around the Mountain: Scenes of Montreal Life."

ABBREVIATIONS

30h Using abbreviations with time and symbols

Some abbreviations are standard in all writing circumstances. In some situations, you may choose whether to abbreviate or spell out a word. When choosing, consider your purpose for writing° and your audience°. Then be consistent in each piece of writing.

❖ PUNCTUATION ALERT: Most abbreviations call for periods: *Mr., R.N., a.m.* Some do not, including names of organizations and government agencies (see 39a): *IBM, CBC.* When the period of an abbreviation falls at the end of a sentence, the period serves also to end the sentence.❖

TIME
The abbreviations a.m. (A.M.) and p.m. (P.M.) can be used only with exact times, such as *7:15 A.M., 7:15 a.m.; 3:47 P.M., 3:47 p.m.* You can use capital or lower-case letters, but be consistent in each piece of writing.

❖ USAGE ALERT: Use *a.m.* and *p.m.* only with numbers indicating time. Do not use them instead of the words *morning, evening,* and *night.*❖

In abbreviations for years, A.D. precedes the year: *A.D. 977.* Conversely, B.C. (or B.C.E.) follows the year: *12 B.C.* (or 12 B.C.E.).

SYMBOLS
Symbols are seldom used in the body of papers written for courses in the humanities, but they are used in charts or similar format. Also, symbols can be appropriate in the sciences.

In the humanities, spell out *percent* and *cent* rather than using the symbols % and ¢. You can use a dollar sign with specific dollar amounts: *$23 billion, $7.85.* Let common sense and your readers' needs guide you.

30i Using abbreviations with titles, names and terms, and addresses

TITLES
Use either a title of address before a name (***Dr.** Daniel Gooden)* or an academic degree after a name *(Daniel Gooden, **Ph.D.**)* Do not use both. Because *Jr., Sr., II, III,* and the like are considered part of the name, they can be used with both titles of address and academic degree abbreviations: *Dr. Martin Luther King, Jr.; Arthur Wax, Sr., M.D.* (The title *Professor* is usually not abbreviated.)

❖ COMMA ALERT: When you use an academic degree or *Jr.* or *Sr.,* insert a comma both before it and after it if it falls before the end of a sentence: *Martin Luther King, Jr., was a superb orator.*❖

NAMES AND TERMS

If you use a long name or term frequently in a paper, you may abbreviate it using these guidelines: The first time, give the full term, with the abbreviation in parentheses immediately after the spelled-out form. After that, you can use the abbreviation alone.

> Spain voted to continue as a member of the **North Atlantic Treaty Organization (NATO),** to the surprise of other **NATO** members.

You can abbreviate *U.K.* as a modifier (*the U.K. skating team*), but spell out *United Kingdom* when you use it as a noun. The same rule applies for *U.S.* and *United States.*

NO	The **U.K.** has many art galleries and museums.
YES	The **United Kingdom** has many art galleries and museums.

ADDRESSES

If you include a full address—street, city, and province—in the body of a paper, you can use the abbreviation for the province name. Both two-letter postal code abbreviations (e.g., AB) and traditional abbreviations (Alta.) are used in writing in Canada. (Only the two-letter abbreviations should be used to address envelopes.) For a list, see Chart 127. Spell out any other combination of a city and a province or a province by itself.

❖ COMMA ALERT: Use a comma before *and* after the province. ❖

NO	Wilfrid Laurier University in **Waterloo, Ont.,** used to be called Waterloo Lutheran University.
YES	Wilfrid Laurier University in **Waterloo, Ontario,** used to be called Waterloo Lutheran University.
YES	Wilfrid Laurier University in **Ontario** used to be called Waterloo Lutheran University.

30j   Using abbreviations in documentation according to standard practice

Documentation means giving the source of any material that you quote (see 31c), paraphrase (see 31d), or summarize (see 31e).

Styles of documentation are discussed in Chapter 33. Chart 125 gives scholarly abbreviations that you might find in the sources that you consult, as well as those that you need for documentation in your writing.

COMMON SCHOLARLY ABBREVIATIONS			125
anon.	anonymous	i.e.	that is
b.	born	ms.,	manuscript, manu-
c. *or* ©	copyright	mss.	scripts
c. *or* ca.	about (with dates)	n.b.	note carefully
cf.	compare	n.d.	no date (of publication,
col., cols.	column, columns		for a book)
d.	died	p., pp.	page, pages
ed.; eds.	edited by; editors	pref.	preface
e.g.	for example	rept.	report, reported by
esp.	especially	sec.,	section, sections
et al.	and others	secs.	
f., ff.	and the following page	v. *or* vs.	versus (legal case)
	or pages	vol., vols.	volume, volumes

MONTH ABBREVIATIONS USED IN MLA STYLE DOCUMENTATION						126
Jan.	January	May	(none)	Sept.	September
Feb.	February	June	(none)	Oct.	October
Mar.	March	Jl.	July	Nov.	November
Apr.	April	Aug., Ag.	August	Dec.	December

POSTAL ABBREVIATIONS			127
CANADA			
AB	Alta.	Alberta	
BC	B.C.	British Columbia	

POSTAL ABBREVIATIONS (*continued*)

MB	Man.	Manitoba
NB	N.B.	New Brunswick
NF	Nfld.	Newfoundland
NS	N.S.	Nova Scotia
NT	N.W.T.	Northwest Territories
ON	Ont.	Ontario
PE	P.E.I.	Prince Edward Island
QC *or* PQ	Que. *or* P.Q.	Quebec
SK	Sask.	Saskatchewan
YT	Y.T.	Yukon Territory

UNITED STATES

AL	Alabama	MT	Montana
AK	Alaska	NB	Nebraska
AZ	Arizona	NV	Nevada
AR	Arkansas	NH	New Hampshire
CA	California	NJ	New Jersey
CO	Colorado	NM	New Mexico
CT	Connecticut	NY	New York
DE	Delaware	NC	North Carolina
DC	District of Columbia	ND	North Dakota
FL	Florida	OH	Ohio
GA	Georgia	OK	Oklahoma
HI	Hawaii	OR	Oregon
ID	Idaho	PA	Pennsylvania
IL	Illinois	RI	Rhode Island
IN	Indiana	SC	South Carolina
IA	Iowa	SD	South Dakota
KS	Kansas	TN	Tennessee
KY	Kentucky	TX	Texas
LA	Louisiana	UT	Utah
ME	Maine	VT	Vermont
MD	Maryland	VA	Virginia
MA	Massachusetts	WA	Washington (state)
MI	Michigan	WV	West Virginia
MN	Minnesota	WI	Wisconsin
MS	Mississippi	WY	Wyoming
MO	Missouri		

30k Using *etc.*

The abbreviation *etc.* is from Latin *et cetera,* which means "and the rest." Do not use *etc.* in writing in the humanities. Acceptable substitutes are *and the like, and so on,* and *and so forth.*

EXERCISE 30-3

Consulting sections 30h, 30i, and 30j, revise this material so that abbreviations are used correctly.

1. The U of M in Winnipeg, Man., was the first institution of higher education to be established in western Can.
2. The first swim across the Eng. Channel took twenty-one hrs., forty-five mins.
3. According to most drs., one of the best places in N.A. for allergy sufferers to live in the AZ desert.
4. Jeanne Sauvé was the first woman to be speaker of the House of Com. and the first woman to be appt. Gov. Gen. of Can.
5. Many coll. students today are required to take courses in lit., soc. sci., and lang.
6. U.S. tourists driving in Can. used to have difficulty realizing that 100 km/h is roughly the equivalent of their own former natl. speed limit of 55 mph.
7. It seems ironic that the paintings of Vincent van Gogh, who died penniless, now sell for millions of $.
8. The route of the Boston Marathon, run every Apr., covers twenty-six mi. between Hopkinton, MA, and Boston, MA.
9. At fifty mins. before the liftoff, the Sat. launch was postponed.
10. The UN bldg. in NYC has been a popular tourist attraction for yrs.

NUMBERS

30l Using spelled-out numbers

Depending on how often numbers occur in a paper and what they refer to, you will sometimes express the numbers in words and sometimes in figures. The guidelines here, like those in the *MLA*

Handbook for Writers of Research Papers, Third Edition, are suitable for writing in the humanities. For the guidelines other disciplines follow, consult their style manuals (for a list, see 33a).

If conveying numerical exactness to your readers is not a prime purpose in your paper, and if you mention numbers only a few times, spell out numbers that can be expressed in one or two words: *Iceland's population increases by more than* **one** *percent a year, but that gain translates into fewer than* **three thousand** *individuals.*

❖ HYPHENATION ALERT: Use a hyphen between spelled-out two-word numbers from *twenty-one* through *ninety-nine* (see 22d-2).❖

If you use numbers fairly frequently in a paper, spell out numbers from *one* to *nine,* and use figures for numbers *10* and above. In the humanities, never start a sentence with a figure; spell out the number. In practice, you can usually revise a sentence so that the number does not come first.

> **Three hundred seventy-five dollars** per credit is the tuition rate for nonresidents.

> The tuition rate for nonresidents is **$375** per credit.

If you are using specific numbers often in a paper (temperatures in a paper about climate, for example, or percentages, or any specific measurements of time, distance, or other quantities) use figures. If you are using an occasional approximation, spell out the numbers: *about nine centimetres of snow.*

Do not mix spelled-out numbers and figures in a paper when they both refer to the same thing.

NO	In four days, our volunteers increased from **five** to **eight** to **17** to **233**.
YES	In four days, our volunteers increased from **5** to **8** to **17** to **233**. [All the numbers referring to volunteers are given in figures, but *four* is still spelled out because it refers to a different quantity—days.]

30m Using numbers according to standard practice

Standard practice requires figures for numbers in the cases covered in Chart 128.

GUIDE FOR USING SPECIFIC NUMBERS	128

DATES	August 6, 1941; 1732-1845; 34 B.C. to A.D. 230
ADDRESSES	10 Downing Street 237 North 8th Street London, ON N6A 3K7
TIMES	8:09 A.M.; 6:00 P.M.; six o'clock, *not* 6 o'clock; four in the afternoon (or 4 P.M.), *not* four P.M.
DECIMALS AND FRACTIONS	5.55; 98.6; 3.1416; 7/8; 12-1/4; three quarters, *not* 3 quarters; one-half
CHAPTERS AND PAGES	Chapter 27, page 245
SCORES AND STATISTICS	a 6–0 score; a 5 to 3 ratio *or* a 5:3 ratio; 29 percent
IDENTIFICATION NUMBERS	94.4 on the FM dial; call 1-416-555-XXXX
MEASUREMENTS	2 cm; 100 kilometres per hour; 90 km/h; 1.5 L; 2 mL; 3 litres; 8-1/2" x 11" paper, *or* 8-1/2 x 11-inch paper
ACT, SCENE, AND LINE NUMBERS	act II, scene 2, lines 75-79
TEMPERATURES	43°F; 4°C; 7.5°C
MONEY	$1.2 billion; $3.41; 25 cents *or* 25¢

EXERCISE 30-4

Consulting sections 30l and 30m, revise this material so that the numbers are in correct form, either spelled out or in figures.

1. The film *Quo Vadis* used thirty thousand extras and 63 lions.
2. The best time to use insecticides is four p.m. because that is when insects are most susceptible.
3. The Canadian government spent over one hundred sixty thousand dollars on museums between 1990 and 1991.

4. 4/5 of everything alive on this earth is in the sea.

5. The first baseball game on record in the United States was played in 1846 on June nineteenth for a final score of 23 to one in 4 innings; an earlier variation of baseball was played on June fourth, 1838, in Beachville, Ontario.

6. The first Birks store was opened on March first, eighteen seventy-nine, on St. James Street in Montreal, not far from the firm's current headquarters at twelve-forty Phillips Square.

7. The record for a human's broad jump is eight point five metres (about twenty-eight feet, one-quarter inch), and the record for a frog's broad jump is just over 4 metres (13 feet, 5 inches).

8. 250 words per minute is the reading speed of the typical reader.

9. The average family income in Nova Scotia in nineteen ninety-one was more than forty-five thousand dollars.

10. 3 out of 4 people who wear contact lenses are between 12 and 23 years of age.

11. There were six hundred four bands of Status Indians in Canada in 1992.

12. The average temperature in July is about 3-3/4°C cooler in Vancouver than it is in Quebec City.

13. Her date of birth may have been twenty-seven B.C.E.

14. 5 millilitres of baking soda will neutralize the acid in the 350 millilitres of lemon juice.

15. They were born at three seventeen a.m. in nineteen hundred.

PART

VII Writing Research

When you write research, you engage in two processes: doing research and writing a research paper. Part Seven explains how to find, evaluate, and write from sources; how to conduct research, understand its results, and write a paper based on your findings; and how to document your sources completely and accurately. As you use Chapters 31 through 35, be aware that writing research fosters habits of mind to draw upon in your studies and throughout your life.

31 Using Sources: Avoiding Plagiarism and Quoting, Paraphrasing, and Summarizing

In writing essays and other papers outside your personal experience, you are usually expected to consult such sources as books, articles, videos, interviews, or even computer bulletin boards. Your assignment might require you to analyze, summarize, synthesize (see 5b and 5f), and react to a single source, in which case you drawn on only that one source; or your assignment might require you to write a research paper, in which case you draw on many sources. Using outside sources well takes practice, so become familiar with what is involved. And then get started. The more you follow the guidelines in Chart 129, the better you will meet the challenge.

31a Avoiding plagiarism

To plagiarize is to present another person's words or ideas as if they were your own. Plagiarism is like stealing. The word *plagiarize* comes from the Latin word for kidnapper and literary thief. Plagiarism is a serious offence that can be grounds for failing a course or expulsion from a college or university. Plagiarism can be intentional, as when you submit as your own work a paper you did not write. Plagiarism is also intentional when you deliberately incorporate the work of other people in your writing without acknowledging those sources and the use you have made of them. Plagiarism can also be unintentional—but no less serious an offence—if you are unaware of what must be acknowledged and how to do it. College and university students are expected to know what plagiarism is and how to avoid it.

---

*Throughout this book, a degree mark (°) indicates that you can find the definition of the word in the Glossary of Terms in this handbook.

540

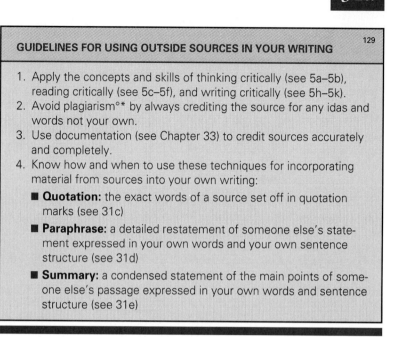

129

GUIDELINES FOR USING OUTSIDE SOURCES IN YOUR WRITING

1. Apply the concepts and skills of thinking critically (see 5a–5b), reading critically (see 5c–5f), and writing critically (see 5h–5k).
2. Avoid plagiarism°* by always crediting the source for any idas and words not your own.
3. Use documentation (see Chapter 33) to credit sources accurately and completely.
4. Know how and when to use these techniques for incorporating material from sources into your own writing:

   ■ **Quotation:** the exact words of a source set off in quotation marks (see 31c)

   ■ **Paraphrase:** a detailed restatement of someone else's statement expressed in your own words and your own sentence structure (see 31d)

   ■ **Summary:** a condensed statement of the main points of someone else's passage expressed in your own words and sentence structure (see 31e)

---

1 Knowing what not to document

When you write a paper that draws on outside sources, you are not expected to document common knowledge (if there is any on your topic) or your own thinking about the subject.

Common knowledge

You do not have to document common knowledge. Common knowledge is information that most educated people know, although they might need to remind themselves of certain facts by looking up information in a reference book. For example, every educated person knows that the U.S. space program included moon landings. Even though you might have to look in a reference book to recall that Neil Armstrong, the first man to set foot on the moon, landed on July 20, 1969, those facts are common knowledge and do not have to be documented. You move into *the realm of research and the need to document* as soon as you get into less commonly known details about the moon landing: the duration of the stay on the moon, the size and capabilities of the spaceship, what the astronauts ate during their journey, and similar details. If you feel that you are walking a thin line between knowledge held in common and knowledge learned from research, be safe and document.

Sometimes, of course, a research paper does not happen to contain common knowledge. For example, Amy Brown, whose research paper appears in Chapter 34, had no common knowledge about her topic of personal space. (In fact, Brown deliberately chose to write about a subject new to her.) Brown's research paper, therefore, consists of documented material from sources and her own thinking about the subject.

Your own thinking

You do not have to document your own thinking about your subject. As you conduct your research, you learn new material by building on your *prior knowledge*—what you already know. You are expected to think about that new material, using the sequence for critical thinking in Chapter 5 and summarized in Chart 28. It is your thinking when you synthesize what you have learned from the sources you are using. But it is your sources' material that you must document. When in doubt, document.

Be particularly careful about allowing plagiarism to slip into a thesis statement° and topic sentences°. It is plagiarism to put a source's main idea into your words and pass that off as your thesis statement or topic sentences. Similarly, it is plagiarism to combine the main ideas of several sources, put them into your own words, and pass that off as your own idea. Your thesis statement and topic sentences must reflect your synthesis of material to make them into your own thinking..

Here are illustrations of a student's own thinking, drawn from the research paper by Amy Brown in Chapter 34:

- the thesis statement: see paragraph 1
- most topic sentences: see, for example, the opening sentences of many paragraphs after paragraph 2; also see comment F
- comments: see, for example, the sentence in paragraph 1 after the parenthetical reference; also the sentence in paragraph 4 introducing the quotation from pact W.H. Auder.
- transitional sentences (for example, the sentence in paragraph 13 after the summary of information from Remland, Jones, and Brinkman and the parenthetical reference)
- the conclusion: see paragraph 14

2

Knowing what to document

What should you document? Everything that is not common knowledge or your own thinking. Document any material that you quote (see 31c), paraphrase (see 31d), or summarize (see 31e). Remember that writing the words of others in your own words does not release you from the obligation to document.

To prevent plagiarism in your writing, take careful notes as you conduct research using outside sources. Here are practices that help researchers avoid plagiarism.

■ **Record complete documentation information.** Become entirely familiar with the documentation style you will use in your paper (see 31b) so that you know what information you will need and in what form.

Make a master list of the documentation facts required for each type of source. For example, a master list for recording the data needed to document articles in print (not electronic) academic journals includes (1) author or authors' names; (2) article title; (3) journal title; (4) journal volume number; (5) issue number, if any; (6) date of publication; (7) page numbers. For an electronically accessed version, the master list has at least four more items: (8) database title; (9) publication medium; (10) name of CD-ROM producer or of online computer service or network; (11) publication date of CD-ROM or online access date. (For more about the categories of information needed for master lists, see Chapter 33.)

Write a bibliography card for each source, recording on it all the information on the master list for the type of source, as well as any information you might need to locate the source again (see 33b).

■ **Record documentation information as you go along.** Never forget to write down complete documentation facts. Use your clearest, most readable handwriting. *When you write a research paper, your chances of unintentional plagiarism decrease sharply if you can easily figure out what you found and where you found it. Never expect to relocate your sources (others might be using them) or to reconstruct what came from the source and what is the result of your own thinking.*

■ **Use a consistent notetaking system.** Always use different colours of ink or a code system to keep three things separate: (1) material paraphrased or summarized from a source; (2) quotations from a source; and (3) your own thoughts. For quotations, always write clear, perhaps oversize, quotation marks so that you are certain to see them later.

31b   Understanding the concept of documentation

Documentation means acknowledging your sources by giving full and accurate information so that readers can find your sources if they choose to. This information includes the author, title, publication information or electronic accessing information, and related facts. Whenever you quote (see 31c), paraphrase (see 31d), or summarize (see 31e), you must document your source correctly according to the documentation style° you are using.

Documentation styles vary among the academic disciplines. When you write using outside sources, ask your instructor what documentation style you are expected to use. Chapter 33 explains and illustrates four documentation styles: Modern Language Association (MLA) style; American Psychological Association (APA) style; Chicago Manual (CM) style; and Council of Biology Editors (CBE) style.

31c   Using quotations effectively

Quotations are the exact words of a source set off in quotation marks (see 28a). In contrast to paraphrases (see 31d) and summaries (see 31e), which present your sources' ideas in your owrds, quotations give your reader the chance to encounter your source's words directly. Chart 130 gives guidelines for using quotations.

Two conflicting demands confront you when you use quotations in your writing. Along with the effect and support of quotations, you also want your writing to be coherent and readable. You might seem to gain authority by quoting experts on your topic, but if you use too many quotations, you lose coherence as well as control of your own paper. If more than a quarter of your paper consists of quotations, you have written what some people call a "scotch tape special." Having too many quotations gives readers—including instructors—the impression that you have not synthesized what your sources say and are letting other people do your talking. Use quotations sparingly, therefore. When you draw on support from an authority, rely mostly on paraphrase (see 31d) and summary (see 31e).

GUIDELINES FOR USING QUOTATIONS

1. Use quotations from authorities in your subject to *support* what you say, not for your thesis statement° or main points.
2. Select quotations that fit your message.
3. Choose a quotation only if
   a. its language is particularly appropriate or distinctive;
   b. its idea is particularly hard to paraphrase accurately;
   c. the authority of the source is especially important to support your material;
   d. the source's words are open to more than one interpretation, so your reader needs to see the original.
4. Do not use quotations for more than a quarter of the text of your paper; rely mostly on paraphrase and summary.
5. Quote accurately.
6. Integrate quotations smoothly into your prose (see 31c-4), paying special attention to the verbs that help you to do so effectively (see 31f).
7. Avoid plagiarism (see 31a). Always document your source. Enclose quotations in quotation marks. Even if you do not use the entire quotation in your paper, the quotation marks signal that all words they enclose are words quoted directly from a source.

---

1 **Quoting accurately**

When you use quotations, be very careful to quote a source exactly. Always check your quotations against the originals—and then recheck. Mistakes are extremely easy to make when you are copying from a source into your notes or from your notes into your paper. If you can do so, photocopy a source's words that you think you might want to quote. If you photocopy material that you intend to quote directly, mark off on the copy the exact place that caught your attention; otherwise, you might forget your impressions and have to spend time trying to reconstruct your thought processes.

If you have to add a word or two to a quotation so that it fits in with your prose, put those words in brackets (see 29c). Make sure that your additions do not distort the meaning of the quotation. The quotation below is taken from original material shown in section 31d-2. The bracketed material replaces the word *he* in the original quotation.

The meaning of *he* is clear in the context of the original source but would not be clear as excerpted here. The bracketed information supplies words to clarify the material.

"If you hail from western Europe, you will find that [the person you are talking to] is at roughly fingertip distance from you" (Morris 131).[*]

If you delete a portion of a quotation, indicate the omission with an ellipsis (see 29d). When using ellipses, make sure that the remaining words accurately reflect the source's meaning. Also, make sure that your omission does not create an awkward sentence structure.

ORIGINAL

Like the porcupines in Schopenhauer's fable, people like to be close enough to obtain warmth and comradeship but far enough away to avoid pricking one another. Personal space is not necessarily spherical in shape, nor does it extend equally in all directions. (People are able to tolerate closer presence of a stranger at their sides than directly in front of them.) It has been likened to a snail shell, a soap bubble, an aura, and "breathing room" (Sommer 26).

WITH ELLIPSES

Like the porcupines in Schopenhauer's fable, people like to be close enough to obtain warmth and comradeship but far enough away to avoid pricking one another. Personal space ... has been likened to a snail shell, a soap bubble, an aura, and "breathing room" (Sommer 26).

---

2 | **Selecting quotations from accepted authorities that fit your meaning**

Quotations from authorities on your subject can bring credibility to your discussion. You must be able to justify every quotation that you decide to use. If you are unsure whether to quote, follow the criteria in Chart 130, item 3. If you decide not to quote, either paraphrase (see 31d) or summarize (see 31e) the material. For example, Amy Brown, author of the student research paper in Chapter 34 about personal space, quoted from Edward T. Hall because he is an accepted authority on her topic. (See Chart 138 in 32f-3).

Similarly, choose words to quote that fit your context. If you force a quotation to fit your material, most readers will quickly discern the manipulation. Also, if you have to hunt for a quotation simply because you want to include a particular authority's words, chances are that the quotation will seem tacked on, not integrated.

---

[*]Source information is in MLA style throughout this chapter (see 33c).

3 Keeping long quotations to a minimum

When you use a quotation, your purpose is to supply evidence or support your assertion, not to reconstruct someone else's argument. If you need to present a complicated argument in detail and thus quote long passages, make absolutely *sure* every word in the quotation counts. Edit out irrelevant parts (using an ellipsis to indicate deleted material; see 31c-1).

If you quote a long passage, you should be able to defend your decision to use it by explaining the quotation's significance. Otherwise, your readers will likely skip over the long quotation—and your instructor will assume that you did not want to take the time to paraphrase (see 31d) or summarize (see 31e) the material.

✤ FORMAT ALERT: For instructions on how to format the layout of a prose quotation more than four lines long (or more than three quoted lines of poetry) in "MLA style," see page 607. For formatting more than 40 quoted words in "APA style," see page 634. ✤

4 Integrating quotations smoothly into your prose

When you use quotations, you *must* integrate them smoothly into your sentences to avoid choppy, incoherent sentences in which quotations do not mesh with the grammar, style, or logic of your prose. Consider these examples based on the original material in section 31c-1.

NO Sommer says personal space for people "like the porcupines in Schopenhauer's fable, people like to be close enough to obtain warmth and comradeship but far enough away to avoid pricking one another" (26). [grammar problem]

YES Sommer says concerning personal space that "like the porcupines in Schopenhauer's fable, people like to be close enough to obtain warmth and comradeship but far enough away to avoid pricking one another" (26).

Perhaps the biggest complaint instructors have about student research papers is that sometimes quotations are simply stuck in without any reason for their inclusion. Without context-setting information, the reader cannot know how the writer connects the quotation with its surroundings. When words are placed between quotation marks, they take on special significance concerning message as well as language.

Also, make sure your readers know *who* said the quoted words; otherwise, you have disembodied quotations (some instructors call them "ghost quotations"). Revise so that more than quotation marks differentiates a quotation from your prose. A quotation seldom should begin a paragraph; rely on your own topic sentence° to begin. Then use the quotation if it supports or extends what you have said.

Citing the author's name and the title of the work as you introduce a quotation helps to create a context for the quotation. Moreover, if the author is noteworthy, you give additional authority to your message by referring to his or her credentials as part of this introduction. Consider the following treatments of source material:

SOURCE

Hall, Edward T. *The Hidden Dimension.* New York: Doubleday, 1966: 171.*

ORIGINAL MATERIAL

Therefore, people from different cultures, when interpreting each other's behavior, often misinterpret the relationship, the activity, or the emotions.

AUTHOR'S NAME

Edward T. Hall claims that "people from different cultures, when interpreting each other's behavior, often misinterpret the relationship, the activity, or the emotions" (171).

AUTHOR'S NAME AND SOURCE TITLE

Edward T. Hall claims in *The Hidden Dimension* that "people from different cultures, when interpreting each other's behavior, often misinterpret the relationship, the activity, or the emotions" (171).

AUTHOR'S NAME, CREDENTIALS, AND SOURCE TITLE

Edward T. Hall, an anthropologist who was a pioneer in the study of personal space, claims in *The Hidden Dimension* that "people from different cultures, when interpreting each other's behavior, often misinterpret the relationship, the activity, or the emotions" (171).

Occasionally quotations speak for themselves, but at times they do not. Usually the words you are quoting are part of a larger piece, and you know the connection that the quotation has to the original material. Your reader may puzzle over why you included the quotation, so a brief introductory remark provides the needed information.

---

*Source information is in MLA style throughout this chapter (see 33c).

31c

AUTHOR'S NAME AND INTRODUCTORY ANALYSIS

Anthropologist Edward T. Hall believes that people from different societies perceive personal space in varying ways, claiming that "people from different cultures, when interpreting each other's behavior, often misinterpret the relationship, the activity, or the emotions" (171).

Another technique for fitting a quotation into your own writing involves interrupting the quotation with your own words.

✤ ALERT: To insert bracketed words into a quotation to make the grammar of the quotation fit the structure or your sentence, see 29c. ✤

"Therefore," claims Edward T. Hall, "people from different cultures, when interpreting each other's behavior, often misinterpret the relationship, the activity, or the emotions" (171).

✤ ALERT: After using an author's full name in the first reference, in subsequent references you can use the author's last name only, unless another source has that same last name. ✤

EXERCISE 31-1

Read the original material. Then evaluate the passages that show unacceptable uses of quotations. Describe the problems, and then revise each passage. End the quotations with this MLA parenthetical reference: (Siwolop 111).

ORIGINAL MATERIAL

This is from "Helping Computer Chips to Keep Their Cool" by Sana Siwolop in *Business Week,* January 25, 1988.

Engineers could improve the efficiency of engines, chemical reactors, furnaces, and other equipment if only they could supply them with electronic sensors. But computer chips can't take the heat. Most microchips develop amnesia long before the temperature climbs to the boiling point of water. But that may change. Researchers at North Carolina State University in Raleigh have successfully made microelectronic transistors that operate at temperatures of up to 1,200 F. The key: using silicon carbide, a material familiar to most people as the grit on sandpaper, instead of the crystalline silicon usually used for computer chips.

UNACCEPTABLE USES OF QUOTATIONS

A. Many problems are caused when sensitive equipment overheats. "Most microchips develop amnesia long before the temperature climbs to the boiling point of water" (Siwolop 111).

B. Many researchers believe that they would be able to "improve the efficiency of engines and other equipment if only they could supply them with electronic sensors" (Siwolop 111).

C. Several new developments have taken place at North Carolina State University in Raleigh "have successfully made microelectronic transistors that operate at temperatures of up to 1,200 F" (Siwolop 111).

D. In the past, there have been serious problems with sensors designed to detect heat. Until recently, "computer chips can't take the heat" (Siwolop 111), but now that problem may be solved.

E. One of the problems in designing a heat sensor is that many "microchips develop amnesia before the temperature climbs up to the boiling point of water" (Siwolop 111).

EXERCISE 31-2

A. For a paper describing the importance of ritual, write a three- to four-sentence passage that includes your own words and a quotation from this material. After the quoted words, use this parenthetical reference: (Visser 11).

The Aztec cared intensely *how* they ate people and also who they ate, when, and where. Every gesture of the sacrifice was laid down as ritual: architecture, costumes, sacred weapons, and utensils were carefully prescribed and prepared. People were allowed to eat only the portions of meat assigned to them by their status. In fact the Aztec were terrified by the idea of human sacrifice carried out in chaotic disorder; it could only mean darkness (the failure of the power of the Sun), and destruction: the gods would become violent and brutish themselves, descend to earth, and eat people just as indiscriminately and with as little regard for protocol and etiquette as people had shown earlier. There were a thousand meanings and emotions associated with the sacrifice, besides the wish to eat and enjoy. Eating people was hedged about with ceremony and elaborate care; what they saw as neatness and propriety governed every gesture.

—Margaret Visser, *The Rituals of Dinner*

B. For a paper arguing that writers of children's books should not impose their own views on their readers, quote from the Landsberg material in Exercise 31-6. Be sure to include in your quotation some of the strengths that Landsberg sees in the novel she is discussing, in addition to one or more of its weaknesses.

C. Write a three- to four-sentence passage that includes your own words and a quotation from a source you are using for a paper assigned in one of your courses. If you have no such assignment, choose any material suitable for a college-level or university-level paper. Your instructor might request a photocopy of the material from which you are quoting.

31d Paraphrasing accurately

When you paraphrase, you precisely restate in your own words a passage written (or spoken) by another person. The word *paraphrase* combines the Greek word for "tell" with the Greek prefix *para-*, meaning "alongside." Thus, *paraphrase* describes a parallel text, one that goes alongside an original writing. Your paraphrases offer an account of what various authorities have to say, not in their words but in yours. The ideas of authorities can give substance and credibility to your message and can offer support for your material. Equally important, the process of writing a paraphrase helps you untangle difficult passages and come to understand them. Paraphrasing forces you to read closely and to extract precise meaning from complex passages. Guidelines for writing a paraphrase are in Chart 131.

GUIDELINES FOR WRITING A PARAPHRASE 131

1. Say what the source says, but no more.
2. Reproduce the source's emphases.
3. Use your own words, phrasing, and sentence structure to restate the message. If certain synonyms are awkward, quote the material—but resort to quotation very sparingly.
4. Read over your sentences to make sure that they do not distort the source's meaning.
5. Expect your material to be as long as, and possibly longer than, the original.
6. Use verbs that help you integrate paraphrases smoothly into your prose (see 31f).
7. Avoid plagiarism (see 31a).
8. As you take notes, record all documentation facts about your source so that you can acknowledge your source accurately to prevent plagiarism.

---

1 Restating material completely using your own words

When you paraphrase, restate the material—and no more. Do not skip points. Do not guess at meaning. Do not insert your own opinions or interpretations. If the source's words trigger your own thinking, preserve your thought right away because you might not recall it later. However, *when you write down your thought, make sure it is physically separate from your paraphrase:* in the margin, in a different colour ink, or circled.

As you paraphrase, use your own words; otherwise you will be quoting. Use synonyms wherever you can, and use your own sentence structures. When you finish, read over your paraphrase to check that it makes sense and does not distort the meaning of the source.

In paraphrasing, the farther you get from the original phrasing, the more likely you are to sound like yourself. Do not be surprised to find that when you change language and sentence structure you might also have to change punctuation, verb tense°, and voice°.

Sometimes, synonyms or substitute phrases are not advisable. Consider how each synonym fits into the flow of your sentence. For example, for a basic concept such as *people,* the phrase *homo sapiens* might make the material seem strained. Also, do not rename terms that the author identifies as coined; quote them. For example, in the student research paper in Chapter 34, no synonym appears for Edward Hall's word "proxemics" because Hall originated it.

---

2 | **Avoiding plagiarism when you paraphrase**

You must **avoid plagiarism** (see 31a) when you paraphrase. Even though a paraphrase is not a direct quotation, you *must* use documentation° to credit your source. Also, you *must* reword your source material, not merely change a few words. Compare these passages, based on a source used in the student research paper in Chapter 34:

SOURCE

Morris, Desmond. *Manwatching.* New York: Abrams, 1977: 131.*

ORIGINAL

Unfortunately, different countries have different ideas about exactly how close is close. It is easy enough to test your own "space reaction": when you are talking to someone in the street or in any open space, reach out with your arm and see where the nearest point on his body comes. If you hail from western Europe, you will find that he is at roughly fingertip distance from you. In other words, as you reach out, your fingertips will just about make contact with his shoulder. If

---

*Source information is in MLA style throughout this chapter (see 33c).

you come from eastern Europe, you will find you are standing at "wrist distance." If you come from the Mediterranean region, you will find that you are much closer to your companion, at little more than "elbow distance."

Unacceptable Paraphrase (Underscored Words Are Plagiarized)

Regrettably, different nations think differently about <u>exactly how close is close.</u> Test yourself: <u>When you are talking to someone in the street or in any open space,</u> stretch your arm out to measure how close that person is to you. If you are from western Europe, you will find that <u>your fingertips will just about make contact with the person's shoulder.</u> If you are from eastern Europe, your wrist will reach the person's shoulder. If you are from <u>the Mediterranean region, you will find that you are much closer to your companion,</u> when your elbow will reach that person's shoulder (Morris 131).

Acceptable Paraphrase

People from different nations think that "close" means different things. You can easily see what your reaction is to how close to you people stand by reaching out the length of your arm to measure how close someone is as the two of you talk. When people from western Europe stand on the street and talk together, the space between them is the distance it would take one person's fingertips to reach to the other person's shoulder. People from eastern Europe converse at a wrist-to-shoulder distance. People from the Mediterranean, however, prefer an elbow-to-shoulder distance (Morris 131).

The first attempt to paraphrase is not acceptable. All that the writer has done is simply change a few words. What remains is plagiarized because the passage keeps most of the original's language, has the same sentence structure, and uses no quotation marks. The documentation is correct, but its accuracy does not make up for the unacceptable paraphrasing.

The second paraphrase is acceptable. It captures the essence of the original in the student's own words.

EXERCISE 31-3

Read the original material and then the unacceptable paraphrase. Point out each example of plagiarism. Then write your own paraphrase. End it with this parenthetical reference: (Jacobs 141).[*]

Original Material

This paragraph is from *The Death and Life of Great American Cities* by Jane Jacobs, published by Random House in 1961, page 141.

A good street neighborhood achieves a marvel of balance between its people's determination to have essential privacy and their simultaneous wish for differing degrees of contact, enjoyment, or help from the people around. This balance is largely made up of small, sensibly managed details, practiced and accepted so casually that they normally seem taken for granted.

UNACCEPTABLE PARAPHRASE (PLAGIARIZES)

A good neighbourhood maintains an impressive balance between the people being determined to have privacy and wishing for varying degrees of contact, pleasure, or assistance from others nearby. People manage this with small details that are normally taken for granted (Jacobs 141).

EXERCISE 31-4

A. For a paper on economic conditions in Third World countries, paraphrase this paragraph. End your paraphrase with this parenthetical reference: (Ehrenreich and Fuentes 87).

For many Third World women, electronics is a prestige occupation, at least compared to other kinds of factory work. They are unlikely to know that in the United States the National Institute on Occupational Safety and Health (NIOSH) has placed electronics on its select list of high health-risk industries using the greatest number of toxic substances. If electronics assembly work is risky here, it is doubly so in countries where there is no equivalent of NIOSH to even issue warnings. In many plants toxic chemicals and solvents sit in open containers, filling the work area with fumes that can literally knock you out.

—BARBARA EHRENREICH AND ANNETTE FUENTES, "Life on the Global Assembly Line"

B. Write a paraphrase of a paragraph of at least 150 words from one of the sources you are using for a paper assigned in one of your courses. If you have no such assignment, choose any material suitable for a college-level or university-level paper. Your instructor may request that you submit a photocopy of the original material to accompany your paraphrase.

31e Summarizing accurately

A summary reviews the main points of a passage and gets at the gist of what an author or speaker says. A summary condenses the essentials of someone else's thought into a few general statements. Guidelines for writing a summary are found in Chart 132.

Summaries and paraphrases (see 31d) differ in one primary way. A paraphrase restates the original material completely; a summary is much shorter and provides only the main point of the original source.

GUIDELINES FOR WRITING A SUMMARY   132

1. Identify the main points and condense them without losing the essence of the material.
2. Use your own words to condense the message.
3. Keep your summary short.
4. Use verbs effectively to integrate summaries into your prose (see 31f).
5. Avoid plagiarism (see 31a).
6. As you take notes, record all documentation facts about your source so that you can acknowledge your source accurately to prevent plagiarism.

Here is a summary based on the original material shown in section 31d-2. Compare it with the acceptable paraphrase in that section.

SUMMARY

Expected amounts of space between people when they are talking differs among cultures: in general, people from western Europe prefer fingertip to shoulder distance, from eastern Europe wrist to shoulder, and from the Mediterranean elbow to shoulder (Morris 131).*

Summarizing forces you to read closely and to comprehend clearly. By writing summaries, you can learn the material because that process helps lock information into your memory. Summarizing is probably the most frequently used technique for taking notes and for incorporating sources into papers.

1 | Isolating the main points and condensing without losing meaning

A summary captures the entire sense of a passage in very little space, so you must read through all the content before you write. Then isolate the main points by asking these questions: What is the subject? What is the central message on the subject? A summary excludes more than it includes, so you must make substantial deletions.

*Source information is in MLA style (see 33c).

As you summarize, you trace a line of thought. Doing this involves deleting less central ideas and sometimes transposing certain points into an order more suited to summary. A summary should reduce the original by at least half. In summarizing a longer original—about ten pages or more—you may find it helpful to first divide the original into subsections and summarize each. Then group your subsection summaries and use them as the basis for further condensing the material into a final summary. Until you are experienced at writing summaries, you will likely have to revise them more than once. Always make sure that a summary accurately reflects the source and its emphases.

Condensing information into a table is another option for summarizing, particularly when you are working with numerical data. (For an example, see the student research paper in Chapter 34: Table 1 summarizes ten pages of a source.)

As you summarize, you may be tempted to interpret something the author says or make a judgment about the value of the author's point. Your own opinions do not belong in a summary, but do jot them down immediately so that you can recall your reactions later. *Be sure to place your ideas in your notes so that they are physically separate from your summary:* in the margin, in a different colour ink, or circled.

---

2 Avoiding plagiarizing when you summarize

Even though a summary is not a direct quotation, you *must* use documentation° to credit your source. Also, you *must* use your own words. Compare these passages, based on a source used in the student research paper in Chapter 34.

SOURCE

Hall, Edward T. *The Hidden Dimension.* New York: Doubleday, 1966: 109.*

ORIGINAL

The general failure to grasp the significance of the many elements that contribute to man's sense of space may be due to two mistaken notions: (1) that for every effect there is a single and identifiable cause; and (2) that man's boundary begins and ends with his skin. If we can rid ourselves of the need for a single explanation, and if we can think of man as surrounded by a series of expanding and contracting fields which provide information of many kinds, we shall

---

*Source information is in MLA style (see 33c).

begin to see him in an entirely different light. We can then begin to learn about human behavior, including personality types.... Concepts such as these are not always easy to grasp, because most of the distance-sensing process occurs outside the awareness. We sense other people as close or distant, but we cannot always put our finger on what it is that enables us to characterize them as such. So many different things are happening at once it is difficult to sort out the sources of information on which we base our reactions.

UNACCEPTABLE SUMMARY (UNDERSCORED WORDS ARE PLAGIARIZED)

<u>Concepts such as</u> identifying causes and determining boundaries <u>are not always easy to grasp</u> (Hall 109).

ACCEPTABLE SUMMARY

Human beings make the mistake of thinking that an event has a "single and identifiable cause" and that people are limited by the boundaries of their bodies. Most people are unaware that they have a sense of interpersonal space, which contributes to their reactions to other people (Hall 109).

The unacceptable summary does not isolate the main point, and it plagiarizes by using almost all language used in the source.

The second summary is acceptable because it not only isolates the main idea but also recasts it in the student's words. One phrase (*single and identifiable cause*) is borrowed, but it is set off in quotation marks. No one would charge this student with plagiarism.

EXERCISE 31-5

Read the original material and then the unacceptable summary because it plagiarizes. Point out each example of plagiarism. Then write your own summary. End it with this parenthetical reference: (Friedman 69).[*]

ORIGINAL MATERIAL

This is from *Overcoming the Fear of Success* by Martha Friedman, published by Seaview Books in 1980, page 69.

The manner in which we respond to negative criticism is a clue to the level of our self-esteem, which in turn is a good index to the degree of our fear of success. If we harbor a feeling of inadequacy, as many of us do, about something, no matter how slight, negative criticism can wipe us out. Many of us carry too many internalized low-esteem messages from the past, negative things our parents or siblings or teachers or schoolday peers said to us.

[*]Source information is in MLA style (see 33c).

UNACCEPTABLE SUMMARY

Many people harbour feelings of low self-esteem as a result of internalized negative messages from the past, and if people respond badly to negative criticism, no matter how slight, it indicates a low level of self-esteem, which is also an excellent index of their fear of success (Friedman 69).

EXERCISE 31-6

A.   For a paper examining the author's point of view in Canadian children's literature, summarize this material. End your summary with this parenthetical reference: (Landsberg 109).*

One-sidedness is a sore (and fatal) temptation for a novelist, to which too many of Canada's accomplished storywriters have succumbed—particularly, alas, those of dissenting views. Perhaps they have been provoked by the national complacency that smothers critics of the status quo like a monstrous clammy blanc mange. Silver Donald Cameron's novel, *The Baitchopper*, about a Nova Scotia fishermen's strike, has a memorable title, an exciting climactic scene at sea in a storm, and some fine salty local language. Unfortunately, it is weakened by a black-and-white finality about heroic proletarian strikers versus the smug establishment. I would share Cameron's conclusions about the rights and wrongs of the strike and about the base self-interest of those who opposed it, but the writer's fixed viewpoint robs his young characters of the opportunity to come to these conclusions for themselves. Ironically, the drama of that inner struggle would have been far more effective in making the point.

—MICHELE LANDSBERG, *Michele Landsberg's Guide to Children's Books*

B.   Write a summary of your paraphrase of the Ehrenreich and Fuentes material in Exercise 31-4. End it with the parenthetical reference given.

C.   Write a one- or two-paragraph-long summary of a source you are using for a paper assigned in one of your courses, or select material suitable for a college-level or university-level paper. Your instructor may request that you submit a photocopy of the original material to accompany your summary.

31f   Using verbs effectively to integrate source material into your prose

Many verbs can help you work quotations, paraphrases, and summaries smoothly into your writing. They are listed in Chart 133. Always try to use them without any strain of style. Also, be aware that some of

*Source information is in MLA style (see 33c).

these verbs imply your position toward the source material (for example, *argue, complain, concede, deny, grant, insist,* and *reveal*); others are general or neutral in meaning (*comment, describe, explain, note, say,* and *write*). Choose them according to the meaning that you want your sentences to deliver. (For examples of verbs being used well in student research papers, see Chapters 34, 35, and 38.)

VERBS USEFUL FOR INTEGRATING QUOTATIONS, PARAPHRASES, AND SUMMARIES 133

agree	complain	emphasize	note	see
analyze	concede	explain	observe	show
argue	conclude	find	offer	speculate
ask	consider	grant	point out	state
assert	contend	illustrate	refute	suggest
believe	declare	imply	report	suppose
claim	deny	insist	reveal	think
comment	describe	maintain	say	write

---

32 The Processes of Research Writing

32a Understanding research writing

Research writing involves three processes: conducting research, understanding the results of your research, and writing a paper on your understanding. The processes of researching, understanding, and writing are interwoven throughout a research project; they utilize all the skills of critical thinking, critical reading, and critical writing discussed in Chapter 5. The **writing process** for a research paper is much like that for all academic papers (see Chapters 1–3), but the **research process** adds a new dimension. In planning, you choose a suitable topic; refine the topic into a research question; use a search strategy to locate, understand, and evaluate sources; and take notes. In drafting and revising, you present your synthesis (see sections 5b and 5f) of the material and support it by quoting, paraphrasing, and summarizing your sources (see Chapter 31).

Research writing seeks to answer questions. Few research assignments are stated as questions, but all assignments imply the need to search for answers. Seeing research as a quest for answers makes clear that you cannot know whether you have located useful material unless you know what you are looking for. Research questions, whether stated or implied, and the processes needed to answer them vary widely. You might explain or otherwise present information: "How does penicillin destroy bacteria?" You might be asked to argue one side of an issue: "Is Parliament more important than the Supreme Court of Canada in setting social policy?" To attempt to find answers, you must track down information from varied sources. *Attempt* is an important word in relation to research. Some research questions lead to a final, definitive answer, but some do not. In the preceding paragraph, the question about penicillin leads to a definitive answer (the antibiotic destroys the cell walls of some bacteria); the question about social policy, on the other hand, leads not to a definitive answer but rather invites an informed opinion based on information gathered from research.

Research can be an engrossing, creative activity. By gathering information, analyzing its separate components, and composing a synthesis of it, you can come to know your subject deeply. As you write, you can make fresh connections and gain unexpected insights. Equally important, you can sample the pleasures of being a self-reliant learner, someone with the self-discipline and intellectual resources to locate and learn information independently.

If you are among those who feel overwhelmed by the prospect of research writing, you are not alone. Many researchers, whether inexperienced or experienced, share such feelings. When you break research writing into the series of steps described in this chapter, however, the project becomes far less intimidating.

32b Scheduling for research writing

Research writing takes time. Once you are aware of what is involved, you can plan ahead and budget your time intelligently. As soon as your instructor gives a research-paper assignment, work out a schedule for finishing each step. You might need only one day for some steps but two weeks each for others.

The more you do research-paper projects, the more skilled you will become at scheduling the work and handling it efficiently. The schedule in Chart 134 lists typical research steps (the parentheses give the section in which each step is discussed). No two research-paper projects are alike, so adapt the schedule to your needs. Also, you might find that all steps might not proceed in a straight line, but rather loop back and forth. Be flexible, but always keep an eye on the calendar.

SAMPLE SCHEDULE FOR A RESEARCH PAPER PROJECT	134
Assignment received (date)	**FINISH BY**
PLAN	
1. Keep a research log (see 32c).	_____
2. Choose a suitable topic (see 32d).	_____
3. Decide on purpose and audience (see 32e).	_____
4. Gather needed equipment (see 32f-1).	_____
5. Know how to evaluate sources (see 32f-3).	_____
6. Determine documentation style (see 32f-4).	_____
7. Decide whether to do field research (see 32g).	_____ →

SAMPLE SCHEDULE FOR A RESEARCH PAPER PROJECT *(continued)*

SEARCH

8. Use a search strategy (see 32h) to compile a working bibliography (see 32j-1). _____

9. Consult the LCSH (Library of Congress Subject Headings) and start compiling a list of key words (see 32i). _____

10. Know how to make bibliographic cards (see 32j-1 and 33a) and take content notes (see 32j-2). _____

11. Draft a preliminary research question or thesis statement (see 32r). _____

12. Use general reference works (see 32k) and specialized reference works (see 32l). _____

13. Use the book catalogue and read books (see 32m). _____

14. Use indexes to periodicals and read periodicals (see 32n). _____

15. Use electronic resources (see 32o). _____

16. Know what resources are available in government documents (see 32p). _____

17. Know how to interview an expert (see 32q). _____

WRITE

18. Draft and revise a final thesis statement (see 32r). _____

19. Outline as required (see 32s). _____

20. Draft paper (see 32t). _____

21. Use accurate and appropriate in-text citations (see 33c through 33f). _____

22. Revise paper (see 32t). _____

23. Compile a final Works Cited or References list (see 33c through 32f). _____

Assignment due (date) _____

32c Using a research log

A research log is like a diary. It becomes a record of your research process, especially your evolving thoughts about your work. Start a research log as soon as you get your assignment. Begin by entering the schedule (see 32b) you intend to follow. Use a separate notebook for the log, one that you can take to the library and wherever else you conduct research.

Although much of your research log will never find its way into your research paper itself, its entries become invaluable aids as you progress from choosing a topic to gathering material to organizing information and finally to writing the paper. As a student expected to concentrate simultaneously on various courses, you can use a research log to enhance your efficiency. A well-kept log traces your line of reasoning as your project evolves, tells where you ended each work session, and suggests what your next steps should be. Such a record means much less wasted time retracing a research path or reconstructing your thinking. Also, a research log serves as a journal (see section 2e) in which you can "think on paper" by using the critical-thinking sequence in Chart 28, section 5b. Most particularly, as you seek to synthesize the various elements in your material, your log helps you discover insights that only the physical act of writing makes possible. The excerpts from a research log shown here are by Amy Brown, the student whose research paper about personal space appears in Chapter 34.

Nov. 1: The assigned subject is communication. Must narrow! I've always wondered about "unspoken" communication, like the messages of body language or the idea of being comfortable when I have "my own space." My psychology textbook has the term "nonverbal communication." Check what it means.

Nov. 15: Found Sommer's book, made a biblio- card, and photocopied p. 26. Excellent source. He is an environmental psychologist. Tone is calm; seems unbiased. I see I was overlapping two concepts: territory and personal space. Territory refers to places we carve out as our own — a chair in a classroom, a room in a house. Personal space is the "bubble" of space we carry around with us. We don't like intrusions in our bubbles.

Excerpts from Amy Brown's Research Log

32d   Choosing and narrowing a topic for research writing

Instructors assign topics for research papers in a variety of ways. Some assign the specific topic. Others assign a general subject area and require you to narrow it to a topic that can be researched within the constraints of time and length imposed by the assignment. Still other instructors expect you to choose a topic on your own.

What if you have free choice of a research topic, but you develop what might be called "research topic block" because the task seems overwhelming? First, stay calm so that you can think clearly. Next, force yourself to get started. One way is to use the "BLB" system, explained in Chart 135.

OVERCOMING RESEARCH TOPIC BLOCK USING "BLB"   135

Use this system by taking one step at a time, without focusing on the entire project right away. Think positively and assure yourself that you can find a topic in the allotted time. For best results, if you do not already know how your school's library is organized, devote one visit to learning where things are (see 32i).

1. **B-B**ROWSE for a subject where ideas can be found.

- The **Library of Congress Subject Headings (LCSH)** is a multi-volume collection that shows the terms used to classify and organize information in the library. LCSH is in conventional books and/or online. The headings are updated frequently, so most current topics are listed. Browsing the LCSH lists is a first-rate way to get ideas for topics—and to see how topics are broken down into subcategories. LCSH also tells you what terms librarians use for various subjects, knowledge that helps you to communicate with librarians about your topic. LCSH lists each subject's call letters and numbers, information that makes you more efficient in locating library sources.

- **General encyclopedias** contain articles on many subjects. Most college and university libraries maintain up-to-date editions of general encyclopedias with articles on current topics. Skimming articles may stimulate you to think about a variety of research topic ideas. The index volume of a general encyclopedia is also a good place to browse for topics because it lists every subject covered in the encyclopedia and also cross-references information.

OVERCOMING RESEARCH TOPIC BLOCK USING "BLB" *(continued)* ¹³⁵

- **Specialized or subject encyclopedias** frequently have chapter headings that read like titles, which can sometimes help you identify issues and controversies that might be interesting to research in particular fields.

- **"Open stacks"** are book collections that libraries give users free access to. You can also try the library's book catalogue (see 32m) or indexes to periodicals (see 32n).

- **Textbooks**—especially in subjects that relate to an assigned research topic—can be helpful. (College and university libraries sometimes have copies of textbooks on reserve, or you might look at one in the bookstore.)

- A **"vertical file"** in some college, university, and public libraries stores materials too short or informal to be catalogued. The file may also contain reports from nonprofit organizations and government offices.

2. **L-L**OOK OVER all the items that interest you. Focus especially on major headings (often in larger and/or darker print than the rest of the material) and the first few pages. To avoid too broad a topic, look at its subdivisions in LCSH. If there are many, the subject is probably too broad. You can use one of the subdivisions marked NT (for "narrower topic") in LCSH to suggest an aspect for you to research.

3. **B-B**RAINSTORM as soon as you think that an idea might have potential. Use the techniques for gathering ideas explained in sections 2d through 2j: freewrite, make lists, draw clusters of ideas, or whatever else helps you scan ideas in what you have found or what comes to mind. Also, carry pen and paper at all times so that you can jot down thoughts if a topic or related ideas suddenly occur to you.

Before deciding on a topic, check it using the guidelines for choosing a topic in Chart 136.

What if you have been assigned a general subject area for your research, but you are not sure how to narrow the subject into a topic appropriate for a research paper? Use the guidelines in Chart 136.

Communication was the general topic assigned to Amy Brown, the student whose research paper appears in Chapter 34. Her instructor required a paper of 1800 to 2000 words to be written in six weeks based on about fifteen sources. To get started, Brown borrowed two textbooks from a friend, one an introduction to psychology and the other an introduction to business communication. Browsing through the textbooks helped Brown make her first major choice. She decided to focus on *nonverbal communication.* To further narrow her topic, Brown went to her university library and looked up the term *nonverbal communication* in the LCSH. She discovered several subdivisions under *Nonverbal communication,* including *personal space,* a topic that particularly caught her interest. Her next step was to check the general encyclopedias and specialized encyclopedias for further information on her topic. She was fascinated to learn that cultures have unspoken standards for the accepted distances between people who are conversing and interacting. Brown also liked the topic of personal space because her university had many sources to which she could refer. As she began to read closely on the topic, Brown evolved her research question: "How do standards for personal space differ among cultures?" The flow chart below illustrates Brown's process of narrowing the topic. Although each decision seems to flow smoothly from the one before, the process is rarely neat and tidy. It looks clearcut only after all the thinking, debating, and choosing end. Do not be surprised if you back out of dead ends and make some sharp turns as you define your choices and find a suitable path to a research question. To clarify your thinking, try charting your decision process as you go along.

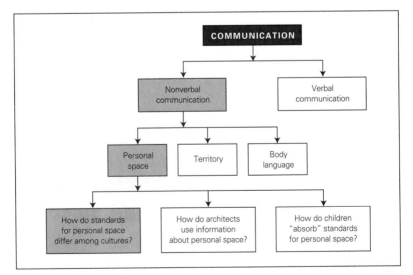

Flow Chart of Amy Brown's Narrowing Process

GUIDELINES FOR CHOOSING A TOPIC FOR A RESEARCH PAPER

1. **Expect to think through various topics before making your final choice.** Avoid rushing; give yourself time to think. Keep your mind open to flashes of insight and to alternative ideas. Conversely, do not allow indecision to block you.

2. **Be practical.** Plan to do the work within the established time limit and paper length. Be sure that sufficient resources on your topic are available and accessible to you.

3. **Choose a topic worth researching.** Trivial topics prevent you from doing what student researchers are expected to do—use critical thinking. Investigate related ideas; analyze, summarize, and interpret them; synthesize complex, perhaps conflicting, concepts; and assess them critically.

4. **Try to select a topic that interests you.** Know that your topic will be a companion for a while, sometimes most of a semester. Select a topic that arouses your interest and allows you to sample the pleasure of satisfying your intellectual curiosity.

5. **Narrow the topic sufficiently.** Avoid topics that are too broad, such as *communication* or even *nonverbal communication*. Conversely, avoid topics that are too narrow to allow a suitable mix of generalizations and specific details.

6. **Confer briefly with a professor in your field of interest.** Ask for advice in narrowing your topic. Also, ask for the names of the major books and authorities on your topic.

32e Determining the purpose and audience for your research paper

The question that guides your research process (see 32a) can help you determine your paper's purpose. If your question asks for facts, information and/or explanation, your purpose is to inform. For example, the question "How do standards for personal space differ among cultures?" requires an answer that calls for informative writing.

On the other hand, if the question raised by a topic asks for an informed opinion based on information and other evidence, your purpose is to persuade (see 1b-2). For example, the question "Why should people be aware of intercultural differences in standards for personal space?" calls for persuasive writing. You may find that your paper's purpose shifts during the research process, as Amy Brown's purpose changed (see 34a). Remain open-minded as you work. By the time you are writing your paper, however, be sure to have defined your purpose.

The **audience** for your academic writing is primarily, but perhaps not exclusively, your instructor (see section 1c). When you think of writing for your instructor, remember that he or she plays two roles: a surrogate for the general reading public or a specialized reader, and a person responsible for judging how well you have understood your material and the forms for presenting it. Sometimes the audience for a research paper includes other people—students in your class or perhaps specialists on your topic. Your reader's expertise on your topic helps you make decisions about content, specific details in explanations, and word choice.

32f Preparing to undertake research

1 Gathering equipment needed for research

Experienced researchers use equipment that helps them work efficiently. Gather the materials listed in Chart 137. Keep them separate from your regular books and materials so that you can locate them easily.

Colour coding helps researchers organize categories of information. For example, you might use one colour of index cards or coloured clips for notes and another for bibliographic information. You might use one colour ink for quotations (see 31c), another for paraphrases and summaries (see sections 31d and 31e), and a third for your thoughts about and synthesis of sources.

2 Learning how the library is organized

Before you begin researching a subject, familiarize yourself with your school's library. Although public and community libraries often provide additional sources for student researchers, their mission is nonacademic, so plan to do the bulk of your research at your college or university library. Some academic libraries provide in-class tours, others offer training sessions, and some distribute informative pamphlets

---

BASIC EQUIPMENT FOR CONDUCTING RESEARCH 137

1. A copy of your assignment.

2. A separate notebook for your research log (see 32c).

3. Pens of several different colours for taking notes. (Pencil tends to blur when notes are shuffled and handled often.)

4. Index cards to give you flexibility in moving information around. Use one index card per source to record bibliographic data (see 33a). Always use a separate index card for each idea you take down in notes.

5. This handbook, the *Simon & Schuster Handbook for Writers, First Canadian Edition.* Refer to sections 32j-1 and 33a when you make bibliographic cards. Write down bibliographic information while you have your sources in hand.

6. Whatever coins you need for the library's copy machines or downloading from a database to a printer.

7. Paper clips, a small stapler, and rubber bands to help you organize index cards and other papers.

8. A separate book bag for you to check out books from the library. Librarians joke about researchers with wheelbarrows. You might need a backpack.

---

to help you learn the library layout and materials. Regardless of the size of your library, be sure to get the answers to these basic questions:

1. Where is the general reference collection?

2. Where is the special reference collection? Is the book catalogue computerized or on cards? (Some libraries use both systems.)

3. What periodical indexes does the library have, and are they print or electronic?

4. Are the book and journal stacks open (you can go where materials are shelved and can browse) or closed (you must request each shelved or archived item, which library personnel obtain for you)?

5. How are the magazines and journals stored? At some libraries, current periodicals published in the last year are usually on display in bins or racks for easy browsing. Older issues may be put into binders and shelved with the book collection.

6. Does the library have any special collections such as newspapers on microfilm, local historical works, and provincial and federal government documents? Remember, using the library takes time, so before you start a project that involves library research, become familiar with the library's possibilities.

3 Being ready to evaluate sources

A **source** can be a book, article, videotape, or any other form of communication. Sources are rarely equally valuable. Before you start to gather information from sources, learn the criteria for evaluating research material given in Chart 138. Evaluate them with a critical eye. Also, as you read, apply the principles of critical reading discussed in sections 5d and 5e.

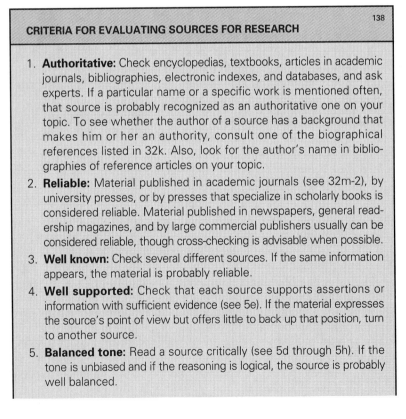

138

CRITERIA FOR EVALUATING SOURCES FOR RESEARCH

1. **Authoritative:** Check encyclopedias, textbooks, articles in academic journals, bibliographies, electronic indexes, and databases, and ask experts. If a particular name or a specific work is mentioned often, that source is probably recognized as an authoritative one on your topic. To see whether the author of a source has a background that makes him or her an authority, consult one of the biographical references listed in 32k. Also, look for the author's name in bibliographies of reference articles on your topic.

2. **Reliable:** Material published in academic journals (see 32m-2), by university presses, or by presses that specialize in scholarly books is considered reliable. Material published in newspapers, general readership magazines, and by large commercial publishers usually can be considered reliable, though cross-checking is advisable when possible.

3. **Well known:** Check several different sources. If the same information appears, the material is probably reliable.

4. **Well supported:** Check that each source supports assertions or information with sufficient evidence (see 5e). If the material expresses the source's point of view but offers little to back up that position, turn to another source.

5. **Balanced tone:** Read a source critically (see 5d through 5h). If the tone is unbiased and if the reasoning is logical, the source is probably well balanced.

CRITERIA FOR EVALUATING SOURCES FOR RESEARCH *(continued)*

6. **Current:** Check that the information is up-to-date. Sometimes long-accepted information is replaced or modified by new research. Check indexes to journals or computerized databases to see if anything newer has come along.

As you evaluate sources, be aware of the difference between **primary** and **secondary sources**. Secondary sources report, describe, comment on, or analyze someone else's work. The information comes to you secondhand, influenced by the intermediary between you and the primary source. Secondary sources explain events, analyze information, and draw conclusions. Consulting secondary sources gives you the opportunity to understand what scholars and other experts know about your subject.

Primary sources include original works—novels, poems, short stories, autobiographies, diaries, firsthand reports of observations and of research, and so on. When you use primary sources, no one comes between you and your direct exposure to the author's own words. Also, you can create a primary source by conducting primary research such as a scientific experiment or an observation, survey, or interview of field research (see 32g).

4   Determining your documentation style

The term **document style** refers to a specific system for providing information about each source you have used in a research paper. Documentation styles vary among the disciplines. The **Modern Language Association (MLA)** has developed a style often used in the humanities (see 33c). The **American Psychological Association (APA)** has developed a style often used in the social sciences (see 33d). **Chicago Manual (CM)** style is used in the humanities and other disciplines (see 33e), and **Council of Biology Editors (CBE)** style is used in the life and physical sciences and in mathematics (see 33f).

Before you start consulting sources, know what documentation style you need to use. (If your assignment does not specify a documentation style, ask your instructor which to use.). Then as you take notes on each source, you will know precisely what sorts of information your documentation style demands so you will write down the correct, full facts from the start.

32g Deciding whether to conduct field research

Field research is primary research. It involves going "into the field" to observe, survey, interview, or engage in other activities. Field research yields original (primary) data. It is not the same as library research, in which you assimilate data and information that others have gathered. Information produced by your observations, questionnaires, or surveys is primary data. Unlike secondary data, primary data do not require documentation with these exceptions: Interviews (see 32q) and some performances involve other people's words, which must be documented if you use them. The guidelines in Chapter 31 for documenting quotations, paraphrases, and summaries apply to spoken as well as written words.

If you intend to do field research, plan time to gather the original (primary) data or information you need as well as to analyze your gathered information and to synthesize (see sections 5b and 5f) it with any other material. Also allow extra time if you think you might want to interview an expert on your topic. First, you must gain enough control of your topic to learn who the authorities are and whom you might be able to interview. Then, you must have your research question in clear focus so that you can ask worthwhile questions of an expert during the interview. For detailed information about conducting an interview, see 32q.

If you want to survey a group of people on an issue your topic involves, allow time to write, reflect on, and revise a questionnaire. Test the questionnaire on a few people you do not intend to survey so that you can revise any ineffective or ambiguous questions. For detailed information on creating a questionnaire, see Chart 150 in section 38a.

If you need to get tickets to an event such as a concert or play, plan ahead. Be ready to suggest alternative dates if you cannot get your first choice. If you need to visit a museum, plan the dates right away.

Field research often involves events that cannot be revisited, so expect to record detailed information during an observation or interview and to decide later whether to use the information. If conditions make it impossible to take notes (for example, darkness in a performance hall), as soon as you have an opportunity, find a quiet place and write down notes as fully as you can.

Decide what is important in your notes. Often, field research conditions make selective note-taking difficult, so go over your notes while your memory is fresh to highlight major categories of information. Again, take the opportunity to fill in details.

32h Using a search strategy for conducting research

A **search strategy** is an organized procedure that leads step-by-step from general to specific sources that can help you answer your research question (see 32a). A productive search allows you to compile a **working bibliography**. A working bibliography is a list of possible sources, which may or may not be usable for your paper or available to you at the time you do your research. A working bibliography is generally about twice as long as the list of sources that you actually refer to in your finished paper. If your assignment is to write an 8- to 10-page paper with a minimum of 10 to 12 sources, then your working bibliography should be at least 20 to 25 items.

When you search for sources according to a plan, you can avoid feeling either at a loss for useful sources or overwhelmed by a seemingly limitless choice of sources. When your search strategy is effective, it structures your work so that you do not mistake activity for productivity. Spending days in the library to locate anything even remotely related to a topic is as fruitless as it is exhausting. No two research processes are exactly alike, so expect to adapt the search strategy explained in this section through section 32q to your needs. As you work, be aware that search strategy is rarely as tidy as it seems it will be when described in this handbook.

Useful search strategies include the "expert" method, which starts with an expert in the field; the "chaining" method, which uses bibliographies from current articles to "chain" back to older sources; and the "layering" method, which layers information from general sources to increasingly specific sources. The layering method is especially useful for student researchers and for anyone researching in an unfamiliar field; it is discussed below and illustrated on the next page.

The **layering strategy** moves from general to specialized reference materials to uncover the most credible authors and sources in a specific subject area. Each time you locate a source about your topic, try to use it to find other sources, so that you layer the information from one source to another. You want the most credible authors and articles to help you answer your research question.

Moreover, having background information and possible author names from general and specialized reference articles makes your searches in the catalogues, indexes, and computer databases faster and more purposeful. Remember, you should complete this phase of the research project as soon as possible after the research paper assignment has been given. Discovering early in the process which sources you need allows you time to find those that are hard to locate, to use interlibrary loan, and to wait for others to return books that you want.

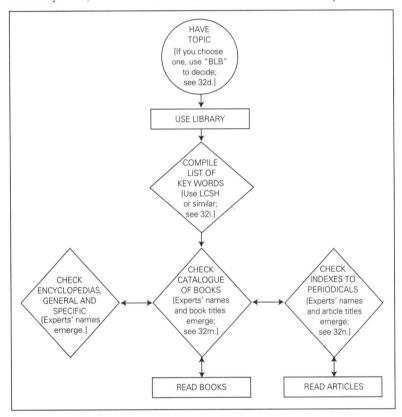

One Option for a Search Strategy: The Layering Method

32i Using LCSH and compiling a list of headings or key words

The Library of Congress cataloguing system is one widely used system for organizing a library's materials. The categories into which this system groups materials are laid out in the *Library of Congress Subject Headings* (LCSH). LCSH is a multivolume catalogue available online or in book form in the reference section of the library. This valuable resource is a catalogue of subject headings only—not authors and titles. Beginning a search strategy with the LCSH can help you narrow your topic (see 32d). Also, in LCSH you find the words and library codes used to organize and classify relevant source materials. LCSH is one of the best places to look for the **search keys** that you need to look for other sources, because many computer catalogues and indexes classify their contents by subject with LCSH terms. You may need specific LCSH words and phrases to access computerized information. The National Library of Canada uses the Library of Congress system except for specifically Canadian subjects. If you are researching a Canadian topic, consult the National Library's *Canadian Subject Headings*.

May Subdivide Geographically

Nonverbal communication (Psychology)

indicates that a
geographic ———————————— *(May Subd Geog)*
location may   Call number ———— *BF637.N66*
follow the   Used for ——— UF Body language
heading or   Kinesics
subdivision   Broader topic——— BT Interpersonal communication
                     Narrower topic——— NT Eye contact
                                                       Gaze—Psychology aspects
                                                       Hugging
                                                       Personal space ——— Amy Brown selected the
                                                                                        narrower topic of
                                                                                        Personal Space for her
                                                                                        research paper that
                                                                                        appears in Chapter 34.

Excerpt from Library of Congress Subject Headings

Amy Brown, whose research paper appears in Chapter 34, found the LCSH excerpt shown below when she looked up *nonverbal communication*. In addition to the subject headings, you can find related headings that can lead to additional sources marked with such codes as RT (related topic), BT (broader topic), and NT (narrower topic).

Researchers use headings and key words to look up information. **Headings** are subject categories in books and periodicals. **Key words**, sometimes called descriptors or identifiers, identify subject categories in periodicals and electronic databases. Knowing how to locate headings and key words is central to the research process. The people who compile reference books, library catalogue information, and indexes to periodicals cannot accommodate an infinite number of headings, so they group information into categories and then base the retrieval systems on key terms.

As you search for sources, you have to compile a list of the headings and key words that will lead you to books and articles on your topic. For example, the topic *nuclear energy* is identified with various headings or key words: *energy, nuclear; atomic energy; energy, atomic; nuclear power; power, nuclear;* and so on. You have to "break the code" to figure out what words identify the category you are seeking in each source. As you work on your research, keep an ongoing list in your research log of headings and key words that relate to your topic. Then whenever you approach a new source, you can use it efficiently.

32j Understanding how to take notes

Your research process includes taking notes as you consult sources. Notetaking has two phases. First, you write preliminary bibliography and summary cards when you think you have located a useful source for your working bibliography. Second, you write content notes once you have moved from searching to reading your selected sources carefully.

Notetaking is a decision-making process. The criteria in Chart 138 in 32f can help you decide if a particular source is worth notetaking—or photocopying, or printing out from the computer. Even if the source does not appear to be useful, note it in your research log with the title, author, date, and call number. Add a message to yourself about why you rejected it. What seems useless one day might have potential if you revise the focus of your paper or slightly reshape your topic.

1 Taking preliminary notes

As you find usable sources, write bibliography cards for them immediately while you have each source in front of you (see 33b). For greatest efficiency, record the information exactly as it will be listed in your finished paper in the documentation style that your instructor has specified (see 32f-4). Doing this can save endless hours of grief later on, because when you compile the list of sources you have referred to in your paper, you have only to put the cards in alphabetical order and type directly from them.

Also, each time you find a useful source, at the bottom of its bibliography card summarize briefly according to the criteria for evaluating sources in Chart 138. An evaluation might read: "This article is by one of the most credible authors writing about my subject" or "Although this book is old, it has good background information and gives good definitions and interesting historical data" or "This article was published only two months ago—it appeared in a scholarly journal and answers my research question perfectly!" Such evaluative statements can provide direction later for your reading and for further notetaking.

2

Taking content notes

In content notes, record information and ideas that relate specifically to your paper. Also, record any understanding you have gained from your readings, using a different colour ink so you do not confuse an author's ideas with yours (see below). Although researchers vary in the approaches and methods they use in taking content notes, they agree that it is essential to have a reliable system for synthesizing information. Use your critical reading skills (see 5d) to sort important information from less important information as it related to your topic.

One option is to decide to take content notes as you go along, right after making a bibliography card for a source and before you try to locate another source. By the time you have worked through the entire layering strategy, you have isolated usable sources, created a working bibliography, and completed a major part of your reading and notetaking.

Another option is to use the layering strategy as a survey process to find out what is available on a particular subject before you commit to extensive reading and notetaking. For this process, set aside two to three hours to go through all the collections on a given subject, writing data and information in your research log and creating an index of available materials on your topic. If you feel comfortable in the early stages of searching that your topic is going to work, you can begin to photocopy useful articles and make preliminary notecards as you go along. Also, keep an author list and a title list to look for specific authors and sources in the catalogues and periodical indexes. The goals for this first block of time in the library are to have a complete working bibliography and perhaps a few articles and books and to know which sources, if any, you need to get through interlibrary loan or from a community library. Researching this way, you start compiling content notes only after the library search is almost complete.

Whatever method works best for you, remember that notetaking has a threefold purpose: first, to help you understand and narrow your topic; second, to find answers to your research question; and third, to help you guard against plagiarism. The third matter is so important that Chapter 31 is devoted to **avoiding plagiarism** and to the skills of quoting, paraphrasing, and summarizing. To **plagiarize** is to steal someone else's words and pass them off as your own. To avoid the risk of plagiarism, take notes in such a way that you will always be able to tell from your notes what is yours and what belongs to a source. You might want to use one colour ink for your thoughts and another colour ink for words that you take from sources in the form of quotations, paraphrases, or summaries.

Use index cards for content notes. In contrast to pages in a note-book, cards provide flexibility for organizing material to use in writing your paper. Never put notes from more than one source on the same index card. If your notes on a source require more than one index card, number the cards sequentially. Using such labels as "1 of 2" for the first card on a source and "2 of 2" for the second card on that same source helps you to work efficiently from your content notecards. If you take notes on more than one idea or topic from a particular source, start a new card for each new area of information. Put a heading on each index card that shows a precise link to one of your bibliographic cards (see section 33a). Include in your content notes the source's title and the number of the page or pages from which you are taking notes. Also, clearly identify the type of note on the card: quotation, para-phrase, or summary. A summary notecard written by Amy Brown, the student whose paper is in Chapter 34, is shown below.

Hall and Hall, *Understanding*, p. 39
Cultural variations in amounts of touching

SUMMARY: Germans keep eye contact but avoid any deliberate or unintentional touching.

Notecard Summarizing a Source

Photocopying can save you time, and having the original copy of articles or book chapters in your research file can be helpful. For instance, you might have paraphrased in your notes and then revised what you have said in later drafts of your paper. Having the original source allows you to check how close your revised comments are to the actual writing, and whether you have inadvertently plagiarized by restating the information. Also, some instructors require you to submit copies of any material you have used in your research. Be sure each photocopied source is labelled with the author's name and other bibliographic information.

Sommer, p. 26

　　The best way to learn the location of invisible ⎱ *J'll*
boundaries is to keep walking until somebody complains. ⎰ *paraphrase*
Personal space refers to an area with invisible boundaries ⏋ *this*
surrounding a person's body into which intruders may ⎤
not come. [Like the porcupines in Schopenhauer's fable, ⎟ *J'll*
people like to be close enough to obtain warmth and ⎟ *quote*
comradeship but far enough away to avoid pricking one ⎬ *this*
another. Personal space ~~is not necessarily spherical in~~ ⎟ *with*
~~shape, nor does it extend equally in all directions. (People~~ ⎟ *ellipses*
~~are able to tolerate closer presence of a stranger at their~~ ⎟
~~sides than directly in front.)~~ It has been likened to a snail ⎦
shell, a soap bubble, an aura, and "breathing room."]
There are major differences between cultures in the
distances that people maintain—Englishmen keep
further apart than Frenchmen or South Americans.

Photocopy of Source, with Annotations

Many students try to substitute underlining and annotating on
photocopied articles for more detailed notetaking on notecards, only to
find that synthesizing the material into their research papers at the
drafting stage is far more difficult without paraphrases and summaries
to work with. Taking short cuts on notetaking also risks inadvertent
plagiarism.

32k Using general reference works

The general reference collection is the starting point for many
research studies. The works in this collection are interdisciplinary; they
provide basic summaries on vast amounts of information. This collection
is also one of the best places to learn the search key words that are so
critical to the successful use of the modern library. You will be hearing
a great deal about "search keys," also called "key words," as we work
through the different library collections.

Most widely used reference works are available in computerized
CD-ROM versions. Many libraries give students access to computer-
based dictionaries, thesauruses, encyclopedias, bibliographies, and
even atlases. Almanacs and statistical works on computer often are
kept more up-to-date than their printed counterparts and can often
present information in several different ways.

General Encyclopedias

General encyclopedia articles can help you get started but usually
are not suitable as major sources for postsecondary-level papers. Articles
in general encyclopedias such as *Encyclopedia Britannica* summarize

579

information about a wide variety of subjects. The articles can give you background information and authors' names. General encyclopedias are not the place to look for information on recent events or current research, although sometimes controversies in the field are summarized. Many articles end with a brief bibliography of major works on the subject, which may lead you to the authors' names and their most current works. To locate the information, start with the Index volume, which will give you volume and page numbers related to your topic. The letters "bib" at the end of an index listing mean that article contains a bibliography and so might be worth checking. If you cannot find what you are looking for, try alternative headings or key words.

One-volume general encyclopedias, such as *The New Columbia Encyclopedia* or the *Random House Encyclopedia,* may cover subjects very briefly. For postsecondary-level work these sources are useful only for you to see whether a general subject area interests you enough for further research.

The brief, multivolume *Canadian Encyclopedia* and the one-volume *Colombo's Canadian References,* an encyclopedic dictionary, are important sources of information on Canadian topics.

Almanacs, Yearbooks, Fact Books

Almanacs—books such as *The Canadian Global Almanac* and *The World Almanac and Book of Facts*—briefly present a year's events and data in government, politics, sports, economics, demographics, and many other categories. *Facts on File* covers world events in a weekly digest and in an annual one-volume Yearbook.

Sources of Canadian information include *Canada Year Book, Canadian Almanac and Directory,* and *Canadian News Facts.* The *Statistical Abstract of the United States* contains a wealth of data about the United States. *Demographic Yearbook* and *United Nations Statistical Yearbook* carry world-wide data. (Other specialized yearbooks and handbooks are named in 32l.) These reference books provide additional resources for key word lists as well as give statistical data that can verify or support the problem you may be investigating.

Atlases

Atlases contain maps—and remember that seas and skies and even other planets have been mapped. These comprehensive books contain many kinds of geographic information: topography, climates, populations, migrations, natural resources, crops, and so on. Examples include *Canada Gazetteer Atlas, The Historical Atlas of Canada,* and *The National Atlas of Canada.*

Dictionaries

Dictionaries define words and terms (see Chapter 20). In addition to general dictionaries, specialized dictionaries exist in many academic disciplines to define words and phrases specific to a field (see 32l). Examples include the *Gage Canadian Dictionary* and *A Dictionary of Canadianisms on Historical Principles.* Many dictionaries are available on computer.

Biographical Reference Works

Biographical reference books give brief factual information about many famous people. They are good places to find dates and brief listings of major events or accomplishments in noted people's lives. (Do not confuse these works with full-length biographies or bestseller accounts about noted people.) Various *Who's Who,* including *Canadian Who's Who,* series cover noteworthy people. *Current Biography: Who's News and Why* is published monthly, with six-month and annual cumulative editions. *Dictionary of Canadian Biography, Dictionary of American Biography* and *Webster's Biographical Dictionary* are also widely available. These sources, as well as specialized biographical reference works on famous people in various fields, also list Nobel Peace Prize and Pulitzer Prize winners.

Because of the many different biographical sources, you may want to ask a librarian for assistance in locating biographical references.

Bibliographies

Bibliographies list books. *Books in Print* and *Canadian Books in Print* list all books that are available through their publishers and sometimes other sources in the United States and Canada. These multivolume works classify their entries by author name, title, and general subject headings, but they do not describe a book's content.

The *Book Review Digest* and the *Canadian Book Review Annual* excerpt book reviews that have appeared in major newspapers and magazines. These excerpts of critics' opinions can help you evaluate a source (see 32g). These digests are published every year. The reviews appear in the volume that corresponds either to the year a book was published or to the one immediately following. The *Book Review Index* lists where reviews have appeared but does not carry the actual reviews. Other book reviews are available in specialized areas, and some book reviews are available as computerized sources.

Consulting specialized bibliographies—ones that list many books on a particular subject—can be very helpful in your research process (see 32l). Annotated or critical bibliographies describe and evaluate the works that they list and are therefore especially useful.

321 Using specialized reference books

Specialized or subject encyclopedias, which provide more authoritative and specific information than general reference works, are usually appropriate for postsecondary-level research. As you work with the layering strategy (see 32h) in your search for sources, you will soon need to become more focused in your research. The specialized reference collection can assist you at this point. It is an area many students overlook in their preliminary searches. Specialized encyclopedias usually contain short summaries that introduce you to the controversies, the experts, and the key words for searching that are specific to your topic. Be sure to look for authors' names in the article or in the bibliography so that you can begin to accumulate a list of credible authors. Those names become invaluable as you search book and periodical catalogues. You may wish to photocopy articles you find, and in particular, any bibliographies that are listed. You will want to start your notetaking process with these sources. Here are selected titles of some of the more commonly used specialized materials categorized by subject area.

BUSINESS AND ECONOMICS
A Dictionary of Economics
Canadian Business Index
Encyclopedia of Advertising
Encyclopedia of Banking and Finance
Handbook of Modern Marketing
The McGraw-Hill Dictionary of Modern Economics
Survey of Economic and Social History in Canada

FINE ARTS
Crowell's Handbook of World Opera
Encyclopedia of Music in Canada
International Cyclopedia of Music and Musicians
The McGraw-Hill Dictionary of Art
The New Grove Dictionary of Music and Musicians
The New Oxford History of Music
Oxford Companion to Art
Oxford Companion to Music

HISTORY

Dictionary of American Biography
Dictionary of Canadian Biography
Encyclopedia of American History
An Encyclopedia of World History
New Cambridge Modern History

LITERATURE

Cassell's Encyclopedia of World Literature
Contemporary Authors
Dictionary of Literary Biography
A Dictionary of Literary Terms
Letters in Canada
The Literary History of Canada
*MLA International Bibliography of Books and Articles on the
      Modern Languages and Literature*
The Oxford Companion to American Literature
The Oxford Companion to Canadian Literature
The Oxford Companion to English Literature
A Reference Guide to English, American and Canadian Literature

PHILOSOPHY AND RELIGION

Dictionary of the Bible
Eastern Definitions: A Short Encyclopedia of Religions of the Orient
Encyclopedia of Philosophy
Encyclopedia of Religion

POLITICAL SCIENCE

The Canadian Annual Review of Politics and Public Affairs
Foreign Affairs Bibliography
Political Handbook and Atlas of the World
Political Science Bibliographies

SCIENCE AND TECHNOLOGY

Encyclopedia of Chemistry
Encyclopedia of Computer Science and Technology
Encyclopedia of Physics
The Encyclopedia of the Biological Sciences
The Larousse Encyclopedia of Animal Life
The McGraw-Hill Encyclopedia of Environmental Science
The McGraw-Hill Encyclopedia of Science and Technology

SOCIAL SCIENCES

The Canadian Education Index
Dictionary of Anthropology
Dictionary of Education
Encyclopedia of Psychology
International Encyclopedia of the Social Sciences

FILM, TELEVISION, THEATRE

Canada on Stage: Canadian Theatre Review Yearbook
Film Canadiana
International Encyclopedia of Film
International Television Almanac
The Oxford Companion to Canadian Theatre
The Oxford Companion to the Theatre

❖ ALERTS: (1) Very specific one-volume works are available that have not been listed here. For example, under Social Science you would find the *Encyclopedia of Divorce, Encyclopedia of Aging,* or *The Encyclopedic Dictionary of Psychology.* (2) New specialized reference works are published throughout the year. Find the call number for your subject area and browse the collection to see what special references are available in your own library. ❖

32m Using a library's book catalogue

A book catalogue is a list of all the books in a library. Years ago, all libraries used a card catalogue to list all their holdings. Then some libraries switched to microfiched catalogues. Today, most libraries have computerized the catalogue.

An online catalogue typically can be accessed in three ways: by author, by title, and by subject. The layering strategy helps you find names of specific authors and titles to use in an online catalogue. To use the subject listings, you must use the correct words as search keys. Usually, these are the ones listed in the LCSH (Library of Congress Subject Headings). Many students become discouraged when they type in a topic on a computerized catalogue only to have "nothing on this subject" appear on the computer screen. For instance if you type "ghost towns" into the computer, the screen might read "no works found." Under "ghost towns," The LCSH says "see Cities and Towns: Ruined and Extinct." Unless you use the specific phrase a topic is classified under in the system, you might not be able to access the information you are looking for. If you are having difficulty in locating key words, ask a reference librarian to help you.

Many libraries are connected electronically to other libraries' catalogues, giving you access to the holdings of those libraries. The online REFCATSS system, which links the catalogues of many university and other large libraries throughout Canada, is used for interlibrary loans. The Internet gives direct access to the catalogues of many large libraries world-wide. If you need materials not available in your own library, you may be able to find them by accessing these networks or other, similar ones.

Whether a catalogue is on cards, microfiche, or computer, the same information is offered. Catalogue information is organized alphabetically in three categories: authors' names, book titles, and subjects. In some libraries, authors and titles are in one file, subjects in another. In other libraries, the three types of information are filed together.

Each card in the card catalogue or on microfiche contains much useful information. The call number is most important. Be sure to copy it down exactly as it appears, with all numbers, letters, and decimal points. The call number tells where the book is located in the stacks. If you are researching in a library with open stacks (you can go where

Library of Congress Catalogue Cards

books are shelved), the call number leads you to the area in the library where all books on the same subject can be found. Being there can help you search for sources, even though some books might have been checked out and other books might be at the reserve desk. The call number is also crucial in a library with closed stacks, where, to get a book, you must fill in a call slip, hand it in at the call desk, and wait for the book to arrive. If you fill in the wrong number or an incomplete number, your wait will be in vain. No matter what medium is used for the book catalogue, write down all call number information on your preliminary notecards to make it easier to locate your books and periodicals.

Tracings are an important feature of card-catalogue cards. Tracings are words, numbered and in fine print below a book's publication data, that give other headings used to classify information related to the subject of the card. Tracings are valuable hints for other topics to look up in the subject file of the card catalogue when you want to find more about a subject. As you find tracings, be sure to add them to your list of headings and key words (see 32i).

32n Using periodicals

Periodicals are magazines and journals published at set periods during a year. The key to using periodicals is to locate **indexes to periodicals.** These indexes list articles written between the dates listed on the cover on each edition. Many indexes are kept up-to-date with supplements between editions. Some but not all indexes include abstracts, which are brief summaries of each article. Classification systems vary among indexes, so take time to learn how to decipher the codes and abbreviations in the index that you need. Most indexes include a guide for readers in the front or back of each volume and supplement, and the guide is usually also in a computerized database, if available. As you learn to use an index, update your list of headings and key words (see 32i) for future reference.

Indexes are packaged in a variety of ways. Some indexes are in yearly bound volumes and interim paperback updates. Depending on the systems at your library, some indexes may be on microfilm or microfiche. These may have to be accessed through computer terminals. Before you start using periodicals, get to know the systems at your library.

Almost all periodical indexes are available on computerized databases, either locally on CD-ROM or through remote access via the

Internet. Most of the systems have different access methods. To access the computer indexes, it is essential to have the specific key words for your topic. A list of author names can also be useful.

1 Using general indexes to periodicals

General indexes list articles in magazines and newspapers. Headings and key words on the same subject vary among indexes, so think of every possible way to look up the information you seek. Large libraries have many general indexes, among them these two major ones.

- The *New York Times Index* catalogues all articles that have been printed in this encyclopedic newspaper since 1851. Supplements are published every two weeks in paperbound volumes. The supplements are organized into volumes (bound, in computerized databases, or on microfilm) periodically.

- The *Readers' Guide to Periodical Literature* is the most widely used index to over 100 magazines and journals for general (rather than specialized) readers. Paperback supplements are published every two weeks. These supplements are organized into volumes (bound, in computerized databases, or on microfilm) periodically. This index does not include scholarly journals, so its uses are often very limited for postsecondary-level research. It can be useful for getting a broad overview and for thinking of ways to narrow a subject. An entry from *Readers' Guide* showing listings for Communication, the subject of Amy Brown's research paper assignment, appears on the next page.

For research in Canadian periodicals, see also *A Bibliography of Canadian Bibliographies, A Guide to Basic Reference Materials for Canadian Libraries, Canadian Newspaper Index,* and *Canadian Periodical Index.*

Computerized general indexes include the *Academic Abstracts* and *Info-trac.* Although they sometimes list more scholarly articles and journals, the majority of these listings serve broad general subjects. *Academic Abstracts* might be compared to a computerized version of *Reader's Guide.* These indexes will print out the information listed on the screen. Some articles are available from the computer in whole text form.

COMMUNICATION, Nonverbal —————— Subject heading
Does your body *parle français?*/French body —— Title of article
  language; teaching methods of (L. Wylie) pors —— Author
  (Time) 113:107 + My 14 '79 ————————— Periodical title
Watching your every move: what you reveal
  about yourself without saying a word. J. Marks.
  Teen (23:36 + Jl '79) ————————————— Vol. 23, p. 36 +, July 1979
When tensions talk—listen! Subtle motion tells a
  story. E. Hamilton. (por) Sci Digest 85:30–2 + Ap ——— Has portrait
  '79
Women smile less for success; study of job success
  by Wendy McKenna and Florence Denmark.
  M. B. Parlee, Psychol Today 12:16 Mr '79
    See also
Eye—Movements
Gesture ——————————————————— Related subject
Sign language   headings
Touch

Annotated Excerpt from *Readers' Guide to Periodical Literature*

2   Using specialized indexes to periodicals

Specialized indexes are much more helpful for most post-secondary-level research than are general indexes (see 32m). Specialized indexes help a researcher become a specialist in a particular topic. These indexes list articles published in academic and professional periodicals. Many specialized indexes carry an abstract (a summary) of each listed article.

Depending on their resources, libraries have many or few specialized indexes in book form and in paperback supplements. Some libraries make available a computerized database that includes many different, specialized indexes. Specialized indexes are usually classified under the same subject headings as the specialized encyclopedia. In larger libraries, both print and computer indexes will be located on the floors with other materials for that subject area. Commonly available specialized indexes (some on CD-ROM or online) include:

BUSINESS AND ECONOMICS
Business Periodicals Index
ABI-Inform

HUMANITIES AND FINE ARTS
Art Index
Essay and General Literature Index

Humanities Index
*MLA International Bibliography of Books and Articles in the
    Modern Languages and Literatures*
Music Index

MEDICINE AND NURSING
Cum Index of Nursing and Allied Health Lit (CINAHL)
Medline (computer only)

RELIGION AND HISTORY
Religious Index
Historical Abstracts
America: History and Life

SOCIAL SCIENCE
Education Index
Psychological Abstracts
Social Science Index
PAIS (Public Affairs Information Service)

SCIENCE AND TECHNOLOGY
General Science Index
Applied Science and Technology Index
Biological Abstracts
Biological and Agricultural Index

Here is an entry from the *Humanities Index* that Amy Brown
used in her research for the paper in Chapter 34. The abbreviations
have the same meaning as those in the excerpt from the *Readers' Guide
to Periodical Literature*. Entries from the computerized edition of the
Humanities Index will appear a little different on the screen, but the information given will be similar.

Nonverbal communication
        See also
    Expression
    Gesture
Background to kinesics. R. L., Birdwhistell. *Etc* 40:352-61
    Fall '83
Mediated interpersonal communication: toward a new
    typology. R. Cathcart and G. Gumpert. *QJ Speech*
    69:267-77 Ag '83

Excerpt from *Humanities Index*

Few libraries subscribe to all the periodicals that are listed in these specialized indexes. Most libraries list the periodicals they carry; some libraries list the titles of their magazines on their computer catalogue under the title access key. Consult those lists to find out if your library has the magazine or journal you are looking for.

Although it may not be possible to locate every article you find listed in the indexes, Internet and interlibrary loan systems allow you to request articles from other locations. Check your library to see what services are available. Many colleges and universities have reciprocal agreements to allow students access to each other's libraries. Find out what major colleges and universities are in your area.

Other places to look include the many community libraries and professional agencies that subscribe to assorted periodicals. Some professional agencies permit students to use their facilities. When you know a book or periodical is just what you need to pull your paper together, take the time to try to find it. The longer you give yourself to complete the process, the more opportunity there will be for tracking down good sources.

320 Using electronic resources

1 Knowing about online and CD-ROM databases

Electronic databases include bibliographic files of articles, reports, and—less often—books. Each item in these databases provides information about title, author, and publisher. If a database catalogues articles from scholarly journals, the entry might also provide an abstract (a summary) of the material. Once you locate an entry that seems promising for your research, however, you must then track down the source itself. Some databases, including ERIC and NEWSBANK, provide the full texts of cited articles on microfiche. With such a system, each citation contains an abstract as well as a catalogue number (for example, ERIC ED 139 580) which allows you to look up the microfiche—ask a librarian where this is stored—that contains the entire article. ERIC is also online now.

Key words are essential for searching electronic databases, some of which contain as many as 100 million references. You must, therefore, choose which databases will be most helpful before you can begin to search. The DIALOG Information System, one of the largest databases, is a compilation of over 200 smaller databases in the humanities, the social sciences, business, science and technology, medicine, economics, and current events. Restrict your search to one database at a time. A reference librarian usually can help you choose the databases best suited to your research, but first you must be able to provide a specific, not vague, description of your research.

Electronic databases may be online (such as DIALOG) or on CD-ROM. CD-ROM is cheaper and easier to use—generally an inexperienced user may follow simple on-screen instructions to search for entries. In contrast, online systems often must be used by trained librarians. Online databases require the library to pay a fee for the time used and the number of entries requested, and your library may pass the fee on to you when you use such a system. Find out whether the service is free for students and, if not, what the charge is. (Some charges are a dollar or more per entry.) Narrowing your search with key words is important to avoid having to pay for a list of useless sources.

Recently, many databases previously available only online have been transferred to CD-ROM. The most popular databases on the DIALOG system (such as the business, psychology, and scientific databases) are now available in this format. CD-ROM databases tend to be smaller than those online and are updated less frequently.

Amy Brown, the student who wrote the research paper in Chapter 34, used a CD-ROM database to search for sources. After consulting a librarian and determining which specific databases were available at her school's library, she decided to use the PsychLIT database (a computerized version of *Psychological Abstracts*, which includes about a dozen major journals related to psychology). With the help of a librarian, Brown chose key words such as *cross cultural differences, social perception,* and *labour force.* She combined these words with others to come up with a list of citations that she could manage to look up in a reasonable amount of time. One of those she found is shown on page 592; its numbered parts are explained on page 593. In addition to the specific databases Amy Brown was able to access, many traditional print indexes such as the *Wilson Indexes for Humanities, Social Science, and Business* are now available in electronic forms.

| 2 | Knowing about the Internet |

The **Internet** is a network of networks linking computers at universities, research centres, government facilities, and businesses around the world. People with personal computers, modems, and a connecting service can also access the Internet. Nicknamed "the information highway," the Internet contains vast numbers of databases that offer a wide variety of information, from company reports, statistical information, and copies of speeches to treaties and government documents. **Gophers** are menus of databases that can be accessed

(1) Silver Platter 2.01   (2) PsycLIT Disc 2 (1/83 9/91)
TI DOCUMENT TITLE: Culture and the Self: Implications for
cognition, emotion, and motivation.
AU AUTHOR(S): Marcus, Hazel R., Kitayamo, Shinobu
IN INSTITUTIONAL AFFILIATION OF FIRST AUTHOR: U Michigan,
Research Ctr for Group Dynamics, Ann Arbor, US
(3) JN JOURNAL NAME: PSYCHOLOGICAL REVIEW, 1991 Apr
Vol 88(2) 224 253
(4) CC CODEN: PORVAX
(5) IS ISSN:0033295X
LA LANGUAGE: English
PY PUBLICATION YEAR: 1991
(6) AB ABSTRACT: People in different cultures have strikingly
different construals of the self, of others, and of the
interdependence of the 2. These construals can influence, and
in many cases determine, the very nature of the individual
experience, including cognition, emotion, and motivation. Many
Asian cultures have distinct conceptions of individuality that
insist on the fundamental relatedness of individuals to each
other. The emphasis is on attending to others, fitting in, and
harmonious interdependence with them. American culture neither
assumes nor values such overt connectedness among individuals.
In contrast, individuals seek to maintain that independence
from others by attending to the self and by discovering and
expressing their unique inner attributes. As proposed herein,
these construals are even more powerful than previously
imagined. Theories of the self from both psychology and
anthropology are integrated to define in detail the difference
between a construal of the self as independent and a construal
of the self as interdependent. Each of these divergent
construals should have a set of specific consequences for
cognition, emotion, and motivation; these consequences are
proposed and relevant empirical literature is reviewed.
(PsycLIT Database Copyright 1991 American Psychological Assn,
all rights reserved)
(7) KP KEY PHRASE:cultural construals of self and others;
individual experience and cognition and emotion and motivation
(8) DE DESCRIPTORS: <u>CROSS CULTURAL DIFFERENCES; SELF PERCEPTION;</u>
SOCIAL PERCEPTION; COGNITION; EMOTIONAL STATES; LIFE
EXPERIENCES; MOTIVATION
(9) CC CLASSIFICATION CODE(S): 2830
(10) PO POPULATION: Human
(11) UD UPDATE CODE: 9109
(12) AN PSYC ABS. VOL. AND ABS. NO.: 78 23878
(13) JC JOURNAL CODE: 1838

A CD-ROM Database Entry

through the Internet. As a researcher, you can use gopher menus to do subject searches.

Also, the Internet carries e-mail and bulletin boards, and permits other public access between individuals. It contains numerous discussion groups and newsgroups that you can browse or query.

The **World Wide Web** is another Internet function connecting computers around the world. It has the capability to transmit graphics and other images as well as text.

Most important, the Internet is developing and changing very quickly. If you are interested in exploring this resource, ask a reference librarian for assistance. Many colleges and universities offer training courses on how to navigate the Internet, and dozens of books have

(1) The brand name of the CD-ROM system. Another common name is DIALOG OnDisc.

(2) The name of the database. The dates in parentheses list the earliest and latest dates covered on the disk.

(3) The journal name, date, and volume, and inclusive page numbers for the full text of the article.

(4) Numerical codes for the journal in which the article appears.

(5) The journal's standard identification number.

(6) The abstract of the article. An abstract provides just enough information to let a researcher decide whether to read the article itself. As a responsible researcher, you should always read an article yourself, quoting from it or paraphrasing or summarizing it in your own words, rather than quoting an abstract of the article.

(7) The key phrases that very briefly sum up what the article is about and that can be very useful for scanning through large numbers of database entries for useful material.

(8) The descriptors, or subject words under which the entry is listed, like subject cards in a card catalogue. The underlined descriptors cross cultural differences and self perception are the words that were entered to start the search that found this entry.

(9) A code for the subject of the article.

(10) The group to which the article applies. This article is about humans in general. Other articles may be about more specific groups, such as Americans, dysfunctional families, paranoid schizophrenics, etc.

(11) A code for when this article was added to the database.

(12) The volume and abstract number where this entry can be found in the print version of *Psychological Abstracts*.

(13) Numerical codes for the journal in which the article appears.

A Key for the CD-ROM Database Entry

been published about getting into and around it. This network can be your path into a vast world of electronic information.

32p Using the government documents collection

Canadian government publications are available in astounding variety. Information is available on population figures, weather patterns, agriculture, national parks, education, welfare, and many other topics. Government document collections are available in reference libraries throughout the country. Ask your reference librarian if your library contains government publications; and if not, ask what library nearest you houses government documents.

You can order government publications that are not available to you through your library system by consulting one of the directories below. Many of these publications are now also available on either computer databases or CD-ROM. Using a computer will eliminate the mailing time and can provide you with the most current information available. Ask a reference librarian if the publications you need are accessible by computer.

- *Government of Canada Publications: Quarterly Catalogue* ceased publication in 1992; it has been replaced by a cataloguing service available through the Internet. The *Weekly Checklist of Canadian Government Publications* is kept up-to-date and is still available in print. Government Telecommunications and Informatics Services, a federal agency, has set up a World Wide Web home page to provide access to federal departments, boards, and agencies, public records, including parliamentary debates and hearings, and government data banks.

- The *Canadian Research Index* (formerly the *Microlog Index*) is a monthly index of material selected from the publications of every level of government in Canada, including parliamentary committees. Also indexed are government-sponsored scientific and technical research reports, statistical reports, and academic theses. Most citations include abstracts. The index is available in print, online, and on CD-ROM and microfiche. It is put out by a private publisher.

- Many federal and provincial government departments, and most provinces and territories, issue catalogues of their publications.

- Statistics Canada collects and analyzes a wide range of data. It publishes an annual *Statistics Canada Catalogue* and releases daily statistical updates, available online, known as *The Daily.* CANSIM, Statistics Canada's online time-series database retrieval system, is updated continually and is accessible through the *CANSIM Directory.*

32q Interviewing an expert

An expert can often offer valuable information, points of view concerning your topic, or advice. The faculty at your school or nearby schools have special expertise in many topics. Corporations and professional organizations can often suggest experts in many fields; a customer service department or public relations office is a good place to begin. Public officials are sometimes available for interviews. Many federal and provincial government offices have employees who specialize in providing information to the public. If your topic relates to an event that your family or friends experienced, they qualify as experts.

If you think you might want to interview other people, plan ahead. It takes time to set up appointments and fit your research needs into other people's schedules. You may not always be granted the interviews you seek, but many people remember their own experiences doing academic research and try to help. If you are following the layering strategy, conduct an interview only after you have solid control of your topic. The layering strategy leads you from the most general to the most specific sources on your topic, and you gradually become an expert on your research question. Wait to interview an expert until you have a solid foundation of knowledge about your topic and you know the specific focus your paper is going to take. Do not expect an interview with an expert to save you the work of researching your topic.

Know why you are interviewing the person and what you want to know. Ask questions that elicit information, not merely a "yes" or "no" answer. Be constructive; avoid language that shows bias or a hostile attitude. Keep in mind some basic rules to follow in arranging an interview:

1. Call for an appointment during office hours.

2. Ask permission to use a tape recorder at the time you make the appointment.

3. Be on time for the interview.

4. If you are tape recording, know your equipment and have it ready when you arrive. Set it up and leave it running until the end of the interview. (No periodic checks to see if it is running.)

5. Go to the appointment prepared with specific questions. The more you know about the subject already, the more specific your questions can be.

6. Pace the interview to the time you have been allotted. Be courteous and appreciative and be prepared to leave promptly at the end of your appointment time.

7. Ask permission to use quotations in your paper.

8. If a secretary or other assistant set up the interview for you, thank him or her at the end of the interview.

9. Follow up an interview, no matter how short, with a brief thank-you note. A note is not just polite; it helps pave the way for the next student who might ask for an interview.

10. After the interview, allow yourself time to fill in any notes you didn't have time to finish. Write a bibliography entry, and on notecards summarize and evaluate your experience. An expert may have a slanted point of view in line with vested interests.

For details about creating and using questionnaires to gather research data, see section 38a.

32r Drafting a thesis statement for a research paper

Drafting a **thesis statement** for a research paper is the beginning of the transition between the research process and the writing process. A thesis statement in a research paper is like the thesis statement in any essay: It tells the central theme (see 2n, especially Chart 10). Any paper must fulfil the promise of its thesis statement. Because readers expect unified material, the theme of the thesis must be sustained throughout a research paper.

Most researchers draft a **preliminary thesis statement** before or during their research process. They expect that they will revise the thesis somewhat after their research, because they know that the sources they will consult will enlarge their knowledge of a subject. Other researchers draft a thesis statement after the research process.

No matter when you draft your thesis statement, expect to write many alternatives. Your goal is to draft the thesis carefully so that it delivers the message you intend. In writing a **revised thesis statement,** take charge of your material. Reread your research log (see 32c). Reread your notes (see 32i). Look for categories of information. Rearrange your notecards into logical groupings. Begin to impose a structure on your material. As you draft a thesis statement, remember that one of your major responsibilities in a research paper is to support the thesis. Be sure that the material you gathered during the research process offers effective support. If it does not, revise your thesis statement, or conduct further research, or both.

Amy Brown, whose research paper appears in Chapter 34, drafted two different preliminary thesis statements before she composed one that worked well with her material.

FIRST PRELIMINARY VERSION	Standards for personal space vary among cultures.
NEXT PRELIMINARY VERSION	These different norms can lead to intercultural misunderstandings when people from different

countries come together unaware of how their expectations concerning interpersonal distances can affect their reactions to each other.

FINAL VERSION   Everyone has expectations concerning the use of personal space, but accepted distances for that space are determined by each person's culture.

Brown knew that the first version of her thesis statement was too broad. Still, she used it as she wrote the first draft of her paper because she knew she would revise it once she saw how the material from her research would come together in her paper. Brown wrote the second version of her thesis statement in the middle of her revising process, after she had written a few drafts of her paper. She knew that her second version was wordy and complicated. She composed her final thesis statement after she put her drafts aside for a few days and got some distance from her material.

As you revise your thesis statement, go back to the research question that guided your research process (see 32a). Your thesis statement should be one answer to the question. Here are examples of subjects narrowed to topics, focused into research questions, and then cast as thesis statements.

SUBJECT   *Rain Forests*

TOPIC   The importance of rain forests

RESEARCH QUESTION   What is the importance of rain forests?

THESIS STATEMENT INFORMATIVE   Rain forests provide the human race with many irreplaceable resources.

THESIS STATEMENT PERSUASIVE   Rain forests must be preserved because they offer the human race many irreplaceable resources.

SUBJECT   *Nonverbal Communication*

TOPIC   Personal space

RESEARCH QUESTION   How do standards for personal space differ among cultures?

THESIS STATEMENT INFORMATIVE   Everyone has expectations concerning the use of personal space, but accepted distances for that space are determined by each person's culture.

THESIS STATEMENT PERSUASIVE   To prevent intercultural misunderstandings, people must be aware of cultural differences in standards for personal space.

SUBJECT	*Smoking*
TOPIC	Curing nicotine addiction
RESEARCH QUESTION	Are new approaches being used to cure nicotine addiction?
THESIS STATEMENT INFORMATIVE	Some approaches to curing nicotine addiction are themselves addictive.
THESIS STATEMENT PERSUASIVE	Because some methods of curing addiction are themselves addictive, doctors should prescribe them with caution.

Outlining a research paper

Some instructors require an outline of a research paper. To begin organizing your material for an outline, you might write an **informal outline.** Group the subcategories in your material until you are ready to write a formal outline.

A **formal outline** should be in the form discussed in section 2o. Head it with the paper's thesis statement. You can use a **topic outline** (a format that requires words or phrases for each item) or a **sentence outline** (a format that requires full sentences for each item). Do not mix the two types. For a sentence outline of the student's research paper, see Chapter 34.

32t Drafting and revising a research paper

Drafting and revising a research paper have much in common with the writing processes for writing any type of paper (see Chapters 2 and 3). But more is demanded. You must demonstrate that you have followed the research steps in this chapter. You must demonstrate an understanding of the information you have located, and you must organize for effective presentation. Additionally, you must integrate sources into your writing without plagiarizing (see section 31a) by properly using the techniques of quotation (see section 31c), paraphrase (see section 31d), and summary (see section 31e). Also, you must use parenthetical references (see section 33b) to document your sources. So many special demands take extra time for drafting, thinking, redrafting, and rethinking.

Expect to write a number of drafts of your research paper. Successive drafts help you gain authority over the information that you have learned from your research. The **first draft** is your initial attempt to structure your notes into a unified whole. It is also a chance to discover new insights and fresh connections. Only the act of writing makes such discovery possible. A first draft is a rough draft. It is a prelude to later work at revising and polishing. Chart 139 suggests some alternative ways to write the first draft of a research paper.

SUGGESTIONS FOR DRAFTING A RESEARCH PAPER   139

- Some researchers work with their notes in front of them. They use the organized piles made for drafting a thesis statement (see 32r) and for outlining (see 32s). They spread out each pile and work according to the categories of information that have emerged from their material. They proceed from one pile to the next. They expect this process to take time, but they are assured of a first draft that includes much of the results of their research.

- Some researchers gather all their information and then set it aside to write a **partial first draft,** a quickly written first pass at getting the material under control. Writing this way helps researchers get a broad view of the material. The second step is to go back and write a **complete first draft** with research notes at hand. The researchers go over their partial draft slowly to correct information, add material left out, and—most important—insert parenthetical references (see Chapter 33).

- Some researchers write their first draft quickly to get words down on paper when they feel "stuck" about what to say next. When they have a clear idea of how to proceed, they slow down and use their notes. These researchers draw on their experiences with gathering ideas (see 2d through 2k), shaping ideas (see 2l), getting started (see 3a), and drafting (see 3b).

- Some researchers photocopy their first drafts and cut up the paper to move paragraphs and sentences around. If a new order suggests itself, the researchers tape the paper together in its new form. Researchers who have access to a computer will find this process considerably easier (see Appendix A).

A **second and subsequent drafts** are the results of reading your first draft critically and revising it. If at all possible, get some distance from your material by taking a break of a few days (or a few hours, if you are pressed for time). Then, reread your first draft and think how it can be improved. You also might ask friends or classmates to read it and react.

As you work, pay attention to any uneasy feelings you have that hint at the need to rethink or rework your material. Experienced writers expect to revise; they know that writing is really rewriting. Research papers are among the most demanding composing assignments, and most writers have to revise their drafts more than a few times. As you revise, consult the Revision Checklists in section 3c to remind yourself of general principles of writing. Also, consult the special revision checklist in Chart 140 for a research paper.

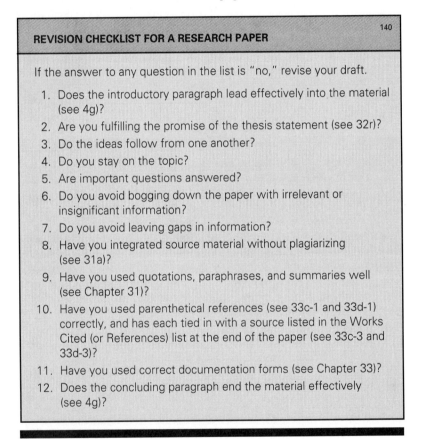

REVISION CHECKLIST FOR A RESEARCH PAPER   140

If the answer to any question in the list is "no," revise your draft.

1. Does the introductory paragraph lead effectively into the material (see 4g)?
2. Are you fulfilling the promise of the thesis statement (see 32r)?
3. Do the ideas follow from one another?
4. Do you stay on the topic?
5. Are important questions answered?
6. Do you avoid bogging down the paper with irrelevant or insignificant information?
7. Do you avoid leaving gaps in information?
8. Have you integrated source material without plagiarizing (see 31a)?
9. Have you used quotations, paraphrases, and summaries well (see Chapter 31)?
10. Have you used parenthetical references (see 33c-1 and 33d-1) correctly, and has each tied in with a source listed in the Works Cited (or References) list at the end of the paper (see 33c-3 and 33d-3)?
11. Have you used correct documentation forms (see Chapter 33)?
12. Does the concluding paragraph end the material effectively (see 4g)?

The **final draft** shows that you have revised well. It shows also that you have edited (see section 3d) and proofread (see section 3e) for correct grammar, spelling, and punctuation. No amount of careful research and good writing can make up for a sloppy manuscript. Strive to make the paper easy to read. If any page is messy with corrections, retype it. If your instructor accepts handwritten papers, use ruled white paper that has *not* been torn out of a spiral notebook. (If at all possible, however, type your work because it will present itself better.) Use black or blue ink and write very legibly.

For a case study of a student writing an MLA-style research paper, including a narrative of the writing process in action, and a sample student research paper, see Chapter 34. For a case study and a sample student research paper using APA style, see Chapter 35.

33 Documenting in MLA, APA, CM, and CBE Styles

When you write a research paper, you must **document** your sources. If you do not, you are plagiarizing, which is a serious offence (see 31a). The purpose of documenting sources is to inform your reader of exactly which sources you have taken information from. To prepare to document, you want to create a working bibliography on cards (see 33a), to keep careful track of all the sources on which you take notes. In your research paper itself, you are expected to use the style of documentation required by your instructor—four major styles are presented in this chapter.

33a Understanding the concept of documentation

Documentation involves marking the exact place in a paper where source material has been used *and* presenting bibliographic information (for example, a book's author, title, year of publication, publisher, and any other required information). Although *bibliography* literally means "description of books," for your research projects you might find yourself compiling a list of sources that includes live interviews, CDs, online information, and films, as well as books and articles.

Bibliographic information is given in a **list of sources** at the end of the paper or in bibliographic notes. When a list of sources includes only the sources actually referred to in a paper, it is called *Works Cited* or *References*. A source list that includes all the works a writer looks at, not just those referred to in the paper, is called *Works Consulted, Bibliography,* or *References*.

Four documentation styles are featured in this chapter. Never mix documentation styles. The most frequently used style in the humanities was developed by the Modern Language Association (**MLA**). It is a **parenthetical citation system** that calls for a source name and page reference to be entered at each place you use a source in your paper. Also, at the end of your paper you include a Works Cited list giving full bibliographic details about each cited source. For full coverage of MLA documentation based on the Fourth Edition of the *MLA Handbook for Writers of Research Papers* by Joseph Gibaldi (1995), see section 33c.

The documentation style used in most social sciences was developed by the American Psychological Association (**APA**). It is a parenthetical citation system that calls for a source name and a publication year, and sometimes a page reference, to be entered at each place you use a source in your paper. Also, at the end of your paper, you include a References list of all cited and "recoverable" sources. (A recoverable source is one that a reader can expect to be able to locate, like a book, and unlike a personal letter.) For full coverage of APA documentation based on the Fourth Edition of the *Publication Manual of the American Psychological Association* (1994), see section 33d.

A third style, also used in the humanities and other disciplines, is described in the style manual of the University of Chicago Press and is known as Chicago Manual (**CM**) style. *The Chicago Manual of Style* describes two very different documentation systems: (1) a name-year parenthetical citation system and References list similar to APA's, and (2) a system using bibliographic notes containing full source information. (A separate list of references is usually unnecessary with bibliographic notes.) For full coverage of the CM bibliography, note style of documentation as described in the Fourteenth Edition of *The Chicago Manual of Style* (1993), see section 33e.

The Council of Biology Editors (**CBE**) has compiled a manual, *Scientific Style and Format*, of style and documentation guidelines for mathematics, the physical sciences, and the life sciences. In it, the CBE describes two documentation systems: (1) a **name-year parenthetical citation system** and References list, and (2) a **"numbered reference" system** using numbers in the paper to cite a source and a numbered References list giving full bibliographic details for each source. For coverage of CBE recommendations for citing sources in a paper and for a References list as described in the Sixth Edition of *The CBE Manual for Authors, Editors, and Publishers* (1994), see section 33f.

Careful, responsible documentation is an academic obligation. To help you fulfil this obligation, this handbook presents MLA, APA, CM, and CBE documentation guidelines in separate sections. Chart 141 gives a handy list of where in this handbook you can find information on each style.

33b Creating a working bibliography

To create a working bibliography, write out a bibliographic card for every source you take notes on. Include all the information you need to fulfil the requirements of the documentation style you are using. Also, for each card on a library source, write the call number in the upper left-hand corner, being careful to copy it exactly. (Depending on how recent they are and how the library you are using stores them, magazines and journals may not have call numbers.) If you conduct research at more than one library, also note on the card the library where you found each source.

Be especially careful with online sources: Include on the bibliographic card for each online source the date on which you access the material. Because some information in online databases is updated periodically, documentation for an online source must include both any date related to the source (such as the date of publication for a print form or the source, if any) and the date you access the material. If you download the source, the date you download is the access date to use even if you take notes on it later. If you take notes from the screen, use the date you take notes.

When the time comes to compile bibliographic information for your research paper, you can easily arrange your bibliographic cards in the order required by your documentation style (for example, in alphabetical order for an MLA-style Works Cited list). The bibliographic cards shown here are for a source cited in the research paper in Chapter 34.

Kenner, Andrew N., and George
Katsimaglis. "Gender Differences in
Proxemics: Taxi-Seat Choice."
Psychological Reports 72 (1993):
625-626.
(I found this in Social Science
Index.)

HD31. H229-1990
Hall, Edward, and Hall, Mildred Reed.
Understanding Cultural Differences:
Germans, French, and Americans.
Yarmouth, ME: Intercultural
Press, 1990.

33c   Using MLA-style documentation

In MLA (Modern Language Association) documentation, you are expected to document any source that you quote, paraphrase, or summarize with a two-part system.

1. Within the body of the paper, use in-text citations, as described in 33c-1.

2. At the end of the paper, provide a list of sources titled Works Cited; see 33c-2 and 33c-3.

(For information about using notes for additional content or for extensive citations of sources when you are using MLA-style parenthetical citations, see 33c-4.)

1 Citing sources in the body of a paper in MLA style

For most in-text citations, wherever you use ideas or information you have found in a source, you give a name or a title (whichever is the first information in the source's entry in the Works Cited list) to identify the source and page numbers to show the exact location in the source of the material you are using. In your sentences that set the context for your use of source material, try to include author names and, when relevant, credentials of authors who are authorities. In such cases, the only part of a citation to put in parentheses is the page number(s). If you cannot incorporate author names into your sentences, give them as part of the parenthetical citation. In a parenthetical citation, use one space between an author name (or title) and page number; do not use a comma or other punctuation between name and page number.

❖ MLA FORMAT ALERT: Position a parenthetical citation at the end of the material it refers to, even at the end of a sentence, if that is not too far away from the material. At the end of a sentence, place a parenthetical reference before the sentence's end punctuation. ❖

The examples in this section show how to handle various parenthetical citations in the body of your paper. Remember, however, that you can usually integrate the names and titles of sources into your sentences.

1. CITING A PARAPHRASED OR SUMMARIZED SOURCE—MLA

Desmond Morris notes that people from the Mediterranean prefer an elbow-to-shoulder distance from each other (131). [Author name cited in text; page number cited in parentheses.]

In <u>Manwatching: A Field Guide to Human Behavior,</u> zoologist Desmond Morris notes that people from the Mediterranean prefer an elbow-to-shoulder distance from each other (131). [Title of source, author name, and author credentials cited in text; page number cited in parentheses.]

On the other hand, people from the Mediterranean prefer an elbow-to-shoulder distance from each other (Morris 131). [Author name and page number cited in parentheses.]

2. CITING THE SOURCE OF A SHORT QUOTATION—MLA

Hall observes that "if you are interested in something, your pupils dilate; if I say something you don't like, they tend to contract" (47), thus suggesting why in some cultures people stand close to each other when they speak. Personal space "moves with us," according to Fisher, Bell, and Baum, "expanding and contracting according to the situation in which we find ourselves" (149).

❖ MLA FORMAT ALERT: When a quotation is no longer than four hand-written or typed lines, enclose the quoted words in quotation marks to distinguish them from your own words in the sentence. Place the parentheses after the closing quotation mark but before sentence-ending punctuation. If a quotation ends in an exclamation point or a question mark, however, put that punctuation mark before the closing quotation mark, put the parenthetical citation next, and then put a period after the parenthetical citation. ❖

Coles asks, "What binds together a Mormon banker in Utah with his brother, or other coreligionists in Illinois or Massachusetts?" (2).

3. CITING THE SOURCE OF A LONG QUOTATION—MLA

Robert Sommer, an environmental psychologist, uses literary and personal analogies to describe personal space:

Like the porcupines in Schopenhauer's fable, people like to be close enough to obtain warmth and comradeship but far enough away to avoid pricking one another. Personal space...has been likened to a snail shell, a soap bubble, an aura, and "breathing room." (26)

❖ MLA FORMAT ALERT: When a quotation is longer than four hand-written or typed lines, do not put quotation marks around the quoted words. Instead, set the quoted words off from your own words by in-denting each line of the quotation. In a typed paper, use a 10-space indent for each line of a quotation longer than four lines. If you are handwriting or using a computer, indent each line of the quotation one inch (about 2.5 cm). Put one space after the last punctuation mark of the quotation, and then put in the parenthetical citation. For other examples of long quotations, of prose and of poetry, see Amy Brown's research paper in Chapter 34. ❖

4. CITING ONE AUTHOR—MLA

Give an author's name as it appears on the source: for a book, the title page; for an article, directly before the title or at the end of the

607

article. Many nonprint sources also name an author: for a CD, cassette, tape, or software, for example, check the printed sleeve or cover. For an online source, identify an author as he or she is identified online.

```
Males in Germany and the United States stand farther apart and
touch less when they talk to other males than when they talk to
females (Shuter 305).
```

5. CITING TWO OR THREE AUTHORS—MLA

Give the names in the order they have in the source. Spell out *and.* For three authors, use a comma between the first- and second-named authors.

```
As children get older, they become more aware of standards for
personal space (Worchel and Cooper 536).
```

```
Personal space gets larger or smaller depending on the circumstances
of the social interaction (Fisher, Bell, and Baum 149).
```

6. CITING MORE THAN THREE AUTHORS—MLA

With three or more authors, you can name them all or use the first author's name only, followed by *et al.,* either in a parenthetical reference or in your sentence. Do not underline *et al.* No period follows *et,* but do use a period after *al.*

❖ USAGE ALERT: The abbreviation *et al.* stands for "and others"; when an author's name followed by *et al.* is a subject, use a plural verb. ❖

```
Fisher et al. have found that personal space gets larger or smaller
depending on the circumstances of the social interaction (158).
```

```
Personal space gets larger or smaller depending on the circum-
stances of the social interaction (Fisher et al. 158).
```

7. CITING MORE THAN ONE SOURCE BY AN AUTHOR—MLA

When you use two or more sources by an author, include the relevant title in each citation. In parenthetical citations, use a shortened version of the title. For example, in a paper using as sources Edward T. Hall's *The Hidden Dimension* and "Learning the Arabs' Silent Language," parenthetical citations use *Hidden* and "Learning." Shorten the titles as much as possible, keeping them unambiguous to readers and starting them with the word by which you alphabetize the works in Works Cited. Separate the author's name and the title with a comma, but do not use punctuation between the title and page number.

Although most people are unaware that interpersonal distances exist and contribute to people's reactions to one another (Hall, <u>Hidden</u> 109), Arabic males seem to understand the practicality of close conversational distances (Hall, "Learning" 41).

When you incorporate the title into your own sentences, you can omit a subtitle, but do not shorten it more than that.

8. CITING TWO OR MORE AUTHORS WITH THE SAME LAST NAME—MLA

Use each author's first and last name in each citation, whether in your sentences or in parenthetical citations.

According to British zoologist Desmond Morris, conversational distances vary between people from different countries (131). If a North American backs away from an Arab, the North American is considered cold, the Arab pushy (Charles G. Morris 516).

9. CITING A WORK WITH A GROUP OR CORPORATE AUTHOR—MLA

When a corporation or other group is named as the author of a source you want to cite, use the corporate name just as you would an individual's name.

In a five-year study, the Canadian Institute of Child Health reported that these tests are usually unreliable (11).

A five-year study shows that these tests are usually unreliable (Canadian Institute of Child Health 11).

10. CITING A WORK BY TITLE—MLA

If no author is named, use the title in citations. In your own sentences, use the full main title and omit a subtitle, if any. For parenthetical citations, shorten the title as much as possible (making sure the shortened version refers unambiguously to the correct source), and always make the first word the one by which you alphabetize it. The following citation is to an article fully titled "Are You a Day or Night Person?"

The "morning lark" and "night owl" connotations typically are used to categorize the human extremes ("Are You" 11).

11. CITING A MULTIVOLUME WORK—MLA

When you cite more than one volume of a multivolume work, include the relevant volume number in each citation. (In the Works Cited list, list the multivolume work once and give the total number of volumes;

see item 9 in the Works Cited examples in 33c-3). Give the volume number first, followed by a colon and one space, followed by the page number(s).

By 1900, the Amazon forest dwellers had been exposed to these viruses (Rand 3: 202).

Rand believes that forest dwellers in Borneo escaped illness from retroviruses until the 1960s (4: 518-19).

12. CITING MATERIAL FROM A NOVEL, PLAY, OR POEM—MLA

When you cite material from literary works, part, chapter, act, scene, canto, stanza, or line numbers usually help readers trying to locate what you refer to more than page numbers do. Unless your instructor tells you not to, use arabic numerals for these references, even if the literary work uses roman numerals.

For novels that use them, give part and/or chapter numbers after page numbers. Use a semicolon after the page number but a comma to separate a part from a chapter.

Flannery O'Connor describes one character in <u>The Violent Bear It Away</u> as "divided in two—a violent and a rational self" (139, pt. 2, ch. 6).

For plays that use them, give act, scene, and/or line numbers. Use periods between these numbers.

Among the most quoted of Shakespeare's lines is Hamlet's soliloquy beginning "To be, or not to be: that is the question" (3.1.56).

For poems and plays that use them, give canto, stanza, and/or line numbers. Use periods between these numbers.

In "To Autumn," Keats's most melancholy image occurs in the lines "Then in a wailful choir the small gnats mourn / Among the river swallows" (3.27-28).

❖ MLA ABBREVIATION ALERT: The *MLA Handbook* advises spelling out the word *Line* (or *Lines*) the first time you cite a line reference because the abbreviation for line (l., plural ll.) can so easily be misread as the numeral 1. After the first citation, you can omit the word. ❖

13. CITING A WORK IN AN ANTHOLOGY OR OTHER COLLECTION—MLA

You may want to cite a work you have read in a book that contains many works by various authors and that was compiled, written, or edited by someone other than the person you are citing. For example, suppose you want to cite "When in Rome" by Mari Evans, which you have read in a literature text by Pamela Annas and Robert Rosen. Use Evans's name and the title of her work in the in-text citation and as the first block of information for the entry in the Works Cited list (see item 10 in the list of MLA Works Cited examples).

```
In "When in Rome," Mari Evans uses parentheses to enclose lines
expressing the houseworker's thoughts as her employer offers
lunch, as in the first stanza's "(an egg / or soup / there ain't
no meat)" (688-89).
```

14. CITING AN INDIRECT SOURCE—MLA

When you want to quote words that you found quoted in someone else's work, put the name of the person whose words you are quoting into your own sentence. Indicate the work where you found the quotation either in your sentence or in a parenthetical citation beginning with "qtd. in."

❖ RESEARCH ALERT: When it is possible to do so, find the primary source for words that you want to quote rather than taking a quotation from a secondary source. ❖

```
Martin Scorcese acknowledges the link between himself and his
films: "I realize that all my life, I've been an outsider. I
splatter bits of myself all over the screen" (qtd. in Giannetti
and Eyman 397).
```

```
Giannetti and Eyman quote Martin Scorcese as acknowledging the
link between himself and his films: "I realize that all my life,
I've been an outsider. I splatter bits of myself all over the
screen" (397).
```

15. CITING TWO OR MORE SOURCES IN ONE REFERENCE—MLA

If more than one source has contributed to an idea, opinion, or fact in your paper, acknowledge all of them. In a parenthetical citation, separate each block of information with a semicolon followed by one space.

```
Once researchers agreed that these cultural "distance zones"
existed, their next step was to try to measure or define them
(Hall 110-20; Henley 32-33; Fisher, Bell, and Baum 153).
```

Because long parenthetical citations can disturb the flow of your paper, consider using an endnote or footnote for citing multiple sources; see 33c-4.

16. Citing an Entire Work—MLA

References to an entire work usually fit best into your own sentences.

In `The Clockwork Sparrow,` Sue Binkley analyzes studies of circadian rhythms undertaken between 1967 and 1989.

17. Citing an Electronic Source with a Name or Title and Page Numbers—MLA

The principles that govern in-text citations of electronic sources are exactly the same as the ones that apply to books, articles, letters, interviews, or any other source you get information from on paper or in person. You put in your own sentences or in parenthetical references enough information for a reader to be able to locate full information about the source in the Works Cited list.

When an electronically accessed source identifies its author, use the author's name for in-text citations. If an electronic source does not name the author, use its title for in-text citations and for the first block of information in that source's Works Cited entry. (See item 10 above for an example of a work cited by its title and for advice about shortening a title for an in-text citation.)

When an electronic source has page numbers, use them exactly as you would the page numbers of a print source.

18. Citing an Electronic Source that Numbers Paragraphs—MLA

When an electronic source has numbered paragraphs (instead of page numbers), use them for in-text references as you would page numbers, with two differences: (1) Use a comma followed by one space after the name (or title); and (2) use the abbreviation *par.* for a reference to one paragraph or *pars.* for a reference to more than one paragraph, followed by the number(s) of the paragraphs you are citing.

Artists seem to be haunted by the fear that psychoanalysts might destroy creativity while it reconstructs personality (Francis, pars. 22-25).

19. Citing an Electronic Source Without Page or Paragraph Numbers—MLA

Many online sources do not number pages or paragraphs. In the Works Cited entry for such a source, include the abbreviation *n. pag.* ("no pagination"). This abbreviation serves to explain to readers why in-text references to this source do not cite page numbers. Here is an example from an online source without page numbers or paragraph numbers.

From March to April in 1994, violations of this important
disclosure regulation increased 123 percent (Pessan).

2 Compiling an MLA-Style Works Cited List

In MLA documentation, in-text citations must be accompanied
by a list of all the sources referred to in your paper. In a Works Cited
list, include only the sources from which you quote or paraphrase or
summarize. Do not include sources that you have consulted but do
not refer to in the paper unless your instructor asks for a Works
Consulted list (which follows the same format as a Works Cited list).
Chart 142 gives general information about a Works Cited list.

GUIDELINES FOR COMPILING AN MLA-STYLE WORKS CITED LIST   142

■ **TITLE**
Works Cited

■ **PLACEMENT OF LIST**
Start a new page numbered sequentially with the rest of the
paper, after Notes pages, if any.

■ **CONTRAST AND FORMAT**
Include all sources quoted from, paraphrased, or summarized in
your paper. Start each entry on a new line and at the regular left
margin. If the entry uses more than one line, indent all lines but
the first five spaces (or one-half inch—about 1.25 cm) from the
left margin. Double-space all lines.

■ **SPACING AFTER PUNCTUATION**
In the Fourth Edition of the *MLA Handbook*, examples of Works
Cited entries use one space after a period at the end of an
information unit such as the author name(s), the title of the cited
source, and the publication information. (In the past, MLA specified
two spaces after these periods.) Unless your instructor tells you to
use two spaces after a period, one space is acceptable.
Put one space after a comma.
Put one space after a colon.

■ **ARRANGEMENT OF ENTRIES**
Alphabetize by author's last name. If no author is named,
alphabetize by the title's first significant word (not *A, An,* or *The*).

➜

GUIDELINES FOR COMPILING AN MLA-STYLE WORKS CITED LIST ¹⁴²
(continued)

- **AUTHORS' NAMES**
  Use first names and middle names or middle initials, if any, as
  given in the source. Do not use initials for any name that is given
  in full. For one author or the first-named author in multiauthor
  works, give the last name first. Use the word *and* with two or
  more authors. List multiple authors in the order given in the
  source. Use a comma between the first author's last and first
  names and after each complete author name except the last.
  After the last author name, use a period: `Fein, Ethel Andrea,`
  `Bert Griggs, and Delaware Rogash.`

  Include *Jr., Sr., II, III,* but do not include other titles and degrees
  before or after a name. For example, an entry for a work by
  Edward Meep, III, M.D., and Sir Feeney Bolton, would start like
  this: `Meep, Edward, III, and Feeney Bolton.`

- **CAPITALIZATION OF TITLES**
  Capitalize all major words in titles.

- **SPECIAL TREATMENT OF TITLES**
  Use quotation marks around titles of shorter works (poems, short
  stories, essays, articles). Underline titles of longer works (books,
  names of newspapers or journals containing cited articles). For underlining, <u>use an unbroken line like this</u> (unless you use software
  that underlines only with a <u>broken</u> <u>line,</u> <u>like</u> <u>this</u>).

  When a book title includes the title of another work that is usually
  underlined (such as a novel, play, or long poem), do not underline
  the incorporated title: <u>Decoding</u> `Jane Eyre.`

  If the incorporated title is usually enclosed in quotation marks
  (such as a short story or short poem), keep the quotation marks
  and underline the complete title of the book (do not underline the
  period): <u>Theme and Form in "The Waste Land</u>`."`

  Drop *A, An,* or *The* as the first word of a periodical title.

- **PLACE OF PUBLICATION**
  If several cities are listed for the place of publication, give only the
  first. If a city name alone would be ambiguous, also give the two-
  letter postal abbreviation for the province or U.S. state, or an abbreviated country name, if necessary.

- **PUBLISHER**
  Use shortened names as long as they are clear: *Prentice* for
  Prentice Hall, Simon for *Simon & Schuster.* For university presses,

GUIDELINES FOR COMPILING AN MLA-STYLE WORKS CITED LIST 142
(continued)

use the capital letters *U* and *P* (without periods): for *Oxford University Press* and the *University of Chicago Press*, respectively, `Oxford UP; U of Chicago P`.

■ **PUBLICATION MONTH ABBREVIATIONS**
Abbreviate all publication months except *May, June,* and *July.* Use the first three letters followed by a period: `Dec., Feb.`

■ **PARAGRAPH NUMBERS IN ELECTRONIC SOURCES**
For electronic sources that number paragraphs instead of pages, give the total number of paragraphs followed by the abbreviation *pars.*: `77 pars.`

■ **INCLUSIVE PAGE NUMBERS**
Use inclusive page numbers to give the starting page number and the ending page number of any paginated electronic source and any paginated print source that is part of a longer work (for example, a chapter in a book, an article in a journal). Inclusive page numbers signal that the cited work is on those pages and all pages in between. If that is not the case, use the style shown below for discontinuous page numbers. In either case, give numerals only, without the words *page* or *pages* or the abbreviations *p.* or *pp.*

Use the full second number through 99. Then use only the last two digits for the second number unless unclear: 103-04 is clear, but 567-602 requires full numbers.

■ **DISCONTINUOUS PAGES**
Use the starting page number followed by a plus sign (+): 32+.

■ **WORKS CITED ENTRIES: BOOKS**
Citations for books have three main parts: author, title, and publication information (place of publication, publisher, and date of publication).

AUTHOR	TITLE	PUBLICATION INFORMATION

`Dudek, Louis. Collected Poetry. Montreal: Delta, 1971.`

■ **WORKS CITED ENTRIES: PRINT ARTICLES**
Citations for periodical articles contain three major parts: author, title or article, and publication information (usually the periodical title, volume number, year of publication, and inclusive page numbers).

→

615

AUTHOR   ARTICLE TITLE

Shuter, Robert   "A Field Study of Nonverbal Communication

in Germany, Italy, and the United States."

JOURNAL TITLE   PUBLICATION
                  INFORMATION

Communication Monographs.   44 (1977): 298-305.

ARTICLE   JOURNAL   PUBLICATION
TITLE   TITLE   INFORMATION

"A Start."   New Republic   2 May 1994: 7+.

■ **WORKS CITED ENTRIES: ELECTRONIC SOURCES**

Citations for electronic sources contain at least six major parts: author, publication information, title of database, publication medium, name of vendor or computer service, electronic publication date or access date. Electronic versions of sources that also appear in print start with information about the print version. Here is an entry for a journal article accessed through a computer service; it also has a print version.

ARTICLE AUTHOR   ARTICLE TITLE

Sheridan, Peter M., and Sandra W. Pike.   "Predictors of

Time to Completion of Graduate Degrees."

                   PUBLICATION INFORMATION
TITLE OF PRINT JOURNAL   FOR PRINT JOURNAL

Canadian Journal of Higher Education   24.2 (1994): 68-88.

ELECTRONIC
PUBLICATION   COMPUTER   ACCESS
MEDIUM   NETWORK   DATE

Online.   ERIC, BRS 123678.   21 June 1994.

Here is an entry for an article from a CD-ROM encyclopedia.

ARTICLE   ARTICLE   CD-ROM
AUTHOR   TITLE   TITLE

Regan, Robert.   "Poe, Edgar Allan."   Academic American

33c
MLA

ELECTRONIC	CD-ROM
PUBLICATION	PUBLICATION
MEDIUM	INFORMATION

<u>Encyclopedia</u>. `CD-ROM`. `Grolier Electronic`

`Publishing, 1993.`

---

3   **Following models for an MLA-style Works Cited list**

Directory

PRINT SOURCES: BOOKS

1. Book by One Author—MLA
2. Book by Two or Three Authors—MLA
3. Book by More than Three Authors—MLA
4. Two or More Books by the Same Author(s)—MLA
5. Book by Group or Corporate Author—MLA
6. Book with No Author Named—MLA
7. Book with an Author and an Editor—MLA
8. Translation—MLA
9. Work in Several Volumes or Parts—MLA
10. Anthology or Collection—MLA
11. One Selection from an Anthology or Collection—MLA
12. More than One Selection from an Anthology or Collection—MLA
13. Signed Article in a Reference Book—MLA
14. Unsigned Article in a Reference Book—MLA
15. Edition—MLA
16. Introduction, Preface, Foreword, or Afterword—MLA
17. Unpublished Dissertation—MLA
18. Reprint of an Older Book—MLA
19. Book in a Series—MLA
20. Book with a Title Within a Title—MLA

617

21. Government Publications—MLA
22. Published Proceedings of a Conference—MLA

PRINT SOURCES: ARTICLES AND OTHER SHORT DOCUMENTS

23. Signed Article from a Daily Newspaper—MLA
24. Editorial, Letter to the Editor, Review—MLA
25. Unsigned Article from a Daily Newspaper—MLA
26. Signed Article from a Weekly or Biweekly Magazine or Newspaper—MLA
27. Signed Article from a Monthly or Bimonthly Periodical—MLA
28. Unsigned Article from a Weekly or Monthly Periodical—MLA
29. Article from a Collection of Reprinted Articles—MLA
30. Article from a SIRS Collection of Reprinted Articles—MLA
31. Article in a Journal with Continuous Pagination—MLA
32. Article in a Journal That Pages Each Issue Separately—MLA
33. An Abstract from a Collection of Abstracts—MLA
34. Published and Unpublished Letters—MLA
35. Map or Chart—MLA

NONPRINT SOURCES

36. Interview—MLA
37. Lecture, Speech, Address—MLA
38. Film or Videotape—MLA
39. Recording—MLA
40. Live Performance—MLA
41. Work of Art or Musical Composition—MLA
42. Radio or Television Program—MLA

ELECTRONIC SOURCES

43. CD-ROM Database: Abstract with a Print Version—MLA
44. Online Database: Abstract with a Print Version—MLA
45. CD-ROM: Article from a Magazine with a Print Version—MLA
46. CD-ROM: Selection from a Book with a Print Version—MLA
47. CD-ROM: Material with No Print Version—MLA
48. CD-ROM: Nonperiodical Publication—MLA
49. Work in More than One Publication Medium—MLA
50. Online: Article from a Newspaper with a Print Version—MLA
51. Online: Article from a Magazine with a Print Version—MLA
52. Online: Material with No Print Version—MLA
53. Online: Material from an Electronic Newsletter—MLA

54. Online: An Electronic Text—MLA
55. Online: A Public Message—MLA

PRINT SOURCES: BOOKS

1. BOOK BY ONE AUTHOR—MLA

Trudeau, Pierre E. Federalism and the French Canadians. Toronto:
    Macmillan Canada, 1968.

2. BOOK BY TWO OR THREE AUTHORS—MLA

Scardamalia, Marlene, Carl Bereiter, and Bryant Fillion. Writing
    for Results: A Sourcebook of Consequential Composing
    Activities. Toronto: OISE Press, 1981.

3. BOOK BY MORE THAN THREE AUTHORS—MLA

Cameron, Deborah, et al. Researching Language: Issues of Power and
    Method. London: Routledge, 1992.

4. TWO OR MORE BOOKS BY THE SAME AUTHOR(S)—MLA

Atwood, Margaret. The Handmaid's Tale. Toronto: McClelland &
    Stewart, 1985.

---. Survival. Toronto: Anansi, 1972.

---. True Stories. Toronto: Oxford UP, 1981.

5. BOOK BY GROUP OR CORPORATE AUTHOR—MLA

Environmental Defense Fund. Recycling and Incineration: Evaluating
    the Choice. Washington, DC: Island, 1990.

American Psychological Association. Publication Manual of the
    American Psychological Association. 4th ed. Washington, DC:
    APA, 1994.

6. BOOK WITH NO AUTHOR NAMED—MLA

The Chicago Manual of Style. 14th ed. Chicago: U of Chicago P, 1993.

7. BOOK WITH AN AUTHOR AND AN EDITOR—MLA

If your focus is on Eudora Welty as the author of the reviews in *A
Writer's Eye* and your paper refers to her and/or her words, put her
name first in the Works Cited entry:

Welty, Eudora. <u>A Writer's Eye: Collected Book Reviews</u>. Ed. Pearl A.
  McHaney. Jackson: UP of Mississippi, 1994.

If your focus is on Pearl A. McHaney's work as the editor of this
collection of reviews and your paper refers to her and/or her words, put
her name first in the Works Cited entry:

McHaney, Pearl A., ed. <u>A Writer's Eye: Collected Book Reviews</u>. By
  Eudora Welty. Jackson: UP of Mississippi, 1994.

8. Translation—MLA

Maillet, Antonine. <u>La Sagouine</u>. Trans. Luis de Cespedes. Toronto:
  Simon & Pierre, 1979.

9. Work in Several Volumes or Parts—MLA

When you use more than one volume of a multivolume work, after
the title give the total number of volumes. In each parenthetical citation,
give both volume and page numbers (see item 11 in 33c-2).

Rand, Enid. <u>Virology</u>. 5 vols. Philadelphia: Lippincott, 1979.

When you use only one volume, instead of the total number of
volumes, give the number of the volume you used. In parenthetical
citations, give page numbers only; do not repeat the volume number.

Rand, Enid. <u>Virology</u>. Vol. 2. Philadelphia: Lippincott, 1979.

When you use only one volume of a multivolume work in which
each volume is titled separately, you can list it as you would any book,
using its individual title and not referring to the rest of the volumes.

Goldman, L. H., Gloria L. Cronin, and Ada Aharoni. <u>Saul Bellow: A</u>
  <u>Mosaic</u>. New York: P. Lang, 1992.

If you want to include information about the set of volumes, put
it after the basic information about the volume you used.

Goldman, L. H., Gloria L. Cronin, and Ada Aharoni. <u>Saul Bellow: A</u>
  <u>Mosaic</u>. New York: P. Lang, 1992. Vol. 2 of <u>Twentieth Century</u>
  <u>American Jewish Writers</u>. 14 vols.

10. Anthology or Collection—MLA

When your paper is about a collection of works rather than about the
individual selections in an anthology or collection, use this form. Also
see item 15 below.

New, W. H., ed. <u>Canadian Short Fiction: From Myth to Modern</u>.
    Scarborough, ON: Prentice, 1986.

11. ONE SELECTION FROM AN ANTHOLOGY OR COLLECTION—MLA

Morriseau, Norval. "The Indian That Became a Thunderbird." <u>Canadian</u>
    <u>Short Fiction: From Myth to Modern</u>. Ed. W. H. New. Scarborough,
    ON: Prentice, 1986. 26-29.

12. MORE THAN ONE SELECTION FROM AN ANTHOLOGY OR COLLECTION—MLA

When you use more than one selection from one anthology, in the
Works Cited list you can give one entry for the anthology and separate
brief entries for each selection cited from the anthology. This plan is
more efficient than using the form shown in item 10 for each selection
you use. Give full details about the anthology or edited collection, with
the editor's name as the first item of information. For each selection
cited in your paper, give the name of the selection's author and title. End
this information with a period, and then give the name that starts the
entry for the anthology and inclusive pages on which the specific
selection falls. For citations in your paper, use the name of the author
of the selection, not the editor of the anthology. The following entries
show first an entry for an anthology followed by entries for two
selections in the anthology. Readers who look at the Davies and Engel
entries are directed to the Ioannou entry for full information about the
anthology and see that the cited material is on pages 40 and 113
respectively.

Ioannou, Greg, and Lynne Missen, eds. <u>Shivers: An Anthology of</u>
    <u>Canadian Ghost Stories</u>. Toronto: McClelland-Bantam, 1989.

Davies, Robertson. "The Charlottetown Banquet." Ioannou and Missen.
    40.

Engle, Marian. "The Country Doctor." Ioannou and Missen. 113.

13. SIGNED ARTICLE IN A REFERENCE BOOK—MLA

Shadbolt, Doris. "Emily Carr." <u>The Canadian Encyclopedia</u>. 2nd ed.

Alphabetically arranged collections such as the encyclopedias in
this model and the next one do not contain page numbers.

14. UNSIGNED ARTICLE IN A REFERENCE BOOK—MLA

"Russia." <u>Encyclopedia Britannica</u>. 1994 ed.

15. EDITION—MLA

When a book is in some edition other than the first, the edition number appears on the title page. Include this information after the title. Use *2nd ed., 3rd ed., Rev. ed.* (for *Revised edition*), and so on. Put a period after *ed.*, which also acts as the period at the end of the information block.

Buckley, Joanne, and David Gates. <u>Put It in Writing</u>. 2nd ed.
Scarborough, ON: Prentice, 1995.

Books are also "editions" when an editor has made an important contribution, such as in selecting works and writing background material about them for an anthology. In this sort of edition, the editor's name (or editors' names) comes first. Also see item 10 above.

Lantolf, James P., and Gabriela Appel, eds. <u>Vygotskian Approaches
to Second Language Research</u>. Norwood, NJ: Ablex, 1994.

Spear, Thomas, and Richard Waller, eds. <u>Being Masai: Ethnicity and
Identity in East Africa</u>. Athens, Ohio UP, 1993.

16. INTRODUCTION, PREFACE, FOREWORD, OR AFTERWORD—MLA

Burton, Lydia, et al. Preface. <u>Editing Canadian English</u>. By Burton
et al. Vancouver: Douglas & McIntyre, 1987. vii-viii.

Allmand, Warren. Foreword. <u>The Life and Death of Anna Mae Aquash</u>.
By Johanna Brand. Toronto: Lorimer, 1993. v-ix.

When you cite an introduction, preface, foreword, afterword, or appendix, give first the name of the person who wrote it. Then give the name of the cited part, capitalizing it and using a period after it; do not underline it or put it in quotation marks. Then give the title of the book. If the preface, introduction, foreword, afterword, or appendix was written by someone other than the author of the book, give the word *By* and the name of the book's author(s), in normal order. If the book's author wrote the part you are citing, after *By* repeat only the last name or names. After publication information, give inclusive page numbers. If a cited preface or introduction uses roman numerals for page numbers, use roman numerals.

17. UNPUBLISHED DISSERTATION—MLA

Buckley, Joanne. "An Assessment of Kieran Egan's Theory of
Educational Development." Diss. U of Western Ontario, 1991.

18. Reprint of an Older Book—MLA

Lampman, Archibald. <u>Lyrics of Earth</u>. 1895. Ottawa: Tecumseh, 1978.

A republished book may be the paperback version of a book originally published as a hardbound, or it may be the reissue of a book. Republishing information can be found on the copyright page. Give the date of the original version before the publication information for the version you used.

19. Book in a Series—MLA

Courchene, Thomas J. <u>In Praise of Renewed Federalism</u>. The Canada
    Round. Toronto: C. D. Howe Institute, 1991.

Give the book title, underlined, after the author name. Put the series title, neither underlined nor in quotation marks, after the book title.

20. Book with a Title Within a Title—MLA

Hayes, Keith J., ed. <u>The Critical Response to Herman Melville's</u>
    Moby Dick. Westport, CT: Greenwood, 1994.

When a book title includes the title of another work that is usually underlined (such as a novel, play, or long poem), do not underline the incorporated title. When a book title includes a title enclosed in quotation marks (such as of a short story or most poems), keep the quotation marks and underline the entire title.

21. Government Publications—MLA

For most government publications, use the name of the government as the first information unit (such as Canada). If no author is named, give the name of the branch of government or the government agency next (such as Department of Finance or Task Force on Program Review).

Canada. Royal Commission on Bilingualism and Biculturalism.
    <u>Preliminary Report</u>. Ottawa: Queen's Printer, 1965.

Canada. Indian and Northern Affairs Canada. <u>The Inuit</u>. Ottawa:
    Supply and Services Canada, 1986.

22. Published Proceedings of a Conference—MLA

Pavlyshyn, Marko, and J. E. M. Clarke, eds. <u>Ukraine in the 1990s.</u>
    <u>Proc. of the First Conference of the Ukrainian Studies</u>
    <u>Association of Australia</u>. Melbourne: Monash University, 1992.

623

If the title of the publication of the conference proceedings includes the name and location of the conference, do not repeat that information after the title. Just give author(s), title, and publication details.

PRINT SOURCES: ARTICLES AND OTHER SHORT DOCUMENTS

23. SIGNED ARTICLE FROM A DAILY NEWSPAPER—MLA

Tebbutt, Tom. "Showman Agassi Lightly Frolics to Canadian Title."
Globe and Mail 1 Aug. 1994: D1.

24. EDITORIAL, LETTER TO THE EDITOR, REVIEW—MLA

"A Black Mark on Local Government." Editorial. London Free Press 27
July 1994: B8.

Hurka, John. Letter. Calgary Sun 5 July 1994: A18.

Toews, Wendy. "Politics of the Mind." Rev. of They Say You're Crazy
by Paula J. Caplan. Winnipeg Free Press 26 Aug. 1995: C3.

25. UNSIGNED ARTICLE FROM A DAILY NEWSPAPER—MLA

"Canadian Adds Flights." Globe and Mail 1 Aug. 1994: B2.

26. SIGNED ARTICLE FROM A WEEKLY OR BIWEEKLY MAGAZINE OR NEWSPAPER—MLA

Wood, Chris. "Storm Clouds over Quebec." Maclean's 6 Nov. 1989: 16-17.

27. SIGNED ARTICLE FROM A MONTHLY OR BIMONTHLY PERIODICAL—MLA

O'Malley, Sean. "Make-It-Happen Kinda Dreamer: Theatre Director
Diane Dupuy Is Nobody's Puppet." Chatelaine Aug. 1994: 36+.

The O'Malley article runs on pages 36-39 and 90. The + sign is sufficient to show that it runs past page 36.

Bell, Jim. "Kingdom Come: Canada's Inuit Finally May Be Getting Their
Own Homeland, But at What Price?" Earthwatch Sept./Oct.: 10-11.

28. UNSIGNED ARTICLE FROM A WEEKLY OR MONTHLY PERIODICAL—MLA

"10 Ways to Sleep Easy." Canadian Living Aug. 1994: 19.

29. ARTICLE FROM A COLLECTION OF REPRINTED ARTICLES—MLA

Brumberg, Abraham. "Russia after Perestroika." New York Review of
Books 27 June 1991: 53-62. Rpt. in Russian and Soviet History.

Ed. Alexander Dallin. Vol. 14, The Gorbachev Era. New York: Garland, 1992. 300-320.

30. ARTICLE FROM A SIRS COLLECTION OF REPRINTED ARTICLES—MLA

Curver, Philip C. "Lighting in the 21st Century." Futurist
Jan./Feb. 1989: Energy. Ed. Eleanor Goldstein. Vol. 4. Boca
Raton: SIRS, 1990. Art. 84.

Social Issues Resources Series (SIRS) articles are looseleaf collections of reprints from many sources. Give information about the original publication before the information about the article's publication in SIRS. Use the abbreviation *Art.* before the SIRS article number.

31. ARTICLE IN A JOURNAL WITH CONTINUOUS PAGINATION—MLA

A journal that pages continuously throughout a volume (usually one year's publication) does not begin each issue with page 1. If the first issue in the volume ends on page 160, for example, the second issue starts on page 161. A reader who has the volume number, the year, and the page numbers can locate the correct issue of a continuously paged journal. Give the volume number in arabic numerals (without an abbreviation before it such as *vol.* or *Vol.*) immediately after the journal name. Include the year in parentheses. Give inclusive page numbers unless the article is printed on consecutive pages; in that case, give the article's first page number followed by a plus sign (+).

LaFollette, M. C. "The Politics of Research Misconduct:
Congressional Oversight, Universities, and Science." Journal of
Higher Education 65 (1994): 261-85.

32. ARTICLE IN A JOURNAL THAT PAGES EACH ISSUE SEPARATELY—MLA

If each issue in a year's issues of a scholarly journal starts on page 1, give an issue number after the volume number. Use arabic numerals. Separate the two numbers with a period but with no space before or after the period. For example, in the model, 30.10 signifies that the Hancock article is in volume 30, number 10 of *IEEE Spectrum.*

Hancock, D. "Prototyping the Hubble Fix." IEEE Spectrum 30.10
(1993): 34-39..

If a journal uses issue numbers but not volume numbers, give the issue number after the journal name.

33. AN ABSTRACT FROM A COLLECTION OF ABSTRACTS

To cite an abstract, first give information for the full work: the author's name, the title of the article, and publication information about the full article. If a reader could not know that the cited material is an abstract, give the word *Abstract*, not underlined, followed by a period. Give publication information about the collection of abstracts. For abstracts identified by item numbers rather than page numbers, use the word *item* before the item number.

```
Marcus, Hazel R., and Shinobu Kitayamo. "Culture and the Self:
    Implications for Cognition, Emotion, and Motivation.
    Psychological Review 88 (1991): 224-53. Psychological Abstracts
    78: item 23878.
```

34. PUBLISHED AND UNPUBLISHED LETTERS—MLA

If you cite a letter from a published source, name the author of the letter first. Identify the letter as such, and give its date, if available. Then give publication information.

```
Lapidus, Jackie. Letter to her mother. 12 Nov. 1975. Between
    Ourselves: Letters Between Mothers and Daughters. Ed. Karen
    Payne. Boston: Houghton, 1983. 323-26.
```

If you cite a personal letter that is not in a published source, give the letter writer's name as author, and put *Letter to the author* after the letter writer's name. Then give the date on the letter.

```
Reilly, Gary Edward. Letter to the author. 26 Dec. 1994.
```

You can document electronic mail in a similar way.

```
Putnam, Christopher. E-mail to the author. 6 June 1996.
```

35. MAP OR CHART—MLA

```
Russia and Post-Soviet Republics. Map. Moscow: Mapping Production
    Association, 1992.
```

NONPRINT SOURCES

36. INTERVIEW—MLA

```
Friedman, Randi. Telephone interview. 30 June 1992.
```

For a face-to-face interview, use `Personal interview` instead of `Telephone interview`. For a published interview, give the name of the interviewed person first, identify the source as an interview, and then give details as for any published source: author (preceded by the word *By*), title, publication details.

For a radio or television interview, give the name of the interviewed person first, the name of the interviewer next, and then information about the program on which the interview was broadcast.

Gellhorn, Martha. Interview with Daniel Richler. <u>Imprint</u>.
    TVOntario, Toronto. 7 Dec. 1992.

37. Lecture, Speech, Address—MLA

Barlow, Maud. Address. League of Canadian Poets. Toronto, 25 May
    1991.

38. Film or Videotape—MLA

<u>A World of Gestures: Cultural and Nonverbal Communication</u>.
    Writ./Dir. David Archer. Berkeley: U of Cal. Extension Media
    Center, 1992.

39. Recording—MLA

In a citation of a recording, put first the information important to your
use of the source. Here is an entry with the focus on the director of the
choral group.

De la Cuesta, Ismael Fernando, dir. Benedictine Monks of Santo
    Domingo de Silos. <u>Chant</u>. Angel, 1994.

If the use of this source in the paper focused on the performers
and the music, the entry would look like this:

Benedictine Monks of Santo Domingo de Silos. <u>Chant</u>. Dir. Ismael
    Fernando de la Cuesta. Angel, 1994.

If you are citing a recording in some medium other than a compact disk, name the medium. To cite a specific song, give the song
title in quotation marks before the title of the recording.

Cohen, Leonard. "Tower of Song." <u>I'm Your Man</u>. Audiocassette.
    Columbia, 1988.

40. Live Performance—MLA

<u>Long Day's Journey into Night</u>. By Eugene O'Neill. Dir. Diane
    Leblanc. With Martha Henry and William Hutt. Tom Patterson
    Theatre, Stratford, ON, 4 June 1994.

41. Work of Art or Musical Composition

Pratt, Christopher. <u>Shop on an Island</u>. London Regional Art Gallery,
    London, ON.

Gershwin, George. <u>Porgy and Bess</u>.

```
Schubert, Franz. Symphony no. 8 in B minor.
```

```
Schubert, Franz. Unfinished Symphony.
```

For musical compositions, give composer and title of work. Underline the title of an opera, ballet, or descriptive word title for music. But if a composition is identified only by musical form, number, and key, do not underline it and do not put it in quotation marks. See the entries for Schubert, which show two ways of identifying the same composition.

42. RADIO OR TELEVISION PROGRAM—MLA

For programs that title both the series and each episode, give the episode title first in quotation marks, and then give the series title underlined. If your use of the program focuses on a participant (such as a performer, writer, or director), give that name first, an abbreviated indication of that person's role (perf., writ., dir.), and then the programming information. Include the network, the local station and its city, and the date of the broadcast.

```
"Friends and Relations." The Road to Avonlea. CBC. CBLT, Toronto.
    22 Feb. 1992.
```

ELECTRONIC SOURCES

The objectives for documenting electronic sources are the same as those for print sources: giving information so that a reader understands what sources you have used and can find those sources that are generally available. The 1995 edition of the *MLA Handbook for Writers of Research* makes two major distinctions that affect the information you put in a Works Cited entry for an electronic source. One is whether the database is "portable," such as those on CD-ROM or diskette, or online; each Works Cited entry names the electronic medium, and the ones you are most likely to encounter are portable databases on CD-ROM and online databases. The second is whether the source has a print version or exists only in an electronic version; each Works Cited entry for a source that also has a print version starts out with information about the print version. For such sources, follow the information in the entries above for printed documents, and then add the necessary information about your electronic access of the source.

In general, the basic information needed for an electronic source is name of author (if any), publication information for a print version (if any), database title, publication medium, name of the producer (for "portable" databases) or computer network or service (for online databases), electronic publication date ("portable") or date of access (online).

To see the differences in an entry for a portable and an online source, compare items 43 and 44. They show a Works Cited entry for the same abstract from *Psychological Abstracts*. Item 43 documents the source accessed through PsycLIT, a CD-ROM version, and item 44 documents online access.

43. CD-ROM Database: Abstract with a Print Version—MLA

Marcus, Hazel R., and Shinobu Kitayamo. "Culture and the Self:
Implications for Cognition, Emotion, and Motivation."
Psychological Abstracts 78 (1991): item 23878. PsycLIT. CD-ROM.
SilverPlatter. Sept. 1991.

This model shows a portable database of information that also appears in a print version and that is updated from time to time. The information units for such a source start with the print version, followed by information about the electronic version. This source is an abstract from *Psychological Abstracts*. The information following the title *Psychological Abstracts* is the volume number and year and the item number of the abstract in the print version. PsycLIT is the name of the CD-ROM database, and SilverPlatter is the name of the producer of the CD-ROM. The database was issued in September 1991. Compare this entry with item 44, for this source accessed online.

44. Online Database: Abstract with a Print Version—MLA

Marcus, Hazel R., and Shinobu Kitayamo. "Culture and the Self:
Implications for Cognition, Emotion, and Motivation."
Psychological Abstracts 78 (1991): item 23878. PsycINFO.
Online. DIALOG. 10 Oct. 1991.

This entry is for the same abstract from *Psychological Abstracts* shown in item 43 but accessed online. This model notes PsycINFO, the name of the online database, where item 43 notes PsycLIT, the name of the CD-ROM database. It uses Online where the model in item 43 uses CD-ROM. Access was through a computer service, so this model uses DIALOG where item 43 uses SilverPlatter. In both entries, *78* is the volume number of the print version of *Psychological Abstracts*, and *item 23878* is the abstract number in the print version. The date on which the abstract was accessed is 10 Oct. 1991.

45. CD-ROM: Article from a Magazine with a Print Version—MLA

"The Price is Right." Time. 20 Jan. 1992: 38. Time Man of the Year.
CD-ROM. Compact Publishing, Inc. 1993.

The information common to both the CD-ROM version and the print version comes first. After the publication date for the print version comes a colon followed by the page number for the print version, *38*. The title of the CD-ROM is *Time Man of the Year*, its producer is Compact Publishing, Inc., and its copyright year is 1993. Underline both the title of the print publication and the title of the CD-ROM.

46. CD-ROM: Selection from a Book with a Print Version—MLA

"Prehistoric Humans: Earliest Homo Sapiens." <u>The Guinness Book of
Records</u> 1994. Guinness Publishing, Ltd. 1994. The <u>Guinness
Multimedia Disk of Records</u>, 1994 Edition. Version 2.0. CD-ROM.
Grolier Electronic Publishing, 1994.

The information about the book version ends after the publisher and year and information about the CD-ROM version begins. Version 2.0 signals that this CD-ROM is updated periodically; the producer changes version numbers rather than giving update dates.

47. CD-ROM: Material with No Print Version—MLA

"Spanish Dance." <u>Encarta</u> 1994. CD-ROM. Redmond, WA: Microsoft, 1993.

Encarta is a CD-ROM encyclopedia with no print version. "Spanish Dance" is the title of an article in this encyclopedia.

48. CD-ROM" Nonperiodical Publication—MLA

Wick, James, and Dave Jackson. <u>Wayzata World Factbook</u> 1993 Edition.
CD-ROM. Wayzata Technology, 1992.

When authors are named, treat the name(s) as for a print publication.

<u>World Atlas MPC</u>. Version 3.2. CD-ROM. Novato: Software Toolworks,
1992.

49. Work in More than One Publication Medium—MLA

Some sources come in more than one medium: a book and a CD, a disk and a video, a CD and a laserdisk. As for other electronic sources, give as much information as available, separating it into information blocks for each medium.

Clarke, David James, IV. <u>Novell's CNE Study Guide</u>. Book. <u>Network
Support Encyclopedia</u>. CD-ROM. Alameda: Sybec, 1994.

This book and CD-ROM come together. The book and the CD-ROM have different titles, but the publication information—Alameda: Sybex, 1994—applies to both.

Diskettes and magnetic tape are two other "portable" electronic media. For them, use the same kinds and patterns of information shown for CD-ROMs, except list *Diskette* or *Magnetic tape* for the publication medium.

The next section shows Works Cited entries for online sources.

50. Online: Article from a Newspaper with a Print Version—MLA

Kapor, Mitchell, and Jerry Berman. "A Superhighway Through the
    Wasteland?" <u>New York Times</u>. 24 Nov. 1993: Op-ed page. <u>New York
    Times Online</u>. 5 May 1995.

Information applying to the print version of this article in the *New York Times* ends at *Op-ed page.* Online is the publication medium and *New York Times Online* is the name of the database. The date 5 May 1995 tells when the article was accessed.

51. Online: Article from a Magazine with a Print Version—MLA

"Homeowners Insurance." <u>Consumer Reports</u>. October 1993: n. pag.
    Online. CompuServe. 5 May 1995.

When an online source does not show page numbers even though a source has a print version, at the end of the information about the print version, put *n. pag.*, an abbreviation meaning "no pagination." This abbreviation in a Works Cited entry signals readers why page numbers are not given in parenthetical references to the source in your paper.

52. Online: Material with No Print Version—MLA

"Athenian-Spartan Rivalry." <u>Academic American Encyclopedia</u>. Online.
    CompuServe. 3 Feb. 1995.

53. Online: Material from an Electronic Newsletter—MLA

"Microsoft Licenses OSM Technology from Henter-Joyce." <u>Microsoft®</u>"
    <u>WinNews Electronic Newsletter</u>. 2:6 (1 May 1995): n. pag.
    Online. Internet. 15 May 1995.

The numerals 2:6 mean volume 2, number 6 of this electronic newsletter.

54. ONLINE: AN ELECTRONIC TEXT—MLA

```
Herodotus. The History of Herodotus. Trans. George Rawlinson.
    Online. Book Stacks Unlimited. Internet. 1 Jun. 1995.
```

Book Stacks Unlimited is where the electronic text "resides." You access this "location" through the Internet network. Here is an entry for the same source showing how to include an electronic address, in this case for a location on the Internet. Start an electronic address with `Available FTP` (which stands for "file transfer protocol") followed by a colon and the address.

```
Herodotus. The History of Herodotus. Trans. George Rawlinson.
    Online. Book Stacks Unlimited. 1 Jun. 1995. Available FTP:
    books. com.
```

55. ONLINE: A PUBLIC MESSAGE—MLA

Be skeptical about using an online posting as a source. Some of them contain cutting-edge information from experts; some of them contain trash. To cite one, give the author name (if any), document title, and then Online posting. Then give location information, network name, and the date that you accessed the message.

---

4 Using content or bibliographic notes in MLA style

In MLA style, footnotes or endnotes serve two specific purposes: (1) You can use them for content (ideas and information) that does not fit into your paper but is still worth relating; and (2) you can use them for bibliographic information that would intrude if you were to include it in your text.

TEXT OF PAPER

```
Eudora Welty's literary biography, One Writer's Beginnings, shows
us how both the inner world of self and the outer world of family
and place form a writer's imagination.¹
```

CONTENT NOTE—MLA

```
¹Welty, who values her privacy, has resisted investigation of her
life. However, at the age of 74, she chose to present her own auto-
biographical reflections in a series of lectures at Harvard
University.
```

TEXT OF PAPER

Barbara Randolph believes that enthusiasm is contagious (65).[1] Many psychologists have found that panic, fear, and rage spread more quickly in crowds than positive emotions do, however.

BIBLIOGRAPHIC NOTE—MLA

[1]Others who agree with Randolph include Thurman 21, 84, 155; Kelley 421-25; and Brookes 65-76.

❖ MLA FORMAT ALERT: Place a note number at the end of a sentence, if possible. Put if after any punctuation mark except the dash. Do not put any space before a note number, and put one space after it. In typed papers, raise the note number a little above the line of words. In word processing programs, use superscript numbers. ❖

For more examples of MLA-style content notes and to see page format for endnotes, see the student research paper in section 34b.

33d Using APA-style documentation

The American Psychological Association (APA) endorses a name-year parenthetical reference documentation system that is used in its journals and has come to be used by students in the social sciences and some other disciplines. APA in-text citations alert readers to material you have used from outside sources. These citations function with an alphabetical **References list** at the end of your paper containing information that enables readers to retrieve the sources you have quoted from (see 31c), paraphrased (see 31d), or summarized (see 31e).

1 Citing sources in the body of a paper in APA style

In-text citations identify a source by a name (usually an author name) and a year (for copyrighted sources, usually the copyright year). You can often incorporate the relevant name, and sometimes the year, into your sentence. Otherwise, put this information in parentheses, placing the parenthetical reference so that a reader knows exactly what it refers to and is distracted by it as little as possible.

The APA *Publication Manual* recommends that if you refer to a work more than once in a paragraph, you give the author name and date the first time that you mention the work, and then give only the name after that. There is one exception: If you are citing two or more works by the same author, each citation must include the date so that a reader knows which work is being cited.

APA style requires page numbers for direct quotations* only (not for paraphrases or summaries). However, some instructors expect page references for any use made of sources, so find out your instructor's preference. Put page numbers in parentheses, using the abbreviation *p.* before a single page number and *pp.* when the material you are citing falls on more than one page.

1. Citing a Paraphrased or Summarized Source—APA

People from the Mediterranean prefer an elbow-to-shoulder distance from each other (Morris, 1977). [Name and date cited in parentheses.]

Desmond Morris notes that people from the Mediterranean prefer an elbow-to-shoulder distance from each other (1977, p. 131). [Name cited in text, date and page cited in parentheses.]

2. Citing the Source of a Short Quotation—APA

A recent report of reductions in SAD-related "depression in 87 percent of patients" (Binkley, 1990, p. 203) reverses the findings of earlier studies. [Name, date, and page reference in parentheses immediately following the quotation.]

Binkley reports reductions in SAD-related "depression in 87 percent of patients" (1990, p. 203). [Name incorporated into the words introducing the quotation and date and page number in parentheses immediately following the quotation.]

3. Formatting a Long Quotation and Citing Its Source—APA

Incorporate a direct quotation of fewer than 40 words into your own sentence(s) and enclose it in quotation marks. Place the parenthetical citation after the closing quotation mark and, if the quotation falls at the end of the sentence, before the sentence-ending punctuation. When you use a quotation longer than 40 words, set it off from your words by starting it on a new line and by indenting each line of the quotation 5 spaces from the left margin. Do not enclose it in quotation marks. Place the parenthetical citation 2 spaces after the end punctuation of the last sentence.

---

*When a source is no more than one page long, the page number is included in information about the source in the References list. Therefore, it is unnecessary to repeat the page number in in-text citations.

DISPLAYED QUOTATION (40 OR MORE WORDS)

Jet lag, with its characteristic fatigue and irregular sleep
patterns, is a common problem among those who travel great
distances by jet airplane to different time zones:

> Jet lag syndrome is the inability of the internal body rhythm
> to rapidly resynchronize after sudden shifts in the timing. For
> a variety of reasons, the system attempts to maintain stability
> and resist temporal change. Consequently, complete adjustment
> can often be delayed for several days-sometimes for a week-
> after arrival at one's destination (Bonner, 1991, p. 72).

Interestingly, this research shows that the number of flying hours
is not the cause of jet lag.

The following examples show how to handle parenthetical citations for various sources. Remember, though, that you often can introduce source names, including titles when necessary, and sometimes
even years in your own sentences.

4. CITING ONE AUTHOR—APA

One of his questions is "What binds together a Mormon banker in
Utah with his brother, or other coreligionists in Illinois or
Massachusetts?" (Coles, 1993, p. 2)

In a parenthetical reference in APA style, a comma and a space
separate a name from a year and a year from a page reference.
(Examples 1 through 3 above also show citations of works by one
author.)

5. CITING TWO AUTHORS—APA

If a work has two authors, give both names in each citation.

One report describes 2123 occurrences (Krait & Cooper, 1994).

The results Krait and Cooper (1994) report would not support the
conclusions Davis and Sherman draw in their review of the literature
(1992).

When citing two (or more) authors, use an ampersand (&)
between the (final) two names for parenthetical references, but use
the word *and* for references in your own sentences.

6. CITING THREE, FOUR, OR FIVE AUTHORS—APA

For three, four, or five authors, use all the authors' last names in the first reference. In all subsequent references, use only the first author's last name followed by *et al.*

FIRST REFERENCE

In one anthology, 35 percent of the selections had not been anthologized before (Elliott, Kerber, Litz, & Martin, 1992).

SUBSEQUENT REFERENCE

Elliott et al. (1992) include 17 authors whose work has never been anthologized.

7. CITING SIX OR MORE AUTHORS—APA

For six or more authors, use the name of the first author followed by *et al.* for all references, including the first.

8. CITING AUTHOR(S) WITH TWO OR MORE WORKS IN THE SAME YEAR—APA

If you use more than one source written in the same year by the same author(s), alphabetize the works by their titles for the References list, and assign letters in alphabetical order to the years—(1996a), (1996b), (1996c). Use the year-letter combination in parenthetical references. Note that a citation of two or more of such works lists the years in alphabetical order.

Most recently, Jones (1996c) draws new conclusions from the results of 17 sets of experiments (1996a, 1996b).

9. CITING TWO OR MORE AUTHORS WITH THE SAME LAST NAME—APA

Use first- and middle-name initials for every in-text citation of authors who share a last name.

R. A. Smith (1997) and C. Smith (1989) both confirm these results.

These results have been confirmed independently (C. Smith, 1989; R. A. Smith, 1997).

10. CITING A GROUP OR CORPORATE AUTHOR—APA

If you use a source in which the "author" is the name of a corporation, agency, or group, an in-text reference gives that name as author. Use the full name in each citation unless an abbreviated version of the name is likely to be familiar to your audience. In that case, use the full name and give its abbreviation at the first citation; then use the abbreviation for subsequent citations.

```
After 1949 the federal government took over responsibility for most
public housing projects (Canada Mortgage and Housing Corporation
[CMHC], 1990).
```

In subsequent citations, you can then use the abbreviated form.

11. CITING WORKS BY TITLE—APA

If no author is named, use a shortened form of the title in citations. Ignoring *A, An,* or *The,* make the first word the one by which you alphabetize the title in References. The following citation is to an article fully titled "Are You a Day or a Night Person?"

```
The "morning lark" and "night owl" connotations typically are used to
categorize the human extremes ("Are You," 1989).
```

12. CITING MORE THAN ONE SOURCE IN A PARENTHETICAL REFERENCE—APA

If more than one source has contributed to an idea or opinion in your paper, cite the sources alphabetically in one set of parentheses; separate each block of information with a semicolon.

```
Conceptions of personal space vary among cultures (Morris, 1977; Worchel
& Cooper, 1983).
```

13. CITING A PERSONAL COMMUNICATION—APA

Telephone calls, personal letters, and interviews are "personal communications" that your readers do not have access to. Acknowledge personal communications in parenthetical references but do not include them in your References list.

```
Recalling his first summer at camp, one person said, "The proximity
of 12 other kids made me—an only child with older, quiet parents—
frantic for the entire eight weeks" (A. Weiss, personal communication,
January 12, 1996).
```

14. CITING GRAPHICS—APA

If you include in your paper a graphic from another source, give a note in the text at the bottom of the table or graphic crediting the original author and the copyright holder. Here are examples of two source lines, one for a graphic from an article, the other for a graphic from a book. (If you plan to publish your document, you will need copyright permission from the copyright holder in order to reproduce the table or graphic. You will also have to add a line such as *Reprinted* [or *Adapted*] *with permission.*

GRAPHIC FROM AN ARTICLE

Note. From "Bridge over troubled waters? Connecting research and pedagogy in composition and business/technical communication" by J. Allen, 1992, <u>Technical Communication Quarterly</u>, 1(4), p. 9. Copyright 1992 by the Association of Teachers of Technical Writing.

GRAPHIC FROM A BOOK

Note. From <u>Additive Alert: A guide to food additives for the Canadian consumer</u> (p. 28) by Linda R. Pim, 1979, Toronto: Doubleday. Copyright 1979 by Pollution Probe Foundation.

2 Compiling an APA-style References list

In APA documentation, in-text citations must be accompanied by a list of sources referred to in your paper. Include in this References list the "recoverable" sources that you quote from, paraphrase, or summarize. A recoverable source is one that another person could retrieve with reasonable effort. Do not include in the References list any source not available to others, such as personal letters and other personal communications. (To alert readers to your use of such sources, you use a parenthetical citation marking the source as a personal communication; see, for example, item 34 about personal interviews.) Chart 143 summarizes information about the References list.

GUIDELINES FOR COMPILING AN APA-STYLE REFERENCES LIST

143

■ **TITLE**

References.

■ **PLACEMENT OF LIST**

Start a new page numbered sequentially with the rest of the paper, after Notes page(s), if any.

■ **CONTENTS AND FORMAT**

Include all quoted, paraphrased, or summarized sources in your paper that are not personal communications, unless your instructor tells you to include all the references you have consulted, not just those you have referred to. Start each entry on a new line, and double-space all lines. Check which of the following indent styles your instructor wants you to use.

1. First line of each entry indented, other lines full width. This style is shown in the APA *Publication Manual*. Indent the first line of each entry 5 to 7 spaces (or 1 default tab, which is about an inch or 2.5 cm in most word-processing programs). If an entry has more than one line, make all lines after the first full width.

   Shuter, R. (1977). A field study of nonverbal communication in Germany, Italy, and the United States. <u>Communication Monographs,</u> 44, 298-305.

2. First line of each entry full width, other lines indented. This "hanging indent" style makes source names and dates prominent. Type the first line of each entry full width, and indent an entry's subsequent lines 5 to 7 spaces (or 1 tab).

   Shuter, R. (1977). A field study of nonverbal communication in Germany, Italy, and the United States. <u>Communication Monographs, 44,</u> 298-305.

■ **SPACING AFTER PUNCTUATION**

The 1994 APA *Publication Manual* calls for one space after most punctuation marks: periods at the ends of information units in references (and at the ends of sentences in your paper), commas, semicolons, and colons (except in ratios in your paper [2:1, 100:1]).

■ **ARRANGEMENT OF ENTRIES**

Alphabetize by author's last name. If no author is named, alphabetize by the first significant word (not *A, An,* or *The*) in the title of the work. →

GUIDELINES FOR COMPILING AN APA-STYLE REFERENCES LIST ¹⁴³
(continued)

■ **AUTHORS' NAME**

Use last names, first-name initials, and middle initials if any. Reverse the order for all author names, and use an ampersand (&) between the second-to-last and last authors. `Mills, J. F., & Holahan, R. H.`

Give names in the order used on the work (title page of book, usually under the article or other printed work). Use a comma between the first author's last name and first initial and after each complete author name except the last. After the last author name, use a period.

■ **DATE**

Put date information after name information, enclosing it in parentheses and using a period followed by one space after the closing parenthesis.

For books, articles in journals that have volume numbers, and many other print and nonprint sources, the year of publication or production is the date to use. For articles from most magazines and newspapers, use the year followed by a month and sometimes day-date. Individual entries later in this chapter show how much information to give for various sources.

■ **CAPITALIZATION OF TITLES**

For books, capitalize the first word, the first word after a colon between a title and subtitle, and any proper nouns. For names of journals and proceedings of meetings, capitalize the first word, all nouns and adjectives, and any other words five or more letters long.

■ **SPECIAL TREATMENT OF TITLES**

Use no special treatment for titles or shorter works (poems, short stories, essays, articles). Underline titles of longer works (books, names of newspapers or journals containing cited articles). For underlining, use an unbroken line if possible.

Do not drop *An, An,* or *The* from the titles of periodicals (such as newspapers, magazines, and journals).

■ **FORM DESCRIPTION**

When a source is not a book or an article, a statement about its form is often useful for a reader who wants to retrieve the source. Enclose "form" information in brackets, and include it after a title and before a period at the end of the block of title information. Do not underline it. Electronically accessed sources should always have a form statement: for example, `[Online]` or `[CD-ROM]`. Also see items 36-43.

GUIDELINES FOR COMPILING AN APA-STYLE REFERENCES LIST 143
(continued)

■ **PUBLISHER**
Use the full name of a publisher, but drop *Co., Inc., Publishers,* and the like.

■ **PLACE OF PUBLICATION**
For publishers in the United States, give city and state (use 2-letter postal abbreviations) for all but the largest U.S. cities (such as Boston, Chicago, Los Angeles, and New York). For other countries, give city and country.

Canadian students and writers publishing in Canada normally use the 2-letter postal abbreviations for Canadian provinces as well as U.S. states.

■ **PUBLICATION MONTH ABBREVIATIONS**
Do not abbreviate publication months.

■ **PAGE NUMBERS**
Use the full second number. Use *p.* and *pp.* before page numbers. List all discontinuous pages, with number separated by commas: `pp. 32, 44–45, 47–49, 53.`

■ **REFERENCES ENTRIES: BOOKS**
Citations for books have four main parts: author, date, title, and publication information (place of publication and publisher).

AUTHOR	DATE	TITLE	PUBLICATION INFORMATION
Dudek, L.	(1971).	Collected poetry.	Montreal: Delta.

■ **REFERENCES ENTRIES: ARTICLES**
Citations for periodical articles contain four major parts: author, date, title of article, and publication information (usually the periodical title, volume number, and page numbers).

AUTHOR	DATE	ARTICLE TITLE
Shuter, R.	(1977).	A field of study of nonverbal communication in

PERIODICAL TITLE

Germany, Italy, and the United States. Communication Monographs,

VOLUME NUMBER	PAGE NUMBERS
44,	298–305.

➜

GUIDELINES FOR COMPILING AN APA-STYLE REFERENCES LIST 143
(continued)

■ **REFERENCES ENTRIES: ELECTRONIC SOURCES**

Because standards for citing electronic sources are still being developed, APA recommends giving information for print forms of sources when print and electronic forms are the same. For widely available online sources, include path information. The basic elements of an electronic reference include author(s), date, title and form description (such as [*Online*] or [*CD-ROM*]), periodical title and other information about a print version, location information (such as an availability statement and path for an online source or the producer and database name for a CD source). Here is an entry for an abstract on CD-ROM.

AUTHORS	DATE	ARTICLE TITLE

Marcus, H. R., & Kitayamo, S. (1991). Culture and the self:

	FORM DESCRIPTION	JOURNAL TITLE AND PUBLICATION INFORMATION

Implications for group dynamics. [CD-ROM]. Psychological Review,

LOCATION INFORMATION

88(2), 224, 253. Abstract from: SilverPlatter File: PsycLIT

Item: 78-23878.

---

3 **Following models for an APA-style References list**

Directory

PRINT SOURCES: BOOKS

ELECTRONIC SOURCES

41. Online Document Without a Print Version—APA
42. Computer Software—APA
43. Abstract on CD-ROM—APA
44. Information Service: ERIC and NewsBank—APA.

PRINT SOURCES: BOOKS

1. BOOK BY ONE AUTHOR—APA

```
Trudeau, P.E. (1968). Federalism and the French Canadians.
Toronto: Macmillan Canada.
```

2. BOOK BY TWO AUTHORS—APA

```
Smith, R. J., & Gibbs, M. (1994). Navigating the Internet.
Indianapolis, IN: Sams.
```

3. BOOK BY THREE OR MORE AUTHORS—APA

```
Scardamalia, M., Bereiter, C., & Fillion, B. (1981). Writing
for results: A sourcebook of consequential composing activities.
Toronto: OISE Press.

Cameron, D., Frazer, E., Harvey, P., Rampton, M. B. H., &
Richardson, K. (1992). Researching language: Issues of power and
method. London: Routledge.
```

In an APA References list, include the last names and initials of all authors, even though in your paper you use only the first author's name when a work has six or more authors.

4. TWO OR MORE BOOKS BY THE SAME AUTHOR(S)—APA

```
Atwood, M. (1972). Survival. Toronto: Anansi.

Atwood, M. (1981). True stories. Toronto: Oxford University Press.

Atwood, M. (1985). The handmaid's tale. Toronto: McClelland &
Stewart.
```

Repeat the author name(s) for each entry. Arrange the entries by date, from least recent to most recent. To cite two or more works by the same author(s) in the same year, arrange those entries in alphabetical order by title, and then assign a letter to each year (for example, 1993a, 1993b, 1993c). In parenthetical citations, the letter following the year distinguishes one same-year source from another.

5. Book by Group or Corporate Author—APA

Environmental Defense Fund. (1990). <u>Recycling and incineration: Evaluating the choice</u>. Washington, DC: Island.

American Psychological Association. (1994). <u>Publication manual of the American Psychological Association</u> (4th ed.). Washington, DC: Author.

When a book is in an edition other than the first, include the edition number in parentheses after the title. Put the period at the end of the block of title information after the closing parenthesis (also see item 6).

6. Book with No Author Named—APA

<u>The Chicago manual of style</u> (14th ed.). (1993). Chicago: University of Chicago Press.

In your paper, use a shortened version of the title in parenthetical references (drop *A, An,* or *The* from a shortened title). Underline the words you use for a book title, and capitalize each significant word, even ones that start with lower-case letters in the References list: (Chicago Manual, 1993).

7. Book with an Author and an Editor—APA

Welty, E. (1994). <u>A writer's eye: Collected book reviews</u> (P. A. McHaney, Ed.). Jackson, MI: University Press of Mississippi.

In an APA References list, always capitalize the abbreviation *Ed.* when it stands for the word *Editor* (or *Editors*). (Use a lower-case letter when *ed.* stands for *"edition,"* as in *Rev. ed.* or *2nd ed.*)

8. Translation—APA

Maillet, A. (1979). <u>La Sagouine</u>. (L. de Cespedes, Trans.). Toronto: Simon & Pierre.

9. Work in Several Volumes or Parts—APA

Goldman, L. H., Cronin, G. L., and Aharoni, A. (1992). <u>Saul Bellow: A mosaic:</u> Vol. 2. <u>Twentieth century American Jewish writers</u>. New York: P. Lang.

10. Anthology or Edited Book—APA

Lantolf, J. P., & Appel, G. (Eds.). (1994). <u>Vygotskian approaches to second language research</u>. Norwood, NJ: Ablex.

Spear, T., & Waller, R. (Eds.). (1993). <u>Being Masai: Ethnicity and identity in East Africa</u>. Athens: Ohio University Press.

The abbreviation OH (for Ohio) does not follow Athens in this entry because Ohio University Press identifies the state.

11. ONE SELECTION FROM AN ANTHOLOGY OR AN EDITED BOOK—APA

Savitch, W. J. (1991). Infinity is in the eye of the beholder. In C. Georgopoulos, & R. Ishihara (Eds.), <u>Interdisciplinary approaches to language: Essays in honor of S. Y. Kuroda</u> (pp. 487-500). Boston: Kluwer Academic.

12. TWO SELECTIONS FROM ONE ANTHOLOGY OR AN EDITED BOOK—APA

Blank, C. (Ed.). (1992). <u>Language and civilization: A concerted profusion of essays and studies in honor of Otto Heitsch</u>. Frankfort-on-Main, Germany: P. Lang.

Middleton, M. (1992). A note on computer jargon. In C. Blank (Ed.), <u>Language and civilization: A concerted profusion of essays and studies in honor of Otto Hietsch</u> (pp. 732-739). Frankfort-on-Main, Germany: P. Lang.

Give full publication information in each entry, whether for a selection or for the whole work. In selection entries, after the title of the main work, enclose page numbers for the selection in parentheses, followed by a period. In the main entry, the first information unit is the name of the editor or compiler of the collection. In an entry for each selection entry, the first unit is the name of the author of the selection.

13. SIGNED ARTICLE IN A REFERENCE BOOK—APA

Shadbolt, D. (1988). Emily Carr. In <u>The Canadian encyclopedia</u> (2nd ed.) (Vol. 1, p. 366). Edmonton: Hurtig.

14. UNSIGNED ARTICLE IN A REFERENCE BOOK—APA

Russia. (1994). In <u>The new encyclopedia Britannica</u> (15th ed.) (Vol. 10, pp. 253-255). Chicago: Encyclopedia Britannica.

15. EDITION—APA

Buckley, J., & Gates, D. (1995). <u>Put it in writing</u> (2nd ed.). Scarborough, ON: Prentice Hall.

**33d
APA**

16. INTRODUCTION, PREFACE, FOREWORD, OR AFTERWORD

If the part of the book you are citing was written by the person who wrote the book, do the entry as you would for the entire work with these exceptions. If the part you are citing has a title, give it, without quotation marks or underlining, after the year (for example, a chapter title or the words *Preface, Foreword, Introduction, Afterword,* and *Appendix*). Then, give the title of the book, followed by parentheses enclosing the page numbers of the cited part and ending with a period after the closing parenthesis. Then give publication information.

Troyka, L. (1996). Preface for ESL students. In <u>Simon & Schuster</u> <u>Handbook for Writers, First Canadian Edition</u> (pp. 780-782). Scarborough, ON: Prentice Hall Canada Inc.

Page numbers can follow an edition number or a volume number in one set of parentheses; use a comma between the sets of information.

If the part you are citing does not have a special title, do the entry as you would for any book, but include page numbers in parentheses after the title. If the part you are citing was written by someone other than the person(s) who wrote the book, first give the name of the person who wrote the part, then give the date, then give the title of the part. Then put the word *In* followed by the name(s) of the book's author(s) or editor(s) in normal order, not reversed. Then give the title of the book, page numbers in parentheses of the relevant part, and publication information.

Allmand, W. (1993). Foreword. In J. Brand, <u>The life and death</u> <u>of Anna Mae Aquash</u> (pp. v-ix). Toronto: Lorimer.

17. UNPUBLISHED DISSERTATION OR ESSAY—APA

Buckley, J. (1991). <u>An assessment of Kieran Egan's theory of</u> <u>educational development</u>. Unpublished dissertation, University of Western Ontario, London.

The abbreviation ON (for Ontario) does not follow London in this entry because the name of the university identifies the province.

Stafford, K. M. (1993, January). <u>Trapped in death and enchantment:</u> <u>The liminal space of women in three classical ballets</u>. Paper presented at the annual meeting of the American Comparative Literature Association Graduate Student Conference, Riverside, CA.

18. REPRINT OF AN OLDER BOOK—APA

Lampman, A. (1985/1978). <u>Lyrics of earth</u>. Ottawa: Tecumseh Press.

19. BOOK IN A SERIES—APA

Courchene, T. J. (1991). <u>In praise of renewed federalism. The Canada Round</u>. Toronto: C. D. Howe Institute.

20. BOOK WITH A TITLE WITHIN A TITLE—APA

Hayes, K. H. (Ed.). (1994). <u>The critical response to Herman Melville's</u> Moby Dick. Westport, CT: Greenwood Press.

21. GOVERNMENT PUBLICATIONS—APA

Royal Commission on Bilingualism and Biculturalism. (1965). *Preliminary report*. Ottawa: Queen's Printer.

Indian and Northern Affairs Canada. (1986). <u>The Inuit</u>. Ottawa: Supply and Services Canada.

22. PUBLISHED PROCEEDINGS OF A CONFERENCE—APA

Pavlyshyn, M., & Clarke, J. E. M. (Eds.). (1992). <u>Ukraine in the 1990s: Proceedings of the first conference of the Ukrainian Studies Association of Australia</u>. Melbourne: Monash University.

PRINT SOURCES: ARTICLES AND OTHER SHORT DOCUMENTS

23. ARTICLE FROM A DAILY NEWSPAPER—APA

Tebbutt, T. (1994, August 1). Showman Agassi lightly frolics to Canadian title. <u>The Globe and Mail</u>, p. D1.

24. EDITORIAL, LETTER TO THE EDITOR, OR REVIEW—APA

A black mark on local government. (1994, July 27). [Editorial]. <u>The London Free Press</u>, p. B8.

Hurka, J. (1994, July 5). [Letter to the editor]. <u>The Calgary Sun</u>, p. A18.

Toews, W. (1995, August 26). Politics of the mind. [Review of <u>They say you're crazy</u>]. <u>Winnipeg Free Press</u>, p. C3.

Form descriptions—[Editorial], [Letter to the editor], and [Review of *They say you're crazy*]—are enclosed in brackets because they are form descriptions given in the words of the person who used the sources and inserted into the blocks of title information (see 29c-1).

Descriptions of form are not titles; do not put titles of special documents or of parts of works in brackets (see item 16).

25. UNSIGNED ARTICLE FROM A DAILY NEWSPAPER—APA

Canadian adds flights. (1994, August 1). The Globe and Mail, p. B2.

26. ARTICLE FROM A WEEKLY OR BIWEEKLY MAGAZINE OR NEWSPAPER—APA

Wood, C. (1989, November 6). Storm clouds over Quebec. Maclean's, pp. 16-17.

27. ARTICLE FROM A MONTHLY OR BIMONTHLY PERIODICAL—APA

When material is not on consecutive pages, give all page numbers.

O'Malley, S. (1994, August). Make-it-happen kinda dreamer: Theatre director Diane Dupuy is nobody's puppet. Chatelaine, pp. 36-39, 90.

Bell, J. (1992, September/October). Kingdom come: Canada's Inuit finally may be getting their own homeland, but at what price? Earthwatch, pp. 10-11.

28. UNSIGNED ARTICLE FROM A WEEKLY OR MONTHLY PERIODICAL—APA

10 ways to sleep easy. (1994, August). Canadian Living, p. 19.

29. ARTICLE FROM A SIRS COLLECTION OF REPRINTED ARTICLES—APA

Curver, P. C. (1990). Lighting in the 21st century. In Social issues resources series. Energy (Vol. 4, Article 84). Boca Raton, FL: Social Issues Resources.

30. ARTICLE IN A JOURNAL WITH CONTINUOUS PAGINATION—APA

LaFollette, M. C. (1994). The politics of research misconduct: Congressional oversight, universities, and science. Journal of Higher Education, 65, 261-85.

31. ARTICLE IN A JOURNAL THAT PAGES EACH ISSUE SEPARATELY—APA

Hancock, D. (1993). Prototyping the Hubble fix. IEEE Spectrum, 30 (10), 34-39.

32. LETTERS—APA

Orlyansky, V. (1991). Letter to the Soviet President. In R. McKay (Ed.), Letters to Gorbachev: Life in Russia through the postbag of "argumenty i fakty" (pp. 120-121). London: Michael Joseph.

An *unpublished* letter is not available to your readers. Treat it as a personal communication, acknowledging it in a parenthetical reference in your paper but not including it in the References list.

33. MAP OR CHART—APA

Russia and post-Soviet republics [Map]. (1992). Moscow: Mapping Production Association.

NONPRINT SOURCES

34. INTERVIEW—APA

A personal interview is not available to your readers. Treat it as a personal communication, acknowledging it in a parenthetical reference in your paper but not including it in the References list.

Randi Friedman (personal communication, June 30, 1992) endorses this view.

35. LECTURE, SPEECH, ADDRESS—APA

Barlow, M. (1991, May 25). Address. Speech presented to League of Canadian Poets, Toronto.

36. FILM OR VIDEOTAPE—APA

Archer, D. (Writer/Director). (1992). A world of gestures: Cultural and nonverbal communication [Videotape]. Berkeley: Univ. of Cal. Extension Media Center.

37. RECORDING—APA

De la Cuesta, I. F. (Director). (1994). Chant [CD]. The Benedictine Monks of Santo Domingo de Silos. (Recording No. CDC 724355513823). Madrid, Spain: Angel Records.

38. LIVE PERFORMANCE—APA

O'Neill, E. (Author), Leblanc, D. (Director), Henry, M. (Performer), & Hutt, W. (Performer). (1994, June 4). Long day's journey into night [Live performance]. Stratford, ON: Tom Patterson Theatre.

39. WORK OF ART OR MUSICAL COMPOSITION—APA

Pratt, C. Shop on an island [Art work]. London, ON: London Regional Art Gallery.

33d
APA

40. Radio or Television Program—APA

Richler, D. (Interviewer). (1992, December 7). Interview with
Martha Gellhorn. _Imprint_ (Show #72) [Television program]. Toronto:
TVOntario.

Electronic Sources

For electronic sources not covered here, the APA _Publication Manual_ suggests consulting Li and Crane's (1993) _Electronic Style: A Guide to Citing Electronic Information._

41. Online Document Without a Print Version—APA

Wallach, D. S. (1993, September 22). FAQ: Typing injuries (2/5):
General Info. [Online]. Available FTP: rtfm.mit.edu Directory:
pub/usenet/news.answers File: typing-injury-faq/general.z

Keep capitalization the same as you find it in the source. Avoid punctuating the availability, directory, and file statements to separate the information units because extra punctuation marks can be mistaken as part of the address. In the example, end punctuation has been omitted for that reason.

42. Computer Software—APA

Transparent Language Presentation Program (Ver. 2.0 for Windows)
[Computer software]. (1994). Hollis, NH: Transparent Language.

43. Abstract on CD-ROM—APA

Marcus, H. R., & Kitayamo, S. (1991). Culture and the self:
Implications for group dynamics [CD-ROM]. _Psychological Review,_
_88_(2), 224, 253. Abstract from: SilverPlatter File: PsycLIT Item:
78-23878.

44. Information Services: ERIC and NewsBank—APA

Chiang, L. H. (1993). Beyond the language: Native Americans'
nonverbal communication. (ERIC Document Reproduction Service No. ED 368
540).

Wenzell, R. (1990). Businesses prepare for a more diverse work
force. (NewsBank Document Reproduction Service N. EMP 27:D12).

<table>
<tr><td>

4

</td><td>

Writing an abstract and using notes in APA style

</td></tr>
</table>

You may be asked to include an abstract at the start of a paper you prepare in APA style. An abstract, as described in the 1994 edition of the APA *Publication Manual,* is "a brief, comprehensive summary" (p. 8). Make this summary accurate, objective, and exact.

❖ APA FORMAT ALERT: If you include an abstract in an APA-style paper, put it on page 2, a separate page after the title page. For an example of an abstract, see the student paper on biological clocks in section 35b. ❖

Content notes can be used in APA-style papers for additional relevant information that cannot be worked effectively into a text discussion. Use consecutive arabic numerals for note numbers, both within your paper and on a separate page following the last text page of your paper. Using the heading *Notes* on this page, number it with your paper, and double-space the notes themselves.

33e Using CM-style documentation

The style manual of the University of Chicago Press endorses two styles of documentation. One is a "name-year" style, similar to APA's system, using in-text citations that direct readers to an alphabetical References list containing full bibliographic details about each source. Parenthetical references commonly contain an author name and a publication year, separated by a space but no punctuation: `(English 1995)`.

The other style of CM (for *Chicago Manual*) documentation is a note system often used in the disciplines of English, humanities, and history. The CM note system gives complete bibliographic information within a footnote or endnote the first time a source is cited. If that source is cited again, less information is given because the source has already been fully described. A separate bibliography is usually unnecessary.

TEXT

`Welty also makes this point.`[1]

NOTE

`    1. Eudora Welty, `*`One Writer's Beginnings`*` (Cambridge: Harvard University Press, 1984), 17.`

Notes may be either at the end of a paper (endnotes) or at the foot of the page on which a citation falls (footnotes). Endnotes are usually easier to format, especially is you are handwriting or typing your paper. Popular

33e
CM

word processing programs can format either endnotes or footnotes easily.

Section 33e focuses primarily on the CM bibliographic note system of documentation. Several of the models in section 33e-2 show References list entries as well as bibliographic note entries.

1 | Creating CM-style bibliographic notes

Chart 144 gives general guidelines for the content and format of CM-style bibliographic notes.

GUIDELINES FOR COMPILING CM-STYLE BIBLIOGRAPHIC NOTES
144

■ **TITLE**
For endnotes, Notes, on a new page numbered sequentially with the rest of the paper, after the last text page of the paper. (Footnotes appear at the bottom of the pages where sources are cited.)

■ **FORMAT**
Place endnotes after the text of your paper, on a separate page entitled Notes. Centre the word Notes about an inch from the top of the page. Double-space after the word Notes. Single-space the notes themselves. Indent each note's first line about 3 characters (or 1 tab space in your word-processing program); do not indent a note's subsequent lines.

In the body of your paper, use raised (superscript) arabic numerals for the note numbers. Note numbers should be positioned after any punctuation marks except the dash, preferably at the end of a sentence. On the Notes pages, superscript and note should be the same type size, and a period should follow the superscript. (Not all word-processing programs allow you to observe these guidelines.)

■ **SPACING AND PUNCTUATION**
No special requirements.

■ **ARRANGEMENT OF NOTES**
Numerical order.

■ **AUTHORS' NAMES**
Give the name in standard (not inverted) order, with names and initials as given in the original source. Use the word *and* between (the last) two authors.

→

GUIDELINES FOR COMPILING CM-STYLE BIBLIOGRAPHIC NOTES 144
(continued)

■ **CAPITALIZATION OF TITLES**
Capitalize the first word and all major words.

■ **SPECIAL TREATMENT OF TITLES**
Underline the titles of long works, and use quotation marks around the titles of shorter works.

Omit *A, An,* and *The* from the titles of newspapers and periodicals. For an unfamiliar newspaper title, in parentheses, give the city (and province or state, if the city is not well known): for example, (Prince Albert, Saskatchewan) *Herald.*

■ **PUBLICATION INFORMATION**
Enclose publication information in parentheses. Use a colon and one space after the city of publication. Give complete publishers' names or abbreviate them according to standard abbreviations in *Books in Print.* Omit *Co., Inc.,* and *Ltd.* Use *Press* (spelled out, not abbreviated). Use *Univ.* for University.

Do not abbreviate publication months.

■ **PAGE NUMBERS**
In inclusive page numbers, give the full second number for 2 through 99. For 100 and beyond, give the full second number if a shortened version is ambiguous.

List all discontinuous page numbers.

Use a comma to separate page numbers for a cited part of a book from the parenthetical publication information.

Use the abbreviations *p.* and *pp.* with page numbers for material from journals that do not use volume numbers.

■ **SECOND CITATIONS**
After giving full bibliographic information in the first note citing a source, subsequent citations can be brief. In short papers, author name(s) and a page reference is usually sufficient information. If you have used more than one work by the author(s), give a shortened title as well.

■ **CONTENT NOTES**
Try to avoid using content notes. If you must use one or two, make them footnotes and use symbols (* and † are standard) rather than numbers. You can repeat these footnote symbols on every page.

GUIDELINES FOR COMPILING CM-STYLE BIBLIOGRAPHIC NOTES 144
(continued)

■ **BIBLIOGRAPHIC NOTES: BOOKS**
Citations for books include the author, title, publication information, and page numbers if applicable. Note 1 is for the first citation of a book; note 2 is for its second citation in a paper that cites two works by Welty, *One Writer's Beginnings* and *"A Worn Path."*

| AUTHOR | TITLE | PUBLICATION INFORMATION |

1. Eudora Welty, One Writer's Beginnings (Cambridge: Harvard

PAGE
NUMBERS

University Press, 1984), 15.

2. Welty, <u>One</u>, 21.

■ **BIBLIOGRAPHIC NOTES: ARTICLES**
Citations for articles include the author, article title, journal title, volume number, year, and page numbers. Note 1 shows the first citation of an article, and note 2 shows the second citation for the article in a paper citing only one work by these authors.

AUTHORS

1. D. D. Cochran, W. Daniel Hale, and Christine P. Hissam,

ARTICLE TITLE

"Personal Space Requirements in Indoor versus Outdoor Locations,"

| JOURNAL TITLE | VOLUME NUMBER | YEAR | PAGE NUMBERS |

Journal of Psychology 117 (1984): 132–33.

2. Cochran, Hale, and Hissam, 133.

→

655

2 | Following models for CM-style documentation

PRINT SOURCES: BOOKS

1. BOOK BY ONE AUTHOR—CM

1. Pierre E. Trudeau, <u>Federalism and the French Canadians</u>
Toronto: MacMillan Canada, 1968).

2. Giuliana Prata, M.D., <u>A Systematic Harpoon into Family Games:
Preventive Interventions in Therapy</u> (New York: Brunner/Mazel
Publishers, 1990).

Here are References list forms for books by one author.

Prata, Giuliana, M.D. <u>A systematic harpoon into family games:
    Preventive interventions in therapy.</u> New York: Brunner/Mazel, 1990.

Trudeau, Pierre E. <u>Federalism and the French Canadians.</u> Toronto:
    Macmillan Canada, 1968.

2. BOOK BY TWO OR THREE AUTHORS—CM

1. Marlene Scardamalia, Carl Bereiter, and Bryant Fillion,
<u>Writing for Results: A Sourcebook of Consequential Composing
Activities</u> (Toronto: OISE Press, 1981).

2. Richard J. Smith and Mark Gibbs, <u>Navigating the Internet,</u>
(Indianapolis: Sams Publishing, 1994).

Here are References list entries. A parenthetical citation lists two
or three authors: (Scardamalia, Bereiter, and Fillion 1981).

Scardamalia, Marlene, Carl Bereiter, and Bryant Fillion. 1981. <u>Writing</u>
<u>for results: A sourcebook of consequential composing activities</u>.
Toronto: OISE Press.

Smith, Richard J., and Mark Gibbs. 1994. <u>Navigating the Internet</u>.
Indianapolis: Sams Publishing.

3. BOOK BY MORE THAN THREE AUTHORS—CM

1. Deborah Cameron et al., <u>Researching Language: Issues of</u>
<u>Power and Method</u> (London: Routledge Publishers, 1992).

Here is a References list entry. A parenthetical citation also uses
et al. for more than three authors: (Cameron et al. 1992).

Cameron, Deborah, et al. 1992. <u>Researching language: Issues of</u>
<u>power and method</u>. London: Routledge.

4. MULTIPLE CITATION OF A SINGLE SOURCE—CM

Second and subsequent notes use shortened forms (see Chart 144).
Ibid. can be used when the information in a note is exactly the same
as the information in the immediately preceding note. If only the page
references differ in two successive notes, you can use *Ibid.* with the respective pages.

2. Schaller, 33.

3. Ibid., 37.

5. BOOK BY GROUP OR CORPORATE AUTHOR—CM

1. Environmental Defense Fund, <u>Recycling and Incineration:</u>
<u>Evaluating the Choices</u> (Washington, D.C.: Island Press, 1990).

2. American Psychological Association, <u>Publication Manual of</u>
<u>the American Psychological Association</u>, 4 ed. (Washington, D.C.:
American Psychological Association, 1994).

Here are References list entries. A parenthetical citation uses the
group name as though it were an individual's name: (Environmental
Defense Fund 1990).

Environmental Defense Fund. 1990. <u>Recycling and incineration:</u>
<u>Evaluating the choice</u>. Washington, D.C.: Island Press.

American Psychological Association. 1994. <u>Publication manual of the</u>
<u>American Psychological Association</u>, 4th ed. Washington, D.C.:
A.P.A.

6. Book with No Author Named—CM

1. <u>The Chicago Manual of Style</u>, 14th ed. 1993. Chicago: University of Chicago Press.

7. Book with an Author and an Editor—CM

When the focus in your paper is on Welty and her reviews, use this form:

1. Eudora Welty, <u>A Writer's Eye: Collected Book Reviews</u>, ed. Pearl Amelia McHaney (Jackson, Mississippi: University Press of Mississippi, 1994).

When your focus is on McHaney's work as editor, use this form:

1. Pearl Amelia McHaney, ed., <u>A Writer's Eye: Collected Book Reviews</u>, by Eudora Welty (Jackson, Mississippi: University Press of Mississippi, 1994).

Here are the References list entries for each focus, first on Welty as author and second on McHaney as editor. Parenthetical citations use the name that begins the References entry.

Welty, Eudora. 1994. <u>A writer's eye: Collected book reviews</u>. Edited by P. A. McHaney. Jackson: University Press of Mississippi.

McHaney, P. A., ed. 1994. <u>A writer's eye: Collected book reviews</u>, by Eudora Welty. Jackson: University Press of Mississippi.

8. Translation—CM

1. Antonine Maillet, <u>La Sagouine</u>, trans. Luis de Cespedes (Toronto: Simon & Pierre, 1979).

Maillet, Antonine. 1979. <u>La Sagouine</u>. Translated by Luis de Cespedes. Toronto: Simon & Pierre.

9. A Work in Several Volumes or Parts—CM

1. L. H. Goldman, Gloria L. Cronin, and Ada Aharoni, <u>Saul Bellow: A Mosaic</u>, vol. 3 of <u>Twentieth Century American Jewish Writers</u> (New York: P. Lang Publishers, 1992).

10. One Selection from an Anthology or an Edited Book—CM

1. Walter J. Savitch, "Infinity Is in the Eye of the Beholder," in <u>Interdisciplinary Approaches to Language: Essays in Honor of S. Y.</u>

Kuroda, ed. Carol Georgopoulos and Roberta Ishihara (Boston: Kluwer
Academic, 1991), 487-500.

11. TWO SELECTIONS FROM ONE ANTHOLOGY OR AN EDITED BOOK—CM

If you cite two or more selections from the same anthology or edited
book, give complete bibliographical information in the first note for
each selection.

12. SIGNED ARTICLE IN A REFERENCE BOOK—CM

1. Doris Shadbolt, "Emily Carr," in <u>The Canadian Encyclopedia,</u>
2nd ed.

13. UNSIGNED ARTICLE IN A REFERENCE BOOK—CM

1. <u>Encyclopedia Britannica,</u> 15th ed., s.v. "Russia."

14. EDITION—CM

1. Joanne Buckley and David Gates, <u>Put It in Writing,</u> 2nd ed.
(Scarborough, Ontario: Prentice Hall, 1995).

15. ANTHOLOGY OR EDITED BOOK—CM

1. James P. Lantolf and Gabriela Appel, eds., <u>Vygotskian
Approaches to Second Language Research</u> (Norwood, New Jersey: Ablex
Publishing Corporation, 1994).

16. INTRODUCTION, PREFACE, FOREWORD, OR AFTERWORD—CM

1. Warren Allmand, foreword to <u>The Life and Death of Anna Mae
Aquash,</u> by Johanna Brand (Toronto: Lorimer, 1993).

17. UNPUBLISHED DISSERTATION OR ESSAY—CM

1. Joanne Buckley, "An Assessment of Kieran Egan's Theory of
Educational Development" (diss., University of Western Ontario,
1991), 33-42.

State the author's name first, the title in quotation marks (not
underlined), then a description of the work (such as *Ph.D. diss.* or
master's thesis), then the degree-granting institution, and the date.

18. REPRINT OF AN OLDER BOOK—CM

1. Archibald Lampman, <u>Lyrics of Earth</u> (1895; reprint, Ottawa:
Tecumseh Press, 1978).

33e CM

19. Book in a Series—CM

1. Thomas J. Courchene, *In Praise of Renewed Federalism,* The Canada Round (Toronto: C. D. Howe Institute, 1991).

20. Book with a Title Within a Title—CM

1. Kevin J. Hayes, ed., *The Critical Response to Herman Melville's* Moby Dick (Westport, Connecticut: Greenwood Press, 1994).

21. Secondary Source—CM

1. Mary Wollstonecraft, *A Vindication of the Rights of Woman* (1792), 90, quoted in Caroline Shrodes, Harry Finestone, and Michael Shugrue, *The Conscious Reader,* 4th ed. (New York: Macmillan Publishing, 1988), 282.

When you quote one person's words, having found them in another person's work, give information as fully as you can about both sources. Note 1 shows the form when the focus of your citation is Mary Wollstonecraft's words. If your focus is on what Shrodes, Finestone, and Shugrue have to say about Wollstonecraft's words, handle the information as shown in note 2.

2. Caroline Shrodes, Harry Finestone, and Michael Shugrue, *The Conscious Reader,* 4th ed. (New York: Macmillan Publishing, 1988), 282, quoting Mary Wollstonecraft, *A Vindication of the Rights of Woman* (1792), 90.

22. Government Publications—CM

1. Royal Commission on Bilingualism and Biculturalism, *Preliminary Report* (Ottawa: Queen's Printer, 1965), 127.

2. Indian and Northern Affairs Canada, *The Inuit* (Ottawa: Supply and Services Canada, 1986), 46.

When a government department, bureau, agency, or committee produces a document, cite that group as the author.

23. Published Proceedings of a Conference—CM

1. Marko Pavlyshyn and J. E. M. Clarke, eds., *Ukraine in the 1990s: Proceedings of the First Conference of the Ukrainian Studies Association of Australia* (Melbourne: Monash University, Slavic Section, 1992).

Pavlyshyn, M., and J. E. M. Clarke, eds. 1992. <u>Ukraine in the</u>
<u>1990s: Proceedings of the first conference of the Ukrainian</u>
<u>Studies Association of Australia</u>. Melbourne: Monash University.

PRINT SOURCES: ARTICLES

24. ARTICLE FROM A DAILY NEWSPAPER—CM

Tom Tebbutt, "Showman Agassi Lightly Frolics to Canadian Title,"
<u>Globe and Mail</u> 1 August 1994, sec. D, p. 1.

Here is the References list entry. A parenthetical citation uses
name and year: (Tebbutt 1994).

Tebbutt, T. 1994. Showman Agassi lightly frolics to Canadian title.
<u>Globe and Mail</u>, 1 August.

25. EDITORIAL, LETTER TO THE EDITOR, OR REVIEW—CM

1. "A Black Mark on Local Government," editorial, <u>London Free</u>
<u>Press</u> 27 July 1994, sec. B, p. 8.

2. John Hurka, letter, <u>Calgary Sun</u> 5 July 1994, sec. A, p. 18.

3. Wendy Toews, "Politics of the Mind," review of <u>They Say You're</u>
<u>Crazy</u>, by Paula J. Caplan, <u>Winnipeg Free Press</u> 26 August 1995, p. C3.

Here are the References list entries:

A black mark on local government. 1994. Editorial in <u>London Free</u>
<u>Press</u>. 27 July.

Hurka, John. 1994. Letter. <u>Calgary Sun</u>. 5 July.

Toews, Wendy. 1995. Politics of the mind. Review of <u>They say you're</u>
<u>crazy</u>, by Paula J. Caplan. <u>Winnipeg Free Press</u>. 26 August.

26. UNSIGNED ARTICLE FROM A DAILY NEWSPAPER—CM

1. "Canadian Adds Flights," <u>Globe and Mail</u> 1 August 1994, sec. B,
p. 2.

27. ARTICLE FROM A WEEKLY OR BIWEEKLY MAGAZINE OR NEWSPAPER—CM

1. Chris Woods, "Storm Clouds over Quebec," <u>Maclean's</u> 6 November
1989, 16–17.

Here is the References list entry.

Wood, Chris. 1989. Storm clouds over Quebec. <u>Maclean's</u>. 6 November.

28. ARTICLE FROM A MONTHLY OR BIMONTHLY PERIODICAL—CM

1. Jim Bell, "Kingdom Come: Canada's Inuit Finally May Be Getting Their Own Homeland, But at What Price?" <u>Earthwatch</u>, September/October 1992, 10-11.

Here is the References list entry:

Bell, J. 1992. Kingdom come: Canada's Inuit finally may be getting their own homeland, but at what price? <u>Earthwatch</u>. September/October.

29. UNSIGNED ARTICLE FROM A WEEKLY OR MONTHLY PERIODICAL—CM

1. "10 Ways to Sleep Easy," <u>Canadian Living</u>, August 1994, 19.

30. ARTICLE FROM A COLLECTION OF REPRINTED ARTICLES—CM

1. Abraham Brumberg, "Russia after Perestroika," <u>The Gorbachev Era</u>, Articles on Russian and Soviet History, vol. 14 (New York: Garland Publications, 1992).

31. ARTICLE IN A JOURNAL WITH CONTINUOUS PAGINATION—CM

1. Marcel C. LaFollette, "The Politics of Research Misconduct: Congressional Oversight, Universities, and Science," <u>Journal of Higher Education</u> 65 (1994): 261-85.

Here is the References list entry:

LaFollette, Marcel C. 1994. The politics of research misconduct: Congressional oversight, universities, and science. <u>Journal of Higher Education</u>. 65: 261-85.

32. ARTICLE IN A JOURNAL THAT PAGES EACH ISSUE SEPARATELY—CM

1. Dennis Hancock, "Prototyping the Hubble Fix," <u>IEEE Spectrum</u>, 30, no. 10 (1993): 34-39.

NONPRINT SOURCES

33. PERSONAL INTERVIEW—CM

1. Randi Friedman, interview by author, Fredericton, New Brunswick, 30 June 1992.

For an unpublished interview, give the name of the interviewee, identify the interviewer, and then give location and date.

34. LETTERS—CM

Treat a published letter like any other published document. For an unpublished letter, give the name of the writer, the name of the recipient, and the date of the letter.

> 1. Gary Edward Reilly, letter to author, 26 December 1994.

35. FILM OR VIDEOTAPE—CM

> 1. Dane Archer, <u>A World of Gestures: Cultural and Nonverbal Communication</u> (Berkeley: The University of California Extension Media Center, 1992), videocassette.

Here is the References list entry:

> Archer, Dane. 1992. <u>A world of gestures: Cultural and nonverbal communication</u>. Berkeley: Univ. of Cal. Extension Media Center. Videocassette.

36. RECORDING—CM

> 1. Ismael Fernandes de la Cuesta, <u>Chant,</u> Benedictine Monks of Santo Domingo de Silos, Angel CDC 724355513823.

ELECTRONIC SOURCES

37. COMPUTER SOFTWARE—CM

> 1. Transparent Language Presentation Program, ver. 2.0 for Windows, Transparent Language, Inc., Hollis, New Hampshire.

Here is the References list entry:

> Transparent Language Presentation Program Ver. 2.0 for Windows. Transparent Language, Inc., Hollis, New Hampshire.

38. ERIC INFORMATION SERVICE—CM

> 1. Linda H. Chiang, <u>Beyond the Language: Native Americans' Nonverbal Communication</u> (Anderson, IN: Midwest Association of Teachers of Educational Psychology, 1993) ERIC ED 368540.

Here is the References list entry:

> Chiang, Linda H. 1993. <u>Beyond the language: Native Americans' nonverbal communication</u>. Anderson, IN: Midwest Association of Teachers of Educational Psychology, ERIC, ED 368540.

33f
CBE

39. ELECTRONIC DOCUMENTS—CM

Until uniform standards for documenting electronic sources exist, the *Chicago Manual* recommends following documentation guidelines of the International Standards Organization (*ISO*). Follow the source for capitalizing and punctuating, since these usually mechanical operations can affect the ability to locate material. In general, the information units are author(s) if any; title, database medium; information about a print version; access or update dates; item or access numbers, if any; paging or other description of length, if any; and location information. The ISO recommends putting information about the database medium, access dates, and length in brackets.

```
     1. Dan S. Wallach, "FAQ: Typing Injuries (2/5): General Info.,"
in typing-injury-faq/general.z [USENET newsgroup], 1993 [cited 14
Nov. 1993]; available from mail-server @@ rtfm.mit.edu; INTERNET.
```

33f **Using CBE-style documentation**

In its 1994 style manual, *Scientific Style and Format,* the (U.S.) Council of Biology Editors (**CBE**) endorses two documentation systems widely used in mathematics and the physical and life sciences. The first system uses name-year parenthetical citations in the text of a paper together with a References list that gives full bibliographic information for each source. The second system uses numbers to mark references to sources in the paper. These numbers correlate with a numbered References list that gives full bibliographic information for each source.

Each of these styles uses a slightly different format for entries in the References list. With the name-date parenthetical system, a name and a date are the first two units of information in each References entry. When in-text citations are numbers referring to the numbered entries in the References list, the first two units of information in References entries are usually a name and title.

This handbook focuses mainly on CBE's numbered reference system. Here is the way it works:

- The first time you cite each source in your paper, assign it a number in sequence, starting with 1.
- In your References list, list and number each entry in the order of its appearance in your paper, starting with 1.

CBE recommends using superscript numbers for marking source citations in your paper, although numbers in parentheses are also acceptable. Here is a brief example showing two sources cited in a paper and a References list arranged in citation sequence.

IN-TEXT CITATIONS

Sybesma[1] insists that this behaviour occurs periodically, but Crowder[2] claims never to have observed it.

REFERENCES LIST

1. Sybesma C. An introduction to biophysics. New York: Academic Press; 1977. 648 p.

2. Crowder, W. Seashore life between the tides. New York: Dodd, Mead & Co.; 1931. New York: Dover Publications Reprint; 1975. 373 p.

Each citation of Sybesma's *Introduction to Biophysics* is followed by a superscript 1, and each citation of Crowder's *Seashore Life* is followed by a superscript 2 in this paper.

1 Compiling a CBE style References list

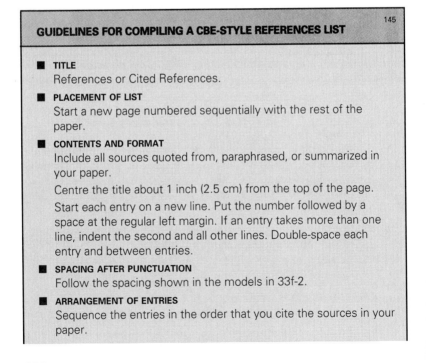

GUIDELINES FOR COMPILING A CBE-STYLE REFERENCES LIST

145

■ **TITLE**
References or Cited References.

■ **PLACEMENT OF LIST**
Start a new page numbered sequentially with the rest of the paper.

■ **CONTENTS AND FORMAT**
Include all sources quoted from, paraphrased, or summarized in your paper.
Centre the title about 1 inch (2.5 cm) from the top of the page.
Start each entry on a new line. Put the number followed by a space at the regular left margin. If an entry takes more than one line, indent the second and all other lines. Double-space each entry and between entries.

■ **SPACING AFTER PUNCTUATION**
Follow the spacing shown in the models in 33f-2.

■ **ARRANGEMENT OF ENTRIES**
Sequence the entries in the order that you cite the sources in your paper.

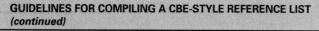

33f
CBE

■ **AUTHORS' NAMES**
Invert all author names, giving the last name first. You can give first names or use only initials of first and middle names. If you use initials, do not use a period or a space between first and middle initials. If you use full first names, separate the names of multiple authors with a semicolon (without the word or symbol for *and*). Use a period after the last author's name.

■ **CAPITALIZATION OF TITLES**
Capitalize a book or an article title's first word and any proper nouns. Do not capitalize the first word of a subtitle unless it is a proper noun.

Capitalize the titles of academic journals. If the title of a periodical is one word, give it in full; otherwise, abbreviate it according to recommendations established by the *American National Standard for Abbreviations of Titles of Periodicals*.

Capitalize a newspaper title's major words, giving the full title, including a beginning *A, An,* or *The.*

■ **SPECIAL TREATMENT OF TITLES**
Do not underline titles or enclose them in quotation marks.

■ **PLACE OF PUBLICATION**
Use a colon after the city of publication. Add a provincial or state postal abbreviation or a country name to a city that might be ambiguous.

■ **PUBLISHER**
Give publishers' names in full, including *Co., Inc., Press, Ltd.,* and so on. Use a semicolon after the publisher's name.

■ **PUBLICATION MONTH ABBREVIATIONS**
Abbreviate publication months.

■ **INCLUSIVE PAGE NUMBERS**
Shorten the second number as much as possible while keeping it unambiguous: for example, 233-4 for 233 to 234; 233-44 for 233 to 244; 234-304. Use the abbreviation *p* without a period or underlining with designations of pages. Follow the guidelines in the models.

■ **DISCONTINUOUS PAGE NUMBERS**
Give the full numbers of all discontinuous pages, preceding the first number with the *p* abbreviation.

→

GUIDELINES FOR COMPILING A CBE-STYLE REFERENCE LIST 145
(continued)

■ **TOTAL PAGE NUMBERS**
When citing an entire book, for the last information unit give the total pages followed by the abbreviation *p* and a period to end the information unit.

■ **REFERENCES ENTRY: BOOK**
Citations for books usually list author(s), title, publication information, and pages (either total pages when citing an entire work or inclusive pages for citing part of a book). Each unit of information ends with a period.

1. Stacy RW, Williams DT, Worden RE, McMorris RO. Essentials of biological and medical sciences. New York: McGraw-Hill Book Company, Inc.; 1955. 727 p.

■ **REFERENCES ENTRY: ARTICLE**
Citations for articles usually list author(s), article title, journal name and publication information, each section followed by a period. Sci Am is the abbreviated form of Scientific American. The volume number is 269, and the issue number in parentheses, is (3).

1. Weissman IL, Cooper MD. How the immune system develops. Sci Am 1993 Mar;269(3):65-71.

---

2   Following models for a CBE-style References list

Directory

PRINT SOURCES: BOOKS

PRINT SOURCES: BOOKS

1. BOOK BY ONE AUTHOR—CBE

1. Hawking SW. Black holes and baby universes and other essays. New York: Bantam Books; 1993. 320 p.

Use one space but no punctuation between an author's last name and the initial of the first name. Do not put punctuation or a space between a first and a middle initial.

2. BOOK BY MORE THAN ONE AUTHOR—CBE

1. Wegzyn, S, Gille J-C, Vidal P. Developmental systems: at the crossroads of system theory, computer science, and genetic engineering. New York: Springer-Verlag; 1990. 595 p.

3. BOOK BY GROUP OR CORPORATE AUTHOR—CBE

1. Canadian Institute of Child Health. Family-centred maternity and newborn care. Ottawa: CICH; 1980.

Use a two-letter postal abbreviation enclosed in parentheses after the name of a city that might be unfamiliar to your readers.

4. ANTHOLOGY OR EDITED BOOK—CBE

1. Heerman B, Hummel S, editors. Ancient DNA: recovery and analysis of genetic material from paleontological, archeological, museum, medical, and forensic specimens. New York: Springer-Verlag; 1994. 1029 p.

5. One Selection or Chapter from an Anthology or Edited Book—CBE

1. Basov NG, Feoktistov LP, Senatsky YV. Laser driver for inertial confinement fusion. In: Brueckner, KA, editor. Research trends in physics: inertial confinement fusion. New York: American Institute of Physics; 1992: p 24-37.

6. All Volumes of a Multivolume Work—CBE

1. Crane FL, Morre DJ, Low HE, editors. Oxidoreduction at the plasma membrane: relation to growth and transport. Boca Raton (FL): Chemical Rubber Company Press; 1991. 2 vol.

7. Unpublished Dissertation or Thesis—CBE

1. Baykul MC. Using ballistic electron emission microscopy to investigate the metal-vacuum interface. [dissertation]. Orem (UT): Polytechnic University; 1993. 111 p.

Print Sources: Articles

8. Published Article from Conference Proceedings—CBE

1. Tsang CP, Bellgard MI. Sequence generation using a network of Boltzmann machines. In: Tsang CP, editor. Proceedings of the 4th Australian Joint Conference on Artificial Intelligence; 1990 Nov 8-11; Perth, Australia. Singapore: World Scientific; 1990: p 224-33.

9. Signed Newspaper Article—CBE

1. Hoke F. Gene therapy: clinical gains yield a wealth of research opportunities. Scientist 1993 Oct 4;Sect A:1, 5, 7.

Sect stands for Section.

10. Unsigned Newspaper Article—CBE

1. [Anonymous]. Arctic drilling study. The Globe and Mail 1995 Sept 2;Sect D:8.

11. Article in a Journal with Continuous Pagination—CBE

1. Scott ML, Fredrickson RJ, Moorhead BB. Characteristics of old-growth forests associated with northern spotted owls in Olympic National Park. J Wildlf Mgt 1993;57:315-21.

Give only the volume number before the page numbers.

12. ARTICLE IN A JOURNAL THAT PAGES EACH ISSUE SEPARATELY—CBE

1. Weissman IL, Cooper MD. How the immune system develops. Sci Am 1993
   Mar;269(3):65-71.

Give both the volume number and the issue number (here, 269 is the volume number and 3 is the issue number). *Sci Am* is the abbreviation for *Scientific American* based on the standards established by the *American National Standard for Abbreviations of Titles of Periodicals*.

13. JOURNAL ARTICLE ON DISCONTINUOUS PAGES—CBE

1. Richards FM. The protein folding problem. Sci Am 1991
   Nov;246(1):54-7. 60-6.

14. ENTIRE ISSUE OF A JOURNAL—CBE

1. Whales in a modern world: a symposium held in London, November
   1988. Mamm Rev 1990 Jan;20(9).

November 1988, the date of the symposium, is part of the title of the issue in this case.

OTHER SOURCES

15. SLIDE SET—CBE

1. Human parasitology [slides]. Chicago (IL): American Society of
   Clinical Pathologists Press; 1990: colour. Accompanied by:
   guide.

16. ELECTRONIC SOURCES—CBE

In general, to cite electronic sources, start with a statement of the type of document, and then give the information you would give for a print version. Then give information that would help a reader to locate the electronic source. End with a date: your access date for online sources or the date of the update you used for CD-ROM databases that are updated periodically.

Case Study: A Student Writing an MLA Research Paper

34

This chapter presents a case study of a student, Amy Brown, going through the processes of conducting research and writing a paper based on her findings. Section 34a narrates the processes. Section 34b shows the final draft of Brown's paper, along with commentary on the paper's key elements. The commentary includes Process Notes explaining many of Brown's decisions during her writing process.

> *Amy Brown was given this assignment for a research paper:* Write a research paper on the general subject of "communication." The paper should be 1800 to 2000 words long and should be based on a variety of sources. The final paper is due in six weeks. Interim deadlines for parts of the work will be announced. To complete this assignment, you need to engage in three interrelated processes: conducting research, understanding the results of that research, and writing a paper based on the first two processes. Consult the *Simon & Schuster Handbook for Writers,* First Canadian Edition, especially Chapter 32, which gives you practical, step-by-step guidance on what this assignment entails.

34a Observing the processes of researching and writing an MLA-style research paper

Amy Brown faced many challenges as she worked on her assignment. Some decisions did not come easily, especially in the early stages of her research process. Brown expected the process to lead to a few puzzles and frustrations, and she resolved to remain patient with herself and the project.

Narrowing the subject of communication to a more **suitable topic** proved the most difficult challenge. Because the idea of unspoken messages among people interested her, Brown decided to concentrate on *nonverbal communication.* She used that term to start compiling a list of **headings and key words** (see 32i). Making her first trip to the library for this research project, she looked for the term *nonverbal communication* in the Library of Congress Subject Headings (LCSH). *Nonverbal communication* was there, listed with its call number—BF637.N66—which Brown copied down immediately. The letters *BF* would help her locate sources on nonverbal communication in any library using the Library of Congress (LC) system to catalogue its materials.

One of the LCSH subdivisions under nonverbal communication was especially meaningful to Brown: *personal space.* She knew that personal space concerns the physical distance people expect to maintain between themselves and others. Brown had become aware of the concept when a cousin who was job hunting lived with Brown and her family for three weeks. Although Brown and her cousin liked each other, Brown became cranky toward her as time went on, feeling that she had lost her "space." Discovering the idea of personal space as a part of communication intrigued Brown. Here was a topic she wanted to research.

Brown then browsed the general encyclopedia collection. Most discussed nonverbal communication in their entries on communication. In the *Encyclopaedia Britannica,* Brown found an entry for *personal space,* but it was about the biological topic of distances between plants. Afraid she might have come to a dead end, she decided to look in one more general encyclopedia, the 1993 edition of *Academic American.* It was a lucky choice: She found a very short article on nonverbal communication with a bibliography at the end. It listed the book *Body Language* by Julius Fast. Brown began an Author Names section in her **research log,** making Fast the first entry.

Heading next for specialized encyclopedias, Brown discovered that her library shelved all specialized reference materials by call number. She located the reference books with the *BF* call letters she had copied down from LCSH. Looking first in *The Encyclopedia of Psychology,* Brown found an article called "Nonverbal Behavior" that summarized various aspects of nonverbal communication and introduced two pieces of information that turned out to be crucial: the term *proxemics,* a synonym for personal space, and the name of an early researcher into personal space, Edward T. Hall. Hall's book *The Hidden Dimension* was cited in the bibliography of the article. Brown now had the name of an **authority** and of a book that ultimately turned out to be a **major source** of her topic.

Pleased with her discovery, Brown wrote about it in her research log, including all the information that she might need to find Hall's *The Hidden Dimension.* She also added Hall to her Author Names list, along with the names of two other experts mentioned in the encyclopedia article: Desmond Morris for studies of multicultural aspects and Judith Hall for research on gender differences in personal space. Brown made a bibliography card in MLA format for the "Nonverbal Behavior" article in *The Encyclopedia of Psychology* and then photocopied the article.

In a second specialized encyclopedia, *The Encyclopedic Dictionary of Psychology,* Brown found an article on proxemics, which named Edward T. Hall as the main authority on the subject and defined proxemics in detail.

Brown next used her **library catalogue.** This computerized system let her search by author, title, and subject. Using the names in her Author Names list, she located books by Morris, Fast, Edward Hall, and Judith Hall. When she searched by subject, her library's system accepted only *nonverbal communication* (rather than *proxemics* or *personal space*). From the 25 or 30 listings that appeared on the screen, Brown chose works whose titles or authors she recognized from the research she had done so far. Using the key word *personal space* during the title search, Brown discovered an important title that would also turn out to be a key source: *Personal Space* by Robert Sommer. The catalogue also listed several other works by Edward Hall, including a 1990 book written with Mildred Hall.

Over the next few days, Brown skimmed the books she had checked out. She felt that they provided her with a solid foundation. She also watched two videos that had been on the printout from her catalogue searches but, deciding that they were too general to be useful, returned them.

The next challenge Brown faced was to find the most **current information** about personal space. Because *nonverbal communication* was catalogued under a social science call number, Brown chose the *Social Science Periodical Index* to find current scholarly articles. *Proxemics* was listed with the cross-reference "See personal space." Brown found numerous articles exploring personal space, many of them with bibliographies that listed her older sources. Seeing their names reassured her that she had uncovered some of the authorities on her topic. Brown decided to read several articles. Because some of them were unavailable to her university library, she arranged to get them through interlibrary loan.

As a last step in gathering current sources, Brown consulted a **periodicals database** her library had recently acquired. She took a few minutes to learn the computer access codes and then searched using the narrower key term *personal space*, as well as the more general key term *nonverbal communication*. Under nonverbal communication she found 68 listings, many of them available in full-text print form (available for complete versions to be called up onscreen or printed out). Being familiar with the names of credible authorities in the field and keeping her narrowed topic of personal space in mind, Brown felt she was equipped to choose worthwhile articles from the database. She scanned the available articles onscreen and printed out those that she felt fairly sure would be relevant.

During this search for materials, Brown was slowly formulating a **research question** that would help to focus her use of the sources she had gathered. Because Edward Hall's discussion of different standards for personal space in different cultures interested her, Brown brainstormed by posing research questions related to that aspect. "What is personal space?" was too broad and lacked focus. "How do North Americans' and Arabs' standards for personal space differ?" was too narrow for the resources available in her school's library. Widening this too specific idea to "How do standards for personal space differ among cultures?" Brown was now ready to focus her exploration of her sources. (For a flow chart that shows Brown's narrowing process, see page 566.)

Now Brown was ready to think about her purpose and audience (see 1b, 1c, and 32e). For an audience, she chose a **general reader—** rather than a specialized reader—because she wanted to assume that the audience would know little about the topic of personal space. Deciding on a purpose proved more complicated. Brown started by wanting to write with a persuasive purpose, but she soon switched to an informative purpose. At first, she wanted to argue that people from different countries have serious trouble with crosscultural communication unless they are aware of varying expectations concerning personal space. While reading and taking notes to answer her research question, however, Brown realized that she could not explain basic crosscultural concepts *and* argue a position within the time and length limits of the assignment. She settled on an informative purpose.

Brown now had a working bibliography. Using MLA documentation style (see section 33c), she had made bibliography cards (see 33b) on key books and articles. It was time to read closely and take notes. Brown carefully headed each index card with the author of the source. Making sure to avoid plagiarism, she paraphrased, summarized, and copied quotations according to the techniques described in Chapter 31. Whenever she copied an author's exact words, Brown enclosed them in oversized quotation marks to alert herself to be especially careful to avoid plagiarism when writing from these notes.

While taking notes, Brown rejected a few sources that duplicated what she already had. Later, as she was writing her paper, she dropped a few other sources that were related to personal space but not to her paper. Her final version uses sixteen sources.

In organizing her paper, Brown looked through her notes and saw that they fell into two piles: standards for personal space in North America and standards in other countries. She tried to outline the material and quickly realized that she would need to start with a definition of personal space. Going back through her cards, she created a third pile for definitions.

Composing her thesis statement was next. Brown wanted her thesis statement to be the last sentence of her introductory paragraph. She drafted a preliminary thesis statement to use as she wrote the first full draft of her paper. Later she revised the thesis statement (for a description of the evolution of her final thesis statement, see 32r). Here is an early draft of Brown's introductory paragraph; the last sentence contains the preliminary thesis statement.

> People know unconsciously what close is when they stand near other people during conversations. This relates to the concept of personal space—the amount of physical distance people expect during social interaction. Standards for personal space vary among cultures.

Brown knew that this early draft was flawed. It lacked interest, the word "this" was a vague pronoun reference, and the thesis statement did not give a full picture of the paper. She showed her draft to three friends and asked them to react. One friend, a major in psychology, had a newspaper clipping in his files that Brown thought would be a good source to draw on for introducing her essay. For Brown's final draft, see page 1 of her paper in 34b.

In writing her paper, Brown composed three drafts. In addition to rewriting her opening paragraph, Brown made other improvements as she revised. Her first draft lacked clear signals to readers about the material's organization. In her second draft, Brown worked hard to craft topic sentences to start many of her paragraphs, realizing that these sentences showed the structure she had imposed on the topic as she synthesized what she had learned from her various sources. Also, Brown felt that her first draft relied too much on quotations, and so she paraphrased (see 31d) and summarized (see 31e) some of the material for the second draft. She kept quotations only when an author's language carried some special significance (see, for example, Brown's third and fourth paragraphs) or helped establish the credibility of the information. In the third draft, Brown polished her word choice, corrected her grammar and spelling, and reworked her conclusion. She decided that the conclusion should be a call to action (see 4g), urging people to become sensitive to the concept of personal space and thereby avoid intercultural misunderstandings. Brown's first draft of a concluding paragraph was only one sentence long, so she knew it needed work.

Brown's final draft appears in 34b. A commentary explaining elements of the paper accompanies each page of this final draft. Process Notes, a special feature of the commentary, narrate Brown's thinking and writing processes as she made choices and decisions.

34b Analyzing an MLA-style research paper

Amy Brown followed MLA style for format decisions on this paper.

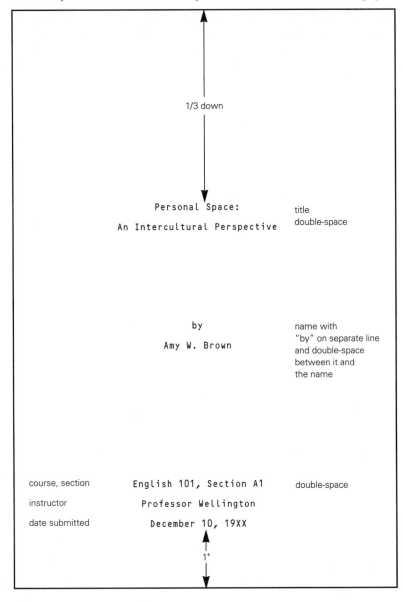

1/3 down

Personal Space:
An Intercultural Perspective

title
double-space

by
Amy W. Brown

name with
"by" on separate line
and double-space
between it and
the name

course, section   English 101, Section A1   double-space

instructor   Professor Wellington

date submitted   December 10, 19XX

1"

34b

Title page and first page of essay with a title page. If your instructor requires a title page, you can use the format and types of information shown on page 678 for Amy Brown's title page. Then, on page 1 of your paper, put your last name followed by a space followed by the numeral 1 in the upper right corner 1/2 inch (about 1.75 cm) below the top edge of the page. Double-space below this heading, and then type the paper's title, centring it. Double-space after the title, and then start your paper, indenting the first line of each paragraph 5 characters. The first page of Amy Brown's paper, on page 682, follows this format.

First page without a title page. If your instructor does not require a title page, follow MLA format style, shown below, for the first page of your paper.

FIRST PAGE FOR A PAPER WITHOUT A TITLE PAGE   1/2"

Brown 1

Amy W. Brown   name

Professor Wellington   instructor

English 101, Section A1   course, section

10 December, 19XX   date submitted

double-
space   Personal Space:

An Intercultural Perspective

When she returned home after a year in South

America, Judith Martin, a North American writer,

began to have a problem. People kept interpreting

her behaviour as flirtatious, but she was not

flirting. Fairly soon she figured out what was

happening. When most South Americans talk to each

other face-to-face, they stand closer together

than do most people from Canada or the United

States. Martin had not readjusted from South

American distances (9). Apparently, she had

forgotten about the phenomenon known as personal

space—the amount of physical distance people

expect during social interaction. Everyone has

expectations concerning the use of personal space,

Brown i

Outline

Thesis statement: Everyone has expectations concerning the use of personal space, but accepted distances for that space are determined by each person's culture.

I. Research on personal space began in the 1960s.

    A. Most people are unaware that interpersonal distances exist.

    B. Personal space depends on invisible boundaries.

    C. Personal space moves with people as they interact.

    D. People do not like anyone to trespass on their personal space.

II. Research reveals North Americans' expectations for personal space.

    A. Hall identifies four zones for personal space.

    B. Subcultures help determine expectations for personal space.

    C. Gender influences people's use of personal space.

III. Research reveals standards for personal space in countries other than Canada and the United States.

    A. Conversational distances vary by cultures.

        1. Western Europeans use fingertip-to-shoulder distance.

        2. Eastern Europeans use wrist-to-shoulder distance.

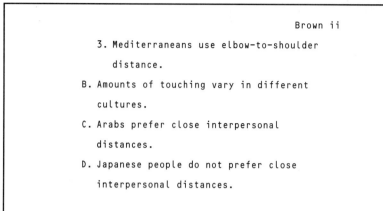

> 3. Mediterraneans use elbow-to-shoulder
> distance.
> B. Amounts of touching vary in different
> cultures.
> C. Arabs prefer close interpersonal
> distances.
> D. Japanese people do not prefer close
> interpersonal distances.

Name and page-number heading. Except for a title page, give each page of a paper you prepare according to MLA format guidelines a heading in the upper right corner 1/2 inch (about 1.75 cm) below the top edge of the paper. Use your last name, followed by a space, followed by the page number. Number pages that come before your essay begins, such as outline pages, with lowercase roman numerals (see Amy Brown's outline). Use arabic numeral 1 on the page on which your essay begins, and then number each page consecutively through to the last page of Works Cited. Double-space below the name and page number to whatever comes next on the page.

Outline. Brown's instructor required a formal outline in the final draft of each student's research paper. To format her outline, Brown referred to sections 2o and 32s in this handbook. In the upper right corner heading consisting of her last name and the page number, she used lowercase roman numerals for the page numbers, a conventional way of showing that the outline comes before the first page of the essay itself. She double-spaced below the name-number heading and then centred the word "Outline," using a capital letter to start it. She double-spaced and then typed the words "Thesis statement" at the left margin, underlining them. The thesis statement matches the last sentence of the first paragraph of her paper.

Brown used a **sentence outline,** not a topic outline (see 2o). To reflect the organization of her paper, she divided the material in the outline into three major parts, numbered I, II, and III. Each item in the three major parts she numbered A, B, etc. Part III-A needed more detail, so the added items are numbered 1, 2, and 3. The items in the outline are in parallel form: Each starts with a subject followed by a verb in the present tense°.

Brown 1 A

Personal Space:

An Intercultural Perspective

1 When she returned home after a year in South
America, Judith Martin, a North American writer, began B
to have a problem. People kept interpreting her
behaviour as flirtatious, but she was not flirting.
Fairly soon she figured out what was happening. When
most South Americans talk to each other face-to-face,
they stand closer together than do most people from
Canada or the United States. Martin had not readjusted
from South American distances (9). Apparently, she had
forgotten about the phenomenon known as personal space—
the amount of physical distance people expect during
social interaction. Everyone has expectations concerning C
the use of personal space, but accepted distances for
that space are determined by each person's culture.

2 Observations about personal space began about thirty
years ago. Anthropologist Edward T. Hall was a pioneer in
the field. He became very interested in how interpersonal
distances affected communication between people. In his D
aptly titled book <u>The Hidden Dimension</u>, Hall coined the
word "proxemics" to describe people's use of space as a
means of communication (1). When <u>The Hidden Dimension</u> was E
published in the 1960s, most people were unaware that
interpersonal distances existed and contributed to
people's reactions to one another. Today, even though
people may be generally more sensitive to multicultural
issues, the cultural differences and expectations Hall
described (109) can still be misunderstood and can still E
affect people's reactions to one another.

COMMENTARY

A. **Title.** Brown's title prepares readers for her paper by giving the paper's major term (personal space) and the focus of her paper's discussion (more than one culture). ◆ PROCESS NOTE: In an earlier draft, Brown's title was "Proxemics: An Intercultural Perspective on the Need for Space." She rejected it because "space" was too general and "proxemics" was too technical. She then tried "Being Close: An Intercultural Perspective," but she revised the first half to avoid multiple meanings. ◆

B. **Introductory device.** Brown uses an anecdote. (See 4g.) She wanted it to serve four functions: to make the abstract concept of personal space concrete and familiar; to tie into the paper's title; to lead into the thesis statement; and to capture readers' interest. ◆ PROCESS NOTE: For an early draft of Brown's introductory paragraph, see page 676. ◆

C. **Thesis statement.** The last sentence of Brown's introductory paragraph is her thesis statement. Emerging from the paper's title and opening anecdote, the thesis prepares readers for what to expect. Brown's thesis developed from her synthesis of the information and ideas she encountered as she conducted her research. ◆ PROCESS NOTE: For the evolution of Brown's thesis statement, see 32r. ◆

D. **Evaluation of source.** Brown established Edward T. Hall as an expert by identifying him as an anthropologist and as a pioneer on the subject of personal space. ◆ PROCESS NOTE: Brown confirmed that Hall was an authoritative, reliable source by finding his name and his work mentioned in articles and listed in bibliographies with articles in reference works such as *The Encyclopedia of Psychology* and *The Encyclopedic Dictionary of Psychology* (see 34a). ◆

E. **Parenthetical page reference for author and book named in the text.** Brown uses two sources by Edward T. Hall in her paper. (His other work is cited in paragraph 10.) Also, she uses a source by Judith Hall (see paragraph 7). To identify the source here unmistakably, she uses Hall's full name and the work title; the parenthetical references include only the page numbers. (Brown also uses a work by Edward T. Hall and Mildred Reed Hall, but that source is always cited as Hall and Hall.) Brown uses quotation marks for the coined word "proxemics." Also, she inserts the first parenthetical reference before the period, at the end of the sentence, because the entire sentence refers to information in Hall. She inserts the second parenthetical reference after "Hall described," not before the sentence-ending period, signalling to readers that Hall's description of cultural differences and expectations is the material on page 109. Brown, not Hall, is saying that even today misunderstandings can still occur and "can still affect people's reactions to one another."

Brown 2

3   Personal space depends on invisible
boundaries. Those boundaries move with people as
they interact. Personal space gets larger or
smaller depending on the circumstances of the
social interaction at any moment (Fisher, Bell,
and Baum 149). Robert Sommer, an environmental
psychologist, uses literary and visual analogies
to describe personal space:

> Like the porcupines in Schopenhauer's fable,
> people like to be close enough to obtain warmth
> and comradeship but far enough away to avoid
> pricking one another. Personal space ... has
> been likened to a snail shell, a soap bubble,
> an aura, and "breathing room." (26)

4   People can react strongly to trespassers on
their personal space. In a textbook, social
psychologists Stephen Worchel and Joel Cooper
supplied one literary version. The poet W. H.
Auden describes his own personal space and
threatens a uniquely negative reaction to
intrusions in his space:

> Some thirty inches from my nose
> The frontier of my person goes
> And all the untilled air between
> Is private pagus or demesne
> Stranger, unless with bedroom eyes
> I beckon you to fraternize
> Beware of rudely crossing it
> I have no gun but I can spit.
> (qtd. in Worchel and Cooper 539)

F

G

H

I

J

J

K

COMMENTARY

F. **Topic sentence.** Brown uses a topic sentence (see 4a) to start many of her paragraphs. ◆ PROCESS NOTE: Brown's topic sentences in this paper emerged from her reflecting on what she learned about personal space as she conducted her research and came to understand what she read. Her topic sentences are the result of her thinking critically, most especially by making connections among ideas as she synthesized all her material (see 5b and 5f). ◆

G. **Paraphrase of original source.** ◆ PROCESS NOTE: In an earlier draft, Brown quoted the material and worked it into her prose. In her final draft, she used a paraphrase because it was not worded memorably enough to warrant quotation. ◆

H. **Parenthetical reference to authors not named in the text.** Authors' names and source page are in parentheses.

I. **A long quotation.** A quotation of more than four typewritten lines is set off from the rest of the text. Brown introduces it with a colon because she has written a complete sentence (compare with paragraph 12). She indents the material (10 characters or 1 inch) on the left and does not paragraph-indent the first line. In the fifth line, Brown uses a three-dot ellipsis where she omitted words (the full original source is shown in 32j-2). The words "breathing room" are in quotation marks because they appear this way in the original source. The parenthetical page reference is placed after the punctuation that ends the quotation.

J. **Use of an unusual source.** ◆ PROCESS NOTE: Although W. H. Auden is not a likely expert on personal space, Brown was delighted to use his poem. Because she had found the poem quoted in a discussion of personal space by social psychologists, she felt justified in using it. Also, it expressed a truth about personal space in exceptionally memorable language. She decided that this poem would be especially meaningful to the nonspecialist readers in her first-year English class. ◆

K. **Parenthetical reference for an indirect source.** Brown had to rely on an indirect source because her efforts to locate the poem in Auden's collected works were unsuccessful. (Brown found that for his later collections, Auden revised and even removed some poems from earlier collections.) She wanted to include the poem (see comment J above). In her parenthetical reference, she used *qtd. in*, the abbreviation for "quoted in," to show the quoted words are Auden's and can be found on page 539 of a work by Worchel and Cooper.

Brown 3

5   Research provides information about the distances that North Americans prefer when interacting. The pioneering work was done by Edward T. Hall. He observed the behaviour of a group of middle-class adults in business and professions in the northeastern United States. He saw four zones of personal space; they are summarized and explained in Table 1.

Table 1

Hall's "Distance Zones"[a]   L

	Intimate	Personal	Social	Public
Close	0 to 6"	$1\frac{1}{2}$ to $2\frac{1}{2}$'	4' to 7'	12' to 25'
Far	6" to $1\frac{1}{2}$'	$2\frac{1}{2}$' to 4'	7' to 12'	25'+

Source: Discussion in Edward T. Hall, <u>Hidden</u> 110-20; M
also Stewart 4-5; Fisher, Bell, and Baum 153.

    [a]Selected illustrations of each zone are: N
<u>Close Intimate</u>: lovers, children with parents; <u>Far Intimate</u>: strangers in crowds; <u>Close Personal</u>: husband and wife talking on the street; <u>Far Personal</u>: friends talking on the street; <u>Close Social</u>: boss and subordinate at a meeting; <u>Far Social</u>: receptionist and people in a waiting room; <u>Close Public</u>: teacher and students in a classroom; <u>Far Public</u>: actors or public speakers with audiences.

COMMENTARY

L. **Table.** A table is an excellent way to summarize complex or extensive information that involves numbers and/or repeated categories. In MLA style°, a table should be placed as close as possible to the paragraph in which it is first mentioned. If a table cannot fit in the space remaining on the page, it can be placed on the next page after the end of the first paragraph on that page. Some instructors permit students to put tables on a separate page, titled Appendix, at the end of the paper, but before pages for notes (if any) and the Works Cited list. Brown uses the format suggested in the *MLA Handbook for Writers of Research Papers*, 4th edition: table number and title at the left margin above the body of the table, lowercase letter to signal a note, source information immediately below the data, and note below source information. In MLA style, table notes are indicated by lowercase letters, and text notes by numbers (see paragraphs 9 and 10). ◆ PROCESS NOTE: In an early draft, Brown wrote sentences to present the information now in this table. She did not think of using a table until she showed her early draft to a friend who said that the material was hard to follow and boring. She then tried to condense the material and, as she was writing, decided that a table would be clearer and more concise. ◆

M. **Source identification.** Because Brown uses two works by Edward T. Hall, she includes a shortened title (*Hidden*) here so that readers will know which of his works she is referring to. (She uses his first name to distinguish him from Judith Hall, author of another source Brown uses; see paragraph 7. The other work by Edward T. Hall is cited in paragraph 10.) Brown uses semicolons to separate each item in a series of multiple references.

N. **Choice of examples.** ◆ PROCESS NOTE: In writing the footnote to the table, Brown had many choices of illustrations for each zone. She chose the ones that seemed to her the most familiar and therefore effective examples. ◆

Brown 4

6   Researchers working with Edward T. Hall's data found that accepted interpersonal distances in North America also depend on other factors. For example, subcultures help determine expectations concerning personal space. Fisher, Bell, and Baum report that groups of Hispanic-Americans generally interact more closely within their subculture than Anglo-Americans do within theirs. They further explain that "in general subcultural groups tend to interact at closer distances with members of their own subculture than with nonmembers" (158).

O

7   Gender also influences people's sense of personal space. In her book <u>Nonverbal Sex Differences</u>, Judith Hall says that women stand closer to another person than men do. In general, two women stand closest to each other, a woman and a man stand somewhat farther apart than two women, and two men stand farthest apart from each other (85-105). The effect of gender can produce the opposite result, however. A study of taxicab passengers in Australia found that 86 percent of women passengers riding alone sat in the back left seat of the taxi, as far from the driver as possible. (The driver sits on the right side in Australia.) Ninety-five percent of men riding alone, on the other hand, chose to ride in the front left seat, next to the driver (Kenner and Katsimaglis 625). Gender also seems to affect people's decisions to trespass on others' personal space. If two women are talking to each other while standing on opposite sides of a corridor, both men and women tend to walk between them. In contrast, both men and women walk around a pair of men or a man and a woman conversing (Lomax et al. 3).

P
Q

R

COMMENTARY

O. **Quotation within sentence.** Brown fits a quotation into her prose, using quotation marks to avoid plagiarism. The parenthetical reference goes immediately after the end of the material from the source (after a closing quotation mark, not before it). ◆ PROCESS NOTE: Brown used a quotation because she felt that the material comparing one subgroup with another might be sensitive. She wanted her readers to have particular confidence in her presentation of the information. This is the third quotation in Brown's paper; the other two (paragraphs 3 and 4) are long quotations, which are displayed. This is a short run-in quotation, which Brown felt covered the material well and offered a change of pace in ways to integrate quotations. ◆

P. **Word choice.** Brown uses *gender*, not *sex* here. ◆ PROCESS NOTE: As Brown read journal articles, she noted that most of them used "gender" rather than "sex," although Judith Hall uses both "sex" and "gender" in *Nonverbal Sex Differences*. Brown chose "gender" because it was used by a greater number of the sources she consulted. ◆

Q. **Author with same last name as another source author.** Brown uses the full name Judith Hall to distinguish this citation of a source from references to Edward T. Hall, who is cited in paragraphs 2, 5, 10, and 12.

R. **Paraphrase of an original source.** ◆ PROCESS NOTE: As Brown paraphrased her source, she did not include all the data in the original. She paraphrased the general observations about men and women mentioned in the article by Kenner and Katsimaglis, but she did not include all their specific details. Brown chose details relating to her focus on men and women riding alone. In choosing, she checked carefully that her choices did not distort the source's meaning and the overall conclusions of the study. ◆

Brown 5

8   Expectations concerning personal space exist   S
in all cultures, but such expectations vary
greatly from culture to culture (Fast 29).
Research reveals standards for personal space in
countries other than Canada and the United States.
For example, conversational distances vary between
people from different countries, according to
Desmond Morris, a British zoologist. He notes that
when people from western Europe stand on the
street and talk, the space between them is the
distance it would take one person's fingertip to
reach the other's shoulder. People from eastern
Europe converse at a wrist-to-shoulder distance.
People from the Mediterranean, however, prefer
elbow-to-shoulder distance (131).

9   Permitted amounts of touching also illustrate
intercultural differences in standards for
personal space. Touching while conversing differs
in Germany, France, and North America. Hall and
Hall report that Germans keep eye contact but
avoid any deliberate or unintentional touching
(39). They describe the French, in contrast, as   T
gesturing, handshaking, and embracing, although
the intensity of touching in France varies from
region to region (92). North Americans, like the   T
French, shake hands when greeting people and
indicate their openness by smiling frequently, but
they seem to prefer a comfortable conversational
distance without any physical contact (142).[1]   T,U

COMMENTARY

S. **Summary of original source.** Brown uses a summary to condense a source. ◆ PROCESS NOTE: Although Brown liked the informal tone of Morris's material, she did not quote it. She found it easy to summarize. Here is the original: ◆

Unfortunately, different countries have different ideas about exactly how close is close. It is easy enough to test your own "space reaction": When you are talking to someone in the street or in any open space, reach out with your arm and see where the nearest point on his body comes. If you hail from western Europe, you will find that he is at roughly fingertip distance from you. In other words, as you reach out, your fingertips will just about make contact with his shoulder. If you come from eastern Europe you will find you are standing at "wrist distance." If you come from the Mediterranean region you will find that you are much closer to your companion, at little more than "elbow distance."

T. **Use of sources.** ◆ PROCESS NOTE: Brown wondered whether she needed to use three separate parenthetical references (after the second, third, and fourth sentences). Her instructor explained that naming the source of all the information cited—Hall and Hall—is required only once as long as Brown mentions these authors in her own sentence. Because the details about German, French, and North American behaviour are in three different places in Hall and Hall, however, three parenthetical citations give the page references. ◆

U. **Related information in a note.** Brown uses a content note (see 33c-4) for related information here and in paragraph 10. A note number is raised slightly above the line after the period ending the sentence. (These raised numbers are called superscripts in word processing programs.) Endnotes are placed at the end of a paper, on a separate sheet of paper titled Notes; see Brown's page 9 for her two content notes.

Brown 6

Arabs prefer close interpersonal distances. Polhemus explains that Arab students move close together more often, confront each other directly, and touch each other more frequently when talking than do North American students (21). In an interview called "Learning the Arabs' Silent Language," Edward T. Hall claims that Arabs know the practicality of close conversational distances: "If you are interested in something, your pupils dilate; if I say something you don't like, they tend to contract" (47).[2] Hall goes on to explain that conversational distances of two feet—preferred by many Arabs—permit people to see each other's pupils better than does the typical North American distance of five feet (48).

COMMENTARY

V. **Word choice.** ◆ PROCESS NOTE: In an early draft, Brown used the words "says" and "say" in most places where she presented information from a source. When she revised, Brown wanted to vary her word choice. She looked at Chart 133 in section 31f to get ideas for different words. In her final draft Brown varies the verbs she uses to include *claim, describe, explain, note, report,* and *observe.* ◆

W. **Quotation from an interview.** Brown quotes what Hall said in an interview. She can be sure of the exact wording because the interview is reported in a respected magazine. In general, professional writers check the wording of a quotation before they use it in print. When material is even slightly controversial, professional writers usually also reconfirm all paraphrases and summaries with the source. Some of the most highly respected publications have a staff whose sole job is to verify information and reconfirm quoted material. Some instructors require students to follow these practices. Also, some instructors prefer that material from an interview be paraphrased or summarized, unless a student has tape-recorded the interview. ◆ PROCESS NOTE: While reading her sources, Brown repeatedly was impressed with Edward T. Hall's language. She kept feeling that her paraphrases and summaries could not possibly do justice to Hall. But she resisted the temptation to quote him extensively. She was aware that a student research paper is, in one sense, an exercise in which a student is expected to demonstrate the ability to paraphrase and summarize well. She quoted Hall here and in paragraph 12 because he is a major reference for her paper and Brown felt that this material helped establish the credibility of her information. ◆

X. **Word choice.** Brown originally wrote "Hall explains that," but when she was revising, she changed the verb to "goes on to explain." This change creates a link to the preceding sentence, helping readers to know that Edward T. Hall (not Judith Hall) is the source.

Brown 7

11   The Japanese traditionally do not prefer close interpersonal distances. Because the island of Japan is quite small for its population, public places are often very crowded. To cope, the people remain formal and aloof even when in very close proximity to one another (Fast 38). More recently, however, many Japanese have lived and worked in Western countries, as well as having seen Western movies and television programs in Japan. As a result, the younger Japanese are beginning to perceive personal space more as Westerners do. Sometimes, conflicts arise between younger and older Japanese, whose cultural experiences have been much less modified by exposure to Western perceptions of personal space (Herlivi).

Y

12   Anyone can easily be misunderstood who is insensitive to the ways that people from other cultures—or, as Herlivi suggests, within a changing culture—use personal space. Clearly, what is considered obnoxious in one culture might be considered polite in another (Fisher, Bell, and Baum 167). As Edward T. Hall says, virtually everything people are and do

> is associated with the experience of space.... Therefore, people from different cultures, when interpreting each other's behavior, often misinterpret the relationship, the activity, or the emotions. This leads to alienation in encounters or distorted communications. (<u>Hidden</u> 171)

Z

COMMENTARY

Y. **Summary of a personal interview.** Brown interviewed Kyoko Herlivi, a student at her university, who was born and had lived most of her life in Japan. ◆ PROCESS NOTE: Brown relies on Fast, a respected authority, for the background information about Japanese behaviour regarding personal space. Although Herlivi confirmed the general information that Brown had read in Fast about Japanese attitudes in the past, what Brown summarizes from the interview is Herlivi's insights into changing behaviour and a plausible reason for the change. ◆

Z. **Combined quotation from two paragraphs in original sources.** Brown combines into one quotation material from two paragraphs in Edward T. Hall. She needs no punctuation to lead into the quotation (compare with the lead-in to the poem quoted after paragraph 4, where a colon is used) because her lead-in is an incomplete sentence. She uses a four-dot ellipsis to show that the quotation is taken from two paragraphs. Here is the original source (Hall, *Hidden* 171):

> This book emphasizes that virtually everything that man is and does is associated with the experience of space. Man's sense of space is a synthesis of many sensory inputs: visual, auditory, kinesthetic, olfactory, and thermal. Not only does each of these constitute a complex system—as, for example, the dozen different ways of experiencing depth visually—but each is molded and patterned by culture. Hence, there is no alternative to accepting the fact that people reared in different cultures live in different sensory worlds.
>
> We learn from the study of culture that the patterning of perceptual worlds is a function not only of culture but of relationship, activity, and emotion. Therefore, people from different cultures, when interpreting each other's behavior, often misinterpret the relationship, the activity, or the emotions. This leads to alienation in encounters or distorted communications.

Brown 8

13   In the next few years, more studies should be undertaken to uncover information about cultural differences in matters of personal space. Such information will be important to help us understand personal space in all cultures (Remland, Jones, and Brinkman 215-17, 30). International understanding cannot thrive unless people recognize and accept such cultural disparities.

AA

14   As international travel and commerce increase intercultural contact is becoming commonplace. Soon, perhaps, cultural variations in expectations for personal space will be as familiar to everyone as are cultural variations in food and dress. Until then, people need to make a special effort to learn one another's expectations concerning personal space. Once people are sensitive to such matters, they can stop themselves from taking the wrong step: either away from or toward a person from another culture.

BB

COMMENTARY

AA. **Concluding device.** In paragraphs 13 and 14, Brown concludes her paper with a call for action (for concluding devices, see 4g). ◆ PROCESS NOTE: In early drafts, Brown's concluding paragraph was quite long. In her final draft, Brown divided it into two paragraphs and added a relevant citation. (See also Comment BB.) ◆

BB. **Revising a concluding paragraph.** ◆ PROCESS NOTE: Brown rewrote her paragraph 14 almost as many times as she did her introductory paragraph. She wanted to get some punch into the ending. After many revisions, she wrote a last sentence that delivered the impact she was searching for. She also consulted Chart 27 in section 4g to remind herself what to avoid in conclusions and then decided to get rid of the phrase "of the sort discussed in this paper." The idea of using steps as a metaphor came to her nearly at the last minute, and she quickly worked it into her final draft. Here is one early draft of paragraph 14. ◆

> Contact between cultures is happening more frequently. After all, international travel and commerce increase daily. It is urgent, therefore, for everyone to realize that there are lots of variations among cultures in personal space. That means there are more differences than those in food and dress. Researchers' observations of the sort discussed in this paper help people understand more about the wide variety of expectations concerning proper amounts of interpersonal closeness and distance.

Brown 9

CC

Notes

double-space

DD

¹Hall and Hall point out that "space is sacred" to Germans, and privacy is extremely important. North Americans often feel lonely when they live and work in Germany. They miss the close association with next-door neighbours, and they often feel that Germans are aloof and inhospitable.

²This might explain why some Arab leaders wear sunglasses indoors.

COMMENTARY

CC. **Endnotes.** On a separate numbered page titled Notes, Brown provides commentary that does not fit into the text of her paper. Content notes in MLA style comment upon, explain, or clarify material written in the text. Each note starts with a number raised slightly (or a superscript number in word-processing programs) and indented five spaces or one-half inch (about 1.75 cm). Double spacing is used within and between all notes. The format of the page is the same as for the other pages. The name-number page line is one-half inch from the top edge of the page, in the upper right corner. The word *Notes*, with the first letter capitalized, is centred a double-space below the name/page line.

DD. **Comments in endnotes.** ◆ PROCESS NOTE: Brown used notes to include this material. She found the information in the first note, about the loneliness of North Americans living in Germany, very interesting and decided that her readers would, too. She used a note for this detail because it did not fit neatly into the logic of her paragraphs. The second note developed when Brown was thinking about the information she had read in the Edward T. Hall interview. A picture flashed into her mind of a man in Arab dress wearing sunglasses. Her insight makes an appropriate and interesting comment in a note. ◆

699

Brown 10

Works Cited

Fast, Julius. <u>Body Language</u>. New York: Evans,   EE
    1970.

Fisher, Jeffrey D., Paul A. Bell, and Andrew Baum.   FF
    <u>Environmental Psychology</u>. 2nd ed. New York:
    Holt, 1984.

Hall, Edward T. <u>The Hidden Dimension</u>. New York:
    Doubleday, 1966.

---. Interview. "Learning the Arabs' Silent   GG,
    Language." With Kenneth Friedman. <u>Psychology</u>   HH
    <u>Today</u> Aug. 1979: 44-54.

Hall, Edward T., and Mildred Reed Hall.
    <u>Understanding Cultural Differences: Germans,</u>
    <u>French, and Americans</u>. Yarmouth, ME:
    Intercultural Press, 1990.

Hall, Judith. <u>Nonverbal Sex Differences:</u>
    <u>Communication Accuracy and Expressive Style</u>.
    Baltimore: Johns Hopkins UP, 1984.   II

Herlivi, Kyoko. Personal interview. 2 Jan. 1995.   JJ

Kenner, Andrew N., and George Katsimaglis. "Gender
    Differences in Proxemics: Taxi-Seat Choice."
    <u>Psychological Reports</u> 72 (1993): 625-26.

Lomax, Crystal M., et al. "Proxemics in Public: KK
    Space Violations as a Function of Dyad
    Composition." ERIC ED 367 940.

Martin, Judith. "Here's Looking at You." <u>Newsday</u>   LL
    27 Jan. 1981, sec. 2: 9+.

Morris, Desmond. <u>Manwatching: A Field Guide to</u>
    <u>Human Behavior</u>. New York: Abrams, 1977.

COMMENTARY

General Format. An alphabetically arranged list of all the sources referred to in the paper, called Works Cited, is used; it follows MLA documentation style (see 33c). Entries are alphabetized by each author's last name; if no author's name is given, the work's title is the first information unit and is alphabetized by its first word (excluding *A, An,* or *The*). Any entry more than one line long has a five-space (or one-half inch) indent for each line after the first. Double spacing is used within and between entries, including after the name/page line to the title, Works Cited.

EE. **Entry for book by one author.**

FF. **Entry for book by three authors.** Inverted order (last name, first name) for name of first author, but regular order for others. *Second edition* abbreviated to *2nd ed.* Publisher abbreviated from *Holt, Rinehart and Winston* to *Holt.* (*Note:* In a work with three or fewer authors, all names are listed; see the Lomax entry for a work by four or more authors.)

GG. **Second work by same author.** Three hyphens and a period stand for the repetition of the preceding author's name. (*Note:* In such instances, works by the same author are listed alphabetically by title, not chronologically according to date of publication.)

HH. **Entry for an interview published in a magazine.** Entry listed by person interviewed, not by the person doing the interviewing. The page numbers are not preceded by *pp.*

II. *University Press* abbreviated *UP.*

JJ. **Entry for a personal (face-to-face) interview.** The date given is the date on which the interview took place.

KK. **Entry for material from an information service.** ERIC stands for Educational Resources Information Center. The number is the ERIC document number.

LL. **Entry for an article in a daily newspaper.** Title of article in quotation marks. Name of newspaper, *Newsday,* underlined. Date of newspaper in this order: day, month (abbreviation permitted), year. Then newspaper section and page numbers without *pp.* The + symbol is used only for newspaper articles when material continues on another page.

Brown 11

Polhemus, Ted. "Social Bodies." The Body as a   MM
    Medium of Expression. Ed. Jonathan Benthall
    and Ted Polhemus. New York: Dutton, 1975.
    13-35.

Remland, Martin S., Tricia S. Jones, and Heidi   NN
    Brinkman. "Proxemic and Haptic Behavior in
    Three European Countries." Journal of
    Nonverbal Behavior 15 (1991): 215-32.

Sommer, Robert. Personal Space: The Behavioral   OO
    Bases of Design. Englewood Cliffs: Prentice,
    1969.

Stewart, Susan. "Too Close for Comfort?" Current
    Health 2 Dec. 1992: 4-5.

Worchel, Stephen, and Joel Cooper. Understanding   PP
    Social Psychology. 3rd ed. Homewood, IL:
    Dorsey, 1983.

COMMENTARY

MM. **Entry for article in a book.** Author of article heads the entry. Editors of book, with names in regular order, follow book title. Title of article in quotation marks. Title of book underlined. Page numbers—without *pp.*—after city of publication and publisher.

NN. **Entry for an article in a journal with continuous pagination.** Article title in quotation marks. Journal title underlined. Then volume number, year in parentheses, and page numbers without the abbreviation *pp.*

OO. Publisher abbreviated from *Prentice Hall* to *Prentice*.

PP. **Entry for book by two authors.** Inverted order (last name, first name) for name of first author, but regular order for second name. Place of publication includes city *and* two-letter postal abbreviation for U.S. state because many readers might not know that Homewood is in Illinois.

35

Case Study: A Student Writing an APA Research Paper

This chapter presents a student research paper written in the documentation style° of the American Psychological Association (APA). Section 35a discusses the researching (see Chapter 32), planning (see Chapter 2), drafting (see 3b and 32t), and revising (see 3c and 32t) processes of the student, Samuel Fung. Section 35b shows the final draft of the paper, including its abstract.

Samuel Fung was given this assignment for a research paper in a course called Introduction to Psychology: Write a research paper of 1800-2000 words about an unconscious process in humans. For guidance, refer to the *Simon & Schuster Handbook for Writers,* First Canadian Edition, Chapters 31 through 33. Use the documentation style of the American Psychological Association (APA) explained in Chapter 33. Your topic and working bibliography are due in two weeks. An early draft of your paper is due two weeks later (try to get it close to what you hope will be your last draft, so that comments from me and your peers can concretely help you write an excellent final draft). Your final draft is due one week after the early draft is returned to you with comments.

35a Observing the processes of researching and writing an APA-style research paper

After Samuel Fung read his assignment, he started **planning** by listing various unconscious processes in humans so that he could pick the one most interesting to him. Referring to his class notes and the textbook from his psychology course, he found these topics: sleep, dreams, insomnia, biological clocks, daydreams, hypnosis, and meditation. He favoured biological clocks because of his experiences with jet lag whenever he travelled between his home in Vancouver and his grand-parents' home in Hong Kong.

Fung then checked to see whether the library at his university had enough sources useful for research on biological clocks. He was pleased to find books, journal articles, magazine and newspaper articles, and even a videotape of a U.S. Public Broadcasting System program on the subject. So that he could compile a working bibliography (see 33b) and, at the same time, try to find an approach to the topic suitable for a paper of 1800-2000 words, Fung began to read and take notes (see 32j). He saw entire books about biological clocks, so he realized that he would need to narrow the topic (see 32d) sufficiently to shape a thesis statement° (see 32r and 2n). The narrowing process worried him because he had been told in other courses that his topics for research papers were too broad. He was determined this time to avoid that same problem.

The working bibliography that Fung submitted consisted of twenty-two sources, though he had read and rejected about six others as inadequate. (He knew that this represented real progress for him.) He did not intend to use them all in his paper, but he wanted them available as he wrote his early drafts. Not surprisingly, his instructor urged him to reduce the list by half once drafting began; otherwise Fung would risk writing too little about too much. He redoubled his efforts to read even more critically to evaluate his sources (see 32f-3) and weed out material. He got his list down to nineteen sources, took detailed notes (see 32j) on each, and began to group his material into emerging subtopics.

To start **drafting** his paper, Fung spread his notecards around him for easy reference, but he felt somewhat overwhelmed by the amount of information at hand, and he wrote only a few sentences. To break through, he decided to write a "discovery draft" (see 3b) to see what he had absorbed from his reading and notetaking. That very rough draft became his vehicle for many things, including creating an effective thesis statement°, inserting source information according to APA documentation style, and checking the logical arrangement of his material.

Revising for Fung started with his thesis statement°, a process that helped him further narrow his focus. He started with "Biological clocks are fascinating," which expressed his feelings but said nothing of substance. His next version served well as he revised his discovery draft into a true first draft: "Biological clocks, our unconscious time keepers, affect our lives in many ways including compatibility in marriage, family life, jet travel, work schedules, illnesses, medical treatments, and the space program." That version proved to Fung that he was covering too much for an 1800-2000-word research paper, and he wanted to drop material. He decided first to inform his readers about the phenomenon of biological clocks and then to discuss the effects of those clocks on people's alertness in the morning and later in the day, on travellers on jet airplanes, and on workers' performance. For his final draft, Fung used this more focused thesis statement: "Biological clocks, which are a significant feature of human design, greatly affect personal and professional lifestyles."

Using APA documentation style made Fung attend very closely to the details of correct parenthetical references (see 33d-1) within his paper and a correct References list (see 33d-2 and 33d-3) at the end. Because he had used MLA documentation style° in other courses, he made sure not to confuse the two styles. For example, he saw that APA-style parenthetical citations require a page reference for a quotation but not for a paraphrase or summary (whereas MLA style requires a page reference for all three). For format and style details of the References list at the end of his paper, he found Chart 143 in section 33d-2 especially helpful.

As Fung checked the logical arrangement of his material, he realized that because he had dropped some aspects of biological clocks when he finally narrowed his topic sufficiently, he needed a little more depth about those aspects that he was retaining. A few hours back in the library gave him what he needed. Having to retrace his steps had a dramatic impact on Fung: Now he saw the difference between researching a topic too broadly (and therefore gathering too many sources for the assignment) and researching a few aspects of a topic in depth by focusing on selected sources. His final draft, which appears in 35b, draws on thirteen sources, a number that is down drastically from the twenty-two with which he started.

Looking at the final draft of an APA-style research paper

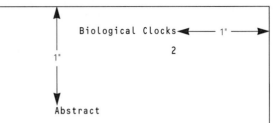

Biological Clocks ◄——— 1" ———►

2

1"

Abstract

double-space

Circadian rhythms, which greatly affect human lives, often suffer disruption in technological societies, resulting in such disorders as jet lag syndrome and seasonal affective disorder (SAD). With growing scientific awareness of both natural circadian cycles and the effects of disturbances of these cycles, individuals are learning how to control some negative effects.

Biological Clocks:

The Body's Internal Timepieces

Life in modern, technological societies is built around timepieces. People set clocks on radios, microwave ovens, VCRs, and electric coffee makers. Students respond to bells that start and end the school day as well as dividing it into blocks of time. Almost everyone relies on clocks to manage time well. While carefully managing the minutes and hours each day, individuals are often encouraged or forced by current styles of family and work life to violate another kind of time: their body's time. Biological clocks, which are also known as circadian cycles, are a significant feature of human design that greatly affect personal and professional lifestyles.

The term "circadian," which is Latin for "about a day," describes the rhythms of people's internal biological clocks. Circadian cycles are in tune with external time cycles such as the 24-hour period of the earth's daily rotation as signalled by the rising and setting of the sun. Usually, humans set their biological clocks by seeing these cycles of daylight and darkness. Carefully designed studies conducted in caves or similar environments that let researchers control light and darkness have shown that most people create cycles slightly over 24 hours when they are not exposed to natural cycles of day and night (Allis & Haederle, 1989; Enright, 1980). Human perception of the external day-night cycle affects the production and release of a brain hormone, melatonin, which is important in initiating and regulating the sleep-wake cycle, as Alfred Lewy and other scientists at the National Institute of Health in Bethesda, Maryland, have found (Winfree, 1987). During the winter, female melatonin secretion increases at night. However, the amount of melatonin secreted by females during the night decreases once summer arrives (Angier, 1995).

An individual's lifestyle reflects that person's own circadian cycle. Scientists group people as "larks" or "owls" based on whether individuals are more efficient in the morning or at night. The idea behind the labels is that "in nature certain animals are diurnal, active during the light period; others are nocturnal, active at night. The 'morning lark' and 'night owl' connotations typically are used to categorize the human extremes" ("Are You," 1989, p. 11).

"Larks" who must stay up late at night and "owls" who must awaken early in the morning experience mild versions of the disturbances, called "jet lag," that time-zone travellers often encounter. Jet lag, which is characterized by fatigue and irregular sleep patterns, results from disruption of circadian rhythms, a common problem among those who travel great distances by jet airplane to different time zones:

> Jet lag syndrome is the inability of the internal body rhythm to rapidly resynchronize after sudden shifts in the timing. For a variety of reasons, the system attempts to maintain stability and resist

temporal change. Consequently, complete adjustment can often be delayed for several days—sometimes for a week—after arrival at one's destination. (Bonner, 1991, p. 72)

Interestingly, research shows that the number of flying hours is not the cause of jet lag. Rather, "the number, rate, and direction of time-zone changes are the critical factors in determining the extent and degree of jet lag symptoms," according to Richard Coleman (1986, p. 67) in <u>Wide Awake at 3 a.m.: By Choice or by Chance?</u> Eastbound travellers find it harder than westbound travellers to adjust, because travelling east forces people to go to bed before their biological clocks are ready for them to do so (Coleman).

Another group that suffers greatly from biological clock disruptions consists of people whose livelihoods depend on erratic schedules. This situation affects 20- to 30-million U.S. workers whose work schedules differ from the usual morning starting time and afternoon or early evening ending time (Weiss, 1989). Charles Czeisler, director of the Center for Circadian and Sleep Disorders at Brigham and Woman's Hospital in Boston, reports that 27 percent of the U.S. workforce does shift work (Binkley, 1990). Shift work can mean, for example, working from 7:00 a.m. to 3:00 p.m. for six weeks, from 3:00 p.m. to 11:00 p.m. for six weeks, and from 11:00 p.m. to 7:00 a.m. for six weeks. Many shift workers endure stomach and intestinal-tract disorders, and, on average, they have a three times higher risk of heart

disease than non-shift workers (Bingham, 1989). In a
1989 report to the American Association for the
Advancement of Science, Czeisler states that "police
officers, [medical] interns, and many others who work
nights perform poorly and are involved in more on-the-
job accidents than their daytime counterparts" (Binkley,
p. 26).

Other researchers confirm that safety is at risk
during late-shift hours (Chollar, 1989). In a study of
28 medical interns observed during late night shifts
over a one-year period, 25 percent admitted to falling
asleep while talking on the phone, and 34 percent had at
least one accident or near-accident during that period
(Weiss, 1989). Investigations into the Challenger
Shuttle explosion and the nuclear-reactor disasters at
Three-Mile Island and Chernobyl reveal critical errors
made by people undergoing the combined stresses of lack
of sleep and unusual work schedules (Toufexis, 1989).

One especially negative effect of an upset
biological clock is a syndrome increasingly recognized
as a medical problem: the disorder known as Seasonal
Affective Disorder (SAD). Dr. Thomas W. Wehr of the
(U.S.) National Institutes of Mental Health, who first
discovered the circadian rhythm differences between
genders, is conducting further research to explain why
more women than men suffer from SAD (Angier, 1995).
Table 1 lists some of the major symptoms of SAD.

Table 1

Common Symptoms of Seasonal Affective Disorder

Sadness	Later waking
Anxiety	Increased sleep time
Decreased physical	Interrupted,
activity	unrefreshing sleep
Irritability	Daytime drowsiness
Increased appetite	Decreased sexual drive
Craving for carbohydrates	Menstrual problems
Weight gain	Work problems
Earlier onset of sleep	Interpersonal problems

Note. From The Clockwork Sparrow (p. 204) by S. Binkley, 1990, Englewood Cliffs, NJ: Prentice Hall. Copyright 1990 by Prentice Hall, Inc.

SAD appears to be related to the short daylight (photoperiod) of winter in the temperate zones of the northern and southern hemispheres. The phenomenon of SAD not only illustrates the important role of circadian rhythms, but also it dramatically proves that an understanding of circadian principles can help scientists to improve the lives of people who experience disruptions of their biological clocks. Binkley claims that exposure to bright light for periods of up to two hours a day during the short photoperiod days of winter reduces SAD-related "depression in 87 percent of patients ... within a few days; relapses followed" (pp. 203-204) when light treatment ended.

Biological Clocks

8

Exposure to long periods of bright light is not, however, an appropriate solution for people whose safety is at risk because of continual assaults on their circadian cycles by shift schedules at work. Establishing work schedules more sensitive to biological clocks could reduce certain safety hazards. A group of police officers in Philadelphia were studied while on modified shift schedules (Locitzer, 1989; Toufexis, 1989). These officers changed between day shifts and night shifts less frequently than they had on former shift schedules; they rotated forward rather than backward in time; and they worked four rather than six consecutive days. Officers reported 40 percent fewer patrol-car accidents and decreased use of drugs or alcohol to get to sleep. Overall, the police officers preferred the modified shift schedules. Charles Czeisler, who conducted the study, summarizes the importance of these results: "When schedules are introduced that take into account the properties of the human circadian system, subjective estimates of work schedule satisfaction and health improve, personnel turnover decreases, and worker productivity increases" (Locitzer, 1989).

Scientists like Charles Czeisler are beginning to help individuals live harmoniously with their biological clocks. Growing awareness of the effects of such situations as shift work and travel across time zones is one significant step toward control. The use of light to manipulate the body's sense of time is another. As more

people become aware of how circadian rhythms affect
lifestyles, the day might soon come when we can fully
control our biological clocks instead of their
controlling us.

Biological Clocks

10

References

Allis, T., & Haederle, M. (1989, June 12). Ace in the
    hole: Stefania Follini never caved in. People, p. 52.

Angier, N. (1995, March 14). Modern life suppresses an
    ancient body rhythm. The New York Times, pp. C1, C3.

Are you a day or night person? (1989, March). USA Today
    Magazine, p. 11.

Bingham, R. (Writer & Director). (1989). The time of our
    lives [Television production]. KCET Commercial
    Television of Southern California, PBS.

Binkley, S. (1990). The clockwork sparrow. Englewood
    Cliffs, NJ: Prentice Hall.

Bonner, P. (1991, July). Travel rhythms. Sky Magazine,
    pp. 72-73, 76-77.

Chollar, S., (1989, November). Safe solutions for night
    work. Psychology Today, p. 26.

Coleman, R. (1986). Wide awake at 3:00 a.m.: By choice
    or by chance? New York: W. H. Freeman.

Enright, J. T. (1980). The timing of sleep and
    wakefulness. Berlin: Springer-Verlag.

Locitzer, K. (1989, July/August). Are you out of sync
    with each other? Psychology Today, p. 66.

Toufexis, A. (1989, June 5). The times of your life.
    Time, pp. 66-67.

Weiss, R. (1989, January 21). Safety gets short shrift
    on long night shift. Science News, p. 37.

Winfree, A. (1987). The timing of biological clocks. New
    York: W. H. Freeman.

PART

VIII

Writing Across the Curriculum

When you write for the different disciplines that you encounter during your college or university years, you become familiar with the perspectives and assumptions that underlie each discipline. Part Eight compares and contrasts the various disciplines so that you can respond effectively to the major types of writing assignments in each discipline. As you use Chapters 36 through 40, be aware that the information in this handbook serves as a resource for your entire academic career and beyond.

36 Comparing the Different Disciplines

36a Recognizing similarities and differences among the disciplines

The humanities, the social sciences, and the natural sciences each have their own perspectives on the world and their own philosophies about academic thought and research. To understand some of the differences among the disciplines, consider these three quite different paragraphs about a mountain.

HUMANITIES

The mountain stands above all that surrounds it. Giant timbers—part of a collage of evergreen and deciduous trees—conceal the expansive mountain's slope, where cattle once grazed. At the base of the mountain, a cool stream flows over rocks of all sizes, colours, and shapes. Next to the outer bank of the stream stands a shingled farmhouse, desolate, yet suggesting its active past. Unfortunately, the peaceful scene is interrupted by billboards and chairlifts, landmarks of a modern, fast-paced life.

SOCIAL SCIENCES

Among the favourite pastimes of Canadian city dwellers is the "return to nature." Many outdoor enthusiasts hope to enjoy a scenic trip to the mountains, only to be disappointed. They know they have arrived at the mountain that they have travelled hundreds of kilometres to see because huge billboards are directing them to its base. As they look up the mountain, dozens of people are riding over the treetops in a chairlift, littering the slope with paper cups and food wrappers. At the base of the mountain stands the inevitable refreshment stand, found at virtually all Canadian tourist attractions. Land developers consider such commercialization a way to preserve and utilize natural resources, but environmentalists are appalled.

NATURAL SCIENCES

The mountain is approximately 2100 metres in height. The underlying rock is igneous, of volcanic origin, composed primarily of granites and feldspars. Three distinct biological communities are present on the mountain. The community at the top of the mountain is alpine in nature, dominated by very short grasses and forbs. At middle altitudes, a typical northern boreal coniferous forest community is present, and at the base and lower altitudes, deciduous forest is the dominant community. This community has, however, been highly affected by agricultural development along the river at its base and by recreational development.

These examples illustrate that each discipline has its writing traditions and preferences. The paragraph written for the humanities describes the mountain from the individual perspective of the writer—a perspective both personal and yet representative of a general human response. The paragraph written for the social sciences focuses on the behaviour of people as a group. The paragraph written for the natural sciences reports observations of natural phenomena.

As you study and write in each of the academic disciplines, you become familiar with alternative ways of thinking. As you come to know the habits of mind that characterize each discipline, you develop specialized vocabularies that allow you to participate in the conversations of each discipline. As your perspectives are broadened, you gain lifelong access to the pleasures of informed insight—among the major benefits of a postsecondary education.

No matter what differences exist among the academic disciplines, all subject areas interconnect and overlap. Chart 146 lists similarities and differences.

For example, in a humanities class you might read *Lives of a Cell,* by Lewis Thomas, a collection of essays about science and nature written by the late noted physician and prize-winning author. As you consider the art of the writer, you will also be thinking deeply about biology and other sciences.

The four differences listed in Chart 146 are discussed in detail here.

1	Conducting research and selecting sources according to each discipline

Primary sources offer you first-hand exposure to information. No one comes between you and the exciting experience of discovering and confronting material on your own. Research methods differ among the disciplines when primary sources are used. In the humanities,

SIMILARITIES AND DIFFERENCES IN WRITING ACROSS THE DISCIPLINES	146

SIMILARITIES

1. Consider your purpose, audience, and tone. — Chapters 1–2
2. Use the writing process to plan, shape, draft, revise, edit, and proofread. — Chapters 2–3
3. Develop a thesis. — Chapters 2–3
4. Arrange and organize your ideas. — Chapter 2
5. Use supporting evidence. — Chapters 2–4
6. Develop paragraphs thoroughly. — Chapter 4
7. Critically think, read, and write, and use correct reasoning and logic. — Chapter 5
8. Argue well. — Chapter 6
9. Write effective sentences. — Chapters 16–19
10. Choose words well. — Chapters 20–21
11. Use correct grammar. — Chapters 7–15
12. Spell correctly. — Chapter 22
13. Use correct punctuation and mechanics. — Chapters 23–30

DIFFERENCES

1. Conduct research and select sources according to each discipline (see 36a-1).
2. Select a style of documentation appropriate to each discipline (see 36a-2 and Chapter 33).
3. Follow manuscript format requirements, if any, in each discipline (see 36a-3).
4. Use specialized language, when needed, in each discipline (see 36a-4).

existing documents are primary sources; the task of the researcher is to analyze and interpret these primary sources. Typical primary-source material for research could be a poem by Dylan Thomas, the floor plans of Egyptian pyramids, or early drafts of music manuscripts. In the social and natural sciences, primary research entails the design and undertaking of experiments involving direct observation. The task of the researcher in the social and natural sciences is to conduct the experiments or to read the first-hand reports of experiments and studies written by people who conducted them.

Secondary sources—articles and books about a primary source—are also important in all disciplines. In the humanities, you can learn much from the examples of others who have analyzed and interpreted primary sources. In the social and natural sciences, secondary sources can usefully synthesize findings in many areas and draw parallels that offer new insights.

2 | Selecting a style of documentation appropriate to each discipline

Writers use **documentation** to give credit to the sources they have used. A writer who does not credit a source is guilty of **plagiarizing**—a serious academic offence (see 31a). Styles of documentation differ among the disciplines.

In the humanities, many fields use the documentation style of the Modern Language Association (MLA). MLA documentation style is explained and illustrated in section 33c. The student research paper in Chapter 34 and the student literary analysis in Chapter 37 use MLA documentation style. CM (Chicago Manual) style, also used in the humanities, is described in 33e. In the social sciences, most fields use the documentation style of the American Psychological Association (APA). APA documentation style is explained and illustrated in 33d. The student research paper in Chapter 35 uses APA documentation style. In the natural sciences, documentation styles vary, as is explained in 33f and 38g.

3 | Following manuscript format requirements, if any, in each discipline

As a reflection of the differences among academic disciplines, different formats are sometimes expected for presentation of material. These special formats have evolved to communicate a writer's purpose, to emphasize content by eliminating distracting variations in format, and to make the reader's work easier. Writing in the humanities is less often subject to set formats, although the writing is expected to be well organized and logically presented. Writing in the social and natural sciences often calls for set formats for specific types of writing.

<table>
<tr><td>4</td><td>**Using specialized language, when needed, in each discipline**</td></tr>
</table>

Specialized language is often referred to as **jargon**. Jargon is useful when it helps people who are specialists communicate easily with each other in a kind of "verbal shorthand." When specialized material is communicated to the general reading public, however, any jargon has to be defined so that everyone can understand the message. Jargon is not useful when it is unnecessarily obscure and overblown (see 21e-2).

All disciplines use specialized language to some extent. The specialized terms in the social and natural sciences are generally more technical and less accessible to nonspecialists than are those in the humanities. The more important that exactness is to a discipline, the more likely that many words will have specialized meanings. For example, consider the word *niche*. It has two generally known meanings: "a place particularly suitable to the person or thing in it," and "a hollowed space in a wall for a statue or vase." Niche in the natural sciences, however, has a very specialized meaning: "the set of environmental conditions—climate, food sources, water supply, enemies—that permit an organism or species to survive."

❖ USAGE ALERT: Many writers in scientific disciplines make a habit of writing in the passive voice. Yet style manuals for scientific writing agree with the advice you will find in 8o: Use the active voice except for purposes best fulfilled by the passive.* ❖

36b Using collaborative writing in various disciplines

If you are told to engage in **collaborative writing,** you will be expected to work with others in your class on a project. A collaborative writing group consists of two or more people, according to the instructor's directions. (Be aware that in many classes your instructor might prefer that you work alone on projects. To avoid any risk of charges of cheating or plagiarism, get permission from your instructor if you want to work collaboratively with other students.)

Many professions require people to serve on committees, to reach general agreement, and to write reports of their deliberations and recommendations. Many businesses and academic fields require people

---

*You may want to look at section 2.06 in the *Publication Manual of the American Psychological Association,* Fourth Edition (36).

to work together on reports or papers that draw upon the different skills and information each person in the group can contribute. Some college and university courses incorporate the experience of writing collaboratively. For example, in a marketing course, each of several groups might be expected to develop a new product, conduct research for marketing the product, and write a paper explaining their plan. Similarly, in a science course, a collaborative project might consist of jointly conducting an experiment, assessing its results, and writing a report.

Collaborative writing gives you the advantage of being able to share your knowledge and hear what others know. "Two heads are better than one" often proves true. Still, working with others on writing projects demands patience and graciousness. You have to work along with the pace of the group, listen carefully as you consider closely what others are saying, and contribute your part to the endeavour. Chart 147 gives guidelines to help you function productively when writing collaboratively. Use them in conjunction with Guidelines for Being an Effective Peer Critic, given in Chart 18 in section 3c-5.

GUIDELINES FOR COLLABORATIVE WRITING 147

GETTING UNDERWAY

1. Get to know each other's names. If you exchange phone numbers; you can be in touch outside of class.
2. Participate in the group process. During discussions help to set a tone that encourages everyone to participate, including people who do not like to interrupt, who want time to think before they talk, or who are shy. If you are not used to contributing in a group setting, try to take a more active role.
3. Facilitate the collaboration. As a group, assign work to be done between meetings. Distribute the responsibilities as fairly as possible. Also, decide whether to choose one discussion leader or to rotate leadership.

PLANNING THE WRITING

4. After discussing the project, brainstorm (see 2g) or use other techniques to think of ideas (see 2d through 2j).
5. As a group, choose the ideas that seem best. Incubate (see 2j), if time permits, and discuss the choices again.
6. As a group, divide the project into parts and distribute assignments as fairly as possible.

→

GUIDELINES FOR COLLABORATIVE WRITING *(continued)*

7. As you work on your part of the project, take notes so that you can be ready to report to the group.
8. As a group, sketch an overview (if you choose to outline, see 2o) of the paper to get a preliminary idea of how best to use the material contributed by individuals.

DRAFTING THE WRITING

9. Draft°* a first paragraph or two. This material sets the direction for the rest of the paper. Each member of the group can draft a version, but agree on one draft for these paragraphs before getting too far into the rest of the draft. Your group might rewrite once the whole paper has been drafted, but a preliminary beginning helps to focus everyone.
10. Work on the rest of the paper. Decide whether each member of the group should write a complete draft or a different part of the whole. Use photocopies to share work.

REVISING THE WRITING

11. Read over the drafts. Check that everything useful has been incorporated into the draft.
12. Use the Revision Checklists in section 3c-3 to decide on revisions. Work as a group, or assign sections to subgroups. Use photocopies to share work.
13. Agree on a final version. Assign someone to prepare it in final form and make photocopies.

EDITING THE WRITING

14. As a group, review photocopies of the final version. Do not leave the last stages to a subgroup. Draw on everyone's knowledge of grammar, spelling, and punctuation. And use everyone's eyes to proofread.
15. Use the Editing Checklist in section 3d to make sure that the final version has no errors. If necessary, retype. No matter how well the group has worked collaboratively, or how well the group has written the paper, a sloppy final version reflects negatively on the entire group.

---

* Throughout this book, a degree mark (°) indicates that you can find the definition of the word in the Glossary of Terms in this handbook.

37 Writing About Literature

Literature, which includes **fiction** (novels and stories), **drama** (plays and scripts), and **poetry** (poems and lyrics), has developed from age-old human impulses to discover and communicate meaning by telling stories, re-enacting events, and singing or chanting. Reading and then writing about literature can deliver a related satisfaction: You have the chance to think about meaning and to tell others what you have found.

37a Understanding methods of inquiry into literature

All questions about literature require you to read a work closely. Some questions then ask you to deal with the material on a literal level (see 5d-1). You might be asked to explain the meaning of a passage in a novel, or to find out what historical events were going on when the work was written or what other scholars have said about some element of the work.

Other questions call for inferential reasoning (see 5d-2) and evaluative thinking (see 5d-3). You might be asked to discuss the effect of sound or rhythm or rhyme in a poem, or to compare characters in two plays by a particular playwright. Unlike inquiry in many other disciplines, you might also be asked to describe your response or reaction to a work of literature after a close, careful reading.

In each case, your answers must be thorough, well reasoned, well supported with evidence, and informed by knowledge of the work.

37b
Understanding purposes and practices in writing about literature

The general purposes of writing about literature are to inform and to persuade (see 1b). **Informative writing** includes explaining what a passage means or what constitutes a particular work's key elements. **Persuasive writing** includes arguing the merits of an evaluation or an interpretation. Reaction papers (see 37d-1) often combine informative and persuasive purposes. All writing about literature calls for you to analyze, synthesize, and assess critically (see Chart 28 in section 5a).

1 | Using first and third person appropriately

Instructors usually have students use the first person° (*I, we, our*) to write about their points of view or personal evaluations, and the third person° (*he, she, it, they*) for other assignments. Be sure to inquire about and adapt to your instructor's requirements. In research papers, the first person is usually acceptable only when you present your personal experience, your own conclusions, or your personal views contrasted with those of the sources that you have consulted and documented°.

2 | Using verbs in the present tense and the past tense correctly when writing about literature

When you describe or discuss a literary work or any of its elements, use the present tense°: *In the play* Blood Relations, *Sharon Pollock **undertakes** a metaphysical healing of the accused axe murderer Lizzie Borden.* The present tense is also correct for discussing what the author has done in a specific work: *Pollock **addresses** the questions of Lizzie's guilt or innocence through the use of a play within a play in which "the Actress," and not Lizzie, **re-enacts** the events of the day of the murders.*

If you are discussing events that take place before the action of a literary work begins, a past-tense° verb is correct: *In refusing to face the events until the re-enactment, Lizzie **has protected** [before the action starts] herself from "the Actress," from Emma's constant prodding, and from herself.* Also use past tenses, as appropriate, to discuss historical events or biographical information: *Actresses **had** a bad reputation, for their career **was considered** promiscuous, just slightly higher on the social scale than prostitution.*

---

3 | Using your own ideas and using secondary sources

Some assignments call only for your own ideas about the subject of your essay. Other assignments ask you to support your analysis with **secondary sources.** Secondary sources include books and articles in which an expert discusses material related to your topic. You can locate secondary sources by using the research process discussed in Chapter 32.

Whenever you use secondary sources, **avoid plagiarism** (see 31a). So that no reader thinks that the ideas of another person are yours, always document your sources (see 31b and Chapter 33). Also, to work material from secondary sources skilfully and gracefully into your writing, use the techniques of quotation (see 31c), paraphrase (see 31d), and summary (see 31e).

37c Using documentation style for writing about literature

If you use secondary sources° when you write about literature, you are required to credit your sources by using documentation. Many instructors require their students to use the documentation style of the Modern Language Association (MLA), an organization of scholars and teachers of language and literature. MLA documentation style is described in Section 33c. Two other documentation styles sometimes required in the humanities are APA (American Psychological Association), presented in Section 33d, and CM (Chicago Manual), presented in Section 33e.

37d Writing different types of papers about literature

Before you write a paper in which you refer or react to a literary work, be sure to read the work closely. To read well, use your understanding of the reading process (see 5b) and engage in critical reading (see 5d).

1 Writing reaction papers

In a paper in which you react to a work of literature, you might ask and try to answer a central question that the work made you think about, criticize a point of view in the work, or present a problem that you see in the work. For example, if you are asked to respond to a play, you might write about why you did or did not enjoy reading the play, how the play does or does not relate to your personal experience or to your view of life, what the play made you think about and try to puzzle through. You can focus on the entire play or on a particular scene, character, or set of lines.

2 Writing book reports

A book report informs readers about the content of a book—by summarizing its plot and its theme and by discussing (1) the significance and purpose of the book, (2) how the book presents its content, and (3) who might be most interested in the book. When you discuss the significance of the book, try to relate it to your field of study. For example, if the book is a classic in children's literature, your focus for a literature class would differ somewhat from your focus for a course in psychology or education.

3 Writing interpretations

An interpretation discusses either what the author means by the work or what the work means personally to the reader. When you are writing an interpretation paper, always consider the questions in Chart 148.

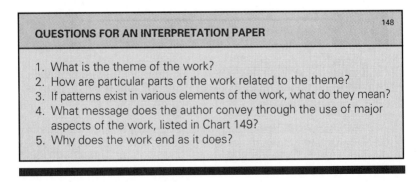

QUESTIONS FOR AN INTERPRETATION PAPER 148

1. What is the theme of the work?
2. How are particular parts of the work related to the theme?
3. If patterns exist in various elements of the work, what do they mean?
4. What message does the author convey through the use of major aspects of the work, listed in Chart 149?
5. Why does the work end as it does?

4   **Writing analyses**

Analysis is the examination of the relationship of a whole to its parts. In a **literary analysis,** you are expected to discuss your well-reasoned ideas about a work of fiction, poetry, or drama. To get to know the work well and to gather ideas for your analysis, read the work thoroughly, again and again. Watch for patterns in the aspects of literary analysis listed in Chart 149. Write notes as you go along so that you have a record of two important resources for your writing: the patterns you find in the material, and your reactions to the patterns and to the whole work.

MAJOR ASPECTS OF LITERARY WORKS TO ANALYZE   149

PLOT	The events and their sequence
THEME	Central idea or message
STRUCTURE	Organization and relationship of parts to each other and to the whole
CHARACTERIZATION	Traits, thoughts, and actions of the people in the plot
SETTING	Time and place of the action
POINT OF VIEW	Perspective or position from which the material is presented—sometimes by a narrator or a main character
STYLE	How words and sentence structures present the material
IMAGERY	The pictures created by the words (similes, metaphors, figurative language) [for a list and definitions, see Chart 100 in section 21c]
TONE	The attitude of the author toward the subject of the work—and sometimes toward the reader—expressed through the choice of words and through the imagery
FIGURES OF SPEECH	Includes metaphor and simile
SYMBOLISM	The meaning beneath the surface of the words and images
RHYTHM AND RHYME	Beat, metre, repetition of sounds, etc.

37e Three case studies of students writing about literature

This section includes three student essays of literary analysis. The last two essays use secondary sources°, and all three use MLA documentation style (see sections 33c and 37c).

---

1 | Student essay interpreting a plot element in a short story

The following essay interprets a plot element in Edgar Allan Poe's story "The Tell-Tale Heart."

Born in 1809, Edgar Allan Poe was an important American journalist, poet, and fiction writer. In his short, dramatic life, Poe gambled, drank, lived in terrible poverty, saw his young wife die of tuberculosis, and died himself under mysterious circumstances at age 40. He also created the detective novel and wrote brilliant, often bizarre short stories that still stimulate the reader's imagination.

When the student who wrote this essay read Poe's "The Tell-Tale Heart," first published in 1843, she was fascinated by one of the plot elements: the sound of a beating heart that compels the narrator of the story to commit a murder and then to confess it to the police. In the following paper, the student discusses her interpretation of the source of the heartbeat.

```
          The Sound of a Murderous Heart

     In Edgar Allan Poe's short story "The Tell-Tale

Heart," several interpretations are possible as to the

source of the beating heart that causes the narrator-

murderer to reveal himself to the police. The noise

could simply be a product of the narrator's obviously

deranged mind. Or perhaps the murder victim's spirit

lingers, heart beating, to exact revenge upon the

narrator. Although each of these interpretations is
```

possible, most of the evidence in the story suggests that the inescapable beating heart that haunts the narrator is his own.

The interpretation that the heartbeat stems from some kind of auditory hallucination is flawed. The narrator clearly is insane--his killing a kind old man because of an "Evil Eye" demonstrates this--and his psychotic behaviour is more than sufficient cause for readers to question his truthfulness. Even so, nowhere else in the story does the narrator imagine things that do not exist. Nor is it likely that he would intentionally attempt to mislead us since the narrative is a confessional monologue through which he tries to explain and justify his actions. He himself describes his "disease" as a heightening of his senses, not of his imagination. Moreover, his highly detailed account of the events surrounding the murder seems to support this claim. Near the end of the story, he refutes the notion that he is inventing the sound in his mind when he says, "I found that the noise was not within my ears" (792). Although the narrator's reliability is questionable, there seems to be no reason to doubt this particular observation.

Interpreting the heartbeat as the victim's ghostly retaliation against the narrator also presents difficulties. Perhaps most important, when the narrator first hears the heart, the old man is still alive. The structure of the story also argues against the retaliation interpretation. Poe uses the first-person point of view to give readers immediate access to the narrator's strange thought processes, a choice that suggests the story is a form of psychological study. If

➜

"The Tell-Tale Heart" were truly a ghost story, it would probably be told in the third person, and it would more fully develop the character of the old man and explore his relationship with the narrator. If the heartbeat that torments the narrator is his own, however, these inconsistencies are avoided.

The strongest evidence that the tell-tale heart is really the narrator's is the timing of the heartbeat. Although it is the driving force behind the entire story, the narrator hears the beating heart only twice. In both of these instances, he is under immense physical and psychological stress--times when his own heart would be pounding. The narrator first hears the heartbeat with the shock of realizing that he has accidentally awakened his intended victim:

> Meantime the hellish tattoo of the heart increased. It grew quicker and quicker, and louder every instant. The old man's terror must have been extreme! It grew louder, I say, louder every moment!--do you mark me well? I have told you that I am nervous: so I am. And now at the dead hour of the night, amid the dreadful silence of that old house, so strange a noise as this excited me to uncontrollable terror. (791)

As the narrator's anxiety increases, so does the volume and frequency of the sound, an event easily explained if the heartbeat is his own. Also, the sound of the heart persists even after the old man is dead, fading slowly into the background, as would the murderer's own heartbeat after his short, violent struggle with the old man. This reasoning can also explain why the narrator did not hear the heart on any of the seven previous nights when he looked into the old man's bedchamber. Because the old man slept and the "Evil Eye" was closed, no action was necessary (according to the narrator-murderer's twisted logic), and therefore he did not experience the rush of adrenaline that set his heart pounding on the fatal eighth visit.

The heart also follows a predictable pattern at the end of the story when the police officers come to investigate a neighbour's report of the dying old man's scream. In this encounter the narrator's initial calm slowly gives way to irritation and fear. As he becomes increasingly agitated, he begins to hear the heart again. The narrator clearly identifies it as the same sound he heard previously, as shown by the almost word-for-word repetition of the language he uses to describe it, calling it "<u>a low, dull, quick sound--much such a sound as a watch makes when enveloped in cotton</u>" [Poe's italics] (792). As the narrator-murderer focuses his attention on the sound, which ultimately overrides all else, his panic escalates until, ironically, he is betrayed by the very senses that he boasted about at the start of the story.

Work Cited

Poe, Edgar Allan. "The Tell-Tale Heart." <u>American Literature: A Prentice Hall Anthology</u>. Vol. 1. Ed. Emory Elliott, Linda K. Kerber, A. Walton Litz, and Terence Martin. Englewood Cliffs: Prentice, 1991. 789-92.

2

Student essay analyzing a play

The following essay examines *Blood Relations,* a play about Lizzie Borden, written by Canadian playwright Sharon Pollock. The play won the Governor General's Literary Award for Drama in 1981. The student's paper explores Pollock's treatment of Lizzie's guilt or innocence and its relation to the use of metadrama in the play.

The Function of Metadrama in Sharon Pollock's <u>Blood Relations</u>

In the play <u>Blood Relations,</u> Sharon Pollock undertakes a metaphysical healing of the accused axe murderer Lizzie Borden through the use of metadrama--a play within a play. Pollock addresses the question of Lizzie's guilt· or innocence through the use of a play within a play in which "the Actress," and not Lizzie, re-enacts the events of the day of the murders. The past reality is thrown into question as a result of the script being based on the Actress's conjectures about Lizzie's actions.

Built into the metadramatic function is a constant awareness of the script itself and of the expectation that Lizzie will be proven guilty. Ultimately, what the script underlines through the use of this self-conscious form is the silencing of Lizzie: through society's image of her, through social mores, and through language itself. Since she chooses to remain enigmatic, Lizzie protects herself from her friend, the Actress, and even from her own darker side. Through this voluntary suppression of her own voice, Lizzie's mysteriousness is reinforced, and we are constantly reminded that she is a character being played by the Actress within the play itself. Strangely enough, it is this re-enactment that finally allows Lizzie to

---

undertake a healing journey, as it gives a medium within which to confront her fears.

The history of metadrama is almost as old as drama itself. Metadrama begins with the emergence of the single playwright (as opposed to a collective troupe) shaping a piece of drama. Once there is an individual author, then there is room and reason to reflect on the creative act itself. Just as the soliloquy calls attention to the audience as players within the drama, so references to theatre in characters' lives draw parallels with the theatre of life. Shakespeare was a frequent user of such reflexive drama, and it is interesting to note that <u>Blood Relations</u> begins with a reference to Shakespeare's <u>Winter's Tale</u>:

> Since what I am about to say must be but that
> Which contradicts my accusation, and
> The testimony on my part no other
> But what comes from myself, it shall scarce
>   boot me
> To say "Not guilty".
> But, if Powers Divine
> Behold our human action as they do,
> I doubt not than but innocence shall make
> False accusation blush and tyranny
> Tremble at . . . at . . . [Patience] (3.1.21–
>   25,27–31, quoted in Pollock 14)

Thus, very neatly, Pollock sums up the questions she seeks to address through the metadramatic function of the play. Shakespeare's innocent Hermione is an interesting choice for comparison with Lizzie Borden, who was not so clearly guiltless. But Pollock presents Lizzie as innocent in so far as she was a victim of the circumstances of the time.

➡

While <u>Blood Relations</u> does examine the question of Lizzie Borden's guilt or innocence, it is ultimately the Actress's beliefs and feelings in the re-creation of events that are presented. The play within the play evolves because the Actress will not accept Lizzie's patient refusal to answer her question as to whether Lizzie "did" or "didn't." Like Hermione, Lizzie finds that her answer to the question is irrelevant because the Actress will not believe either answer and asks the question out of enjoyment rather than for truth's sake. While Lizzie toys with the Actress, refusing to answer her questions, the Actress in turn toys with the known historical events, and translates them into theatre.

The play thereby systematically and self-consciously draws attention to its ability to query the difference between fiction and reality. This tactic liberates Pollock from following a strictly historical approach and allows her to introduce an interrogative viewpoint. It also allows a perspective on Lizzie's situation that makes it universal, for Pollock sets out to demonstrate that anyone trapped in circumstances as constricting as Lizzie's would be driven to commit at the very least suicide or, more likely, murder.

The use of metadrama in <u>Blood Relations</u> "explicitly and overtly lays bare its condition of artifice" (Waugh 4) in the space created between what the Actress says and does and what Lizzie will not say. Only in Lizzie's silence is the truth to be found. The gap between the silence and the words forms "an arena of conflict between two voices" (Waugh 5). Lizzie's silence is the focus of the play, for it reveals the causes of the crimes: aided by the Actress, Lizzie does not have to commit herself to the telling. Yet, although Lizzie does not tell her own story, she is no mere spectator during its retelling, either: she assumes the role of Bridget the maid. When family ties failed in the events leading up to the trial and during the trial iself, Bridget's testimony gave Lizzie an alibi. But Bridget is a creation of Lizzie's own making; the words she speaks to the Defense are given her by Lizzie. So when Lizzie does speak, it is only in echoes of her own words. The Actress, on the other hand, deals with the failed relationships: with Lizzie's father Andrew Borden, a man who cannot choose between his wife and his daughter; with Abigail Borden, her step-mother, who jealously views Lizzie as a rival; with Emma, Lizzie's sister, who flees when tensions mount, rather than act as mediator; with Dr. Patrick, Lizzie's only friend, who is more concerned with appearances than with feelings.

Lizzie's very powerlessness silences her. Bound by the dictates of a society that refuses to allow women choices, Lizzie is faced with either a life of servitude to a widower and his children, or to a life ruled by Abigail's whims and hatred. At no time is Lizzie allowed to choose a future life on her own terms. She does not wish to marry, but that is not a decision she is allowed to make. When Andrew Borden signs over the farm where Lizzie spent her childhood, Lizzie loses her only possible avenue of peaceful escape. For a woman to have freedom in 1892, she needed money, and Lizzie sees more and more of her father's fortune being consumed by her step-family. Her universe continually narrows.

The silencing of Lizzie is threefold: Her tongue is tied by the language deemed appropriate for a woman

➡

of her day; her actions are confined by social mores that dictate her every move; she is restrained by an image that reduces her to a helpless creature, incapable of making decisions. When Lizzie's birds are brutally slaughtered by her father, the stage is set for the only possible means of liberation available to her: murder.

The reasons for Lizzie's refusal to address the question of her guilt or innocence are not specifically spelled out in the script, and these motivations have been viewed differently by various directors. In the premiere production in Edmonton, Lizzie participates in the game in order to keep the Actress interested in her. The National Arts Centre production viewed Lizzie's motives quite differently: Lizzie angrily suggests playing the game in order to stop the Actress from endlessly questioning her (Wallace and Zimmerman 124). So even the relationship between Lizzie and the Actress remains undefined, and only Lizzie's silence is consistent. Lizzie remains enigmatic, her mysteriousness reinforced through the suppression of her voice as a character in the play. Finally, the audience comes to understand Lizzie's time and the Actress, but Lizzie remains a puzzle. The audience never learns the true events, but does become acquainted with Lizzie's possible motivations as experienced by the Actress.

In an interview about her play <u>Saucy Jack</u>, Pollock stated that what interested her about people was how they react in extreme circumstances, because that helped explain their everyday behaviour. Pollock seeks to illuminate, both in <u>Saucy Jack</u> and in <u>Blood Relations</u>, women who face terrible things and who are ultimately empowered by them, not victimized. Lizzie Borden is strengthened in this way by the healing journey of the re-enactment.

Lizzie's dangerousness is not that she has been acquitted of a murder or even that she was probably a murderer. Her ultimate dangerousness in the play is a result of her double, or perhaps triple, construct as a virginal, seductive, and possibly lesbian character. Lizzie, as a spinster, is virginal and hence untamed and potentially threatening. The seductive aspect of her character is seen through her flirtations and game playing with the married Dr. Patrick. With him, she becomes a temptress who behaves shamefully, and those around her feel she should be married off to a suitable man so that she can fulfil her supposedly proper destiny. Her relationship with the Actress is yet another indication of her dangerousness. For, although the relationship is ambiguous, there is undeniably a sexualized element in their "liaison" (18). The threat of her personality leaves her secluded outside the realm of normal and accepted behaviour and, naturally, invites rumour. Actresses had an equally bad reputation, for their career was considered promiscuous, just slightly higher on the social scale than prostitution. As Lizzie sardonically notes, however, this is irrelevant given the damage done to her reputation by the murders of her father and step-mother and the subsequent trial:

> EMMA. That . . . actress who's come up from
> Boston.
> MISS LIZZIE. What about her?
> EMMA. People talk.
> MISS LIZZIE. You needn't listen.

→

> EMMA. In your position you should do nothing
> to <u>inspire talk</u>.
>
> MISS LIZZIE. People need so little in the way
> of inspiration. And Miss Cornelia's
> classes didn't cover "Etiquette for
> Acquitted Persons". (68-69)

Lizzie's sarcastic mask is meant to conceal the pain of
her situation. For her, there is no escape. In order to
live free, she has had to sacrifice her respectable
position in society. Lizzie is nevertheless unhappy with
her sexual self and with her place in the world. She
admits that she wonders if she was born defective:

> Do you suppose . . . do you suppose there's a
> formula, a magic formula for being "a woman"?
> Do you suppose every girl baby receives it at
> birth, it's the last thing that happens just
> before birth, the magic formula is stamped
> indelibly on the brain--Ka Thud!! . . .
> and . . . through some terrible
> oversight . . . perhaps the death of my
> mother . . . I didn't get that Ka Thud!! (36)

As the scenes are re-enacted, Lizzie begins to examine
her pain and to gain some perspective on her life. The
Actress says as Lizzie, "I'm supposed to be a mirror.
I'm supposed to reflect what you want to see, but
everyone wants something different. If no one looks in
the mirror, I'm not even there, I don't exist" (39). As
Lizzie relives the events, the process enables her to
face her fears and define herself. She tells the Actress
of a dream on a carousel where she's wearing a mask that
conceals the fact that she has no eyes beneath it. This
"eyelessness" or "I-lessness" is reflected throughout

the play in references to eyes, in Lizzie's habit of staring right through people, and in references to images retained on the retina of the eye when people die. Here eyelessness is also an indication of her lack of ability to determine her own destiny. In refusing to face the events until the re-enactment ten years after the murders, Lizzie has been protecting herself from the Actress, from Emma's constant prodding, and from herself. Only when the retelling is complete does Lizzie realize that she alone does not bear all the guilt. Her sister Emma is in part responsible for the events of the day, as she comments:

> Did you ever stop and think that I was like a puppet, your puppet. My head your hand, yes, your hand working my mouth, me saying all the things you felt like saying, me doing all the things you felt like doing, me spewing forth, me hitting out, and you, you--! (70)

When Emma fled on the day of the murders and abandoned her self-appointed role as mediator, she must have known that she was abdicating responsibility for Lizzie's inevitable violence. Truly, it seems in the re-enactment that Emma fled precisely because violence was inevitable. It also becomes clear over the course of the play that Lizzie had already been considered a killer by the society of her time: the killer of her own mother in childbirth (57).

The play eases Lizzie's pain by transferring the agonies of her constricting life to the Actress. The Actress is consistently beaten down by the oppressive forces that have ruled Lizzie's early life, until the Actress is finally driven to the point of breakdown and ➔

a willingness to commit murder in her re-enactment. In fact, the Actress seems to have assumed Lizzie's damaged self by the end of the play. The implication is that anyone, given the right set of circumstances, would be capable of murder. Lizzie's circumstances were more than sufficient to drive her to the crime; she was a woman faced with no palatable alternatives in her life. To survive, Lizzie is forced to kill.

The role-playing throughout the script becomes a moral exploration posing the question, "Was Lizzie justified in killing her father and step-mother (if she did)?" Pollock depicts the circumstances that would provide a strong-willed, intelligent woman in the repressive New England of 1892 with a motive for murder, but Pollock does not leave Lizzie alone to shoulder the guilt. She implicates all of society (and the audience) in the crime with her ambiguous ending:

> EMMA. You didn't . . . did you?
>
> MISS LIZZIE. Poor . . . Emma.
>
> THE ACTRESS. Lizzie. (She takes the hatchet from Miss Lizzie.) Lizzie, you did.
>
> MISS LIZZIE. I didn't. (The Actress looks to the hatchet--then to the audience.) You did. (70)

While the fiction is left carefully intact (for it was the Actress who has acted out the events of the day), Lizzie is absolved of her guilt through the circumstances of a multiplicity of failed relationships and the mores of the time. Lizzie has been healed and the true guilty parties are handed the burden of the murders. The gap continues to resonate between the fact and the fiction, the silence and the words, and the true nature of the events will never be known. A plausible explanation has, however, been offered, and Lizzie finds peace.

Pollock also ably demonstrates why such a society could not convict Lizzie of a brutal and violent murder. Lizzie was acquitted precisely because the men of the jury could not believe a woman capable of such a crime under the prescribed norms of female behaviour in turn-of-the-century New England. In fact, those very codes of behaviour gave Lizzie no other alternative, as Pollock envisions the story.

The use of the metadramatic script allows Pollock to introduce the theme of Lizzie's healing and to update the perspective of her story so that its topic is of interest to current audiences. Through the revelations of the play, Pollock exposes the true perpetrators of the crime: a society that treated women like children or animals and that confined women to narrow lives.

Works Cited

Pollock, Sharon. _Blood Relations and Other Plays_. Edmonton: NeWest Press, 1981.

---. Interview with Sheila Rogers. _The Arts Tonight_. CBC Radio. 7 Dec. 1993.

Shakespeare, William. _The Winter's Tale_. Ed. Baldwin Maxwell. _The Complete Pelican Shakespeare_. Baltimore: Penguin, 1972. 1337-68.

Wallace, Robert, and Cynthia Zimmerman, eds. "Sharon Pollock." _The Work: Conversations with English-Canadian Playwrights_. Toronto: Coach House Press, 1982. 115-26.

Waugh, Patricia. _Metafiction: The Theory and Practice of Self-Conscious Fiction_. London: Methuen, 1984.

3

Student research paper analyzing a poem

The following essay is a literary analysis of a poem. It uses secondary sources°. E. J. Pratt, a major figure in Canadian poetry, was born in 1882 in Western Bay, Newfoundland. Pratt's narrative poetry attempts to mythologize Canadian history, a subject he takes up in *Towards the Last Spike,* for which he won his third Governor General's Award. In this paper, the student discusses Pratt's reconciliation of epic tradition and modern Canadian historical events. (Note that the title of a long poem is given in italics, not in quotation marks.)

Towards the Last Spike: A Canadian Epic?

In a review of Towards the Last Spike that appeared in the University of Toronto Quarterly, Northrop Frye made this comment: "The poem is in the epic tradition, without any of the advantages of epic to sustain it" (270). Pratt took a subject that was "epic" in scope and size, and created instead the "verse panorama," as he called it in its lengthy subtitle. It can be argued that Canadian poets lack the poetic tradition that would turn their history into epic poetry. Pratt comes close to the epic in Towards the Last Spike, but through his choice of dramatic technique, he has, in effect, originated a style of narrative poetry that works against the ultimately unifying vision of the epic. The poem anthologizes the past in a series of vignettes linked by historical "progress reports." This structure enables Pratt to achieve variety and contrast without distorting the remainder of the poem; the work ultimately has the cumulative effect of richness and a textured quality. At the same time, the fragmentation of the narrative mirrors the political divisiveness and lack of national unity that the poem portrays, finally subverting Pratt's epic aim.

In keeping with his panoramic vision, Pratt sets up a complex web of themes through the course of the poem. The poem has two protagonists, mankind and nature. Not only do these two contend with each other, but man also quarrels with man, and natural elements are in conflict with each other as well. The two protagonists are equated as "two fortresses: the mind, the rock" (65). The conflicts take place in two different worlds, each carefully characterized by Pratt: the political realm of Macdonald and the natural one of the nameless Canadian workers and the landscape--the "Laurentian monster."

The poem is as much a reflection of how politicians operate as it is an account of the building of the railroad. In his political sections, Pratt illustrates

> . . . the battle of ideas and metaphors
> And kindred images called by the same name
> Like brothers who with temperamental blood
> Went to it with their fists. (51)

This political struggle is waged between the imaginative, emotional man represented by Macdonald and Van Horne, and the cerebral, practical man typified by Blake and Mackenzie. The characterization is not as simple as this opposition would imply, however, for Macdonald in his own way is as calculating as Blake. One of Pratt's major accomplishments in this poem is the credible portrait of the political consciousness in action. Pratt describes Macdonald's political awareness at length in the section entitled "The Gathering" and shows the politician at work concocting his platform:

> He could make use of that--just what he needed
> A Western version of the Arctic daring,

➜

Romance and realism, a double dose. (43)

Pratt continually emphasizes the power of metaphors and
words in the political context. Macdonald recognizes the
potency of Blake's phrase "To build a Road over that sea
of mountains" (53), with its implication that the task
is impossible. This idea frightens Macdonald more than
the rest of Blake's massive rhetoric, for

> This carried more than argument. It was
> A flash of fire which might with proper kindling
> Consume its way into the public mind. (53)

The theme of control runs as a corollary to
Pratt's concept of words and metaphors. Macdonald is
able to gain control in the House of Commons through his
vision and his use of words, while Blake, "the homicidal
master of the opiates," loses his audience and therefore
his support through boredom (53). Van Horne is shown to
be a master of control to rival Macdonald, since he is
able to manage both the resources of nature and the
inventions of man:

> . . . Electricity
> And rock, one novel to the coiling hand,
> The other frozen in the lap of Age,
> Were playthings for the boy, work for the man. (57)

Macdonald and Van Horne also share the passion of
the visionary man; symbolically each spends a sleepless
night gazing at the stars and at the landscape. Blake,
in ironic comparison, needs help to see the country
around him:

> Though with his natural eyes
> Up to this time he had not sighted mountains
> He was an expert with the telescope. (52)

At the same time Pratt undercuts the vision of Macdonald

because it originates in liquor, "his medicine":

> A blessed sleep fell like a dew upon him,
> And soon, in trance, drenched in conciliation,
> He hiccupped gently--"Now let S-S-Stephen come!" (76)

Pratt's ability and craftsmanship as a poet are reflected clearly in the poem. He uses various patterns of images to draw the poem together: The metaphor of music is one example of this technique and further elaboration of the drive to control. The image is first applied to the vision of the railroad:

> The airs had long been mastered like old songs
> The feet could tap to in the galleries.
> But would they tap to a new rhapsody,
> Whose ear could be assured of absolute pitch
> To catch this kind of music in the West? (49)

Political language is equated with music as well, so that the battle between Blake and Macdonald is not just of rival visions, but also of rival musical expressions:

> Blake had returned to the attack and given
> Sir John the ague with another phrase
> As round and as melodious as the first:
> "The Country's wealth, its millions after millions
> Squandered--LOST IN THE GORGES OF THE FRASER":
> A beautiful but ruinous piece of music
> That could only be droned with drums and fifes. (65)

Pratt also uses the image of the orchestra as a description of the Conservatives in defeat, with Macdonald shown as the "old conductor off the podium" (50). The metaphor returns to conclude the poem effectively, as the completion of the railroad becomes the new beginning for the young nation: "Merely the tuning-up!" (80). The image is appropriate in this

➔

context, for it implies that the railroad has finally organized Canada into a new harmony. The tone rises in the last section to a pitch of excitement and optimism in its celebration of the achievement. Occasionally, like Macdonald, Pratt uses a phrase that provides a striking visual image for the reader. An example of this occurs in his treatment of Blake, in the expression "Rumours he heard had gangrened into facts" (46).

The elemental conflict between humans and the landscape is contrasted with the sophisticated battle of political visions. The landscape is splendidly characterized by Pratt as a primeval reptile whose primary weapon is its immense size:

> Whose tail had covered Labrador and swished
> Atlantic tides, whose body coiled itself
> Around the Hudson bay, then curled up north
> Through Manitoba and Saskatchewan
> To Great Slave Lake. In continental reach
> The neck went past the Great Bear Lake until
> Its head was hidden in the Arctic Seas. (61)

Traditionally, the epic hero battles the monster to defend or reach his home; here, however, the homeland is the monster. The characterization of home as alien or "other" makes identification with the land in the interests of a national vision impossible and undercuts the poet's epic ambition. In addition, Pratt points to the apparently indissoluble link between terror and beauty in the Canadian scene:

> They needed miles to render up their beauty
> As if the gods in high aesthetic moments
> Resenting the profanity of touch
> Chiselled this sculpture for the eye alone. (64)

Here Pratt would seem to be anticipating the ambivalent relationship to the natural world, at once home and enemy, illustrated in the work of later writers like Margaret Atwood in <u>The Journals of Susanna Moodie</u> or Charles Lillard and Barry McKinnon in their "Bushed" poems.

The landscape is a living thing that wrestles not only with man, but with itself as well. The conflict exists on many levels at one time:

The men were fighting foes which had themselves

Waged elemental civil wars and still

Were hammering one another at this moment. (65)

Although the men are ultimately successful in the combat, and the poem is, in part, a celebration of the triumph of human will over nature, Pratt, in concluding his poem, chooses to focus on the landscape rather than on his "hero." The "Laurentian monster" endures and has the ability to adapt to the new conditions that humans have imposed on it:

. . . To drown

The traffic chorus, she must blend the sound

With those inaugural, narcotic notes

Of storm and thunder which would send her back

Deeper than ever in Laurentian sleep. (80)

Pratt makes certain, though, that the reader is aware of the cost of the railroad in terms of human life and strength. His interlude "Ring, Ring the Bells" underlines this by illustrating the process of metamorphosis that changes men into landscape.

The title <u>Towards the Last Spike</u> emphasizes not the final event, but rather the movement toward the climax. This is reflected in the anticlimactic treatment

➡

of the driving of the last spike, which undercuts the epic and heroic quality of the previous events. Pratt creates a realistically human scene. Donald Smith does not drive the spike home with one superhuman or legendary blow: He fumbles it.

The poem is uneven in quality, and Pratt can be amazingly trite in some of his images. The following part of his description of Van Horne can be cited as an example of Pratt's verse at its most overworked:

Here he could clap the future on the shoulder

And order Fate about as his lieutenant

For he would take no nonsense from a thing

Called Destiny--the stars had to be with him. (57)

These are understandable flaws in a work of this range, and Pratt is for the most part successful in bringing his immense work and all its characters vividly to life. He can write convincingly as an observer of Canadian nature or as a political cartoonist in his depiction of British Columbia as "the Lady" wavering between the respective lures of Macdonald and the Americans. Pratt's modern awareness of discords and divisions admits irony into the poem and diminishes its epic world view. His diversity becomes in itself an impediment to the realization of epic coherence. The question that the poem, with its contradictory impulses, asks is whether epic form and feeling can be sustained in the twentieth century.

Towards the Last Spike is epic in proportions and in its universal theme, but it lacks the conventions and formulaic devices that characterize the earlier epic style. It moves toward the epic vision just as the country moves toward national unity with the creation of

the railroad, but the conflicts that are still
unresolved prohibit anything beyond a momentary glimpse
of a binding national identity, one of the prerequisites
of epic vision. <u>Towards the Last Spike</u> is unique in
Canadian poetry, for it is a compendium of our
historical experience, and as such, it becomes almost by
default our Canadian "epic."

Works Cited

Frye, Northrop. "Poetry." <u>University of Toronto
Quarterly</u> 22 (1953): 270-73.

Pratt, E. J. <u>Towards the Last Spike</u>. Rpt. in <u>Poets
Between the Wars</u>. Ed. ---. Toronto: McClelland &
Stewart, 1967.

38
Writing in the Social Sciences and Natural Sciences

38a
Understanding methods of inquiry in the social sciences

Disciplines in the **social sciences** include subject areas such as economics, education, geography, political science, psychology, and sociology. At some colleges and universities, history is included in the social sciences; at others it is included in the humanities. The social sciences focus on the behaviour of people as individuals and in groups.

Observation is a common method for inquiry in the social sciences. To make observations, take along whatever tools or equipment you might need: writing or sketching materials, and perhaps recording or photographic equipment. As you make observations, take very accurate and complete notes. If you use abbreviations to speed your notetaking, make sure you will later understand them when you need to write up your observations. In a report of your observations, tell what tools or equipment you used, because your method might have influenced what you saw (for example, your taking photographs may make people act differently than usual).

Interviewing is another common technique that social scientists use. Interviews are useful for gathering people's opinions and impressions of events. If you interview, remember that interviews are not always a completely reliable way to gather factual information, because people's memories are not precise. If your only source for facts is interviews, try to interview as many people as possible so that you can cross-check the information. Before you interview anyone, practise with whatever notetaking tools you might need, so that they do not intrude on the interview process (see also 32h-1).

Questionnaires can be useful for gathering information in the social sciences. When you administer a questionnaire, be sure that you ask a sufficient number of people to respond, so that you do not reach conclusions based on too small a sample of responses. To write questions for a questionnaire, use the guidelines in Chart 150.

GUIDELINES FOR WRITING QUESTIONS FOR A QUESTIONNAIRE   150

1. First, define what you want to find out, and then write questions that will elicit the information you seek.
2. Phrase questions so that they are easy to understand.
3. Use appropriate language (see 21a), and avoid artificial language (see 21e).
4. Be aware that how you phrase your questions will determine whether the answers that you get truly reflect what people are thinking. Make sure that your choice of words does not imply what *you* want to hear.
5. Avoid questions that invite one-word answers about complex matters that call for a range of responses.
6. Test a draft of the questionnaire on a small group of people before you use it. If any question is misinterpreted or hard to understand, revise and retest it.

38b Understanding writing purposes and practices in the social sciences

Social scientists write to inform readers by presenting and explaining information (see 1b-1) or to persuade readers by arguing a point of view (see 1b-2).

Analysis (see 4f-6 and 5a) helps social scientists write about problems and their solutions. For example, an economist writing about a major automobile company in financial trouble might first break the situation into parts, analyzing employee salaries and benefits, the selling price of cars, and the costs of doing business. Next, the economist might show how these parts relate to the financial status of the whole company. Then the economist might speculate about how specific changes would help solve the company's financial problems.

Social scientists are particularly careful to **define their terms** when they write, especially when they discuss complex social issues. For example, if you are writing a paper on substance abuse in the medical profession, you first have to define what you mean by the terms *substance abuse* and *medical profession.* By *substance* do you mean alcohol and drugs or only drugs? How are you quantifying *abuse?* When you refer to the medical profession, are you including nurses and lab technicians or only doctors? Without defining these terms, you can confuse your readers or lead them to wrong conclusions.

Social scientists often use **analogy** (see 4f-8) to make unfamiliar ideas clear. When an unfamiliar idea is compared to one that is more familiar, the unfamiliar idea becomes easier to understand. For example, sociologists may talk of the "culture shock" that some people feel when they enter a new society. The sociologists might compare this "shock" to the reaction that someone living today might have if suddenly moved hundreds of years into the future or the past.

In college and university courses in the social sciences, some instructors ask students to write their personal reactions to information or experiences, in which case the first person (*I, we, our*) is acceptable. In most writing for the social sciences, however, writers use the third person (*he, she, it, one, they*). Also, because the emphasis is on people or groups being observed rather than on the person doing the observing, some social scientists use the passive voice° (see 8n and 8o) rather than the active voice°. The *Publication Manual of the American Psychological Association,* the most commonly used style manual in the social sciences (see 38c), however, recommends the active voice whenever possible.

38c Using documentation style in the social sciences

If you use secondary sources° when you write about the social sciences, you are required to credit these sources by using documentation°. The most commonly used documentation style° in the social sciences is that of the American Psychological Association (APA). The APA documentation style uses parenthetical references in the body of a paper and a References list at the end of a paper. APA documentation style is described in section 33d. For an example of a student research paper that uses APA documentation style, see Chapter 35.

The *Chicago Manual* (CM) style of documentation is sometimes used in the social sciences. CM bibliographic note style is described in section 33e.

38d Writing different types of papers in the social sciences

Two major types of papers in the social sciences are case studies and research papers.

1 Writing case studies in the social sciences

A **case study** is an intensive study of one group or individual. It is usually presented in a relatively fixed format, but the specific parts and order of case-study formats vary. Most case studies contain the following components: (1) basic identifying information about the individual or group; (2) a history of the individual or group; (3) observations of the individual's or group's behaviour; and (4) conclusions and perhaps recommendations as a result of the observations.

In writing a case study, describe situations; do not interpret them unless your assignment allows you to interpret *after* you report. Be sure to differentiate between fact and opinion (see 5d-3). For example, you may observe nursing-home patients lying in bed on their sides facing the door. Describe exactly what you see; do not interpret this observation as, say, patients watching for visitors. Perhaps medicines are injected in the right hip, and patients are more comfortable lying on their left side, thus facing the door.

2 Writing research papers in the social sciences

You may be assigned a **research paper** in the social sciences for which you must consult secondary sources°. (See 32l on using specialized reference books and 32m-2 on using specialized indexes.) These sources are usually articles and books that report, summarize, and otherwise discuss the findings of other people's research. For an example of a student research paper written for an introductory psychology course, see Chapter 35.

38e   Understanding methods of inquiry in the sciences

Disciplines in the **natural sciences** include astronomy, biology, chemistry, geology, and physics. The sciences focus on natural phenomena. The purpose of scientific inquiry is discovery. Scientists formulate and test hypotheses in order to explain cause and effect (see 5f) systematically and objectively.

The **scientific method,** commonly used in the sciences to make discoveries, is a procedure for gathering information related to a specific hypothesis. The scientific method is the cornerstone of all inquiry in the sciences. Guidelines for using the scientific method are shown in Chart 151.

GUIDELINES FOR USING THE SCIENTIFIC METHOD   151

1. Formulate a tentative explanation—known as a **hypothesis**—for a scientific phenomenon. Be as specific as possible.
2. Read and summarize previously published information related to your hypothesis.
3. Plan and outline a method of investigation to uncover the information needed to test your hypothesis.
4. Experiment, exactly following the investigative procedures you have outlined.
5. Observe closely the results of the experiment, and write notes carefully.
6. Analyze the results. If they prove the hypothesis to be false, re-work the investigation and begin again. If the results prove the hypothesis to be true, say so.
7. Write a report of your research. At the end, you might suggest additional hypotheses that might be investigated.

38f   Understanding writing purposes and practices in the natural sciences

Scientists usually write to inform their audiences about factual information.

Exactness is extremely important in scientific writing. Readers expect precise descriptions of procedures and findings, free of personal biases. Scientists expect to be able to *replicate*—repeat step-by-step—the experiment or other process and get the same outcome as the writer.

Completeness is also essential in scientific writing. Without complete information, the reader might come to wrong conclusions. For example, a researcher may investigate how different types of soil affect plant growth. The researcher should report not only the analysis of each soil type, but also the amount of daylight each plant receives, the moisture content of the soil, the amount and type of fertilizer used, and all other related facts. Having all this information may lead the researcher to unexpected insights. For instance, plant growth may be less dependent on soil type than on a combination of soil type, fertilizer, and watering. This observation could be made only if the researcher had carefully noted all the facts.

The sciences generally focus on the experiment rather than the experimenter and on objective observation rather than subjective interpretation. Unless you are writing a personal-reaction paper, generally avoid using the first person (*I, we, our*) in writing science papers.

When writing for the sciences, often you are expected to follow fixed formats, which are designed to summarize a project and present its results efficiently. In your report, organize the information to achieve clarity and precision. Writers in the sciences sometimes use charts, graphs, tables, diagrams, and other illustrations to present material. In fact, illustrations can sometimes explain complex material more clearly than words can.

38g Using documentation style in the natural sciences

If you use secondary sources° when you write about the sciences, you are required to credit your sources by using documentation°. Documentation styles° in the various sciences differ somewhat. Ask your instructor which style you should use. If your instructor has no preference, consult 33g for a list of available style manuals in the sciences, and try to locate the manual you need. If you cannot locate the manual, or if the science you are writing in does not have a style manual, find a journal that publishes research in that science and imitate its documentation style.

The Council of Biology Editors (CBE) has compiled style and documentation guidelines for the life sciences, the physical sciences, and mathematics in *Scientific Style and Format: The CBE Manual for Authors, Editors, and Publishers,* 6th edition (1994). CBE documentation guidelines are described in section 33f.

38h Writing different types of papers in the natural sciences

Two major types of papers in the sciences are reports and reviews.

1 Writing science reports

Science reports tell about observations and experiments. Such reports may also be called "laboratory reports" when they describe laboratory experiments. Formal reports include the eight sections (including the title) described in Chart 152. Less formal reports, which are sometimes assigned in introductory courses, might not include an abstract or a review of the literature. Ask your instructor which sections to include in your report.

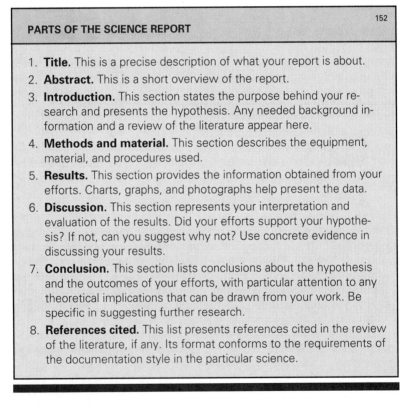

PARTS OF THE SCIENCE REPORT   152

1. **Title.** This is a precise description of what your report is about.
2. **Abstract.** This is a short overview of the report.
3. **Introduction.** This section states the purpose behind your research and presents the hypothesis. Any needed background information and a review of the literature appear here.
4. **Methods and material.** This section describes the equipment, material, and procedures used.
5. **Results.** This section provides the information obtained from your efforts. Charts, graphs, and photographs help present the data.
6. **Discussion.** This section represents your interpretation and evaluation of the results. Did your efforts support your hypothesis? If not, can you suggest why not? Use concrete evidence in discussing your results.
7. **Conclusion.** This section lists conclusions about the hypothesis and the outcomes of your efforts, with particular attention to any theoretical implications that can be drawn from your work. Be specific in suggesting further research.
8. **References cited.** This list presents references cited in the review of the literature, if any. Its format conforms to the requirements of the documentation style in the particular science.

SAMPLE SCIENCE REPORT (EXCERPTS)

An Experiment to Predict Vestigial Wings
in an F_2 <u>Drosophila</u> Population

INTRODUCTION

The purpose of this experiment was to observe second
filial generation (F_2) wing structures in <u>Drosophila.</u> The
hypothesis was that abnormalities in vestigial wing
structures would follow predicted genetic patterns.

METHODS AND MATERIALS

On February 7, four <u>Drosophila</u> (P_1) were observed.
Observation was made possible by etherizing the parents
(after separating them from their larvae), placing them
on a white card, and observing them under a dissecting
microscope. The observations were recorded on a chart.

On February 14, the larvae taken from the parents
on February 7 had developed to adults (F_1), and they
were observed using the same methods as on February 7.
The observations were recorded on the chart.

On February 19, the second filial generation (F_2)
was supposed to be observed. This was impossible because
they did not hatch. The record chart had to be
discontinued.

RESULTS

No observations of F_2 were possible. For the F_1
population, according to the prediction, no members
should have had vestigial wings. According to the
observations, however, some members of F_1 did have
vestigial wings.

➔

[DISCUSSION SECTION OMITTED]

CONCLUSIONS

Two explanations are possible to explain vestigial wings in the F_1 population. Perhaps members from F_2 were present among the F_1 generation. This is doubtful since the incubation period is 10 days, and the time between observations was only 8 days. A second possible explanation is that the genotype of the male P_1 was not WW (indicating that both genes were for normal wings) but rather heterozygous (Ww). If this were true the following would be the first filial products in a 1:1 ratio:

$$P_1 \ Ww \ x \ ww$$
$$F_1 \ Ww \ ww$$

Thus, the possibility for vestigial wings would exist. The problem remains, however, that the ratio was not 1:1 2:1 (i.e., 24 normal to 12 abnormal). One explanation could be that the total number was not large enough to extract an average.

The hypothesis concerning predicted genetic patterns in F_2 could not be confirmed because the F_2 generation did not hatch. This experiment should be repeated to get F_2 data. A larger F_1 sample should be used to see if the F_1 findings reported here are repeated.

---

2 | Writing science reviews

A **science review** is a paper discussing published information on a scientific topic or issue. The purpose of the review is to gather together for readers the current knowledge about the topic or issue.

Sometimes the purpose of a science review is to suggest a new interpretation of the old material. Any reinterpretation is based on a synthesis of old information with new, more complete information. In such reviews, the writer must marshal evidence to persuade readers that the new interpretation is valid.

If you are required to write a science review, (1) choose a very limited scientific issue currently being researched; (2) use information that is current—the more recently published the articles, books, and journals you consult, the better; (3) accurately summarize and paraphrase material—as explained in 31e and 31d; (4) document your sources (see Chapter 33). If your review is more than two or three pages, you might want to use headings to help your reader understand the organization and idea progression of your paper. See Chapter 32 for advice on finding sources.

39 Business Writing

Business writing requires of you what other kinds of writing call for: understanding your audience and your purpose. This chapter explains how to write business letters (see 39a), job application letters (see 39b), and résumés (see 39c). As you write for business, use the guidelines listed in Chart 153.

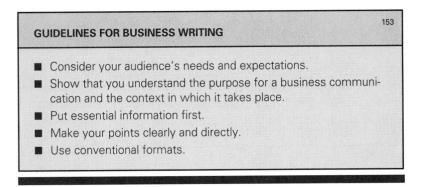

GUIDELINES FOR BUSINESS WRITING 153

- Consider your audience's needs and expectations.
- Show that you understand the purpose for a business communication and the context in which it takes place.
- Put essential information first.
- Make your points clearly and directly.
- Use conventional formats.

39a Writing and formatting a business letter

Business letters are written to give information, to build goodwill, or to establish a foundation for discussions or transactions. Experts in business and government agree that the letters likely to get results are short, simple, direct, and human. Here is good, basic advice: (1) Call the person by name; (2) tell what your letter is about in the first paragraph; (3) be honest; (4) be clear and specific; (5) use correct English; (6) be positive and natural; (7) edit ruthlessly.

762

For business letters, use the guidelines in Chart 154 and the format on page 764. Note the use of the abbreviation *PC,* meaning that a *photocopy* has been sent in place of the customary *cc,* which refers to a *carbon copy.* To avoid sexist language in the salutation of your letter, use the guidelines in Chart 155. For a business envelope, see page 768.

GUIDELINES FOR BUSINESS LETTERS	154
LETTERHEAD	If printed stationery is not available, type the company name and address centred at top of white paper, 8 1/2 x 11".
DATE	Put the date at the left margin under the letterhead, when typing in block form as shown in the example. When using paragraph indentations, type the date so that it ends at the right margin.
INSIDE ADDRESS	Direct your letter to a specific person. Be accurate in spelling the name and the address. If unsure of your information, telephone and ask questions of a secretary or other assistant.
SUBJECT LINE	Place at the left margin. In a few, concise words state the letter's subject.
SALUTATION	Use a first name only if you personally know the person. Otherwise, use *Mr.* or *Ms.* or whatever title is applicable with the person's last name. Avoid sexist language.
CLOSING	*Sincerely* or *Sincerely yours* are generally appropriate, unless you know the person very well and wish to use *Cordially.* Leave about four lines for your signature.
NAME LINES	Type your full name and title below your signature. The title can be on the same line as your name or on the next line.
SECOND PAGE	Head a second page with three items of information: the name of the person or company to which your letter is addressed, the number 2 or page 2, and the date. Place the information on three lines at the top left margin or on one line spaced across the top of the page.

BUSINESS LETTER FORMAT

letterhead

AlphaOmega Industries, Inc.
1234 Emily Carr Blvd.
Vancouver BC V6M 2C3

date

December 28, 19XX

inside
address

Ron R. London, Sales Director
Seasonal Products Corp.
270 18th St.
Brandon MB R7A 6A9

subject line

Subject: Spring Promotional Effort

salutation

Dear Ron:

message

Since we talked last week, I have completed
plans for the spring promotion of the
products that we market jointly.
AlphaOmega and Seasonal Products should
begin a direct mailing of the enclosed
brochure on January 28.

I have secured several mailing lists that
contain the names of people who have a
positive economic profile for our products.
The profile and the outline of the lists are
attached.

Do you have additional approaches for the
promotion? I would like to meet with you on
January 6 to discuss them and to work out the
details of the project.

Please call me and let me know if a meeting
next week at your office accommodates your
schedule.

closing

Sincerely,

Alan Stone

name, title

Alan Stone, Director of Special Promotions

writer's/
typist's
initials

AS/kw

copies

PC: Yolanda Lane, Vice President, Marketing
enclosures

enclosures

ENC: Brochure; Mailing Lists;
Customer Profile

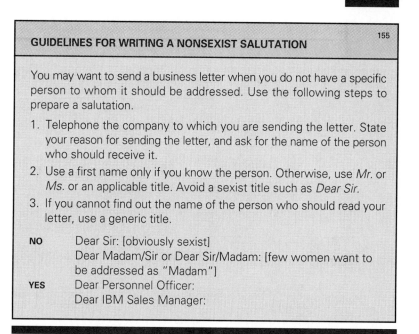

In addressing an envelope, remember that the best-written letter means nothing if it does not reach its destination. In the illustration on page 768, you will see the Canada Post guidelines for addressing envelopes so that they can be processed by machine. (Envelopes that must be sorted by hand add several days to mail-delivery time.)

39b Writing and formatting a job application letter

Chart 156 gives guidelines for a job application letter. A sample job application letter appears on page 767.

156

GUIDELINES FOR JOB APPLICATION LETTERS

YOUR ADDRESS	Type your address in block style as you would on an envelope. Use as your address (with a postal code) a place where you can be reached **by letter.**
DATE	Put the date below your address. Make sure that you mail the letter on either the same day or the next day; a delayed mailing can imply lack of planning.
INSIDE ADDRESS	Direct your letter to a specific person. Telephone the company to find out the name of the person to whom you are writing. Be accurate. A misspelled name can offend the receiver. A wrong address usually results in a lost letter.
SALUTATION	Be accurate. No one likes to see his or her name mis-spelled. In replying to an ad that gives only a post-office box number, omit the salutation and start your opening paragraph directly below the inside address. To avoid sexist language, use Chart 155.
INTRODUCTORY PARAGRAPH	State your purpose for writing and your source of information about the job.
BODY PARAGRAPH(S)	Interest the reader in the skills and talents you offer by mentioning whatever experience you have *that relates to the specific job.* Mention your enclosed résumé, but do *not* summarize it.
CLOSING PARAGRAPH	Suggest an interview, stating that you will call to make arrangements.
CLOSING	*Sincerely* or *Sincerely yours* is generally appropriate.
NAME LINES	Type your full name below your signature. Leave about four lines for your signature.
NOTATION	If you are enclosing any material with your letter, type *ENC:* and briefly list the items.

JOB APPLICATION LETTER

```
                      248 Woodbridge Hall
                      Wilfrid Laurier University
                      75 University Ave. W
                      Waterloo ON   N2L 3C5
                      May 15, 19XX
```

Rae Clemens, Director of Human Resources
Taleno, Ward Marketing, Inc.
1471 Summit Blvd.
London ON   N6G 1E9

Dear Ms. Clemens:

I am answering the advertisement for a marketing trainee
that Taleno, Ward placed in today's <u>London Free Press</u>.

Marketing has been one of the emphases of my course work
here at Wilfrid Laurier University, as you will see on
my enclosed résumé. This past year, I gained some
practical experience as well, when I developed marketing
techniques that helped to turn my typing service into a
busy and profitable small business.

Successfully marketing the typing service (with flyers,
advertisements in university publications, and even a
two-for-one promotion) makes me a very enthusiastic
novice. I can think of no better way to become a
professional than working for Taleno, Ward.

I will be here at Laurier through August 1. You can
reach me by phone at (519) 555-1976. Unless I hear from
you before, I'll call on May 25 about setting up an
interview.

```
                      Sincerely yours,

                      Lee Chen

                      Lee Chen
```

ENC: Résumé

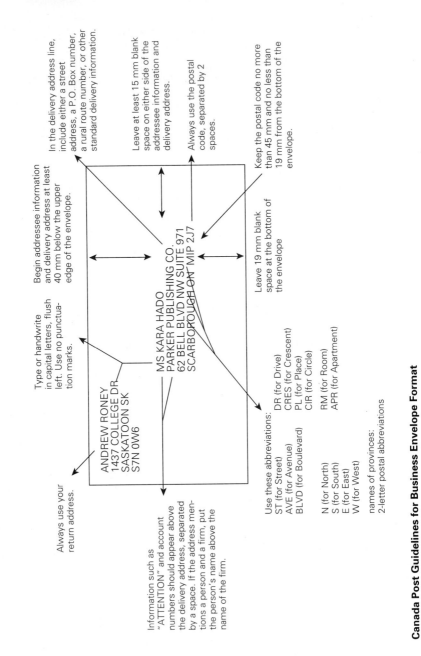

In the delivery address line, include either a street address, a P.O. Box number, a rural route number, or other standard delivery information.

Leave at least 15 mm blank space on either side of the addressee information and delivery address.

Always use the postal code, separated by 2 spaces.

Keep the postal code no more than 45 mm and no less than 19 mm from the bottom of the envelope.

Begin addressee information and delivery address at least 40 mm below the upper edge of envelope.

Type or handwrite in capital letters, flush left. Use no punctuation marks.

Leave 19 mm blank space at the bottom of the envelope

ANDREW RONEY
1437 COLLEGE DR
SASKATOON SK
S7N 0W6

MS KARA HADO
PARKER PUBLISHING CO.
62 BELL BLVD NW SUITE 971
SCARBOROUGH ON M1P 2J7

Always use your return address.

Information such as "ATTENTION" and account numbers should appear above the delivery address, separated by a space. If the address mentions a person and a firm, put the person's name above the name of the firm.

Use these abbreviations:
ST (for Street)   DR (for Drive)
AVE (for Avenue)   CRES (for Crescent)
BLVD (for Boulevard)   PL (for Place)
                         CIR (for Circle)

N (for North)   RM (for Room)
S (for South)   APR (for Apartment)
E (for East)
W (for West)

names of provinces:
2-letter postal abbreviations

Canada Post Guidelines for Business Envelope Format

39c Writing and formatting a résumé

A **résumé** is an easy-to-read, factual document that presents your qualifications for employment. All résumés cover certain standard items: name, address, phone number; education; past experience; skills and talents; publications, awards, honours, membership in professional organizations; a list of references or a statement that they are "available upon request."

A résumé gives you an opportunity to present a positive picture of yourself to a prospective employer. Employers understand that college and university students may have limited experience in the business world. Think of headings that allow you to emphasize your strengths. For example, if you have never done paid work, do not use *Business Experience*. You can use *Work Experience* if you have done volunteer or other unpaid work. If the experience you offer an employer is that you have run school or social events, you might use *Organizational Experience*. If your greatest strength is your academic record, put your educational achievements first.

You may choose to arrange your résumé in emphatic order with the most important information first and the least important last. Or you may choose to arrange information in chronological (time) order, a sequence that is good for showing a steady work history or solid progress in a particular field. Lee Chen's résumé, which was sent with the job application letter on page 767, is on page 770. It uses emphatic order. Stephen Schmit's résumé, on page 771, uses chronological order.

When you are applying for a specific job, modify your basic résumé to emphasize your qualifications for that job. Lee Chen added the *Marketing Trainee* heading and the statement about relevant experience for becoming a marketing trainee to her basic résumé and positioned the *Marketing Experience* section first. These modifications help to send a message that Chen's qualifications for the marketing trainee position are better than other applicants'. If you keep your résumé on computer, you can easily tailor it to specific job opportunities.

Your résumé usually has to fulfil only one purpose: It has to convince the person who first looks at it to put it into the "Call for an interview" pile rather than into the wastebasket. To do that best, a résumé should be eye-catching and informative, and it should make its readers think, "We should talk to this person; seems like someone who would be an asset to our business."

EMPHATIC RÉSUMÉ

MARKETING TRAINEE

Lee Chen
248 Woodbridge Hall
Wilfrid Laurier University
75 University Ave. W
Waterloo ON N2L 3C5
519-555-1976

The experience I acquired marketing my typing service
provided me with a good practical background for a
position as a marketing trainee.

MARKETING EXPERIENCE (program for campus typing service)
    Evaluated typing-service capabilities; analyzed
    market for service; drew up and implemented marketing
    plan; produced 2-colour flyer, designed print ads and
    wrote copy, developed and ran special promotion.
    August 19XX to February 19XX.

BUSINESS EXPERIENCE
    Type-Right Typing Service: Ran campus typing service
    for two years. Duties included word processing (Word,
    PageMaker, WordPerfect), proofreading, billing and
    other financial record-keeping, and customer contact.
    August 19XX to present.

    Archer & Archer Advertising: Worked as general
    assistant in the copy department under direct
    supervision of John Allen, Director. Duties included
    proofreading, filing, direct client contact. June
    19XX to August 19XX.

ADDITIONAL EXPERIENCE
    Coordinated student-employment service at Pauline
    Johnson High School, Brantford, Ontario. Duties
    included contacting students to fill jobs with local
    employers, arranging interviews, and writing follow-
    up reports on placements.

EDUCATION
    Wilfrid Laurier University
    B.A. May 19XX, Psychology, Marketing

EXTRACURRICULAR
    Marketing Club, Computer Graphics Society

References available upon request.

CHRONOLOGICAL RÉSUMÉ

Stephen L. Schmit
5163 Duke St.
Halifax NS   B3J 3J6

(902)555-8165

CAREER QUALIFICATIONS   Technical writer trained in
    preparation of manuals, catalogues, and instructional
    materials. Experienced in writing computer
    documentation containing syntax formats.

WORK EXPERIENCE   Dalhousie University, Halifax, NS,
    Reading and Writing Specialist, English Language
    Centre, March-July 19XX, January-March 19XX.

    Created individual lesson plans for each student
    assigned to the Reading and Writing Laboratory
    and developed materials for use in Laboratory
    programs. Ran the Laboratory for approximately 100
    students 20 hours a week. Kept all records of
    students' work and prepared written and oral
    reports on student progress and laboratory
    operations.

    Tutor of International Students, September 19XX-
    present. Integrated students into an urban school
    and community and was a positive role model
    educationally and socially.

    W. M. Mercer, Inc., Halifax, NS, September-December
    19XX.
    Data processing and general office duties. Created
    and implemented a CRT search system for office
    personnel.

SPECIAL SKILLS   C programming language; Word,
    WordPerfect, Lotus 1-2-3, Excel.

EDUCATION   Dalhousie University, Halifax, NS, Bachelor
    of Arts, June 19XX.

    Concentration: English with minors in Economics and
    Technical Communications.

    Activities: Selected to serve on the Residence
    Judicial Board, a faculty-staff-student group that
    adjudicates residence-hall disputes; campus newspaper
    reporter; yearbook staff.

40 Writing Under Pressure

When you write under the pressure of time constraints, you are expected to write as completely and clearly as possible. The demands of writing under pressure can sometimes seem overwhelming, but if you break the challenge into small, sequential steps and then focus on each step in turn, you can succeed. If you tend to freeze under pressure, force yourself to take some slow, deep breaths and use a relaxation technique such as counting backwards from ten. When you turn to the task, remember to break the whole into parts so that the process is easier to work through.

Writing answers for essay tests is one of the most important writing tasks that you face in your postsecondary education. Common in the social sciences and humanities, essay tests are becoming increasingly common in the natural sciences as well. Essay tests give you the chance to synthesize and apply your knowledge, thereby helping your instructor determine what you have learned. Essay tests demand that you recall information and also put assorted pieces of that information into contexts that lead to generalizations you can support.

40a Understanding cue words and key words

Most essay questions contain what is sometimes called a **cue word,** a word of direction that tells what the content of your answer is expected to emphasize. Knowing the major cue words and their meanings can increase your ability to plan efficiently and to write effectively. Be guided by the list of cue words and sample essay-test questions in Chart 157.

Each essay question also has one or more **key words** that tell you the information, topics, and ideas you are to write about. For example, in the question "Criticize the architectural function of the modern football stadium," the cue word is "criticize," and the key words are "architectural function" and "football stadium." To answer the question successfully, you must define "architectural function," then describe the typical modern football stadium (mentioning major variations when important), and then discuss how well the typical modern football stadium fits your definition of "architectural function."

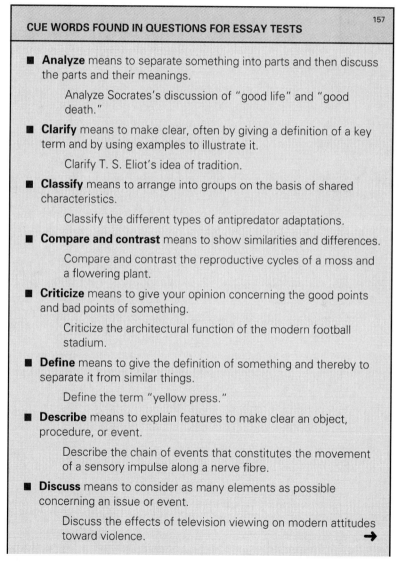

CUE WORDS FOUND IN QUESTIONS FOR ESSAY TESTS

157

- **Analyze** means to separate something into parts and then discuss the parts and their meanings.

  Analyze Socrates's discussion of "good life" and "good death."

- **Clarify** means to make clear, often by giving a definition of a key term and by using examples to illustrate it.

  Clarify T. S. Eliot's idea of tradition.

- **Classify** means to arrange into groups on the basis of shared characteristics.

  Classify the different types of antipredator adaptations.

- **Compare and contrast** means to show similarities and differences.

  Compare and contrast the reproductive cycles of a moss and a flowering plant.

- **Criticize** means to give your opinion concerning the good points and bad points of something.

  Criticize the architectural function of the modern football stadium.

- **Define** means to give the definition of something and thereby to separate it from similar things.

  Define the term "yellow press."

- **Describe** means to explain features to make clear an object, procedure, or event.

  Describe the chain of events that constitutes the movement of a sensory impulse along a nerve fibre.

- **Discuss** means to consider as many elements as possible concerning an issue or event.

  Discuss the effects of television viewing on modern attitudes toward violence. ➔

CUE WORDS FOUND IN QUESTIONS FOR ESSAY TESTS *(continued)*

- **Evaluate** means to give your opinion about the value of something.

  Evaluate Nellie McClung's contribution to feminism in Canada.

- **Explain** means to make clear or intelligible something that needs to be understood or interpreted.

  Explain how the amount of carbon dioxide in the blood regulates rates of heartbeat and breathing.

- **Illustrate** means to give examples of something.

  Illustrate the use of symbolism in Thomas King's novel *Green Grass, Running Water.*

- **Interpret** means to explain the meaning of something.

  Give your interpretation of Margaret Avison's poem "The Swimmer's Moment."

- **Justify** means to show or prove that something is valid or correct.

  Justify the existence of labour unions in today's economy.

- **Prove** means to present evidence that cannot be refuted logically or with other evidence.

  Prove that smoking is a major cause of lung cancer.

- **Relate** means to show the connections between two or more things.

  Relate increases in specific crimes in 1932–33 to the prevailing economic conditions.

- **Review** means to re-examine, summarize, or reprise something.

  Review the structural arrangements in proteins to explain the meaning of the term *polypeptide.*

- **Show** means to point out or demonstrate something.

  Show what effects pesticides have on the production of wheat.

- **Summarize** means to repeat briefly the major points of something.

  Summarize the major benefits of compulsory education.

- **Support** means to argue in favour of something.

  Support the position that destruction of rain forests is endangering the planet.

40b Writing effective responses to essay-test questions

An effective response to an essay-test question is complete and logically organized. Here are two answers to the question "Classify the different types of antipredator adaptations." The first one is successful; the second is not. The sentences are numbered for your reference, and they are explained on page 776.

ANSWER 1

(1) Although many antipredator adaptations have evolved in the animal kingdom, they all can be classified into four major categories according to the prey's response to the predator. (2) The first category is hiding techniques. (3) These techniques include cryptic coloration and behaviour in which the prey assumes characteristics of an inanimate object or part of a plant. (4) The second category is early enemy detection. (5) The prey responds to alarm signals from like prey or other kinds of prey before the enemy can get too close. (6) Evasion of the pursuing predator is the third category. (7) Prey that move erratically or in a compact group are displaying this technique. (8) The fourth category is active repulsion of the predator. (9) The prey kills, injures, or sickens the predator, establishing that it represents danger to the predator.

ANSWER 2

(1) Antipredator adaptations are the development of the capabilities to reduce the risk of attack from a predator without too much change in the life-supporting activities of the prey. (2) There are many different types of antipredator adaptations. (3) One type is camouflage, hiding from the predator by cryptic coloration or imitation of plant parts. (4) An example of this type of antipredator adaptation is the praying mantis. (5) A second type is the defence used by monarch butterflies, a chemical protection that makes some birds ill after eating the butterfly. (6) This protection may injure the bird by causing it to vomit, and it can educate the bird against eating other butterflies (7) Detection and evasion are also antipredator adaptations.

Here is an explanation of what happens, sentence by sentence, in the two answers to the question about antipredator adaptations.

	ANSWER 1	**ANSWER 2**
Sentence 1	Sets up classification system and gives number of categories based on key word	Defines key word
Sentence 2	Names first category	Throwaway sentence—accomplishes nothing
Sentence 3	Defines first category	Names and defines first category
Sentence 4	Names second category	Gives an example for first category
Sentence 5	Defines second category	Gives an example for second (unnamed) category
Sentence 6	Names third category	Continues to explain example
Sentence 7	Defines third category	Names two categories
Sentence 8	Names fourth category	
Sentence 9	Defines fourth category	

Answer 1 sets about immediately answering the question by introducing a classification system as called for by the cue word, *classify*. Answer 2, on the other hand, defines the key word, a waste of time on a test that will be read by an audience of specialists. Answer 1 is tightly organized, easy to follow, and to-the-point. Answer 2 rambles, never manages to name the four categories, and says more around the subject than on it.

40c Using strategies when writing under pressure

If you use specific strategies when writing under pressure, you can be more comfortable and your writing will likely be more effective. As you use the strategies listed in Chart 158, remember that your purpose in answering questions is to show what you know in a clear, direct, and well-organized way.

The more you use the strategies in the chart and adapt them to your personal needs, the better you will use them to your advantage. Try to practise them, making up questions that might be on your test and timing yourself as you write the answers. Doing this offers you another benefit: If you study by anticipating possible questions and writing out the answers, you will be very well prepared if one or two of them show up on the test.

STRATEGIES FOR WRITING ESSAY TESTS	158

1. Do not start writing immediately.
2. If the test has two or more questions, read them all at the start. Determine whether you are supposed to answer all the questions. Doing this gives you a sense of how to budget your time either by dividing it equally or by allotting more for some questions. If you have a choice, select questions about which you know the most and can write about most completely in the time limit.
3. Analyze each question that you answer by underlining the cue words and key words (see 40a) to determine exactly what the question asks.
4. Use the writing process as much as possible within the constraints of the time limit. Try to allot time to plan and revise. For a one-hour test of one question, take about 10 minutes to jot down preliminary ideas about content and organization, and save 10 minutes to reread, revise, and edit your answer. If you suddenly are pressed for time—but try to avoid this—consider skipping a question that you cannot answer well or a question that counts less toward your total score. If you feel blocked, try free writing (see 2f) to get your hand and your thoughts moving.
5. Support any generalizations with specifics (see 4c about using the formula RENNS for being specific).
6. Beware of "going off the topic." Respond to the cue words and key words (see 40a) in the question, and do not try to reshape the question to conform to what you might prefer to write about. Remember, your reader expects a clear line of presentation and reasoning that answers the given question.

EXERCISE 40-1

Look back at an essay that you have written under time pressure. Read it over and decide whether you would change the content of your answer or the strategies you used as you were writing under pressure. List these specific strategies, and, if you think they were useful, add them to Chart 158.

PART

IX

Writing When English Is a Second Language

 When English is your second language, you face the special challenge of needing to learn characteristics of English that native-born writers take for granted. Part Nine begins with a special ESL Preface to set the context for your using the rest of Part Nine, which explains the features of English that tend to give non-native writers the most trouble. As you use Chapters 41 through 46, remember that learning to write English involves much more than studying separate features. As for writers in any language, the more time you spend actually writing, the faster you can become a fluent writer.

Preface for ESL Students

Do you sometimes worry when you write in English? If you ever do worry about your English writing, let me assure you that you have much in common with me and with many college and university students. But as an ESL writer, you face a special challenge because you must attend to every word, every phrase, every sentence, and every paragraph in a way that native speakers of English do not.

You may be reassured to know that any errors you make as an ESL writer indicate that you are progressing through necessary stages of second-language development. Eventually, when you have passed through all the stages that all language learners must, you should be a proficient writer of English.

Unfortunately, there are no shortcuts. As with progress in speaking, listening, and reading comprehension in a new language, passing through the various stages of language development takes time. Some students have more available time than others, and some students have a home or study environment that enables faster learning of a new language. However, no matter how fast a language skill is learned, all the stages of language development must be experienced. Just as most adults make mistakes when they learn to play a new sport, few people write fluently and without error when they compose a first draft of a piece of writing. In fact, only rarely have even the most noted and experienced writers ever written something perfectly the first time.

What can you do to progress as quickly as possible from one writing stage to another? You might start by trying to remember what the typical school writing is like in your first language. Try to recall how ideas are presented in writing in your native language, especially when information has to be explained and when a matter of opinion has to be argued.

In recalling the typical style of school writing in your native language, compare it with what you are learning about writing style in English. For example, most college and university writing has a very direct, straightforward basic structure. In a typical essay or research paper, the reader expects to find a **thesis statement**°,* which clearly states the overall message of the piece of writing, by the end of the first or second paragraph. Usually, each paragraph that follows relates directly to the thesis statement and starts with a sentence, called a **topic sentence**°, that tells the point of the paragraph. The rest of each paragraph usually supports the point by using reasons, examples, and other specific details. The final paragraph brings the essay or research paper to a reasonable, logical conclusion.

This handbook contains many examples of writing by college and university students. For essays, see sections 3f, 6h, and 37e. For research papers, see Chapters 34 and 35 and section 37e. Also, this handbook explains paragraph structures typically expected in college and university writing; see Chapter 4. By the way, these typical academic structures do not apply to novels, plays, poems, or articles in most newspapers and magazines.

Writing structures typical of your native language probably differ from those in this country. Always honour your culture's writing traditions and structures, for they reflect the richness of your heritage. At the same time, try to adapt to and practise the academic writing style characteristic of English-speaking Canada. Later, when you are writing fluently, your instructors likely will encourage you to practise other writing styles that are less common and that allow greater liberty in organization and expression.

Over the past twenty years, many interesting observations have been made about the distinctive variations in school writing styles among people of different cultures and language groups. Research about these contrasts is ongoing, so scholars hesitate to generalize about them. Even so, interesting differences seem to exist. Traditional French school essays usually begin with a series of points that are discussed in the body of the essay and then repeated in reverse order in the conclusion. Japanese school writing customarily begins with references to nature. In some African nations, a ceremonial, formal opening is expected to start school writing as an expression of respect for the reader.

The ESL chapters following this special ESL Preface are designed to help you focus on errors that many ESL writers make. I hope that Chapters 41 through 46 can be of great use to you.

I hope also that the rest of this handbook will become your trusted companion. Throughout its pages, ESL Notes (signalled by the symbol ◆ preceding and following them) and various kinds of Alerts (signalled by the symbols ❖ and ✦ preceding and following them) present information in related contexts that can help you as you acquire Canadian English-language writing skills. A directory of selected ESL

Notes and Alerts follows this Preface to help you locate ones that may be especially useful to you.

Lynn Quitman Troyka

DIRECTORY OF ESL NOTES AND SELECTED ALERTS

- Recognizing noun suffixes: ESL Note, page 175
- Recognizing adjective suffixes: ESL Note, page 178
- Not repeating a subject with a personal pronoun in the same clause: ESL Note, page 185
- Using *to* and *for* with indirect objects: ESL Note, page 186
- Phrasing indirect questions: ESL Note, page 195
- Changing verb form in only one verb in a verb phrase: ESL Note, page 210
- Not omitting pronoun subjects: ESL Note, page 244
- Not omitting *it* included in an expletive (subject filler): ESL Note, page 248
- Revising long sentences: ESL Note, page 360
- Using computerized thesauruses cautiously: Computer Alert, page 402
- Using only one end-punctuation mark: Punctuation Alert, page 441

41 ESL Singulars and Plurals

How to Use Chapter 41ESL Effectively

1. Use this chapter together with these handbook sections:
   - 7a nouns°
   - 8c -*s* forms of verbs°
   - 11a–11l subject–verb agreement°
   - 12f nouns as modifiers°
2. Remember that throughout this handbook, a degree mark (°) after a word indicates that you can find the definition of the word in the Glossary of Terms toward the back of the book.
3. Use any **cross-references** (often given in parentheses) to find full explanations of key concepts.

This chapter can help you choose between using singulars° (one) and plurals° (more than one). Section 41a discusses the concept of count and noncount nouns°. Section 41b discusses determiners° and nouns. Section 41c discusses particularly confusing instances of the choice between singular and plural. Section 41d discusses some nouns with irregular plural forms.

41a Understanding the concept of count and noncount nouns

Count nouns name items that can be counted: *radio, street, idea, fingernail.* Count nouns can be singular° or plural° (*radios, streets*).

Noncount nouns name things that are thought of as a whole and not separated into separate, countable parts: *rice, knowledge, traffic.* Two important rules to remember about noncount nouns are that (1) they are never preceded by *a* or *an,* and (2) they are never plural.

783

Chart 159 lists eleven categories of uncountable items, giving examples in each category.

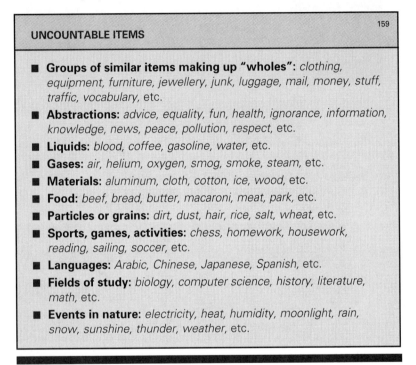

UNCOUNTABLE ITEMS 159

- **Groups of similar items making up "wholes":** *clothing, equipment, furniture, jewellery, junk, luggage, mail, money, stuff, traffic, vocabulary,* etc.
- **Abstractions:** *advice, equality, fun, health, ignorance, information, knowledge, news, peace, pollution, respect,* etc.
- **Liquids:** *blood, coffee, gasoline, water,* etc.
- **Gases:** *air, helium, oxygen, smog, smoke, steam,* etc.
- **Materials:** *aluminum, cloth, cotton, ice, wood,* etc.
- **Food:** *beef, bread, butter, macaroni, meat, park,* etc.
- **Particles or grains:** *dirt, dust, hair, rice, salt, wheat,* etc.
- **Sports, games, activities:** *chess, homework, housework, reading, sailing, soccer,* etc.
- **Languages:** *Arabic, Chinese, Japanese, Spanish,* etc.
- **Fields of study:** *biology, computer science, history, literature, math,* etc.
- **Events in nature:** *electricity, heat, humidity, moonlight, rain, snow, sunshine, thunder, weather,* etc.

Some nouns can be countable or uncountable depending on their meaning in a sentence. Most of these nouns name things that can be meant either individually or as "wholes" made up of individual parts.

COUNT	You have a **hair** on your sleeve. [In this sentence, *hair* is meant as an individual, countable item.]
NONCOUNT	Kioko has black **hair**. [In this sentence, *hair* is meant as a whole.]
COUNT	The **rains** were late last year. [In this sentence, *rains* is meant as individual, countable occurrences of rain.]
NONCOUNT	The **rain** is soaking the garden. [In this sentence, particles of *rain* are meant as a whole.]

When you are editing your writing (see Chapter 4), be sure that you have not added a plural *-s* to any noncount nouns, for they are always singular in form.

41b
ESL

❖ VERB ALERT: Be sure to use a singular verb with any noncount noun that functions as a subject° in a clause. ❖

To check whether a noun is count or noncount, look it up in a dictionary that notes the distinction. For example, in the *Longman Dictionary of American English,* count nouns are indicated by [C] and noncount nouns are indicated by [U] (for uncountable). Nouns that have both count and noncount meanings are marked [C;U].

41b Using determiners with singular and plural nouns

Determiners, also called *expressions of quantity,* are used to tell "how much" or "how many" about nouns. Other names for determiners include *limiting adjectives°, noun markers,* and *articles°.* (For information about articles—the words *a, an,* and *the*—see Chapter 42ESL.)

Choosing the right determiner with a noun can depend on whether the noun is noncount° or count° (see 41a). For count nouns, you must also decide whether the noun is singular or plural. Chart 160 lists many determiners and the kinds of nouns that they can accompany.

DETERMINERS TO USE WITH COUNT AND NONCOUNT NOUNS 160

GROUP 1: DETERMINERS FOR SINGULAR COUNT NOUNS

With every **singular count noun**, always use one of the determiners listed in Group 1.

a, an, the

| **a house** | **an egg** | **the car** |

one, any, some, every, each, either, neither, another, the other

| **any house** | **each egg** | **another car** |

my, our, your, his, her, its, their, nouns with *'s* or *s'*

| **your house** | **its egg** | **Connie's car** |

this, that

| **this house** | **that egg** | **this car** |

one, no, the first, the second etc.

| **one house** | **no egg** | **the fifth car** |

➔

GROUP 2: DETERMINERS FOR PLURAL COUNT NOUNS

All the determiners listed in Group 2 can be used with **plural count nouns**. Plural count nouns can also be used without determiners, as discussed in section 42b.

the

the bicycles	**the rooms**	**the ideas**

some, any, both, many, more, most, few, fewer, the fewest, a number of, other, several, all, all the, a lot of

some bicycles	**many rooms**	**all ideas**

my, our, your, his, her, its, their, nouns with 's or s'

our bicycles	**her rooms**	**students' ideas**

these, those

these bicycles	**those rooms**	**these ideas**

no, two, three, four, the first, the second, the third, etc.

no bicycles	**four rooms**	**the first ideas**

GROUP 3: DETERMINERS FOR NONCOUNT NOUNS

All the determiners listed in Group 3 can be used with noncount nouns (always singular). Noncount nouns can also be used without determiners, as discussed in section 42b.

the

the porridge	**the rain**	**the pride**

some, any, much, more, most, other, the other, little, less, the least, enough, all, all the, a lot of

enough porridge	**a lot of rain**	**more pride**

my, our, your, his, her, its, their, nouns with 's or s'

their porridge	**India's rain**	**your pride**

this, that

this porridge	**that rain**	**this pride**

no, the first, the second, the third, etc.

no porridge	**the first rain**	**no pride**

❖ USAGE ALERT: The phrases *a few* and *a little* convey the meaning "some": *I have **a few** rare books* means "I have *some* rare books." *They are worth **a little** money* means "They are worth *some* money."

786

Without the word *a*, the words *few* and *little* convey the meaning "almost none": *I have **few*** [or *very few*] *books* means "I have *almost no* books." *They are worth **little** money* means "They are worth *almost no* money." ♣

Using correct forms in *one of* constructions, for nouns used as adjectives, and with *States* in names or titles

One of *constructions*

One of constructions include *one of the* and a noun° or *one of* followed by an adjective°-noun combination (*one of my hats, one of those ideas*). Always use a plural noun as the object° when you use *one of the* with a noun or an adjective-noun combination.

NO	One of the **reason** to live here is the beach.
YES	One of the **reasons** to live here is the beach.
NO	One of her best **friend** has moved away.
YES	One of her best **friends** has moved away.

The verb° in these constructions is always singular because it agrees with the singular *one*, not with the plural noun: *One of the most important inventions of the twentieth century **is*** [not *are*] *television*.

For advice about verb forms that go with *one of the . . . who* constructions, see section 11k.

Nouns used as adjectives

Adjectives° in English do not have plural forms. When you use an adjective with a plural noun, make the noun plural but not the adjective: *the **green*** [not *greens*] *leaves*. Be especially careful when you use as an adjective a word that can also function as a noun.

The bird's wingspan is 25 **centimetres**. [*Centimetres* is functioning as a noun.]

The bird has a 25-**centimetre** wingspan. [*Centimetre* is functioning as an adjective.]

Do not add *-s* (or *-es*) to the adjective even when it is modifying a plural noun or pronoun.

NO	Many **Canadians** students are avid fans of off-road racing.
YES	Many **Canadian** students are avid fans of off-road racing.

Names or titles that include the word States

States is a plural word. However, names such as the *United States* or the *Organization of American States* refer to singular things—one country and one an organization, even though made up of many states. When *States* is part of a name or title referring to one thing, the name is a singular noun and therefore requires a singular verb.

NO   The United **States** have a large entertainment industry.

          The United **State** has a large entertainment industry.

YES   The United **States has** a large entertainment industry.

41d Using nouns with irregular plurals

Some English nouns have irregular spellings. In addition to those discussed in chart 101 in section 22c, here are others that often cause difficulties.

Plurals of foreign nouns and other irregular nouns

Whenever you are unsure whether a noun is plural, look it up in a dictionary. If no plural is given for a singular noun, add an *-s*.

Many nouns from other languages that are used unchanged in English have only one plural. If two plurals are listed in the dictionary, look carefully for differences in meaning. Some words, for example, keep the plural form from the original language for scientific usage and have another English-form plural for nonscientific contexts: *formula, formulae, formulas; appendix, appendices, appendixes; index, indices, indexes; medium, media, mediums; cactus, cacti, cactuses;* and *fungus, fungi, funguses.*

Words from Latin that end in *-is* in their singular form become plural by substituting *-es: parenthesis, parentheses; thesis, theses; oasis, oases,* for example.

Other words

Medical terms for diseases involving an inflammation end in *-itis: tonsillitis, appendicitis.* They are always singular.

The word *news,* although it ends in *s,* is always singular: *The **news is** encouraging.* The words *people, police,* and *clergy* are always plural even though they do not end in *s: The **police are** prepared.*

EXERCISE 41-1

Consulting Chapter 41, select the correct choice from the words in parentheses and write it in the blank.

EXAMPLE   In the United States and Canada, the (popularities, popularity) **popularity** of cats as pets (are, is) **is** rapidly outstripping that of dogs.

1.   One of the main (reason, reasons) _____ may be the recent change in (North American, North Americans) _____ lifestyles.

2.   Many people in Canada and the (United State, United States) _____ are moving from big houses with large yards to small apartments with (three-metres, three-metre) _____ balconies.

3.   Dogs must be walked, even in (rain, rains) _____ and (snow, snows) _____ .

4.   People also are spending (many, much) _____ time away from home.

5.   As long as they have sufficient (food, foods) _____ and (waters, water) _____ , cats can safely be left alone for a few days.

42 ESL Articles

42 Articles

How to Use Chapter 42 ESL Effectively

1. Use this chapter together with these handbook sections.
    - 7a articles° and nouns°
    - 41a singulars° and plurals° with count nouns° and non-count nouns°
    - 41b determiners° with count and noncount nouns
2. Remember that throughout this handbook, **a degree mark (°)** after a word indicates that you can find the definition of the word in the Glossary of Terms toward the back of the book.
3. Also, use any **cross-references** (usually given in parentheses) to find full explanations of key concepts.

This chapter gives you guidelines for using articles. Section 42a discusses using articles with singular count nouns. Section 42b discusses using articles with plural count nouns and with noncount nouns (which are always singular). Section 42c discusses using articles with proper nouns° and with gerunds°.

42a Using *a, an,* or *the* with singular count nouns

The words *a* and *an* are called **indefinite articles.** The word *the* is called a **definite article.** Articles are one type of determiner. (For other determiners, see Chart 160 in 41b.) Articles signal that a noun will follow and that any modifiers between the article and the noun refer to that noun.

a chair	**the** computer
a cold, metal chair	**the** lightning-fast computer

Every time you use a singular count noun, a common noun that names one countable item, the noun requires some kind of determiner; see Group 1 in Chart 160 (in Chapter 41) for a list. To choose between *a* or *an* and *the*, you need to determine whether the noun is **specific** or **nonspecific**. A noun is considered specific when anyone who reads your writing can understand from the context of your message exactly and specifically to what the noun is referring.

For nonspecific singular count nouns, use *a* (or *an*). When the singular noun is specific, use *the* or some other determiner. Chart 161 can help you decide when a singular count noun is specific and therefore requires *the*.

✤ USAGE ALERT: Use *an* before words that begin with a vowel sound. Use *a* before words that begin with a consonant sound. Words that begin with *h* or *u* can have either a vowel or a consonant sound. Make the choice based on the sound of the first word after the article, even if that word is not the noun.

an idea	**an h**onour	**a u**seless umbrella
an umbrella	**a g**ood idea	**a h**istory book ✤

WHEN A SINGULAR COUNT NOUN IS SPECIFIC AND REQUIRES *THE*   161

- **Rule 1: A noun is specific and requires *the* when it names something unique or generally known.**

    The sun has risen above **the horizon**. [Because *sun* and *horizon* are generally known nouns, they are specific nouns in the context of this sentence.]

- **Rule 2: A noun is specific and requires *the* when it names something used in a representative or abstract sense.**

    I would like to know who chose **the unicorn** to be **the symbolic animal** on Canada's coat of arms. [Because *unicorn* and *symbolic animal* are representative references rather than references to a particular unicorn or animal, they are specific nouns in the context of this sentence.]

- **Rule 3: A noun is specific and requires *the* when it names something defined elsewhere in the same sentence or in an earlier sentence.**

    The ship **St. Roch** was the first vessel to navigate the Northwest Passage. [The name *St. Roch* denotes a specific ship.]

    The carpet in my bedroom is new. [*In my bedroom* defines exactly which carpet is meant, so *carpet* is a specific noun in this context.] ➜

I have **a computer** in my office. **The computer** is often broken. [*Computer* is not specific in the first sentence, so it uses *a*. In the second sentence, *computer* has been made specific by the first sentence, so it uses *the*.]

- **Rule 4: A noun is specific and requires *the* when it names something that can be inferred from the context.**
  Monday, I had to call **the technician** to fix it. [If this sentence follows the two sentences about a computer in Rule 3 above, *technician* is specific in this context.]

One common exception affects Rule 3 in Chart 161. A noun may still require *a* (or *an*) after the first use if one or more descriptive adjectives come between the article and the noun: *I bought* ***a sweater*** *today. It was* ***a*** [not *the*] ***red sweater***. Other information may make the noun specific so that *the* is correct. For example, *It was* ***the red sweater that I saw in the store yesterday*** uses *the* because the *that* clause makes specific which red sweater is meant.

42b Using articles with plural nouns and with noncount nouns

With plural nouns and noncount nouns, you must decide whether to use *the* or to use no article at all. (For guidelines about using determiners° other than articles with nouns, see Chart 160 in 41b.)

What you learned in section 42a about nonspecific and specific nouns can help you make the choice between using *the* or using no article. Chart 161 in section 42a explains when a singular count noun's meaning is specific and calls for *the*. Plural nouns and noncount nouns with specific meanings usually use *the* in the same circumstances. However, a plural noun or a noncount noun with a general or nonspecific meaning usually does not use *the*.

Geraldo grows **flowers** but not **vegetables** his garden. He is thinking about planting **corn** sometime.

Plural nouns

A plural noun's meaning may be specific because it is widely known.

The oceans are being damaged by pollution. [Because the meaning of *oceans* is widely understood, *the* is correct to use. This example is related to Rule 1 in Chart 161.]

A plural noun's meaning may also be made specific by a word, phrase°, or clause° in the same sentence°.

Geraldo sold **the daisies from last year's garden** to the florist. [Because the phrase *from last year's garden* makes *daisies* specific, *the* is correct to use. This example is related to Rule 3 in Chart 161.]

A plural noun's meaning usually becomes specific by being used in an earlier sentence.

Geraldo planted **tulips** this year. **The tulips** will bloom in April. [*Tulips* is used in a general sense in the first sentence, without *the*. Because the first sentence makes *tulips* specific, *the tulips* is correct in the second sentence. This example is related to Rule 3 in Chart 161.]

A plural noun's meaning may be made specific by the context.

Geraldo fertilized **the bulbs** when he planted them last October. [In the context of the sentences about tulips, *bulbs* is specific and calls for *the*. This example is related to Rule 4 in Chart 161.]

Noncount nouns

Noncount nouns are always singular in form (see 41a). Like plural nouns, noncount nouns use either *the* or no article. When a noncount noun's meaning is specific, use *the* before it. If its meaning is general or nonspecific, do not use *the*.

Kalinda served **rice** to us. She flavoured **the rice** with curry. [*Rice* is a noncount noun. This example is related to Rule 3 in Chart 161: By the second sentence, *rice* has become specific, so *the* is used.]

Kalinda served us **the rice that she had flavoured with curry.** [*Rice* is a noncount noun. This example is related to Rule 3 in Chart 161: *Rice* is made specific by the clause *that she had flavoured with curry*, so *the* is used.]

Generalizations with plural or noncount nouns

Rule 2 in Chart 161 tells you to use *the* with singular count nouns used in a general sense. With generalizations using plural or noncount nouns, omit *the*.

NO	**The tulips** are **the flowers** that grow from **the bulbs.**
YES	**Tulips** are **flowers** that grow from **bulbs.**
NO	**The dogs** require more care than **the cats** do.
YES	**Dogs** require more care than **cats** do.

42c Using *the* with proper nouns and with gerunds

Proper nouns

Proper nouns name specific people, places, or things (see 7a). Most proper nouns do not require articles°: *We visited **Lake Rossignol** with **Asha** and **Larry**.* As shown in Chart 162, however, certain types of proper nouns do require *the*.

Gerunds

Gerunds are present participles (the *-ing* form of verbs°) used as nouns: ***Skating** is invigorating.* Gerunds usually are not preceded by *the*.

PROPER NOUNS THAT USE *THE*   162

- **Nouns with the pattern *the* ... *of* ...**
  - **the** Dominion **of** Canada   **the** eleventh **of** November
  - **the** President **of** Mexico   **the** University **of** Paris
- **Plural proper nouns**
  - **the** United Arab Emirates
  - **the** Johnsons
  - **the** Rocky Mountains [but Mount Fuji]
  - **the** Vancouver Canucks
  - **the** Falkland Islands [but Long Island]
  - **the** Great Lakes [but Lake Louise]
- **Collective proper nouns (nouns that name a group)**
  - **the** Modern Language Association
  - **the** Society of Friends
- **Some (but not all) geographical features and regions**
  - **the** Amazon   **the** Gobi Desert   **the** Indian Ocean
  - **the** Beauce   **the** Outback   **the** Lake District
  - [Quebec]
- **A few countries and cities**
  - **the** Congo   **the** Sudan
  - **the** Hague   **The** Pas
  - [capital of the Netherlands]

NO   The **constructing** new bridges is necessary to improve traffic flow.

YES   **Constructing** new bridges is necessary to improve traffic flow.

Use *the* before a gerund when two conditions are met: (1) the gerund is used in a specific sense (see 42a) and (2) the gerund does not have a direct object°.

NO   **The designing** fabric is a fine art. [*Fabric* is a direct object of *designing*, so *the* should not be used.]

YES   **Designing** fabric is a fine art. [*Designing* is a gerund, so *the* is not used.]

YES   **The designing of fabric** is a fine art. [*The* is used because *fabric* is the object of the preposition° *of* and *designing* is meant in a specific sense.]

EXERCISE 42-1

Consulting Chapter 42, select the correct choice from the words in parentheses and write it in the blank.

EXAMPLE   For centuries, (a, an, the) **the** heart was regarded with awe by physicians.

1. As (a, an, the) _____ result, (a, an, the) _____ first surgeon to cut into (a, an, the) _____ human heart had to overcome many fears and superstitions.
2. Asked to guess when this surgery was first tried, most people would say in (a, an, the) _____ middle of (a, an, the) _____ twentieth century.
3. Heart surgery actually was first performed in 1893 by (a, an, the) _____ African-American surgeon named Daniel Hale Williams.
4. (A, An, The) _____ injured young man was brought to (a, an, the) _____ Chicago hospital with (a, an, the) _____ knife wound in (a, an, the) _____ heart.
5. Surgeon Williams cast aside age-old taboos and dared to operate—successfully—on (a, an, the) _____ heart.

Word Order

1. Use this chapter together with these handbook sections:
    - 7k–7o sentence° patterns
    - 7e adjectives°
    - 7p sentence types
    - 7f adverbs°
    - 7m modifiers°
    - 11f verbs° in inverted word order
    - 7o clauses°
2. Remember that throughout this handbook, **a degree mark (°)** after a word indicates that you can find the definition of the word in the Glossary of Terms toward the back of the book.
3. Also, use any **cross-references** (usually given in parentheses) to find full explanations of key concepts.

This chapter can help you with several issues of word order in sentences. Section 43a discusses standard word order for English sentences and important variations. Section 43b discusses the placement of adjectives. Section 43c discusses the placement of adverbs.

43a Understanding standard and inverted word order in sentences

In **standard word order**, the most common pattern for declarative sentences in English, the subject° comes before the verb°. (To better understand these concepts, review sections 7k–7o.)

SUBJECT   VERB

That book   was heavy.

With **inverted word order**, the main verb° or an auxiliary verb° comes before the subject. The most common use of inverted word order in English is forming **direct questions**. Questions that can be answered with "yes" or "no" begin with a form of *be* used as a main verb, or with an auxiliary verb (*be, do, have*), or with a modal auxiliary (*can, should, will*, and others—see Chapter 46ESL).

QUESTIONS THAT CAN BE ANSWERED WITH "YES" OR "NO"

MAIN VERB *BE*   SUBJECT

Was   that book heavy?

AUXILIARY
VERB   SUBJECT   MAIN VERB

Have   you   heard the noise?

MODAL
AUXILIARY
VERB   SUBJECT   MAIN VERB

Can   you   lift the book?

To form a yes/no question with a verb other than *be* as the main verb and when there is no auxiliary or modal as part of a verb phrase, use the appropriate form of the auxiliary verb *do*.

AUXILIARY
VERB   SUBJECT   MAIN VERB

Do   you   want me to put the book away?

A question that begins with a **question-forming word** like *why, when, where,* or *how* cannot be answered with "yes" or "no": **Why *did the book fall?*** Some kind of information must be provided to answer such a question; the answer cannot be "yes" or "no." Information is needed: for example, *It was too heavy for me.*

Most information questions follow the same rules of inverted word order as yes/no questions.

INFORMATION QUESTIONS: INVERTED ORDER

QUESTION
WORD   MAIN
         VERB *BE*   SUBJECT

Why   is   that book open?

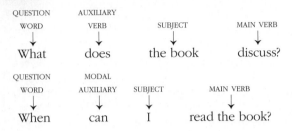

QUESTION WORD	AUXILIARY VERB	SUBJECT	MAIN VERB
↓	↓	↓	↓
What	does	the book	discuss?

QUESTION WORD	MODAL AUXILIARY	SUBJECT	MAIN VERB
↓	↓	↓	↓
When	can	I	read the book?

When *Who* or *What* functions as the subject in a question, however, use standard word order.

INFORMATION QUESTIONS: STANDARD ORDER

QUESTION WORD WORD	MAIN VERB
↓	↓
Who	dropped the book?

QUESTION WORD WORD	MAIN VERB
↓	↓
What	was the problem?

❖ ALERT: When a question has more than one auxiliary verb, put the subject after the first auxiliary verb.

FIRST AUXILIARY	SUBJECT	SECOND AUXILIARY	MAIN VERB
↓	↓	↓	↓
Would	you	have	replaced the book ❖

The same rules apply to emphatic exclamations: ***Was*** *that book heavy!* ***Did*** *she enjoy that book!*

Also, when you use negatives such as *never, hardly, ever, seldom, rarely, not only,* or *nor* to start a clause, use inverted order. These sentence pairs show the differences.

I have never seen a more exciting movie. [standard order]

Never have I seen a more exciting movie. [inverted order]

She is not only a talented artist **but also** an excellent musician.

Not only is she a talented artist, but **she is also** an excellent musician.

I didn't like the book, and **my husband didn't either.**

I didn't like the book, and **neither did my husband.**

❖ USAGE ALERT: With indirect questions, use standard word order: *She asked **how I dropped the book*** (not *She asked **how did I drop the book***). ❖

❖ STYLE ALERT: Word order deliberately inverted can be effective, when used sparingly, to create emphasis in a sentence that is neither a question nor an exclamation (also see 19f). ❖

43b **Understanding the placement of adjectives**

Adjectives modify—that is, they describe or limit—nouns°, pronouns°, and word groups that function as nouns (see section 7e). In English, an adjective comes directly before the noun it describes. However, when more than one adjective describes the same noun, several sequences may be possible. Chart 163 shows the most common order for positioning several adjectives.

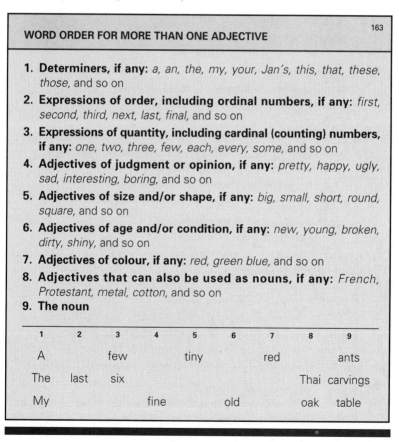

| | | | | **WORD ORDER FOR MORE THAN ONE ADJECTIVE** | | | | 163 |

WORD ORDER FOR MORE THAN ONE ADJECTIVE

1. **Determiners, if any:** *a, an, the, my, your, Jan's, this, that, these, those,* and so on
2. **Expressions of order, including ordinal numbers, if any:** *first, second, third, next, last, final,* and so on
3. **Expressions of quantity, including cardinal (counting) numbers, if any:** *one, two, three, few, each, every, some,* and so on
4. **Adjectives of judgment or opinion, if any:** *pretty, happy, ugly, sad, interesting, boring,* and so on
5. **Adjectives of size and/or shape, if any:** *big, small, short, round, square,* and so on
6. **Adjectives of age and/or condition, if any:** *new, young, broken, dirty, shiny,* and so on
7. **Adjectives of colour, if any:** *red, green blue,* and so on
8. **Adjectives that can also be used as nouns, if any:** *French, Protestant, metal, cotton,* and so on
9. **The noun**

1	2	3	4	5	6	7	8	9
A		few		tiny		red		ants
The	last	six					Thai	carvings
My			fine		old		oak	table

43c
Understanding the placement of adverbs

Adverbs modify—that is, describe or limit—verbs°, adjectives°, other adverbs, or entire sentences (see section 7f). Adverbs are usually positioned first, in the middle, or last in clauses. Chart 164 summarizes adverb types, what they tell about the words they modify, and where each type can be placed.

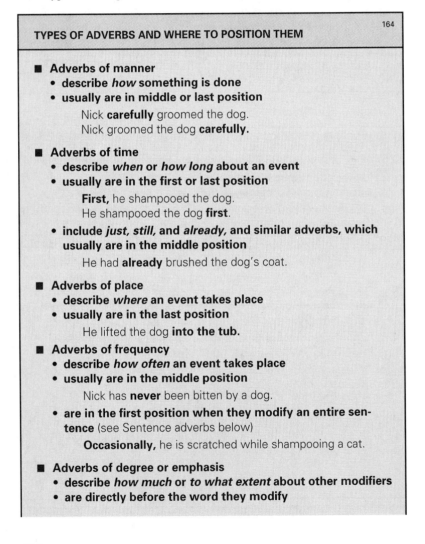

164

TYPES OF ADVERBS AND WHERE TO POSITION THEM

- **Adverbs of manner**
  - describe *how* something is done
  - usually are in middle or last position
    > Nick **carefully** groomed the dog.
    > Nick groomed the dog **carefully.**

- **Adverbs of time**
  - describe *when* or *how long* about an event
  - usually are in the first or last position
    > **First,** he shampooed the dog.
    > He shampooed the dog **first**.
  - include *just, still,* and *already,* and similar adverbs, which usually are in the middle position
    > He had **already** brushed the dog's coat.

- **Adverbs of place**
  - describe *where* an event takes place
  - usually are in the last position
    > He lifted the dog **into the tub.**

- **Adverbs of frequency**
  - describe *how often* an event takes place
  - usually are in the middle position
    > Nick has **never** been bitten by a dog.
  - are in the first position when they modify an entire sentence (see Sentence adverbs below)
    > **Occasionally,** he is scratched while shampooing a cat.

- **Adverbs of degree or emphasis**
  - describe *how much* or *to what extent* about other modifiers
  - are directly before the word they modify

TYPES OF ADVERBS AND WHERE TO POSITION THEM *(continued)*

Nick is **extremely** calm around animals. [*Extremely* modifies *calm*]

- **include** *only*, which is easy to misplace (see 15b-1)

■ **Sentence adverbs**
  - **modify the entire sentence rather than just one word or a few words**
  - **include transitional words and expressions** (see 4d-1) **as well as *maybe, probably, possibly, fortunately, unfortunately, incredibly,* and others**
  - **are in first position**
    Incredibly, he was once asked to groom a rat.

❖ PUNCTUATION ALERT: Unless they are very short (fewer than five letters), adverbs in the first position are usually followed by a comma. ❖

❖ USAGE ALERT: Do not let an adverb in a middle position separate a verb from its direct object° or indirect object° (see section 15b-3). ❖

EXERCISE 43-1

Consulting Chapter 43, find and correct any errors in word order.

1. The antique glass beautiful vase shattered on the floor.
2. Lu Mi had not meant to break her favourite mother's jar.
3. She was so upset that almost she cried.
4. When Lu Mi's mother heard the sound of shattering glass, she ran into the room asking, ``You are all right?''
5. Knowing that Lu Mi had broken accidentally the vase, her mother was not angry extremely.

Prepositions

How To Use Chapter **44 ESL** Effectively

1. Use this chapter together with these handbook sections.
   - 7g prepositions°
   - 21a using appropriate language
2. Remember that throughout this handbook, **a degree mark (°)** after a word indicates that you can find the definition of the word in the Glossary of Terms toward the back of the book.
3. Also, use any **cross-references** (usually given in parentheses) to find full explanations of key concepts.

Prepositions function with other words in prepositional phrases°. Prepositional phrases usually indicate **where** (direction or location), **how** (by what means or in what way), or **when** (at what time or how long) about the words they modify.

This chapter can help you with several uses of prepositions, which function in combination with other words in ways that are often idiomatic. An idiom's meaning differs from the literal meaning of each individual word (see 20a). For example, *Yao-Ming* ***broke into*** a smile means that a smile appeared on Yao-Ming's face. However, the dictionary definitions of *break* and *into* imply that *broke into a smile* means "shattered the form of" a smile. Knowing which preposition to use in a specific context takes much experience reading, listening to, and speaking the language. A dictionary like the *Longman Dictionary of Contemporary English* or the *Oxford Advanced Learner's Dictionary* can be especially helpful when you need to find the correct preposition to use in cases not covered by this chapter. Section 44a lists many common prepositions. Section 44b dicusses prepositions with some expressions of time and place. Section 44c discusses combinations of verbs and prepositions called phrasal verbs°. Section 44d discusses common expressions using prepositions.

44a Recognizing prepositions

Chart 165 shows many common prepositions.

COMMON PREPOSITIONS				165
about	before	except for	near	through
above	behind	excepting	next	throughout
according to	below	for	of	till
across	beneath	from	off	to
after	beside	in	on	toward
against	between	in addition to	onto	under
along	beyond	in back of	on top of	underneath
along with	but	in case of	out	unlike
among	by	in front of	out of	until
apart from	by means of	in place of	outside	up
around	concerning	inside	over	upon
as	despite	in spite of	past	up to
as for	down	instead of	regarding	with
at	during	into	round	within
because of	except	like	since	without

44b Using prepositions with expressions of time and place

Chart 166 shows how to use the prepositions *in, at,* and *on* to deliver some common kinds of information about time and place. The chart, however, does not cover every preposition that indicates time or place, nor does it cover all uses of *in, at,* and *on.* For example, it does not explain the subtle difference in meaning delivered by the prepositions *at* and *in* in these two correct sentences: *I have a chequing account **at***

803

that bank and *I have a safe-deposit box **in** that bank.* Also, the chart does not include expressions that operate outside the general rules. (Both these sentences are correct: *You ride **in** the car* and *You ride **on** the bus.*)

USING *IN, AT,* AND *ON* TO SHOW TIME AND PLACE 166

TIME

- ***in*** **a year or a month** (*during* is also correct but less common)

    in 1995   **in** May

- ***in*** **a period of time**

    in a few months (seconds, days, years)

- ***in*** **a period of the day**

    in the morning (afternoon, evening)
    in the daytime (morning, evening) *but* **at** night

- ***on*** **a specific day**

    on Friday   **on** my birthday

- ***at*** **a specific time or period of time**

    at noon   **at** 2:00   **at** dawn   **at** nightfall
    at takeoff (the time a plane leaves)
    at breakfast (the time a specific meal takes place)

PLACE

- ***in*** **a location surrounded by something else**

    in Alberta
    in Utah
    in downtown Bombay
    in the kitchen
    in the apartment   **in** the bathtub

- ***at*** **a specific location**

    at your house   **at** the bank
    at the corner of Third Avenue and Main Street

- ***on*** **the top or the surface of something**

    on page 20
    on the second floor, but **in** the attic or **in** the basement
    on Wellington Street
    on the mezzanine
    on street level

44c Using prepositions in phrasal verbs

Phrasal verbs, also called *two-word verbs* and *three-word verbs,* are verbs° that combine with prepositions to deliver their meaning.

In some phrasal verbs, the verb and the preposition should not be separated by other words: ***Look at** the moon* [not ***Look** the moon **at**]*. In **separable phrasal verbs,** other words in the sentence can separate the verb and the preposition without interfering with meaning: *I **threw away** my homework* is as correct as *I **threw** my homework **away**.*

Here is a list of some common phrasal verbs. The ones that cannot be separated are marked with an asterisk (*).

LIST OF SELECTED PHRASAL VERBS

ask out	get along with*	look into
break down	get back	look out for*
bring about	get off*	look over
call back	go over*	make up
drop off	hand in	run across*
figure out	keep up with*	speak to*
fill out	leave out	speak with*
fill up	look after*	throw away
find out	look around	throw out

Position a pronoun° object° between the words of a separable phrasal verb: *I threw **it** away.* Also, you can position an object phrase of several words between the parts of a separable phrasal verb: *I threw **my research paper** away.* However, when the object is a clause, do not let it separate the parts of the phrasal verb: *I threw away **all the papers that I wrote last year**.*

Many phrasal verbs are informal and are used more in speaking than in writing. For academic writing, a more formal verb may be more appropriate than a phrasal verb. In a research paper, for example, *propose* or *suggest* might be better choices than *come up with*. For academic writing, acceptable phrasal verbs include *believe in, benefit from, concentrate on, consist of, depend on, dream of* (or *dream about*), *insist on, participate in, prepare for,* and *stare at.* None of these phrasal verbs can be separated.

EXERCISE 44-1

Consulting Chapter 44 and using the list of phrasal verbs in section 44b, write a one- or two-paragraph description of a typical day at work or school in which you use at least five phrasal verbs. After checking a dictionary, revise your writing, substituting for the phrasal verbs any more formal verbs that you think may be more appropriate for academic writing.

44d Using prepositions in common expressions

In many common expressions, different prepositions convey great differences in meaning. For example, four prepositions can be used with the verb *agree* to create five different meanings.

agree to = to give consent [I cannot **agree to** buy you a new car.]

agree about = to arrive at a satisfactory understanding [We **agree about** your needing a car.]

agree on = to arrive at a satisfactory understanding [You and the seller must **agree on** a price for the car.]

agree with = to have the same opinion. [I **agree with** you that you need a car.]

agree with = be suitable or healthful [The idea of such a major expense does not **agree with** me.]

You can find entire books filled with English expressions that include prepositions. The list below shows a few that you are likely to use often.

LIST OF SELECTED EXPRESSIONS WITH PREPOSITIONS

ability in	different from	involved with [*someone*]
access to	faith in	knowledge of
accustomed to	familiar with	made of
afraid of	famous for	married to
angry with *or* at	frightened by	opposed to
authority on	happy with	patience with
aware of	in charge of	proud of
based on	independent of	reason for
capable of	in favour of	related to
certain of	influence on *or* over	suspicious of
confidence in	interested in	time for
dependent on	involved in [*something*]	tired of

45
ESL

Gerunds, Infinitives, and Participles

How to Use Chapter 45ESL Effectively

1. Use this chapter together with these handbook sections:
   - 7d verbals°
   - 11a subject–verb agreement°
   - 7k and 7l subjects° and objects°
   - 18a–18c parallelism
   - 8b principal parts° of verbs

2. Remember that throughout this handbook, a degree mark (°) after a word indicates that you can find the definition of the word in the Glossary of Terms toward the back of the book.

3. Also, use any **cross-references** (usually given in parentheses) to find full explanations of key concepts.

Participles are verb forms (see 8b). A verb's -*ing* form is its present participle. The -*ed* form of a regular verb is its past participle; irregular verbs form their past participles in various ways (for example, *bend, bent; eat, eaten; think, thought*—for a complete list, see Chart 59 in section 8d). Participles can function as adjectives° (*a **smiling** face, a **closed** book*).

A verb's -*ing* form can also function as a noun (***Sneezing*** *spreads colds*), which is called a **gerund**. Another verb form, the infinitive, can also function as a noun. An **infinitive** is a verb's simple or base form usually preceded by the word *to* (*We want everyone **to smile***). Verb forms—participles, gerunds and infinitives—functioning as nouns or modifiers are called **verbals**, as explained in section 7d.

This chapter can help you make the right choices among verbals. Section 45a discusses gerunds and infinitives used as subjects. Section 45b discusses verbs that are followed by gerunds, not infinitives. Section 45c discusses verbs that are followed by infinitives, not gerunds. Section 45d discusses meaning changes depending on whether certain verbs are followed by a gerund or an infinitive. Section 45e explains that meaning does not change for certain sense verbs° no matter whether they are followed by a gerund or an infinitive. Section 45f discusses differences in meaning between the present-participle form and the past-participle form of some modifiers.

45a Using gerunds and infinitives as subjects

Gerunds are used more commonly than infinitives as subjects. Sometimes, however, either is acceptable.

Choosing the right health club is important.

To choose the right health club is important.

❖ VERB ALERT: When a gerund or an infinitive is used alone as a subject, it is singular° and requires a singular verb. When two or more gerunds or infinitives create a compound subject°, they require a plural verb. (See sections 7k and 11d.) ❖

45b Using a gerund, not an infinitive, as an object after certain verbs

Some verbs° must be followed by gerunds° used as direct objects°. Other verbs must be followed by infinitives°. Still other verbs can be followed by either a gerund or an infinitive. (A few verbs can change meaning depending on whether they are followed by a gerund or an infinitive; see 45d.) Chart 167 lists common verbs that must be followed by gerunds, not infinitives.

Yuri **considered** *calling* [not *to call*] the mayor.

He **was having trouble** *getting* [not *to get*] a parking permit.

Yuri's boss **recommended** *taking* [not *to take*] someone who speaks English and Russian to the office that issues the permits.

Gerund after go

Go is usually followed by an infinitive: *We can go to see* [not *go seeing*] *a movie tonight*. Sometimes, however, *go* is followed by a gerund in phrases such as *go swimming, go fishing, go shopping,* and *go driving: I will go shopping* [not *go to shop*] *after work*.

45b
ESL

VERBS AND EXPRESSIONS THAT USE GERUNDS AFTER THEM		
acknowledge	detest	mind
admit	discuss	object to
advise	dislike	postpone
anticipate	dream about	practise
appreciate	enjoy	put off
avoid	escape	quit
cannot bear	evade	recall (remember)
cannot help	favour	recommend
cannot resist	finish	regret
complain about	give up	resent
consider	have trouble	resist
consist of	imagine	risk
contemplate	include	suggest
delay	insist on	talk about
deny	keep (on)	tolerate
deter from	mention	understand

Gerund after be + complement + preposition

Many common expressions use a form of the verb *be* plus a complement° plus a preposition. In such expressions, use a gerund, not an infinitive, after the preposition. Here is a list of some of the most frequently used expressions in this pattern.

LIST OF SELECTED BE + COMPLEMENT + PREPOSITION EXPRESSIONS

be (get) accustomed to   be interested in
be angry about   be prepared for
be bored with   be responsible for
be capable of   be tired of
be committed to   be (get) used to
be excited about   be worried about

We **are excited about *voting*** [not *to vote*] in the next election.

Who will **be responsible for *locating*** [not *to locate*] our polling place?

❖ USAGE ALERT: Always use a gerund, not an infinitive, as the object of a preposition. Be especially careful when the word *to* is functioning as a preposition in a phrasal verb (see 44c): *We are **committed to changing*** [not *to change*] *the rules.* ❖

45c **Using an infinitive, not a gerund, as an object after certain verbs**

Chart 168 lists selected common verbs° and expressions that must be followed by infinitives°, not gerunds°, as objects°.

She **wanted *to go*** [not *wanted going*] to the lecture.

Only three people **decided *to question*** [not *decided questioning*] the speaker.

168
VERBS AND EXPRESSIONS THAT USE INFINITIVES AFTER THEM

afford	claim	hope	promise
agree	consent	intend	refuse
aim	decide	know how	seem
appear	decline	learn	struggle
arrange	demand	like	tend
ask	deserve	manage	threaten
attempt	do not care	mean	volunteer
be left	expect	offer	vote
beg	fail	plan	wait
cannot afford	give permission	prepare	want
care	hesitate	pretend	would like

Infinitives after **be + complement**

Gerunds are common in constructions that use forms of the verb *be,* a complement°, and a preposition° (see 45b). However, use an infinitive, not a gerund, when *be* plus a complement is not followed by a preposition.

We **are eager *to go*** [not *going*] camping.

I **am ready *to sleep*** [not *sleeping*] in a tent.

Infinitives to indicate purpose

Use an infinitive in expressions that indicate purpose: *I read a book to learn more about Mayan culture.* This sentence means "I read a book for the purpose of learning more about Mayan culture." *To learn* delivers the idea of purpose more concisely (see Chapter 16) than expressions such as "so that I can" or "in order to."

Infinitives with the first, the last, the one

Use an infinitive after the expressions *the first, the last,* and *the one:* Soon-yi is **the first to arrive** [not *arriving*] *and the last to leave* [not *leaving*] *every day.*

Unmarked infinitives

Infinitives used without the word *to* are called **unmarked infinitives** or **bare infinitives**. An unmarked infinitive may be hard to recognize because it is not preceded by *to*. Some common verbs followed by unmarked infinitives are *feel, have, hear, let, listen to, look at, make* (meaning "compel"), *notice, see,* and *watch.*

> Please let me **take** [not *to take*] you to lunch. [unmarked infinitive]
>
> I want **to take** you to lunch. [marked infinitive]
>
> I can have Kara **drive** [not *to drive*] us. [unmarked infinitive]
>
> I will ask Kara **to drive** us. [marked infinitive]

The verb *help* can be followed by either a marked or an unmarked infinitive. Either is correct: *Help me **put** [or **to put**] this box in the car.*

❖ USAGE ALERT: Be careful to use parallel structure (see Chapter 18) correctly when you use two or more gerunds or infinitives after verbs. If two or more verbal objects° follow one verb, put the verbals into the same form.

NO	We went **sailing** and **to scuba dive**.
YES	We went **sailing** and **scuba diving**.
NO	We heard the wind **blow** and the waves **crashing**.
YES	We heard the wind **blow** and the waves **crash**.
YES	We heard the wind **blowing** and the waves **crashing**.

Conversely, if you are using verbal objects with compound predicates°, be sure to use the kind of verbal that each verb requires.

NO	We enjoyed **scuba diving** but do not plan **sailing** again. [*Enjoyed* requires a gerund object and *plan* requires an infinitive object; see Charts 166 and 167.]
YES	We enjoyed **scuba diving** but do not plan **to sail** again. ❖

45d Knowing how meaning changes when certain verbs are followed by a gerund or an infinitive as an object

With stop

The verb *stop* followed by a gerund° means "finish, quit." *Stop* followed by an infinitive means "stop or interrupt one activity to begin another."

> We **stopped eating**. [We finished our meal.]
>
> We **stopped to eat**. [We stopped another activity, such as driving, in order to eat.]

With remember *and* forget

The verb *remember* followed by an infinitive means "not to forget to do something": *I must* **remember to talk** *with Isa*. *Remember* followed by a gerund means "recall a memory": *I* **remember talking** *in my sleep last night*.

The verb *forget* followed by an infinitive means "to not do something": *If you* **forget to put** *a stamp on that letter, it will be returned*. *Forget* followed by a gerund means "to do something and not recall it": *I* **forget having put** *the stamps in the refrigerator*.

With try

The verb *try* followed by an infinitive means "make an effort": *I* **tried to find** *your jacket*. Followed by a gerund, *try* means "experiment with": *I* **tried jogging** *but found it too difficult*.

45e Understanding that meaning does not change whether a gerund or an infinitive follows certain sense verbs

Sense verbs° include words such as *see, notice, hear, observe, watch, feel, listen to,* and *look at*. The meaning of these verbs is usually not affected whether they are followed by a gerund° or an infinitive° as an object°. *I* **saw** *the water* **rise** and *I* **saw** *the water* **rising** both have the same meaning in English.

812

**45f
ESL**

EXERCISE 45-1

Consulting sections 45b, 45c, 45d, and 45e, write the correct form of verbal object (either a gerund or an infinitive) for each verb in parentheses.

EXAMPLE   Everyone would like (find) **to find** easier ways to use computers.

1. Think about (hold) _____ a computer on your lap and (write) _____ on its screen with a pen.
2. Several new computers will let you (do) _____ just that.
3. Engineers have developed these new machines, called "pen-based" computers, (replace) _____ pencil and paper.
4. No bigger than spiral notebooks and called electronic notebooks, pen-based computers have a special stylus for (write) _____ directly onto the flat screen.
5. No (train) _____ or (type) _____ is required.
6. Manufacturers hope (open) _____ up whole new markets.
7. Pen-based computers will help (revive) _____ slow sales of computers.
8. Many people who never considered (buy) _____ a computer before are starting (look) _____ seriously at the pen-based computer.
9. People who cannot be tied to a desk by a computer cord can now enjoy the convenience and power of a computer simply by (put) _____ down their clipboard and (pick) _____ up an electronic notebook.
10. I remember (wish) _____ for a notebook computer myself.

45f Choosing between -*ing* forms and -*ed* forms for adjectives

Deciding whether to use the -*ing* from (present participle°) or the -*ed* form (past participle° of a regular verb°) as an adjective° in a specific sentence can be difficult. For example, *I am **amused*** and *I am **amusing*** are both correct in English, but their meanings are very different. To make the right choice, decide whether the modified noun° or pronoun° is causing or experiencing what the participle describes.

Use a present participle (-*ing*) to modify a noun or pronoun that is the agent or the cause of the action.

> Mica described your **interesting** plan. [The noun *plan* causes what its modifier describes—interest; so *interesting* is correct.]
>
> I find your plan **exciting**. [The noun *plan* causes what its modifier describes—excitement; so *exciting* is correct.]

Use a past participle (-*ed* in regular verbs) to modify a noun or pronoun that experiences or receives whatever the modifier describes.

An **interested** committee wants to hear your plan. [The noun *committee* experiences what its modifier describes—interest; so *interested* is correct.]

Excited by your plan, I called a board meeting. [The pronoun *I* experiences what its modifier describes—excitement; so *excited* is correct.]

Here are frequently used participles that convey very different meanings, depending on whether the -*ed* or the -*ing* form is used.

amused, amusing	frightened, frightening
annoyed, annoying	insulted, insulting
appalled, appalling	offended, offending
bored, boring	overwhelmed, overwhelming
confused, confusing	pleased, pleasing
depressed, depressing	reassured, reassuring
disgusted, disgusting	satisfied, satisfying
fascinated, fascinating	shocked, shocking

EXERCISE 45-2

Consulting section 45f, choose the correct participle.

EXAMPLE: It can be a (satisfied, satisfying) **satisfying** experience to learn about the lives of artists.

1. Artist Frida Kahlo led an (interested, interesting) _____ life.
2. When she was 18, (horrified, horrifying) _____ observers say Kahlo (injured, injuring) _____ in a streetcar accident.
3. A (disappointed, disappointing) _____ Kahlo had to abandon her plan to study medicine.
4. Instead, she began to create paintings filled with (disturbed, disturbing) _____ images.
5. Some art critics consider Kahlo's paintings to be (fascinated, fascinating) _____ works of art even though many people find them (overwhelmed, overwhelming) _____ .

46 ESL | Modal Auxiliary Verbs

How to Use Chapter 46ESL Effectively

1. Use this chapter together with these handbook sections.
   - 7c recognizing verbs°
   - 8j progressive tenses°
   - 8e auxiliary verbs°
   - 8g verb tense°
   - 8l and 8m subjunctive mood°

2. Remember that throughout this handbook, **a degree mark (°)** after a word indicates that you can find the definition of the word in the Glossary of Terms toward the back of the book.

3. Also, use any **cross-references** (usually given in parentheses) to find full explanations of key concepts.

Auxiliary verbs are known as *helping verbs* because adding an auxiliary verb to a main verb° helps the main verb convey additional information (see 8e). For example, the auxiliary verb *do* is important in turning sentences into questions. *You have to sleep* becomes a question when *do* is added: *Do you have to sleep?* The most common auxiliary verbs are forms of *be, have,* and *do.* (Charts 60 and 61 in section 8e list the forms of these three verbs.)

Modal auxiliary verbs are one type of auxiliary verb. They include *can, could, may, might, should, had better, must, will, would,* and others discussed in this chapter. They have only two forms: the present-future and the past. Modals differ from *be, have,* and *do* used as auxiliary verbs in the ways discussed in Chart 169.

> **SUMMARY OF MODALS AND THEIR DIFFERENCES FROM OTHER** 169
> **AUXILIARY VERBS**
>
> - Modals in the present or future are always followed by the simple form of a main verb: *I might* **go** *tomorrow.*
>
> - One-word modals have no *-s* ending in the third-person singular: *She* **could** *go with me, you* **could** *go with me, they* **could** *go with me.* (The two-word modal *have to* changes form to agree with its subject: I **have to** leave, she **has to** leave.) Auxiliary verbs other than modals usually change form for third-person singular: *I* **have** *talked with her, he* **has** *talked with her.*
>
> - Some modals change form in the past. Others (*should, would, must,* which convey probability, and *ought to*) use *have* + a past participle. *I* **can** *do it* becomes *I* **could** *do it* in past-tense clauses about ability. *I* **could** *do it* becomes *I* **could have** *done it* in clauses about possibility.
>
> - Modals convey meaning about ability, necessity, advice, possibility, and other conditions: For example, *I can go* means "I am able to go." Modals do not indicate actual occurrences.

This chapter can help you use modals to convey shades of meaning. Section 46a discusses using modals to convey ability, necessity, advisability, possibility, and probability. Section 46b discusses using modals to convey preferences, plans or obligations, and past habits. Section 46c introduces modals in the passive voice°.

46a Conveying ability, necessity, advisability, possibility, and probability with modals

Conveying ability

The modal *can* conveys ability now (in the present), and *could* conveys ability before (in the past). These words deliver the meaning of "able to." For the future, use *will be able to.*

> We **can** work late tonight. [*Can* conveys present ability.]
>
> I **could** work late last night, too. [*Could* conveys past ability.]
>
> I **will be able to** work late next Monday. [*Will be able* is future; *will* here is *not* a modal.]

Adding *not* between a modal and the main verb makes the clause° negative: *We **can not*** (or ***cannot***) *work late tonight; I **could not** work late last night; I **will not be able** to work late next Monday.*

❖ USAGE ALERT: You will often see negative forms of modals turned into contractions°: *can't, couldn't, won't, wouldn't,* and others. Because contractions are considered informal usage by some instructors, you will never be wrong if you avoid them in academic writing except for reproducing spoken words. ❖

Conveying necessity

The modals *must* and *have to* convey the message of a need to do something. Both *must* and *have to* are followed by the simple form of the main verb. In the present tense, *have to* changes form to agree with its subject.

You **must** leave before midnight.

She **has to** leave when I leave.

In the past tense, *must* is never used to express necessity. Instead, use *had to.*

PRESENT TENSE

We **must** study today.

We **have to** study today.

PAST TENSE

We **had to** [not *We must*] take a test yesterday.

The negative forms of *must* and *have to* also have different meanings. *Must not* conveys that something is forbidden; *do not have to* conveys that something is not necessary.

You **must not** sit there. [Sitting there is forbidden.]

You **do not have to** sit there. [Sitting there is not necessary.]

Conveying advisability or the notion of a good idea

The modals *should* and *ought to* express the idea that doing the action of the main verb is advisable or is a good idea.

You **should** go to class tomorrow morning.

In the past tense, *should* and *ought to* convey regret or knowing something through hindsight. They mean that good advice was not taken.

You **should have** gone to class yesterday.

I **ought to have** called my sister yesterday.

The modal *had better* delivers the meaning of good advice or warning or threat. It does not change form for tense.

You **had better** see the doctor before your cough gets worse.

Need to is often used to express strong advice, too. Its past-tense form is *needed to.*

You **need to** take better care of yourself.

Conveying possibility

The modals *may, might,* and *could* can be used to convey an idea of possibility or likelihood.

We **may** become hungry before long.

We **could** eat lunch at the diner next door.

The past-tense forms for *may, might,* and *could* use these words followed by *have* and the past participle of the main verb.

I **could have studied** German in high school, but I studied Spanish instead.

Conveying probability

In addition to conveying the idea of necessity (see Conveying Necessity, p. 817), the modal *must* also can convey probability or likelihood. It means that a well-informed guess is being made.

Marisa **must** be a talented actress. She has been chosen to play the lead role in the school play.

When *must* conveys probability, the past tense is *must have* plus the past participle of the main verb.

I did not see Boris at the party; he **must have left** early.

EXERCISE 46-1

Consulting section 46a, fill in the blanks with the past-tense modal that expresses the meaning given in parentheses.

EXAMPLE   I (advisability) **should have** gone to bed at the regular time last night.

1.   I (advisability) _____ learned my lesson after what happened in class today.

2. Because I (necessity, no choice) _____ finish writing a paper, I stayed up until 3:00 a.m.

3. In class today, I (ability) _____ not stay awake.

4. The instructor (making a guess) _____ seen my eyes close.

5. I woke up instantly when I heard him say, "You (advice, good idea) _____ stayed in bed if you (necessity, no choice) _____ sleep, Mr. Lee."

46b Conveying preferences, plans, and past habits with modals

Conveying preferences

The modals *would rather* and *would rather have* express a preference. *Would rather* (present tense°) is used with the simple form° of the main verb° and *would rather have* (past tense°) is used with the past participle° of the main verb.

We **would rather see** a comedy than a mystery.

Carlos **would rather have stayed** home last night.

Conveying plan or obligation

A form of *be* followed by *supposed to* and the simple form of a main verb delivers a meaning of something planned or of an obligation.

I **was supposed to meet** them at the bus stop.

Conveying past habit

The modals *used to* and *would* express the idea that something happened repeatedly in the past.

I used to hate going to the dentist.

I would dread visiting the dentist each time.

❖ USAGE ALERT: Both *used to* and *would* can be used to express repeated actions in the past, but *would* cannot be used for a situation that lasted for a duration of time in the past.

NO	I **would** live in Corner Brook.
YES	I **used to** live in Corner Brook. ❖

46c Recognizing modals in the passive voice

Modals use the active voice°, as shown in sections 46a and 46b. In the active voice, the subject does the action expressed in the main verb° (see 8m–8o).

Modals can also use the passive voice°. In the passive voice, the doer of the main verb's action is either unexpressed or is expressed as an object° in a prepositional phrase° starting with the word *by*.

PASSIVE	The waterfront **can be seen** from my window.
ACTIVE	I **can see** the waterfront from my window.
PASSIVE	The tax form **must be signed by** the person who fills it out.
ACTIVE	The person who fills out the tax form **must sign** it.

EXERCISE 46-2

Consulting Chapter 46, select the correct choice from the words in parentheses and write it in the blank.

EXAMPLE I (would, used to) **used to** collect stamps.

1. Devi (should have, should have been) _____ hired by the bookstore manager.
2. The plane (must be landed, must have landed) _____ on time.
3. You (ought not to have, ought not have) _____ said that.
4. I am going to have some ice cream even though I (cannot, should not) _____ .
5. You (might not have been, might not have) _____ left your chequebook at home.

Usage Glossary

This usage glossary presents the customary manner of using particular words and phrases. *Customary manner*, however, is not as firm in practice as the term implies. Usage standards change. If you think a word's usage might differ from what you read here, consult a dictionary published more recently than this book.

As used here, *informal* indicates that the word or phrase occurs commonly in speech but should be avoided in academic writing. *Nonstandard* indicates that the word or phrase should not be used in standard spoken English and in writing.

Some commonly confused words appear in this Usage Glossary. For an extensive list of homonyms and other commonly confused words, see 22b. Parts of speech, sentence structures, and other grammatical terms mentioned in this Usage Glossary are defined in the Terms Glossary, which follows this Glossary.

a, an Use *a* before words beginning with consonants (*a dog, a grade, a hole*) or consonant sounds (*a one-day sale, a European*). Most North American English uses *a*, not *an*, with words starting with a pronounced *h*: *a* [not *an*] *historical event.*

accept, except *Accept* means "agree to; receive." As a verb, *except* means "exclude, leave out"; as a preposition, *except* means "leaving out": *Except* [preposition] *for one detail, the striking workers were ready to accept* [verb] *management's offer: They wanted the no-smoking rule excepted* [verb] *from the contract.*

advice, advise *Advice,* a noun, means "recommendation"; *advise,* a verb, means recommend; give advice": *My advice is to do what your physician advises.*

affect, effect As a verb, *affect* means "cause a change in; influence" (*affect* also functions as a noun in the discipline of psychology). As a noun, *effect* means "result or conclusion"; as a verb, it means "bring about": *Many groups effected* [verb] *amplification changes at their concerts after discovering that high decibel levels affected* [verb] *their hearing. Many fans still choose to ignore sound's harmful effects.*

aggravate, irritate *Aggravate* is used colloquially to mean "irritate." Use *aggravate* to mean "intensify; make worse." Use *irritate* to mean "annoy; make impatient."

all ready, already *Already* means "before; by this time"; *all ready* means "completely prepared": *The ballplayers were **all ready** and the manager had **already** given the lineup card to the umpire.*

all right Two words, never one (not *alright*).

all together, altogether *All together* means "in a group, in unison"; *altogether* means "entirely, thoroughly": *The sopranos, altos, and tenors were supposed to sing **all together**, but their first attempt was not **altogether** successful.*

allude, elude *Allude* means "refer to indirectly or casually"; *elude* means "escape notice": *They were **alluding** to budget cuts when they said that "constraints beyond our control enabled the suspect to **elude** us."*

allusion, illusion An *allusion* is an indirect reference to something; an *illusion* is a false impression or idea.

a lot Informal for *a great deal* or *a great many*; avoid it in academic writing.

a.m., p.m. (or **A.M., P.M.**) Use only with numbers, not as substitutes for the words *morning, afternoon,* or *evening*: *We will arrive in the **afternoon*** [not *in the p.m.*].

among, between Use *among* for three or more items and *between* for two items: *My roomates and I discussed **among** ourselves the choice **between** staying in school and getting full-time jobs.*

amount, number Use *amount* for uncountable things (*wealth, work, corn, happiness*); use *number* for countable items: *The **amount** of rice to cook depends on the **number** of dinner guests.*

and/or Appropriate in business and legal writing when either or both items it connects can apply: *This process is quicker if you have a modem **and/or** a fax machine.* Writing in the humanities usually expresses alternatives in words: *This process is quicker if you have a modem, a fax machine, or **both**.*

anymore Use *anymore* with the meaning "now, any longer" in negations or questions only: *No one knits **anymore**. For positive statements, use an adverb such as now: Summers are so hot **now*** [not anymore] *that holding yarn is unbearable.*

anyplace Informal for *any place* or *anywhere.*

anyways, anywheres Nonstandard for *anyway, anywhere.*

apt, likely, liable *Apt* and *likely* are used interchangeably. Strictly, *apt* indicates a tendency or inclination: *Allen is **apt** to leave early on Friday.* *Likely* indicates a reasonable expectation or greater certainty than *apt*: *I will likely go with him to the party.* (Some authorities in Canada do not allow this use of *likely* and prefer to use *probably* here.) *Liable* denotes legal responsibility or implies unpleasant consequences: *Maggie and Gabriel are **liable** to be angry if neither of us shows up.*

as, like, as if, as though Use *as*, not *like*, as a subordinating conjunction introducing a clause: *This hamburger tastes good, **as*** [not *like*] *a hamburger should.* Use *as if* (or *as though*), not *like*, to introduce a subjunctive or other conditional clause. *That hamburger tastes **as if*** [not *like*] *it had been grilled all day. As* and *like* can both function as prepositions in comparisons. Use *like* to suggest a point of similarity or an area of resemblance, but not complete likeness, between nouns or pronouns: *Mexico,* **like** [not *as*] *Argentina, belongs to the United States.* Use *as* to show equivalence: *Beryl acted **as*** [not *like*] *the moderator of our panel.* Also if the items are in prepositional phrases, use *as* even if you are suggesting only one point of similarity: *In Mexico, **as*** [not *like*] *in Argentina, Spanish is the main language.*

assure, ensure, insure *Assure* means "promise, convince"; *ensure* means "make certain or secure," *insure* means "indemnify or guarantee against loss" and is reserved for financial or legal certainty, as in insurance: *The agent **assured** me that he could **insure** my rollerblades but that only I could **ensure** that my elbows and knees would outlast the skates.*

as to Avoid as a substitute for *about: They answered questions **about*** [not *as to*] *their safety record.*

awful, awfully The adjective *awful* means "causing fear." Avoid it as a substitute for intensifiers such as *very* or *extremely.* In academic writing, also avoid the informal usage of the adverb *awfully* for *very* or *extremely.*

a while, awhile As two words, *a while* is an article and a noun that can function as a subject or object. As one word, *awhile* is an adverb; it modifies verbs. In a prepositional phrase, the correct form is *a while: for a while, in a while, after a while.*

bad, badly *Bad* is an adjective; use it after linking verbs. (Remember that verbs like *feel* and *smell* can function as either linking verbs or action verbs.) *Badly* is an adverb and is nonstandard after linking verbs; see 12d: *Farmers feel **bad** because a **bad** drought has **badly** damaged the crops.*

been, being *Been* is the past participle of the verb *be; being* is the present participle of *be,* used in the progressive form: *You **are being** [not *been*] silly if you think I believe you **have been** [not *being*] to Sumatra.*

being as, being that Nonstandard for *because* or *since: We forfeited the game **because** [not *being as* or *being that*] our goalie has appendicitis.*

beside, besides *Beside* is a preposition meaning "next to, by the side of": *She stood **beside** the new car, insisting that she would drive.* As a preposition, *besides* means, "other than, in addition to": *No one **besides** her had a driver's licence.* As an adverb, *besides* means "also, moreover": ***Besides**, she owned the car.*

better, had better Used in place of *had better, better* is informal: *We **had better** [not *We better*] be careful.*

breath, breathe *Breath* is a noun; *breathe* is a verb.

bring, take Use *bring* for movement from a distant place to a near place or to the speaker; use *take* for movement from a near place or from the speaker to a distant place: *If you **bring** a leash when you come to my house, you can **take** Vicious to the vet.*

but, however, yet Use *but, however,* and *yet* alone, not in combination with each other: *The economy is strong, **but** [not *but yet* or *but however*] unemployment is high.*

calculate, figure, reckon Informal or regional for *estimate, imagine, expect, think,* and similar words.

can, may *Can* indicates ability or capacity; *may* requests or grants permission. In negations, however, *can* is acceptable in place of *may: You **cannot** [or *may not*] leave yet.*

can't hardly, can't scarcely Nonstandard; double negatives.

censor, censure The verb *censor* means "delete objectionable material; judge"; *censure* means "condemn; reprimand officially."

chairman, chairperson, chair Many writers and speakers prefer the gender-neutral terms *chairperson* and *chair* to *chairman*; *chair* is more common than *chairperson*.

choose, chose *Choose* is the simple form of the verb; *chose* is the past-tense form: *I* **chose** *the movie last week, so you* **choose** *it tonight.*

cloth, clothe *Cloth* is a noun meaning "fabric"; *clothe* is a verb meaning "cover with garments or fabric; dress."

complement, compliment *Complement* means "bring to perfection, go well with; complete"; *compliment* means "praise; flatter": *They* **complimented** *us on the design of our experiment, saying that it* **complemented** *work done twenty years ago.*

conscience, conscious The noun *conscience* means "a sense of right and wrong"; the adjective *conscious* means "being aware or awake."

consensus of opinion Redundant; use *consensus* only.

continual(ly), continuous(ly) *Continual* means "occurring repeatedly"; *continuous* means "going on without interruption": *Intravenous fluids were given* **continuously** *for three days after surgery; nurses were* **continually** *hooking up new bottles of saline.*

data Plural of *datum*, a rarely used word. Informal usage commonly treats *data* as singular, but it should be treated as plural in academic writing.

different from, different than *Different from* is preferred for formal writing; *different than* is common in speech.

disinterested, uninterested *Disinterested* means "impartial"; *uninterested* means "indifferent; not concerned with."

emigrate from, immigrate to *Immigrate to* means "enter a country to live there"; *emigrate from* means "leave one country to live in another."

enthused Nonstandard substitution for the adjective *enthusiastic: Are you* **enthusiastic** [not enthused] *about seeing a movie?*

etc. Abbreviation for the Latin *et cetera*, meaning "and the rest." For writing in the humanities, avoid in-text use of *etc.*; acceptable substitutes are *and the like, and so on, and so forth.*

everyday, every day The adjective *everyday* means "daily" and modifies nouns; *every day* is an adjective-noun combination that functions as a subject or object: *I missed the bus* **every day** *last week. Being late for work has become an* **everyday** *occurrence.*

explicit, implicit *Explicit* means "directly stated or expressed"; *implicit* means "implied, suggested": *The warning on cigarette packs is* **explicit:** *"Smoking can kill you." The* **implicit** *message is "Don't smoke."*

fewer, less Use *fewer* for anything that can be counted (with count nouns): **fewer** *dollars,* **fewer** *fleas,* **fewer** *haircuts.* Use *less* with collective or other noncount nouns: **less** *money,* **less** *scratching,* **less** *hair.*

former, latter When two items are referred to, *former* signifies the first one and *latter* signifies the second. Do not use *former* and *latter* for references to more than two items.

go, say *Go* is nonstandard for *say, says,* or *said: After he stepped on my hand, he **said*** [not *he goes*], *"Your hand was in my way."*

good and Nonstandard intensifier: *They were exhausted* [not *good and tired*].

good, well *Good* is an adjective (***good*** *idea*). Using it as an adverb is non-standard. *Well* is the equivalent adverb: *run **well*** [not *run good*].

got, have *Got* is nonstandard in place of *have: What do we **have*** [not *got*] *for supper?*

have, of Use *have,* not *of,* after such verbs as *could, should, would, might, must: You should **have*** [not *should of*] *called first.*

have got, have got to Avoid using *have got* when *have* alone delivers your meaning: **I have** [not *have got*] *two more sources to read.* Avoid *have got to* for *must: I **must*** [not *have got to*] *turn in a preliminary thesis statement by Monday.*

hopefully An adverb meaning "with hope, in a hopeful manner" or "it is hoped that," *hopefully* can modify a verb, an adjective, or another adverb: *They waited **hopefully** for the plane to land. Hopefully* is commonly used as a sentence modifier with the meaning "I hope," but you should avoid this usage in academic writing: *I **hope*** [not *Hopefully*] *the plane will land safely.*

if, whether Use either *if* or *whether* at the start of a noun clause: *I don't know **if*** [or *whether*] *I want to dance with you.* In conditional clauses, use *whether* or (or *whether or not*) when alternatives are expressed or implied: *I will dance with you **whether or not** I like the music.* Similarly: *I will dance with you **whether** the next song is fast or slow.* Use *if* in a conditional clause that does not express or imply alternatives: ***If** you promise not to step on my feet, I will dance with you.*

imply, infer *Imply* means "hint or suggest without stating outright"; *infer* means "draw a conclusion from what is being expressed." A writer or speaker implies; a reader or listener infers: *When the Member of Parliament implied that she might begin taking intensive French lessons, reporters **inferred** that she had decided to run for leader of her party.*

incredible, incredulous *Incredible* means "extraordinary; not believable"; *incredulous* means "unable or unwilling to believe." A person would be *incredulous* in response to finding something *incredible: Listeners were **incredulous** as the freed hostages described **incredible** hardships they had experienced.*

inside of, outside of Nonstandard for *inside* or *outside: She waited **outside*** [not *outside of*] *the dormitory.*

irregardless Nonstandard for *regardless.*

is when, is where Avoid these constructions in giving definitions: *Defensive driving **involves drivers' staying alert*** [not *is when drivers stay alert*] *to avoid accidents that other drivers might cause.*

its, it's *Its* is a personal pronoun in the possessive case: *The dog buried **its** bone. It's* is a contraction of *it is* or *it has* (***It's** a hot day; **it's** hotter than usual because the humidity is high.*

kind, sort Use *this* or *that* with these singular nouns; use *these* or *those* with the plural nouns *kinds* and *sorts*. Also, do not use *a* or *an* after *kind of* or *sort of: Drink* **these kinds** *of fluids* [not this kind of fluids] *on* **this sort** *of* [not sort of a] *day.*

kind of, sort of Informal as adverbs meaning "in a way; somewhat": *The hikers were* **somewhat** [not kind of] *dehydrated by the time they got back to camp.*

later, latter *Later* means "after some time; subsequently"; *latter* refers to the second of two: *The college library stays open* **later** *than the town library; also, the* **latter** *is closed on weekends.*

lay, lie *Lay (laying, laid)* means "place or put something, usually on something else" and needs a direct object; *lie (lying, lay, lain)*, meaning "recline," does not take a direct object; see 8f. Substituting *lay* or *lie* is nonstandard: *Lay* [not lie] *the blanket down, and then* **lay** *the babies on it so they can* **lie** [not lay] *in the shade.*

leave *Leave* means "depart"; *let* means "allow, permit." *Leave* is nonstandard for *let*: *Let* [not leave] *me use your car tonight.*

lots, lots of, a lot of Informal for *many, much, a great deal:* **Many** [not A lot of] *bees were in the hive.*

may be, maybe *May be* is a verb phrase; *maybe* is an adverb: Our team **may be** tired, but **maybe** we can win anyway.

media Plural of *medium.* In most cases, a more specific word is preferable: *Television reporters offend* [not The media offend] *viewers by shouting questions at grief-stricken people.*

morale, moral *Morale* is a noun meaning "a mental state relating to courage, confidence, or enthusiasm." As a noun, *moral* means "ethical lesson implied or taught by a story or event"; as an adjective, *moral* means "ethical": *One* **moral** *to draw from corporate downsizings is that overstressed employees suffer from low* **morale**. *Under such stress, sometimes even employees with high* **moral** *standards steal time, supplies, or products from their employers.*

Ms. A woman's title free of reference to marital status, equivalent to *Mr.* for men.

off of Nonstandard for *off:* Don't fall **off** [not off of] the piano.

OK, O.K., okay All three forms are acceptable in informal writing. In academic writing, try to express meaning more specifically: *The weather was* **satisfactory** [not okay] *for the race.*

on account of Wordy; use *because* or *because of:* **Because of** [not On account of] *the high humidity, paper jams occur in the photocopier.*

percent, percentage Use *percent* with specific numbers: *2 percent, 95 percent.* Use *percentage* when descriptive words accompany amounts that have been expressed as percentages: *Less than* **6 percent** *of Canada's land is legally protected as wilderness, a smaller* **percentage** [not percent] *than is commonly believed.*

plus Nonstandard as a substitute for *and: The band will do three concerts in Hungary,* **and** [not plus] *it will tour Poland for a month.* Nonstandard as well as a substitute for *also, in addition, moreover:* **Also** [not Plus], *it may be booked to do one concert in Vienna.*

precede, proceed *Precede* means "go before"; *proceed* means "advance, go on, undertake, carry on": *Preceded by elephants and tigers, the clowns* **proceeded** *into the tent.*

pretty Informal qualifying word; use *rather, quite, somewhat,* or *very* in academic writing: *The flu epidemic was* **quite** [not *pretty*] *severe.*

principal, principle *Principle* means "a basic truth or rule." As a noun, *principal* means "chief person; main or original amount"; as an adjective, *principal* means "most important": *"During assembly, the* **principal** *said "A* **principal** *value in this society is the* **principle** *of free speech.*

raise, rise *Raise* (*raised, raising*) needs a direct object; *rise* (*rose, risen, rising*) does not take a direct object. Using these verbs interchangeably is nonstandard: *What if the mob* **rises** [not *raises*] *up and runs amok?*

rarely ever Informal; in academic writing, use *rarely* or *hardly ever: The groups* **rarely** [not *rarely ever*] *meet, so they* **hardly ever** [not *rarely ever*] *interact.*

real, really Nonstandard intensifiers.

reason is because Redundant; use *reason is that: One* **reason** *we moved away* **is that** [not *is because*] *we changed jobs.*

reason why Redundant; use either *reason* or *why: I still do not know the* **reason** *that* [or *I still do not know* **why,** not *the reason why*] *they left home.*

regarding, in regard to, with regard to Too stiff or wordy for most writing purposes; use *about, concerning,* or *for: What should I do* **about** [not *with regard to*] *dropping this course?*

respective, respectively The adjective *respective* relates the noun it modifies to two or more individual person or things; the adverb *respectively* refers to a second set of items in a sequence established by a preceding set of items: *After the fire drill, Dr. Pan and Dr. Moll returned to their* **respective** *offices, on the second and third floors,* **respectively.** (Dr. Pan has an office on the second floor; Dr. Moll has an office on the third floor.) Do not confuse *respective* and *respectively* with *respectful* and *respectfully,* which refer to showing regard for or honour to something or someone.

shall, will *Shall* was once used with *I* or *we* for future-tense verbs, and *will* was used with all other persons (*We* **shall** *leave Monday, and he* **will** *leave Thursday*); but *will* is commonly used for all persons now. Similarly, distinctions were once made between *shall* and *should. Should* is much more common with all persons now, although *shall* is used about as often as *should* in questions asking what to do: *Shall* [or *Should*] *I get your jacket?*

should, would Use *should* to express condition or obligation: *If you* **should** *see them, tell them that they* **should** *practise what they preach.* Use *would* to express wishes, conditions, or habitual actions: *If you* **would** *buy a VCR for me, I* **would** *tape all the football games for you.*

sometime, sometimes, some time The adverb *sometime* means "at an unspecified time"; the adverb *sometimes* means "now and then"; *some time* is an adjective-noun combination meaning "an amount or span of time": **Sometime** *next year we have to take qualifying exams. I* **sometimes** *worry about finding* **some time** *to study for them..*

stationary, stationery *Stationary* means "not moving"; *stationery* refers to paper and related writing products.

such Informal intensifier; avoid it in academic writing unless it precedes a noun introducing a *that* clause: *That play got terrible* [not *such bad*] *reviews. It was* **such** *a dull drama that it closed after one performance.*

supposed to, used to The final *d* is essential: *We were **supposed to*** [not suppose to] *leave early. I **used to*** [not use to] *wake up as soon as the alarm rang.*

sure Nonstandard for *surely* or *certainly: I was **certainly*** [not *sure*] *surprised at the results.*

than, then *Than* indicates comparison: *One is smaller **than** two. Then* relates to time: *He tripped and **then** fell.*

that, which Use *that* with restrictive (essential) clauses only; *which* can be used with both restrictive and nonrestrictive clauses, but many writers reserve *which* for nonrestrictive clauses only. *The house **that** Jack built is on Beanstalk Street, **which** [not that] runs past the reservoir.*

their, there, they're *Their* is possessive; *there* means "in that place" or is part of an expletive; *they're* is a contraction of *they are:* ***They're*** *going to their accounting class in the building **there** behind the library. **There are** twelve sections of Accounting 101.*

theirself, theirselves, themself Nonstandard for *themselves.*

thusly Nonstandard for *thus.*

till, until Both are acceptable; except in expressive writing, avoid the contracted form *'til* in academic writing.

to, too, two *To* is a preposition; *too* is an adverb meaning "also; more than enough"; *two* is the number: *When you go **to** Prince Edward Island, visit Green Gables. Go **to** one of the seaside restaurants for dinner, **too**. It won't be **too** expensive, because **two** people can share a lobster.*

toward, towards Both are acceptable; *toward* is somewhat more common in North America.

try and, sure and Nonstandard for *try to* and *sure to: If you **try to*** [not try and] *find a summer job, be **sure to*** [not sure and] *list on your résumé all the software programs you can use.*

unique An absolute adjective; use it without *more, most,* or other qualifiers, or use a different adjective: *Solar heating is **uncommon*** [not *rather unique*] *in northern latitudes. In only one home in Vermont, a **unique*** [not *very unique*] *heating system uses hydrogen for fuel.*

wait on Informal for *wait for*; appropriate in the context of persons giving service to others: *I had to **wait** a half hour for that clerk to **wait on** me.*

where Nonstandard for *that: I read in the newspaper **that*** [not where] *Michael Jordan might retire from basketball again.*

-wise The suffix *-wise* means "in a manner, direction, or position." Be careful not to attach *-wise* indiscriminately to create new words rather than using good words that already exist. When in doubt, check your dictionary to see that a *-wise* word you want to use is acceptable.

your, you're *Your* is possessive; *you're* is the contraction of *you are:* ***You're*** *generous to share **your** Internet time with us.*

Terms Glossary

This glossary defines important terms used in this handbook, including the ones marked with a degree symbol (°). Many of these glossary entries end with parenthetical references to the handbook section(s) or chapters where the specific term is most fully discussed.

absolute phrase A phrase containing a subject and a participle and modifying an entire sentence: *The semester* [subject] *being* [present participle of *be*] *over, the campus looks deserted.* (7n)

abstract noun A noun that names things not knowable through the five senses: **idea**, *respect.* (7a)

active voice An attribute of verbs showing that the action or condition expressed in the verb is done by the subject, in contrast with the passive voice, which conveys that the action or condition of the verb is done to the subject (8n and 8o)

adjective A word that describes or limits (modifies) a noun, a pronoun or a word group functioning as a noun: *silly, three.* (12).

adjective clause A dependent clause also known as a *relative clause.* An adjective clause modifies a preceding noun or pronoun and begins with a relative word (such as *who, which, that,* or *where)* that relates the clause to the noun or pronoun it modifies. Also see *clause.* (7o-2)

adverb A word that describes or limits (modifies) verbs, adjectives, other adverbs, phrases, or clauses: *loudly, very, nevertheless, there.*

adverb clause A dependent clause beginning with a subordinating conjunction that establishes the relationship in meaning between the adverb clause and its independent clause. An adverb clause modifies the independent clause's verb or the entire indepdendent clause. Also see *clause, conjunction.* (7o-2)

agreement The required match of number and person between a subject and verb or a pronoun and antecedent. A pronoun that expresses gender must match its antecedent in gender also. (11)

analogy An explanation of the unfamiliar in terms of the familiar. Like a simile, an analogy compares things not normally associated with each other;

but unlike a simile, an analogy does not use *like* or *as* in making the comparison. Analogy is also a rhetorical strategy for developing paragraphs. (21c, 4f-8)

analysis A process of critical thinking that divides a whole into its component parts in order to understand how the parts interrelate. Sometimes called division, analysis is also a rhetorical strategy for developing paragraphs. (5, 4f-6)

antecedent The noun or pronoun to which a pronoun refers. (10, 11m–11r)

antonym A word opposite in meaning to another word. (20a)

APA style See *documentation style.*

appositive A word or group of words that renames a preceding noun or noun phrase: *my favorite month,* **October.** (7m-3)

argument A rhetorical attempt to convince others to agree with a position about a topic open to debate. (1b, 6)

articles Also called *determiners* or *noun markers,* articles are the words *a, an,* and *the. A* and *an* are indefinite articles, and *the* is a definite article; also see *determiner.* (7a, 42)

assertion A statement. In developing a thesis statement, an assertion is a sentence that makes a statement and expresses a point of view about a topic. (2n)

audience The readers to whom a piece of writing is directed. (1c)

auxiliary verb Also known as a *helping verb,* an auxiliary verb is a form of *be, do, have, can, may, will,* and others, that combines with a main verb to help it express tense, mood, and voice. Also see *modal auxiliary verb.* (8e)

base form See *simple form.*

bibliography A list of information about sources. (33)

brainstorming Listing all ideas that come to mind on a topic, and then grouping the ideas by patterns that emerge. (2g)

case The form of a noun or pronoun in a specific context that shows whether it is functioning as a subject, an object, or a possessive. In modern English, nouns change form in the possessive case only (*city* = form for subjective and objective cases; *city's* = possessive-case form). Also see *pronoun case.* (9)

cause and effect The relationship between outcomes (effects) and the reasons for them (causes). Cause-and-effect analysis is a rhetorical strategy for developing paragraphs. (5i, 5k, 4f-9)

chronological order Also called *time order,* an arrangement of information according to time sequence; an organizing strategy for sentences, paragraphs, and longer pieces of writing. (4e)

citation Information to identify a source referred to in a piece of writing. See also *documentation.* (31, 33)

clause A group of words containing a subject and a predicate. A clause that delivers full meaning is called an *independent* (or *main) clause.* A clause that lacks full meaning by itself is called a *dependent* (or *subordinate*) clause. See *also, adjective clause, adverb clause, nonrestrictive element, noun clause, restrictive element.* (7o)

Terms-2

cliché An overused, worn-out phrase that has lost its capacity to communicate effectively: *smooth as silk, ripe old age.* (21d)

climactic order Sometimes called *emphatic order,* climactic order is an arrangement of ideas or information from least important to most important. (4e)

clustering See *mapping.*

coherence The clear progression from one idea to another using transitional expressions, pronouns, selective repetition, and/or parallelism to make connections between ideas. (4d)

collective noun A noun that names a group of people or things: *family, team.* (11h, 11r)

comma fault See *comma splice.*

comma splice The error that occurs when only a comma connects two independent clauses. (14)

common noun A noun that names a general group, place, person, or thing: *dog, house.* (7a)

comparative The form of a descriptive adjective or adverb that reflects a different degree of intensity between two: *blue, less blue; more easily, less easily.* See also *positive, superlative.* (12e)

comparison and contrast A rhetorical strategy for organizing and developing paragraphs by discussing a subject's similarities (comparison) and differences (contrast). (4f-7)

complement An element after a verb that completes the predicate, such as a direct object after an action verb or a noun or adjective after a linking verb. Also *see object complement, predicate adjective, predicate nominative, subject complement.*

complete predicate See *predicate.*

complete subject See *subject.*

complex sentence See *sentence types.*

compound predicate See *predicate.*

compound sentence See *sentence types.*

compound subject See *subject.*

concrete noun A noun naming things that can be seen, touched, heard, smelled, or tasted: *smoke, sidewalk.* (7a)

conjunction A word that connects or otherwise establishes a relationship between two or more words, phrases, or clauses. Also see *coordinating conjunction, correlative conjunction,* and *subordinating conjunction.*

coordinating conjunction A conjunction that joins two or more grammatically equivalent structures: *and, or, for, nor, but, so, yet.*

coordination The use of grammatically equivalent forms to show a balance or sequence of ideas. (17a–17d)

correlative conjunction A pair of words that joins equivalent grammatical structures, including *both ... and, either ... or, neither ... nor, not only ... but.*

count noun A noun that names items that can be counted: *radio, street, idea, fingernail.* (41a–41b, 42a–42b)

critical response Formally, an essay summarizing a source's central point or main idea and then presenting the writer's synthesized reactions in response. (5g)

cumulative sentence The most common structure for a sentence, with the subject and verb first, followed by modifiers adding details; also called a *loose sentence.* (19e)

dangling modifier A modifier that attaches its meaning illogically, either because it is closer to another noun or pronoun than to its true subject or because its true subject is not expressed in the sentence. (15c)

declarative sentence A sentence that makes a statement: *Sky diving is exciting.* Also see *exclamatory sentence, imperative sentence, interrogative sentence.*

deduction The process of reasoning from general claims to a specific instance. (5j-2)

definite article See *articles.*

demonstrative pronoun A pronoun that points out the antecedent: *this, these, that, those.*

denotation The dictionary definition of a word. (20a, 20b-2)

dependent clause A clause that cannot stand alone as an independent grammatical unit. See also *adjective clause, adverb clause, noun clause.*

descriptive adjective An adjective that describes the condition or properties of the noun it modifies and (except for a very few such as *dead* and *unique*) has comparative and superlative forms: *flat, flatter, flattest.*

descriptive adverb An adverb that describes the condition of properties of whatever it modifies and has comparative and superlative forms: *happily, more happily, most happily.*

determiner A word or word group, traditionally identified as an adjective, that limits a noun by telling "how much" or "how many" about it. Also called *expression of quantity, limiting adjective,* or *noun markers.* (41b, 42)

diction Word choice. (20, 21)

direct address Words naming a person or group being spoken to; written words of direct address are set off by commas: *The answer,* **my friends**, *lies with you. Go with them,* **Gene**. (24f)

direct discourse In writing, words that repeat speech or conversation exactly, and so are enclosed in quotation marks.

direct object A noun or pronoun or group of words functioning as a noun that receives the action (completes the meaning) of a transitive verb. (7l)

direct question A sentence that asks a question and ends with a question mark: *Are you going?*

direct quotation See *quotation.*

documentation The acknowledgment of someone else's words and ideas used in any piece of writing by giving full and accurate information about the person whose words were used and where those words were found; for example, for a print source, documentation usuallly includes author name(s), title, place and date of publication, and related information. (31, 33)

documentation style Any of various systems for providing information about the source of words, information, and ideas quoted, paraphrased, or summarized from some source other than the writer. Documentation styles discussed in this handbook are MLA, APA, CM, and CBE. (33)

double negative A nonstandard negation using two negative modifiers, rather than one. (12c)

drafting A part of the writing process in which writers compose ideas in sentences and paragraphs. (3b)

edited English English language use that conforms to established rules of grammar, sentence structure, punctuation, and spelling; also called *standard English*. (21a-2)

editing A part of the writing process in which writers check the technical correctness of their grammar, spelling, punctuation, and mechanics. (3d)

elliptical construction A sentence structure that deliberately omits words expressed elsewhere or that can be inferred from the context.

euphemism Language that attempts to blunt certain realities by speaking of them in "nice" or "tactful" words. (21e)

evidence Facts, data, examples, and opinions of others used to support assertions and conclusions.

exclamatory sentence A sentence beginning with *What* or *How* that expresses strong feeling: *What a ridiculous statement!*

expletive The phrase *there is (are), there was (were), it is,* or *it was* at the beginning of a clause, changing structure and postponing the subject: *It is Mars that we hope to reach* (compare *We hope to reach Mars*).

expository writing See *informative writing*.

expression of quantity See *determiner*.

faulty predication A grammatically illogical combination of subject and predicate. (15d-2)

finite verb A verb form that shows tense, mood, voice, person, and number while expressing an action, occurrence, or state of being.

first person See *person*.

freewriting Writing nonstop for a specified time in order to generate ideas by free association of thoughts. Focused freewriting may start with a set topic or may build on one sentence taken from earlier freewriting. (2f)

fused sentence The error of running independent clauses together without the required punctuation that marks them as complete units. (14)

future perfect progressive tense The form of the future perfect tense that describes an action or condition ongoing until some specific future time: *they will have been talking*.

future perfect tense The tense indicating that an action will have been completed or a condition will have ended by a specified point in the future: *they will have talked*.

future progressive tense The form of the future tense showing that a future action will continue for some time: *they will be talking.*

future tense The form of a verb, made with the simple form and either *shall* or *will,* expressing an action yet to be taken or a condition not yet experienced: *they will talk.*

gender Concerning languages, the classification of words as masculine, feminine, or neutral. In English, a few pronouns show changes in gender in third-person singlular: *he, him, his; she, her, hers; it, its its.* A few nouns naming roles change form to show gender difference: *prince, princess,* for example. (11q, 21b)

gerund A present participle functioning as a noun: ***Walking*** *is a good exercise.* Also see *verbal.*

gerund phrase A gerund, its modifiers, and/or object(s), which functions as a subject or an object. (7n)

helping verb See *auxiliary verb.*

homonyms Words spelled differently that sound alike: *to, too, two.* (22b)

idiom A word, phrase, or other construction that has a different meaning from its usual meaning: *He lost his head. She hit the ceiling.*

illogical predication See *faulty predication.*

imperative mood The mood that expresses commands and direct requests, using the simple form of the verb and often implying but not expressing the subject, *you: Go.* (8l)

imperative sentence A sentence that gives a command: *Go to the corner and buy me a newspaper.*

indefinite article See *articles,determiner.*

indefinite pronoun A pronoun such as *all, anyone, each,* and *others,* that refers to a nonspecific person or thing. (11p)

independent clause A clause that can stand alone as an independent grammatical unit. (7o-1)

indicative mood The mood of verbs used for statements about real things, or highly likely ones: *I think Grace is arriving today.* (8l)

indirect discourse Reported speech or conversation that does not use the exact structure of the original and so is not enclosed in quotation marks. (15a-4)

indirect object A noun or pronoun or group of words functioning as a noun that tells to whom or for whom the action expressed by a transitive verb was done. (7l)

indirect question A sentence that reports a question and ends with a period: *I asked if you are going.*

indirect quotation See *quotation.*

induction The reasoning process of arriving at general principles from particular facts or instances. (5j-1)

infinitive A verbal made of the simple form of a verb and usually, but not always, *to,* that functions as a noun, adjective, or adverb.

infinitive phrase An infinitive, its modifiers, and/or object. It functions as a noun, adjective, or adverb.

informal language Word choice that creates a tone appropriate for casual writing or speaking. (21a-1)

informative writing Writing that gives information and, when necessary, explains it; also known as *expository writing*,. (1b)

intensive pronoun A pronoun that ends in *-self* and that intensifies its antecedent: *Vida **himself** argued against it.*

interjection An emotion-conveying word that is treated as a sentence, starting with a capital letter and ending with an exclamation point or a period: *Oh! Ouch!*

interrogative pronoun A pronoun such as *whose* or *what,* that implies a question: ***Who** called?*

interrogative sentence A sentence that asks a direct question: *Did you see that?*

intransitive verb A verb that does not take a direct object. (8f)

invention techniques Ways of gathering ideas for writing.

inverted word order In contrast to standard order, the main verb or an auxiliary verb comes before the subject in inverted word order. Most questions and some exclamations use inverted word order.

irony Words used to imply the opposite of their usual meaning. (21c)

irregular verb A verb that forms the past tense and past participle in some way other than by adding *-ed* or *-d*. (8d)

jargon A particular field's or group's specialized vocabulary that a general reader is unlikely to understand. (21e)

levels of formality The degree of formality reflected by word choice and sentence structure. A highly formal level is used for certain ceremonial and other occasions when stylistic flourishes are appropriate. A medium level, which is neither too formal nor too casual, is acceptable for most academic writing. (21a-1)

levels of generality In grouping information or ideas, moving from the most general to the most specific. (2l)

limiting adjective See *determiner.*

linking verb A main verb that connects a subject with a subject complement that renames or describes the subject. Linking verbs convey a state of being, relate to the senses, or indicate a condition. (8a)

logical fallacies Flaws in reasoning that lead to illogical statements (5k).

loose sentence See *cumulative sentence.*

main clause See *independent clause.*

main verb A verb that expresses action, occurrence, or state of being and that shows mood, tense, voice, number, and person. (8)

mapping An invention technique based on thinking about a topic and its increasingly specific subdivisions; also known as *clustering* and *webbing*. (2i)

mechanics Conventions regarding the use of capital letters, italics, abbreviations, and numbers. (30)

metaphor A comparison implying similarity between two things. A metaphor does not use words such as *like* or *as*, which are used in a simile and which make a comparison explicit: *a mop of hair* (compare the simile *hair like a mop*). (21c)

misplaced modifier Describing or limiting words that are wrongly positioned in a sentence so that their message is either illogical or relates to the wrong word(s). (15b)

mixed construction A sentence that unintentionally changes from one grammatical structure to another, incompatible one, thus garbling meaning. (15d)

mixed metaphors Incongruously combined images. (21c)

MLA style See *documentation style.*

modal auxiliary verbs A group of auxiliary verbs that add information such as a sense of needing, wanting, or having to do something or a sense of possibility, likelihood, obligation, permission, or ability. (46)

modifier A word or group of words functioning as an adjective or adverb to describe or limit another word or word group. (12, 19e)

mood The attribute of verbs showing a speaker's or writer's attitude toward the action by the way verbs are used. English has three moods: imperative, indicative, and subjunctive. Also see *imperative mood, indicative mood, subjunctive mood.* (8l and 8m)

noncount noun A noun that names "uncountable" things: *water, time.* (41, 42)

nonessential element See *nonrestrictive element.*

nonrestrictive element A descriptive word, phrase, or dependent clause that provides information not essential to understanding the basic message of the element it modifies and so is set off by commas. (24e)

nonsexist language See *sexist language.*

nonstandard Language usage other than edited English. Also see *edited English* (21a-2)

noun A word that names a person, place, thing, or idea. Nouns function as subjects, objects, or complements.

noun clause A dependent clause that functions as a subject, object, or complement. (7o-2)

noun complement See *complement.*

noun determiner See *determiner.*

noun phrase A noun and its modifiers functioning as a subject, object, or complement. (7n)

number The attribute of some words indicating whether they refer to one (singular) or more than one (plural).

object A noun, pronoun, or group of words functioning as a noun or pronoun that receives the action of a verb (direct object); tells to whom or for whom something is done (indirect object); or completes the meaning of a preposition (object of a preposition). (7l)

object complement A noun or adjective renaming or describing a direct object after a few verbs including *call, consider, name, elect,* and *think: I call joggers fanatics*.

objective case The case of a noun or pronoun functioning as a direct or indirect object or object of a preposition or of a verbal. A few pronouns change form to show case *(him, her, whom)*. Also see *case*. (9)

paragraph A group of sentences that work together to develop a unit of thought. (4)

paragraph development Using specific, concrete details (RENNS) to support a generalization in a paragraph; rhetorical strategies for arranging and organizing paragraphs. (4f)

parallelism The use of equivalent grammatical forms or matching sentence structures to express equivalent ideas. (18)

paraphrase A restatement of someone else's ideas in language and sentence structure different from those of the original. (31d)

parenthetical documentation See *parenthetical reference*.

parenthetical reference Information enclosed in parentheses following quoted, paraphrased, or summarized material from a source to alert readers to the use of material from a specific source. Parenthetical references function together with a list of bibliographic information about each source used in a paper to document the writer's use of sources. (33c-1, 33d-1)

participial phrase A phrase that contains a present participle or a past participle and any modifiers and that functions as an adjective. See also *verbal*.

passive construction See *passive voice*.

passive voice The form of a verb in which the subject is acted upon; if the subject is mentioned in the sentence, it usually appears as the object of the preposition *by: I was frightened by the thunder* (compare the active-voice version *The thunder frightened me*). The passive voice emphasizes the action, in contrast to the active voice, which emphasizes the doer of the action. (8n, 8o)

past participle The third principal part of a verb, formed in regular verbs, like the past tense, by adding *-d* or *-ed* to the simple form. In irregular verbs, it often differs from the simple form and the past tense: *break, broke, broken*. (8b)

past perfect progressive tense The past perfect tense form that describes an ongoing condition in the past that has been ended by something stated in the sentence: *I had been talking*. (8j)

past perfect tense The tense that describes a condition or action that started in the past, continued for a while, and then ended in the past: *I had talked*.

past progressive tense The past tense form that shows the continuing nature of a past action: *I was talking*. (8j)

past tense form The second principal part of a verb, in regular verbs formed by adding -ed or -d to the simple form. In irregular verbs, the past tense may change in several ways from the simple form.

perfect tenses The three tenses—the present perfect (*I have talked*), the past perfect, (*I had talked*) and the future perfect (*I will have talked*) that help to show complex time relationships between two clauses. (8i)

periodic sentence A sentence that begins with modifiers and ends with the independent clause, thus postponing the main idea—and the emphasis—for the end; also called a *climactic sentence*. (19e)

person The attribute of nouns and pronouns showing who or what acts or experiences an action. First person is the one speaking (*I, we*); second person is the one being spoken to (*you, you*); and third person is the person or thing spoken about (*he, she, it; they*). All nouns are third person.

personal pronoun A pronoun that refers to people or things, such as *I, you, them, it*.)

persuasive writing Writing that seeks to convince the reader about a matter of opinion. (1b)

phrasal verbs A verb that combines with one or more prepositions to deliver its meaning: *ask out, look into.* (44c)

phrase A group of related words that does not contain a subject and predicate and thus cannot stand alone as an independent grammatical unit. A phrase functions as a noun, verb, or modifier. (7n)

plagiarism A writer's presenting another person's words or ideas without giving credit to that person. Documentation systems allow writers to give proper credit to sources in ways recognized by scholarly communities. Plagiarism is a serious offence, a form of intellectual dishonesty that can lead to course failure or expulsion. (31)

planning An early part of the writing process in which writers gather ideas. Along with shaping, planning is sometimes called *prewriting*. (2)

plural See *number*.

positive The form of an adjective or adverb when no comparison is being expressed: *blue, easily*. Also see *comparative, superlative*. (12e)

possessive case The case of a noun or pronoun that shows ownership or possession. Also see *case*. (9, 27a–27d)

predicate The part of a sentence that contains the verb and tells what the subject is doing or experiencing or what is being done to the subject. A *simple predicate* contains only the main verb and any auxiliary verb(s). A *complete predicate* contains the verb and all its modifiers, objects, and other related words. A *compound predicate* contains two or more verbs and their objects and modifiers, if any. (7k)

predicate adjective An adjective used as a subject complement: *That tree is **leafy***.

predicate nominative A noun or pronoun used as a subject complement: *That tree is a **maple***.

premises In a deductive argument expressed as a syllogism, statements presenting the conditions of the argument from which the conclusion must follow. (5j)

preposition A word that conveys a relationship, often of space or time, between the noun or pronoun following it and other words in the sentence. The noun or pronoun following a preposition is called its *object.* (7g, 44)

prepositional phrase See *phrase, preposition.*

present participle A verb's *-ing* form. Used with auxiliary verbs, present participles function as main verbs. Used without auxiliary verbs, present participles function as nouns or adjectives. (8b, 7d)

present perfect progressive tense The present perfect tense form that describes something ongoing in the past that is likely to continue into the future. *I have been talking.*

present perfect tense The tense indicating that an action or its effects, begun or perhaps completed in the past, continue into the present: *I had talked.*

present progressive tense The present tense form of the verb that indicates something taking place at the time it is written or spoken about: *I am talking.*

present tense The tense that describes what is happening, what is true at the moment, and what is consistently true. It uses the simple form (*I **talk***) and the *-s* form in the third person singular, (*he, she it **talks***). (8h)

prewriting A term for all activities in the writing process before drafting. See *planning* and *shaping.* (2)

primary sources "Firsthand" work: write-ups of experiments and observations by the researchers who conducted them; taped accounts, interviews, and newspaper accounts by direct observers; autobiographies, diaries, and journals; expressive works (poems, plays, fiction, essays); also known as *primary evidence.* Also see *secondary source.* (5h, 32g)

progressive forms Verb forms made in all tenses with the present participle and forms of the verb *be* as an auxiliary. Progressive forms show that an action, occurrence, or state of being is ongoing. (8j)

pronoun A word that takes the place of a noun and functions in the same ways that nouns do. Types of pronouns are *demonstrative, indefinite, intensive, interrogative, personal, reciprocal, reflexive,* and *relative.* The word (or words) a pronoun replaces is called its *antecedent.* (9, 10, 11m–11r)

pronoun-antecedent agreement The match in expressing number and person, and for personal pronouns, gender as well, required between a pronoun and its antecedent. (11m–11r)

pronoun case The way a pronoun changes form to reflect its use as the agent of action (subjective case), the thing being acted upon (objective case), or the thing showing ownership (possessive case). (9)

pronoun reference The relationship between a pronoun and its antecedent. (10)

proofreading Reading a final draft to find and correct any spelling or mechanics mistakes, typing errors, or handwriting illegibility; the final step of the writing process. (3e)

proper adjective An adjective formed from a proper noun: *Victorian, Canadian.*

proper noun A noun that names specific people, places, or things and is always capitalized: *Moose Jaw, Eli Mandel, Corvette.*

purpose The goal or aim of a piece of writing: to express oneself, to provide information, to persuade, or to create a literary work. (1b)

quotation Repeating or reporting another person's words. *Direct quotation* repeats another's words exactly and encloses them in quotation marks. *Indirect quotation* reports another's words without quotation marks except around any words repeated exactly from the source. Both direct and indirect quotation require documentation of the source to avoid plagiarism. See also *indirect discourse.* (28a, 31c)

reciprocal pronoun The pronouns *each other* and *one another* referring to individual parts of a plural antecedent: *We respect **each other**.*

References In many documentation styles, including APA, the title of a list of sources cited in a research paper or other written work. (33d, 33e, 33f)

reflexive pronoun A pronoun that ends in *-self* and that reflects back to its antecedent: *They claim to support **themselves**.*

regular verb A verb that forms its past tense and past participle by adding *-ed* or *-d* to the simple form. Most English verbs are regular. (8d)

relative adverb An adverb that introduces an adjective clause: *The lot **where** I usually park my car was full.*

relative clause See *adjective clause.*

relative pronoun A pronoun such as *who, which, that, what,* and *whoever,* that introduces an adjective clause or sometimes a noun clause.

restrictive clause A dependent clause that gives information necessary to distinguish it from others in the same category. In contrast to a nonrestrictive clause, a restrictive clause is not set off with commas. (24e)

restrictive element A word, phrase, or dependent clause that provides information essential to the understanding of the element it modifies. In contrast to a nonrestrictive element, a restrictive element is not set off with commas. (24e)

revision A part of the writing process in which writers evaluate their rough drafts and, based on their decisions, rewrite by adding, cutting, replacing, moving, and often totally recasting material. (3c)

rhetoric The area of discourse that focuses on arrangement of ideas and choice of words as a reflection of the writer's purpose and sense of audience. (1)

Rogerian argument An argument technique adapted from the principles of communication developed by psychologist Carl Rogers. (6c)

run-on (run-together) sentence See *fused sentence.*

secondary source A source that reports, analyzes, discusses, reviews, or otherwise deals with the work of someone else, as opposed to a primary source, which is someone's original work or first-hand report. A reliable secondary source should be the work of a person with appropriate credentials, should appear in a respected publication or other medium, should be current, and should be well reasoned. (5h, 32g)

second person See *person.*

sentence See *sentence types.*

sentence fragment A portion of a sentence that is punctuated as though it were a complete sentence. (13)

sentence types A grammatical classification of sentences by the kinds of clauses they contain. A *simple sentence* consists of one independent clause. A *complex sentence* contains one independent clause and one or more dependent clauses. A *compound-complex sentence* contains at least two independent clauses and one or more dependent clause. A *compound sentence* contains two or more independent clauses joined by a coordinating conjunction. Sentences are also classified by their grammatical function; see *declarative sentence, exclamatory sentence, imperative sentence,* and *interrogative sentence.* (7j, 7p)

sexist language Language that unfairly assigns roles or characteristics to people on the basis of gender. Language that avoids gender stereotyping is called *nonsexist language.* (21b, 11g)

shaping An early part of the writing process in which writers consider ways to organize their material. Along with planning, shaping is sometimes called *prewriting.* (2)

simile A comparison, using *like, or, as,* between otherwise dissimilar things. (21c)

simple form The form of the verb that shows action, occurrence, or state of being taking place in the present. It is used in the singular for first and second person and in the plural for first, second, and third person. It is also the first principal part of a verb. The simple form is also known as the *dictionary form* or *base form.* (8b)

simple predicate See *predicate.*

simple sentence See *sentence types.*

simple subject See *subject.*

simple tenses The present, past, and future tenses, which divide time into present, past, and future. (8g)

singular See *number.*

slang Coined words and new meanings for existing words, which quickly pass in and out of use; not appropriate for most academic writing. (21a-3)

source A book, article, document, other work, or person providing information. (1e, 31, 32, 33)

split infinitive One or more words coming between the two words of an infinitive. (15b-2)

standard English See *edited English.*

standard word order The most common order for words in English sentences: the subject comes before the predicate.

subject The word or group of words in a sentence that acts, is acted upon, or is described by the verb. A *simple subject* includes only the noun or pronoun.

A *complete subject* includes the noun or pronoun and all its modifiers. A *compound subject* includes two or more nouns or pronouns and their modifiers. (7k)

subject complement A noun or adjective that follows a linking verb, renaming or describing the subject of the sentence; also called a *predicate nominative.* (7m-1)

subjective case The case of the pronoun functioning as subject. Also see *case.* (9)

subject-verb agreement The required match between a subject and verb in expressing number and person. (11a–11l)

subjunctive mood The verb mood that expresses wishes, recommendations, indirect requests, speculations, and conditional statements: *I wish you were here.* (8m)

subordinate clause See *dependent clause.*

subordinating conjunction A conjunction that introduces an adverbial clause and expresses a relationship between the idea in it and the idea in the independent clause. (7h)

subordination The use of grammatical structures to reflect the relative importance of ideas. A sentence with logically subordinated information expresses the most important information in the independent clause and less important information in dependent clauses or phrases. (17a–17d)

summary An extraction of the main message or central point of a passage or other discourse; a critical thinking activity preceding synthesis. (5f, 31e)

superlative The form of the adjective or adverb that expresses comparison among three or more things: *bluest, least blue; most easily, least easily.* (12e)

syllogism The structure of a deductive argument expressed in two premises and a conclusion. The *first premise* is a generalized assumption or statement of fact. The *second premise* is a different assumption or statement of fact based on evidence. The *conclusion* is also a specific instance that follows logically from the premises. (5j)

synonym A word that is close in meaning to another word. (20a)

synthesis A component of critical thinking in which material that has been summarized, analyzed, and interpreted is connected to what is already known (one's prior knowledge). (5b, 5f)

tag question An inverted verb-pronoun combination added to the end of a sentence, creating a question, that "asks" the audience to agree with the assertion in the first part of the sentence: *You know what a tag question, **don't you?*** A tag question is set off from the rest of the sentence with a comma. (24f)

tag sentence See *tag question.*

tense The time at which the action of the verb occurs: in the past, present, or future. (8g–8k)

tense sequence In sentences that have more than one clause, the accurate matching of verbs to reflect the logical time relationships. (8k)

thesis statement A statement of an essay's central theme that makes clear the main idea, the writer's purpose, the focus of the topic, and perhaps the organizational pattern. (2n)

third person See *person.*

tone The writer's attitude toward his or her material and reader, especially as reflected by word choice. (1d)

topic The subject of discourse.

topic sentence The sentence that expresses the main idea of a paragraph. (4b-3)

Toulmin model for argument A model that defines the essential parts of an argument as the *claim* (or *main point*), the *support* (or *evidence*), and the *warrants* (or *assumptions behind the main point*). (6e)

transition The connection of one idea to another in discourse. Useful strategies for creating transitions include transitional expressions, parallelism, and planned repetition of key words and phrases. (4d)

transitional expressions Words and phrases that signal connections among ideas and create coherence. (4d-1)

transitive verb A verb that must be followed by a direct object. (8f)

unity The clear and logical relationship between the main idea of a paragraph and the evidence supporting the main idea. (4b)

usage A customary way of using language. (21, Usage Glossary)

valid A term applied to a deductive argument when the conclusion follows logically from the premises. Validity describes the structure of an argument, not its truth. (5j)

verb A class of words that shows action or occurrence or describes a state of being. Verbs change form to show time (tense), attitude (mood), and role of the subject (voice). Verbs occur in the predicate of a clause and can be in verb phrases, which may consist of a main verb, any auxiliary verbs, and any modifers. Verbs can be described as transitive or intransitive depending on whether they take a direct object. (8)

verbal A verb part functioning as a noun, adjective, or adverb. Verbals include *infinitives, present participles* (functioning as adjectives), *gerunds* (present participles functioning as nouns), and *past participles.* (7d)

verbal phrase A group of words that contains a verbal (an infinitive, participle, or gerund) and its modifiers.

verb phrase A main verb, any auxiliary verb(s), and any modifiers.

voice An attribute of verbs showing whether the subject acts (active voice) or is acted upon (passive voice). (8n and 8o)

webbing See *mapping.*

Works Cited In MLA documentation style the title of a list of all sources cited in a research paper or other written work. (33c-2 and 33c-3)

writing process Stages of writing in which a writer gathers and shapes ideas, organizes material, expresses those ideas in a rough draft, evaluates the draft and revises it, edits the writing for technical errors, and proofreads it for typographical accuracy and legibility. The stages often overlap. See *planning, shaping, drafting, revision, editing, and proofreading.* (1, 2, 3)

Index

All entries in boldface italics (***advice***, ***advise***, for example) are discussed in the Usage Glossary and any other place listed. Section numbers are in boldface type and page numbers in regular type. The listing "**30m:** 536" thus refers you to page 536, which is in section **30m**.

Index

Index

Chart
List

CHARTS IN TINTED BOXES

CHARTS IN TINTED BOXES (continued)

CHARTS IN TINTED BOXES (*continued*)

Response Symbols

Here are two lists of symbols your instructor might write on your papers.
The first list shows traditional correction symbols; the second list shows
complimentary symbols. You can find material related to each item by
consulting the handbook sections or chapters given.

CORRECTION SYMBOLS

ab	abbreviation error, **23b, 30h–30k**	*pl*	plural error, **22c**
ad	adjective or adverb error, **12**	*pro ref*	pronoun reference error, **10**
agr	agreement error, **11**	*pro agr*	pronoun agreement error, **11m–11r**
ca	case error, **9**	*pe*	punctuation error, **23–29**
cap	needs capital letter, **30a–30e**	*ref*	pronoun reference error, **10**
cl	avoid cliché, **21d**	*rep*	repetitious (redundant), **16c**
coh	needs coherence, **4d**	*ro*	run-on sentence, **14**
coord	faulty coordination, **17a–17d**	*shift*	shift, **15a**
cs	comma splice, **14**	*sl*	avoid slang, **21a-3**
dev	needs development, **4a, 4c, 4f**	*sp*	spelling error, **22**
dm	dangling modifier, **15c**	*subord*	faulty subordination, **17e–17h**
e	needs exact language, **20b**	*sxt*	sexist language use, **11q, 21b**
emph	needs emphasis, **19**	*t*	verb tense error, **8g–8k**
frag	sentence fragment, **13**	*trans*	needs transition, **4d-1, 4d-5**
fs	fused sentence, **14**	*u*	needs unity, **4b, 4c**
hyph	hyphenation error, **22d**	*us*	usage error, **Usage Glossary**
inc	incomplete sentence, **15e**	*v*	verb form error, **8b–8f**
ital	italics (underlining) error, **30f–30g**	*v agr*	verb agreement error, **11a–11l**
k	awkward construction, **15, 16, 21e**	*var*	needs sentence variety, **19**
		w	wordy, **16**
lc	needs lower-case letter, **30a–30e**	*wc*	word choice error, **20, 21**
		ww	wrong word, **20, 21**
mixed	mixed construction, **15d**	∧	insert
mm	misplaced modifier, **15b**	ℰ	delete
num	number use error, **30l–30m**	∽	transpose
¶	start new paragraph, **4**	#	space needed
no ¶	do not start new paragraph, **4**	◡	close up
//	parallelism, **18**	?	meaning unclear

COMPLIMENTARY SYMBOLS

gd coh	good coherence, **4d**	*gd th*	good thesis statement, **2n, 3c-2, 6b, 32r**
gd coord	good coordination, **17a–17c**	*gd trans*	good transitions, **4d-1, 4d-5**
gd dev	good development, **4c, 4f**	*gd ts*	good topic sentence, **4a, 4b**
gd log	good logic, **5j–5k**	*gd u*	good unity, **4b, 4c**
gd //	good parallelism, **18**	*gd var*	good sentence variety, **19**
gd rea	good reasoning, **5i–5k**	*gd wc*	good word choice, **20, 21**
gd rev	good revising, **3c**	*gd wp*	good writing process, **1, 2, 3**
gd sub	good subordination, **17e–17g**		

How to Use Your Handbook

You can use your *Simon and Schuster Handbook for Writers* as a reference book, just as you use a dictionary or an encyclopedia. At each step, use one or more suggestions to find the information you want.

STEP 1: USE lists to decide where to go.

- Overview of Contents (on inside front cover)
- Scan the longer Contents that starts on page iii.
- Scan the Index at the back of the book for a detailed alphabetical list of all major and minor topics.
- Scan the list of Charts in Tinted Boxes that highlight and summarize all major subjects.

STEP 2: LOCATE the number that leads to the information you seek.

- Find a chapter number.
- Find a number-letter combination for a subsection of a chapter, explaining a rule or guiding principle.
- Find a chart number.
- Find a page number.

STEP 3: CHECK elements on each page to confirm where you are in the book. (See the opposite page.)

- Look for the shortened title at the top of each page (left page for chapter title and right page for section title).
- Look for a chapter number and section number in the blue tab at the top corner of each page.
- Look for a page number at the bottom of the page.

STEP 4: LOCATE and read the information you need. Use special features, illustrated on the opposite page, to help you.

- Use cross-references (usually given in parentheses) to related key concepts.
- Find the definition for any word followed by a degree mark (°) in the Terms Glossary at the back of the book.
- Use ❖ ALERT ❖ notes for pointers about related matters of usage, grammar, punctuation, and writing. Watch for ✚ COMPUTER TIPS ✚ and ◆ ESL NOTES ◆ as well.